THE EVOLUTION OF
REEF COMMUNITIES

THE EVOLUTION OF REEF COMMUNITIES

J. A. Fagerstrom

University of Nebraska
Lincoln, Nebraska
    and
University of Colorado
Boulder, Colorado

A WILEY-INTERSCIENCE PUBLICATION
JOHN WILEY & SONS
NEW YORK · CHICHESTER · BRISBANE · TORONTO · SINGAPORE

Copyright © 1987 by John Wiley & Sons, Inc.

All rights reserved. Published simultaneously in Canada.

Reproduction or translation of any part of this work
beyond that permitted by Section 107 or 108 of the
1976 United States Copyright Act without the permission
of the copyright owner is unlawful. Requests for
permission or further information should be addressed to
the Permissions Department, John Wiley & Sons, Inc.

Library of Congress Cataloging in Publication Data:
Fagerstrom, J. A.
   The evolution of reef communities.

   "A Wiley-Interscience publication."
   Bibliography: p.
   1. Reefs.   2. Animal communities.   3. Paleontology.
I. Title.

QE565.F34 1987   574.5'26367   87-8189
ISBN 0-471-81528-4

Printed in the United States of America

10 9 8 7 6 5 4 3 2 1

To my father, for guidance and inspiration

Preface

Fascination with reefs and reef communities extends from tourists awed by their beauty and diversity to masked and flippered shell collectors to a wide spectrum of scientists. Modern reefs are in *jeopardy* because of overzealous exploitation by treasure hunters, high-impact land "developers," and even by the scores of "free spirits" wishing to emulate the easy-going island life that beguiled the crew of the H.M.S. Bounty and Paul Gauguin.

Scientific reef research extends from the water surrounding modern reefs to their geological foundations and from the thin veneer of living organisms to their evolutionary ancestors extending back in geological history for hundreds of millions of years. The inevitable result of such diversity has been an enormous but highly fragmented reef literature. This volume fills the need for a synthetic approach to the "reef phenomenon"; it integrates the broad scope of research on modern (Holocene) and ancient reefs with consideration of the major environmental factors and processes that influence their success or failure. Despite their great variation in size, shape, location, and biological properties, reef communities have maintained an overall integrity and objectivity that is unmatched by any other type of marine community.

The "reef phenomenon" is chiefly a "biological phenomenon!" Therefore, the book emphasizes the biological aspects of reef evolution. It is the first synthesis of the *complete* (two billion years) geologic history of any marine or terrestrial community type.

The book is divided into three parts. Part I focuses on the environmental factors and processes, especially biological, that control the nature and distribution of Cenozoic reefs, the establishment of models for comparing and interpreting older reefs, and the adequacy of Cenozoic models for such comparisons and interpretations. Part II summarizes the geological history and autecology of the major reef-building higher taxa from algae to crinoids, including several that are extinct or of uncertain biological affinities. Part III summarizes the geological history and synecology of reef communities, including builders, destroyers, and dwellers, on almost a geological stage-by-stage basis from the Late Precambrian through the Cretaceous. The final chapter summarizes the geologic history of reef communities, the extinction/recovery/stabilization events that have shaped this history and establishes a succession of ten major ecological-evolutionary reef community "units" from the Precambrian to the Holocene. These units and their temporal distribution are only indirectly linked to the history of comparable units based on nonreef organisms and communities.

Many aspects of the evolution of reef communities are independent of the rest of the world biota; this evolution has been influenced by global mass extinction events as well as an unpredictable succession of "opportunistic" reef-building higher taxa and communities. It is this succession of reef communities of distinctly different composition and structure that makes the biological aspects of the "reef phenomenon" more complex and interesting than the non-biological, which by contrast are remarkably uniform through time. Global reef extinction brought with it a sharp reduction in biotic diversity and a long *(millions of years)* period of recovery and re-establishment of a new reef community type. Thus, reefs are both durable and fragile when viewed from the perspective of geologic time. The fragility of reef communities should be of sobering concern to the exploiters of modern reefs; unfortunately the short-term benefits (recreation and profit) are seldom weighed against the potential long-term biological hazards of extinction and ecologic instability.

This book is the outgrowth of a series of lectures that I presented to professional geologists and graduate students at Nanjing University, People's Republic of China, in 1983. I have expanded the scope to include the biological attributes of Holocene reef communities that make them unique and of interest to professionals and students in biology. The book is therefore highly interdisciplinary and should be of value in graduate seminars dealing with ecology/paleoecology and evolutionary biology/paleobiology.

One of the most difficult problems in any interdisciplinary study is the "nomenclature gap" that separates the practitioners of each discipline. Reef nomenclature is an excellent example of this problem and has often been the main obstacle to effective communication between biologists and geologists. Geologists have been the chief contributors to the "explosion" of reef terminology; this has even led to intradisciplinary communication problems. To alleviate this nomenclature gap, the main text purposely contains a minimum of specialized terms and avoids the controversy surrounding them. Instead, there is a glossary of selected biological and geological terms designed to bridge the gap; it also includes numerous terms that I regard as non-essential synonyms of basic terms. In addition, the text contains numerous references and cross-references to aspects of reef nomenclature that are clarified by photographs (see Plates 1–51 at end of book) and figures (within each chapter).

This is not a book in "reef nomenclature" and controversy over terms but rather a book of concepts and their application to the study of "The Evolution of Reef Communities."

J.A. FAGERSTROM

Jamestown, Colorado
August 1987

Acknowledgments

A book of this scope requires the encouragement, help, and cooperation of numerous institutions and individuals. It gives me great pleasure to acknowledge the following institutions and individuals for responding, often on short notice, to my various requests:

For review and criticism of early drafts of chapters dealing with their areas of expertise: E. G. Kauffman (Chaps. 1, 10, 14), G. Muller-Parker (Chaps. 2, 5), W. A. Oliver, Jr. (Chap. 9), C. Johnson (Chap. 1), R. Hunt, M. Voorhies, P. Freeman, B. Ratcliffe and C. Lemon (Chap. 15).

For leadership in the field to study reefs in their areas of expertise: Cambrian, S. Rowland, R. Gangloff, W. Ahr; Devonian, P. Playford, A. Cockbain, H. Tsein, W. A. Oliver, Jr., Carboniferous, M. Ota, R. West, G. R. Clark II, J. Wray, J. Harbaugh; Jurassic, C. Gaillard, P. Bernier; Cretaceous, B. Perkins; Cenozoic, G. Multer, L. Montaggioni. I have drawn heavily on field discussions with each in preparing many of the examples used in Part III. My field expenses during 1957–1959 were partially subsidized by the University of Michigan and in 1961–1985 by the University of Nebraska, Sigma Xi, the American Philosophical Society, and the Geological Society of America.

For informal discussions in hallways, offices, or other places where I could "badger" them, for requests for help by mail or phone: my colleagues in geology and biology at the University of Nebraska, especially S. Treves, R. Nelson, R. Hunt, M. Voorhies, N. Lindsley-Griffin, and A. Joern. Ruth Ford, Geology Librarian at Nebraska, responded with grace and humor to my numerous and sometimes frantic calls for help in locating books and maps.

For the opportunity to teach reef community evolution at Nanjing University, People's Republic of China, in 1983: Guo Linzhi (Acting President) and R. Roskins, S. Treves, and R. F. Diffendal, Jr., and especially Zhang Zhongying, my interpreter, who conveyed my approach to reefs to "our students" with skill and patience. The bulk of the text was written in 1985 during a leave of absence from the University of Nebraska arranged by S. Treves.

For the provocative questions and discussions in the classroom, lab, and field concerning my ideas on reef processes and community structure and function: former students. One of the rewarding aspects of teaching is the opportunity to present ideas and observe the way they are ingested and digested by critical students and professional colleagues "in the making." Muddled ideas are soon unmasked, regurgitated, and eventually reformulated in the stimulation of such give and take, student–teacher discusssions. For help translating French: my daughter Christine Howe.

Finally, to my wife, Marilyn, for her encouragement to undertake the book, and once begun, for her patience, compassion, advice, and word processing abilities! She provided "neutral" responses to my numerous questions on form, style, and format and transformed my scribbled notes and drafts into the final manuscript. To her I own my greatest thanks for a big job well done!

Contents

THE EVOLUTION OF
REEF COMMUNITIES

PART I
THE REEF PHENOMENON

1

What is a Reef?

CRITERIA FOR RECOGNITION

> Reefs have been defined and redefined, classified and codified, inspected, dissected, investigated and reinvestigated to the point that it might seem that there is very little else that could be done to them.
>
> (Longman, 1981, p. 10)

Introduction

Reef communities are special communities in many different and interesting ways. For some scientists they are special because they are so very old (at least 2 billion years!) and provide clues about the origin and early evolution of life; for others they are special because of their fantastically abundant and diverse life. For still others the fascination of reefs lies in the rise, proliferation, and fall of a succession of compositionally different but structurally similar biological communities. Reefs are primarily biological phenomena, and, as such, the history of their evolution is intriguing to biologists concerned with the present stage of this history. Paleobiologists are interested in the historical succession of communities and possible causes for their extinction, and petroleum geologists are interested because nearly half the world's crude oil comes from reefs and rocks directly associated with reefs.

General Characteristics

A typical *marine organic reef* is the product of a vigorous biological response to a relatively restricted set of interdependent environmental factors (chemical, physical, geological, and biological). During its growth, a

3

reef progressively alters its local environment, which in turn modifies many aspects of these environmental factors. The chief manifestations of this biological response are the relatively dense packing and rapid growth rates of predominantly sessile, colonial, or highly gregarious organisms.

Typically these organisms secrete calcareous (siliceous in a few taxa) skeletons, which, by virtue of their large size, dense packing, and *in situ* interlocking growth, form a rigid structure having a ridge or moundlike shape and positive topographic relief with respect to the unconsolidated, usually carbonate, sediments of the adjacent seafloor.

During the middle and late Cenozoic, the volumetrically predominant skeletal organisms present in reef structures were "stony corals" and "calcareous algae" *(sensu lato)*. Throughout geologic history numerous other sessile invertebrates have been characterized by their ability to grow rapidly upward in dense associations with a variety of other organisms to maintain an elevated growing surface in turbulent waters. These densely packed, "rapid growers" have included algae, sponges, bryozoans, brachiopods, molluscs, and annelids at varied times and places.

Each aspect of this general characterization will be amplified at several places in the book, but the overall significance of the major ones will be discussed briefly here. Interestingly, virtually all the controversy over what is or is not a reef concerns geologists studying pre-Cenozoic reefs. Biologists studying living reefs are in almost unanimous agreement regarding what constitutes a reef (see Schuhmacher, 1976, p. 12, for a biological definition).

Rigidity

Due to the vigorous growth of organisms with large skeletons and their tendency to become intergrown, the reef structure may have varying degrees of rigidity toward external mechanical stress. This rigidity is usually expressed as topographic relief of the reef surface above the adjacent seafloor or "level-bottom." Such varied relief in turn produces relatively strong gradients in several chemical, physical, and biological factors in the reef environment. These gradients commonly appear as geomorphic and ecologic zonations that are presumably influenced by water depth and such depth-related factors as light intensity, turbulence, and turbidity. These zonations may also be expressed in the nature and distribution of the sediments deposited in and around the reefs and by sharp differences in the biota from the reef to the adjacent sedimentary substrate.

Sizes and shapes of reefs are highly varied in both time and space and depend largely on their location, especially the preexisting geomorphology, hydrologic regime, growth rates of the organisms, crustal subsidence, and longevity of the reef environment. The living part of the reef is a relatively thin veneer of organisms on or attached to a rigid underlying structure that may or may not have formed in an environment similar to the present surface.

Rigidity and topographic relief also give the reef a degree of wave and current resistance that exceeds the resistance of the adjacent unconsolidated sediments to transportation. During times of normal turbulence, the reef stands as a rigid bulwark in a sea of constantly shifting sedimentary grains of varied sizes from mud to pebbles.

During times of abnormally high turbulence, the rigid structure of the reef may undergo varied degrees of destruction to produce grains and blocks as well as cracks (fractures; fissures) within the structure itself that commonly are parallel to the reef front (Pl. 1). Such cracks then become filled with sediment and solidified by encrusting organisms and early cement to form neptunian dikes and sills (Playford et al., 1984a) cross-cutting the general fabric of the reef.

Framework

Rigidity is imparted to reefs by two structural components, both of which are operative in the living reef or very soon after the death of the reef. The first component in time, and commonly also in volume, is the mass of large, colonial or gregarious, intergrown skeletal organisms in general growth position (Pl. 2). The second component is the mass of early, submarine, calcareous cement (Pl. 3b) that unites both the organisms and the sediments within the reef into the reef structure (Pl. 3a). Reefs with frameworks dominated by early diagenetic inorganic cement are almost unknown in the Holocene; some hardened stromatolites (discussed below) may be included here. By contrast, in the Paleozoic and Mesozoic, cement framework reefs were of considerable importance. These two components of the framework act in unison to produce the rigid reef, which may be subdivided into the organic (skeletal) framework and the inorganic (cement) framework (Pl. 1b). The transported sedimentary grains within the framework are *not* part of the framework.

In the study of living reefs, the problem of determining which skeletal organisms are in their living positions is of minor importance. However, in ancient reefs, determination of the relative proportions of *in situ* whole skeletons, transported whole skeletons, and transported skeletal debris (Pl. 4) is crucial to the recognition of reefs and their frameworks; even so, their recognition and distinction may prove very difficult.

Estimation of the *volume* of *in situ* skeletal material strongly depends on the sampling method and area sampled. Samples from living reefs commonly are collected from the upper surface; sampling from ancient horizontal reef surfaces (contemporaneous time planes) is unusual. In recent years, considerable attention has been given to sampling open cracks, crevices, and caves within the reef structure. In contrast, sampling of ancient reefs is usually done from vertical, two-dimensional quarry faces, natural vertical outcrops, and cores. Core samples generally underestimate skeletal volume and overemphasize vertical variation.

The skeletal content of ecologically zoned reefs is highly varied in space and time. James (1983, p. 348) reported the skeletal volume of Holocene Bermudan reefs as 40–80%. From outcrop data, Ginsburg and Choi (1984) estimated the coral content of the Key Largo Limestone (Pleistocene) in southern Florida at 32–46% of the reef volume; of the Pleistocene reefs in Kenya at 18–46%; and of the Pleistocene reefs of Barbados as high as 60%. In the latter case, most of the corals are fragments and not in growth position. In cores from Quaternary reefs in the Great Barrier Reef, Australia, massive and branching corals generally comprise less than 30% of the rock volume, a figure that Ginsburg and Choi regard as typical of most Quaternary reefs. However, Hopley (1982, pp. 221–222) estimated porosities of Great Barrier Reef Holocene corals and sediments at 40–60%. (See Ginsburg and Schroeder, 1973, Figs. 5, 7, 9–14, and Kobluk and James, 1979, Figs. 3, 4, for illustrations of early reef porosity.) On the other hand, Ginsburg (1983, p. 149) estimated the cross-sectional area of cavities in large reef masses at 75–85%. Finally, Piller (1981, p. 287) estimated the volume of the *in situ* organic framework at less than 10% in the Upper Triassic Hochkonig Massif near Salzburg, Austria.

The initial reef pores vary in size from microscopic (algal and fungal borings) to large caves and tunnels up to 5 m high and 10 m long (Ginsburg, 1983, p. 149) and vary from subspherical to highly irregular. During the early postmortem history of the reef framework, there is a progressive decrease in the importance of the organic framework relative to that of the inorganic framework. The relative proportions of organic and inorganic frameworks also have changed considerably and non-systematically through geologic time.

Sediments

The sediments in the reef environment may be subdivided into those deposited within the framework (internal; Pl. 5) and those deposited external to the framework on the adjacent level-bottom. Both the internal and external sedimentary grains generally are calcareous and chiefly of biological origin. Wiens (1962, p. 84) reported that at least 97% of the sediments in the lagoon at Bikini Atoll, Marshall Islands, are calcareous.

Most of the non-calcareous sediments in reef environments have local terrigenous sources (Hayward, 1982; Roberts and Murray, 1983) or consist of minor admixtures of siliceous or phosphatic skeletal grains. Reefs growing near areas of rapid terrigenous deposition are much more strongly influenced by sedimentary (often fluvial) processes and may be subject to more rapid burial than reefs growing in carbonate depositional systems.

However, the skeletal framework, the internal sediments, and the cement of the vast majority of both Holocene and ancient reefs are calcareous. All but the cement is produced primarily by biologic processes operating at or near the site of their final occurrence. Similarly, most of the external sediments are biologically produced within the general reef environment and have undergone only moderate amounts of transport. Extensive lateral and bathymetric transport of external sediment may also occur; however, the net result of such transport is that reef environments are overwhelmingly sediment "producers and exporters," not "importers."

Reefs rarely occur in isolation, regardless of their size, location, or age. Instead, they occur in variously spaced clusters; each cluster is commonly called a "*reef system*" or if the cluster is enormous, such as the Great Barrier Reef, it may be called a "reef province." Reefs plus reef systems (provinces) and the adjacent (external) sediments constitute a "reef complex."

Biotic Diversity

Although rigidity and topographic relief are the chief criteria for the recognition of reefs, most reefs are also characterized by a significantly higher taxonomic diversity than the adjacent level-bottoms. However, there are numerous exceptions among reefs of nearly all stages of ecologic development and geologic age.

The stratigraphic record from the Precambrian to the Holocene contains a variety of structures that in most ways are similar to typical reefs described above but in other features are quite dissimilar. The most common similarities are the dense packing of the *in situ* calcareous skeletons (Pls. 2 and 6a), the overall ridge or moundlike shape of the structures, and their positive topographic relief. The chief dissimilarity is their very low taxonomic diversity (some are almost monospecific); many such Holocene structures are associated with water of non-marine salinity. In addition, there are ancient reefs that lack an organic framework but appear to have had an important inorganic cement framework. Some authors have composed reef definitions in ways that specifically exclude these structures (e.g., Braithwaite, 1973, p. 1109), whereas numerous other authors have regarded them as true (but atypical) reefs.

Low Diversity Organic Skeletal Frameworks

There is a significant number of higher invertebrate taxa that contain species capable of variously cementing their skeletons to (encrusting) the substrate and appear to benefit from the ecological advantages of dense packing. These organisms are not colonial in the sense of genetic identity derived by asexual reproduction; instead, their high density is in large part due to strong larval selection that has attracted numerous generations to the same habitat and rapid postlarval growth rates. Larval sub-

TABLE 1.1. Characteristics and Examples of Holocene Low Diversity Framework Reefs

Framework	
Organic (Skeletal)	Inorganic (Cement)
1. Oyster	1. Stromatolites with early di-agenetic pore cement
2. Vermetid	2. Examples from the Paleozoic and Mesozoic; see Part III
3. Serpulid	
4. Bryozoan	
5. Stromatolites with calcified fil-ament sheaths	

strate selection and rapid growth result in gregarious distributions and may produce almost monospecific frameworks of the same sizes and shapes as more typical reefs. Holocene examples include (Table 1.1, above).

Oyster (Bivalvia) Reefs. Norris (1953), Shier (1969), and Stenzel (1971, pp. 1046–1048) have described Holocene and buried Pleistocene accumulations of the oyster *Crassostrea virginica* from brackish water tidal channels and bays of the Texas and Florida coasts. The largest of these oyster-shell frameworks are elongate parallel to the channels and have linear dimensions of 8–10 km, widths up to 150 m, and are as much as 4 m thick with well-defined steep margins. Most of these structures occur at depths from the low tide line to 2 m, but Caspers (1950) described enormous *Ostrea edulis* frameworks in the North Sea at depths of 23–28 m and in almost normal marine salinity.

Although pre-Pleistocene oyster reefs are relatively uncommon in the stratigraphic record, similar domal structures up to 4.5 m thick and 10 m in diameter have been described from Middle and Upper Triassic rocks in southern Germany (Bachmann, 1979; Geister, 1984). These frameworks were formed by encrusting right valves of the bivalve *Placunopsis ostracina* (Superfamily Pectinacea?). The dense packing of these relatively small (1.5 cm dia) valves virtually excluded all other organisms except for a few foraminifera, brachiopods, other bivalves, gastropods, serpulids, and an unknown borer; Bachmann (1979) estimated the overall composition as 75% *P. ostracina* valves, 5% other sessile benthos, and 20% micritic interstitial mud.

Although these structures apparently were rigid, their stratigraphic relationship with the enclosing rocks indicates that topographic relief was low. Geister (1984) estimated the water depth at 50–100 m.

Vermetid (Gastropoda) Reefs. In Holocene intertidal locations in southwestern Florida, massive aggregations of intergrown and cemented tubular conchs of the vermetid gastropod *Vermetus (Thylaeodus) nigricans* form wave-resistant frameworks up to 3 m thick arranged in elongate barrierlike shapes parallel to the shore (Shier, 1969). The vermetid frameworks began their growth on tidal channel margin *Crassostrea virginica* assemblages but appear to have soon developed into frameworks composed of 20–60% vermetid tubes; the remainder consists of muddy internal sediment. Although gregarious vermetids have been present in the Gulf Coast region at least since the Eocene, apparently they only built large, rigid frameworks during the Holocene. However, Miocene barrierlike structures are known from the Podolian area of the U.S.S.R. and from Poland that were formed by vermetids, algae, and corals with lesser contributions from bryozoans and serpulids (Duncan, 1957, p. 1976; Pisera, 1985).

Serpulid (Polychaeta) Reefs. Serpulids are another important group of tube dwellers living in locally sizable aggregations similar to the vermetids. Their intertwined calcareous tubes form the organic framework of several wave-resistant reefs (Pl. 8) up to several tens of meters long and one meter thick (Andrews, 1964, summarized in Shier, 1969, pp. 500–501; Ten Hove, 1979). Most occurrences are shallow subtidal and lagoonal locations in widely separated, temperate locations; in the bays and lagoons of the Texas Gulf Coast, they thrive in brackish-hypersaline waters.

The factors contributing to mass aggregation of their tubes include certain attributes of the animals themselves (short larval period, high habitat selectivity, and larval gregariousness; Ten Hove, 1979) and lack of competition for space from other organisms.

In both vermetid and serpulid Holocene reefs, the sizes and arrangements of the tubes are similar and the associated low diversity macrofauna includes bivalves (*Crassostrea* and *Mytilus*) and barnacles.

Beus (1980) described small (0.5 m thick; 1.5 m dia) frameworks consisting of intergrown serpulid tubes from Upper Devonian rocks of central Arizona; Burchette and Riding (1977) described their presence in slightly larger reefs in the Carboniferous, Jurassic, and Miocene. Serpulids are also locally abundant in reef-associated Cretaceous limestones in Texas (Pl. 8*b*).

Bryozoan Reefs. In the shallow (<2-m), brackish waters of the Netherlands' coast, reefs built primarily by Bryozoa (*Electra curstulenta* with locally significant contributions by *Alcyonella fungosa*) are present in tidal channels and "lakes." The growth rate of *E. curstulenta* is exceedingly rapid; some zoaria exceed 10 m in diameter and 1 m in thickness and provide shelter and a firm substrate for hydroids, nudibranchs (Gastropoda), polychaetes, crustaceans, and fishes (Boekschoten and Bijma, 1982).

Summary. Most Holocene low diversity reefs with rigid organic frameworks are formed by gregarious animals with calcareous skeletons cemented to the substrate. They are most common in shallow, turbid coastal embayments of non-normal marine salinity where they appear to be protected from destruction by high surf and stenohaline predators. Whether or not these same environmental parameters, especially depth and salinity, can be extrapolated to comparable low diversity fossil reefs remains to be tested.

Stromatolites and Algal Crusts

The roles of blue–green (Cyanophyta) and green (Chlorophyta) algae in the formation of stromatolitic reefs have varied a great deal through geologic history. (The term algae is used here in the informal sense of plants lacking true roots, stems, and leaves.) A major complicating factor in the recognition of such reefs is the degree of rigidity and topographic relief that these organisms can impart to the living structure.

Holocene algae belonging to several higher taxa appear to be incapable of forming a skeleton by precipitation of $CaCO_3$, either on the cell wall or in the mucilaginous sheath surrounding the cells. However, there are a very few living non-marine cyanophytes and perhaps several extinct marine forms whose physiology does include precipitation of calcareous filament sheaths. In addition, the cyanophytes may create microenvironments conducive to inorganic precipitation of tubular sheaths surrounding the cell walls (Pratt, 1979, Fig. 4C) or they may live in environments (especially intertidal to supratidal) where microcrystalline cements are inorganically precipitated in the pore spaces between the algal filaments (Dalrymple, 1965) much like the cement in beachrock (Pratt, 1979, Table 2 and Fig. 4 B,C). The role of cyanophytes in creating calcified filament sheaths may involve either increased pH or reduced CO_2 partial pressure due to photosynthesis (Wray, 1977, pp. 25–26) but these factors may be of less importance in calcification of sheaths than the effects of sulfate-reducing bacteria. Occurrences of inorganic calcification of non-skeletal algal sheaths have been described from shallow, non-marine (usually hypersaline) environments and unusual substrate mineralogy (Lyons et al., 1984).

In both these situations (filament sheaths and pore cements), the structures produced are most commonly small nodules which, as fossils, are known from rocks as old as Precambrian and called *Girvanella* (Rezak, 1957b, Pl. 1), *Sphaerocodium* (Wray, 1977, Figs. 18, 19), *Ortonella* or "Porostromata" by some other authors. The largest pore-cemented Holocene stromatolites are the semilithified club-shaped forms (about 2 m tall) in intertidal locations at Shark Bay, Western Australia (Logan, 1961; Logan et al., 1974). Even larger stromatolites occur in the fossil record (Rezak, 1957a; Playford et al., 1976).

At shallow subtidal depths, dasycladacean and cyanophytic algae are forming rigid, topographically positive stromatolites in water of marine salinity in the Bahama Islands (Dravis, 1983). In this case, ooids in suspension are trapped by the algae in a layered matlike arrangement. Soon after the death of the algae, their filaments are encased in precipitated high-Mg calcite cement which creates the rigid inorganic framework of these stromatolites.

In both the Shark Bay and Bahamas examples of rigid Holocene stromatolites, it is uncertain but quite unlikely that any direct or inconclusive indirect evidence of algal filaments would be present if they were to become fossils. Thus, they would be like the vast majority of fossil stromatolites, which also lack any proof of rigidity achieved by early calcification of either filament sheaths or pores. Typical fossil stromatolites appear only as thinly laminated lime mudstones; because their algal origin is difficult or impossible to determine, some authors have also called them "cryptalgal limestones" or "Spongiostromata" rather than stromatolites (see Glossary). Similarly laminated rocks can also be formed by bacteria or by purely inorganic processes (Multer and Hoffmeister, 1968).

The terminology to distinguish among these highly varied cyanophyte-built structures is quite diverse and not uniform, except for the well-understood stromatolites. In the context of this volume, stromatolites displaying evidence of early rigidity and topographic relief are termed *framework stromatolitic* reefs (Table 1.1). Although the diversity in most Holocene (Ginsburg, 1960; Gebelein, 1969) and in some ancient stromatolites is remarkably high (e.g., Schopf, 1977, Table 2), the vast majority of ancient stromatolites provide no evidence of their original biotic diversity.

Most Holocene stromatolites owe their existence and rigidity to their intertidal location in hypersaline waters and therefore are almost surely not close environmental analogues for many of their fossil counterparts (cf. Playford and Cockbain, 1969; Fagerstrom and Burchett, 1972). Nonetheless, the fossil record contains abundant examples of large, densely packed stromatolite reefs of variable positive relief and uncertain rigidity. In addition, hardened stromatolitic/cryptalgal crusts, in conjunction with a variety of skeletal invertebrates, have been major contributors to numerous other reefs, especially in the late Paleozoic and early Mesozoic.

Stromatolites exemplify the problems created by definitions and classifications aimed at categorizing a natural spectrum. A few Holocene stromatolites have calcified filament sheaths or an inorganically precipitated cement framework, while others have no evidence of any framework; the proportion of framework fossil stromatolites to non-framework stromatolites and cryptalgal limestones appears to be very small. In addition, the restricted environmental settings for virtually all Holocene stromatolites and cryptalgal limestones appear to be refugia to escape herbivore grazing (especially gastropods) and are rather poor analogues for structures formed by skeletal and non-skeletal Cyanophyta and Chlorophyta in the stratigraphic record.

WHAT IS NOT A REEF?

> . . .the word reef in geologic literature means *nothing*, unless each occurrence
> is accurately described, and this is seldom the case.
>
> (Cumings, 1932, p. 332)

Examples

Numerous and varied organic concentrations, both Holocene and ancient,
have been ascribed to reefs but are excluded here for one or more reasons.
These reasons include lack of a rigid framework or topographic relief,
small size, organisms not *in situ* and in growth position, and lack of colonial or gregarious growth habit or of calcareous or siliceous skeletons.

Sabellid "Reefs"

Multer and Milliman (1967), Gram (1968), and Kirtley and Tanner (1968)
have described reefs as structures produced by very dense aggregations
of tube-dwelling polychaetes (Family Sabelliidae; Pl. 6b). These structures
are semirigid, topographically elevated, and nearly worldwide in distribution; the best known are found in western Europe and Florida where
they are largely confined to shallow (<10 m), turbulent, and turbid water.
Near Mont-Saint-Michel, France, such "worm reefs" reach thicknesses of
6 m, cover areas up to 30 km², and locally restrict estuarine tidal flows.

The sabellids capture suspended sand grains (chiefly quartz) and build
their tubes by cementing the grains to the tube aperture with mucus.
Upon death of the worm, the organic cement is destroyed and so these
sabellid-built structures are unknown in the fossil record.

Shell Heaps

Ridge and moundlike heaps or storm beaches of current-transported whole
and fragmented shells are common features of the supratidal to shallow
subtidal zones of many shorelines. The shells may be very densely packed
(coquina). However, such shell heaps lack initial rigidity, are generally
of low taxonomic diversity (because of current sorting), the shells are not
in growth position, and most bivalves are disarticulated.

Mud Mounds

In shallow subtidal locations in the Florida Keys, Florida Bay, and the
Bahamas, where there are local sources of abundant lime mud and restricted water movements, the upright growth of the roots and blades of
mangroves *(Rhizophora)* and grasses *(Thallassia)* reduces current velocities (baffling) and then traps the deposited fine sands and muds among
their roots (Swinchatt, 1965; Scoffin, 1970; Turmel and Swanson, 1976).

The areas of abundant mangroves and grasses contain more mud (up
to 70%) in the surface and near-surface sediment than adjacent areas

(50% sand). The processes of current baffling and sediment trapping have apparently been active for about 10,000 years and have produced frameless, low relief mounds or banks of mud and partially decayed organic matter as much as 7 m thick. The trapped mud, roots, rhizomes, and blades have undergone minimal natural compaction and cementation, but mechanical compaction experiments (Shinn and Robbin, 1983) indicate that the plant materials would produce subhorizontal carbon-rich layers. Upon complete decay, these layers might be lost entirely from the geologic record, leaving only an ill-defined mass of lime mud having varied degrees of increased thickness compared with the adjacent contemporaneous sandier rocks. Hoffmeister and Multer (1965) used the term "reef" to describe a similar accumulation of semi-indurated mud and mangrove roots (dated at 1000–2000 years BP) from southern Florida. This same general baffling and trapping mechanism for lime muds has been invoked to interpret the origin of large numbers of ancient (especially Paleozoic) frameless, mud-rich, fossil-poor mounds and banks commonly called "mud mounds."

Although the time of origin of mangroves and marine grasses is uncertain, it is highly unlikely that they were the baffles and traps in any pre–Late Cretaceous mud mounds. Many of the Paleozoic "mounds" are surprisingly well-defined in outcrop and their stratigraphic relations suggest that they had greater initial topographic relief than their possible Holocene Florida analogues (Pray, 1958). The sediment trapping and binding role of stromatolite-forming blue–green algae has been used by Pratt (1982) in the interpretation of many Paleozoic mud mounds. Kauffman and Sohl (1974, p. 401) have suggested such an origin for all of the "classic examples" of the Cretaceous "rudist reefs" of the Tethyan Realm. Lane (1971, pp. 1438–1440) invoked the same general mode of origin for most of the crinoid-rich lenses (reefs of some authors) of bioclastic debris in the late Paleozoic; in these structures the pelmatozoan columns played the role of baffles.

Typically, ancient mud mounds interfinger with laterally extended "aprons" of skeletal debris that dip as bedded flank deposits away from the topographically positive massive reef core. In many cases it can be demonstrated that the core was the source of the apron skeletal debris as well as any associated larger limestone blocks derived from of the core itself.

Minimum Size

Among Holocene photic and aphotic zone reef systems there is an unbroken size gradation from isolated solitary corals, to weakly colonial, to strongly colonial coralla of various sizes, to clusters of large, massive coralla, to coral knolls, knoll reefs, and patch reefs ending with entire reef systems. The proportion of coral-covered to sediment-covered areas of reef systems is highly varied but seldom exceeds 0.3. Across this size spectrum there is little agreement of a minimum value for use of the term "reef" (cf. coral knoll or reef knoll) among workers studying Holocene reefs and even less among those studying ancient ones (Braithwaite, 1973, p. 1109).

In Squires' (1964, pp. 904–906) discussion of the growth of aphotic zone reefs, size and shape limits for each of his types were not defined; it is possible, though, to make some comparisons from his illustration. These reef types range from about 6 m in diameter and 1 m high ("thicket" of Squires), to about 15 × 1.5 m ("coppice"), to about 20 × 2 m ("bank"), to more than 600 × 15 m ("old bank"). Numerous other authors adopted these same terms but used them for reefs (both Holocene and ancient and photic and aphotic zone) of quite different sizes and shapes. The concept of minimum size and shape for ancient reefs is considerably more subjective than for Holocene reefs because of poor or incomplete exposure (Nelson et al., 1962, pp. 241–242). However, it is clear that the term "reef" has commonly been used for much smaller ancient structures (Pls. 9a; 10a; 40a) than for the Holocene.

There is also a close relation between taxonomic diversity, collecting intensity and sample size, and reef size (discussed in Chap. 5), and all of these factors may be involved in distinguishing reefs from non-reefs. Nonetheless, with comparable collecting intensities and sample sizes, reef diversity is generally higher than level-bottom diversity.

In conclusion, there appears to be no generally accepted minimum size concept for reefs of any age (Holocene/ancient) or location (open ocean/shelf or photic/aphotic) and so no attempt will be made here to define

TABLE 1.2. A Hierarchy of Characteristics of Holocene Reefs and the Nature of Their Expression in "Non-reefs."

Reefs (Including Stromatolites)	"Non-reefs" (Including Cryptalgal Structures)
1. Rigid; framework present	1. Not rigid; framework absent
2. Skeletons or other calcareous microstructures (filaments; pore cement) abundant; skeletons large, colonial, or gregarious; intergrown in living position	2. Nature, abundance, and orientation of skeletons variable
3. Positive topographic relief	3. Topographic relief variable; may be positive
4. Framework organisms have rapid growth rates	4. Growth rates of organisms variable but commonly slow
5. Taxonomic diversity high; includes several ecological functional groups	5. Diversity variable but usually lower than for reefs.

minimum size. Reefs are usually large enough to modify the local environment in ways that will increase diversity to a level higher than the diversity of the adjacent substrate.

Biostrome

The term "biostrome" (Cumings, 1932) is of geological origin and its use is almost always confined to ancient rocks. However, even among geologists there is great lack of uniformity in usage of the terms reef, bioherm (see Glossary), and biostrome.

Cumings defined two attributes of biostromes that are of special importance: (1) they are "distinctly bedded" and (2) "they don't swell into lenslike or reeflike form." Implicit in this definition is that their upper and lower surfaces are flat and parallel; if they had original topographic relief it was minimal. Thus, an ideal biostrome has a shape that is quite different from a reef, but accurate shape determination and stratigraphic relations in both reefs and biostromes strongly depend on the size, shape, and completeness of outcrops; the presence or absence of bedding may be very subjective near the margins of ancient reefs. Furthermore, some biostromes are simply extensions of the concept of transported shell and reef debris to depositional settings at greater distances from reefs than the dipping bedded flanks.

CONCLUSIONS

There is a hierarchy of features that characterize reefs and are generally absent or highly modified in non-reefs (Table 1.2). Numerous aspects of the hierarchy are subjective and the author has no illusions that they will be accepted by all biologists and geologists. If they have value, it may be that they combine characteristics used by both groups of researchers and are predicated on two assumptions: (1) a reef does not cease to be a reef when it dies and is buried in sediment and (2) many features of Holocene reefs are not present in ancient reefs (never were present or were lost during diagenesis) or their expression has changed during their geologic history.

2

Cenozoic Reef Models I

OCCURRENCE

The bathymetric and geographic distribution of reefs are highly dependent on the ways they are defined. There is a strong bias among Holocene workers and many geologists to define reefs in ways that restrict them to structures in the photic zone in warm waters (Point A, Fig. 2.1) of the equatorial realm (Fig. 2.2). However, this restriction is debatable even for the Holocene; it also becomes highly interpretive for ancient reefs and does not accommodate the spectrum of reefs characterized in Chapter 1.

BATHYMETRY AND GEOGRAPHY

The data of Figure 2.1 indicate that Holocene coral-dominated reefs are remarkably broad in their thermal and bathymetric ranges and that their occurrence roughly follows the general bathymetric thermal gradient. It is also important to note that except for Points A–D, these reef areas are located considerably beyond the latitudinal limits of the general tropical photic zone reef belt (Fig. 2.2). Furthermore, the bathymetric ranges of the reef areas in Figure 2.1 show an almost continuous and overlapping succession extending from the low tide line to nearly 1500 m. Also, the apparent bathymetric, and in many cases the thermal tolerance limits for aphotic zone reefs far exceed these parameters for shallow, tropical reefs.

Among photic zone tropical reefs there is an *inverse* relation between the overall vigor of the reef and water depth. Maximum biologic activity takes place in the upper 10 m; most large reefs are in the upper 25 m. At 50 m, the diversity of coral species is decreased to about half the maximum and at 100 m the species reduction is 90%. Thus, there is a gradual

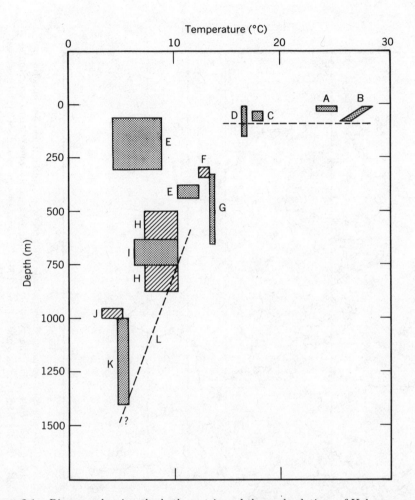

Figure 2.1.   Diagram showing the bathymetric and thermal relations of Holocene coral-dominated reefs. Data for Points A–L as follows: A. Optima for shallow water, tropical; reefs *sensu stricto* of numerous authors; B. Coral Sea Plateau (Orme, 1977); C. A "drowned" Pleistocene reef, Gulf of Mexico (Ludwick and Walton, 1957); D. East coast, Florida (Reed, 1980, 1983); E. Norway (Teichert, 1958); F. Campbell Plateau (Squires, 1965; Maksimova, 1972); G. Mediterranean (Teichert, 1958); H. Blake Plateau (Stetson et al., 1962); I. Florida Strait (Neumann et al., 1977); J. Ireland–France (Teichert, 1958); K. Bahamas (Mullins et al., 1981); L. Eastern Atlantic (Le Danaois, 1948). Maximum reported depth for non-reef corals is 6200 m (Cairns and Stanley, 1981). Dashed line at about 80–90 m marks approximate bathymetric limit for flourishing growth of calcareous algae in tropical and subtropical waters.

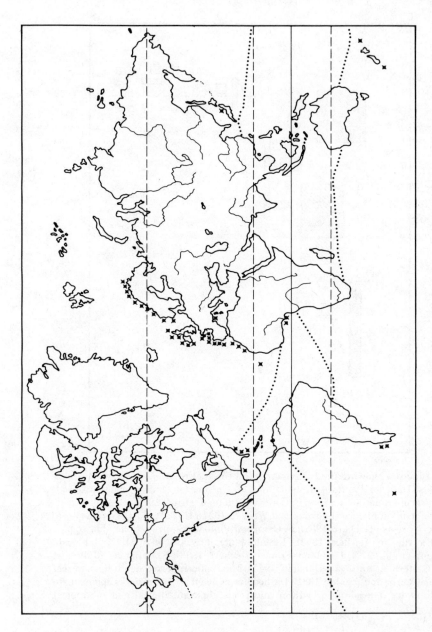

Figure 2.2. Geographic distribution of Holocene coral-dominated photic zone reefs (between dotted lines) and aphotic zone reef areas (crosses). Data sources: (photic zone) Wells, 1957; Emery et al., 1954, Plate 72; (aphotic zone) Cairns and Stanley, 1981, with additions from Pruvot, 1894, 1895, for Mediterranean, and Squires, 1964, for Japanese continental shelf. The decreased width of the tropical photic zone reef belt in the eastern Atlantic and Pacific Oceans is due to the weaker trade winds in these areas (allowing the doldrums to encroach on the equator) and the presence of upwelling cold currents.

18

reduction in vigor rather than a sharp lower bathymetric limit (Wells, 1967, p. 350). Stoddart (1969, pp. 442–443) and numerous other authors regard attenuation of light intensity with depth as the critical control limiting biologic activity in these reefs.

Interestingly, Goreau et al. (1979) have noted that there is a significant difference in the lower limit of active coral growth in photic zone reefs between the Pacific (60 m) and the Caribbean (100 m); they have speculated that the reason is more intense coral predation in the deeper Pacific reef waters.

Coral-dominated reefs in the Red Sea extend from the photic zone to depths of 122 m, where winter temperatures are about 22°C and light intensity is only 0.5% of surface intensity (Fricke and Hottinger, 1983). Although the deep water reefs are small (5 m dia; 2 m high), two coral species have built a rigid framework that provides niches for a diverse benthos, including brown and coralline red algae, foraminifera, sponges, at least five other coral species, bryozoans, vermetids, and barnacles.

Reed (1980) sampled a succession of small coral-dominated reefs growing on ledges and other prominences off the east coast of Florida and found a *direct* relationship between coral vigor and depth; that is, the largest coralla and reefs are present at 101 m where upwelling current velocities are greatest. Both Fricke and Hottinger and Reed concluded that currents, not depth or temperature, control the vigor and distribution of these reefs by providing food to the predominant suspension feeders and mud that settles among the upright invertebrate skeletons to increase their support.

Although corals in the area of the Coral Sea Plateau live only in the upper 50–55 m, there are flourishing reefs with crustose red algae, sponges, and sediment-baffling and trapping antipatharians and gorgonaceans to depths of 140 m (Orme, 1977a). Squires (1965) described large coral-dominated structures up to 40 m tall off New Zealand with their tops nearly 300 m below the surface.

Continuing to progressively deeper water, Neumann et al. (1977) described rigid structures up to 100 m long and 50 m high in the Straits of Florida in water 600–900 m deep that are dominated by varied branching corals, sponges, unstalked crinoids, and alcyonarians. Mullins et al. (1981) recognized mound-shaped coral reefs on the north slope of Little Bahama Bank at depths of 900–1300 m. These structures are covered with at least 16 species of weakly branched and solitary corals and are separated by gravity flow deposits originating near the bank margin.

The most prolific development of aphotic zone coral reefs appears to be along the eastern Atlantic continental shelf margin and upper slope from northern Norway to northwestern Africa (Fig. 2.2). According to Teichert (1958), the minimum depth for reef growth in Norwegian waters is 60 m with the optimum between 200 and 300 m. Joubin (1922) recognized 110 aphotic zone coral reefs in the eastern Atlantic with the maximum depth at 2800 m.

From increased biological sampling from these deep-water coral-dominated reefs has come the realization that algae can survive and locally fluorish at surprising depths and that the bathymetric and thermal limits of some of these corals are enormously greater than for typical photic zone tropical corals. Hillis-Colinvaux (1984) reported living *Halimeda* at 140 m and encrusting red calcareous algae at 200 m on the reefs at Enewetak Atoll, Marshall Islands. Examples of remarkable bathymetric and thermal ranges of some important deep-water coral species include: (1) *Lophelia prolifera* (temperatures: 0.3–13.6°C; Maksimova, 1972, p. 765); (2) *L. pertusa,* 130–400 m (Wilson, 1979, p. 169); (3) *Caryophyllia smithii,* lower shore to at least 230 m (Wilson, 1975, p. 617); (4) species of the delicate, solitary genus *Fungicyathus* range from 60 to 5800 m (temperatures: 0.5–26.5°C; Wells, 1967, p. 353). These data strongly suggest that neither depth nor temperature is the chief control over the occurrence of aphotic zone corals.

Stetson et al. (1962, p. 4) summarized features common to corals that dominate deep-water reefs: (1) they are colonial with individual coralla up to several meters in diameter and height; (2) coralla are branching (arborescent to dendroid) with relatively thin, fragile branches; and (3) branches form by asexually budded polyps growing upward from a single point of attachment to the substrate.

Coates and Kauffman (1973, p. 964) and Squires (1959) have provided some generalizations regarding aphotic zone reefs: (1) they are located near rich sources of suspended biotic nutrients such as upwelling currents; in fact, such currents appear to be the chief control over their occurrences; (2) coral diversity is low; commonly only one or two species dominate the assemblage (most belong to *Lophelia, Dendrophyllia,* and *Madrepora*); (3) their overall rates of accretion are slow but steady compared with photic zone reefs; (4) currents are strong enough to transport suspended mud to be baffled and trapped by the surface organisms but generally too weak to transport the shells of the macrobenthos; (5) physical destruction by currents and biologic destruction by boring organisms is minimal, but there may be significant production of skeletal sediments from grazing by fishes and crustaceans; and (6) death of these reefs may be the result of rapid burial in sediment, rapid temperature change, or development of anoxic conditions.

Causal factors that limit the occurrence of photic zone reefs to low latitudes include temperature, light intensity, and competition from non-skeletal macroalgae. In areas where such reefs encroach upon the latitudinal limits of the tropical reef belt, there appears to be competition for light between the calcareous algae and zooxanthallate corals (see below) of the reef and the large fronds of the macroalgae, such as *Eucheuma, Laurencia, Sargassum,* and *Turbinaria.* Thus, shade from the floating fronds may inhibit vigorous reef growth and may be important in confining reefs to low latitudes (Crossland, 1981; Wiebe et al., 1981). It is clear that coral-dominated reefs have extended bathymetric and geographic ranges and are not confined to the warm, shallow water of the circum-equatorial tropical realm. Coral density in some deep-water reefs is high enough to produce local environmental gradients comparable to those in well-developed shallow, tropical reefs (Squires, 1959, p. 375).

Deep-water coral reefs have rarely been reported from the stratigraphic record; Cairns and Stanley (1981) recognized just eight occurrences from the Triassic to Tertiary. The paucity of these structures may be partly due to the lack of good criteria for their recognition or to the strong bias of most paleoecologists toward shallow tropical reefs. With increasing awareness of the importance of Holocene deep-water reefs and perhaps with more study, some other ancient reefs will be reinterpreted as deep-water. However, at this stage, the paucity of deep-water ancient reefs relative to shallow-water reefs appears to be real.

SYMBIOSIS

Symbiosis is a state of affairs in which organisms live together for mutual benefit in such close relationship that each has lost at least some degree of physiological independence.

(Gotto, 1969, p. 16)

In the sea there is a full spectrum of degrees of physiological union among organisms, but in reef communities they appear to be more common and of greater importance to the success of the community than in other types of marine communities. The symbioses between the vegetative stage of endosymbiotic dinoflagellates commonly called *zooxanthellae* and several higher invertebrate taxa are exceedingly important in photic zone reef ecosystems. The dinoflagellates have been identified as the species *microadriaticum* and variously assigned to the genera *Gymnodinium, Symbiodinium,* and *Zooxanthella* of some authors. Endosymbionts occur in the coccoid vegetative state, whereas cells isolated from hosts and maintained in culture alternate between the coccoid state and a gymnodinoid motile state. Other algal symbionts include cyanophytes and filamentous chlorophytes, but their importance to the success of photic zone reefs is of much less significance than the zooxanthellae.

Zooxanthellae–Scleractinian Symbiosis

In the coral polyp the zooxanthellae are concentrated (up to 30,000 cells/ mm^3) inside the cells of the endoderm. The distribution of zooxanthellae in a colonial coral is not uniform; the whitish tips of actively growing coral branches have far fewer zooxanthellae than the darker, older part of the colony. The abundance of zooxanthellae within the polyps is inversely proportional to depth and also related to coral taxonomy and the apparent "health" of the polyp; physiologically stressed polyps expel zooxanthellae into the coelenteron, and complete loss of zooxanthellae commonly precedes polyp death. Even coral larvae (planulae) contain zooxanthellae!

Odum and Odum (1955) recognized two forms of living algae in the coral polyp and skeleton. They estimated that filaments of chlorophytes in the skeletal pores have a much higher biomass than the zooxanthellae; also, the total algal biomass in the polyp and skeleton exceeds the animal biomass by a factor of 3. In just the polyp tissue, the ratio of animal to plant protein is about 0.7–1.2, which means that the polyp is about half algal (Muscatine, 1973, p. 98). By contrast, Sorokin (1981, Table 1) determined that the zooxanthellae biomass is only about 0.5–3% of the total polyp biomass.

In reef ecosystems, the zooxanthellae play important roles in carbon (inorganic and organic), nitrogen, and phosphorus fixation. The waste products of polyp respiration are used by the zooxanthellae, and the efficiency of this element recycling appears to be one of the keys to the success of the symbiotic association as well as the entire reef ecosystem.

The fixation of carbon is based on the photosynthesis–respiration reaction (metabolism) which in its simplest form can be expressed as

$$6CO_2 + 6H_2O = C_6H_{12}O_6 + 6O_2 \qquad (2.1)$$

The amount of organic carbon fixed by the zooxanthellae exceeds the requirement for their respiration, growth, and reproduction (Muscatine et al., 1981); therefore, part of the surplus (up to half of the photosynthetically fixed carbon; Chalker, 1983, p. 29) is translocated in soluble compounds (chiefly glycerol, alanine, and glucose) to the polyps and is used by them in the synthesis of lipids. The lipids in turn appear to be a major energy source for the polyps. Davies (1984, Figs. 2, 5) has diagrammatically shown the energy pathways and budget of a typical zooxanthellate coral; he estimated that about 51% of the energy fixed by the zooxanthellae is used in respiration by the algal–animal system; 48% is lost from the system as surplus zooxanthellae expelled by the polyp or as mucus; and only 1% is used for growth.

The production of free oxygen is the other aspect of the photosynthetic reaction that is important in symbioses. As long ago as 1932, Yonge et al. demonstrated that the ratio of gross oxygen produced to net oxygen consumed by zooxanthellate corals in shallow water is about 2–3. Net oxygen produced depends on several factors, but especially light intensity (depth) and the areal exposure of the zooxanthellae. Thus, in branching coralla with high surface/volume ratios, light is available to more zooxanthellae. The excess oxygen produced by the zooxanthellae is dissolved in the water for use by the other organisms or, in oxygen-saturated water, the oxygen is lost to the atmosphere. Non-zooxanthellate aphotic zone corals show no effects of oxygen deficiency, so it is reasonable to assume that the importance to the coral of oxygen production by zooxanthellae is less than carbon fixation (equation 2.1).

Zooxanthellae are also indirectly involved in the formation of skeletal $CaCO_3$ by the coral. Apparently, the uptake of CO_2 by the zooxanthellae for photosynthesis increases the rate of $CaCO_3$ precipitation by altering the carbonate–bicarbonate–carbon dioxide system (see Chemical Factors, Chap. 3). The rate of skeleton formation in photic zone zooxanthellate corals in nearly all cases studied exceeds the rate for non-zooxanthellate corals regardless of depth (see Growth Rates, Chap. 3). However, the lack of zooxanthellae in aphotic zone corals does not prevent the formation of deep-water reefs in locations having adequate currents for an abundant and constant supply of suspended zooplankton available to the corals. Understanding the importance of the role of the zooxanthellae in skeleton formation is further complicated by the fact that the non-skeletal jellyfish, anemones (Order Actinaria), and zoantharians in both the shallow-water reef zone and temperate zone contain zooxanthellae, appear to be physiologically similar to the zooxanthellate scleractinians and yet are not involved in skeleton formation.

The system for cycling compounds of nitrogen and phosphorus between the zooxanthellae and the polyps is very efficient, largely due to the absence of a cellulose cell wall in the zooxanthellae and the relatively uniform chemical and physical aspects of the reef environment (Leletkin and Zvalinsky, 1981). In fact, the efficiency of this system is the primary basis for virtually all of the differences between photic and aphotic zone reefs. Corals and other lower invertebrates rely on diffusion to remove their metabolic wastes (soluble CO_2, PO_4, NO_3, SO_4), but in those containing symbiotic algae some of the essential nutrient elements are retained and recycled within the algal–animal system. The polyps' dissolved metabolic wastes are taken up by the zooxanthellae and used in the synthesis of carbohydrates. The carbohydrates then become an energy source for the zooxanthellae to synthesize amino acids, proteins, and fats (including lipids), all potential energy sources for polyp metabolism. Despite the relatively low biomass of the zooxanthellae, they are so productive that they can provide most of the metabolic requirements of the polyps. Sorokin (1981) found that the ratio of photosynthetic oxygen production to zooxanthellae biomass for many common Great Barrier Reef corals is about 2–4/d; that is, carbohydrate production, as measured by oxygen production (equation 2.1), is remarkably high in relation to the low biomass of the producers.

However, the relatively high metabolic rate of the polyps and the loss of polyp metabolites to the seawater require periodic addition of nitrogen and phosphorus from zooplankton sources. Shortages of these nutrient elements for use by the zooxanthellae appear to limit polyp growth more than shortages of either energy or carbon. Thus, the availability of zooplankton to the coral polyp strongly influences the flux of carbon, nitrogen, and phosphorus to the zooxanthellae and thus the growth of the coral polyps and skeleton. Sorokin (1981) estimated that of the total coral energy requirements, 71% comes from photosynthetic fixation by the zooxanthellae, 17% by predation on the zooplankton (carnivory), and 22% from absorption of dissolved organic matter and bacteria (herbivory).

Occasionally, the productivity of the zooxanthellae exceeds the productivity of the polyp and the excess zooxanthellae must either be digested or expelled by the polyp. Numerous authors have suggested that digestion of zooxanthellae may be a major part of the total polyp diet, but no proof of algal digestion has yet been presented. It also has been suggested that the zooxanthellae–coral symbiosis represents a complete autotrophic–heterotrophic system. However, such carbon autotrophy is only possible in shallow water; Davies (1977) found that at depths greater than about 40 m, *Montastraea* spp. could obtain only about 50% of its carbon requirement from zooxanthellate photosynthesis, with the remainder coming from other sources.

The light available for photosynthesis affects the autotrophic input to the polyp. Photoadaptation (increased concentration of photosynthetic pigments in low light) by the zooxanthellae stabilizes this input and also increases the range of environments (especially depth) in which corals can survive.

The concentration of zooxanthellae also appears to change with both biological and physical environmental stresses. Experimental data indicate that when zooplankton in suspension are limiting, the zooxanthellae represent a potential carbon reservoir for the polyp. But when suspended food sources are abundant, the polyps can live very successfully in darkness without zooxanthellae. However, if zooxanthellate corals are deprived of planktonic sources of carbon, nitrogen, and phosphorus, they may extrude the zooxanthellae and die, indicating that the polyps cannot subsist solely on zooxanthellae. Furthermore, stresses due to fluctuating temperature or salinity (Jaap, 1985) result in changes in zooxanthellae concentrations. Therefore, the zooxanthellae–scleractinian symbiosis is not static and changes may have enormous ramifications in shallow-water reef ecosystems. Unfortunately, such changes are difficult to detect in ancient ecosystems.

In summary, the zooxanthellae–scleractinian symbiosis is mutually beneficial and of major importance to the vigorous growth and overall success of photic zone reefs. However, absence of this symbiosis has not prevented the growth of reefs in the aphotic zone. Benefits to the zooxanthellae include protection from herbivores and ready access to sources of carbon, nitrogen, and phosphorus. Benefits to the coral include ready access to sources of oxygen and organic carbon compounds (especially lipids) as well as aid in skeleton formation and perhaps digestion of zooxanthellae as supplemental food.

Hermatypic/Ahermatypic Corals

The term hermatypic . . . is therefore proposed to describe corals of the reef-building type, the living species of which possess symbiotic zooxanthellae within their tissues. In contrast to this term, ahermatypic is proposed to describe the corals of the non-reef-building type, the living forms of which do not possess zooxanthellae and which live under greatly varying conditions of depth, temperature and light.

(Wells, 1933, p. 27)

Ever since this distinction between hermatypic and ahermatypic was proposed, nearly all authors have also accepted what seem to be its logical corollaries, namely: (1) non-zooxanthellate corals do not build reefs; (2) all zooxanthellate corals build reefs; and (3) all coral reefs, both Holocene and ancient, are confined to the photic zone. (This author prefers the "zooxanthellate/non-zooxanthellate" terminology of Rosen [1981, p. 106] to "zooxanthellate/azooxanthellate" of Schuhmacher and Zibrowius [1985, p. 6], for reasons of priority.) Unfortunately, considerable confusion has developed because both Wells' definition and the corollaries are not absolutely true (Schuhmacher and Zibrowius, 1985).

Examples

Although scleractinians containing symbiotic zooxanthellae are concentrated in the geographic areas of photic zone reefs, they are not confined to these areas. Furthermore, many of the zooxanthellate corals in reef areas are quite small, usually solitary, and cannot be regarded as reef-building. Conversely, non-zooxanthellate corals are present in both photic and aphotic zone reef areas and the colonial forms are the most important builders of aphotic zone reefs. In well-lighted water (4–5 m) in the Philippines, the non-zooxanthellate scleractinian *Tubastrea micranthus* grows in arborescent coralla up to 1 m high and 15 cm diameter at the base (Schuhmacher, 1984). Because of the large coralla and their unusual skeletal strength, they are important frame-builders of some reefs (i.e., they are non-zooxanthellate, photic zone hermatypic corals). Thus, although Wells' (1933) distinction between hermatypic/zooxanthellate corals and ahermatypic/non-zooxanthellate corals commonly is true for the Holocene, there are so many exceptions that modification is needed.

Evidence that zooxanthellate corals are not confined to shallow water includes:

a.   The common shallow-water reef-building, zooxanthellate scleractinians *Acropora* sp. and *Leptoseris* sp. are reportedly alive at 180 m in Palau, Caroline Islands, and to at least 460 m (8.5°C) in Hawaii (Wells, 1967, p. 350); both occurrences are within the equatorial reef belt (Fig. 2.2) but far below the base of the photic zone.

b.   At Bikini and nearby atolls, Marshall Islands, maximum generic diversity is 37 and occurs in the upper 10 m, but at 100 m (near base of photic zone) there are 11 genera of zooxanthellate corals; at 180 m, there are 7 or 8 genera; at 200 m, there are 3 genera; and 1 genus is present at 240 m (Rosen, 1975; 1977).

In a bathymetric succession of small reefs off the east coast of Florida, *Oculina varicosa* is present from near-shore (2–6 m depth) to over 100 m (Reed, 1980). During the summer, when light intensity is greatest, a few colonies of *O. varicosa* at 75–80 m contain some zooxanthellae; in deeper water, zooxanthellae are invariably absent and in shallower water they are usually present. Thus, for this species, the presence or absence of zooxanthellae appears to be controlled by depth–light relations. There are about eight or nine genera of Holocene scleractinians that contain both zooxanthellate and non-zooxanthellate species, and at still higher taxonomic levels, the separation is even less clear.

Summary

The presence, concentration, or absence of symbiotic zooxanthellae is not related to taxonomy (e.g., anemones vs. corals or even species in the same genus or individuals in same species) nor are zooxanthellate scleractinians confined to the circum-equatorial reef belt. However, the concentration of zooxanthellae is related to location within the polyp, general state of polyp "health," and the intensity of the sunlight, which, in turn, is related to water depth and turbidity and latitudinal location. Thus, the terms hermatypic and zooxanthellate are not synonyms; hermatypic should be restricted to those corals that build reefs regardless of whether they contain zooxanthellae (Table 2.1). Nonetheless, most photic zone colonial scleractinians in areas of Holocene reefs do contain zooxanthellae and in these areas the non-zooxanthellate corals are commonly small, solitary, or encrusting and are found in sheltered (cryptic) habitats. The maximum diversity of non-zooxanthellate corals is at 50–300 m (Wells, 1967, p. 353) and they rarely build reefs in water shallower than 60 m.

The base of the photic zone for non-symbiotic calcareous algae is considerably deeper than for the zooxanthellae, so that in depths of about

TABLE 2.1. Bathymetric Distribution of Hermatypic and Ahermatypic Scleractinian Corals

Depth	Zooxanthellate Corals	Non-zooxanthellate Corals
Photic zone	1. Hermatypic 2. Ahermatypic	1. Ahermatypic
---------- Approx. 100 m ----------		
Aphotic zone	Absent	1. Hermatypic 2. Ahermatypic

90–200 m the importance of calcareous algae relative to corals may increase. However, calcareous algae are usually subordinate to the non-zooxanthellate corals in aphotic zone reefs at these depths.

Of the approximately 200 genera of Holocene scleractinian corals, approximately half contain zooxanthellate individuals and species and half are non-zooxanthellate; however, of the approximately 550 Holocene species, nearly two-thirds are zooxanthellate. Table 2.2 summarizes data from numerous sources regarding chemical and physical environmental factors considered important in the distribution of Holocene scleractinians. These data clarify the highly stenotopic nature of the zooxanthellate forms compared with the remarkable eurytopism of the non-zooxanthellates. In addition, the endemism of zooxanthellate corals compared with the non-zooxanthellates is well-documented; Cairns (1979) found a direct correlation between depth for non-zooxanthellate corals and their known geographic ranges (i.e., deep-water forms had greater ranges than those in shallow water).

Wells (1967) tested the value of known bathymetric and thermal range data for several genera of Holocene non-zooxanthellate corals to estimate depth–temperature relations of Eocene–Pleistocene fossil assemblages

TABLE 2.2. Comparison of Chemical and Physical Factors Influencing the Distribution of Holocene Zooxanthellate and Non-zooxanthellate Scleractinian Corals

	Zooxanthellate	Non-zooxanthellate
Zooxanthellae	Present	Absent
Salinity (‰)		
Range	27–48	34–36
Optimum	34–36	34–36
Temperature (°C)		
Range	11–40	−1–35
Optimum	23–28	6–10
Depth (m)		
Range	High tide to ~ 150	High tide to 6200
Optimum (highest diversity)	Low tide to ~ 25	60–300
Latitude		
Range	35°N–32°S	70°N–78°S
Optimum	23°N–23°S	?

containing the same genera. The Holocene data suggest that these corals are relatively better estimators of temperature than of depth and that extrapolation of these data to congeneric corals as old as the Eocene produces broad (tens to hundreds of meters) depth estimates but relatively narrow (1–6°C) temperature range estimates.

The least conclusive of Wells' tests was of a Middle Eocene assemblage from Barbados (Fig. 2.3) containing 11 genera that he regarded as non-zooxanthellate, 5 zooxanthellate genera, and 1 genus (*Madracis*) having both non-zooxanthellate and zooxanthellate Holocene species. As expected, the presumed zooxanthellate taxa estimate depth (0–100 m) and temperature (16–27°C) to be vastly different from estimates based on the presumed non-zooxanthellates (depth, 360–400 m; temperature, 14–15°C). There are at least three explanations for this discrepancy. One possibility is that at least some of the corals never actually lived with the others, that is, the zooxanthellates may have been transported to deeper water after death. Secondly, the presumed zooxanthellate versus non-zooxanthellate distinction based on the Holocene analogue is erroneous, that is, some of the genera had different symbiotic or non-symbiotic relationships in the Eocene than now (Buddemier and Kinzie, 1976, call such Holocene taxa "aposymbiotic"). Or perhaps the depth–temperature relationships of

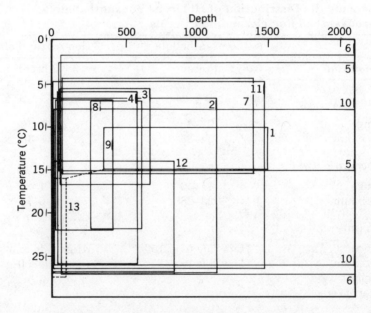

Figure 2.3. Presumed bathymetric and thermal ranges of 11 genera of non-zooxanthellate corals (numbered 1–11), 5 genera of zooxanthellates (dashed line numbered 13), and *Madracis* (numbered 12), a genus with both non-zooxanthellate species and zooxanthellate Holocene species. (From Wells, 1967.)

the Holocene simply do not apply to their Eocene ancestors, that is, the tolerance limits have altered through geologic time.

Other Algal–Animal Symbioses

There are at least 150 genera of non-scleractinian invertebrates that are symbiotic with algae, including foraminifera, sponges, anemones and other coelenterates and bivalves. The algae involved are cyanophytes, chlorophytes (rarely), and zooxanthellae (most common); ingested chloroplasts may also be involved and have been mistaken for zooxanthellae. In these associations, the algal–animal physiology is essentially the same as for the zooxanthellae–scleractinian symbiosis described above, but in a few cases the photosynthetic efficiency and the translocation rates of the metabolites are even higher for the non-scleractinians than for the scleractinians.

Foraminiferida
Several species of both planktic and benthic foraminifera (mostly in the Families Scritidae and Alveolinidae) contain zooxanthellae. C. S. Ross (1972) found that actively swimming (flagellate) *Gymnodinium* spp. appeared to be concentrated in the vicinity of the relatively large foram *Marginopora vertebralis* as if there was perhaps an attraction between them. Non-flagellate ellipsoids of the same general appearance as the external *Gymnodinium* are present in large numbers inside the nearly transparent chamberlets of the foram test. Chalker (1983, p. 36) found a similar relation between the zooxanthellae and *Heterostegina depressa* and believed the symbiosis to be completely autotrophic. Cowen (1983, pp. 454–456) reviewed the evidence for algal symbioses among a variety of "larger" reef-dwelling fossil foraminifera, including the late Paleozoic Fusulinacea and several Cretaceous–Miocene discoidal higher taxa.

Porifera
Among Holocene reefs, sponges are second to corals in terms of their contribution to total benthic faunal biomass; their symbiosis with algae may be nearly as prevalent as in corals. The physiological importance of the symbiosis to the sponges appears comparable to corals except that the symbionts in sponges are only minimally involved in skeletal secretion.

At Davies Reef, Great Barrier Reef, 9 of the 10 most common sponge species contain symbiotic cyanophytes (both uni- and multicellular), about 80% of the individual sponges contain cyanophytes, and cyanophyte–sponge symbionts make up about 80% of the benthic biomass to depths of 20 m (Wilkinson, 1983). At Discovery Bay, Jamaica, Pang (1973) discovered three species of zooxanthellate sponges growing on the two most abundant shallow-water (0–30 m) coral species (*Acropora palmata, A. cervicornis*). Just as in the case of corals, the abundance of sponge symbionts is inversely proportional to depth and directly related to sponge surface area exposed to sunlight. At Discovery Bay, all three zooxanthellate sponges are encrusting forms and two of them commonly overgrow their substrate completely.

At Davies Reef, maximum sponge biomass occurs at 20 m. Of the 10 sponge species investigated by Wilkinson (1983) from this depth, 7 have photosynthesis/respiration ratios greater than 1 (under experimental conditions) and in 6 species the ratio exceeds 3. Furthermore, the phototropic efficiency of symbiotic sponges and corals appears to be nearly the same.

Others

In addition to the zooxanthellate jellyfish, anemones, and zoantharians noted above, zooxanthellae also are present in some Antipatharia and Gorgonacea with calcareous spicules. Flourishing gorgonian growth in shallow water seems to be as dependent on the presence of zooxanthellae as does flourishing coral growth. Just as with corals, non-zooxanthellate gorgonians and antipatharians are very successful inhabitants of aphotic zone reefs but unlike corals, they contribute nothing to the skeletal framework.

Dense concentrations of zooxanthellae within the tissues of the circulatory system of the common shallow-water reef bivalve *Tridacna* provide substantial amounts of photosynthetic carbon and oxygen to the bivalve. Earlier authors believed that the "farmed" zooxanthellae were digested by *Tridacna,* but subsequent studies (e.g., Trench et al., 1981) suggest that this may not be true. In addition, other herbivorous bivalves and gastropods directly acquire chloroplasts which they maintain in the exposed mantle cells or store in leaflike convolutions ("solar collectors") on the exposed dorsal surface.

REEFS NOT DOMINATED BY CORALS

Algae

In the shallow subtidal waters along the margin of the Bermuda Platform, at St. Croix, U.S. Virgin Islands (Bosence, 1984) and elsewhere in the western Atlantic, there are several cup-shaped reefs up to 30 m long and 12 m high that are built by crustose red coralline algae, the encrusting calcareous hydrozoan *Millepora,* and locally by the encrusting foraminifer *Homotrema rubrum* (Ginsburg and Schroeder, 1973). Living organisms on the surface of Bermudan algal reefs are sparce but do include small corals (*Diploria* sp.; *Porites astreoides*) that elsewhere are important framebuilders.

The algal–*Millepora* framework also contains boring vermetid gastropods (two species), bivalves (seven species), and sponges (two species); the larger internal cavities are encrusted by various acorn barnacles, non-zooxanthellate corals, bryozoans, and serpulids and also contain a diverse non-encrusting assemblage of algae, foraminifera, sponges, alcyonaria, crustaceans, and the echinoid *Diadema antillarum*.

Teichert (1958) noted the occurrence of large algal structures in frigid water about 10–20 m deep well inside the Arctic Circle. In Oslo Fiord, the deepest algal crusts are at 48 m, but in the southern temperate regions Teichert remarked that corals and calcareous algae live together at 48–65 m.

In Middle Miocene reefs located east of the Holy Cross Mountains in Poland, coralline algae comprise up to 70% of the rock volume; vermetid gastropods are a distant second in abundance and are followed by bryozoans (Pisera, 1985). The assemblage is remarkably similar to the Bermudan cup reefs.

Porifera

There is no doubt that the Bermudan algal-dominated structures described above are reefs (rigidity, skeletal volume, diversity, relief, etc.), but the case for the sponge-dominated structures described by Wiedenmayer (1978; 1980a) from the Great Bahama Bank, north of Andros Island, Bahamas, is much more equivocal. These "sponge reefs" are up to 10 m in diameter, partly buried in sediment, and lack appreciable topographic relief. Species diversity is high (especially sponges) and includes gorgonians (54 species), corals (9 species), *Millepora alcycornis,* algae (green, brown, and red), foraminifera, and molluscs.

The main problem in determining whether or not these are reefs involves the relative importance of the roles of sponges as rigid framebuilders, sediment traps, and binders and as sites of early inorganic cementation. The sponge fauna includes species that burrow into and bind loose sediment, epifaunal species that bind sediment, and numerous dwelling species that are epifaunal to semi-infaunal. Most of the burrowing and semi-infaunal species have only the oscular chimneys exposed; the buried portions are as much as 2 m below the sediment surface. Sediment is trapped and bound by organisms living on the sediment surface adjacent to the chimneys, so that periodically the buried sponges extend their chimneys, establish a new laterally expanded tissue layer, and incorporate sediment within and below the new layer. The sponges involved in this expansion and sediment accretion process are not rigid, but, as seawater moves through the canal systems of some species, there appears to be very early cementation (inorganic?) so that the more mature, deeply buried sponges are quite well calcified. The final result is a rather discrete mass of non-skeletal and skeletal organisms, trapped and bound calcareous internal sediment, and calcified sponges that are quite similar to some ancient reefs and spicule-rich limestones dominated by sponges (Wieden-mayer, 1980b). Thus, the combination of a fibrous spongin/spicular skeleton, internal sediment, and early calcification may provide enough rigidity and stability to the mass and enough ecologic niches for development of a diverse fauna for the structure to be a reef. In most ancient reefs, the matters of rigidity and topographic relief can be determined by study of the laterally adjacent flanking beds, but such a study has not been completed for the Bahamian "sponge reefs."

The massive calcareous skeletons of ceratoporellid sclerosponges dominate the reef surface and are the main reef frame-builders at depths of 70–105 m at Discovery Bay, Jamaica (Lang et al., 1975; Fagerstrom, 1984). Zooxanthellate corals build the reef framework in shallower water and are present but rare below 70 m. The sclerosponge reefs also contain a diverse assemblage, including skeletal algae (*Halimeda*), encrusting foraminifera, several types of coelenterates, bryozoans, brachiopods, bivalves, serpulids, crustaceans, and echinoderms (Lang, 1974; Lang et al., 1975).

Others

Reefs dominated by masses of serpulid tubes associated with coralline algae, vermetids, barnacles, and corals occur in the Holocene of Bermuda and several localities in the Caribbean (Ten Hove, 1979); fossil reefs up to 2 m thick of the same general composition have also been reported from the Carboniferous, Jurassic, and Miocene. Flügel et al. (1984a) have described Middle Triassic "serpulid/algal/cement" reefs in Spain. Two species of serpulids are the most abundant fossils in the Spanish reefs but also contain Dasycladecea, some other problematic algae, foraminifera, and bivalves; the framework is both organic (serpulids and algae) and early inorganic cement.

In the Gulf of Aqaba on the shelf off the Sinai Peninsula, Egypt, at depths of 130–200 m, the reefs are constructed chiefly by encrusting Bryozoa and associated serpulids (Hottinger, 1984). Other organisms of lesser importance in the framework include encrusting foraminifera, numerous non-zooxanthellate solitary corals, and abundant gorgonians; the internal sediment contains a relatively higher content of planktonic skeletal organisms than in shallow-water reefs.

Bryozoans also constitute about 60–70% of the volume of reefs approximately 2000–3000 years old that occur in a tidal channel at Joulters Cay, Bahamas (Cuffey et al., 1977; Cuffey and Fonda, 1979). At least 14 bryozoan species are present and form sheetlike crusts, thicker multilaminar masses, and porous lumps; the associated organisms include corals, coralline algae, serpulids, the encrusting foram *Homotrema,* and boring sponges and bivalves. In the terminology of Cuffey (1974) the bryozoans performed varied ecological roles of "framebuilders, hidden encrusters, cavity-dwellers and cavity-fillers."

CONCLUSIONS

There is no doubt that coral-dominated reefs are geographically and bathymetrically the most widely distributed Holocene reefs. Although coralline algae, milleporines, sponges, and bryozoans may dominate the organic frameworks in some Holocene reefs, these reefs are confined to very localized areas and are usually smaller than coral-dominated reefs. Not all Holocene reefs are coral reefs; in the examination of pre-Cenozoic reefs in Part III, it will also be conclusively demonstrated that there is considerable taxonomic variation among the dominant organisms in essentially contemporaneous ancient reefs.

3

Cenozoic Reef Models II

CONTROLLING FACTORS

CHEMICAL FACTORS

Salinity

There are no reefs in freshwater; most low diversity reefs occur in brackish water and the great majority of reefs are in normal marine water (34–36‰). In areas of near-shore reefs, it is well-documented that they are absent near the mouths of rivers, but the relative importance of reduced salinity versus increased turbidity as causative factors is uncertain. Most of the variation in salinity in reef areas is related to rainfall, river-water input, and evaporation. In the central area of the Great Barrier Reef where rainfall is highest, the annual variation in salinity is about 3.5‰ (Hopley, 1982, p. 57), whereas at the southern end the variation is less than 0.5‰ and the salinity gradient from the open ocean to the lagoon at Bikini Atoll, Marshall Islands, is only 0.1‰ (Johnson, 1954).

Scleractinians are relatively stenohaline organisms (Table 2.2). Their survival in abnormal salinity depends on the degree of abnormality and the time that they are subject to abnormal salinity. Vaughan (1919) determined experimentally that most species can withstand reduction to 28‰ and that the upper limits vary from about 40 to 48‰ depending on the species. Similarly, 8 coral species from the Great Barrier Reef withstood immersion for 4–5 h in 50% seawater (approx. 16‰), but longer immersion was usually lethal. Exposure to freshwater for more than 30 min is usually lethal, as is exposure to salinity of 52‰ for more than 24 h.

There are thriving small reefs in the Strait of Tiran between the Red Sea and the Gulf of Aqaba in salinity of 40‰ and Kinsman (1964) found large flourishing "heads" of *Porites* in the Persian Gulf at 48‰ and reefs at 42‰.

Dissolved Gases

Oxygen
Photosynthetic/metabolic rates are the chief influences over the concentration of oxygen dissolved in reef waters for use by the organisms, especially animals, in respiration. In short-term upstream–downstream measurements of dissolved oxygen in water flowing across reef systems, there is an increase during the day and a decrease at night that is directly related to the photosynthetic rate. The converse is true for the concentration of dissolved carbon dioxide from animal respiration. But for most reefs, the annual photosynthetic rate exceeds the respiration rate, which means that more carbon dioxide is being converted to organic matter than is released to the water by respiration, or animal metabolism.

However, the photosynthesis/metabolism (P/M) ratio depends on the intensity of the sunlight, which for benthic communities depends on latitude, water depth, and turbidity. At Kaneohe Bay, Hawaii, Henderson (1981) found that in areas of turbid water the P/M ratio ranged from 0.4 to 2.0 but was generally less than 1.0, whereas Mao and Yoshida (1955) found that in the Marshall Islands the shallow waters were saturated with dissolved oxygen. In fact, near oxygen saturation is probably the usual long-term condition of photic zone reef waters.

Carbon Dioxide
The biogeochemical cycles involved in the utilization of respired carbon dioxide are more complex than for photosynthetic oxygen, which either dissolves in the water or escapes to the atmosphere.

The sequence of reactions involving carbon dioxide is as follows:

$$CO_2 + H_2O = H_2CO_3 \qquad (3.1)$$

$$H_2CO_3 = H^+ + HCO_3^- \qquad (3.2)$$

$$HCO_3^- = H^+ + CO_3^{-2} \qquad (3.3)$$

In areas of turbulent water, carbon dioxide produced in excess of the photosynthetic needs of the zooxanthellae and other plants is removed. In quiet water, the removal of carbon dioxide during the day by photosynthesis (equations 2.1 and 3.1) causes the bicarbonate to release additional carbon dioxide by shifting the equilibria (equations 3.2 and 3.3) which is accompanied by a rise in pH. However, at night the production of metabolic carbon dioxide restores pH levels to about 7. Thus, seawater acts as a carbon dioxide reservoir for use in photosynthesis and metabolism (Dawes, 1981, p. 326).

Carbon dioxide can also be removed from the system by increasing the temperature or by the precipitation of calcium carbonate (see Calcification below).

Dissolved Nutrients

Subsequent to the fixation of carbon by photosynthesis, the zooxanthellae and other plants require dissolved nutrient elements for growth, maintenance, and reproduction. The most important of these elements, and the forms in which they are used by the plants, are nitrogen (as NO_2^{-2}, NO_3^{-1}, NH_4^{-1}, and dissolved organic nitrogen) and phosphorus (as PO_4^{-3}, dissolved organic phosphate, and other forms). These elements are non-uniformly distributed in the seas, and because there is generally very little vertical movement of the water column (upwelling) in the tropics to bring dissolved nutrients into the photic zone, the oceanic waters surrounding reefs are notable for their low levels of nutrient concentration and biological production (Crossland, 1983, Table 1). Thus, the limited production that does occur in oceanic plankton ecosystems stems from their success in using, holding, and recycling nutrient elements between the phytoplankton, zooplankton, and decomposers before they sink into the aphotic zone. In contrast, production in reef ecosystems is dominated by the zooxanthellae and other benthic algae, and here the sedimentary substrate acts as a "sink" to hold and recycle the nutrients.

Early efforts to measure changes in concentrations of dissolved nutrients in reef waters (upstream–downstream studies) were based on the unproven assumption that circulation was entirely unidirectional and at a relatively uniform flow rate. Despite these potential inadequacies, it appears as if (1) nutrient concentrations in reef waters are much higher than in the surrounding open ocean (up to 250 times; Crossland, 1983), (2) their concentrations are highly varied in time and space within the same reef system, and (3) that the cycles of the same element also vary within the same reef system (Hatcher and Frith, 1985). However, at Lizard Island, Great Barrier Reef, measurements by Crossland (1983, pp. 62–63) showed that the overall system produced little net change in nutrient chemistry of the surrounding water.

PHYSICAL FACTORS

The physical environment on a coral reef represents both a resource to be partitioned and a stress to be endured.

(Done, 1983, p. 107)

Temperature

General

In low latitudes, there is usually a better developed thermal stratification of the water column than at temperate–polar latitudes. Thus, in the region of the Marshall Islands, Mao and Yoshida (1955, p. 658) recognized three distinct layers: (1) 0–75 m: an isothermal layer due to mixing by waves, currents, and thermohaline convection; (2) 75–300 m: the thermocline with declining temperatures with increasing depth; and (3) 300–1500 m: a layer of low (weak) thermal gradient. In the shallow waters overlying photic zone reefs, the annual temperature range exceeds the range in the near-surface waters of the adjacent ocean (e.g., 8.4°C vs. 5.6°C at Abaco Island, Bahamas; Storr, 1964, p. 32). Similarly, large open ocean reef systems are far less likely to experience temperature extremes near lethal limits of corals than reefs close to continents.

At Low Isles, Great Barrier Reef, Hopley (1982) reported that for about 60% of the time the temperature gradient from the surface to 28 m is less than 0.2°C. At Discovery Bay, Jamaica, Kinzie (1973) reported the annual temperature range as only about 3°C at 15 m, and on the days with the steepest thermal gradient the change from 12 to 73 m is less than 2°C. Thus, among most photic zone reefs, there are neither temperature fluctuations nor steep bathymetric thermal gradients to inhibit reef growth.

It is important to note that the temperature range data of Table 2.2 for zooxanthellate and non-zooxanthellate scleracterinians are based on particular situations and individual taxa and that when two or more taxa live together, as in reefs, these temperature range figures diminish for the species association and approach the optimum values. For example, Squires (1964, p. 907) reported the temperature tolerance limits for the non-zooxanthellate coral *Dendrophyllia* as 7–27.3°C but that when this genus was found in reefs with other species, its temperature range was reduced to as little as 7–10°C. Stetson et al. (1962) noted that the maximum temperature for development of typical non-zooxanthellate coral reefs is 10°C. Similarly, the vast majority of photic zone reefs are found within the optimum temperature range (23–28°C) for zooxanthellate corals. However, at the latitudinal limits for photic zone reefs, winter temperatures may be as low as 18°C.

For most marine poikilotherms, temperature has a much greater influence on coral reproduction (different genera have different temperature minima for breeding; Rosen, 1975, p. 2) and larval survival than on individual adult corals. Thus, the thermal requirements for the recovery of devastated reefs or for the growth of new reefs are more stringent than for the maintenance of established reefs.

Photic Zone Reefs

Holocene. Temperature exerts the major control in determining the latitudinal limits of the world tropical reef belt. As these limits are approached from the equator, the general size and vigor of reefs progressively diminish until, at about the 18–20°C isocryme photic zone, reefs disappear. There is also a progressive increase in both short- and long-term temperature fluctuations toward the latitudinal limits, but absolute minimum temperature appears to be more limiting than temperature changes to reef growth.

The correlation between absolute temperature and reef distribution is particularly evident along north–south trending continental margins. In the region of the Great Barrier Reef, the most vigorous reefs occur equatorward where the mean annual temperature is 27.5°C and the winter minimum is 20°C (Endean, 1982, p. 23). Similarly, in the Gulf of California, mean annual temperatures for surface waters range from 15°C at the north end to 28°C at the south. Several species of zooxanthellate corals form reefs in the southern half of the gulf but are absent in the northern half (Squires, 1959, p. 375).

Among relatively small reefs and their associated lagoons, short-term lateral variations in temperature, even at low tide, are generally small except in very shallow tidepools and subtidal backwaters around islands, where extreme temperature fluctuation can exclude corals (Sargent and Austin, 1954; Wiens, 1962, pp. 222–224).

Pre-Holocene. Determination of long-term climatic changes and their influence on the history and distribution of photic zone reefs has been the focus of considerable research since about the mid-1800s, but the pace of progress has increased considerably since about 1970 with the application of radiometric isotope (to establish absolute age) and oxygen isotope (to establish trends of temperature change and estimate absolute change) methods to the problem.

Several interrelated biological, chemical, and physical factors make these determinations difficult. For example, because corals do not precipitate their skeletons so that the oxygen isotopes are in equilibrium with the adjacent seawater (Swart, 1983; Swart and Coleman, 1980), research has focused on the giant clam *Tridacna* spp. In addition, the isotope ratios of both oxygen (for temperature) and carbon (for age) depend on evaporation/precipitation rates and growth rates as well as temperature. Despite these problems, there is remarkable similarity in the ranges of ^{18}O (PDB) values for seawater and *Tridacna* shells across the reef at Heron Island, Great Barrier Reef (i.e., the water and shell data are mutually reinforcing; Swart et al., 1983; Flood, 1985).

Along the northern coast of Papua, New Guinea, rather continuous diastrophism has produced a succession of uplifted reefs and associated sediments ranging in age from about 140,000 years BP (elevation about + 150 m) to the present. The average temperature of the near-shore surface water is currently about 28.2°C. Aharon (1983) found that maximum ^{18}O-enrichment (coldest water) in *Tridacna* shells occurred about 43,000 years BP and indicated temperatures of about 22.5°C and that maximum ^{18}O-depletion (warmest water) occurred about 133,000 years BP with temperatures similar to the present. Furthermore, his data for the last glacial stage (120,000–18,000 years BP) indicates several older warm interstadials and younger cold interstadials and that during the last approximately 7,000–10,000 years the temperature has risen by about 3°C.

The shells of *Tridacna gigas* that Aharon used were thought to have lived in the very shallow water of the ancient reef crests and adjacent areas. Flood (1985) determined the ^{18}O (PDB) values for a series of *T. maxima* shells taken alive in the shallow waters from near the shore of Heron Island (warmest water) to the marginal reef slope leading to deep water (coldest). He found that the range from greatest enrichment to greatest depletion in ^{18}O among contemporaneous shells (1.4‰) was nearly as great as the range from greatest enrichment to greatest depletion (about 1.8‰) in the reefs studied by Aharon (1983). Flood concluded that the shells of organisms such as *Tridacna* spp. that live near the reef crest were not suited for estimating paleotemperatures because the lateral variation in temperature across a modern reef was nearly as great as the temperature variation due to climatic change from a cold glacial stage to a warm interglacial stage.

In a cooperative effort to determine world climates near the end of the last glacial stage, members of the CLIMAP Project (1976) established a set of parameters and then in a computer simulation experiment used them to prepare two maps: (1) sea-surface temperatures and aspects of continental climate for a typical August about 18,000 years ago and (2) the difference between August sea-surface temperatures 18,000 years ago and modern temperatures (the maps are presented in simplified form in Hopley, 1982, p. 388). So far as effects on the tropical reef belt are concerned, the major conclusions to be made from the CLIMAP Project are

a.   In the eastern Atlantic and central Pacific Oceans, there was marked cooling (up to 6°C colder than today) between the equator and 10°S latitude. In the Pacific, this was due to increased upwelling; in the eastern Atlantic, there was also increased upwelling as well as increased flow of the cold Bengula Current. However, sea-surface temperatures in nearly the entire tropical part of both oceans remained high enough for vigorous coral growth to continue (i.e., overall shrinking of the reef belt was minor).

b.   Sea-surface temperatures 18,000 years ago in the Gulf of Mexico, Caribbean, the western equatorial Atlantic, the western Pacific, and the

Great Barrier Reef were less than 2°C colder than today, and so the impact of thermal stress on reefs here should have been minimal.

c.   Due to increased upwelling and colder sea-surface temperatures along the west coasts of Africa, South America, and Australia, the latitudinal extent of the reef belt in these areas was very restricted (a situation that has persisted to the present).

Summary. It appears as if the cooler temperatures of the Pleistocene must have had only minor and short-term (from the viewpoint of geology) effects on the geographic distribution of reefs. Furthermore, if the magnitude of the temperature changes reported by Aharon (1983) and CLIMAP (1976) is correct, they fall well within the tolerance limits of zooxanthellate corals (Table 2.2) and also within the optimum temperature range for a very large number of species.

Finally, there are considerable data, mostly from temperate–polar regions, suggesting that Cenozoic climatic cooling may have begun as early as the Late Eocene–Early Oligocene. At this time, the long Cenozoic history of scleractinian-dominated reefs was well under way, the evolutionary diversification of scleractinians at the order–family levels continued without interruption (Newell, 1971, Fig. 2), the diversity of reef-living colonial scleractinian genera increased relative to non-reef solitary genera (Coates and Oliver, 1973) and the overall generic diversity of encrusting coralline algae also increased during the Oligocene–Holocene (Adey and Macintrye, 1973). Thus, there are virtually no biological data indicating that temperature stress diminished the vigor or overall success of post-Eocene reefs.

Aphotic Zone Reefs

Unlike equatorial waters, where the upper part of the water column is nearly isothermal throughout the year, there are marked seasonal temperature fluctuations in the upper waters in temperate–polar regions. Near Norway, the seasonal fluctuations extend to depths of 90–100 m and approximately coincide with the base of the permanent thermocline; elsewhere, the base of the zone of temperature fluctuations occurs within the thermocline. The limits of the thermocline are the 10°C and 5°C isotherms and these limits descend in the water column toward the equator.

According to Squires (1964), the upper limit of flourishing coral growth of aphotic zone reefs approximately coincides with the base of the zone of seasonal temperature fluctuations (i.e., in relatively uniform temperatures either within or close to the base of the permanent thermocline). In the eastern Atlantic, these depth limits range from about 60 m (the Norwegian fiords; Point E, Fig. 2.1) to 950 m (Point J, Fig. 2.1).

The aphotic zone reefs of the Blake Plateau in the western Atlantic (Point H, Fig. 2.1) occur below the warmer water of the Gulf Stream, which is responsible for an unusually steep thermocline in this area.

Nonetheless, the reef tops are located within the thermocline just below the depth of seasonal temperature fluctuations (Stetson et al., 1962).

Temperature–Density Relations

The density of seawater is controlled by its temperature and salinity, but because of the remarkable uniformity of salinity, temperature is a far more important control over density in the open ocean. And because density is inversely proportional to temperature, the bathymetric density profile (e.g., Mao and Yoshida, 1955, Fig. 191) is generally a near mirror image of the temperature profile. Thus, warm light water near the surface and progressively colder and heavier water with increasing depth provide an internal stability to open ocean waters (i.e., there is resistance to development of density-driven vertical currents). This reinforces the general concept that upwelling water is generally not an important source for nutrient elements to open ocean reef ecosystems and that the maintenance and growth of these reefs depend instead on highly efficient and conservative internal recycling processes.

Turbulence

General

In the present context, turbulence refers to all forms of water movement, principally waves and currents. In reef systems, the overall effect of the general state of high turbulence is to maintain a remarkable uniformity in salinity, dissolved gases and nutrients, and temperature.

Waves are an important aspect of turbulence for photic zone reefs but do not influence aphotic zone reefs, whereas currents are significant influences in both photic and aphotic zones. Waves may be subdivided into breaking and non-breaking (including swell) types and are primarily wind-driven so that their intensity and direction largely reflect local or regional wind conditions. Currents may be wind-, tide-, or density-driven and their direction and intensity may reflect conditions on scales from local to global. Thus, turbulence at a particular reef is highly varied in time, intensity, and form and is influenced by such local factors as exposure of the reef to the open sea, its proximity to the breaking surf, and water depth.

Photic Zone Reefs

Wind Driven. There is a remarkable overall coincidence in the location of the global trade winds system ("prevailing easterlies") and the distribution of photic zone reefs. In the region of the eastern Atlantic where the belt of the doldrums closely impinges on the equator, the coincidence of the trade winds and reef distribution is readily apparent (Fig. 2.2) and is in turn related to the wind-induced upwelling of cold water and the attendant equatorward shift of the surface water isotherms and isocrymes. Although the trades have an important easterly component, in many areas the northeasterly or southeasterly components may be at least as important. Thus, at most locations within the trade winds system there is a strong unimodal component within the NE–SE quadrant (e.g., Brown and Dunne, 1980, Fig. 3).

Because the tropical open ocean shallow-water currents are primarily wind-driven, there is also a close correspondence between intensity and direction of the trade winds and these water current systems. In situations where the wind and shallow-water currents are not parallel, the difference is usually due to a deflection to the left of the ocean currents in response to the Coriolis force.

Another global effect of the trade winds is the creation of a longitudinal temperature gradient in the tropical waters of both the Atlantic and Pacific Oceans from cooler in the east to warmer in the west. In response, the N–S dimension of the reef belt widens westward (Fig. 2.2) and there is a greater concentration (Emery et al., 1954, Pl. 72) and more luxuriant growth of reefs in the western parts of those oceans than in the east.

In the immediate vicinity of individual photic zone reefs, the complexity of the interrelations among waves and currents increases but can be simplified by considering the parts of typical reef systems separately. Waves that approach reefs from the open ocean typically are non-breaking and have long wavelengths and periods, but as they reach the reef there is a progressive increase in their height (amplitude), and the interplay between waves and currents intensifies.

On the seaward slope of a reef exposed to the open ocean, the water column may be subdivided into four vertically intergrading units based on the nature of the turbulence: (1) the shore surf zone of breaking waves; (2) a zone of oscillating movement with progressive decrease in the diameter of orbital motion with increasing depth; (3) at about 20 m there is a rather abrupt transition from oscillating to unidirectional, 3-dimensional currents moving downslope *near* the bottom; and (4) 2-dimensional currents flowing *at* the bottom. Below about 14 m, turbulence is predominantly by currents and is exclusively by currents below 18 m; above about 10 m, water movement is predominantly oscillatory (Done, 1983, Fig. 17).

There is usually a progressive decrease in water velocity with depth, but Roberts et al. (1975; 1977) have shown that the decrease in wave force (proportional to velocity) with depth may be counterbalanced by increased current force (shallower than about 15 m, wave force is inversely proportional to depth, but at 15–35 m, current force is directly proportional to depth). Thus, at about 15 m, current force and wave force are approximately equal; the current force at 21 m also approximately equals the wave force at 3 m. In the wave-dominated zone above 15 m (above "wave base" of many authors), there is a progressive reduction in energy with decreasing depth due to increased friction with the bottom and refraction and reflection of the waves. Friction is enormously greater in areas where reef relief is about 2 m than in areas of smooth sandy substrates.

Storr (1964, pp. 50–53) closely studied the tidal currents in a complex reef system off the east coast of Great Abaco Island, Bahamas, and found that: (1) current velocity is influenced by numerous factors but is inversely related to depth; (2) during flood tides the current velocities across the reef tops are considerably higher than in the sediment-filled depressions between the reefs; (3) during flood tides crossing the reefs at the top of the seaward slope, the waves acted like a pump, augmenting the tidal current so that the velocity at depths of about 60 cm is more than twice that at 150 cm.

In situations where reefs are elongate parallel to the shore but separated from the shore by a shallow lagoon, the currents crossing the top (crest) of the reef and the part of the lagoon immediately behind the reef are primarily driven by waves breaking at the crest. As waves move up the seaward slope and approach the crest, they increase in height and steepness. They then break as crashing or pounding surf and at this point there is a rapid change in the wave energy into strong surge currents, a reduction in the wave height, and an increase in wave frequency. The degree of modification of the wave energy by this process depends on the (1) overall geometry of the reef, (2) water depth at the reef crest, (3) uniformity of depth along and across the reef, and (4) width and depth of the lagoon (Roberts and Suhayda, 1983). Where the topography of the crest is irregular, current velocities are quite variable due to disruption of flow patterns and diversion of the currents into channels between individual reefs. Current velocities across the crest also depend on the stage of the tidal cycle; at Abaco Island, Storr (1964, p. 54) found the flood tide current velocity more than twice as great as the ebb tide velocity.

Energy loss at the reef crest by incoming waves results from breaking activity and from friction; at low tide the breaking loss is greater than at high tide. Between about 75–95% of incoming kinetic energy is lost on the crest and only about 5–25% reaches the back-reef lagoon (Roberts, 1980; Roberts and Suhayda, 1983). Variation in energy reaching the lagoon also depends on the continuity of the crest and the refraction and diffraction of waves around the ends of the reefs.

Non-storm activity on the reef crest delivers bursts of energy to the lagoon in the form of short-term surge currents. As these currents cross the lagoon, they decrease in velocity and assume complex flows patterns due to irregularities in the substrate topography and finally produce small breaking waves on the shore. Breaking waves in the lagoon and the patterns of lagoon wave trains depend on local conditions of wind direction and intensity and substrate topography.

Tide Driven. Numerous factors influence the frequency and range of tides and hence the currents they produce. However, there are a few simplifying generalizations pertinent to this discussion. In the open oceans, the tides are semidiurnal and generally of low range (about 1–2 m in the Pacific and Caribbean but somewhat greater in the Indian Ocean). During flood tides, water enters the lagoons of open ocean atolls by surge channels and passes between the reefs and by breaking waves and currents crossing the reef crest. During the next ebb tide, approximately 70% of the previous flood tidewater leaves the lagoon by the channels and passes, but the last of the remaining water may have a lagoon residence time up to 1 mo (Lewis, 1977, p. 332). Therefore, there is relatively slow mixing and minimal addition of nutrients to the lagoon from the ocean. On the other hand, only a small amount of the organic production within the lagoon is lost to the ocean.

In reef areas near continents, such as the Great Barrier Reef, tide frequencies are more irregular and ranges generally exceed those of the open ocean. As a consequence, the influence of tide-driven currents is commonly greater than for wind- and wave-driven currents. Tidal currents may therefore enhance or even reverse wave currents, especially in the channels and passes between reefs, the net effect of which is to transport more sediment into the lagoons than is removed. The lagoon as a whole, but especially areas adjacent to elongate reef crests, is a major site of sediment deposition and may be described as a sediment trap or sink. On the seaward slope, the depth at which wave force equals current force (about 15 m; Roberts et al., 1975, 1977) is also a location of important sediment deposition.

Windward/Leeward Reefs. Another common consequence of the location of photic zone reefs in the belt of unidirectional trade winds is the rather striking difference between the geomorphology and organic growth on the windward and leeward sides. Roberts (1974) calculated tht the wave power on the windward side of Grand Cayman Island in the Caribbean was about 80 times greater than on the leeward side. The effects of these strongly unidirectional wind-induced waves and currents are generally more evident on open ocean reefs than near continents, where tidal currents may dampen the effects of wind-driven currents. However, it must be stressed that the overall size and shape of most open ocean reef systems are controlled by major geologic factors rather than by waves and currents.

In typical Indo-Pacific atolls, the windward reef crest is dominated by calcareous algae that may grow to 1 m above the low tide level; there is also a wide lagoon. In contrast, on the leeward side, calcareous algae are of lesser importance, the crest only reaches the low tide level, the lagoon is narrow, but coral growth is more luxuriant. However, at Johnston Island, an atoll located in the Pacific North Equatorial Current, the only reef development is on the leeward side (Emery, 1956); the reason for the absence of windward reefs is uncertain.

Reefs in the western Atlantic are protected by the South American continent from major swells produced by south temperate zone storms, so that the predominant turbulence is wind-driven by the NE trade winds. South of Anegada Island in the British Virgin Islands, the constant unidirectional currents appear to significantly affect the shapes of the numerous small reefs on the leeward side (Brown and Dunne, 1980). The current direction (NW–SE) results from the combined effects of regional and local wind- and ocean-driven currents from the east and northeast and the tidal currents. There is a marked elongation of many of the reefs parallel to the prevailing water currents and at about 45°–60° to the prevailing winds.

Origins of the exceedingly varied sizes and shapes of the reefs of the Great Barrier Reef (excluding outer ribbon reefs) have been controversial for at least 35 years. They are influenced by the S–SE flowing East Australian Current, a SW flowing branch of the Trade Wind Drift (Maxwell, 1968, Figs. 10, 11) and complex local tidal currents driven by unusually great tidal ranges (maximum = 11 m; mean = 3–3.5 m). In the landward part of the reef system, the tidal currents scour channels and transport significant amounts of sediment to offshore areas.

Fairbridge (1950) suggested that the initial location of the reefs was controlled by geologic factors but that once their upward growth reached wave-base, winds and wind-driven currents controlled their growth direction and hence shape. He developed a scheme of reef and island shape evolution and classification based on wave and current erosion on the windward sides and deposition of reef-derived debris on the leeward side. The more detailed genetic classification of reef shapes of Maxwell (1968) also stresses the importance of winds, waves, and currents, but whether these factors are of prime importance has been questioned by Hopley (1982, pp. 247–249).

Both Fairbridge and Maxwell assumed that all reefs in the Great Barrier Reef system were removed by erosion during the low sea-level stages of the Pleistocene; they also assumed that the history of the present living reefs is confined to a stable Holocene sea level or that Holocene sea-level fluctuations were less important than currents in influencing reef/island shapes. By contrast, Hopley (1982, pp. 248–274) places greater importance on other factors such as the geomorphology of the pre-Holocene surface, the nature of the substrate, Quaternary sea-level changes, and variation in the growth rates of the reef organisms in his classification of Great Barrier reefs.

An important characteristic of well-developed windward reef systems is the presence of a lateral succession of geomorphic and ecological zones that are arranged as bands roughly parallel to the reef crest. At least as early as 1950 (Ladd et al., 1950), variation in turbulence was given as a major factor in controlling the character and width of the zones. Numerous subsequent authors (e.g., Geister, 1977, 1984; Graus et al., 1984) have also attributed the zonation to generally greater variation in turbulence across the reef system than in the other chemical and physical factors.

(More detailed discussion of the geomorphic zonation is presented below under Geologic Factors and of the ecologic zonation under Cenozoic Communities.)

Aphotic Zone Reefs

Several authors (e.g., Stetson et al., 1962; Mullins et al., 1981; Cairns and Stanley, 1981) have indicated that the distribution of aphotic zone reefs is strongly influenced by currents; Neumann et al. (1977) noted that the reefs in the Florida Strait (depth = 600–800 m) are elongate parallel to the current direction. In many cases, ripple marks on the adjacent substrate attest to the importance of currents. Mullins et al. (1981) measured current velocities of 50 cm/s at depths of 1000–1300 m and 60 cm/s at 400 m; Shipek (1962) illustrated ripple-marked fine sands at 1100–2000 m on the seaward slope of Enewetak Atoll, Marshall Islands.

J. B. Wilson (1975) reported the depth range of the non-zooxanthellate scleractinian *Caryophyllia smithii* from near the low tide level to at least 230 m and that the substrate and corallum shape were influenced by the turbulence. In areas where the tidal currents are strong (50–150+ m/s), the coralla are low with broad basal attachment to pebbles and cobbles, whereas in weaker currents (<100 m/s) the coralla are higher with narrow basal attachment to sand, polychaete tubes, and shells.

Two interrelated aspects of turbulence influence the development of aphotic zone reefs: (1) currents provide food and (2) organisms act as baffles to reduce current velocity. The sessile benthonic polyps require minimum turbulence to provide them with adequate nutrition from suspended sources, primarily zooplankton. Reed (1983) discovered that *Oculina varicosa* is one of those unusual corals in which the abundance of zooxanthellae is inversely proportional to depth and that in east–central Florida the growth rates of coralla living on the crests of escarpments and promontories at 80 m exceeded those for coralla at 6 m. Reed attributed at least part of the difference to periodic upwelling that brought more food to the coralla at 80 m than to those at 6 m; he also found that higher turbidity and the deposition of sediment on the polyps may also have reduced the growth rates in shallow water. Although not yet proven, the general decrease in turbulence with depth and the resulting reduction in exposure to food sources may well be the primary control on the lower depth limit for some of the aphotic zone reefs indicated in Figure 2.1.

Although the branches of typical dendroid aphotic zone coralla are thin and much weaker than those of their photic zone counterparts, in both cases the branches resist breakage at normal turbulence levels and become major contributors to the frameworks of their respective reef types. Such resistance to turbulence contributes to the progressively increasing size, relief, and steep margins of reefs; the aphotic zone reefs reported by Mullins et al. (1981) have relief of 5–40 m, steep sides, and abrupt changes of slope at the base with coralla lying loose on the adjacent fine-grained substrates as if broken from the sides of the reefs. Within aphotic zone reefs and between the coralla and their branches, there is considerable internal fine-grained sediment that Mullins et al. (1981) and Neumann et al. (1977) thought may have been deposited as a result of current velocity reduction by the branches acting as baffles with the suspended sediment then trapped between the branches and coralla. Such internal sediment may help support the organic framework of these reefs and enable them to grow both vertically and laterally.

The Paleocene (Danian) rocks in Denmark contain several bryozoan-dominated reefs that Thomsen (1983) regarded as analogous to the Holocene aphotic zone reefs described by Mullins et al. (1981) and Neumann et al. (1977). The Danish reefs are similar to the Holocene reefs in size, shape, and overall importance of currents in influencing the nature of their varied faunas (Danian bryozoa; Holocene corals) and in growth of the reefs by skeletal accretion and sediment trapping.

Turbidity and Texture

Turbidity refers to the concentration of suspended solids (inorganic and organic) in a unit volume of seawater; texture refers to the size of these solids (grains) as well as those on or in the substrate. The following discussion deals only with photic zone reefs and with grains in suspension; the grains on the bottom are considered in Chapter 4.

Interrelations among turbulence, turbidity, and texture in all environments are exceedingly complex, but a few simple generalizations that apply to reef environments also prove useful here; most of them will be amplified later. First, reef waters are remarkable for their unusually low levels of turbidity despite the generally high turbulence that in other environments commonly produces higher turbidity. Numerous factors contribute to low reef turbidity but a major one is that turbulence transports virtually all mud from the immediate vicinity of the reefs; substrates adjacent to reefs generally consist of sand and larger sizes of grains. The low turbidity of reef waters has important physical effects and biological consequences (discussed below).

A second group of generalizations that relates to the physical effects arise from the fact that suspended solids reflect and disperse incoming solar radiation. Light intensity is high in tropical reef waters, the depth to the base of the photic zone is unusually great, and determination of the photic zone base is often difficult. In fact, the base of the photic zone varies considerably among major groups of reef plants; for zooxanthellae, it is about 100 m, for encrusting red coralline algae up to about 125 m, for some calcareous greens (i.e., *Halimeda*) up to 150 m, and for blue–greens a few hundred meters.

The biological effects of these turbidity–light interrelations, which are of greatest importance, involve:

a.   Photosynthetic rates and efficiencies. Photosynthetic rates of zoo-xanthellae and other plants in reef environments usually exceed those of non-reef environments.

b.   Relative importance of organisms intolerant to high turbidity. For instance, the importance of sponges is much higher in reef than in non-reef environments.

c.   Bathymetric ranges. Ranges of most corals living on the seaward slope appear to be directly related to light intensity and duration. For zooxanthellate corals, Wells (1967, p. 350) concluded that light attenuation with depth was the chief control over their lower bathymetric limit and showed (Wells, 1957) that the "effective day" for coral growth at 20 m was 11 h but only 40 min at 40 m.

GEOLOGICAL FACTORS

> The number of different kinds of reefs in existence is considerable and the workers on each type have developed a nomenclature which is locally suitable.
> (Stephenson et al., 1931, p. 92)

During the long history of the classification of photic zone reefs, most authors, beginning with Charles Darwin (1842), have emphasized the importance of geological factors in both descriptive and genetic classifications. These factors have included the location of reefs with respect to major global features (ocean basins, continental shelves, and major fracture systems), the presence, proximity, or absence of associated lands, the nature of the underlying rocks, and the diastrophic history of the earth's crust. Other aspects of reef history that have been used in reef classifications include effects of climatic changes and such biological factors as the dominant organisms and their growth rates.

Descriptive Classifications

Based on Location
The most fundamental geological separation of the various reef types is between those that are located in the open ocean and are thus removed from any significant interaction with continental processes and those that are located on continental shelves. Open ocean reefs have structures, shapes, and growth patterns that are largely controlled by the areally limited topographic feature on which they have grown. Continental shelf reefs are less limited areally (and so may be larger and more numerous) but are more likely to be limited by adverse chemical and physical factors resulting from their proximity to a large landmass. Shelf reefs vary considerably more than oceanic reefs in shape and in geomorphic and biologic

structure. Oceanic reefs have foundations of oceanic crust volcanic rocks (especially olivene basalt) and so their location is controlled by the location of their volcanic foundations; these are in turn related to global tectonic features (e.g., oceanic ridges and fracture systems). In contrast, shelf reef foundations are usually continental crust sedimentary rocks of considerable variety.

With regard to the oceanic–shelf distinction described above, the reefs of the Bahama Banks are somewhat of an enigma. They are clearly continental shelf reefs, but the platforms and banks on which they are located are bounded by steep submarine escarpments that lead to deep (600–1800 m), flat-floored channels. Furthermore, the bank sediments and underlying rocks are pure carbonates, lack terrigenous siliciclastics, and date back to at least the Early Cretaceous (Newell, 1955b; Newell and Rigby, 1957).

Numerous authors, beginning with Agassiz (1894), have noted similarities between the location and ringlike arrangement of the Bahamian reefs and some Pacific open ocean reefs. Other authors, beginning with Hess (1933), have debated the geological origin of the banks. More recently, Read (1982) classified the banks as isolated platforms; Mullins and Lynts (1977) interpreted them as fault-bounded horsts on a widening (extensional) continental shelf (cf. Newell, 1955b, p. 305).

Proximity to land, either large continents or small islands, is highly variable for both oceanic and shelf reefs; for both types, there may be no adjacent land to influence either reef location or growth. Thus, reefs are marine biological phenomena, and the presence or absence of nearby land is secondary. Yet our anthropocentric classifications give considerable weight to terrestrial relations.

Oceanic Reefs. Open ocean photic zone reefs and reef systems have been conveniently subdivided into those associated with high islands (usually volcanic), those associated with low islands (usually sedimentary), and those without associated islands. Tahiti in the Society Islands is an example of an unusually large (over 1000 km^2) and high (2241-m) volcanic island. However, just within the Society Islands, other high volcanic islands are as small as 2 km^2 (Meketia) and as low as 380 m (Maupiti). The influence of terrestrial processes on high island reefs is quite limited but nonetheless obvious in the typical black volcanic sand beaches.

Low islands and their associated reefs may occur in isolation, as groups, or in various degrees of proximity to high islands. In any case, there is almost always a clear distinction between those reefs associated with high islands and those associated with low islands. There are numerous, generally small (a few km^2), vegetated, low (<30-m) islands associated with oceanic reefs that have sediments or geologically young sedimentary rocks in their centers and foundations. The subaerically exposed rocks have had varied origins during higher Quaternary sea levels, as evidenced by reef limestones and reef-derived debris piled by the surf in strand-line terraces. Although there are Cenozoic reef limestones present at higher elevations (e.g., +100 m at Makatea Island, Tuamotu Archipelago) and sand dunes at elevations greater than 30 m, in oceanic reef areas there is nearly everywhere a clear-cut geological distinction between high and low islands. This distinction has been recognized in such colloquial terms for low islands as "cay" and "key" in the western Atlantic and "motu" in Polynesia.

Shelf Reefs. On the continental shelves, reefs may be present from the shelf margin (or upper continental slope in the case of aphotic zone reefs), continuously or intermittently across the shelf to locations immediately adjacent to ("plastered against") the continental shoreline. Reefs growing at shelf margins are generally larger and more vigorous than those in more interior shelf locations because they may be adjacent to upwelling, cooler, nutrient-rich water that stimulates both inorganic (by loss of dissolved CO_2) and organic production of $CaCO_3$. In shelf areas, most associated islands are low and composed of sediments or geologically young sedimentary rocks; in such areas, the distinction between high and low island reefs is rarely needed. However, Lizard Island in the Great Barrier Reef is an exception; it is a high island of continental rocks located nearly 50 km from the Australian continent. The degree of influence from terrestrial processes on shelf reefs depends largely on their proximity to the continent and is generally much greater than for oceanic reefs. Such terrestrial influences include a higher proportion of siliciclastic shelf sediments, deceased vigor of reefs living near the mouths of rivers and other areas of high turbidity, and concentrations of dissolved nutrient elements near river mouths. However, on shelves adjacent to arid continents, these influences may be considerably modified. For example, the reef system adjacent to the shore of the Red Sea is virtually unbroken by freshwater influx for a distance of about 4300 km.

The Cenozoic Great Barrier Reef is probably the largest shelf reef complex in the history of the earth; it is nearly 2000 km long, from 21 to 300 km wide, and covers a total area of about 270,000 km^2, of which only about 11,700 km^2 (4.3%) consists of living coral reefs. Some individual reefs rise more than 100 m above the adjacent sedimentary substrate. Maxwell (1968) has subdivided the shelf into a shallower (9.5–39 m) inner part (nearer the continent) and a deeper (39–50 m) marginal part which together contain 2,500 individual reefs.

The locations, sizes, shapes, and concentration of reefs within the complex depend on numerous factors; Maxwell (1973) presented the following generalizations tht give some idea of shelf reef variation:

   a.   In the northern part (9–16°S latitude), reefs are abundant and dispersed across the entire shelf with a nearly continuous line of reefs (ribbon reefs) along the seaward margin.

b.   In the central part (16–20°S), there are no seaward margin reefs, reef density is the lowest in the entire shelf, and most reefs that are present occur adjacent to islands.

c.   The south end (20–22°S) has the best developed seaward margin reefs but the most poorly developed within-shelf reefs.

Ancient Reefs. Geological classifications of ancient reefs, especially pre-Cenozoic, based on location are considerably different from the one presented here. The main reasons for the difference are:

a.   Oceanic reefs seem to be exceedingly rare in the pre-Cenozoic stratigraphic record, especially reefs associated with volcanic rocks. The association of highly recrystallized coral-bearing limestones and blocks of olivene basalt in melange deposits of accretionary continental margins (e.g., early–middle Paleozoic Lovers Leap and Gregg Ranch melanges of northern California; Lindsley-Griffin, 1977 and Lindsley-Griffin and Griffin, 1983) is suggestive of former oceanic reefs. Other ancient oceanic reefs may have been lost by subduction of small volcanic piles beneath continental margins. As a consequence of the paucity of pre-Cenozoic oceanic reefs, geological classifications based on location almost exclusively concern continental margin and interior (platform) reefs.

b.   The fact that ancient continental shelves and margins are thought to have differed significantly from Cenozoic shelves and margins, especially with regard to slope of the continental shelf and continental slope, the rate of shelf subsidence, the nature and distribution of the shelf sediments, and the accretion of oceanic crust plates on continent margins.

c.   A shift to a much more complex terminology for ancient continental shelf reefs with synonymous conflicting and confusing definitions, redefinitions, and usages of the areas and units involved.

d.   The desire to generalize from spatially limited information (drill cores and cuttings from wells that are widely separated) to large areas with the attendant problems of scale. This is the ever-present geological problem of building models on a small scale and then using and comparing these models at different scales.

Despite these differences, nearly all classifications of ancient reefs dealing with location (e.g., Ahr, 1973; Ginsburg and James, 1974; Wilson, 1975, pp. 20–46, 362–364; Read, 1982) concern continental shelf reefs; nearly all factors related to their distribution are homologous with Holocene shelf reefs, especially those in the Great Barrier Reef, Bahama Platform, and the Florida Keys. Unlike Holocene reefs, which seem to have maintained rather constant positions on the shelf, many ancient reefs moved their location laterally on the shelf in response to varied rates of shelf subsidence or uplift (Pl. 11a).

However, there is one aspect of the location of ancient reefs not stressed by most previous authors that does not have a close Cenozoic analogue.

During the Paleozoic, the central parts of most of the continents (interior platform, craton) were submerged by shallow seas which locally or regionally contained numerous small (patch) reefs, many of which, especially in North America, were subjects of classic research on reef paleoecology. Extensive late Mesozoic and Cenozoic diastrophism uplifted the continents and drained these former interior seas to produce Cenozoic reef distributions virtually restricted to the continental shelves and open oceans.

Based on Size and Shape (Form)

> ... of all the forms of coral reefs, the atolls have appeared to men of science to be the richest in mystery and most strange.
>
> (Revelle, 1954, p. III)

Oceanic Reefs. The fundamental importance of geologic factors in controlling reef size, and especially shape, is most apparent in open ocean reefs and reef systems. These close interrelationships result from the fact that most such reefs surround oceanic crust volcanoes in various stages of activity, erosion, and crustal subsidence. Thus, the size and shape of these volcanoes directly control the size and shape of the associated reefs and reef system (i.e., the sizes and shapes of oceanic reef systems reflect the outer submarine contours of their volcanic foundations). The foundation may be a simple, individual volcanic cone or a cluster of cones variably concealed beneath reefs growing on their flanks and summit. If the volcano is geologically young, the volcanic flanks and summit may be subaerially exposed as high islands with relatively small surrounding reefs. Wiens (1962, p. 26) compared the shapes of 162 open ocean reefs and reef systems in the Pacific with the prevailing wind and surface current patterns; he found no relation between the direction of long axes of the reefs and reef systems and the wind and current direction. Instead, the long axes coincided with size, shape, and orientation of submerged geologic features.

The earliest scientific classification of ocean reefs based on shape and origin was presented by Darwin (1842) and, despite its antiquity, it has been the basic system continuously used since. In situations of reefs associated with high islands, Darwin recognized two types: (1) *fringing*: the reefs are located directly on the island shore with no lagoon between and (2) *barrier*: the reefs are separated from the island shore by a lagoon.

The shapes of fringing reefs are exceedingly varied and depend on numerous factors, but their width depends on the slope of the underlying foundation (i.e., if the slope is steep, the reef is narrow). Most fringing reefs are a thin veneer on the volcanic foundation and both the foundation and reefs are geologically young.

Barrier reefs are relatively narrow and elongate and arranged in nearly continuous chains roughly parallel to the high island shore; that is, they are broadly arcuate in map view (Pl. 10*b*). The width of the lagoon varies from a few hundred meters (in which case they almost merge with fringing reefs) to a few kilometers; lagoon depths vary from a few centimeters to a few tens of meters (typically <30 m).

The name *atoll* consideraly pre-dates Darwin's usage; it refers to a sub-circular or ringlike arrangement of narrow, arcuate reefs partially en-closing a shallow-water central lagoon that lacks a volcanic island (Pl. 12). Sizes, shapes, and depths of atoll lagoons are exceedingly variable. The largest is at Kwajalein, Marshall Islands, with maximum and min-imum diameters of about 415 and 94 km; maximum depths are 90–100m. For most atolls, the correlation between their size ("diameter") and depth is quite poor; however, for the Maldive Islands, Indian Ocean, Steers and Stoddart (1977, p. 45) found a rather good exponential relation between size and lagoon depth; the largest Maldive atoll is about 70 km in diameter and 90 m deep.

The highest parts of barrier reefs and atolls may be marked by low islands but the presence or absence of such islands is unrelated to their classification. For example, in the western Caroline Islands, there are 20 submerged atolls having no subaerial expression (Wiens, 1962, p. 28).

So, on the basis of size, shape, and relation to land, the three reef types (fringing and barrier reefs; atolls) described and classified by Darwin (1842) are quite clear-cut and easily recognized in the open oceans. Sub-sequent authors have suggested numerous additional names for other reef types and there are also numerous colloquial names for oceanic reefs, most of which are synonyms or very limited in their application. However, there is one additional reef type not recognized by Darwin that has re-ceived broad acceptance; this is the *patch* reef.

Patch reefs usually: (1) are smaller than fringing and barrier reefs and atolls; (2) lack a lagoon but are located in lagoons of barrier reefs and atolls (Pl. 12b); (3) are submerged, although the tops may reach low tide level; and (4) unlike nearly all other oceanic reefs, have foundations con-sisting of sediments or sedimentary rocks. Lagoons of the largest atolls may contain thousands of patch reefs (2300 at Enewetak; Steers and Stoddart, 1977, p. 46) of highly varied sizes and shapes. Emery (1956, Fig. 2) described typical patch reefs in the lagoon at Johnston Island in the central Pacific as: (1) irregularly flat-topped with an overhanging rim formed by coralline algae; (2) with sides covered with prolific growth of irregular masses of branching corals (primarily *Acropora* spp.), grading at the base into clean, white sand of the lagoon floor; (4) averaging about 3 m in height and 12–13 m in diameter. Elsewhere, the term has been used for structures of quite different sizes, shapes, and organic compo-sitions (e.g., James, 1983, p. 348). Patch reefs are subcircular to irregular in plan view and in their smaller sizes they merge with structures called coral knolls, coral thickets, or coral heads. If the sides are steep, they may be called pinnacle reefs. (For an extended discussion of reef types and classification, see Tayama, 1952, pp. 220–278.)

Thus, there are only four basic types of oceanic reefs: fringing, barrier, atoll, and patch. All others are here regarded as variants of these basic types (see Glossary).

Continental Shelf Reefs. The degree of variation in sizes and shapes of continental shelf reefs exceeds such variation in oceanic reefs due, at least in part, to the greater complexity of factors that control their growth. Nonetheless, the same four basic reef types described above for oceanic reefs can also be recognized (sometimes requiring considerable "stretching") in continental shelf reefs. In fact, use of the term "barrier reef" for reefs of the Great Barrier Reef pre-dates use of the term by Darwin (1842). Despite this priority in usage, and because of the enormous variety of shelf barrier reefs, many workers restrict their use of "barrier reef" to oceanic reefs and use alternative names for reefs of similar shape located on continental shelves. In the northern and southern parts of the Great Barrier Reef, the outermost shelf margin reefs are linear, 300–1000 m wide and many kilometers long. Because of their much greater distance from land, their larger size compared with oceanic barrier reefs, and because they may occur in double lines or as linear reefs within the shelf area, Australians more commonly refer to such linear reefs as *ribbon* rather than barrier reefs.

Among shelf reefs, the term "fringing reef" has been used for all reefs immediately adjacent to land regardless of whether the land is a continent, a bedrock island on the shelf, or a small lagoonal sand cay. Rings of narrow, elongate reefs (atolls) are present but rare on continental shelves and are not founded on oceanic volcanic rocks. Nonetheless, the term "atoll" (or bank atoll, shelf atoll, etc.) has received limited usage in a purely descriptive sense for some ringlike reefs in the Great Barrier Reef, Indonesia, the Caribbean, and the Gulf of Mexico.

Conversely, patch reefs (and all their nomenclatural variants) abound on continental shelves and the term may have been originally used for such reefs. Indeed, most reefs of the Great Barrier Reef are patch reefs (Pl. 16a). Of the nearly 2500 reefs in the Great Barrier Reef complex, most are less than 2 km^2 (cf. Emery, 1956) and only 75 are larger than about 50 km^2 (Maxwell, 1973, p. 300).

The most elaborate descriptive classification (with strong genetic implications) of continental shelf reefs is the one by Maxwell (1968, p. 101) based on the Great Barrier Reef. The numerous reef forms recognized by Maxwell represent stages in the continuous interplay between biological growth and destruction, wind and water turbulence, and sedimentary processes. Relatively elongate forms with cusps, prongs, and meshes are more strongly influenced by turbulence, whereas circular-to-elliptical forms are more strongly influenced by biological factors. The influence of sedimentary processes is most apparent in the later histories of all shelf reef forms (Scoffin et al., 1978). Because of its emphasis on Holocene processes and the geologically ephemeral nature of many of the forms,

Maxwell's classifiction has not been widely used among workers studying continental shelf reefs outside the Great Barrier Reef province.

Some of the earliest classifications based on the varied forms in the Great Barrier Reef concentrated on the nature of the islands (e.g., Steers, 1937; Fairbridge, 1950; Steers and Stoddart, 1977). These classifications have generally stressed the presence/absence and nature of the vegetation (see also Hopley, 1982, pp. 320–349).

Sizes and shapes of ancient continental shelf reefs are nearly as varied as those of Cenozoic reefs. The Late Devonian reefs and adjacent rocks marginal to the Canning Basin, Western Australia, (Pl. 13b) and those of the Late Permian in western Texas and New Mexico are nearly as extensive as the Great Barrier Reef. There also appears to be as much variation in sizes and shapes of ancient patch reefs (Pl. 11b) as in the Holocene. In fact, numerous ancient structures have been called reefs (or bioherms; see Glossary) that would be regarded by workers studying the Cenozoic as too small to be reefs; Gaillard (1983, pp. 115–121) described bioherms as structures less than one meter high and one or more meters in diameter (outcrop length) that occur in coeval clusters in the French Jura Mountains (cf. Pl. 10a).

Some geologists have used a separate terminology (e.g., mound, bank, biostrome) for both shelf and cratonic reefs and for non-reefs such as mud mounds and shell heaps. In many cases, the distinctions between these terms for ancient reefs have been based on shapes (profile) seen in vertical outcrops, in contrast to the distinctions of Maxwell (1968) for Holocene reefs which are based on map (plan) view. Regardless of age, these reefs are regarded here as varied types of patch reefs such as are abundantly represented in Holocene oceanic and shelf lagoons.

Geomorphic Zonation

Large, shallow-water reef systems are characterized by lateral successions of geomorphic zones that are subparallel to the shore of the adjacent land and to the contours of the submerged seaward slope. Lateral variation in turbulence seems to be a major control over the nature of this zonation; the zonation is expressed both geomorphologically and ecologically (see Chap. 5). The geomorphic zones express variation in the balance between aggradation (biological growth; sediment deposition) and degradation (erosion).

In schemes of geomorphic zonation, the reef crest (surf zone; breaker zone) naturally divides the reef system into two units, the outer or seaward part (dominated by waves in water less than 15-m depth; dominated by currents in 15–35-m depth) commonly called the fore-reef, and the inner or landward part (back-reef of many authors) dominated by tidal currents and local turbulence factors (Pl. 10b). The crest marks the shallow-water transition from wave to current dominance (Pl. 14a). The ultimate refinements in geomorphic zonation appear to be those of Clausade et al. (1971), who distinguished 68 zones on an individual reef near Malagasy, and Battistini et al. (1975), who defined 125 geomorphological features for reefs of the Indo-Pacific region.

Indo-Pacific Oceanic Atolls and Barrier Reefs

Geomorphic zonation is better developed on the windward sides of open ocean atolls than on other types of reefs. Despite the considerable morphologic variation among Indo-Pacific atolls (Newell, 1956, p. 332), the following four or five zones (an island may or may not be present) can usually be recognized (Table 3.1; Fig. 3.1; Pl. 12a): lagoon, island, reef flat, algal ridge, and seaward slope. (For excellent illustrations of these zones, see Tracey et al., 1948.)

Lagoon and Island. Lagoon floors consist of an irregular patchwork of large, relatively level areas of slowly deposited, predominantly clean sand substrates, patch reefs, and coral knolls or heads and closed depressions ("blue holes") up to 100 m deep. If there is an island, the slope from the island to the lagoon is commonly steep, especially if there are near-shore lagoonal reefs.

Atoll islands are low aggradational features consisting of poorly sorted sand to boulder-size grains commonly overlying the upper parts of dead reefs. The sedimentary grains are transported from the more seaward parts of the atoll, mostly by hurricanes, and heaped in marginal ramparts and storm beaches so that the island grows by lateral accretion. In situations involving small islands and particularly destructive or repeated

---

TABLE 3.1. Geomorphic Zonation: Windward Side of Indo-Pacific Atolls

   I. Lagoon
       Includes marginal reefs, shelf, slope, floor with patch/pinnacle reefs, and
       depressions (sinks, dolines, blue holes, etc.)
  II. Island (may be absent)
       Includes seaward/lagoonward beaches
 III. Reef flat
       Includes subzones of deeper water (moat) on seaward side and boulders of
       reef rubble (rampart) on landward side; if island present, it divides reef
       flat into seaward and lagoonward parts
  IV. Algal ridge; reef crest
       Includes surge channels, caverns, tunnels, passes; surf breaks against
       seaward edge of algal ridge
   V. Seaward slope
       Includes submarine terrace, spur/buttress and groove system, marginal
       living reefs, and reef-derived sedimentary debris

Source: Modified from Emery et al., 1954; Wells, 1957; Stoddart, 1969.

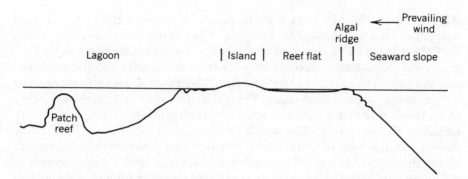

Figure 3.1.   Generalized cross section of the windward side of a typical Indo-Pacific Holocene atoll showing the arrangement of the major geomorphic zones. Cf. Table 3.1. (Modified from Wells, 1957a, Fig. 2; vertical exaggeration 6X.)

storms, sedimentary material may be carried across the island and deposited in the lagoon, or small islands may be removed by erosion. Thus, from a geological point of view, atoll islands are ephemeral features of short duration that are very difficult, if not impossible, to recognize in pre-Quaternary reef systems.

In places, the internal older reef core of a Holocene atoll island may be exposed in elevated ridges or terraces and provides local evidence of former higher sea levels.

Reef Flat. If an island is present, the reef flat extends from the island seaward shore to the landward margin of the algal ridge and is covered by very shallow water (a few centimeters to a few meters); large parts of the reef flat are commonly subaerially exposed at low tide. If an island is absent, the inner or lagoonward margin merges with the seaward margin of the lagoon; the boundary is marked by increased water depth into the lagoon. The outer or seaward margin of the reef flat is often marked by a narrow belt of deeper water (often called the "moat") with somewhat more prolific coral growth.

The width of the reef flat varies from a few tens to a few thousands of meters, averaging about 500 m; reef flats are generally wide if the central lagoon is shallow (and vice versa; Tayama, 1952, pp. 249–250). The reef flat surface is covered by bare rock, including *in situ* erosional remnants as well as rubble blocks up to several meters in diameter transported by storms from the seaward margin of the reef, encrusting algae, loose sand, beds of seagrass, and mats of filamentous algae; living corals may be surprisingly rare. The sandy areas overlie hard, rocklike crusts which in turn overlie thicker, unconsolidated sediments. Scattered pools, tidal channels, and the moat provide a variety of microhabitats for eurytopic algae and infaunal invertebrates.

Algal Ridge. The algal ridge corresponds to the reef crest; its seaward margin is clearly marked by the line of breaking waves and pounding surf (Pl. 14*a*). The top or crest of the ridge is also marked by nearly continuous shallow-water currents crossing from the seaward to the landward margin and continuing to the reef flat. The inner margin is recognized by the steep slope to the moat. Typically, the seaward slope is steeper than the landward slope, but prolific coral growth on the latter may equalize the steepness. The width of the algal ridge varies from a few meters to a few tens of meters and the ridge may rise several centimeters above the high tide level. The surface is irregular and, where exposed to pounding surf, covered by a nearly continuous encrustation of red coralline algae (especially *Porolithon* and *Lithothamnion;* Pl. 14*b*); elsewhere, algal-covered terraced tide pools dot the top of the ridge. Toward the reef flat, there may be progressively increasing importance of erect-growing brown algae (especially *Turbinaria* and *Sargassum*); algal ridges with brown algae are more commonly associated with high island barrier reefs than with atolls (personal communication, M. Pichon, 1985). Algal ridges, best developed in the Pacific trade winds belt, are generally absent from monsoonal and doldrums areas of Indonesia and are of intermediate development in the Indian Ocean.

The algal ridge is usually not a continuous rim around atolls and barrier reefs but is broken at several places by major, deep (navigable) passes (Pl. 13*a*) and smaller surge channels through which a large volume of tide-driven water enters and leaves the lagoon; however, some atolls with shallow, sediment-filled lagoons (e.g., Anaa and Hikueru, Tuamotu Archipelago) lack passes through the continuous algal ridge–island rim.

The surge channels begin at the seaward margin of the ridge, where their width and depth may be as much as 15 m, and become narrower toward the inner margin. Rapid lateral growth of encrusting coralline algae commonly produces surge tunnels by roofing over the channels; such tunnels may connect internal caverns of varied sizes which may be marked at the ridge surface by "blow-holes." Both surge channels and tunnels are lined by current-resistant algae and a few corals.

Seaward Slope. Among *typical* open ocean barrier reefs and atolls, regardless of their location, there are three important geomorphic features on the seaward slope: (1) the steep upper portion leads downslope to a variably developed terrace at 15–20-m depth; a somewhat shallower terrace is present in some atoll lagoons; (2) a lateral succession of elevated spurs or buttresses and depressed grooves; and (3) a deeper-water (below 20 m), rather uniformly sloping (about 30°) algal-, coral-, and sediment-covered surface essentially conforming to the gradient of the underlying volcanic cone. In comparison to the near absence of corals on the algal ridge, corals dominate the seaward slope to about 75–80 m.

The grooves of the spur and groove succession at Bikini Atoll, Marshall Islands, are spaced about 8 m apart, begin in water about 5 m deep, extend down the seaward slope to about 10–15 m deep, and their sediment-filled floors are 1–2 m below the tops of the adjacent spurs (Wiens, 1962, pp. 53–57). On seaward slopes lacking a terrace, spurs and grooves are usually poorly developed or absent. At their upper ends, grooves are generally aligned with the seaward ends of the surge channels of the algal ridge; most of the sand in the grooves has been transported by ebb tide currents from the reef flat, through the surge channels, and moves by gravity down the grooves to the deep seaward slope. Where the seaward slope is steep, the grooves act as sediment chutes leading to debris fans and slump heaps below the terrace level.

In contrast to the near-absence of organisms in the grooves, encrusting coralline algae and corals cover the surface of the spurs; on Indo-Pacific reefs, coralline algae commonly dominate the spurs, whereas in the Atlantic, corals dominate. Thus, strong evidence suggests that the relief from grooves to spurs results from abrasion by downslope sediment movement in the grooves and upward organic growth on the spurs. Whether abrasion or growth is more important is uncertain, but in either case the development of both grooves and spurs is enhanced by exposure to strong and persistent surf on the algal ridge. Spur and groove systems are rather ephemeral geomorphic features but are present (e.g., Pl. 15a; southern Germany, Barthel, 1977) in a few ancient reefs.

Wiens (1962, p. 114) has suggested that in the early history of atoll systems, the growth rate of algae and corals in the algal ridge and upper seaward slope is very high and the depositional rate of lagoonal sediments is very slow. The early upward and later outward growth thus eventually produces a steep or even overhanging algal ridge and upper seaward slope. Those overhangs may be broken by storm waves into rubble boulders which roll downslope under the influence of gravity or may be carried by waves and currents and deposited on the reef flat or island ramparts. In this manner, the sediments on both sides of the reef crest may become quite poorly sorted compared with lagoon sediments.

Most geomorphic features of the windward atoll margin are also present in modified form on the leeward margin, where wave turbulence is less. For example, leeward reef flats are generally narrower, the algal ridge, spurs, and grooves are less well-developed or absent, the upper seaward slope is steeper because of more prolific coral growth, and there are fewer talus deposits on the deeper seaward slope.

In most open ocean barrier reef systems, the same geomorphic zonation can be recognized except that the area between the algal ridge and high island includes both the shallow reef flat and the deeper lagoon (Pl. 10b) and there may be offshore low islands between the lagoon and seaward slope.

Great Barrier Reef

Because of reduced turbulence, the much wider lagoon, and greater dispersion of reefs, geomorphic zonations of Great Barrier reefs are less strikingly developed and more varied than on open ocean reef systems. However, local areas of abnormally high turbulence such as the shelf margin ribbon reefs and some patch reefs (e.g., Heron Island in the Capricorn Group) do have good zonations. Therefore, no attempt will be made here to present a generalized zonation scheme comparable to Table 3.1. Maxwell (1968, Fig. 72) has presented zonations for various reef types in his classification of Great Barrier reefs.

The Great Barrier Reef system has no single, discreet lagoon comparable to oceanic atolls and barrier reefs. Instead, the lagoon is divisible into inner and outer parts with a complex system of passes (up to 40 m deep) between the patch reefs and islands. In many areas, the deepest part of the lagoon is remarkably close to the continent. In addition to the huge general lagoonal area, many of the shelf patch reefs contain small ephemeral lagoons at various stages of infilling by sediment. The sizes and shapes of these lagoons result from a combination of inherited morphology from the pre-Holocene shelf and the growth of organisms on the reef periphery during the Holocene rise in sea level (Hopley, 1982, p. 315).

The patch reef flats are characterized by a radial pattern of reefs and sediments and discontinuous algal–coral ridges elongated parallel to the predominant wave direction (Pl. 16a; Maxwell, 1968, p. 116). Although reef crests contain abundant algae, Great Barrier reefs lack a true algal ridge. Conversely, good spur and groove systems (up to 80 m long) and submerged terraces at several depths are common among Great Barrier reefs, especially where the reef front is steep. Hopley (1982) believes the grooves represent erosional channels formed during Pleistocene emergence and have been maintained by movement of water and sediment at their bases and that the various terrace levels between 18 and 67 m are the result of complex interrelations between various Pleistocene sea levels and levels of upward growth of Pleistocene reefs.

Western Atlantic Fringing and Barrier Reefs

Geomorphic zonations of western Atlantic reefs (atolls are nearly nonexistent) are broadly similar to Indo-Pacific barrier reefs, and because fringing reefs have been more intensely studied in the Caribbean than elsewhere (e.g., Jamaica), their zonation is discussed here in some detail. Unfortunately, the same general uniformity of terminology used for Indo-Pacific atolls and barrier reefs does not exist for Caribbean reefs (Table 3.2; Fig. 3.2). In addition, previous descriptions of Caribbean reefs tend to intermix aspects of geomorphological zonation with aspects of ecological zonations in ways that make them virtually inseparable.

Detailed study of the relatively wide fringing reefs on the north coast

TABLE 3.2. Geomorphic Zonation of Selected Caribbean Fringing and Barrier Reefs

Jamaica; Fringing Reef (After Goreau and Goreau, 1973)		Carrie Bow Cay; Barrier Reef (Rützler and Macintyre, 1982)		General (After James, 1983)	Herein (Generalized) (See also Fig. 3.2)	
Regional Zones	Depth (m)	Major Units	Depth (m)	Zones	Zones	Depth (m)
					(Shore)	Intratidal-Supratidal
Back reef[a,b]						
1. Inshore zone	0.1–3	1. Lagoon	1.5–2	1. Back-reef[b]	1. Lagoon[b]	0.1–5
2. Lagoon zone	0.5–5					
Reef crest						
3. Rear zone	0.2–3	2. Back-reef	0.1–1	2. Reef flat	2. Reef flat	0–1
4. Reef flat zone	0–1					
5. Breaker zone	0–5	3. Reef crest	Intertidal	3. Reef crest	3. Reef crest	Intertidal
6. Moat zone	2–8					
7. Mixed zone	7–15	4. Inner fore-reef	1–12	4. Reef front		
8. Buttress zone	2–20					
Seaward slope						
9. Fore-reef	15–40	5. Outer fore-reef	12–60	5. Fore-reef	4. Seaward slope	0.1–?
10. Fore-reef slope	30–65					
11. Deep fore-reef	>65					

[a]Note variation in terminology.
[b]Narrow–absent in fringing reefs.

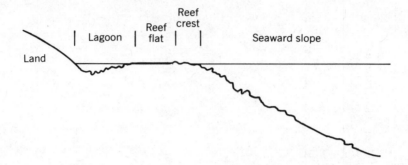

Figure 3.2.   Generalized cross section of a typical Caribbean or Indo-Pacific fringing or barrier reef system showing the arrangement of the major geomorphic zones. Cf. Table 3.2. (Modified from James, 1983, Fig. 14; considerable vertical exaggeration.)

of Jamaica were begun by Goreau (1959) and extended by Goreau and Goreau (1973). These authors recognized and described 3 geomorphic regions and 11 zones (Table 3.2), some of which are based on very local geomorphic and species-level taxonomic differences. (It is interesting to note the use of the term "lagoon" by these authors, a practice unusual for fringing reefs which are usually characterized as lacking a lagoon.)

The fringing reef at Bellairs on the west coast of Barbados was described in nearly as great detail by Stearn et al. (1977, pp. 483–492); they recognized 12 geomorphic/ecologic/sedimentologic zones. Although not stressed by Stearn et al., there is a striking resemblance between their geomorphic, etc., zonation (Fig. 4) and their bathymetric chart (Fig. 3) that suggests a strong local correlation between geomorphology/bathymetry and such interrelated factors as turbulence, substrate, light intensity, and coral ecology; which factor(s) exerts the chief influence is uncertain.

In their comparably detailed study of a 650-m long transect across the barrier reef at Carrie Bow Cay, Belize, Rützler and Macintyre (1982) described five geomorphic/ecologic zones (Table 3.2); in the considerably wider barrier reef system off the east coast of the Florida Keys, Ginsburg (1956) recognized only three subdivisions: fore-reef (= seaward slope), outer reef arc (= barrier reef), and back-reef (= reef flat).

Well-developed spurs and grooves characterize the windward sides of nearly all western Atlantic reefs. They are generally comparable to those on oceanic reefs, except that on Caribbean fringing reefs, they may have even greater relief due to their remarkably steep (clifflike) seaward slopes; the grooves contain lesser amounts of loose sediment and may extend to somewhat deeper water.

Drill cores in the spur and groove succession at Looe Key, Florida (Shinn et al., 1981) indicate that it formed over reef sand at least 5 m thick that in turn overlies a flat Pleistocene surface. These authors concluded that for most western Atlantic reefs, the spurs and grooves are of constructional (biologic) origin and that their occurrence is not controlled by bedrock topography (cf. Hopley, 1982, p. 292). It is unknown whether these data and conclusions also apply to spurs and grooves on oceanic reefs.

Comparison of Indo-Pacific and Western Atlantic Zonations

Several comparisons of the geomorphic zonations of Indo-Pacific and western Atlantic reef systems have noted the near-absence of atolls and of algal ridges in the latter (e.g., Stoddart, 1969, pp. 445–458; Kinsey, 1981). The absence of algal ridges in the western Atlantic has generally been attributed to lower levels of wave turbulence. Another aspect of these geomorphic differences is the fact that algal ridges commonly are not present on Indo-Pacific fringing reefs; most western Atlantic reefs are fringing and so would not be expected to have algal ridges. However, such ridges are present in Panama, Bermuda, St. Croix, the Lesser Antilles, and Brazil (Davies, 1983, p. 70; Adey and Vassar, 1975). Where ridges are present, they do not extend as high into the intertidal zone as the algal ridges of Pacific atolls.

Done (1983) noted that in Caribbean reefs the water over the reef flats is commonly deeper than for Indo-Pacific reefs; this may be due to lower Caribbean tidal ranges. Diagrams in Kinsey (1981) indicate that reefs are wider and seaward slopes steeper for Indo-Pacific reefs; however, at Discovery Bay, Jamaica, the seaward slope is nearly vertical in some places.

Finally, it is important to note that it is common for individual small reefs (patch reefs, coral knolls, etc.) to be unzoned regardless of where they are located. It appears as if their size is inadequate to produce a significant environmental gradient across the structure even where there is considerable turbulence. In other cases, especially in lagoons, the turbulence appears to be uniform around the reef perimeter.

Aphotic Zone Reefs

Largely due to the lack of detailed information on aphotic zone reefs, little attention has been paid to their descriptive classification. However, most of those in the Atlantic Ocean are found in areas of moderate-to-strong bottom currents such as near the deeply submerged (drowned) outer edges of continental shelves or the upper parts of continental slopes (Teichert, 1958; Cairns and Stanley, 1981). In the Pacific, these reefs are on steep-sided, drowned seamounts, and flat-topped platforms (Orme, 1977a, p. 294).

In the region of the Blake Plateau, western Atlantic Ocean, Stetson et al. (1962) recognized over 200 distinct structures (both coral reefs and non-reefs) with relief up to 155 m covering an area of 3100–3900 km^2. In the eastern Atlantic, the largest Norwegian reefs are over 4 km^2 (Dons, 1944) with relief up to 65 m (Teichert, 1958). Teichert also reported a deep-water reef 485 km west of Morocco that is a nearly vertical-sided pillar 700 m tall. Other aphotic zone reefs are much smaller; Wilson (1979) reported coral patches only 10–50 m in diameter west of Scotland.

Many European aphotic zone reefs are elongate parallel to the shelf edge; others are more circular and still others are elongate perpendicular to the shelf edge (Stetson et al., 1962, p. 33). As noted above (Physical Factors: Turbulence), the shapes (and sizes?) of these reefs are more strongly influenced by currents than by their location.

Following Teichert's (1958) suggestion, several authors have used the term "bank" rather than reef for these deep-water (aphotic zone) structures with the rather clear understanding that, if they were to be found in the stratigraphic record, they would be called either reefs, bioherms, or biostromes. Such a shift in terminology from Holocene to ancient is confusing and unnecessary and further complicated by the varied usages of the term "bank" by still other authors (see Glossary). Therefore, all these structures, regardless of location, size, shape, or geologic age, are here considered to be aphotic zone patch reefs and no attempt is made to subdivide or classify them.

Genetic Classifications

Reef Foundations

Interest in determining the geologic nature of the rocks beneath oceanic reefs probably began considerably before Darwin (1842) proposed his "subsidence theory" (discussed below) for the origin of atolls. However, his theory further stimulated this interest (Darwin had even suggested drilling as a way of determining its validity). The first organized attempt to drill a hole through a reef and into its foundation was not begun until 1896–1898, when the Royal Society (London) sponsored such a project at Funafuti Atoll, Ellice Islands. The Funafuti boring reached 340 m; the upper 194 m was entirely coral limestone and the rest was dolomite. No true foundation was reached by this early attempt; later seismic data indicate that the foundation is at about 550–770 m.

The Royal Geographical Society (Australia) sponsored the first attempt (1926) to drill to the foundation of a continental shelf reef (Michaelmas Cay, Great Barrier Reef). This boring penetrated 183 m of reef limestone and a later boring at Heron Island (1937) went to 223 m; neither hole reached the bedrock foundation. Results of other reef drillings prior to 1966 are summarized by Trichet et al. (1984, pp. 241–244). The primary goal of each of these early drilling projects was the resolution of the "coral reef problem" (i.e., was Darwin correct?). Confirmation of Darwin's "subsidence theory" ultimately depended on determining the nature of the bedrock foundation.

Oceanic Reefs. Bikini and Enewetak Atolls, Marshall Islands, are located in an area of numerous submerged volcanic cones (seamounts), most of which rise over 3 km above the adjacent deep seafloor (Emery et al., 1954, Chart 1). Most seamounts were truncated by (early Cenozoic?) erosion to form flat-topped guyots. The age of the volcanic rocks is uncertain (probably late Mesozoic?; Ladd, 1973; Shipek, 1962).

In 1947, two holes were drilled at Bikini, neither of which reached the volcanic foundation. The deepest was abandoned at 780 m. Seismic and magnetic data gathered in 1946, 1947, and 1950 indicate that the depth to the volcanic foundation is at 600–2100 m, averaging about 1300 m.

The first successful drilling to the reef foundation was in 1951 at Enewetak Atoll. At a depth of 1340 m, the contact between underlying volcanic foundation of olivene basalt and Eocene reef limestone was penetrated (Ladd et al., 1953). The sedimentary sequence above the basalt includes photic zone coral–algal frameworks, lagoonal, and other shallow-water carbonate rocks and seaward slope deposits (Ladd, 1973). Subsequent drilling to the foundation of Mururoa Atoll, French Polynesia, was successfully undertaken in 1964–1965 (Trichet et al., 1984).

Significance. In April, 1836, Charles Darwin climbed the central volcanic peak of Tahiti; while observing the nearby island of Moorea and its surrounding lagoon and barrier reef, he "discovered" by induction his classic "subsidence theory" for the origin of atolls (Darwin, 1842). Atolls represent the culmination of a genetic succession of geomorphic reef types that begins with fringing and includes barrier reefs as an intermediate stage (Fig. 3.3). Several interrelated factors influence the rates at which the exposed volcanic cone is eroded and subsides into the oceanic crust. Hence, the developmental rate for atoll formation is highly varied. Nonetheless, drilling into volcanic foundations plus the shallow-water origin of the overlying succession of reefs and reef-related carbonate rocks clearly confirms the basic validity of Darwin's subsidence theory for the origin of oceanic fringing and barrier reefs and atolls.

Cores from the holes drilled at Bikini and Enewetak show evidence of an extended interval (approx. 10 million years?) between the formation of the volcanic cone and the beginning of reef growth. The original height of the volcano and the amount of erosion and subsidence during this interval are unknown. The reef and other shallow-water carbonate rocks above the foundation also contain evidence of periodic subaerial leaching and cementation by meteoric water during the Cenozoic history of predominantly upward reef growth. These leached and cemented zones (unconformities) were formed during the Late Eocene and Oligocene, late Early Miocene, and the Pleistocene; they are related to times when the rate at which sea level dropped exceeded the rate of subsidence of the volcanic foundation. Unconformities also indicate that the Cenozoic sub-

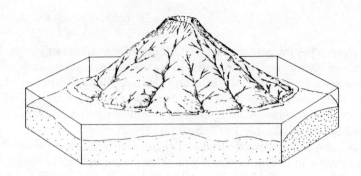

(a)

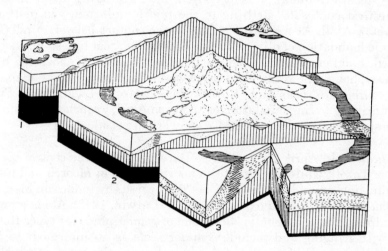

(b) "Hence, if we imagine such an island after long successive intervals, to subside a few feet . . . the coral would be continued upwards, rising from the foundation of the encircling reef."

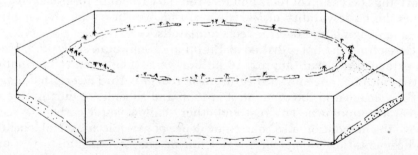

(c) "In time, the central land would sink beneath the level of the sea and disappear but the coral would have completed its circular wall." An atoll island is "a monument raised by myriads of tiny architects to mark the spot where a former land lies buried in the depths of the ocean."

(Quotations from the journal diary of Charles Darwin, 12 April 1836.)

66

sidence rate was not uniform; Ladd (1973) estimated that during the Eocene, the foundation subsided at a rate of about 52 m/million years, during the Miocene at 40 m/million years, and since the Miocene, at only 15 m/million years.

By comparison, radiometric dates of the volcanic foundation at Mururoa Atoll and paleontologic dating of the initiation of reef growth are both Early Miocene. The subsidence rate based on these dates is about 42.5 m/million years. In the shallowest hole (penetrating the summit of the Mururoa volcano), the basalt was dated at 7.2 million years. Trichet et al. (1984) estimated the Late Miocene–Holocene subsidence rate at 80 m/ million years!

Steers and Stoddart (1977) reported a widespread Miocene unconformity within the Coral Sea basin and determined that the oldest basin margin reefs are also Miocene. From their data, they inferred that rates of basin margin subsidence and upward reef growth were approximately equal and estimated them at about 80–110 m/million years.

Continental Shelf Reefs. There is almost no evidence to indicate that Darwin's subsidence theory can also be used to explain the origin and development of continental shelf reefs. The greater size of continental shelves and their slower rates of subsidence are the major differences that preclude the development of same genetic succession in both open ocean and shelf locations. For example, the Australian continent and adjacent Queensland Shelf have been remarkably stable since the Paleozoic. Hopley (1982, p. 28) suggested that the oldest shelf reefs of the Great Barrier Reef system began their growth during the Early Miocene (about 18 million years ago). Since reef growth began, the Queensland Shelf has subsided slowly and intermittently but not as deeply nor as fast as oceanic volcanic reef foundations.

Most continental shelf fringing reefs are relatively thin (5–15 m) and geologically young; those of the Great Barrier Reef were built on Pleistocene–early Holocene unconformities and have extended laterally over adjacent unconsolidated sediments (Hopley, 1982, pp. 356–368). Growth

---

Figure 3.3. Schematic diagrams showing the genetic succession of oceanic reef types based on the "subsidence theory" of Darwin (1842). (*a*) Young volcanic peak surrounded by ring of thin fringing reefs. The ring is broken at mouths of streams where reduced salinity and high turbidity inhibit reef growth. At this early stage in the succession, the volcano may still be active (e.g., Hawaiian fringing reefs and associated islands) and has undergone minimal subsidence. (*b*) Barrier reef stage with clearly defined lagoon. By this stage the volcano is usually inactive, has undergone considerable subsidence, and the reefs are many meters thick (e.g., Tahiti and Moorea). Vertical ruling: volcanic rock; horizontal wavy ruling: reef framework; horizontal dashes: lagoonal sediment; inclined dashes: seaward slope sediment. (*c*) Atoll stage in which no volcanic rocks are exposed in the lagoon (e.g., Bikini and Enewetak Atolls). (Figs. (*a*) and (*c*) from Shepard, 1977; Fig. (*b*) from Kuenen, 1950.)

of fringing reefs begins at or very near the shoreline and formation of a lagoon is precluded by the slow subsidence rate and transportation of sediment from the reef front or crest toward the shore. Sediment deposition occurs between the crest and the shore, filling the potential site for a lagoon.

The elongate shapes of shelf margin photic zone barrier (ribbon) reefs is due to their location parallel to the shelf margin and to their inability to colonize the deep continental slope. Deep-water shelf margins are preferred locations for aphotic zone reefs, many of which are also elongate parallel to the shelf margin. In the case of both photic and aphotic zone shelf margin reefs, their location and elongate shape appear to be controlled largely by strong waves and/or currents which provide nutrients and a physical/chemical environment conducive to vigorous organic production and skeletonization (discussed below).

Davies (1983) has tabulated various estimates of subsidence rates for the foundations of shelf reefs; they range from 20 m/million years for carbonate platforms to 200 m/million years for shelf basins. Hopley (1982, p. 382) has suggested that the average subsidence rate for continental shelves is about 20 m/million years; this rate is half (or less) the rate for oceanic volcanic foundations.

Sea-level Fluctuations

Introduction. Foundation subsidence is not the only factor that influences the size, shape, and genesis of reefs. Other important factors include:

   a.   Diastrophism of the earth's crust. In addition to local subsidence (one form of diastrophism) of individual volcanoes, the crust may warp downward or upward in broad (regional) flexures (McNutt and Menard, 1978), downward by subduction near continental shelf margins, and laterally by seafloor spreading or along transform faults. All of these forms of crustal movement may alter the locations of reefs with respect to sea level.

   b.   Changes in volume of water in the seas (eustasy). In these situations, if there is no diastrophism, sea-level changes result primarily from formation of glaciers (drop in sea level) or their melting (rise in sea level).

In some areas, sea level has been influenced by both diastrophism and eustasy, thus making the history of sea-level fluctuations highly complex. Furthermore, both factors exert considerable influence over the origin, location, and development of photic zone reefs (Chappell, 1980). Their influence over aphotic zone reefs is rather minimal.

Darwin (1842) made no provisions for the effects of eustatic sea-level fluctuations in his "subsidence theory" for the origin of atolls. For the prolonged Cenozoic development of most oceanic reefs, the diastrophic influence is much greater than eustatic influences. Conversely, for the origin and short-term (Neogene) development of thinner and younger continental shelf reefs, eustatic influences exceed diastrophic influences. In areas of active mountain-building (orogeny) and volcanism, elevated reefs and wave-cut terraces show a systematic increase in age with increasing height above sea level. Such reefs have been used effectively to determine the rate of uplift (after compensating for eustatic effects).

Worldwide climatic cooling apparently began during the Early Oligocene, increased during the Miocene and Pliocene, and reached its culmination during the Pleistocene. Superimposed on this overall long-term trend were several shorter-term fluctuations of both warmer and colder thermal regimes that caused emergence and erosion as well as submergence and "drowning" of shallow photic zone reefs. Pre-Pleistocene reefs and beach terraces are found at elevations of 50 m or more above present sea level; Thiel (1962) estimated that if all ice now on the earth were to melt, sea level would rise by about 66 m. Conversely, features that have been judged to be of subaerial or peri-tidal origin (terraces, caves, shallow-water reefs) are present at depths as great as 130 m.

Pleistocene Eustasy. Evidence of Pleistocene glacially induced sea-level fluctuations is widespread and includes:

a.   Elevated (Pl. 2) and submerged photic zone reef frameworks and associated wave-cut benches, terraces, and reef flats (with corals, etc., in growth positions). The quality of preservation of these features and hence the objectivity of their recognition is inversely related to their age, the rate of sea-level change, and on the types, growth forms, and degree of support (resistance to erosion and transportation) of the framework organisms. Old reefs at relatively high elevations that have been alternately exposed and submerged several times and frameworks dominated by branching coralla are usually poorly preserved; reefs 120,000 years old or younger and presently located at lower elevations (+5 to +10 m) are rather well preserved. However, the distinction between very young reefs (less than 5,000 years) at low elevations (1–2 m) and storm-deposited ramparts and shingles composed of branched corals is difficult to make on many shorelines. On the seaward slope of most Indo-Pacific reefs, there is a clearly defined submarine terrace at about 15–20 m depth that probably was formed by wave erosion during the Late Pleistocene; many such reefs also have slightly emergent (+1 m) young wave-cut reef flats (Montaggioni and Pirazzoli, 1984).

b.   The presence of one or more "generations" of framework calcite (rarely dolomite) cements of freshwater (vadose or phreatic) origin. Such cements indicate one or more episodes of emergence and are usually closely associated with leached unconformities; unlike most of the other criteria considered here, meteoric water cements and leached unconformities can be recognized and correlated in subsurface cores (Marshall and Davies, 1984). These cements and leached unconformities indicate Pleistocene emergence of many Pacific oceanic reefs and subsequent differential foundation subsidence rates. For example, the 6000–9000 yr unconformity at 9 m depth (below sea level) in the core from Mururoa Atoll occurs at −10 m and at −20 m at Enewetak Atoll and One Tree Reef, Great Barrier Reef, respectively (Grigg, 1981, p. 689). These cores also contain older unconformities (between 100,000 and 200,000 years old; Veeh and Green, 1977, p. 195).

c.   Notches, caverns, and caves formed by surf erosion and freshwater solution near sea level. These features have been recognized in both emergent (up to +40 m) and submergent (down to −100 m) locations at numerous levels and indicate former episodes of sea-level stability (Pl. 16b; 17a).

d.   Ancient microatolls (Pl. 17b; see Glossary) and algal ridges. These are very precise indicators of former intertidal-to-very-shallow subtidal levels. In fact, the total height of microatolls coincides closely with the water depth at the time of their growth (Scoffin and Stoddart, 1978).

On the basis of these and other criteria for recognizing Pleistocene sea levels, historical successions of fluctuations have been described for numerous tropical coasts. (The methods for dating these features are beyond the scope of this book.) For example, in the West Indies and especially in Jamaica, four levels of emergent reefs were formed during Pleistocene interglacial stages and have been dated at 80,000–200,000 years BP. There is also a succession of drowned reefs and ridges at −24, −40, and −60 m formed during glacial stages and dated at 8,000, 11,000, and 14,000 years BP, respectively (Goreau et al., 1979).

Ideally, eustatic fluctuations and subsequent still-stands of the same age have a global signature when they are formed. However, there is no single global pattern of features at the same elevation comparable to the West Indian succession. In progressively older fluctuations, the global variations resulting from differences in local and regional diastrophism and differences in biological composition and coral growth rates increase in magnitude. The oldest generally agreed-upon emergent features were formed during the last interglacial stage (Sangoman in North American terminology; Riss-Würm in European) about 120,000–125,000 years ago and occur at elevations of +5 to +10 m (Fig. 3.4); all younger features are submarine with the possible exception of much younger features (4,000–6,000 years BP) on some shores at about +1 to +2 m. The best developed submergent features were formed during the last glacial stage (Wisconsinan in North American terminology; Würm in European) about 18,000–20,000 years BP and occur at about −130 to −140 m (Fig. 3.4).

Effects on Reefs. Perhaps the chief geomorphic effects of low Pleistocene sea levels on oceanic barrier reefs and atolls were the formation of the

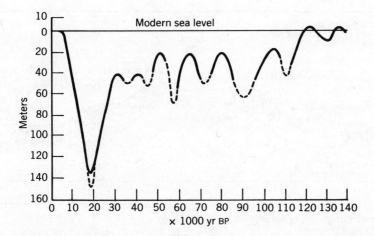

Figure 3.4. Pattern of sea-level changes over the last 140,000 years. The last interglacial stage (Sangoman) is marked by elevated shore features about 120,000 years BP, the last glacial stage (Wisconsinian) by deeply submerged features about 20,000 years BP, the Holocene by rising sea level (Holocene transgression) to about 5,000 years BP, and relatively uniform sea level from 5,000 years BP to the present. (From Hopley, 1982.)

major passes and channels between the reefs by subaerial erosive processes and the leveling of numerous emergent volcanic cones by shallow-water erosive processes. If sea-level drop (regression) occurs slowly and the sloping sides of the volcano are broad, the reefs should also migrate laterally downslope and become reestablished at the level of the lower still-stand (Fig. 3.5a). Subsequent higher sea levels (transgression) brings marine water into the lagoons through the passes, covers the flat-topped cones, and reestablishes growth of the barrier reef and atoll system (Fig. 3.5b).

For continental shelves, the geomorphic effects of lower sea level on subaerially exposed older reef systems are much more drastic. Widespread unconformities are formed on the exposed carbonate substrates; if the climate is humid, the surface may become very uneven by the deep incision of streams and the development of a karst topography consisting of dolines, caverns, and limestone towers (Purdy, 1974, Fig. 30). On wide shelves, there may be limited lateral migration of patch reefs toward the seaward slope and of marginal reefs down the seaward slope. Usually, however, the regression exposes and kills nearly all the reefs so that renewed growth with subsequent rising sea level begins on the unconformity (former land surface) and continues in a dominantly upward direction.

Classification of Shelf Reefs
The origins and development of continental shelf reefs and their genetic classification commonly are more strongly influenced by eustatic factors than by diastrophic factors. In addition, the effects of eustatic changes have been greater on the developmental histories of continental shelf patch

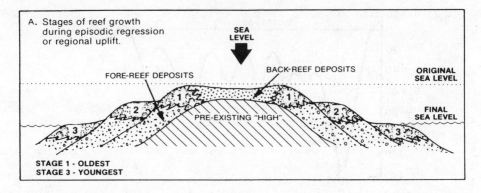

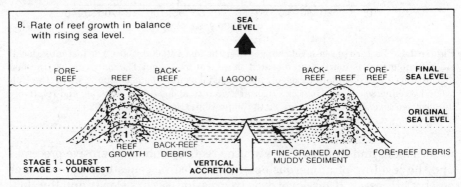

Figure 3.5. Geomorphic changes of reef systems in response to sea-level change. (*a*) Lateral migration down seaward slopes during falling sea level. (*b*) Vertical reef growth during rising sea level. (Modified from Longman, 1981.)

reefs than on either continental margin (barrier) reefs or fringing reefs. As a result, most disagreement over genetic classification of shelf reefs has concerned the exceedingly diverse sizes, shapes, and histories of patch reefs, especially those of the Great Barrier Reef (reviewed in Hopley, 1982, Chap. 1; pp. 247–249).

Foundations. Although reefs have been present and locally very abundant on Cenozoic continental shelves since the Eocene, most of them were alternately killed and revived more than once (Lloyd, 1973; Chappell, 1983) prior to and including the last (Sangoman) interglacial stage (approx. 120,000 years BP). Since the Sangoman high sea-level interglacial stage, sea level has fluctuated several times (Fig. 3.4) and reached a minimum about 20,000 years BP during the Wisconsinan glacial stage. During these and earlier episodes of low sea level, multiple unconformities were formed and provided potential hard surfaces for the foundation and upward growth of reefs.

However, because of the considerably greater drop in sea level during the Wisconsinan glacial stage, it is widely believed that nearly all Holocene continental shelf reefs were founded on and have grown upward from this unconformity (antecedent platform of Hoffmeister and Ladd, 1944). This eroded surface was composed primarily of interspersed older reefs located mostly in elevated positions ("highs") and variously cemented sedimentary substrates. Although the duration of Wisconsinan low sea level was relatively short (<10,000 years), the surface of this unconformity (karst topography) was variously eroded to different shapes, slopes, elevations, and relief (Purdy, 1974; Hopley, 1982, Chaps. 6, 7). As sea level rose during the Holocene and flooded the karst surface, there was preferential reestablishment of young reefs on the "highs" so that most Early Holocene reefs began their growth on the Wisconsinan unconformity above pre-Wisconsinan reefs. Thus, the initial location, size, and shape of Holocene reefs were largely determined by or inherited from pre-Holocene reefs and other topographic "highs" (Searle et al., 1981; Geister, 1983; Fig. 3.6).

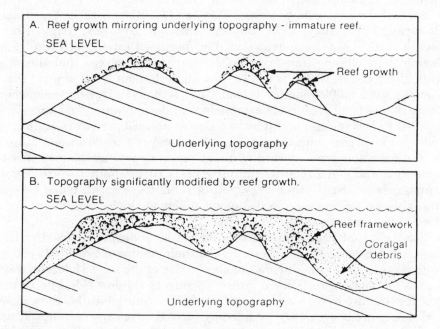

Figure 3.6. Relationship between submarine foundation topography, time, and reef morphology. (a) Soon after the Holocene transgression began, coral knolls and reefs began to grow on the elevated foundation "highs." (b) With continued reef growth, the topographic depressions became filled with reef debris and the reefs reached a common level near the low-tide line. (From Longman, 1981.)

Purdy (1974) emphasized the role of karst topography for the origin and development of oceanic reefs, especially atolls and barrier reefs, as well as for shelf reefs. Others (e.g., Hopley, 1982, pp. 187–195, 216–219; Searle et al., 1981; Choi, 1981) acknowledge the importance of pre-Holocene unconformities as foundations for Early Holocene reefs but would modify the long-term influence of the configuration of the karst surface in the later history of reef development. After establishment of the initial reefs on the karst "highs," subsequent modifications in location, size, and shape were the result of interrelations between rates of sea-level rise and upward reef growth. Many of the disagreements among various genetic classifications of shelf reefs involve differences in the relative influence of the initial foundation topography and these subsequent factors (sea-level rise; reef growth).

Holocene Transgression. Ideally, the rates of sea-level rise during the Holocene were globally uniform during the same time intervals and directly reflect the rate of glacial ice melting. Differences in local and regional diastrophism, the features used to determine ancient sea levels, the rates of erosion of these features, and the ages of these features cause variation in the calculated rates of the Holocene transgression (Fig. 3.7).

Several authors (e.g., Stoddart, 1969, p. 467; Bloom, 1974; Thom and Chappell, 1975; Adey, 1978; Hopley, 1982, pp. 169–184; Grigg, 1981; Lighty et al., 1982) have determined or discussed rates of sea-level rise during the Holocene transgression. It is generally agreed that the rate from about 6,000–18,000 years BP was higher (about 5–10 mm/yr) than the rate since 6,000 years BP (about 0.5–1.5 mm/yr). During the earlier phase of sea-level rise, reefs established in deeper water and therefore exposed to less intense sunlight had slower upward growth rates. Many could not keep pace with the rising sea level and so were "drowned"; those in shallow water grew upward at about the same rate as the rate of sea-level rise and continued as thriving reefs throughout the Holocene transgression. Still other very young reefs were established as the transgression successively flooded new foundation "highs" and maintained their upper surfaces in shallow water.

For reefs that kept pace with rising sea level during the earlier Holocene, there was commonly a change in their dominant growth direction from vertical to lateral during the slower rise of the later Holocene (Fig. 3.8). Most modern reefs have grown upward to the low tide line in the last few hundred years and are presently growing laterally; their sizes and shapes are being slowly modified by surface waves and currents. Thus, reefs that began in shallower water during the Holocene transgression reached the low tide line before those in deeper water; they began their latral growth phase earlier and consequently have quite different shapes than the "late arrivals." The longer the period of lateral growth, the less apparent the influence of the foundation surface. (Factors influencing up-

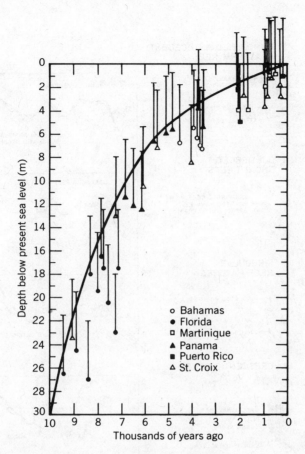

Figure 3.7. Minimum sea-level curve for the last 10,000 years based on 42 *in situ* samples of the very shallow-water (<5 m) framebuilding scleractinian *Acropora palmata* in the western Atlantic. Vertical bars represent ancient water-depth intervals of 0–5 m for each sample. Variation from curve due to numerous factors discussed in text. (From Lighty et al., 1982.)

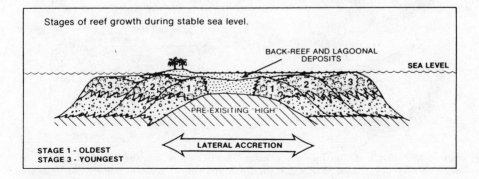

Figure 3.8. During episodes of stable (i.e., the present) or very slowly rising sea level, the dominant direction of reef growth is lateral, and progressively younger reef margins encroach over older reef-derived flank deposits (From Longman, 1981.)

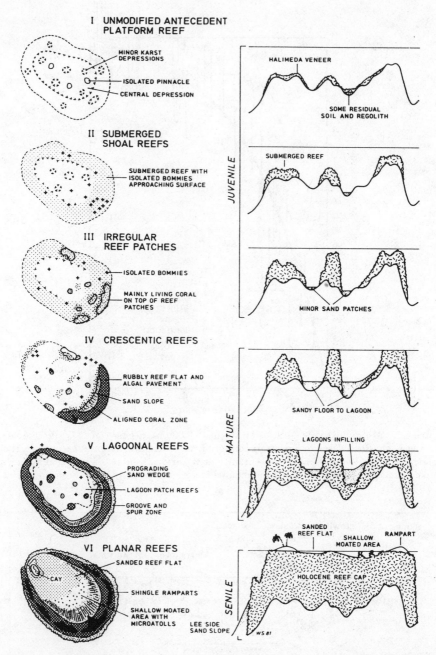

Figure 3.9. Schematic outline of a genetic classification of continental shelf patch reefs based on a medium-sized antecedent platform and time since flooding by the Holocene transgression. "Bommies" is an Australian term for small coral knolls or coral "heads." In the juvenile stages, the rate of sea-level rise exceeds the rate of upward accretion of the reef. With slower rise (mature stages), accretion "catches up," the reef surface reaches sea level, and dominant growth becomes lateral. (From Hopley, 1982.)

ward growth of corals and algae are discussed in Chap. 3: Biological Factors and Accretion of Reefs in Chap. 4.)

In oceanic reefs the probability of "drowning" is somewhat greater than for shelf reefs because of their generally higher rates of foundation subsidence. During the Holocene transgression, upward reef accretion had to nearly equal the combined rates of foundation subsidence and sea-level rise to prevent "drowning." The tops of numerous guyots are covered with dead Late Pleistocene reefs that clearly indicate that these reefs "lost the race." Other seamounts and guyots contain older reefs in which the cause of "death by drowning" was almost wholly due to rapid subsidence.

Summary. Genetic classification of continental shelf reefs is generally more difficult than for oceanic reefs because of greater variation in the locations, sizes, and shapes of their foundations, the greater effects of eustasy on their development, and the greater variation in chemical and physical factors (especially intense storms) and their effects on shelves than in the open ocean. Thus, differences in the ages of shelf reefs, their foundations, response to eustatic fluctuations, storms, etc., strongly affect the growth, geomorphic development, and classification of shelf reefs. These cause-and-effect relationships must be analyzed almost on a reef-by-reef basis to understand their variously different histories before a coherent and broadly accepted genetic classification of shelf reefs is attained. Several such classifications have been proposed with varying emphases on one or more features (e.g., lagoon size or shape) that are locally applicable to particular reefs. However, the crux of the geomorphic classification problem is the relative importance given to the karst-induced size and shape of the foundation, the influence of Holocene sea-level rise, and the effects of shallow-water processes since the reef reached sea level. The shelf patch reefs of the Great Barrier Reef have been the subject of some of these attempts at classification. Most recently, Hopley (1982, pp. 249–255) has outlined a genetic classification (Fig. 3.9) of patch reefs and discussed (pp. 255–274) the problems of using it for some of the reefs of the Great Barrier Reef system.

BIOLOGICAL FACTORS

Biogeography

The chief influences over the distribution and taxonomic composition of the major marine biogeographic units (includes realms and provinces of most authors) are their geologic history, their present large-scale environmental parameters, especially temperature and water circulation patterns and various geological and biological factors (reviewed by Potts, 1985). Within these major units, the distribution and composition of such smaller units as communities and populations in the sea are most strongly influenced by more local environmental parameters such as salinity, substrate, and turbulence. In situations where gradients in these chemical and physical factors are steep or where there is a physical barrier to migration, biogeographic boundaries of varying degrees of objectivity can be determined. The present discussion will concern Holocenc provinces as determined by the distribution of scleractinian corals.

Provinces

The world photic zone reef coral biota is easily subdivided into two self-explanatory biogeographic provinces, the Atlantic and the Indo-Pacific. Prior to the uplift of the Panamian isthmus, there was a single pantropical province with only minor taxonomic differences; the Caribbean and eastern Pacific were connected by the former Bolivar seaway. Dating of the uplift by faunal means gives discrepant results. The corals suggest that separation of the Atlantic and Indo-Pacific Provinces may have begun as early as in the Middle–Late Miocene (approx. 5–15 million years ago; Frost, 1972; Newell, 1971, pp. 23–30; cf. Rosen, 1975, p. 5; Jones and Hasson, 1985, pp. 339–341), whereas land mammals clearly indicate that the Bolivar seaway prevented the migration of North American placentals to South America until the Late Pliocene–Early Pleistocene (2.5–10 million years ago; Patterson and Pascual, 1972; Stehli and Webb, 1985).

One of the most important distinctions between the Atlantic and Indo-Pacific Provinces is the higher diversity at the genus and species levels of both the corals and non-coral taxa in the Indo-Pacific Province. (The gorgonians are a notable exception; the diversity and abundance of tropical western Atlantic gorgonians is the highest in the world; Kinzie, 1973, p. 95.) For example, the highest Indo-Pacific coral diversity is more than 50 genera and 700 species (in Melanesia, southeast Asia; Stoddart, 1969, p. 441), whereas in the Atlantic the comparable figures are 34 and 64 (in Jamaica; Wells and Lang, 1973). On the Atlantic side of Panama, there are 21 genera and only 10 on the Pacific side (Stehli and Wells, 1971).

Atlantic Province. The Atlantic Province includes the reefs in the Caribbean and West Indies, the north and east coasts of South America, Florida, the Bahamas, Bermuda, and the Gulf of Guinea in western Africa (Fig. 2.2); the Indo-Pacific Province occupies the remainder of the tropical reef belt (between the dotted lines, Fig. 2.2).

The most massive Atlantic Province corals are *Montastraea annularis* and *Diploria* spp; shallow seaward slopes of high turbulence are dominated by branching *Acropora palmata,* encrusting *Agaricia,* and the hydrozoan *Millepora.* In protected shallow areas, *A. areolata* and *Cladocora arbuscula* predominate, and, in deeper water, foliaceous corals such as *Agaricia undata.* On the leeward sides of reefs, the dominant genera are *Montastraea, Diploria, Stephanocoenia, Millepora,* and *Agaricia,* with almost no *Acropora* (Stoddart, 1969, p. 458).

In the Atlantic, *Acropora* and *Porites* are among the most important genera and each is represented by three species; in contrast, in the Indo-Pacific Province there are about 150 species of *Acropora* and 30 species of *Porites*. There also are several important Indo-Pacific genera (e.g., *Pocillopora, Stylophora, Seriatopora, Montipora, Goniopora, Goniastrea*) that are now absent in the Atlantic but were present during the Tertiary in both provinces. On the basis of lower diversity and the absence of several important genera in the Atlantic, Wells (1957a, p. 628) characterized this province as "a weakening relict of that of the mid-Tertiary Tethyan seas." The times of extinction of the various genera in the Atlantic are staggered but with maxima at the ends of the Eocene and Oligocene.

Indo-Pacific Province. Because of the much higher diversity and greater taxonomic variation among Indo-Pacific reefs, it is much more difficult to characterize this province. However, the genera noted in the previous paragraph are both abundant and widespread.

In the area of the narrow continental shelf of the eastern Pacific, the relations among water temperature, circulation patterns, and *molluscan* faunal provinces are well-established. The boundary between the California Province (temperate realm) and the Panamic Province (tropical realm) coincides with the 20°C isotherm which occurs about mid-length in the Gulf of California and roughly corresponds with the northern limit of coral reefs. Squires (1959, pp. 403–404) determined that at the species level, the *corals* of the Gulf of California and Panamic Molluscan Province have close Indo-Pacific affinities; of the 22 species in the eastern Pacific, 6 are present in all three areas. Squires concluded that the corals of the Gulf do not constitute a separate province. He also found that the photic zone corals of the eastern Pacific islands (Galapagos, Clipperton, Socorro, Clarion) are more like those of the main Indo-Pacific Province than to those of the continental shelf (Panamic Molluscan Province).

Perhaps the greatest similarity between Atlantic and Indo-Pacific Province reefs is that in areas of high wave turbulence both are dominated by *Acropora* species with branches pointing into the surf. Additionally, numerous non-coral genera and even species are common to both provinces.

The greatest differences revolve around the general lack of algal ridges and their associated biota from Atlantic reefs. Thus, the encrusting coralline algae which are of major importance in Pacific reefs and of less importance in the Indian Ocean are of generally minor importance in the Atlantic Province. Other differences are indicated in Table 3.3 (see also Jones and Hasson, 1985, p. 341).

Cosmopolitanism/Endemism
Among the corals, there is an interesting contrast between the overall within-province cosmopolitanism and between-province endemism.

TABLE 3.3. Taxonomic Comparison of Atlantic Province and Indo-Pacific Province Photic Zone Reef Faunas

Taxa	Atlantic	Indo-Pacific
1. Huge bivalves	Absent	Common, especially *Tridacna, Hippodus*
2. Gall crabs	Absent	Abundant
3. Giant anemones (with communal crustaceans and fish)	Absent	Abundant
4. Cypraeids	Few Species	Many species
5. Conids	Few species	Many species
6. Gorgonacea	*Plexaurella* and *Eunicea* ("sea whips") present.	Uncommon
	Gorgonia ("sea fans") large, abundant, diverse	Uncommon– insignificant
7. Coenothecalia; Stolonifera	Uncommon– insignificant	*Heliopora, Tubipora* ("organ pipes"), *Sarcophyton, Lobophyllum, Xenia* abundant

Source: After Wells, 1957a, p. 628; Stoddart, 1969, p. 459.

Within the Indo-Pacific Province, the taxonomic composition of reef corals, even at the species level, is remarkably similar from the Red Sea and the east coast of Africa through Indonesia to French Polynesia, an equatorial distance of about 22,500 km. This same coral assemblage is clearly recognizable at reduced diversity for another 5000 km in reefs on the east coast of Panama. The Indo-Pacific Province also is clearly recognizable in the Great Barrier Reef (of 320 algal species, only about 2–3% are endemic), whereas south of the reef, algal diversity (>1000 spp.) and endemism (approx. 32%) are much higher (Cribb, 1973, p. 72). In the Marshall Islands, about 84% of the species of Foraminiferida are widely distributed in the tropical Pacific and only 8% are present only in the lagoons (Cushman et al., 1954). Conversely, many aphotic zone corals are among the most cosmopolitan benthic invertebrates known; some species are distributed nearly worldwide. Thus, there is a single global aphotic zone coral province (Stanley, 1980).

It is uncertain how this widespread coexistence of highly diverse competing organisms can be maintained; Levinton (1982, p. 442) suggested that the rates of competitive exclusion among reef organisms are unusually slow or that competition here is so complex that exclusion is inefficient. Furthermore, the data of Scheltema (1972) of long-term survival of planktonic larvae of reef organisms (up to 320 d) and those of Jokiel (1984) on long-distance rafting of mature coral colonies (20,000–40,000 km!) certainly help explain interprovince cosmopolitanism.

The degree of interprovince endemism is very high; Rosen (1975, p. 3) reported that there are only 5 genera common to both provinces and Stehli and Wells (1971, Fig. 6) calculated an overall generic Jaccard Coefficient of Similarity of only about 0.05! Thus, each province appears to have behaved as a separate evolutionary system during the Neogene, resulting in progressively increasing interprovince endemism.

Diversity

Nowhere else in the seas is there such a bewildering range of living things. . .
(Wells, 1957a, p. 609)

The concept, measurement, and interpretation of taxonomic diversity is one of ecology's most interesting problems, and studies of reef communities are commonly cited as examples of high diversity; there are nearly 350 species of scleractinians in the Great Barrier Reef! Regardless of geologic age or location, reef communities nearly always are much more diverse than contemporaneous communities living adjacent to reefs. In the present context, diversity is simply the number of genera or species present in a unit area (Holocene communities) or volume of rock (ancient communities). This usage is comparable to "species richness" of other authors if the measurement is at the species level. However, species diversity of reef communities is only indirectly related to the concept of taxonomic uniformity/equitability because of sampling and area/volume problems of the comparatively large colonial reef organisms. Sampling techniques have varied considerably among different workers, which makes comparing diversity among Holocene and ancient reefs difficult. Such comparisons should be among samples of similar size collected from areas/volumes of similar size, and, to establish meaningful variations or trends in diversity, the samples should be from similar community types (within-habitat diversity). Nonetheless, it is readily apparent to even a casual observer that one of the important characteristics of reef communities is their high diversity. Wells (1957a, p. 625) noted that the total species diversity (Protozoa to fish) of large reef areas was unknown but could reach more than 3000 species (probably a conservative figure); Newell (1971, p. 2) estimated that ". . . the specific diversity of a modern tropical coral reef exceeds by one order of magnitude the diversity of the most nearly comparable other marine community. . . ." Most of the interest in diversity concerns the interpretation of why reefs are so diverse.

Centers of high diversity suggest that they have been centers of rapid evolutionary diversification. If this is correct, the geologic longevity of taxa near these centers should be relatively short with increasing longevity of taxa toward the margins (Stehli and Wells, 1971; cf. Newell, 1971, p. 28). In the Atlantic Province, the center of highest coral diversity is in the western Caribbean and here the average longevity of the genera is the shortest. By contrast, in reefs near the southern latitudinal limit off the east coast of Brazil, species-level diversity is about half that of the Caribbean and consists of dominantly archaic, endemic taxa; millepores and coralline algae are relatively more important here than in the Caribbean reefs.

The same general diversity gradient and longevity pattern also are present in the Indo-Pacific Province but the data are not quite as convincing. In addition, the average longevity of Atlantic Province coral genera is strikingly higher than for the Indo-Pacific, suggesting that lower Atlantic diversity is indeed related to slower evolutionary rates. However, it is important to note that these suggestions are based on indirect evidence; just because the Indo-Pacific highest diversity center contains several endemic genera and species does not prove that they originated there. The fossil record is generally inadequate to prove the location of most speciation events. In both provinces, the highest diversity occurs at about 10–15°N latitude and generally corresponds with the highest surface water temperatures except for an anomalous area of high temperature–low diversity in the eastern Pacific (Stehli and Wells, 1971, Figs. 1–4).

But high species diversity in reefs is not true for all higher taxa nor is the degree of diversity difference from reefs to non-reefs uniform among the higher taxa. For example, the diversity and overall size of plants in reef communities is less than in non-reefs, the abundance and diversity of brown algae in temperate regions is higher than in comparable reef areas, and in the Great Barrier Reef the development of red algae is surprisingly poor relative to non-reef areas in southern Australia. In the latter area, there are eight times as many red as green algal species, whereas in the southern area of the reefs there are only twice as many reds as greens (Cribb, 1973, p. 73).

Even within the same reef system, the pattern of diversity change may be irregular. For example, in the Great Barrier Reef, fringing reefs have higher overall diversity than other reef types (Veron and Pichon, 1976), and in French Polynesia, coral diversity is higher in high island reef systems than in those with lower land-derived nutrient concentrations.

High diversity has two major consequences for the manner in which the community functions: the organisms are highly specialized in their food selection and they occupy more restricted living space. Both of these consequences require special adaptations for survival from competition; the first may be described as fine partitioning of feeding niches and the second as fine partitioning of space into microhabitats. In diverse reef communities, every conceivable food resource is efficiently utilized and every conceivable microhabitat occupied, in many cases by relatively small organisms. However, there are numerous exceptions to these generalizations, some of which are discussed later in this chapter.

Another aspect of diversity that is particularly applicable to reef communities concerns the relatively rapid growth rates of some organisms and their ability to occupy large areas of the reef surface at the expense of other organisms. Thus, "Why doesn't the most rapidly growing species simply crowd out other species and reduce the diversity of mature reefs?" The presumed correct, but certainly not proven, answer is that intense cropping by herbivores and carnivores (Menge and Sutherland, 1976), changes in the chemical and physical factors, and variable success in larval recruitment keep what may appear to be a uniform and stable community in a state of dynamic flux in the relative proportions of the species. Changing biotic and abiotic stresses prevent the domination of reef communities by a few fast-growing species. Sale (1977) attributed high diversity of reef fishes to these same general factors. By contrast, in low wave stress embayments and lagoons, Dollar (1982) found monospecific reefs built by the coral *Porites compressa* and reasoned that it simply displaced its competitors.

Area–Diversity Relations

Sampling problems become readily apparent when diversities are compared from highly discrepant area or volume sizes simply because diversities in large areas are greater than in small areas (Abele and Walters, 1979). In searching for reasons to explain this relation, it must be remembered that diversity is the result of the interrelations between speciation and extinction rates. Thus, in larger areas, gene pools are likely to be larger and more polymorphic and habitats more varied, providing more opportunities for genetic isolation, genetic drift, and allopatric speciation. Conversely, small areas can also become isolated sites of rapid speciation and endemism. For example, the lagoon at Bikini Atoll, Marshall Islands, is quite isolated from the open ocean and Johnson (1954) discovered that the lagoon zooplankton contains several endemic species and is more diverse than the open ocean plankton. By contrast, in French Polynesia, Chevalier (1981) found that in atoll lagoons having open circulation with the ocean, coral diversity was much higher than in nearly closed lagoons.

Theory also suggests that large areas contain more refuges during times of environmental stress, which reduces the probability of extinction. Newell (1971, p. 23) reported that the greatest coral endemism in the

Indo-Pacific Province is in Indonesia and the north end of the Great Barrier Reef and that this condition is geologically young. This suggests that several of the taxa are relicts and that these two high diversity areas may be refugia. The reefs at the north end of the Red Sea may be another isolated refuge of high diversity (58 genera), but in this case it is located at the latitudinal limit of the province.

Newell (1971, pp. 25–26) compared the total areas of the Atlantic and Indo-Pacific Provinces and the generic and species diversities of their corals, molluscs, and fish. He found that the total area of the Indo-Pacific reef province is about 5 times greater than the Atlantic and that taxonomic diversity in the Indo-Pacific is from about 4 to 9 times greater than in the Atlantic; thus, the number of taxa per km^2 is quite similar. Adey and Burke (1977) refined the area–diversity approach by determining the areas of shallow coastal shores available for growth of reefs; they found that this area in the Indo-Pacific is about 14.5 times greater than in the Atlantic. This figure almost exactly coincides with their data on the difference in the diversity of coral *species* in the two provinces and strongly supports the hypothesis of Abele and Walters (1979, pp. 121–125) that area may be the chief control over species diversity.

In both provinces, the highest diversity centers closely coincide with areas of geologically young, volcanically active island clusters located near convergent plate margins. Conversely, lowest diversity coincides with the extensive open ocean, island-poor areas in the eastern part of each province. These geological aspects lend considerable support to the allopatric speciation model for high reef diversity.

Diversity Gradients

The mere presence of centers of high diversity in both the Atlantic and Indo-Pacific Provinces implies that diversity must decrease radially from those centers; numerous examples of such diversity gradients drawn from a wide variety of higher taxa were presented by Fischer (1961). Both the raw data and trend surface maps of Stehli and Wells (1971) confirm the existence of latitudinal and longitudinal diversity gradients in both provinces and that because diversity is higher in the Indo-Pacific, the latitudinal gradient there is much steeper than in the Atlantic; the longitudinal gradients in both provinces appear to be similarly steep. Furthermore, their data rather clearly indicate that the latitudinal diversity gradient closely follows the latitudinal gradient for sea surface temperature; thus, diversity and temperature appear to be positively correlated, but the relationship between the longitudinal diversity gradient and temperature is unclear because the longitudinal temperature gradient is so weak. A further complication is the fact that in many areas of low diversity near the latitudinal limits of coral reefs, not only does the absolute lower temperature fall below the optimum (Table 2.2), but the annual temperature range also exceeds the optimum. In such situations, it is uncertain whether the low coral diversity is more strongly influenced by low absolute temperature or by greater temperature fluctuation.

Previously, Wells (1954) had discovered that in the Indo-Pacific the same genera seem to drop out in the same sequence regardless of the direction from the center of highest diversity (i.e., there is an overall symmetry in the generic composition and diversity of reef communities centered around the diversity maximum). The more recent data of Stehli and Wells (1971, p. 118) suggest that some refinement of Wells' earlier generalization may be necessary. In addition, Yonge (1973) reported that in both the Atlantic and Indo-Pacific no new coral genera or species appear along the latitudinal gradient, so that each taxon present near the province periphery is also present at the high diversity center.

Perhaps the best example of a latitudinal diversity gradient is for coral genera on the east coast of Australia (Wells, 1955, 1957; Squires, 1959, p. 396; Veron, 1974). Here there is a progressive diversity decrease from a maximum of 60 at the north end of the Great Barrier Reef (9°S latitude) to about 20 at the south end (24–25°S), followed by a less steep decline to 7 at Sydney (34°S) and to one genus at Tasmania (41°S). The same general diversity gradient also occurs in much attenuated form in the reefs in the Gulf of California, ending with monospecific "reefs" at the north end (26°N latitude; Squires, 1959, pp. 395–396, 401). In both the Great Barrier Reef and the Gulf of California, the diversity gradients appear to support the close correlation between surface water temperature and coral diversity (Fischer, 1961, Fig. 5).

Latitudinal and longitudinal diversity gradients are not confined to corals; they have also been reported for reef fishes and gastropods of the genus *Conus* (see Levinton, 1982, pp. 427–430), other molluscs (Wiens, 1962, p. 233), and crinoids (Macurda and Meyer, 1983).

Photic zone coral diversity is inversely correlated with depth (Wells, 1957; Rosen, 1977), but determination of the relative importance of the numerous potential causal factors involved is made difficult by the fact that temperature, the amount of sunlight, turbulence, dissolved gases, etc., are also inversely correlated with depth. In addition, the decreasing quality of sampling in progressively deeper water may account for some of the apparent low diversities below 100 m. However, the progressively decreasing coral diversity with depth among photic zone reefs seems to grade rather uniformly into the well-documented low taxonomic diversity of corals in aphotic zone reefs. Rosen (1977) presented a method for using generic diversity in Indo-Pacific shallow photic zone reefs to predict water depth, but diversity alone is a poor predictor of depth in the transition region from deep photic to shallow aphotic zone reefs.

Ecologic Succession

One of the important theoretical aspects of ecologic succession is that the community changes from one of low diversity and high instability (the pioneer stage) to progressively higher diversity levels (intermediate stage), ending with one of high stability and diversity (climax stage). Because the succession may be interrupted, reversed, or set back by catastrophic events of varying severity and the rates of change vary among contemporaneous communities (Knowlton et al., 1981), the duration from pioneer to climax is not very predictable; estimates for reefs are about 10–50 years. Ideally, there is an orderly and predictable sequence of appearances and disappearances of species in the succession: pioneer communities are dominated by hardy species that are the first to appear and the last to disappear as a result of catastrophe, whereas climax community species are the last to appear and the first to disappear during or after a catastrophe.

Many ecologists recognize two intergrading types of succession (Odum, 1971, pp. 54–55). The first type is autogenic, or community controlled, in which the changes are brought about by the activities of the organisms themselves. That is, the organisms in each stage modify the environment in ways that enhance the success of the organisms in the next stage and cause their own demise; many ecologists regard this type as the only "true" succession. Another type of succession is allogenic or physically/chemically induced. Both types of succession occur in reef communities and may alternate in their relative importance.

Connell and Slatyer (1977) proposed three process models of succession:

a.   Facilitation (= autogenic above).
b.   Tolerance; the pioneer species are fast growing, rapid dispersers (opportunists) and the later colonizers (equilibrium species) utilize the environmental resources more efficiently. Bosence (1984) regarded the succession of algal ridge species at St. Croix, U.S. Virgin Islands, as an example of the tolerance model.
c.   Inhibition; no replacement species are added to the community until damage to the community creates an opening which is occupied by more stable, longer-lived taxa.

Walker and Alberstadt (1975) postulated a four-stage autogenic succession for reef communities beginning with the substrate stabilization stage and followed in succession by colonization, diversification, and domination stages. The stabilization and colonization stages are pioneer communities dominated by opportunistic (r-selected) species; the diversification stage is intermediate, and the domination stage is a climax community consisting of equilibrium (k-selected) species. Stabilization chiefly involves the preparation of a hard substrate in an environment suitable for reef growth. Colonization is recognized by the first appearance of large, branching and encrusting colonial organisms and increasing diversity and community complexity. Diversity increases to a maximum, especially at the class–order levels in the diversification stage, with progressively finer niche and habitat partitioning in a fluctuating but non-catastrophic physical environment. Theoretically, diversity should decrease somewhat in the domination stage, with survival of only the best competitors (competitive exclusion), and in long-term stable environments should reach highly stable community structures. The *allogenic* succession described by Grigg and Margos (1974) on Hawaiian lava flows may confirm the postulated decline in diversity in the last two autogenic stages.

Since the 1950s, ecologists have given considerable attention to the effects of catastrophic events, such as hurricanes (cyclones), reef-covering lava flows, and predator outbursts, on reef communities and the subsequent allogenic successions they induce. Before these studies it was generally assumed that virtually all reefs were at the climax stage, but now the effects of intermittent physical–chemical–biological disturbances and the stages involved in recovery are regarded as very important.

Selected Holocene Examples. The literature on reefs contains numerous studies of succession (mostly allogenic) and comparison of them indicates that there is no "universal" sequence for either the Atlantic or Indo-Pacific Province. Furthermore, subsuccessions for various ecological groups (algae, borers, etc.) or for various locations within reef systems have been described.

In cores penetrating Atlantic Province reefs, the Holocene (autogenic?) succession begins with assemblages dominated by head-shaped corals and changes upward to assemblages dominated by branching forms, especially *Acropora palmata* and/or *A. cervicornis*. In the eastern Pacific, branching forms of *Pocillopora* dominate, whereas at Bikini, Marshall Islands, the dominants are head-shaped. In a borehole at Réunion Island, Indian Ocean, branching forms dominate the upper 18 m; very little is known of the vertical succession through Great Barrier Reefs (Davies, 1983, pp. 69–70).

One of the most comprehensive general discussions of autogenic succession is by Pichon (1981, pp. 581–589) for shelf margin reefs; in it, he relates the succession to substrate topography and turbulence but provides no borehole data. According to Pichon, stabilization of the initial substrate requires a hardground; only rarely does a coral larva attach to soft substrates. Most often, the hardground consists of shelled invertebrates such as barnacles, vermetid gastropods, bivalves, or even foraminifora living in moderately deep water of low turbulence; usually within a year the earliest colonial corals arrive (*Stylophora, Pocillopora, Porites* in the Indo-Pacific; *Montastraea annularis, Siderastrea, Porites asteroides, Diploria clivosa* in the Atlantic). During subsequent colonization, diversity increases as well as the percentage of coral-covered substrate until finally space becomes limiting and competition increases and causes a decline in diversity. Growth of the coral-covered structure continues with the addition of coralline algae, pore-filling cements, and deposition of internal sediment until it exceeds the minimum size for a true reef. If the upward growth rate exceeds the rate of sea-level rise or foundation subsidence, increasing turbulence in shallower water causes the replacement of the early massive corals by branching forms, *Millepora,* and progressively increasing numbers of encrusting coralline algae. When the reef reaches the low tide level, the reef flat, dominated at first by branching *Acropora,* begins to form. There is a quite different ecological succession for reef flat patch reefs because they are more strongly affected by shallow-water waves and currents.

Adey and Vassar (1975) have described the ecological succession involved in the development of an algal ridge at St. Croix, U.S. Virgin Islands. The submerged (1–2 m) hardground for the ridge consists of dead branched *Acropora palmata* and *Millepora.* If wave turbulence is relatively low so that fish are able to graze, the dominant coralline algae are *Neogoniolithon* and *Porolithon* which simply overgrow and encrust the *Acropora–Millepora* surface. By studying the algal colonization of freshly broken hardgrounds and the "stratigraphic sequence" of algal growth forms, Bosence (1984) further refined the St. Croix "succession" (or circle) as follows: (1) initial laminar-branched *Lithophyllum;* (2) intermediate overgrowth by laminar and then by columnar *Porolithon;* (3) ending, or returning to *Lithophyllum* crusts. He estimated that the "succession" takes from a few years to a few decades.

Increased research on the very important faunas inhabiting dimly lighted to dark internal cavities of reefs (cryptic habitats) and in piles of storm-transported reef rubble has led to the use of the same "stratigraphic method" to determine ecological successions of organisms (coelobites) in these habitats. In sawed blocks of coral rubble from Florida, Choi (1984) established a three-stage autogenic succession from pioneering forams (*Planorbulina, Gypsina,* and the encrusting *Homotrema rubrum*), boring bivalves and serpulids, and one bryozoan species to a high diversity intermediate assemblage dominated by encrusting bryozoans but including some sponges and ending with overgrowth by the tunicate *Didemnum candidum;* he estimated that it took only three years to complete the succession.

On an even shorter scale, Davies and Hutchings (1983) described *seasonal* (3–16-mo) changes (too short for a true succession) of substrate borers and encrusters at Lizard Island, Great Barrier Reef, and related the changes to seasonal larval recruitment and very short life cycles (*r*-selected species). Risk and MacGeachy (1978) suggested that the autogenic succession of bioeroding organisms penetrating dead coral skeletons begins in a matter of days after death with bacteria, fungi, and algae, followed within weeks by sponges, somewhat later by spionid polychaetes, and ending with sipunculids and bivalves.

The effects of intense storms and other catastrophic events on reef communities and their subsequent recovery are natural experiments in allogenic succession. The nature of these successions is highly varied because they depend on the nature, frequency, and severity of the catastrophes and the nature of the preexisting community (especially the sizes and shapes of the corals) and its location; fringing reefs suffer greater damage from freshwater dilution and high turbidity following hurricanes than barrier reefs and atolls. Immediately following a hurricane in Jamaica, reef areas became a mosaic of nearly destroyed bare patches interspersed with nearly untouched reefs, giving a patchwork of differing successional stages (Woodley et al., 1981). If the destruction of live polyps is nearly complete and coral recolonization depends entirely on resettlement by planulae, the recovery rate is much slower than if surviving polyps on dispersed skeletal fragments are abundant and can repopulate the substrate asexually.

Allogenic successions and recovery rates for different reefs have been described by Woodley et al. (1981; Jamaica), Hopley (1982, pp. 98–100; Great Barrier Reefs) and Dollar (1982, pp. 78–79; Hawaii). In each case, the succession began with mat-forming algae (greens first, then reds and browns) growing rapidly over bare substrates followed by massive or foliaceous corals and then branching *Acropora* and *Porites*. The rate of extension of coral cover over the interreef sediments is very slow. Following complete destruction of the coral surface by a hurricane at Heron Island, Great Barrier Reef, only about 30% recovery of the former coral surface had been attained by coral regrowth five years later. Three years after the 1961 hurricane at Belize, almost the only living corals were survivors (new larval recruitment was almost nil), but large areas were covered by the algae *Padina* (brown) and *Halimeda* (green).

Jackson (1977; 1979) approached the matter of allogenic succession from the study of asbestos plate substrates and relevant ecological theory. Succession on the plates began with solitary serpulids and bivalves which were later supplanted by colonial corals and bryozoans. Among the colonial forms, the early colonizers should be *r*-selected species having growth forms described by Jackson as runners, vines, sheets, mounds, plates, and trees (in order of decreasing fecundity). If physical disturbance is low and food and light are abundant, hard substrates should be overgrown by sheets and mounds, but in the reverse situations plates and trees may dominate. Rapid growth by sheets, mounds, or vines allows them to overgrow (encrust) adjacent bare substrates, whereas plates and trees are established by larval recruitment followed by upward growth.

In cryptic habitats, Jackson's succession begins with runners, vines, and solitary animals and proceeds to sheets and mounds of sponges, ascidians, and cheilostomes (partly confirmed by Choi, 1984). Whether the succession results from differential larval recruitment and colonial growth rates or is truly autogenic is uncertain.

Autogenic ecological successions appear to be as well developed and characteristic of aphotic zone reefs as of photic zone reefs. According to most previous authors, aphotic zone successions are as intimately related to the size and shape of the structure as they are to its taxonomic composition; thus, the terminology for these successions is based primarily on size and shape. In 1958, Teichert proposed the term "bank" for large, aphotic zone, coral-dominated structures to distinguish them from photic zone reefs. Unfortunately, the word has been used in such varied connotations (see Glossary) that the value of Teichert's distinction is doubtful even for aphotic zone Holocene structures and is virtually useless for similar ancient structures. In the present context, these banks and "lithoherms" (Neumann et al., 1977) are simply aphotic zone (non-zooxanthellate) patch reefs.

Subsequent to Teichert's (1958) review, Stetson et al. (1962) and Squires (1964) developed the size/shape terminology currently used for aphotic zone reefs: (from small, flat-topped to large, mound-shaped structures) colony, thicket, coppice, and bank. Whether colonies are sufficiently large to be reefs is doubtful, but the others clearly exceed the usual minimum size concept of reefs; they are also taxonomically diverse and contain baffled and trapped internal sediment much like photic zone reefs. The terminology and descriptions of Squires (1964) were used and amplified by Mullins et al. (1981) for other Holocene aphotic zone reefs, by Coates and Kauffman (1973) for a Cretaceous aphotic zone coral reef, and by Kauffman and Sohl (1974) for Cretaceous *photic zone* bivalve-dominated structures. In each case, the authors stressed the importance of increasing taxonomic diversity through the succession (if they recognized the presence of a succession). However, some of the aphotic zone reefs described by Mullins et al. (1981) have existed for at least 22,000 years! Even if aphotic zone ecologic successions are much longer than those in the photic zone reefs, changes in taxonomic composition extending for periods of thousands of years probably result from immigration and evolution rather than autogenic succession.

At Rockall Bank near Scotland, Wilson (1979) described the ecological succession of an aphotic zone reef using Squires' (1964) terminology. The Rockall Bank structure began by the settlement of a *Lophelia pertusa* (Scleractinia) planula, and this species remained dominant throughout the succession. The pioneer community also contains brachiopods, bivalves, encrusting bryozoans, barnacles, and polychaetes. By the coppice stage, diversity increases to a much higher level spanning the phylogenetic spectrum of macroinvertebrates from sponges to echinoderms. Wilson also stressed the very important role of the boring sponge *Cliona* in weakening the branches of *L. pertusa* so that the coralla break into fragments that in turn become a part of the internal sediment supporting the upper living colony branches.

Ancient Reef Successions. Because the field experience of paleoecologists frequently begins with outcrops at which they emphasize vertical changes in both the fauna and the enclosing limestone, it is only natural that they have accepted and vigorously pursued the recognition and description of ecological successions in ancient reef communities. Although not explicitly stated as a succession, one of the earliest works in this regard was on the Silurian reefs in the north–central United States (Lowenstam, 1957; Nicol, 1962). Before the publication of the important review by Walker and Alberstadt (1975), most descriptions of ancient community successions consisted of three stages (pioneer, intermediate, climax); Lowenstam described these stages as quiet water, semirough water, and wave-resistant in keeping with his earlier (1950) emphasis on wave turbulence in the recognition of reefs. Later authors (e.g., James, 1979, 1983; Méndez-Bedia and Soto, 1984) recognized the four stages (stabilization, colonization, diversification, domination) of Walker and Alberstadt (1975; "bandwagon effect?"). Crame (1980) described a succession in the Pleistocene reefs of Kenya but determined that it was confined to the earliest stages of reef growth; thereafter, the occurrence of the coral species was random and unstructured.

In paleoecological successions, it is difficult to make the distinction between autogenic and allogenic; criteria for recognizing such short-term events as individual storms are poorly understood and yet the effects of intense storms on ancient communities must have been as great as for the Holocene. In addition, the absolute duration of the succession is usually impossible to measure, so the distinction between successional and evolutionary change is also difficult to determine. Nonetheless, most vertical successions in reefs have been attributed to autogenic causes. In Paleozoic and Mesozoic reefs, basal concentrations of pelmatozoan columnals or other shell debris to which small colonies of upright growing organisms are attached have been interpreted as evidence for the stabilization stage. The attached colonial forms begin the colonization stage; they may dramatically increase the overall size of the emerging reef structure, and, at the same time, the size of the individual colonies may also increase, their shapes may undergo progressive change, and the rapid upward component of skeletal growth and trapped internal sediment produces a mound of progressively greater height/width ratios.

Ideally, taxonomic diversity should increase radially from the center and base of the reef (Geister, 1983, Fig. 49) from the stabilization through diversification stages and then decline during the domination stage. However, only unbiased and intense collecting will prove this theory because numerous skeletons of loosely attached forms may be transported after death and become part of the internal sediment at some distance from their living habitat.

There is yet another aspect of vertical change in ancient reef communities that is only rarely considered by paleoecologists but may have considerable bearing on the reason for these changes. The upward and lateral growth of reefs as well as changes in their location are closely related to changes in relative sea level. Thus, reefs are commonly an integral part of transgressive/regressive rock sequences and their taxonomic composition and location reflect these geologically controlled environmental (especially depth, turbulence, turbidity) changes. Vertical changes produced by long-term lateral shifts in environment are known among stratigraphers, sedimentologists, and paleontologists as "Walther's Laws of Succession of Facies and Faunas" (Middleton, 1973); such changes were recognized (but not called Walther's Laws) by Henson (1950) in the Cretaceous–Tertiary reefs of the Middle East.

In transgressive/regressive sequences, the vertical faunal sequence ("stacking") merely represents the superposition of faunas that formerly were living side-by-side in the reef system (Geister, 1983, Fig. 53; see also Figs. 5.1 and 5.2 herein). In this case, the vertical changes in faunal composition and diversity are not related to ecological causes. Instead, the vertical sequence produced by transgression may place a reef crest fauna stratigraphically above a reef flat fauna and stratigraphically below a seaward slope fauna; regression may produce the sequence in reverse. The taxonomic composition of each fauna and the features of the enclosing rocks merely reflect environmental differences in reef flats, crests, and seaward slopes; their superposition in a quarry outcrop or drill hole is not directly related to either ecologic succession or evolution. The relative importance of Walther's Laws, ecological succession, and evolution in controlling the vertical sequence of ancient reef faunas depends on numerous geological and biological factors and the rate at which they operate. Ecological succession is relatively rapid and reversible, whereas evolution is relatively slow and irreversible, and Walther's Laws may intermix the two processes in complex vertical sequences that are exceedingly difficult to interpret.

Cenozoic History
There have been numerous attempts to measure the geological history of diversity of the world biota, or the marine biosphere. Their authors have generally agreed that the overall Phanerozoic trend (with several important "ups and downs") has been one of gradually increasing diversity at the family, genus, and species levels through the Paleozoic and Mesozoic. Cenozoic (especially Holocene) diversity considerably exceeds all previous diversity levels (e.g., Newell, 1967; Bambach, 1977; Sepkoski et al., 1981; Sepkoski, 1982; Signor, 1982; for contrasting opinions, see Raup, 1976; Sheehan, 1977). These measures of diversity are based on organisms with shells, skeletons, and the like or that have left a record of their behavior (trace fossils); in reef communities, the latter consist mainly of cryptalgal stromatolites and borings.

Trends. The trends of early gradual diversity increase and a sudden "jump" in the Cenozoic express the interrelations between the rates of origin of new taxa by evolution and extinction of "old" taxa (often called taxonomic turnover) and the number of "surviving" taxa from one segment of geologic time to the next (cf. Hoffman, 1985). It is also important to realize that during the Cenozoic the overall rate of diversity increase has not been uniform (there also have been "ups and downs"), nor has the amount of increase been similar among the varied marine communities. Reliable estimates of the overall *species* diversity, or even of just coral species, for reef communities in successive intervals during the Cenozoic are woefully inadequate for establishing patterns or trends of diversity change. However, it is clear that reef communities, as well as most non-reef shallow marine communities, are presently at their highest species diversity in the earth's entire history.

During the Eocene, coral generic diversity increased sharply (Newell, 1971, Fig. 5) and Eocene reefs were dominated by mostly cosmopolitan genera. Differentiation of the Atlantic and Indo-Pacific Provinces in the Miocene–Pliocene was accompanied by increased worldwide coral generic diversity as well as the initiation of higher diversity in the Indo-Pacific. For the remainder of the Cenozoic, the difference in provincial diversity continued to increase as a result of much more rapid evolutionary rate in the Indo-Pacific at both the genus and species levels (Stehli and Wells, 1971).

Climatic Effects. Valentine (1984) has discussed some of the possible causal effects of Neogene climates on biogeography and overall taxonomic diversity. He cited evidence for a long Cenozoic history of progressively cooler worldwide temperatures, beginning as early as the Oligocene, to produce progressively steepening latitudinal thermal gradients and thermally induced provincialism. Increased provincialism in turn created opportunities for increased diversity by increased species packing in each province and within ecosystems. In this way, Neogene worldwide shallow marine diversity may have increased by a factor of three. The tropical reef belt (especially the Indo-Pacific) presumably participated in the increased provincialism (Stehli and Wells, 1971, pp. 118–120, present evidence for three Holocene subprovinces) and species packing, as suggested by the data for rapid evolution presented by Stehli and Wells (1971).

The potential effects on diversity produced by Pleistocene sea-level fluctuations were considered by Wise and Schopf (1981). They estimated that the area of the worldwide continental shelves covered by seas varied by a factor of three during the extremes of the Pleistocene fluctuations; from theoretical species-area relations, they predicted that species diversity should increase by about 25% from the lowest to the highest sea levels. Furthermore, with successive fluctuations it might be expected that there might be a progressive "pumping" of diversity ("diversity pump" of Valentine, 1968) to higher and higher levels with extinction of small, local populations on falling seas and speciation into new habitats on rising seas. However, Wise and Schopf found no evidence of large-scale evolutionary replacement of faunas, either reef or non-reef, that coincides with such changes in sea level and concluded that the degree of provincialism was of greater influence over diversity than the size (habitat area) of each province.

Ecologic Effects. The accumulation of data on diversity in the marine biosphere (Sanders, 1968), especially the surprisingly high diversity in the deep sea, as well as indirect support from several aspects of ecological theory dealing with diversity (e.g., Valentine, 1969; Bretsky and Lorenz, 1970; Eldredge, 1974) led to the formulation (Sanders, 1969) of the concept that ecologically old and stable environments were characterized by high diversity and young, unstable environments by low diversity. The concept was generally known as the "time–stability hypothesis"; Sanders (1968, 1969) described the old, highly diverse communities as "biologically accommodated" and the young communities of low diversity as "physically controlled." During the early–mid-1970s, numerous ecologists and paleoecologists accepted the overall concept and applied it to a variety of communities, including Holocene reefs (e.g., Grassle, 1973; Endean, 1976).

The theoretical basis for the time–stability hypothesis was that stability, predictability, and high diversity in communities are advantageous to the organisms and mutually reinforcing (i.e., stability/predictability lead to high diversity and high diversity leads to stability/predictability). High diversity of k-selected, equilibrium species results in complex biological interactions, small niche sizes (specialization), and occupation of microhabitats and is maintained because the trophic and spatial resources of the environment are stable and predictable. These factors may in turn reduce competition and the stability of the environment should lead to reduced extinction rates. Geomorphic subdivision of reef systems (seaward slope, crest, flat, lagoon, etc.) and the resulting lateral variation in physical environmental factors have created a large number of microhabitats and with them special adaptive opportunities for fine niche partitioning. And as former open substrates are progressively subdivided into microhabitats, the predictability of the physical and biological aspects of the environment increases.

In 1978, Connell presented a quite different approach to explain high reef diversity based on the ecological consequences of disturbance and disruption of communities by intense storms, floods, predator outbursts, and the like rather than stability/predictability (see also Levin and Paine, 1974, and excellent summary by Dollar, 1982, pp. 79–80). According to these authors, prolonged periods of environmental stability lead to competitive exclusion; rapid growth of the best competitors should theoretically reduce diversity to quite low levels, as should the converse (frequent, intense disturbance). Connell reasoned that episodes of intermediate frequency and intensity should produce the highest levels of diversity; he cited data from the effects of storm activity on diversity at Heron Island,

Great Barrier Reef (also confirmed by Dollar, 1982, for Hawaiian reefs). Therefore, if periodic hurricanes partially destroy reefs and selectively remove the least hardy species (a type of "species pruning"), they will progressively allow more new microhabitats to be partitioned into more new niches. The most successful operation of such a "diversity pump" requires that the periods between disturbance and disruption exceed the average period of reef recovery but be shorter than the time for community succession to reach and become fully accommodated to the domination stage.

Basically, the distinctions between Sanders' "time–stability," Connell's "intermediate disturbance," and the ideas of dominance by the "fastest growers" hypotheses chiefly hinge on the efficiency of the competitive exclusion process and its effect on community diversity. Competitive exclusion is indeed a highly variable process and operates differently among both modern and ancient communities. Among ancient communities of much lower diversity and broader niches than their Holocene counterparts, the operation of competitive exclusion must surely have been far less efficient.

Huston (1979) discussed the problem of community diversity more from the viewpoint of the maintenance of high diversity than from its origin. He reasoned that environmental fluctuations prevented species populations and communities from reaching size and diversity equilibria; that is, competitor dominance also fluctuates among several species. In addition, if all competitors in highly diverse communities have low fecundity (an important characteristic of k-selected equilibrium species), the efficiency of competitive exclusion should be low, thus allowing the maintenance of high diversity. Thus, with low fecundity of competing populations that are fluctuating in size, diverse communities will approach equilibrium so slowly that they can maintain their high diversity for prolonged periods.

Buss and Jackson (1979) have discussed yet another possible method by which reefs may ameliorate the efficiency of competitive exclusion and maintain high diversity. They suggest that in parts of reef communities, especially cryptic habitats, competition may not be related to a dominance hierarchy (e.g., Species A over species B, B over C) but instead may be more complex, non-hierarchical, or circular (e.g., A over B, B over C, C over A) networks. Such networks may cause oscillations in diversity, alternately favoring one species and then another, resulting in a postponement of competitive exclusion and permitting high diversity to continue almost indefinitely.

Conclusion. It is apparent that the high diversity of Holocene and ancient reef communities is the result of interactions among numerous factors (chemical, physical, geological, biological) and to attempt to identify their relative importance at this time is nearly impossible. And yet high diversity is one of the most obvious attributes of reef communities (especially those in the photic zone). It is difficult to measure objectively; interpretation of its origin, maintenance, and consequences for the success of these communities is uncertain, often confusing, or frustrating, but very interesting.

Community Biomass, Productivity, and Biogeochemistry

> Coral atolls are 'islands' of isolated high productivity in the middle of comparatively barren tropical oceans. . .
>
> (Stoddart, 1969, p. 446)

The high diversity of photic zone reef communities is also accompanied by high biomass and productivity of reefs relative to most non-reef communities (Lewis, 1977, Tables 1, 2; there are no comparable data for aphotic zone reefs) which in turn depend on the efficient utilization and recycling of the dissolved nutrients (= reef biogeochemistry). Thus, biomass, productivity/growth, and biogeochemistry are intimately linked and are fairly good measures of the short-term vigor and functional success of the reef community.

Biomass
Most reef biomass is in coral tissue (10–40%, Sorokin, 1981; 97%, Lewis 1977, Table 3). Wilkinson (1983) estimated that in typical shallow-water reefs, sponge biomass is second, and Hartman (1977, p. 128) reported that at 25–50-m depth in Jamaica, sponge biomass may be higher than the combined total biomass of scleractinians and octocorals. The chief contributors to reef macroalgal biomass are the chlorophytes and rhodophytes, in contrast to temperate zones where various brown algae (Phaeophycophyta) dominate (Wiebe et al., 1981, p. 721). In high island and near-shore continental shelf reefs, brown algae such as *Turbinaria, Sargassum*, and *Padina* and marine grasses are especially important (marine grasses are generally more important in Atlantic than in Indo-Pacific reefs); in some lagoons and reef flats, the latter may comprise most of the biomass (e.g., Frost, 1977b, Fig. 2).

Open ocean plankton communities in the tropics are characterized by relatively uniform and low biomass compared with those in temperate waters. There is also a general shortage of phytoplankton in reef ecosystems, so that the typical phytoplankton–zooplankton biomass relations of other communities are not present in reef waters (Lewis, 1977, p. 327). For example, at French Frigate Shoals, Hawaii, Polovina (1984) found the phytoplankton/zooplankton biomass ratio to be only about 3.7. In other ecosystems, ratios as high as 10 are common; considerable plankton biomass leaves atoll lagoons with the currents. However, high lagoon biomass at Bikini Atoll relative to the adjacent ocean was attributed by

Johnson (1954) to low current dispersal and high lagoonal productivity. In other situations, loss of plankers from lagoons by currents may result in a deficit of gross planktonic production, which is probably offset by high net productivity of corals.

An important factor contributing to the high biomass of reef communities is the occupation by small animals of microhabitats and cryptic habitats in the reef framework. The greater the surface area produced by irregularities, such as internal tunnels, caverns, and spur and groove systems, the higher the potential biomass. Stetson et al. (1962) reported similarly complex microhabitats and high biomass in aphotic zone reefs relative to adjacent level-bottom communities.

There have been several attempts to subdivide total reef biomass into average values for various trophic levels. One of the earliest was a study of the windward reef at Enewetak Atoll, Marshall Islands, by Odum and Odum (1955). They estimated the mean total biomass at 846 g/m^2 for herbivores and 11 g/m^2 for carnivores; by comparison, Polovina (1984) estimated total biomass at French Frigate Shoals, Hawaii, at only 390 g/m^2.

A similar but more detailed study of benthic biomass relationships for four geomorphic zones on Holocene Caribbean reefs was presented by Frost (1977b, pp. 99–101). He recognized 40 "taxa" of varying degrees of informality (e.g., scaphopods; epiphytic "turf" algae) and distributed them among seven major "trophic categories" (one producer; six consumers). In comparing his data to those of Odum and Odum (1955) for Enewetak, Frost found that total producer biomass appears to be much higher in the Caribbean, but that coral polyp (plus associated symbiotic algae) biomass is quite similar in the two areas.

One very important problem in preparing reef biomass pyramids is to apportion the coral polyp biomass into its primary producer (zooxanthellae), primary consumer (herbivore), and secondary consumer (zooplankton, etc., carnivore) components. Odum and Odum (1955, p. 294) estimated that in zooxanthellate corals, the total plant biomass (zooxanthellae + blue–green algae + green algae) exceeded the animal biomass by a factor of three; they were especially impressed by the large biomass of filamentous algae occupying the upper parts of the coral skeleton. Subsequent authors (Kanwisher and Wainwright, 1967; Froelich, 1983; Lewis, 1977, p. 314) have determined other plant/animal biomass ratios for corals and doubted that enough sunlight reaches skeletal algal filaments for them to be regarded as net producers. Biomass data for Caribbean reefs as estimated by Frost (1977b) was also presented as pyramids with *seven* trophic levels (an impossibility if laws of thermodynamics are considered). Frost does not discuss how he apportioned the polyp biomass between the producer (algal) and animal components, but unlike Odum and Odum (1955), seemed to regard the polyps as more animal than plant. Until the plant/animal proportions of coral polyps and the relative contributions of algal and grass macrophytes to total reef biomass have been resolved, the size of the producer step of reef communities is uncertain; this, therefore, makes the relative sizes of herbivore and carnivore steps uncertain. Consequently, the degree of generality of the Odum and Odum (1955) and Frost (1977b) biomass figures is as yet uncertain.

Estimation of the biomass of ancient reef communities is exceedingly difficult and must be based on several assumptions (Powell and Stanton, 1985); the most tenuous are the virtual absence or at best under-representation of the producers, especially the phytoplankton, and the very uncertain relations between skeletal mass and biomass. Estimates of ancient reef biomass are further complicated by their considerable lateral and vertical variations, variable degrees of compaction and dissolution, infilling of former pores by sediment and cement, and, in the case of extinct organisms, the absence of comparable living descendants.

Productivity: Dissolved Nutrients
There are several nutrient elements and compounds necessary for primary productivity of reefs, but only nitrogen (N) and phosphorus (P) will be discussed here. Dissolved N and P are supplied from two general sources: (1) the open ocean and land run-off and (2) recycling from decay of organic matter. Recycling alone cannot provide the nutrients for net primary productivity; conservation of existing nutrients (minimal losses from the system) and input from new sources are both required. New supplies to open ocean atolls are quite modest but may be of considerable importance for fringing and barrier reefs. Once the nutrients have been incorporated into the system as organic material, it is important that they be retained. Nutrients are produced by various means, such as "fecal rain" from pelagic fish, metabolic wastes, and decomposed organic material, and are recycled by the reef system. (Recycling of nutrients by zooxanthellate corals is discussed in Zooxanthellae–Coral Symbiosis, Chap. 2.)

Conservation of the nutrients is enhanced by the limited circulation between the inner parts (e.g., lagoons, caverns) and the open ocean, by nitrogen fixation by filamentous blue–green algae, and oxidation of NO^- by bacteria in the interreef sediments. One important difference between reef ecosystems and the adjacent open ocean planktonic ecosystems is that retention and recycling of nutrients are relatively more complete in photic zone reefs; upon death, oceanic planktonic organisms begin their descent toward the aphotic zone and if they reach it before decay is complete, the nutrients are temporarily "lost" for primary production.

Numerous factors contribute to the high productivity of reef systems, such as the highly efficient zooxanthellae–coral symbiosis, other high rates of nitrogen fixation, and the efficient recycling of phosphorus by the community (Johannes et al., 1972). Bacteria and other microorganisms play a major role in nutrient recycling. Henderson (1981) found distinctly different nutrient element cycles in reef system silt and rubble substrates and attributed some of these differences to microbial processes and to the higher concentrations of infaunal excrement in silt. Endean (1982, p. 214) found the highest bacterial counts in the meshwork of dead coral colonies inhabited by various defecating invertebrates. Thus, microbes produce "pools" of nutrient elements in the pores between sediment particles and in skeletons of dead organisms.

Another approach to the study of the nutrient element cycles in reef systems is to compare the oxygen consumed in relation to the organic phosphorus and nitrogen produced. This relation is approximately stoichiometric in planktonic ecosystems, but Henderson (1981) discovered that the ratio of oxygen consumption to phosphorus and nitrogen production in reefs is about twice as great as in the plankton. The relatively greater oxygen consumption in reefs may be related to the much greater importance of animal respiration than in the plankton, where much of the oxygen is produced. Thus, Grigg et al. (1984) concluded that: (1) although the concentration of nutrients in reef waters was relatively low, the flux of nutrients through the ecosystem was sufficiently rapid to produce and maintain the high biomass and primary productivity that characterize reef ecosystems; (2) reef communities operate at or near the upper metabolic rates associated with the photosynthetic process; and (3) these high metabolic rates are more limiting to primary productivity than low nutrient concentration. Most previous authors regarded low nutrient concentrations as the chief limits to reef biomass and productivity.

Summary. Details of nitrogen and phosphorus fluxes through reef ecosystems are uncertain and problems exist in extending experimental data derived from short-term studies of small areas to longer-term generalizations and conclusions; nonetheless, reefs appear to be highly efficient systems for the production, conservation/storage, and use of these essential chemical elements. Reef systems include localized environments in which organic material accumulates, chiefly in the form of algal and microbial mats; however, the importance of microbial processes in the overall energy budget and nutrient cycles of these systems is uncertain. It now seems as if (1) most reefs are net exportors of nitrogen and so nitrogen input and fixation are very important processes, (2) reefs have only minor effects on concentration of phosphorus in the surrounding water (Johannes et al., 1972; Lewis, 1977; Atkinson, 1981), (3) the availability of phosphorus is more likely to limit biological production than nitrogen, (4) oxygen and carbon are present in copious supply, and (5) high metabolic rates may be the chief limits on total reef productivity.

Productivity: Primary

Primary productivity of reef ecosystems, measured by carbon fixed as $C_6H_{12}O_6$ or oxygen produced (equation 2.1), is nearly as high as for almost any natural ecosystem known. In the sea, the productivity of some marine-grass- or kelp-dominated communities may rival or even exceed reefs, but it is inescapable that one of the important characteristics of "healthy" photic zone reef systems is their high primary production. (By definition, primary productivity is non-existent in the aphotic zone.)

There are numerous potential sources for primary production including zooxanthellae (Muscatine, 1980; see also Symbioses, Chap. 2), filamentous algae within and external to the corals, calcareous and non-calcareous macroalgae, grasses, and the phytoplankton. Neither the filamentous algae within corals nor the phytoplankton are important producers relative to the other sources; reef system phytoplankton production is about the same as in the adjacent open ocean. Primary benthic production in reef communities usually exceeds primary production in open ocean planktonic communities (generally the lowest in the sea; Dawes, 1981, pp. 356–358) by a factor of at least 10.

The chief controls on reef primary production are light, the supply and concentration of nutrients and high metabolic rates. The photosynthetic capacity of the plants and the distribution of their habitats, including water depth and the density and vertical stacking of coral colonies, are important factors influencing the rates of primary production. Primary production commonly is highest on the crests and coral knolls, intermediate on flats and lagoons, and lowest on the deep seaward slope (for absolute values, see Sargent and Austin, 1954; Lewis, 1977, pp. 310–311; Levinton, 1982, p. 436; Grigg et al., 1984; Atkinson and Grigg, 1984).

The biological vigor of all communities is a direct function of the rate of turnover of the primary producers (commonly expressed as the ratio of primary productivity/biomass). Because both productivity and biomass are relatively constant for reef communities, turnover is commonly determined on an annual basis. For the windward reef at Enewetak Atoll, Marshall Islands, Odum and Odum (1955) estimated turnover at 12.5 times/yr. Rapid turnover such as this not only requires rapid metabolic and production rates of the algae but also rapid flux of the nutrient elements through an efficient and conservative ecosystem.

Macintyre et al. (1974) have detailed the complex pathways by which carbon, both organic and inorganic, is exchanged between the reef, sediments, water, and atmosphere. In addition to the carbon fixed in living organisms (biomass), it is also stored as dissolved and particulate organic carbon (chiefly in the water), and as $CaCO_3$ in skeletons, spicules, sediments, and cement. The present discussion concerns only the organic forms; the inorganic are considered later in this chapter.

Kinsey and Davies (1979) indicated that the organic carbon cycle in reef communities is generally in equilibrium (primary production = consumption by respiration + decomposition), that upper seaward slopes and the crest are net producers, and that this surplus is carried into the flat and lagoon as suggested by Smith and Marsh (1973). Conversely, the data of Atkinson and Grigg (1984) indicate that the cycle is *not* in equilibrium;

they estimate that about 10% of the net primary productivity (6% of gross) escapes from the French Frigate Shoals, Hawaii, reef ecosystem (chiefly by burial in the sedimentary substrate or offshore export). Furthermore, Grassle's (1973, pp. 260–262) discussion of the turnover of the opportunistic macroalgae on the reef flat at Heron Island, Great Barrier Reef, indicated that the excess production is carried from the flat to the seaward slope. The whole-reef production of carbon is therefore variable in time and in space and the fate of the surplus (if any) is uncertain.

Productivity: Secondary
The biomass resulting from primary production in reef communities chiefly occurs in three forms: (1) the cells and tissues of living plants, (2) decaying larger to colloidal size particles of organic matter (often called organic detritus), and (3) dissolved organic carbon. Regardless of the apparently high consumer biomass, primary benthic productivity accounts for about 90% of the total productivity of reef ecosystems; planktonic plus secondary production is only about 10% (Atkinson and Grigg, 1984).

Secondary productivity is based on the supply and concentration of these food sources, but their relative importance depends on the consumer (corals appear to use all three sources to varying degrees). Lewis (1977, pp. 320–321) reported that in a study in the Laccadive Islands about 20% of gross primary production ended up as organic detritus; elsewhere there was up to seven times more suspended organic material than substrate organic detritus. He also noted that the biomass (dry weight) of suspended particulates passing over reefs was much greater than the biomass of nettable living plankton; there was also more suspended organic detritus over reefs than in the adjacent open ocean. Hatcher (1983) summarized the relative composition of organic particulates in reef areas as follows: (1) on seaward slopes and crests, organic aggregates and mucus from corals are major constituents; (2) over algal ridges and flats, algal fragments and fecal pellets predominate; and (3) lagoons are enriched in particulates (and zooplankton) but not to the same degree as over the surrounding reefs. Except for a few isolated studies (e.g., Richard, 1982), there are very few data on secondary production by non-corals (which locally may exceed the biomass of corals).

Herbivores in reef communities include both sessile and vagrant animals. Although there are a few deposit-feeding sessile forms, most are suspension feeders which utilize organic particulates. Most vagrant forms are grazers on benthic algae. The importance of various algae as food for grazers partly depends on their morphologies. Littler et al. (1983) have described a hierarchy of algal resistance to mechanical grazing by urchins; this hierarchy goes from: (1) crustose coralline algae (most resistant); (2) foliated calcareous; (3) thick, leathery, and coarsely branched (non-calcareous); (4) filamentous; to (5) sheets (least resistant). Excluding zooxanthellate corals (which are primary producers, herbivores, and carnivores), the biomass of grazers may be the dominant form of animal life in some reef communities.

The grazers promote rapid turnover of the primary producers; Carpenter (1983) estimated that herbivore (mostly grazing molluscs, urchins, and fish) consumption amounted to between about 35 and 85% of daily algal production and that without grazing, algal production might *decrease* by half. However, in algal ridges where turbulence is so high that the common grazing urchins and fish are almost excluded, the encrusting coralline algae out-compete corals for space. By contrast, in deeper, less turbulent water the herbivore grazer biomass is so much higher that they commonly limit algal growth enough for corals to out-compete algae for space.

After posing the question, "Are coral reef ecosystems nutrient limited or predator controlled?", Grigg et al. (1984, p. 24) concluded that, at French Frigate Shoals, Hawaii, "nutrient limitation is of less significance than formerly believed, and predation mortality is the most important factor controlling secondary and higher production." (Predator here includes herbivore + carnivore.) These authors suggest that reef ecosystems contain *six* trophic levels. They also determined that despite their high benthic primary production, reef ecosystems are very inefficient at producing high consumer biomass because of high losses by predation and predator respiration.

Herbivores (especially fish) grazing on calcareous algal crusts affect primary organic production and calcification of algae (Lewis, 1977, p. 325). Steneck (1983, pp. 45–46, 56) concluded that although crustose coralline algae grow slowly and their contribution to total primary production is low, the removal of epiphytes from the crust surface by herbivores is very important to their survival and may actually enhance their productivity; diversity of the corallines is also directly correlated with herbivore grazing intensity.

Productivity: Tertiary

Reef communities contain two main "groups" of carnivores: some corals and some fish. Coral nutrition is very complex (Muscatine, 1973); the nematocysts have two functions: (1) to stun and capture prey (mostly zooplankton) and (2) to repel predators. It is readily apparent from the low productivity of both open ocean and reef planktonic communities that zooplankton biomass is grossly inadequate to supply the energy requirements of corals and other reef carnivores. Odum and Odum (1955) diminished the magnitude of this energy budget problem by emphasizing the autotrophic side of coral metabolism and thereby reduced their estimate of the carnivore biomass to only about 1.3% of the community biomass.

Despite the effectiveness of corals in repelling some potential predators, carnivorous consumers of coral tissue include a variety of fish, gastropods, polychaetes, crustaceans, and starfish (Robertson, 1970; Parker, 1984, p.

159). Much of this grazing mortality is temporary and the polyp cover is regenerated by asexual reproduction from undamaged polyps. However, if grazing is intense, regeneration may be delayed long enough for such encrusters as filamentous algae, sponges, and crustose algae to repopulate the dead coral surface.

Reef fish are highly varied in their food choices. In an east African reef, Talbot (1965) estimated that of the total fish biomass, 19% consists of herbivores feeding on algae and 1% consists of plankton feeders; the remainder are carnivores feeding on corals (20%), other invertebrates (49%), and other fish (11%). Similarly, Sutton (1983) indicated that only 60–80% of reef fish are carnivores; most of these feed on benthic invertebrates, especially crustaceans.

Regardless of the magnitude of carnivore biomass, it must be supported chiefly by benthic and pelagic herbivores. Thus, the high grazer biomass explains the attraction of Holocene reefs for sharks, barracuda, and moreys. By contrast, carnivorous fish are very rare as fossils in ancient reefs, probably as a result of their low preservation potential.

Reef Biogeochemistry

Emphasis so far has been on the constructive aspects (cell and tissue growth) of individual organisms, groups of organisms, and whole reefs (photosynthesis, biomass, productivity) and the factors that most strongly influence them. Measurements of primary production may be made by determining either the amount of oxygen produced or the amount of carbon fixed (equation 2.1). However, all organisms and ecosystems include an equally important destructive aspect (respiration) that can be measured by the amount of oxygen consumed or organic matter destroyed. In living organisms, these processes of construction and destruction are nearly in balance and together are most properly called metabolism. These general concepts and the term "metabolism" have been extended to higher levels of ecological organization (populations, communities, etc.) by many previous authors. Here, the term "reef biogeochemistry" will be used for the totality of the chemical processes in a reef ecosystem that are involved in both organic construction (photosynthesis; calcification) and destruction (respiration; biological erosion).

Photosynthesis/Respiration (P/R) Ratios. The biogeochemistry of parts of reefs or whole reef ecosystems can be determined by measuring oxygen or carbon dioxide produced or carbon fixed as $C_6H_{12}O_6$. For reef communities, most metabolism studies have focused on the oxygen produced by the zooxanthellae–coral polyp symbiosis and most reef biogeochemistry has concerned oxygen production in open ocean atolls. From these measurements, interpretations may be made regarding the overall metabolic/ biogeochemical status of the ecological unit involved and are commonly expressed as the ratio of photosynthesis to respiration (for constraints on the validity of the ratio for algal–polyp symbionts, see Muscatine et al., 1981, pp. 601–602; the chief problem is that in cases where P/R is greater than one, it is uncertain where the fixed carbon is located or whether it is being stored, used, or lost from the system). Therefore, if the P/R ratio exceeds one, the unit is fixing (producing) more organic carbon than it is consuming (and vice versa if the ratio is less than one, a condition that cannot persist very long).

Although the net primary productivity of zooxanthellate corals is highly varied and strongly depends on the intensity of light (up to a point), virtually all measurements of P/R ratios indicate that they are autotrophic (e.g., Muscatine et al., 1981; Sorokin, 1981; McCloskey and Muscatine, 1984). The chief concern is that nearly all such experiments are of short duration and therefore may not reflect seasonal or annual environmental fluctuations and trends.

When measurements of P/R ratios are extended to communities, the generalizations based on them also becomes less certain. So, because of the spatial heterogeneity of reef ecosystems, it becomes even more difficult to extrapolate the data from individual coral colonies or parts of reefs to whole reef systems. For example, in shallow-water areas rich in algae and grasses, such as ridges and some flats, P/R ratios usually exceed one (e.g., Smith and Marsh, 1973; Smith, 1973; Davies, 1983); on the other hand, in areas of level-bottom substrates between reefs (Harrison, 1983) and some lagoons, the ratio is commonly less than one (cf. Sargent and Austin, 1954; Smith, 1983a, Table 1). Furthermore, autotrophic carbon gains in one part of a reef may be offset by heterotrophic losses in another by the transport of both particulate and dissolved organic matter by currents. Even within one part of a reef, fluctuations in population sizes by predation markedly influence P/R ratios through time.

Although these small-scale problems may seem formidable, there have been numerous attempts to monitor changes in P/R for parts of reefs simultaneously (especially open ocean atolls) and then integrate the parts into a combined P/R ratio for whole reef ecosystems (e.g., Sargent and Austin, 1954; Smith, 1983a; Atkinson and Grigg, 1984). For most of these attempts, the ratio falls in the range of 0.95–1.05, that is, on a *very* short-term basis, the biogeochemistry of atoll systems appears to be approximately at equilibrium. Open ocean atolls, at least, thus appear to be self-sustaining ecosystems, producing about as much organic matter as they consume. Although numerous attempts have been made to determine P/R ratios for high island and continental shelf reefs (Kinsey, 1985, Table 3), their interpretation is made more difficult by the greater complexity of the current patterns and the higher supply and concentration of nutrients. Such complexities may be at least part of the cause for the generally greater variation in P/R ratios for near-land reefs compared with open ocean atolls.

Finally, none of these studies are sufficiently long-term to reach any geological conclusions regarding the *in situ* production versus consumption of organic matter. Despite the remarkably high biomass and primary benthic productivity of Holocene photic zone reef communities, their overall P/R ratios are near equilibrium; this, in turn, suggests that these, and perhaps ancient reef ecosystems, lack any large "sinks" of organic matter for conversion to the enormous quantities of petroleum found in ancient reef complexes. It seems as if nearly all organic production in excess of the respiratory requirements of Holocene reef ecosystems is lost as organic material (particulate, colloidal) transported to deeper-water, off-reef ecosystems. Kinsey (1985) concluded a long discussion of P/R ratios with the following: "At this stage the only safe assumption to be drawn from a long-term P/R = 1 would seem to be that import equals export ... P/R = 1.1 should not be interpreted as 10% of P that is available for export, but rather a situation in which potential export exceeds potential import by an amount equal to 10% of P."

Reef Calcification. One of the essential by-products of the metabolism of reef corals, calcareous algae, and many other organisms and of general reef biochemistry is the precipitation of $CaCO_3$, both organically as skeletons and inorganically as sediment (see Sediment Production, Chap. 4). The precipitation of skeletal $CaCO_3$ in prodigious quantities is a major characteristic of both Holocene and ancient reef communities.

Chave et al. (1972) defined gross $CaCO_3$ productivity *(G)* of a reef as the amount of $CaCO_3$ produced per unit area of the reef (usually expressed as kg $CaCO_3/m^2/yr$). Other authors have referred to this as *reef calcification,* and although the positive correlation between *G* and coral or algal growth rates is obvious, measurement of the relationship is difficult. The complex interrelations in reef communities involving the flux of CO_2 are described by Smith (1973) and Barnes and Devereux (1984) among others. (The concept of calcification rates is also applicable to level-bottom substrates; see Depositional [Accumulation] Rates, Chap. 4.)

The mechanisms by which organisms with calcareous skeletons remove Ca^{+2} from seawater and combine it with carbon are uncertain; however, for corals and calcareous algae, calcification rates appear to be positively correlated with photosynthetic rates (cf. Smith, 1973, Fig. 6, and Chalker, 1983, pp. 32–35). Goreau et al. (1979) suggested that removal of dissolved CO_2 from seawater during photosynthesis as well as the precipitation of $CaCO_3$ result in the change of HCO_3- and pH to provide more CO_2 and $CaCO_3$ to the reef system by the following reactions:

$$2HCO_3^- = CO_2 + H_2O + CO_3^{-2} \qquad (3.4)$$

$$Ca^{+2} + CO_3^{-2} = CaCO_3 \qquad (3.5)$$

(see Sediment Production, Chap. 4, for further discussion of these chemical reactions; the role of zooxanthellae in skeletal calcification was discussed above in Symbioses, Chap. 2).

However, when photosynthesis ceases at night, calcification continues at reduced rates and of course day *and* night calcification is an essential feature of aphotic zone reefs. Conversely, there appears to be a negative correlation between the rates of calcification and carbon production (equation 2.1). In the nutrient-rich waters surrounding fringing and near-shore patch reefs, organic carbon production by non-calcareous algae is high and calcification is low; in open ocean atolls, the reverse seems to be true (M. Pichon, personal communication, 1985). Calcification rates also seem to be closely related to the latitudinal limits of the tropical photic zone reef belt. Among Hawaiian reefs (near the northern latitudinal limit), in a distance of 9° latitude, the calcification rate *(G)* decreases from about 15 kg $CaCO_3/m^2/yr$ in lower latitudes to about 0.3 in higher latitudes (Grigg, 1981, Fig. 3), chiefly due to the combined effects of lower incidence of light and cooler temperature. However, regardless of reef location, calcification does not appear to be limited by supplies of either CO_2 or Ca^{+2} (Equation 3.5).

In addition to the probable direct relation between calcification rate of corals and light intensity, several other factors also appear to influence the former. These include differences due to location within the reef system, taxonomy, corallum size and shape, density of colony spacing, and the initial porosity and time of infilling by pore cement (Gladfelter, 1984; for examples of variation in absolute measures of reef calcification rates, see Stearn et al., 1977, p. 507; Smith, 1983b, pp. 243–244; Davies, 1983, pp. 77–80; Kinsey, 1985, Tables 3–5). Smith (1983b, pp. 243–244) and Kinsey (1985) suggested that the average calcification rate is 10 kg $CaCO_3/m^2/yr$ for reef areas of extensive coral cover. Smith (1978) estimated that reef and reef sediment calcification accounts for precipitation of about 50% of the annual calcium ion input by rivers to the world ocean.

Skeletal Growth Rates

In most reefs, the greatest influence over the rate of calcification is the rate of precipitation of $CaCO_3$ into the skeletons of the chief reef framework organisms; for Cenozoic reefs, these are the Scleractinia and the calcareous algae. Both corals and algae are characterized by very rapid growth rates relative to the other shelled organisms inhabiting reefs. Stearn et al. (1977, p. 509) concluded that the precipitation of $CaCO_3$ by just the Scleractinia and coralline algae (excluding sedimentary level-bottom substrates) for a fringing reef at Barbados totals 9–15 kg $CaCO_3/m^2/yr$, which is comparable to the *total* reef calcification *(G)* described above. Numerous factors, both physical and biological, influence skeletal growth rates and it is uncertain which are the most important. Because most of these factors vary seasonally, annually, or irregularly, measurements of growth rates based on several years' duration have the greatest validity; Buddemier and Kinzie (1976, p. 201) reported that variation in intracolony annual coral growth rates and longer-term intercolony variation may each differ by a factor of two. Weber and White (1977, pp. 175–176) found that growth rates for *Montastraea annularis* from British Honduras varied by a factor of about three; in colonies living side by side, there was a significant difference in both annual and longer-term growth rates. Furthermore, much of this variation depends upon how individual corals allocate the available energy to production/consumption, reproduction, and skeletal growth.

Physical Factors

Light intensity and all of its interrelated aspects (depth, latitude, temperature, turbidity) are very important for photic zone organisms but of much less importance to aphotic zone organisms. Goreau et al. (1979) reported that the growth rate of some corals was as much as 14 times faster in sunlight than in darkness! For most corals, optimum growth occurs in shallow (1–10 m), warm (23–28°C), clear water of moderate turbulence; most conspecific variation in growth rates is related to deviations from one or more of these optima.

Within the upper 10–15 m, most variation in coral growth is related to taxonomy and local physical factors; below about 15 m, growth rate drops sharply with increasing depth (Buddemier and Kinzie, 1976, p. 210); at 30 m, *Montastraea annularis* grows at 10% of its optimum and *Porites lutea* at 40% (Hopley, 1982, p. 74). Conversely, Hughes (1983) found that among five species of foliaceous corals in depths of 10–35 m in Jamaica, growth rates "were found to be very weakly dependent on depth." To exemplify the complexity of the depth–growth rate relation further, the data of Weber and White (1977, Table 2) indicate that *M. cavernosa* grows at about the same rate from the surface to 18 m; for *M. annularis,* growth rate is the same from 4.5 to 18 m (Baker and Weber, 1975). These data suggest that some sort of photoadaptation (perhaps by the zooxanthellae) is taking place. Grigg (1982, Fig. 3) reported that in the coral *Porites lobata* in the Hawaiian Islands, skeletal growth (mm/yr) and colony accretion (kg $CaCO_3/m^2/yr$) are negatively correlated with latitude, whereas skeletal density (mg/mm^3) is positively correlated; in a latitudinal difference of 9°, skeletal growth rate differs by a factor of four. However, in a reef in Western Australia at the same *south* latitude as the slowest growing Hawaiian corals, Crossland (1981) reported comparatively high growth rates in two species of branching corals. These rates were still lower than conspecific rates at lower latitude and Crossland attributed the differences to water temperature. Several other authors (e.g., Shinn, 1966; Clauson, 1971; Weber and White, 1977; Dodge and Lang, 1983; Patzold, 1984) have stressed the positive correlation between skeletal growth and temperature.

At Heron Island, Great Barrier Reef, Grassle (1973, pp. 256–258) found that colony sizes among some abundant corals and encrusting algae were smaller on the reef crest than on the seaward slope. He attributed this difference to abrasive destruction in the higher turbulence of the crest.

Biological Factors

Several intrinsic (genetic) and external (ecological) aspects of the life of reef organisms appear to exert considerable influence over their growth rates; these aspects include purely taxonomic differences as well as intraspecific differences in colony size, shape and age, competition for space and food, and injury by predators.

The data of Weber and White (1977, Table 2) clearly indicate that in what appear to be identical physical environments *Montastraea annularis* (Scleractinia) grows at a rate about 30% faster than *M. cavernosa*. Optimum growth rates occur at different depths among closely related species: for *M. annularis,* it is at about 10 m, but for *M. verrucosa* it is at 2 m (Buddemier and Kinzie, 1976, p. 212).

Growth rates are strongly related to overall colony shape in many higher coral taxa but may vary considerably among different parts of the same colony. Thus, linear dimensions increase more rapidly in branching than in massive corals, but the reverse may be true for weight increase. Oliver (1984) reported that among the branches of *Acropora formosa* the tips of some are covered with zooxanthellate polyps and others by non-zooxanthellate polyps; the skeleton in the latter tips is more lightly calcified and the skeletal elements are thinner and more widely spaced than in the former. Furthermore, the non-zooxanthellate tips extend in length, but the zooxanthellate tips only increase in diameter and the latter predominate in the interior parts of the corallum where the branches are crowded and length increase is inhibited by their dense packing.

Growth rates also appear to change during the life of the coral colony. Typically, young colonies grow most rapidly; some corals grow throughout life, whereas others cease growth when they reach a certain size (Endean, 1982, p. 60). Injury to polyps by predation or physical stress also affects growth rates; Hughes (1983) reported that in a four-year study of 883 colonies, over 75% were injured at least once.

Zooxanthellate Corals

Linear Extension. Growth rates of living corals can be measured and expressed in many ways, such as a linear dimension (e.g., length, diameter, circumference, height; expressed as mm/yr), surface area of corallum (mm^2/yr), volume (mm^3/yr), or weight (g/yr), by returning to the same individual over an extended period (the longer, the better) and repeating the same measurement without injury to the polyps. Because of the polyp injury problem, the most reliable data are from linear dimensions (first attempted by Vaughan, 1915, and subsequently used, abused, refined, and criticized by numerous authors; summarized by Buddemier and Kinzie, 1976).

Other methods for determining growth rates are destructive but have the advantage of a much longer (tens of years) and presumably more reliable growth history. They are based on the assumption that once a part of the skeleton has been precipitated by the coral, it is a closed system no longer in contact with seawater and so will retain its chemical and physical identity. Thus, the coral may be repeatedly inoculated with stain to produce internal skeletal color bands or with radioactive isotopes (^{45}Ca) that also become concentrated in bands. Banding based on variation in skeletal density is part of the natural life history of some corals (cf. Gladfelter, 1984, p. 54) and is also useful for determining growth rates (band spacing in mm per growth period). The clarity of density bands can be greatly enhanced by x-radiography (for examples, see Weber and White, 1977, Figs. 1–4). For most corals, the most obvious band development is annual, but the time (season) of deposition of the more dense bands representing slower growth is quite variable; bands may also be influenced by water depth, temperature, and reproductive cycles (Highsmith, 1979).

Buddemier and Kinzie (1976, pp. 212–216) evaluated the then existing data and concluded that: (1) for massive corals in optimal environments, growth rates are about 10–15 mm/yr for their maximum growth dimension; (2) for *Acropora* spp., branch elongation was at the rate of 100–150 mm/yr (several measurements exceed 200 mm/yr); and (3) growth rates for other corallum shapes are between these extremes, that is, >15–<100 mm/yr. The significance of these rapid skeletal extension rates to the success of Cenozoic reef communities is that in coral-dominated frameworks they are the primary basis by which topographic relief is achieved.

Weight. Expressions of coral growth rates based on weight increase ("calcification" of some authors; not to be confused with "reef calcification" discussed above) require measurements of skeletal volume increase as well as the specific gravity of the skeleton. Both measurements are variable among taxa and difficult to determine (Stearn et al., 1977, p. 498). Furthermore, the chief value of rapid weight increase is that it provides enhanced stability to coralla inhabiting areas of high turbulence.

Cyclic Growth. Superimposed on the major (annual; seasonal) growth banding of many corals are more numerous and much more closely spaced minor (daily; monthly) growth bands (Scrutton, 1978); viewed with a microscope, they appear as epithecal ridges parallel to the calyx rim. The significance of epithecal ridges was first recognized by Wells (1963); he also assessed (1970) the probable causes for the episodic growth responsible for the ridges, which included daily fluctuations in nutrient supplies, tides, temperature, and light. Barnes (1972) described ridge formation as the result of daily changes in the shape of the polyp epitheca. Scrutton (1965) noted that in many corals reproductive cycles have a lunar periodicity and also produce epithecal ridges. Thus, growth banding may have periodicities on scales that are daily, monthly, seasonally, or annually and it may be difficult to determine which bands represent which periodicities on any particular coral.

Wells (1963) was able to distinguish major annual growth bands in both Holocene and fossil corals. By counting the number of minor epithecal ridges between each annual band, he determined that the most closely spaced ridges represented daily growth increments (for excellent illustrations of annual bands and daily ridges, see Runcorn, 1966) and that the earth's history was characterized by a regular decrease in the number of days per year from about 425 at the beginning of the Cambrian to the present 365. In addition, Wells (1963) used his growth data to estimate the longevity of large Holocene coralla at around 1000 years and of fossil coralla at more than 200 years.

Scrutton (1965) recognized rather evenly spaced major constrictions of corallite diameter in Devonian corals that he regarded as monthly; within each such monthly cycle, he counted about 30–31 minor epithecal ridges that he regarded as daily. By taking Wells' (1963) Devonian year of 399 days and dividing it by the number of days in a Devonian month, Scrutton estimated that there were about 13 synodic months in a Devonian year, or about 13 lunar reproduction cycles/year (Scrutton's 30–31 days/month were later revised by Runcorn, 1966, to 28–29 days/siderial month).

The same general methods of measuring annual growth bands and counting daily epithecal ridges can also be used to estimate annual growth rates of fossil corals (Table 3.4). Despite the considerable taxonomic and morphological differences and varied number of days in the year, these data suggest that pre-Cenozoic corals grew somewhat more slowly than Holocene corals (cf. Buddemier and Kinzie, 1976, pp. 212–216) but nonetheless much more rapidly than most other invertebrates having calcareous skeletons.

Non-zooxanthellae Corals

In the rather uniformly cold and dark realm populated by most non-zooxanthellate corals, episodic incremental growth and related bands and ridges are generally absent or, at best, poorly developed. Their periodicity and its causes are also quite uncertain (Sorauf and Jell, 1977; cf. Barnes, 1972, p. 347; Reed, 1981). Nonetheless, a few estimates of growth rates have been presented (Table 3.5) and comparison with those for zooxanthellate scleractinians (cf. Buddemier and Kinzie, 1976) clearly indicates much slower growth, except for *Oculina varicosa* and *Tubastraea micranthus* living in shallow water; the discrepancy becomes magnified when it is emphasized that all the non-zooxanthellate coralla are of branching shapes and that branching zooxanthellate coralla increase in length at rates up to 200 mm/yr. Wilson (1979) estimated the longevity of coralla of *Lophelia pertusa* 1.5 m high at 200–350 years.

TABLE 3.4. Annual Growth Rates of Pre-Cenozoic Corals as Determined from Spacing of Epithecal Ridges[a]

Geologic Age	Coral Class; Corallum Shape	Growth Rate (mm/yr)	Ref.
Jurassic			
Oxfordian	S; Massive	1–4	Ali, 1984
Oxfordian	S; Branching	5–12	
Carboniferous			
Dinantian	R	40–60	Ali, 1984
Visean	R; Fasciculate	36–58; $\overline{X} = 53$	Johnson and Nudds, 1975
Visean	R; Varied	42–69; $\overline{X} = 55$	Johnson and Nudds, 1975
Devonian			
Middle	R; Solitary	19	Barnes, 1972
		16–22; $\overline{X} = 19$	From photos in Scrutton, 1964
Silurian			
Middle	T	5–14; 8–18	Scrutton and Powell, 1980

[a]Key: S = Scleractinia; R = Rugosa; T = Tabulata.

TABLE 3.5. Annual Growth Rates of Holocene Non-zooxanthellate Scleractinia

Species	Depth; Temperature	Growth Rate (mm/yr)	Ref.
Oculina varicosa	6 m[a]; $\overline{X} = 25°C$	0–41; $\overline{X} = 11$	Reed, 1981
	80 m; $\overline{X} = 16°C$	0–45; $\overline{X} = 16$	
O. diffusa[a]		7–23	Vaughan, 1915
Tubastrea micranthus	4–50	40	Schuhmacher, 1984
Lophelia prolifera	130–900 m; 4–10°C	6–15	Reed, 1981
		5–7	Cairns and Stanley, 1981
		>6.8	Stetson et al., 1962
		>7.5	Stetson et al., 1962
L. pertusa	800 m	6	Wilson, 1979
	955–1006 m	4.2–7.5	

[a]Contains zooxanthellae in shallow water.

Algae

Unlike the Scleractinia, in which growth rates are influenced by numerous factors whose relative importance is difficult to determine, light intensity and the factors that influence it clearly control algal growth rates; Adey and Vassar (1975) estimated that growth rates of tropical coralline algae are 10–20 times faster than of their high latitude counterparts and attributed the difference to higher incoming light levels. In addition, Goreau and Goreau (1973) determined that from 0.5 to 60 m at Jamaica, the algae can grow much faster than zooxanthellate corals and are able to precipitate skeletal $CaCO_3$ at much lower levels of light intensity; they theorized that the lesser abundance (biomass) and diversity of algae was due to their higher turnover rate. Conversely, the data of Adey and Vassar (1975, Table 2) indicate that the rates of marginal extension for coralline algal crusts at depths of 30–200 cm are only slightly greater than the average optimal extension rates for massive corals and are considerably less than branching coral tip extension rates.

Among the crustose coralline algae, growth rates and colony shape are related to both light and turbulence. Steneck and Adey (1976) found that *Lithophyllum congestum* in moderate turbulence develops branches with maximum growth at the tips (up to 8 mm/yr). Increase in crust thickness strongly depends upon the grazing intensity of herbivores, especially parrot fish, and occurs at rates much slower than marginal extension (approx. 1–5 mm/yr vs. 10–30 mm/yr; Adey and Vassar, 1976; Steneck and Adey, 1976; Stearn et al., 1977).

For the erect-growing calcareous green alga *Halimeda* spp., new branch plates (5–10-mm dia) are added at the rate of about 0.1–1.0 plates/branch/d or several plates/plant/d (Wefer, 1980; Drew, 1983), and for the much more lightly calcified *Pencillus,* Wefer recorded plant height increases of 1–5 mm/d.

Stearn et al. (1977, pp. 505–508) determined the rate of weight increase (calcification), unimpeded by grazing, of the four most common genera of coralline algae on a reef at Barbados. For the genus with the most rapid increase *(Porolithon),* they calculated a rate of about 3.1 kg $CaCO_3/m^2/$yr which is almost exactly one order of magnitude less than the rate of weight increase for the most rapidly calcifying coral *(Porites porites);* if the effects of herbivore grazing had been included, the discrepancy may have been even greater. At Davies Reef (19°S lat.), Great Barrier Reef, Drew (1983) estimated the calcification by *Halimeda* at about 1–3 kg $CaCO_3/m^2/yr$. In comparison, the annual rates of weight increase for *Halimeda* and *Penicillus* in shallow lagoons at Bermuda (32°N lat.), as well as their contribution to total reef calcification, are inconsequential (Wefer, 1980).

Data on the growth rates of other reef-dwelling organisms show that their contributions to overall reef growth and calcification are generally not substantial. Willenz and Hartman (1985) and Benavides and Druffel (1986) measured the annual linear growth increment (about 0.2–0.5 mm/

yr) of a massive calcareous Jamaican sclerosponge species living at 26–30 m. Although calcification rates of the common (up to 1 specimen/100 m^2; Hopley, 1982, p. 79) huge bivalve *Tridacna gigas* are uncertain, they are probably high because of the abundant zooxanthellae in the mantle margin tissues.

Competition

Competition (intraspecific and interspecific) is a *major* biological factor influencing the composition and structure of reef communities (Jackson, 1983, p. 56–70). It operates in conjunction with such other factors as light/nutrients, biomass/productivity, and skeletal growth/predation, all mentioned above. In reef communities, the chief forms of competition are for space and for energy (sunlight; food); the former is far more intense and limiting to the overall "success" for most reef organisms. The very irregular surfaces of reefs and reef systems (spurs, grooves, caves, etc.) tend to decrease the competition for space and enhance the opportunities for reef animals to feed at different levels in relation to the substrate and in the water column (tiering; trophic stratification) to reduce competition for food.

Allocation of Space

The adaptations displayed by Holocene reef organisms to acquire and then hold space are varied and "ingenious"; they include: (1) direct overgrowth of one organism by another; it is usually most intense among horizontally growing encrusting forms, (i.e., "shoulder-to-shoulder" competition); (2) aggressive behavior between adjacent organisms; this is especially important among fish and corals and in corals involves very direct interactions of the polyp tentacles and mesenteries (i.e., "head-to-head" competition); aggressive defense of territory is a common trait of numerous reef fish to reduce space and food competition; (3) indirect overtopping of one organism by another (Levinton, 1982, Fig. 20-7); thus, a faster growing foliaceous coral may shade out a slower growing form, thereby further reducing its growth rate, without ever touching it. To mediate or even eliminate the intensity of direct forms of competition and predation, numerous species have well-developed immunological or allelopathic responses to repel aggressive adults or fouling larvae.

The discovery that numerous corals live in a linear hierarchy ("pecking order"; Sp. A over Sp. B, B over C, C over D, etc.) of levels of aggressive behavior (Lang, 1973) has led to a very different conception of the organization of reef communities (cf. Bak et al., 1982). Aggressive competition for space is most intense in areas of highest coral density and species diversity. It involves the ability to extend specialized "fighting and sweeper" tentacles beyond the basal polyp margin to touch and wound or kill polyps of its competing neighbor (Chornesky, 1983; Hidaka and Yamazato, 1984, Fig. 1) and then extend the marginal fila-

ments of the mesenteries to the wounded or dead tissue and digest it
outside the coelenteron. In this way, the space between adjacent colonies becomes bare of coral tissue and the more aggressive species can
grow over the corallum of the other (Pl. 18a). Interspecific aggression
is more highly developed than intraspecific and its detailed study led
to Lang's hierarchy for Jamaican corals. Intraspecific contacts generally lead to colony fusion, but aggressive behavior may occur between
different morphs of the same species (Hidaka and Yamazato, 1984;
Logan, 1984).

Lang (1973) found that the most aggressive species (mostly in Suborder
Faviina) had massive-encrusting coralla of small size (and slow growth
rates) and were minor components of reef communities; she regarded
aggression as primarily a defense to prevent their own overgrowth by
more rapidly growing ramose-foliose species.

In contrast to Lang's linear hierarchy, Buss and Jackson (1979) proposed that more complex competitive networks or loops (Sp. A over Sp.
B, B over C, but C over A) for space acquisition were also important in
the organization of reef communities, especially in cryptic habitats. They
indicated that the species involved in networks (see their Fig. 4) generally
belong to different genera or families (only partially true of Lang's hierarchy) and that the rate at which dominance is achieved is slower in
networks than in hierarchies.

Sponges appear to be the most successful competitors against corals
for space on reefs, and the degree of their success increases with depth.
Hartman (1977) reported that the oscular chimneys of the common West
Indian boring sponge *Siphonodictyon* extend above the polyp surface of
the coral into which it has bored. Other sponges belonging to various
higher taxa successfully encrust corals by their rapid lateral growth but
are in turn subject to considerable fish predation. A variety of other invertebrates (e.g., zoanthids, gorgonians, anemones, ascidians) are very
successful (aggressive?) competitors for space in shallow, non-cryptic reef
habitats.

Predation by grazing herbivores is a very important limitation on the
space occupied by algae in reef communities and thus helps mediate the
marginal interference and the intensity of direct overgrowth competition
among encrusting algae. Among fish, herbivory on algae is more common
and potentially more damaging than carnivory on coral polyps; fish predation appears to have greater impact on coral larvae than on adult polyps
(Fritz et al., 1983). However, Breitburg (1984) discovered that on rocky
substrates, encrusting coralline algae may be the most resistant organisms
to attack by grazing urchins and that such algae resist larval recruitment
by other sessile species. Although lateral growth rates of such algae are
comparatively rapid, they may be poor space competitors; algae generally
do not overgrow the leading edges of invertebrates, but are readily
overgrown themselves (Breitburg, 1984).

Allocation of Food. A major factor contributing to the competitive success of reef corals is their varied means of capturing food and their highly non-selective diet. Corals are excellent examples of suspension (not filter) feeders; they capture food from water passing over polyps, quickly trap and move food to the mouth, and shed inorganic debris from the polyp surface.

Corals utilize three major sources of food (excluding the possible digestion of symbiotic zooxanthellae): (1) they are nanno-, micro-, and macrophagous carnivores on a variety of pelagic animals, chiefly zooplankton (for taxa consumed, see Yonge, 1930); (2) they absorb dissolved carbohydrates, amino acids, and lipids from either the symbiotic zooxanthellae or from the seawater; and (3) they may occasionally become scavengers. Their means of capturing food include cilia and sticky mucus nets, strands on the tentacles and body wall, and extension through the mouth of filaments along the proximal free margin of the mesenteries (Muscatine, 1973). Thus, by extending the tentacles and the mesenterial filaments, each polyp has a very large food gathering/absorbing surface; this, coupled with their relatively non-discriminatory diet, makes them highly successful food competitors. By comparison, corals are eaten by relatively few animals; their nematocysts provide excellent defense to all but a few molluscs, echinoderms, crustaceans, and fish.

Competitive Exclusion

Although the overall competitive success of corals in reef communities results from the interaction of numerous factors, their highly efficient use of the chemical, physical, and biological resources of the environment to produce rapid growth rates as well as their competitive superiority in acquiring and holding space and food are of prime importance. In view of this situation, it is reasonable to again ask, "Why are reef communities so diverse?" or "Why haven't the fastest growing, or the most aggressive coral species driven the others to extinction or to level-bottoms?" Again, it seems as if complex interrelations among several factors may mediate the efficiency of competitive exclusion.

Buss (1979) discussed the almost self-reinforcing relation between differential growth of space competitors and feeding success (i.e., the overgrowing species also limits the access to food of the overgrown species and is thereby able to enhance its superiority progressively). Goreau and Goreau (1959) found no significant correlation between growth rates among 13 Jamaican corals and their relative abundances; *Montastraea annularis* grows slowly but occupies a high percentage of the reef surface. Conversely, Porter (1974) attributed the dominance of *Pocillopora* in shallow east Pacific reefs to its rapid growth and overtopping ability.

The general inverse relation between growth rate/colony size and the aggressiveness of the polyps prevents the rapid occupation of space by a few successful aggressor individuals or species (Logan, 1984). This is especially true if the basis for aggression is the defense of space already occupied. Finally, the slower developing and more flexible species interactions in competitive networks cause fluctuations in the space mosaic of reef surfaces and enhance the opportunities for coevolutionary relationships (Buss and Jackson, 1979). The origin and maintenance of competitive dominance in relation to high diversity in reef communities are indeed complex problems that are much easier to describe than to interpret.

Coloniality and Gregariousness

There is a virtually unbroken spectrum among reef organisms in the degrees of individuality versus coloniality that they exhibit, and among those that are colonial, there is a similar spectrum in the levels of unification and integration among the different parts of the colony. (For a discussion of this spectrum and terminology to describe different levels of integration, see Boardman et al., 1973; Rosen, 1979.) Organisms that remain entirely separate as adults are here called solitary.

An important aspect of colonial organisms is the physical union and common genetic heritage achieved by means of asexual reproduction among the individuals. Examples of important colonial organisms in reef communities include corals, anemones, hydroids, zoanthids, gorgonians, bryozoans, and ascidians. Sponges have some colonial characteristics but are here regarded as individuals (following Fry, 1979). Coloniality and/or gregariousness is especially important among the various framework organisms in Holocene (Jackson, 1977, Table 2), as well as nearly all ancient reef communities. The incidence of coloniality in higher taxa containing both colonial and non-colonial species (e.g., Anthozoa) is much higher in the shallow tropical reef belt; on hard substrates in both tropical and temperate latitudes, species diversity of colonial forms exceeds the diversity of solitary forms by at least three times (Jackson, 1977, p. 758).

Gregariousness ("discontinuous societies" of Rosen, 1979) is near the center of the individual–colony spectrum; it is the situation in which there is an unusually dense concentration of individuals that lack genetic unity from asexual reproduction but live in close physical union achieved by cementation (oysters), enmeshing of tubular shells (vermetids, serpulids; Pl. 8), or dense packing of robust shells (extinct rudists; Pl. 37). Either alone or in combination, cementing, enmeshing, and packing achieve rigidity and topographic relief.

The duration of the larval period for most invertebrates involves a compromise between the need for extensive dispersal to new habitats to ensure survival and the need to reproduce. Jackson (1979, p. 504) pointed out that larval recruitment is a more risky method of successfully extending local range than truly asexual propagation because of generally high larval (and infant) mortality rates. He also found that in experiments on artificial substrates involving short-term ecological succession in cryptic reef habitats, the earliest recruits were larvae of mostly non-colonial species such as serpulids and bivalves. Soon, these early species were supplanted by a variety of colonial organisms (Jackson, 1977, Fig. 1; "colonial animals" include sponges which were important in overgrowing "solitary animals" and reducing "free space").

There appear to be several advantages of coloniality in reef organisms, including:

a.   Directional growth into spatial refuges (a "safe position" of escape) enhances survival during environmental stress; a runnerlike form appears particularly successful for directional growth. Coloniality spreads the risk of mortality; in cases of partial colony mortality, the survivors can also exploit such refuges with greater success than solitary organisms (Buss, 1979, pp. 459–460).

b.   Among skeletal organisms, coloniality provides mechanical efficiency in the arrangement of structures with minimal expenditure of energy for precipitation of the skeleton (Coates and Oliver, 1973, p. 23).

c.   Coloniality leads to larger and usually stronger skeletons that are more likely to maintain their position in strong currents and survive storms (Coates and Oliver, 1973, p. 22). Robust skeletons enable the suspension feeding individuals in the colony to rise above the substrate, prevent fouling by larvae of other species, and provide volume to the reef framework.

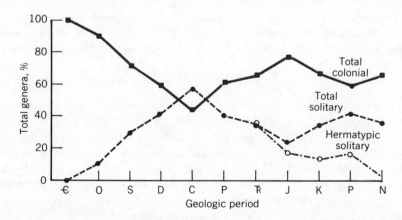

Figure 3.10.   Number of genera of solitary and colonial zoantharian corals per geologic period. Hermatypic solitary = presumed solitary zooxanthellate forms; the difference between "total solitary" and "hermatypic solitary" represents presumed aphotic zone forms; "total colonial" includes both presumed zooxanthellate and non-zooxanthellate forms. Symbols for geological periods conventional; Tertiary Period subdivided into Paleogene (P) and Neogene (N). (From Coates and Oliver, 1973.)

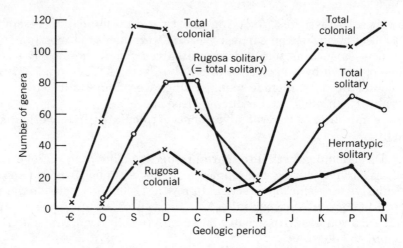

Figure 3.11. Number of solitary and colonial zoantharian corals per geologic period through Phanerozoic time. Hermatypic solitary = presumed solitary zooxanthellate and non-zooxanthellate forms. Late Paleozoic (C + P) decrease in colonial genera due to extinction of Heliolitidae in Devonian and decline in Tabulata. Symbols for geologic periods conventional; Tertiary Period subdivided into Paleogene (P) and Neogene (N). (From Coates and Oliver, 1973.)

    d.   An apparently much greater degree of polymorphism and morphological plasticity among colonial organisms allows them greater adaptability to local environmental variation.

    e.   Coloniality bestows a greater ability to respond to environmental fluctuations by controlling the allocation of energy to each of the essential colony functions, such as feeding, growth, and sexual reproduction in polymorphic colonies.

    During their long geologic history, corals have exhibited great variety in degrees of coloniality from wholly solitary individuals and simple quasi-colonies joined only by skeletal material (with presumed wholly sexual reproduction) to very highly integrated, asexually produced soft parts and skeletons all functioning in a communal manner. Coates and Oliver (1973, p. 24) indicated that highly integrated colonies are metabolically more efficient than solitary and weakly integrated colonies but that not all colony types have strong, rapidly precipitated skeletons that are needed to build reef frameworks. They have also traced the geologic history of zoantharian coloniality (Figs. 3.10 and 3.11) and noted that only once (in the Carboniferous) have the solitary corals been generically more diverse than the colonial ones. Other trends in *coral coloniality* during geologic history include (Coates and Oliver, 1973, p. 10):

a. Reduced polyp sizes with increasing coloniality which leads to reduced colony mortality with increasing polyp predation.
b. Increasing development of the coenosarc (non-polyp tissue) and accompanying strengthening of the corallum.
c. Increasing budding from the coenosarc rather than from only the polyps.
d. Increasing fusion of polyps and calyxes with the formation of polyps with multiple mouths and gullets and increasing integration of colony metabolism.

SUMMARY

Environments conducive to the origin and vigorous growth of reefs consist of a relatively restricted set of controlling environmental factors. These factors are here combined into four categories: chemical, physical, geological, and biological (Fig. 3.12; Table 3.6). In a flourishing reef, these factors are integrated into an ecologically coherent, self-reinforcing functional unit (community) that is resistant to change and possesses remarkable abilities to recover from stress. Yet, a reef and its environment are much more than an enumeration of a set of limiting parameters. A reef is dynamic and by its growth it also molds its environment in ways that are unique and make it readily distinguishable from adjacent environments.

Because the unique aspects of reefs chiefly concern their skeletal framework, reefs are primarily biological phenomena. Thus, where the non-biological factors are less than optimal (e.g., deep, cold, brackish, hypersaline, etc., water) the vigor of this phenomenon is diminished and reefs lose their unique characteristics. They become gradational with level-bottoms which are controlled by a different and less restricted set of factors in which the non-biological factors may be more influential than the biological.

The biological factors that contribute to the overall success of Cenozoic reefs are centered around their high metabolic rates and efficiencies, which are expressed as high biomass (dense packing of organisms) and rapid growth of cells, tissues (high productivity), and skeletons (calcification). The skeletons of the framework organisms are large, colonial, and strong to provide volume and rigidity to the reef structure and, when combined with rapid upward growth, result in topographic relief. Growth and periodic destruction of the framework appear to modify several aspects of the environment in ways that open new habitats and niches, which generally lead to higher species diversity in reef communities than in adjacent level-bottom and pelagic marine communities.

TABLE 3.6. The Chief Environmental Factors That Control the Origin and Growth of Reefs Arranged by Categories Indicated in Figure 3.12

Chemical	Physical	Geological	Biological

1. Salinity
2. Dissolved nutrients
	1. Temperature
	2. Turbulence
		1. Location
		2. Form
		  a. Descriptive classifications
		  b. Geomorphic zonation
			1. Biogeography
			2. Diversity

3. Dissolved gases	3. Turbidity/ substrate	3. Genetic classifications	3. Biomass, productivity, geochemistry 4. Competition 5. Coloniality/ gregariousness

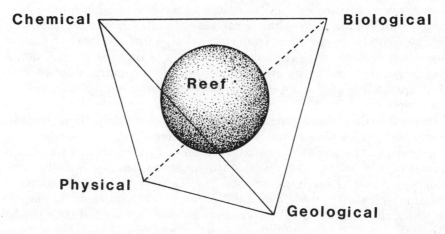

Figure 3.12. Schematic representation of the four major categories (corners of tetrahedron) of environmental factors that control origin and growth of a reef (sphere within tetrahedron). Individual factors listed by category in Table 3.6.

4

Cenozoic Reef Models III
SIMULTANEOUS PROCESSES

The discussion so far has emphasized numerous *factors* and their complex interrelations that influence the overall success of reefs rather than the *processes* that operate simultaneously to make reefs the most dynamic ecosystems in the sea. Reefs can be subdivided into functional units (both topographic and biologic); the processes operate somewhat differently in each unit to produce what may appear to be quite different results. And yet there is unity of factors, processes, and results that makes reef communities so unique. Chapter 3 emphasized the *factors* and their general long-term stability; this chapter will emphasize shorter-term dynamic *processes* and will expand the scope to include the sediments of reef complexes. Chapter 5 will emphasize the biologic *results*.

PROCESSES

The most important process in all Holocene and ancient reefs is the construction of the framework by skeletal organisms (Fig. 4.1). This framework is unique to reefs and gives them their rigidity and topographic relief. Almost as soon as the skeletons and organisms have constructed the organic framework, numerous processes of destruction begin to break it down into skeletal grains of various sizes and shapes. These grains are immediately subject to the overall hydrodynamic regime of the reef complex; if there is sufficient turbulence, the grains are subjected to the process of transportation, either in suspension or by traction, from the reef to the reef complex. If turbulence is too low to transport the grains, they settle into the framework and become internal sediment. Eventually, the transporting currents lose their velocity and ability to transport, either by en-

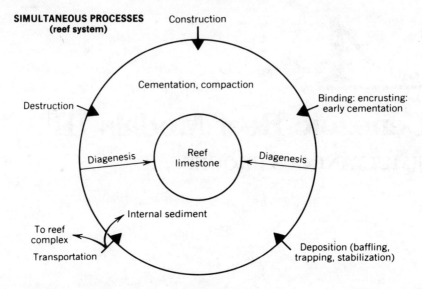

Figure 4.1. The simultaneous operation of the five basic processes (outer circle) during the living stage of reef development; see text for complete discussion. Construction and binding/encrusting processes are chiefly biological and produce or "build" (*sensu lato*) the reef framework; destruction, transportation, and deposition deal with origin and fate of reef-derived skeletal grains in reef and reef complex. Diagenetic processes (cementation, compaction) transform the semi-consolidated reef framework and internal sediment into reef limestone.

countering an obstacle or by abatement of their driving force (wind, tide, gravity, etc.), with the result that deposition of the grains occurs. At this stage, the reef consists of a living organic framework in some degree of partial destruction with voids between the skeletons partially filled with unconsolidated internal sediment and surrounded by an apron of reef-derived skeletal grains. The next process involves the binding or unification of the organic framework and the internal sediment to form a relatively solid and immobile mass of semiconsolidated reef materials.

It is important to reemphasize that all five of these processes (Fig. 4.1) operate simultaneously, either while the veneer of frame-building organisms is still alive or immediately after the death of part or all of the reef. These processes fluctuate in their relative importance over short time intervals. During periods of normal turbulence, construction and binding predominate, whereas during and following storms or other catastrophic events, destruction, transportation, and deposition predominate. The overall form (size and shape) of the reef depends on the interrelations between these processes which in turn are controlled by the interrelations among the factors discussed in Chapter 3. Both the factors and processes vary across the different geomorphic zones of the reef, and the reef organisms respond in different ways to these variations. Thus, factors, processes, and biological responses interact to produce the varied forms of the reef framework as well as the taxonomic composition and structure of the reef community.

The final process is the geologically prolonged conversion of the recently dead semiconsolidated reef mass into a lithified (hard) reef limestone by the multiple changes called *diagenesis*. In reefs, the rigid framework minimizes the effects of sediment compaction during diagenesis and the relatively large voids maximize the importance of cementation.

CONSTRUCTION PROCESS

The organic framework of Cenozoic reefs consists of an intergrown mass of large colonial/gregarious organisms and their skeletons, chiefly scleractinians, that are buried to some degree in sediment. The skeletons are in their growth positions and are therefore presumed to be sufficiently large and strong to resist normal turbulence. Chamberlain (1978), Schuhmacher and Plewka (1981) and Schuhmacher (1984) have experimentally compared the strength parameters (i.e., porosity, compressive strength, compressive elastic modulus, and abrasive wear) for several Holocene hermatypic corals and one ahermatypic sclerosponge. They found that despite the generally high porosity of the corals (about 30–85%), their skeletons are remarkably strong but that the skeleton of the sclerosponge was much stronger than any of the corals for every parameter measured. Furthermore, the skeletal resistance to abrasion of the one non-zooxanthellate coral studied was higher than for most zooxanthellate corals. Unfortunately, there are no measurements of skeletal strength for any pre-Cenozoic reef-building taxa for comparison with the Holocene data. However, Schuhmacher and Plewka (1981) regarded the Holocene sclerosponges and the extinct stromatoporoids as similarly strong. In Holocene reefs, the living cells and tissues form a thin veneer on the surface of a framework that may be several hundred or thousands of years old and several meters thick. (Growth rates of the frame-building corals and some calcareous algae are discussed in Biological Factors, Chap. 3.)

The reef framework is porous and so may appear to lack strength and rigidity; in addition to high skeletal porosity, there is considerable void space between the skeletal elements of the framework. In boreholes drilled at Bikini and Enewetak Atolls, Marshall Islands, during the 1950s, there was no "tidal lag" in the water levels, and in older parts of the framework there is a porosity decrease due to infilling by sediment and pore cement.

These same framework characteristics (large, strong skeletons in growth position; dense packing) apply to both photic and aphotic zone Holocene reefs and to most pre-Cenozoic reefs except that the taxa involved in the construction process are different and their skeletons are generally smaller and less rigid. One of the important characteristics of Cenozoic photic zone reefs is their overall domination by large, colonial scleractinians.

DESTRUCTION PROCESS

The processes of destruction can be divided into those that are physical and those that are biological. The intensity, immediate impact, and duration of the impact of the physical processes are usually greater and our awareness of them is heightened by the short-term damage they can inflict on reefs. In contrast, biological destruction is subtle, methodical, and relentless, but its overall, long-term effects may be just as great as the physical processes. Davies (1983, Table 1) has compiled estimates of rates of gross (physical and biological) destruction of the surface of reef limestones from several sources; they vary from 0.05 to 4 mm/yr. Although submarine chemical solution of reef carbonates may occur, the effects are very local and the rates are usually so slow that they can be ignored; conversely, freshwater (vadose and phreatic) solution is very important (see Geological Factors, Chap. 3).

Physical

Physical processes include: (1) mechanical disruption, breakage, and abrasion of organisms and skeletons by the pounding surf; (2) death by desiccation, salinity, or temperature change, or by high turbidity and subsequent sediment suffocation. These processes are usually related to storms, earthquakes, or volcanic activity. Storm-induced high turbulence causes most short-term reef destruction; it varies from very slight to complete. A 1961 hurricane at Belize destroyed nearly the entire reef over an area exceeding 300 km². Whole coral colonies were detached and transported onshore to form boulder ramparts, carried offshore to form debris fans, or broken *in situ* by the waves into rubble piles (Stoddart, 1969, p. 451). Considerable damage is inflicted on undisrupted organisms by rolling coral skeletons, other large fragments, and moving, abrasive sand grains. The extent of damage is variable on different parts of the reef, especially if the normal lee side becomes the windward side during a storm. Damage is usually selective on the smaller, weaker, and more exposed organisms. Delayed mortality may continue for several months after the original cause of the destruction has ended (Knowlton, 1981); in ancient reefs, if death has been catastrophic, the effects of destruction may outweigh the effects of prior construction processes (i.e., the reef decreases in size).

Physical destruction of aphotic zone reefs is much less intense than of those in the photic zone because turbulence is less and the products of destruction are more likely to be retained by the reef as internal sediment (Squires, 1964).

Biological

The biological processes of removing pieces of hard substrates by means of scraping, rasping, grinding, or boring are called *bioerosion;* dead skeletal substrates are far more susceptible to bioerosion than surfaces covered by living organisms. The overall importance of bioerosion is inversely related to depth; it is most intense in the intertidal zone.

Scraping and rasping are processes attributed to fish, especially parrot fish, and radula-bearing molluscs (Pl. 19*b*). Scraping and grinding are attributed to echinoids with well-developed Aristotle's Lanterns; the results include elongate scratches (Pl. 19*a*) and shallow, cup-shaped depressions of similar or larger size than the maker. Annual bioerosion rates per individual for scraping/rasping gastropods are about 0.4–5 cm^3, for chitons about 8–13 cm^3, and for grinding echinoids about 14–18 cm^3.

Borers are mostly sessile, range in size from a few microns to several centimeters in diameter (Pl. 20*a*), and are attributed to a large variety of taxa. The borings are usually cylindrical (Pl. 18*b*) and penetrate both the skeletal reef framework and early cemented internal sediment; repeated boring, sediment filling, cementation, and reboring can replace up to 50% of the original framework (Ginsburg and Schroeder, 1973, Fig. 22).

Numerous authors have estimated bioerosion rates for various taxa (tabulated by Davies, 1983, p. 72; Davies and Hutchings, 1983; Hutchings, 1986), but the factors involved are so complex that no general pattern emerges. Nonetheless, it is apparent that the processes of bioerosion may destroy a very significant part of the skeletal framework or reduce a reef to rubble unless the processes are stopped by burial, cementation, or overgrowth by encrusting or binding organisms. Furthermore, the processes of bioerosion often weaken the framework to the point that it simply collapses from its own weight or becomes much more susceptible to destruction by the physical process described above.

Once skeletal sediments have been formed by the numerous processes of destruction, they then become subject to repeated boring, churning (bioturbation), resuspension, and transportation before they are finally deposited as internal sediment and bound or cemented to the constructed framework or transported to the reef complex.

Sediment Production

Shallow-water reef environments characteristically differ from nearly all other benthic marine environments in the very high proportion of sedimentary material that is of local (endogenous) origin and the comparatively small amount that is transported to reefs from distant sources (exogenous). Among sedimentary grains for which the origin can be determined, it is commonly true that over 90% are endogenous whole or fragmented skeletons. Well over half of typical Holocene reef sediments are aragonite and most of the remainder are high-Mg calcite; low-Mg calcite, dolomite, silica, and terrigenous siliciclastic grains are rare except for fringing reefs. Reef systems produce far more sediment than they are able to retain as internal sediment (Stoddart, 1969); the surplus is transported by waves and currents to the reef complex substrate or out of the general reef environment. Thus, reefs are major net "exporters" of carbonate sediment, in contrast to most other benthic environments, which are net sediment "importers."

Because most of the sediment produced by reefs is of skeletal origin (Orme, 1977b, Table 1), the reef crest, with its high density of rapidly growing corals, and the lagoon-reef flat areas, with an abundance and high turnover rates of skeletal algae, are the main local sediment sources. The mechanical disruption of skeletons by the pounding surf produces grains that include both whole skeletons and skeletal fragments of highly disparate sizes, from large blocks to sand. A large proportion of the pebble-sand fraction is derived by physical abrasion of dead skeletons and by chipping and fracturing of larger grains.

Folk and Robles (1964) determined the size–frequency distributions of the Isla Pérez, Alacran Reef in the Gulf of Mexico and discovered six relatively discrete modal classes: the largest were blocks, with the progressively smaller classes dominated by coral "sticks" (two classes), bivalve and gastropod shells, *Halimeda* flakes, and fine coral sand. The sizes, shapes, and relative abundances of grains larger than silt depend primarily on the contributing organisms (corals, molluscs, *Halimeda*) and the structure of their skeletons, which in turn strongly influence the process and rate of sediment production. In areas of considerable turbulence, sediments consist of grains of mixed sources; in lower turbulence areas, the sediments are dominated by shells of very local origin.

Role of Bioerosion

Bioerosion, probably at least as important in sediment production as physical abrasion, primarily produces skeletal fragments of pebble and smaller sizes; Glynn and Stewart (1972, p. 513) estimated that sediment of sand-pebble size fragments of the coral *Pocillopora* spp. produced by the combined activity of four bioeroding species (two small crustaceans, a gastropod, and a tetraodontid fish) amounted to more than 6 metric tons/hectare/yr. Sediment production by parrot fish at Saipan, Mariana Islands, amounts to about 3 mm/yr of fine substrate sand; at Barbados, however, the reef erosion and sediment production by parrot fish were regarded by Frydl and Stearn (1978) as minor relative to echinoids and macroborers. Elsewhere in the Caribbean, Ogden (1977) compared the rates of sediment production by parrot fish and echinoids and found echinoids to be the more effective bioeroders by at least one order of magnitude. But because echinoids are restricted to shallow parts of the reef, their total effect may be less than for the wider-ranging parrot fish.

The effects on the reef of sediment production by bioerosion depend upon the organisms involved, their abundance, and distribution. As the bioeroders crop the reef surface, they may break the skeletons of their prey and discard the fragments or they may ingest them along with the living tissues. Ingested fragments may then be assimilated and degraded before they are defecated on or above the substrate. The relative proportion of discarded to defecated fragments varies among the various species involved in the prey/predator relationship; it is further complicated by the fact that both discarded and defecated fragments may pass through several cycles of ingestion before they finally enter the stratigraphic record. In level-bottom sediments between reefs, holothurians and parrot fish are particularly important in the ingestion–degradion–defecation process and may recycle the same grain numerous times each year.

Typically, size–frequency distributions of sediments produced by bioerosion are bimodal. The larger clasts consist of relatively complete skeletons or fragments that have been so weakened by bioerosion that they eventually collapse and move by gravity to locations near their life habitat. Loose sediment in sheltered depressions on the reef surface consists of coarse gravel to sand-size skeletal fragments of local origin that eventually may become part of the reef's internal sediment. The small-size clasts (mostly sand, silt, and clay) are removed from the excavations produced by the grazing, rasping, grinding, and boring process and may be easily transported great distances by currents. The relative weight percent of each of these size fractions is quite variable but usually the larger clasts outweigh the smaller.

The whole tests of Foraminiferida are extremely important constituents of beach, lagoonal, and reef flat sands; locally, large forams such as *Marginopora* may also provide a significant part of the gravel fraction (C. S. Ross, 1972). At Oahu, Hawaii, Muller (1974) calculated the production of skeletal $CaCO_3$ by *Amphistegina madagascariensis* as 500 $g/m^2/yr$ with growth rates of about 7 $\mu m/d$. Other major biogenic sources of sand in reef systems include grains produced by boring, grinding, and grazing by echinoids and fish; minor sources are calcareous spicules released by decay of gorgonians and alcyonaceans, which are very abundant in western Atlantic reefs.

Determination of the origin of grains smaller than sand ($<$1/16-mm dia) is much more difficult because their morphology is less distinctive than for larger grains. A large proportion represent the late stages in the mechanical abrasive breakdown of skeletal fragments. Another major source of silt-size grains is the ejected chips from the boring activities of sponges; because most sponges lack zooxanthellae and so their biomass increases with depth relative to algae and corals, the effects of sponge boring also increase with depth.

Boring by sponges is mechanical, not chemical; bacteria, filamentous algae, and fungi are the chief chemical microborers in skeletal materials (Golubic et al., 1975). The basal layer of sponge cells in contact with the hard substrate expand and contract during boring to produce chips of about 15–80 μm that are expelled through the excurrent canals. The chips have uniquely sculptured, curved surfaces (Wilkinson, 1983) and so can be recognized in the fine sediments. Sediment production by sponges at Barbados is estimated at 5–10 metric tons/hectare/yr (Hunter, 1977); estimates of the proportion of sponge chips in the silt fraction of lagoonal and reef flat sediments vary from 20 to 40% (Futterer, 1974; Halley et al., 1977).

In view of the generally high biomass of siliceous demosponges in reef communities and the abundance of sponge-boring chips, the very low content of siliceous spicules in level-bottom sediments (<2%) is very surprising. Hartman (1977) attributed this difference to the slow growth, turnover rates, and long life span of these sponges; rapid dissolution of siliceous spicules in carbonate materials is also an important factor (Land, 1976). The contribution of siliceous skeletons of diatoms and nannoplankton to reef substrates is negligible.

Roles of Codiacean Algae

Various codiacean (green) skeletal algae are exceedingly important in the production of several types of sediments in reef environments. Although the quantitative significance of some of these sediments is controversial, the rapid growth and high turnover rates of these plants make their potential contributions enormous. The most common Holocene reef-dwelling codiaceans are species of the erect-growing genera *Halimeda*, *Penicillus*, *Udotea*, and *Rhipocephalus*.

Halimeda. The role of *Halimeda* is less controversial than the others because its skeleton consists of heavily calcified plates about 2–15 mm in diameter that fall to the substrate upon death of the plant; the plates are easily identified on the basis of their size, shape, and internal structure even after they have been abraided. They are ubiquitous in sediments associated with Cenozoic reefs.

Halimeda spp. grow in abundance in virtually all parts of the reef environment except the most turbulent; the plants attach by holdfasts to both hard and soft substrates. They are most abundant in the lagoons and flats. At Enewetak Atoll, Marshall Islands, they extend down the seaward slope to depths of about 140 m; at 90 m *Halimeda* covers up to 50% of the hard substrate (Hillis-Colinvaux, 1986).

At Belize, *Halimeda* is the major contributor to substrate sediments from the lagoon to depths of at least 200 m on the seaward slope (Rützler and Macintyre, 1982), and in the lagoon at Davies Reef, Great Barrier Reef, the *actual* sediment production by *Halimeda* alone amounts to 185 $g/m^2/yr$ or about 0.13 mm/yr (Drew, 1983); Chave et al. (1972) estimated the *potential* $CaCO_3$ production by *Halimeda* at $10^4 g/m^2/yr$!

Others. The importance of the other codiaceans noted above to the production of sediment is much more difficult to determine because they produce clay-size (about 4–10 µm) needles of aragonite that are morphologically indistinguishable from needles produced by abiotic processes (see Cloud et al., 1962, Pls. 3–5). Aragonite and calcite clay of non-needle shapes are also produced by physical abrasion of skeletal grains, ingestion–degradation–defecation of grains by deposit feeders, and by bacteria and microborers. Thus, the real problem is to determine the relative contribution of each of these potential sources to the total clay-size fraction.

Numerous authors have supported the potential of codiaceans (especially *Penicillus*) to contribute significantly to the production of reef flat and lagoonal aragonite clays (e.g., Stockman et al., 1967; Neumann and Land, 1975; Wefer, 1980; Rützler and Rieger, 1973) by generally stressing the high density of these plants and their rapid growth and turnover rates.

The most probable alternative to the codiacean origin of the aragonite needle clay involves physical–chemical reactions in the following succession:

$$CO_2 + H_2O = H_2CO_3 \qquad (4.1)$$

$$H_2CO_3 = H^+ + HCO_3^- \qquad (4.2)$$

$$HCO_3^- = H^+ + CO_3^{-2} \qquad (4.3)$$

$$2HCO_3^- = CO_2 + H_2O + CO_3^{-2} \qquad (4.4)$$

$$Ca^{+2} + CO_3^{-2} = CaCO_3 \qquad (4.5)$$

Precipitation of $CaCO_3$ as aragonite needles requires lowering the partial pressure of CO_2 in the seawater–sediment system. This may be done by either physical means (increased heat and evaporation; decreased pressure in shallower water) or biological means (consumption of CO_2 by photosynthesis). Proponents of the non-algal origin for most of the shallow-water needles include Cloud et al. (1962) and Liebezeit et al. (1984).

In the large area of the Great Bahama Bank west of Andros Island, about 95% of the sediments are endogenous; of those grains larger than silt, about 10–20% can be recognized as skeletal (4–12% are algal, predominantly *Halimeda*). The controversy surrounds the remaining 75%, of which about 95% of the clay fraction and more than 50% of the silt consist of aragonite needles and laths. Cloud et al. (1962) believe that virtually all of these needles and laths are of physical–chemical origin.

Aphotic Zone Reefs

In aphotic zone reefs, the proportion of exogenous sediment, especially fine siliciclastics, is generally higher than in shallow-water lagoons and flats; it is still much less than the endogenous skeletal carbonate component.

The upper surface of the Blake Plateau is nearly 800 m deep and in these quiet waters there is virtually no breakdown of the large coral skeletons comprising these reefs (Stetson et al., 1962). Sediment accumulates slowly among the corallum branches and supports them essentially in growth position. In the sediments surrounding the aphotic zone reefs studied by Mullins et al. (1981), the sand-gravel fraction is dominated by endogenous calcareous skeletons and the fine fraction by calcareous tests of planktonic foraminifera and pteropods; none of the grains appear to have had a shallow-water source. However, Neumann et al. (1977) recognized *Halimeda* fragments and oolites of shallow-water origin in the sand surrounding deep water (600–700 m) reefs in the Straits of Florida.

In the deep-water reefs of the Norwegian fiords and in the eastern Atlantic (Fig. 2.2), the spaces between the coral branches are filled with skeletal debris from asteroids, ophiuroids, gorgonians, bryozoans, and the like. The adjacent sediment consists mostly of terrigenous silt and clay (i.e., in the stratigraphic record, they would appear as calcareous reefs in a shale matrix; Teichert, 1958, p. 1072).

Conclusions

It is readily apparent that the many processes involved in destruction of the organic framework of reefs powerfully influence their sizes, shapes, and the nature of the internal and external sediment. The skeletons of the frame-building organisms are major constituents of reef sediments of all sizes and in all locations across the reef system from the lagoons and flats to the seaward slopes. However, in the flats and lagoons adjacent to photic zone reefs, the contribution of non-frame-builders, especially codiacean algae and foraminifera, is potentially far more important than skeletons of frame-builders.

SEDIMENT TRANSPORTATION

Following sediment production, the next process to become operative in reef systems is the removal (transportation) of the excess sediment (i.e., does not become internal sediment) from its place of origin to a place of deposition in the reef complex (Fig. 4.1). The main transporting forces involved in moving reef sediments are: (1) the wind-driven, shallow-water waves and currents that generally move across the reef from the open ocean toward the reef flat and lagoon; (2) the tide-driven currents moving across the reef in both the lagoonward and oceanward directions; and (3) the gravity-driven movements of grains to shallow sediment surface depressions, internal cavities, and down the seaward slope. The strength of these forces is affected by the size, location, and geometry of the reef complex.

Although the strength of these forces and their importance in sediment transport are highly varied, they can be subdivided into two types: those that occur during the "normal" or prevailing operation of the reef system and those of short-term duration that result from intense storms. Even casual observation of interreef substrates during normal conditions of turbulence shows essentially continuous movement of the sand and smaller grains; each passing wave throws some of the "fines" into suspension and shifts the larger grains along the bottom by traction and saltation.

Catastrophic storms introduce an enormous volume of heterogeneous sediment into reef systems in a short time. The bulk of this sediment consists of coral fragments derived from the reef crest and upper seaward slope that is transported to and across the reef flat, island, or lagoon. Particularly intense storm waves are remarkably successful at dislodging large fracture-bounded blocks from the reef crest and then transporting them across the flat to the beach ramparts. Other sediment sources include the passes, surge channels, caverns, and grooves of the reef complex that are scoured of loose material which is moved lagoonward by the storm waves and currents.

Following these storms, this new wave of sediment input is slowly redistributed through the reef system by the "normal" processes; the coarse skeletal debris may remain as lag deposits, whereas the finer sands and muds are moved to more sheltered locations on the flats and lagoons or down the seaward slope. During these prolonged periods, tidal currents play major roles in sediment redistribution on the flat and lagoon as well as in transporting former crest, flat, and lagoon sediments back into passes, surge channels, and grooves. Gravity flow then carries some of the sediment down the seaward slope. In fact, abrasion by sediment carried by tidal and gravity currents *may* enlarge some of the passes, channels, and grooves (Wiens, 1962, pp. 120–126); coral construction of the spurs appears to exceed sediment erosion in the grooves in producing the relief of the upper seaward slope (Shinn et al., 1981).

Gravity is also responsible for local transport of a significant part of the internal sediment retained within the reefs themselves. Skeletal breakdown at the reef surface produces grains of diverse sizes and shapes that fall into spaces between the *in situ* organic framework and settle into stable locations. Other internal sediment is driven into these spaces by waves and currents and is derived from adjacent level-bottoms.

Although the physical transport of sediment by waves, currents, and gravity predominates, there may also be locally significant biological transport by vagile bioeroders and deposit feeders (fish are especially important) by the process of ingestion at a different location than defecation.

Bardach (1961) estimated that in Bermuda the sediment transport by fish amounted to 2.3 metric tons/hectare/yr; a single storm moves several times this amount in a few hours. Comparable figures for other vagile deposit feeders are not available, but for invertebrates the transport distance is rather inconsequential.

The interrelations among grain size and shape, specific gravity, and current velocity required to move sediment are complex. Roberts and Suhayda (1983) recognized two fundamentally different velocities governing the transportation of granular sediments: (1) the minimum, or threshold, velocity required to lift sediments from the bottom and put them into suspension; and (2) the gravity-induced velocity at which suspended grains settle through the water column. The threshold velocities for clay and silt considerably exceed those for sand; clay has an even greater velocity than pebbles. By contrast, the settling velocities of sand and pebbles are several orders of magnitude greater than for clay and silt. This fact simply means that it requires strong currents to suspend clay and silt, but once these grains are in suspension, relatively weak currents may transport them for considerable distances.

Under "normal" wind, wave, and current conditions at the reef crest, clay-through-pebble sizes can all be suspended together. The coarse sediments produced at the crest and upper seaward slope are moved only short distances before they settle to the substrate near the reef crest–reef flat boundary; at this point, there is rapid attenuation of current velocity and the sediments remain in place until storm waves and currents resuspend and transport them lagoonward. The transport of suspended "fines" is much more complex. "Normal" flood tides crossing the crest carry the fines well into the flats and lagoons and ebb tides remove them to the seaward slope through the passes. Storms create abnormally high water levels in the flats and lagoons; this water recedes rapidly as the storm abates and produces enormous sediment flushing in these areas and sediment dumping on the seaward slope.

Burrowing and bioturbation by the infauna of the flat and lagoonal level-bottom community are especially important in resuspending clay and silt in areas where currents are too weak to suspend them but still adequate to transport and redistribute them. Roberts et al. (1981) estimated that the burrowing shrimp *Callianassa* at St. Croix, U.S. Virgin Islands, eject up to 3.9 kg/m^2/d of sediment 5–10 cm into the water; this sediment is then redistributed within the central lagoon.

The reef crest is also a critical demarcation between the two main directions of sediment transport: either from the crest toward the flat and lagoon or from the crest down the seaward slope. Although the crest is an area of major sediment production, only a small part of the coarse material and almost none of the "fines" are retained there as internal sediment. In atolls, reef crest- and flat-derived sediment enters the complex circulation pattern of the lagoon. Whether this sediment, as well as that produced by lagoonal processes, remains in the lagoon or is removed depends on the interrelations among the volume of sediment carried in or produced there, lagoonal circulation, and subsidence of the lagoon floor. Efficient removal of sediment requires numerous, large passes relatively uniformly spaced around the perimeter. In Indo-Pacific atolls, there is a *general* relationship between lagoon diameter, depth, and passes; large atolls have deep lagoons and numerous passes. For example, Kwajalein Atoll, Marshall Islands, is both the largest and has the greatest number of passes (28) of any Holocene atoll (Tayama, 1952, p. 247). Deep lagoons with poor circulation are sediment "sinks," and if subsidence rates are slow, they may turn into hypersaline evaporite pans with low islands.

Gravity-induced sediment transport down the seaward slope is highly episodic and the grains vary in size from suspended muds to huge, tumbling blocks loosened at the reef crest. Receding normal tides bring a slow "rain" of fine materials, especially near the mouths of passes, whereas storm-flushed heterogeneous sediment from lagoons, flats, and upper seaward slopes literally cascades down the middle and lower slopes in torrents. There is also rapid movement of bored corals, especially the laterally extended foliaceous forms, that simply collapse of their own weight and dislodge sediment and living organisms as they tumble downslope.

Short-term observations of sediment transportation on reef crests and flats during "normal" conditions generally indicate that the net movement is toward the shore and/or lagoon. In view of the high rates of sediment production on the crest and flat, long-term onshore transport would result in rapid filling of the flats and lagoons. Because such filling is slow, it is readily apparent that there is compensating offshore sediment transport in the passes and surge channels, especially during and after storms.

Geological data are also useful for comparing the relative long-term importance of onshore versus offshore sediment transport. In nearly all ancient reef complexes, the volume of rocks deposited on seaward slopes and basins greatly exceeds the thickness and volume of the chronologically equivalent rocks of reef flats and continental shelves. The two most important factors responsible for this difference are depositional rate and substrate subsidence rate; the former depends upon the rate at which sediment is transported to the final site of deposition. Although these data are indirect measures of the relative importance of onshore versus offshore transport, they strongly suggest that the offshore is much more important and that ancient basins are the recipients of most of the excess carbonate production in photic zone reef systems. Before final basin deposition has occurred, many of the individual grains have taken a rather circuitous route. They typically begin as reef crest skeletons to be broken by the waves, only to be transported shorewards by currents, repeatedly deposited–transported–redeposited in the flat or lagoon before being carried seaward by tidal currents and then down the seaward slope by gravity flows to mix with pelagic sediments of the open ocean. The pelagic component progressively increases in importance away from the base of the seaward slope.

Aphotic Zone Reefs

Deep-water currents are primarily driven by gravity and arise from density differences in the water column (i.e., cold, dense sediment-rich water moves down slope beneath warmer, lighter water); the greater the density difference, the stronger the current. Mullins et al. (1981, p. 1001) summarized some of the current velocity data for eastern Atlantic aphotic zone reefs as follows:

    a.   At 830 m in the Blake Plateau: up to 41 cm/s.

    b.   At 400 m in the Straits of Florida: 60 cm/s.

    c.   At 1000–1300 m north of Little Bahama Bank: up to 50 cm/s.

    d.   At 650 m in the Straits of Florida just west of Little Bahama Bank: 2–7 cm/s.

In all but the last case, the currents are more than sufficient to suspend and transport sands (Roberts and Suhayda, 1983, Table 1); because their movement begins in more turbid shallow water, these currents can easily transport their clay-sand size material for great distances. Other evidence for current sediment transport in deep water adjacent to reefs include well-developed, large (wave height: 2–15 cm; wave length: 15–50 cm) ripple-marks in sand and gravel (reef debris of shallow-water origin) at depths of 1100–2000 m on the slope of Enewetak Atoll, Marshall Islands (Shipek, 1962).

SEDIMENT DEPOSITION AND ACCUMULATION

In shallow-water reef environments, sediments of the level-bottom are repeatedly deposited, moved, and redeposited, whereas in deeper water, deposition is commonly the final event of a more sustained transportation process. This section is only concerned with final sediment deposition and subsequent entry into the geological stratigraphic record (accumulation); deposition begins when transportation ends, and this occurs when the settling velocity finally exceeds the current velocity. In shallow water, this simply means that the wind- and tide-driven waves and currents have been dissipated and that in deep water, density differences and substrate slope are no longer adequate to sustain the currents required to transport the available sediments. In reef flats and lagoons, depositional sites are mostly located in substrate depressions and the leeward sides of current obstructions; in deeper water, deposition occurs mostly at the base of the seaward slope on reef-derived debris fans that extend into the adjacent basins.

The overall depositional process can be subdivided into two stages: (1) baffling of the currents to reduce their velocity and (2) trapping and stabilization of sediments after deposition to prevent their continued movement by traction or resuspension. Benthic reef and level-bottom organisms play important roles in both of these stages.

Baffling

baffle: a) to check or break the force of: to deflect or stop the flow of; to interfere with the free or straight motion of; to disperse the effective force of; a verb; b) something for deflecting, checking or otherwise regulating flow as a plate or wall; a noun.

(Webster's 3rd New International Dictionary, 1976)

The Process

Anything extending above the general level of the substrate is a baffle; because of the characteristically irregular surface of reefs and their topographic relief, baffles and the baffling process are much more important in reef environments than elsewhere in the sea. Baffles also play an indirect role in protecting reefs from wave and current destruction by reducing current velocity and absorbing the force of the surf.

Klement (1967) seems to have been the first to recognize the sedimentologic significance of baffles in reef environments; he stressed the role of organisms as baffles but did not separate the baffling from the trapping/ stabilizing processes or the organisms involved in each. In the present usage, this distinction is considered to be important because baffles do not always reduce turbulence; locally, they may produce eddies and cause resuspension, scouring, and sediment transport. Furthermore, quite different organisms may be involved in baffling and trapping. For example, an erect, bladelike coenosteum of *Millepora* oriented perpendicularly to the prevailing currents is a very effective baffle but does not trap or hold sediment. The enmeshed filaments in an algal mat trap sediment but do not baffle currents. And the *Thalassia* plant is both a baffle and a trap: the blades baffle and the roots trap. Thus, final sediment deposition in reef environments is a two-step process: first comes current reduction and gravity-induced dropping of the grains to the substrate, and second, the holding and prevention of the grains from continued transport.

Photic Zone

Baffling occurs on scales from whole reef systems to individual organisms. For example, by reducing wave and current force and thereby creating and maintaining flats and lagoons, elongate shelf margin reefs (barrier reefs; ribbon reefs) and algal ridges are protective baffles for both open ocean and continental shelf reef systems. Such reefs absorb wave shock, deflect currents into passes and surge channels, and create local scouring eddies; their overall effect, however, is to reduce current velocities enough for sediment deposition to occur on the reef flats. Similarly, displaced large blocks act as baffles on seaward slopes and in basins.

On progressively smaller scales, the spurs and grooves on the upper seaward slope form baffles for the dissipation of wave energy. Patch reefs, reef knolls, coral skeletons, and even such soft-bodied structures as the blades, leaves, and "props" of macroalgae, marine grasses, mangroves, sponges, anemones, and the like are effective obstructions to the force of currents. Scoffin (1970) noted that currents of 30 cm/s above the level of the mangrove and eel-grass baffles in Bimini Lagoon were reduced to zero at the water–sediment interface.

All these factors may produce eddy-scoured depressions at the sides and leeward margin of baffling structures, but their overall effect is to reduce current velocities at and near the sediment–water interface and promote sediment deposition. Such baffles may occur on both sedimentary and hard substrates; the reef as a whole is a baffle, as well as the individual organisms growing upward from its surface.

The effectiveness of the baffling and sediment deposition process is directly related to the size and spacing density of the baffles. In a forest and in a reef (the analogy is direct), the larger the baffle and the closer its spacing to neighboring baffles, the greater the effective reduction in current velocity. Isolated baffles bear the full force of the current; closely spaced baffles, such as tree trunks in a forest or coral branch "thickets," gorgonian "fans," or alcyonarian "whips" in a reef, are mutually supportive during storms. In addition, the more effective the baffles, the more rapid the current reduction and sediment deposition; if upstream sorting has been poor, the more heterogeneous the sizes of the deposited sediments. In mud-rich reef frameworks, the rather clear inference is that the currents were not transporting heterogeneous grains; current reduction by semieffective baffles should produce a concentration of larger clasts relative to small ones. In ancient reefs, it is rare to find the baffling organisms in their growth positions unless they have strong, firmly attached skeletons and the depositional rate has been slow and uniform enough to "drown" them in the sedimentary matrix.

Aphotic Zone

Baffling by reefs and organisms is apparently as important for sediment deposition in the aphotic zone as in the photic zone. Bottom currents carrying fine sediment encounter the reef baffles and the meshwork of the live branching corals and fragments trap and hold it (Stetson et al., 1962,

p. 32). Mullins et al. (1981) reported that the sediments within the deep-water, coral-dominated reefs north of Little Bahama Bank are finer-grained than those between the reefs and suggested that the interreef sediments were current-winnowed but that the reefs acted as current baffles and sediment traps. They and Neumann et al. (1977) reasoned that after reef growth has begun, the baffle/trap process operates in a feedback manner; coral growth, baffling, and trapping of sediment near the bases of the branches lead to a progressive increase in the size of the structure and hence its effectiveness to continue the overall accretion process. The result is a coral-dominated framework supported by an infilling of fine-grained carbonate mud, plus the skeletons of *in situ* reef dwellers and a smaller component of pelagic organisms and sediment from the water column.

Squires (1964, p. 906) noted that in comparisons of deep- and shallow-water reefs, the volume of live coral required to construct a deep-water reef is less because of the greater effectiveness of the baffle/trap process, especially as the size of the structure increases. Furthermore, because of effective baffling, corallum fragments undergo minimal removal from aphotic zone reefs.

Trapping and Stabilization

In areas of moderate-to-high turbulence such as reefs, after the sedimentary particles have been deposited it is generally also necessary to hold them if there is to be net accumulation; otherwise, transporting currents remove them to other potential depositional sites. The holding process is here called trapping and stabilization. On Holocene level-bottom substrates, soft-bodied organisms or their mucous secretions are commonly involved. In reefs, however, the various surficial and internal cavities, voids, and other spaces in the framework are the sites of internal sediment accumulation.

The organisms, or parts of organisms, of the level-bottom community that are involved in trapping and stabilization are (1) filamentous algae growing in laterally expanded mats and stromatolites, (2) the strands of the holdfasts of erect-growing chlorophytes, (3) the surficial mucus of isolated corals, and (4) the tangles of exposed grass and mangrove roots. Laterally expanded skeletal organisms are uncommon members of the level-bottom community and are only minimally involved in the trapping and stabilization process. Effective and prolonged trapping and stabilization of level-bottom sediments by non-skeletal organisms produces mud mounds rather than reefs.

On hard substrates such as dead corals and beach rampart rubble, algae may form mats which trap and stabilize sediment; algae may also enhance later carbonate cementation to form beachrock. These algal mats retain seawater in their pores and, by photosynthesis, raise the pH to about 10, at which point both high-Mg calcite and aragonite precipitate (Epstein and Friedman, 1982, p. 158).

Surficial Sediments

Level-bottom

The nature and distribution of sediment within and adjacent to shallow-water reefs have attracted the attention of numerous sedimentologists and carbonate petrologists for over a century. The pace of this research accelerated quickly during the 1950s for two quite different reasons. First, there was increased support of basic reef research by the U.S. government in the Marshall and other Pacific Islands (see *U.S. Geological Survey, Professional Paper 260*). Second, there was an increasing awareness of vast quantities of hydrocarbons that are present in ancient reefs and their associated rocks. This latter interest has been a matter of continuing intense research by petroleum geologists during the ensuing years. The result of all this attention has been the accumulation of an enormous amount of local and regional sedimentologic data (Table 4.1, A, B) as well as numerous attempts at synthesis to produce facies models for petroleum exploration in ancient reef complexes (Table 4.1, C).

Among the early attempts to unite the study of Holocene reefs and their associated sediments with the search for petroleum, the work in Guadalupe Mountains in the southwestern United States must be regarded as classic. The pioneering field studies by Philip King (especially his 1948 monograph) and Norman Newell (especially Newell et al., 1953) provided the basis for continuously accelerating research in this area.

The nature and distribution of surface and near-surface sediments in reef complexes are influenced by so many local and regional factors (Chap. 3) and processes that it is very difficult to determine the relative importance of the factors or to generalize about the operation of the processes. The situation is even more difficult to understand and interpret because all the factors and processes shift in location and intensity over time spans varying from ephemeral (a storm) to geologically prolonged. Prolonged environments, either shifting or stable, produce three-dimensional rock bodies arranged in various lateral and vertical relations called *facies*. The abiotic aspects of these rocks are *lithofacies* and the biotic aspects are *biofacies*.

In many ways, each reef complex is unique, and few, if any, can adequately serve as models for comparison with other complexes. Conversely, synthetic models commonly have significant flaws when they are applied to particular reef complexes. Thus, the inductive–deductive method must be used with caution in studies of reefs and their sediments.

The emphasis here will be on those aspects of the surficial sediments

TABLE 4.1. Selected References Pertaining to the Nature and Distribution of Holocene Surficial Sediments in Diverse Reef Complexes

A. Detailed local studies
   1. Western Atlantic Ocean
     a. Abaco Island, Bahamas: Storr, 1964
     b. Great Bahama Bank: Newell et al., 1951; Cloud et al., 1962
     c. Florida Keys: Ginsburg, 1956; Swinchatt, 1965
     d. Reef pinnacles, Gulf of Mexico: Ludwick and Walton, 1957
   2. Bikini Atoll, Marshall Islands: Emery et al., 1954 and other parts of *U.S. Geol. Surv., Prof. Pap. 260*
   3. Saipan, Mariana Islands: Cloud, 1959
   4. Kapingamarangi Atoll, Caroline Islands: McKee et al., 1959
   5. Great Barrier Reef
     a. Howick Group: Flood et al., 1978
     b. Heron Island: Maxwell et al., 1961 and 1964
B. Regional studies
   1. Indo-Pacific atolls: Wiens, 1962
   2. Great Barrier Reef: Maxwell, 1968, 1973
C. General syntheses
   1. Cloud, 1952
   2. MacNeill, 1954
   3. Stoddart, 1969
   4. Ahr, 1973
   5. Orme, 1977 a and b
   6. Longman, 1981
   7. James, 1983

that appear to influence the nature and distribution of the level-bottom organisms and communities adjacent to reefs (Chap. 5). As is generally the case in soft substrate communities dominated by infaunal taxa, grain size and sorting are especially important.

Substrate Grain Size
The size and composition of the particles on the substrate surface in any particular area are affected by the interrelations among numerous processes beginning at their source (sediment production discussed above) and continuing through the processes of transportation, baffling, and trapping. Accumulations of transported dead skeletons are very characteristic of island beaches (Pl. 4*a*) and the seaward slope; they constitute the "transported assemblages" of Fagerstrom (1961). In reef flats and lagoons, the substrate grains may be a heterogeneous mixture of both endogenous (mostly whole skeletons) and exogenous materials (mostly skeletal fragments and mud) with highly varied predepositional histories ("mixed assemblages" of Fagerstrom, 1961). Orme (1977b, Table 1) has

summarized the relative abundance of various skeletal components of numerous reef complexes but made no attempt to distinguish the endogenous from the exogenous grains. The variation in these data is considerable and reflects global biogeographic differences as well as local differences in sample location.

Subsequent burial and incorporation into the sedimentary record initiate additional chemical (dissolution; cementation), physical (compaction), and biological (ingestion; bioturbation) processes that may cause additional in grain-size changes before and during very early diagenesis.

On some reef flats, there is a general concentric zonal arrangement in sizes of substrate grains from coarsest adjacent to the high turbulence of the reef crest to progressively smaller grains toward the beach or lagoon (McKee et al., 1959). These sedimentologic zones generally correspond with the geomorphic zonations of the associated reef systems; they are, however, less well-defined and are better developed on windward than on leeward shores. Similar sediment zonations are present across whole reef complexes. Table 4.2 is a synthesis for Jamaican reef complexes and summarizes the interrelations among the geomorphic zones, substrate lithology or sediments, sediment production, and sediment source. It also shows the importance of the area of the reef crest as a source of transported skeletal grains to both onshore and offshore depositional sites. Evident too is the mixing of endogenous (local) and exogenous (transported) grains in all parts of the complex except the crest; the taxonomic diversity of skeletal grains involved also varies considerably across the reef complex.

Large, deep, open ocean atoll lagoons act as sediment traps or "sinks" for the overproduction of sediment on the crest and flat; their substrate sediments are also characterized by a lateral zonation (or concentric rings) consisting of transported foraminiferal beach sands, coarse coral debris (mostly transported from the crest and flat) in the shallowest water to *Halimeda* plates (mixed endogenous and exogenous), to deepest water sands and muds dominated by endogenous foraminifera, and debris from coral knolls and knoll reefs. In the lagoon at Kapingamarangi Atoll, Caroline Islands, the base of the *Halimeda*-dominated substrate is at about 38 m (Stoddart, 1969, pp. 473–474).

There is a bathymetric gradient in grain sizes in the seaward slope sediments from large blocks loosened from the reef crest and upper slope by the waves to coarse fragments of corals and *Halimeda* derived from shallow water at intermediate depths to sands and finally muds in very deep water. At Bikini Atoll, Marshall Islands, the transition from sands dominated by planktonic foraminifera (especially *Globigerina*) to red clay occurs at about 3900 m on the seaward slope (Ladd, 1973).

Substrate Sorting

Numerous processes (both physical and biological) also influence the degree of sorting of level-bottom sediments; despite the generally high tur-

TABLE 4.2. Sediments of Jamaican Reef Complexes[a]

Reef Zones	Zone 1 (Inshore)	Zone 2 (Lagoon)	Zones 3–8 (Reef Crest)	Zones 9–11 (Seaward Slope)
Substrate lithology/ sediments	Rock (occasional imbricate ramparts); beach rubble; sand	Sand, mud; some rubble; coral heads	Reef framework; some sand patches, alternating grooves	Sand, mud; talus cones; coral outcrops, mud flows
Producing organisms	Corals, calcareous algae, echinoderms, worms, arthropods	Algae, sponges, gorgonians, forams, corals, molluscs, arthropods, echinoderms, fish	Corals, milleporas, algae, echinoderms, molluscs, forams	Algae, corals, antipatharians, sponges, gorgonians, thin-shelled molluscs, echinoderms, bryozoans, arthropods, worms, forams
Source (point of origin) of grains	Some terrigenous siliciclastics; others transported from Zones 3–8	Local; others transported from Zones 3–8	Local	Local; others transported from Zones 3–8

Source: Modified from Goreau and Goreau, 1973.
[a]Zones and their geomorphic characteristics are given in Table 3.2.

bulence of reef complexes and its importance in producing good sorting, reef complexes are notable for their poor sorting. The chief reasons for this are: (1) the great diversity of sediment sizes produced by the reef complex; (2) the relatively rapid rates of sediment breakdown, transport, and deposition. Level-bottom reef flat sediments typically favor a preponderance of gravel and sand, whereas grass-covered areas and lagoons contain poorly sorted sand and mud.

Poor sorting is especially characteristic of seaward slopes where debris fans consist of exogenous blocks, skeletal gravels, and sands and pelagic muds mixed with the skeletons of various endogenous organisms. For example, in the deep-water (2500–5000-m) basin north of St. Croix, U.S. Virgin Islands, skeletal sands of shallow-water derivation are ubiquitous and contain heterogeneous admixtures of tumbled blocks from the reef crest, planktonic foraminifera and pteropods, and pelagic mud (Hubbard et al., 1981).

The movement of sediments by fish and benthic animals may be only locally important, but the sorting and volume of sediment involved are very important. Bioturbation probably plays as large a role in homogenizing the substrate and thus decreasing sorting as it does in enhancing selective winnowing and increasing sorting.

Internal Sediments

The emplacement of sediments in the internal cavities and other water-filled voids in the reef framework is by gravitational settling of locally derived whole skeletons as well as fragments and exogenous sediment (mostly skeletal sand and gravel and small amounts of "fines") carried by wind-driven waves and currents. Thus, the origins and sizes of the grains may be heterogeneous and sorting very poor. Ginsburg and Schroeder (1973, pp. 589–595) recognized fragments of exogenous coralline algae, the encrusting foraminifer *Homotroma rubrum,* molluscs, *Halimeda,* echinoids, and such pelagic forms as coccoliths, diatoms, and pteropods in mixed association with cavity-dwelling encrusters and borers in the pores of Bermudan algal reefs. Conversely, Bosence (1984) found that the internal sediments of the algal reefs at St. Croix, U.S. Virgin Islands, more accurately reflect the local biological composition of the reef than of the interreef sediments; however, they are generally finer-grained due to the exclusion of coarse materials from small pores and the high silt content from boring sponges. The texture and sorting of the internal sediment are controlled by the sizes of both the cavities and their openings to other cavities as well as to the reef surface.

In shallow-water Jamaican reefs, the broad base of the reefs is composed of very large, hemispherical coralla of *Montastraea annularis* to which are attached smaller, branching coralla of *Porites furcata* and *Acropora cervicornis.* The internal sediment consists predominantly of large branch fragments of the latter species (Goreau, 1959; Goreau and Goreau, 1973), many of which have been previously killed or weakened by bioerosion.

Summary

The processes of transportation and deposition are largely physical and are most strongly influenced by turbulence. They involve the origin of grains and their subsequent deposition, primarily in the level-bottom and seaward slope environments by sedimentologic processes (Fig. 4.1). The reef and the sediments, later to become rocks, constitute the reef complex.

Excellent general syntheses (Table 4.1, C) of these reef processes, the factors influencing them and their importance in different parts of reef complexes, and the varied sedimentologic results (sediments; rocks) of the processes may be found in J. L. Wilson (1975), Orme (1977b, especially Table 2), Longman (1981, especially pp. 21–35), and James (1983, pp. 347–378).

BINDING AND EARLY CEMENTATION

The process of construction produces the organic framework of reefs while those of destruction, transportation, and deposition produce and distribute the loose internal reef sediments and the extremely greater volume of sediments to the reef complex. As these four processes operate, the rigidity and topographic relief of the reef framework are enhanced by the process of binding, encrusting, and early cementation (Fig. 4.1). This process unites the various parts of the organic framework (*in situ* whole skeletons joined and firmly held together) and the internal sediments (grains joined to grains or to *in situ* skeletons) and in this way contributes to the overall building and stabilization of the reef framework. Rapid upward growth by large skeletons constructs the organic framework, whereas rapid lateral growth by sheetlike skeletons binds the organic framework and internal sediment. Binding and cementation slowly reduce the volume of pore space in the framework. Binding is a biologic process that contributes to the organic framework. Early cementation is a physical–chemical process that forms the inorganic framework and, upon death of the reef, continues directly to later diagenetic cementation.

By enhancing the rigidity of the reef framework, binding and cementation also enhance its resistance to physical and biological destruction. Early cements are suitable substrates for encrusters as well as for borers, but overall, these cements increase the strength of the framework.

Binding

In one way, the functional role of binding in reef communities corresponds to trapping and stabilization in level-bottom communities (i.e., the holding of transported grains), but binding also involves holding, supporting, and bracing of large, whole *in situ* skeletons. Another major difference is that binding organisms are skeletal, mostly colonial and of sheetlike morphology, whereas many level-bottom trappers and stabilizers are non-skeletal, mostly non-colonial, and grow in elongate strands. Finally, binding can be accomplished by organisms growing on the surface of the unconsolidated internal sediment as well as on hard substrates such as whole skeletons or large fragments (commonly called *encrusting*). In either case, the significance of the binding/encrusting process lies in the uniting of skeletons and grains to enhance the rigidity of the reef framework.

Because the general level of turbulence in photic zone reefs is so much higher than in aphotic zone reefs, the importance of binding in the enhancement of rigidity is much more critical for the success of photic zone reefs. In addition, the most common Cenozoic binding organisms are skeletal algae, which, by definition, are absent from aphotic zone reefs.

Early Cementation

The late 1960s and early 1970s was a period of discovery of the very important role that early (synsedimentary; syndepositional of some authors) submarine high-Mg calcite and aragonite cements play in the formation of the inorganic framework of Holocene photic zone reefs. These cements are most often present in the cavities, voids, and pores that also contain internal sediment. Early cement at the surface of living reefs is indeed rare, except for some stromatolites; subaerial "laminated crusts" attributed to early cementation have been described from the Holocene (Multer and Hoffmeister, 1968) and from ancient reef limestones ("Spongiostromata" of some authors).

Recognition of early cements in ancient reef limestones pre-dates these Holocene cement discoveries; the Late Permian rocks of the Guadalupe Mountains reefs are particularly important in this regard. Parts of the massive Capitan Limestone consist of up to 75% radial fibrous calcite that was regarded by Newell (1955a) as early cement. Furthermore, the origin of this cement has been central to the long-running debate as to whether the massive Capitan Limestone is in fact a reef (discussed in Chap. 6).

The early cements in Holocene reefs include various crystal forms. High-Mg calcite is usually more abundant than aragonite; it occurs as: (1) spherical–subspherical "peloids," 20–60 μm in diameter, composed of an inner mass of micrite with an outer rim of pseudospar; (2) isopachous rinds of bladed spar around grains; (3) cavity linings; or (4) intraskeletal pore cement. The cement commonly occurs as two distinct layers: an inner micrite envelope and an outer crust of bladed spar with the long crystal axes perpendicular to the grain surface or cavity wall. Aragonite occurs as: (1) needlelike, spherulitic masses in syntaxial contact with skeletal or non-skeletal aragonite crystals; (2) micrite envelopes around aragonite; and (3) larger botryoidal masses (Marshall, 1983; James, 1983, p. 368; Ginsburg and Schroeder, 1973; Ginsburg, 1983).

These early cements are important because they are best developed within cavities and pores in areas of high turbulence (i.e., near the crests and upper seaward slopes of reefs facing the open ocean) and thus further protect the framework from physical destruction. Bosence (1984, Table 1) estimated, from the study of slabs of shallow-water coralline algal reefs at St. Croix, U.S. Virgin Islands, that early cemented internal sediments comprise up to 20% of the rock volume. Such cements are also present in reef flats and lagoons, where there is less need for framework protection (Rützler and Macintyre, 1982, p. 43; Macintyre, 1984; Marshall, 1983).

Evidence for early cementation may begin within a few centimeters of the living reef surface; there is a progressive increase in importance deeper into the reef. At Bermuda, rocks only 1 m from the surface are thoroughly indurated (Ginsburg and Schroeder, 1973) reef limestones consisting of an algal–*Millepora*–vermetid gastropod organic framework, cemented internal sediments, and voids lined with *in situ* encrusting organisms and cement. The most abundant cement is high-Mg calcite pseudospar; next is aragonite needles lining the vermetid tubes. There may be several layers (or "generations") of internal sediment alternating with cavity encrusters and/or rinds of early cement (Ginsburg, 1983, p. 151). Matthews (1974, p. 234) suggested that a common paragenetic sequence for early cements begins with aragonite, usually as micrite followed by high-Mg calcite, usually as bladed pseudospar; silts in internal cavities are usually cemented by bladed pseudospar before sands.

Corals have taxonomically controlled varying amounts and sizes of intraskeletal pore space and permeability. After death, the pores in the outer parts of the aragonite skeletons become lined with micrite envelopes (either high-Mg calcite or aragonite). The subsequent cement nucleates directly on either the coral skeleton or the micrite as aragonite or high-Mg calcite or as mineralogic mixtures of both. Intraskeletal early cements generally become more important toward the center of the skeleton and may reduce the original porosity by 75% (Goreau et al., 1979). Evidence that cementation is submarine includes: (1) high-Mg calcite is known only from marine water and although aragonite forms elsewhere, it is very rare; (2) ratios of the carbon and oxygen isotypes; and (3) cementation within 1 cm of reef surface in seawater 8 m deep precludes any freshwater influence (Ginsburg and Schroeder, 1973). Although the details of the precipitation process are still uncertain, it basically involves reduction in the partial pressure of CO_2 dissolved in the seawater (equations 4.1–4.5) in contact with the growing cement crystal. Such reduction can occur by both physical or chemical mechanisms (e.g., increased temperature; decreased pressure in shallower water) or by withdrawal of CO_2 in photosynthesis. Seawater is commonly supersaturated with CO_2, but to produce volumetrically significant $CaCO_3$ requires flushing the pores with large volumes of water (Matthews, 1974, p. 234); this partly explains the positive correlation between abundant cements, high turbulence, and shallow water (Ginsburg, 1983, p. 152). The physical–chemical mechanism is based on changes in the CO_2 partial pressure in internal cavities and pores due to wave surge. The relatively great importance of early cements in these locations lends considerable credence to this mechanism.

Alternatively, algal photosynthesis may raise the pH levels and reduce the CO_2 partial pressure to induce cement precipitation. The significance of early cements in algal-dominated reefs supports this mechanism (Ginsburg and Schroeder, 1973; Bosence, 1984). Epstein and Friedman (1982) suggest a cause-and-effect relation between high pH, dissolution of SiO_2, and $CaCO_3$ pore cement precipitation which is controlled by diurnal fluctuation in light intensity.

Having established plausible mechanisms for submarine cementation, the next problem is to establish whether it occurs before the death of the reef surface organisms. Evidence to support this theory includes (Ginsburg and Schroeder, 1973, pp. 597, 610; Marshall, 1983, p. 232):

a.   Holocene age of well-cemented fossils embedded as deeply as 3.5 m below the reef surface.

b.   The interlayering of cemented internal sediment, *in situ* cavity dwelling organisms, and pore/cavity lining cements. These relations imply sequential episodes of sediment deposition, cementation, and biologic repopulation while the cavity was still connected to and flushed by seawater (i.e., there is an internal cavity stratigraphy that is very young). Fissure fillings in some pre-Cenozoic reefs contain similar multiple organic/inorganic layerings (Pl. 3) which have been used as evidence for closely spaced episodes of early cementation.

c.   At Barbados, the overall composition (12% micritized skeletal material; 10% internal sediment; 5% calcite cement; 3% aragonite cement) of the products of early diagenesis and cementation is similar from the reef surface to 1–1.5 m; thus, the near-surface cementation must be essentially contemporaneous with the living reef surface (Boucher, 1977, as reported by Hopley, 1982, p. 145).

Fluctuations in sea level during the Pleistocene exposed and submerged older Cenozoic and Pleistocene reefs several times to produce complex cementation, dissolution, and recrystallization histories that have obscured the earliest submarine cements. In many such reefs, low-Mg calcite of freshwater or even hypersaline vadose and phreatic zone origin simply continued the *pore-reduction* process begun by submarine cements. Elsewhere, and in some cases simultaneously, there was pore and cavern *enlargement* by freshwater vadose zone leaching.

Early cementation is not confined to photic zone reefs. Neumann et al. (1977) coined the term *lithoherm* partly to emphasize the indurated nature of the surface of some deep-water reefs in the Straits of Florida. In these reefs, there is no doubt that the cementation process is wholly physical–chemical; Neumann et al. attributed the cementation to the reduced pressure and increased temperature of ascending currents moving through the surficial pores of the reefs.

REEF ACCRETION ("GROWTH")

For reefs to achieve positive *topographic relief*, their long-term upward accretion ("growth") rate must exceed the accumulation rate of sediments on the adjacent level-bottom. Reef accretion may be expressed in terms of either linear reef extension rates (similar to corallum growth rates; see Chap. 3) or as the net (gain minus loss) rate of skeletal precipitation of $CaCO_3$ per unit area (the rate of early cementation is so poorly known that it is usually omitted from these determinations). Nearly all the processes discussed earlier in this chapter influence reef accretion and level-bottom depositional rates; their interactions are very complex, but the result is either net reef accretion or destruction.

The construction process attaches cardinal importance to assessing reef accretion and in turn depends directly on the rates of skeletal growth (linear extension) and of total or gross $CaCO_3$ precipitation *(G)* by the constructing organisms; the factors influencing these rates are discussed in Chapter 3. Construction is continuously retarded by the physical and biological processes of destruction and sediment production but is enhanced by the processes of binding and early cementation. All these processes and their physical and biological manifestations strongly depend on water depth, which in turn depends on the interrelations among foundation subsidence, sea-level change, and biological construction. These interdependencies among numerous factors and processes and the nature of the end result are not unique to reef ecosystems; they are, however, more highly integrated in reefs than in other marine ecosystems.

So long as a reef remains wholly submerged, the main growth direction is upward, but when the upper surface reaches the low tide level, lateral growth replaces upward growth (Fig. 3.8). At this stage in Holocene reefs, on the windward, open ocean side of the reef crest, construction and destruction are approximately in balance; most of the accretion then takes place on the leeward side of the crest and on the reef flat. However, for many ancient shelf margin reefs, accretion was most important on the basin side of the reef (Pl. 11*a*).

Rates of reef accretion can be assessed in terms of an excess of $CaCO_3$ input or production over loss by the removal of skeletal sediment and dissolution. This excess was defined as net $CaCO_3$ production *(N)* by Chave et al. (1972, p. 124) and *mass accretion* by Smith (1983); Stearn et al. (1977, Fig. 1) and Davies (1983, Fig. 14) have diagrammatically shown the complex "flow patterns" by which $CaCO_3$ cycles into and out of reef complexes. Thus, because of losses from the reef framework, reef accretion rates, whether measured as linear extension or net $CaCO_3$ production

(N), are never as high as skeletal growth rates of the frame-constructing organisms or as gross *(G)* CaCO₃ production (Buddemier and Kinzie, 1976, pp. 216–217; Wilkinson, 1983, p. 268; Wulff, 1984).

Linear Extension Rates

Numerous authors have measured or summarized the measurements of vertical and lateral linear extension rates of Pleistocene and Holocene photic zone reefs (e.g., Hopley, 1982, p. 224; Davies, 1983, pp. 75, 79; Hopley, 1983, p. 194; Hopley et al., 1983, p. 159; Macintyre et al., 1981; Lewis, 1977, p. 330; Bosence, 1984, p. 558; Adey and Vassar, 1975; Marshall and Jacobson, 1985; Storr, 1964, p. 19; Orme, 1977b, p. 147; Ginsburg and Schroeder, 1973, p. 601). From these data a few generalizations emerge:

a. Vertical extension rates for most reefs are in the range of 1–15 mm/yr; lateral extension rates are less (0.2–2.5 mm/yr). There are very few comparative data for ancient reefs; the mean Eocene–Holocene vertical extension rate for the reefs at Bikini and Enewetak Atolls, Marshall Islands, is only 2 mm/yr (Stoddart, 1969, p. 465), and for an English Jurassic reef, about 3.7 mm/yr (Ali, 1984). Teichert (1958, p. 1067) reported a vertical extension rate for a Holocene aphotic zone reef in Trondheim Fiord of 16 mm/yr!

b. Some of the highest vertical accretion rates occurred during the postglacial sea-level rise (18,000–5,000 years BP), when most reefs successfully "struggled" to remain in the photic zone (i.e., actual extension rates approximated potential rates). Lateral reef accretion has been most rapid during the last 5,000 years, when vertical extension rates have exceeded the rate of sea-level rise.

Drill hole data from Tarawa Atoll, Kirabati (formerly Gilbert Islands), indicate that the modern reef began to grow about 8,000 years BP and accreted rapidly (about 10 mm/yr) until about 7,000 years BP. Between 6,000 and 4,500 years BP, sea-level stabilized and vertical accretion decreased to about 1–2 mm/yr (Marshall and Jacobson, 1985). The higher vertical accretion rate at Tarawa is more comparable to those for shelf reefs such as the Great Barrier Reef than it is to other open ocean atolls such as Enewetak, Bikini, or Mururoa.

In their study of the accretion of the algal ridges at St. Croix, U.S. Virgin Islands, Adey and Vassar (1975, p. 68) determined that the process begins on highly turbulent, coral-dominated pavements less than 1.2 deep. The early coralline algae are crustose (primarily *Neogoniolithon* sp. and *Porolithon pachydermum*) and are subject to considerable grazing during calm water periods; other members of this early association include other red algae (Peyssonneliaceae), the encrusting foraminifer *Homotrema rubrum*, corals, and *Millepora*. This association accretes upwardly at about

5–6 mm/yr (intense grazing may limit accretion to only 0.5 mm/yr); when accretion reaches sea level, the early crustose corallines are replaced by a branching form *(Lithophyllum)* which rapidly builds the ridge to +20– +30 cm. With slowly rising or stable sea level, *Porolithon pachydermum* is capable of building the ridge to as high as +50 cm. Adey and Vassar concluded that the sizes and shapes of algal ridges are primarily controlled by grazing intensity and the rate of sea-level rise.

Net CaCO₃ Production Rates

Chave et al. (1972) estimated the overall net production rate *(N)* for Holocene reef systems at about 1 kg $CaCO_3/m^2/yr$; they regarded this rate as just adequate to keep the reef surface in the same water depth during the postglacial sea-level rise. (For comparison, they estimated the gross production *(G)* at about 10 kg $CaCO_3/m^2/yr$; thus, $G - N$ = production used in lateral reef accretion + skeletal sediments transported into the reef complex or into deep water basins + dissolution of $CaCO_3$ in seawater.)

Subsequently, other authors (summarized by Smith, 1983b, Table 1) have discounted the importance of losses of skeletal sediments and estimated the value of "net calcification" for numerous individual reef environments; their results suggest that in areas of dense coral and algal cover near the reef crest, N = 8–12 kg $CaCO_3/m^2/yr$ and in reef flats and coral–algal pavements, N = 1.5–6.5. These same data (now discounting the importance of lateral accretion) have been translated from net calcification rates to vertical accretion rates (Smith, 1983b, Fig. 1). From the geological viewpoint, the assumptions upon which both the net calcification rates and the vertical accretion rates are based (reviewed by Smith, 1983b, pp. 241–244) are very uncertain (see especially Sediment Transportation and Early Cementation above). However, Smith's overall conclusions regarding the relative magnitudes of reef and reef flat/pavement accretion rates seem intuitively reasonable from a biological viewpoint.

Level-bottom Sediment Accumulation

The rates at which level-bottom sediments accumulate and permanently enter the stratigraphic record depend on the quantitative relations between sediment production, texture, transportation, substrate erosion and deposition, substrate subsidence or sea-level rise, and location within the reef complex. With so many processes and factors involved, it is readily clear why the rates are so variable (Table 4.3); nonetheless, they fall roughly within a range of one order of magnitude (0.3–3 mm/yr).

Comparison of these level-bottom accumulation rates with the upward accretion rates of whole reefs described above (1–15 mm/yr) indicates why

TABLE 4.3. Mean (Range) Accumulation Rates of Holocene Level-bottom Carbonate Sediments at Selected Locations[a]

Location	Depositional rate (mm/yr)	General grain size	Ref.
1. Crane Key, Florida Bay	0.6	Mud	Hoffmeister and Multer, 1964
2. Great Bahama Bank	⩾0.8	Mud	Cloud et al., 1962
3. Redbill (reef flat), GBR	0.33		Hopely, 1982, p. 226
4. One Tree (windward reef flat), GBR	3.2		Hopley, 1982, p. 226
5. One Tree (lagoon), GBR	1.7	Sand	Hopley, 1982, p. 226
6. GBR	Mean = 2.62 (0.34–5.91)		Hopley, 1982, p. 226
7. GBR (lagoons)	Up to 5.9	Mixed	Hopley, 1982, p. 309
8. One Tree, GBR	1.7	Sand	Marshall and Davies, 1982
9. Northern GBR	1.0	Mixed; *Halimeda* plates and mud	Davies and Marshall, 1985
10. Davies (lagoon), GBR	0.5	*Halimeda* and mixed sediment	Drew, 1983
11. Pacific Atolls (lagoon)	>3.8	Mixed	Wiens, 1962, p. 105
12. Réunion Island (lagoon)	0.2	Mixed (intertidal)	Montaggioni, 1977

[a]GBR = Great Barrier Reef.

reefs have topographic relief (i.e., reefs accrete at 3–5 times the rate at which the adjacent level-bottom sediments accumulate). Because reef destruction produces the vast majority of the sediments that flank small reefs, it is also obvious why these sediments slope or dip away from reef margins as "aprons." The angle of slope or original dip of these flanking deposits approximately coincides with the angle of repose of their constituent sediments. This angle depends primarily on the porosity of the sediments, which in turn depends on grain-size, sorting, and depositional rate. The angle of repose for poorly sorted carbonate sand and gravel is about 30–35° and for well-sorted mud is 2–5°.

Sediment Compaction

Dipping flank beds are an important feature of most ancient reefs and have been used to estimate relative reef accretion/sediment accumulation rates and amounts of topographic relief for these reefs. Ancient flank beds typically decrease in mean grain size and increase in thickness away from reefs; angles of dip frequently exceed expected angles of repose for sediments of which they were originally composed. The usual reason for such "over-steepened" dips is the greater compaction of the level-bottom sediments relative to the rigid reef framework. Sedimentologic evidence of flank and level-bottom bed compaction includes the presence of pressure solution stylolites, flattened burrows, and tilted geopetal structures.

Shinn and Robbin (1983) suggested that compaction of carbonate sediments proceeds in two overlapping phases: an early mechanical stage and a later chemical one. The latter includes some pressure solution that may provide carbonate ions for diagenetic cements. Their mechanical compression equipment simulated sediment burial to 3900 m and at these pressures the reduction in both thickness and porosity of original muds is about 50–60%.

Topographic Relief

Features of small ancient reefs that may be used (with some caution) to determine the amount of original relief between their crests and the immediately adjacent reef flat include:

a.   The relief on bedding planes that can be traced from the reef crest down the flanks to the level-bottom, or the relief on thin "clay or mud seams and stringers" that can be traced through the core of the reef and down the flanking beds (Pl. 9b) to the adjacent level-bottom (Abbott, 1976, pp. 2122–2123; Narbonne and Dixon, 1984, p. 39). If there is general parallelism among several such beds, if texture, stylolitization, and burrow compaction are similar from the reef crest to the level-bottom, and if the geopetal structures do not indicate any postdepositional tilting, then the effects of differential compaction would appear to be minimal. Conversely, if beds below the reef dip toward the reef and become thinner (Pl. 10a), they indicate considerable differential compaction, and if the beds covering the reef crest thicken toward the level-bottom, they may indicate either slower accumulation rates or greater compaction on the crest relative to the level-bottom. All evidence of greater compaction of the level-bottom sediments relative to the reef framework leads toward overestimating the original topographic relief unless steps are taken to compensate for it.

b.   The relief on bedding planes that interfinger with the margin of the reef framework and can be traced down the flanks to the level-bottom. If the flank beds thicken downslope (the usual case), and if evidence of differential compaction does not increase downslope, then the present relief approximates the original relief. The low angle of dip of the flank beds adjacent to Triassic oyster-built reefs in southern Germany was used by Geister (1984b) as evidence for very low original topographic relief of these structures (i.e., the reefs and the level-bottom sediments have undergone similar amounts of compaction). This evidence is also supported by the apparently slow rate of accretion (1 mm/yr).

c.   On a regional scale, abrupt and distinct changes in the thickness of reefs relative to the coeval level-bottom rocks. However, if the reef framework is rigid limestone and the level-bottom is shale, the thickness differences are commonly due to differential compaction. Ball et al. (1977, pp. 256–258) determined that lateral thickness changes from algal-rich limestones to the intervening shale and fine-grained sandstone were very gradual (about 6–8 m in 8–97 km); they concluded that the relief from the original algal lime mud to the adjacent terrigenous level-bottom sediment surface was no more than several *centimeters* and that the shapes of the algal limestones are broadly lenticular–tabular and not comparable to typical reefs.

d.   Also on a regional scale, Newell et al. (1953, pp. 187–191) determined varying amounts of topographic relief from the reef-rimmed margin to the center of the Delaware Basin, southwestern United States, during the Late Permian by "measuring the vertical distance from the reef top to a stratigraphically equivalent horizon in the basin in front of the reef escarpment." They also concluded that "no significant exaggeration of the depositional relief was accomplished by differential compaction." In these same rocks, Klement (1968, p. 43) observed a distinct break in the depositional slope from the nearly horizontal rocks of the "reef core" to the steeply dipping (30°) beds of the basinward slope. Extension of this dip angle from the reef crest to stratigraphically equivalent basin slope rocks provides reasonable estimates of relief down the slope (Playford and Cockbain, 1969), but because the dip angle decreases into the basin, this method overestimates the maximum crest-to-basin relief.

In some reef complexes, the topographic relief of the crest is sufficient to restrict the circulation of oceanic water toward the reef flat or lagoon (Kirkland et al., 1966). Under suitably arid conditions, the salinity of the flat/lagoonal water may rise enough to cause the precipitation of evaporite minerals (Fisher, 1977; Sarg, 1981). Mixed carbonate and evaporite minerals may also mark the final stages of infilling of atoll lagoons.

Summary

The more rapid accretionary rates of reefs relative to the slower accumulation rates of adjacent level-bottom sediments accounts for the characteristic topographic relief of reefs and the original dip of the flanking deposits. Topographic relief implies rigidity and resistance to waves and currents (shallow water) or just currents (deep water). Evidence of partial resistance includes the abundance of reef-derived skeletal fragments in the flanking deposits. But topographic relief and dipping flanks are not unique to reefs; they are also characteristic of some non-reefs (carbonate build-ups; Heckel, 1974) such as shell heaps, oolite shoals, and mud mounds. In some situations, the dipping flanks between ancient rocks of different lithologies are due entirely to differential compaction. In mud mounds, the overthickening of the "core" may be entirely the consequence of current baffling and sediment trapping by non-frame-building organisms. Geologists often discover that it is as difficult to determine the cause for the dips of flank beds as it is to determine whether the "core" of the structure is indeed a reef (Pray, 1958, presents a careful analysis of the problems involved). A few geologists have regarded relief and dipping flanks as the chief criteria for recognition of ancient reefs; they have thereby altered the concept of reef (or bioherm) to include such "build-ups" or "overthickenings" of non-biologic origin.

Some ancient biostromal limestones lack dipping flank beds and thereby also seem to have lacked original dip and topographic relief (Pl. 9a).

5

Cenozoic Reef Models IV

COMMUNITIES

WHAT IS A COMMUNITY?

The Community Concept

Defining the term *community* is at least as difficult as defining the term *reef* (see Chap. 1). Many ecologists and paleoecologists strongly doubt the validity of the community as an ecological unit and no longer use the term (e.g., Hoffman, 1979, 1982); others, including the present author, regard the community as the basic descriptive unit in synecology. To the "believers" in the reality of communities (sometimes called organismic communities), they are like a superorganism consisting of numerous interacting species, having a broadly predictable composition, and occupying a broadly predictable habitat. The interspecific interactions provide a general cohesion to the community. The *ecosystem* is the companion basic functional unit, but in practice, the terms community and ecosystem are often used almost interchangeably. For example, in any shallow neritic shelf area, the species found in the benthic and pelagic realms are almost wholly different and are therefore commonly regarded as different communities. However, from the functional viewpoint, the benthic animals are dependent on the pelagic (planktonic) plants and so both the animals and plants are parts of the same ecosystem. Therefore, no attempt is made here to produce a concise and inevitably controversial definition of community; some important aspects of the general community concept are discussed (see Kauffman and Scott, 1976, for an excellent review), with an attempt to apply them in particular to reef communities.

Because communities are fundamentally descriptive, having attributes that are influenced by many complex variables, their recognition may be

154

quite subjective. Modern statistical methods and data handling techniques are exceedingly valuable in characterizing certain aspects of communities such as composition and distribution; these methods are of more limited value for other essential attributes (Table 5.1).

The distribution of organisms in nature is not only influenced by measurable and predictable chemical, physical, and biological factors, but also by numerous stochastic processes that produce nonpredictable results. In reef communities, such processes include planktonic larval recruitment, infant mortality, and various catastrophic events. Thus, one of the most difficult aspects in both theoretical and field community ecology is the almost universal "patchy" distribution of communities and the clumped–dispersed distributions of the organisms of which they are composed. Patchiness and clumping lie at the heart of most sampling problems, and sample quality determines the validity of such essential attributes of communities as their composition, structure, and distribution. (For an example of sampling problems in patchy reef-associated level-bottom habitats and their interpretation, see Jones, 1984.) Finally, there are the human factors of sample bias, collecting intensity (influenced by numerous factors, e.g., attitude, time, and finances), and in many geological situations the physical impossibility of collecting "proper and adequate" sam-

TABLE 5.1. Important Characteristics for the Recognition and Description of Holocene Marine Benthic Communities

I. Dominantly biological (discussed in Chap. 5)
  A. Compositional/taxonomic
    1. Similarity among samples[a]
    2. Diversity; species richness[a]
    3. Biomass[a]
    4. Interspecific interactions (competition, symbioses, commensalism, etc.)
  B. Distributional (habitat; range)
    1. Recurrent in space and time
    2. Mappable (objectivity of boundaries)
  C. Structural
    1. Equitability/dominance[a]
    2. Trophic structure; energy flow and biomass dominance by trophic level[a]
    3. Guild structure
    4. Niche structure
II. Dominantly non-biological (discussed in Chap. 3)
  A. Chemical factors[a]
  B. Physical factors[a]
  C. Geological factors[a]

[a]Amenable to quantitative/statistical description and analysis in reef communities.

ples. (For recent discussions of ecological field sampling methods in general and reefs in particular, see Stoddart and Johannes, 1978, Weinberg, 1978, and Done, 1983, pp. 122–129, and references therein; for examples of Holocene reef sampling, see also Rützler and Macintyre, 1982, pp. 14, 40–43 and Marsh et al., 1984, pp. 175–178; for problems in sampling ancient reefs, see Scoffin, 1971, pp. 176–177.)

Sampling methods and the data thereby obtained are strongly influenced by field conditions. The biological data from shallow-water reefs are not gathered in the same way as those for deep-water reefs and are therefore not easily amenable to sophisticated statistical comparison. Furthermore, the data from the reef surface are not comparable for statistical purposes to the paleobiological data from a quarry face or core; nor are data from a quarry comparable to those from a core. Ecological interpretations must be based on comparable samples obtained by comparable methods (otherwise it may be "apples versus oranges").

Important Community Characteristics; Criteria for Recognition

Regardless of their location, communities can be recognized on the basis of a relatively few fundamental characteristics (Table 5.1). Data gathering for determination of some characteristics is relatively simple and thus much more emphasis has been placed on these, whereas for others, data gathering may be laborious, tedious, and/or expensive. Only rarely are all of the data listed in Table 5.1 available for any one community.

Compositional/Taxonomic. The quickest way to recognize particular communities and distinguish them from other communities is to determine and compare their species compositions (this implies that the ranges of the component species are not random) and the non-biological habitat factors. Experienced field ecologists commonly do not need to proceed any further to recognize major communities; in some cases, the objectivity of communities is so great that on the basis of a description of the chemical, physical, and geological factors (including latitude and longitude), a specialist can successfully predict the biological characteristics of the community without going to the field. In the sea, this method is often all that is necessary to recognize reef communities (*sensu lato*) and to distinguish them from non-reef communities.

However, virtually all modern studies of the composition and distribution of Holocene communities involve much more than these simple observations, especially if the conclusions are to have more than just local significance. For example, Done (1982) analyzed the occurrences of 94 scleractinian species and varieties, 3 species of *Millepora,* and 1 alcyonarian at 175 collecting sites on 10 different reefs spread over an area of nearly 10,000 km^2 of the Great Barrier Reef and Coral Sea platform. On the basis of the similarity of taxonomic association ("togetherness"), he recognized and described the composition of 17 different coral communities; nearly all the species occurred in more than 1 community and most species were represented in more than 5 communities. At each of the 10 reefs, he recognized several communities, each of which had a characteristic depth and geomorphic location. Done (1982) also increased the level of synthesis by grouping the 17 communities into 3 "classes" of communities (or supercommunities). Each community was present in more than 1 class, the same class is present on more than 1 reef and also in more than 1 of Done's major divisions of the study area (i.e., his Class III consists of 5 communities; 1 or more of these 5 are present at reefs distributed from near the mainland coast, across the Great Barrier mid- and outer shelf reefs to the Coral Sea, a distance of about 200 km).

The composition of communities can also be expressed in terms of tax-onomic diversity (at any level, but most frequently species–genus and commonly excluding microorganisms), total community biomass, or bi-omass at any trophic level. In the organismic view of communities, they are more than just a random association of individuals and species; these species interact in various ways (some are highly interdependent; others are quite passive) that provide an internally controlled cohesion to the overall composition of the community. Although the species composition of simple, low diversity communities is relatively easy to determine, the higher degree of cohesion among species in complex communities such as reefs gives them greater long-term stability and hence greater objectivity in recognition.

Distributional/Boundaries.

> Recognition of contiguous ecological field units within a given environment amounts to designating segments of a continuously variable sequence. Such units in large part express real central tendencies, but boundaries are most indefinite and to draw boundaries at all may be misleading.
>
> (Cloud, 1952, p. 2135)

Perhaps the most controversial aspect of the community concept is its objectivity, which in turn leads to controversy over the nature of the boundaries between adjacent communities. In areas where there are strong gradients in the non-biological factors or in the biological interactions and where cohesion is strong, community recognition and boundary mappability are quite objective (as is the case of boundaries between reefs and adjacent level-bottom communities; see also Turmel and Swanson, 1976). Where these environmental gradients are weak and biological cohesion is also weak, the degree of objectivity is low (in a transect, species seem to come and go in an almost random sequence). Despite these prob-lems of objectivity, communities are recurrent in space and through lim-ited intervals of time. Recovery from catastrophic destruction eventually reproduces essentially the same original community and happens in a predictable succession of stages.

Structural. There are also fundamental structural aspects of communities used for their recognition. Equitability is related to diversity (but not sample size) and expresses the relative proportion of the individual organisms in the community belonging to each species. In highly equitable communities, the individuals are evenly distributed among the species present and in communities of at least moderate complexity, each trophic level has one dominant and one or more subdominant species. Loss of any of the dominant species results in major reorganization of the community structure.

Trophic structure expresses the functional attributes of the individuals and species in terms of their production and/or consumption of energy and their chief source of energy (Scott, 1976, pp. 29–46) and therefore involves the ecosystem aspect of ecology. In complex communities such as reefs, assignment of individuals, species, and higher taxa to particular trophic levels or categories may be difficult, but their assignment to a particular guild is usually much easier. Trophic structure emphasizes community organization with respect to the feeding/energy characteristics of individuals and species, whereas guild structure in reef communities refers to broad spatial aspects of ecological groupings composed of several species. Because of their high diversity and structural complexity, the guild structure of reef communities is usually more easily determined than the trophic structure.

Guild structure in reef communities expresses their organization with regard to differences in the utilization of substrate space. Trophic structure and guild structure are comparable levels of synthesis; the former is based on utilization of energy and the latter on utilization of space. In each trophic level and in each guild there are several species. In complex ancient communities such as reefs, trophic structures are especially tenuous if important higher taxa are "soft-bodied" and therefore not preserved, or are extinct or phylogenetically controversial (e.g. stromatoporoids). In most cases, however, such taxa can be readily assigned to a particular guild.

Community Comparisons

Despite the lack of consensus on the existence of numerous types of communities, their boundaries, and the particular criteria by which they may be recognized, it is inescapable that reefs, at least, are outstanding examples of the reality of the community concept. When the characteristics listed in Table 5.1 are measured and described for reef communities and then compared with non-reef communities, the differences are enormous; also, the boundaries between reefs and adjacent level-bottom communities are frequently so objective that even a non-specialist can easily recognize and map them on an aerial photograph or base map.

The degree of endemism between reef communities and adjacent level-bottoms (a *between* habitat comparison) is generally so high that there are very few species or even genera in common. Reef communities are dominated by sessile, epifaunal, suspension feeding, skeletonized macroinvertebrates; level-bottoms are dominated by vagile, infaunal, deposit feeding, skeletal, and soft-bodied, micro and macroinvertebrates.

In a study of the molluscan fauna (282 gastropod species, 99 bivalves, 2 Polyplacophora, and 1 cephalopod) from the lagoon at Peros Banhos Atoll, Indian Ocean, across the flat and island and down the seaward slope to a depth of 40 m, Sheppard (1984) found that the species were distributed into 3 intertidal to shallow subtidal hard substrate (reef surface) assemblages (or subcommunities), 1 intertidal island beach, and 1 lagoonal level-bottom assemblage. Among the hard substrate assemblages, water depth appears to be the main influence on species distribution. The level of *within* habitat endemism is very high; of the 384 molluscan species, only 25 (6%) are present in more than 1 of the 5 assemblages and none are present in more than 2. Between-habitat level-bottom endemism is also very high; of the 76 lagoonal species, only 2 (2.6%) are also present in any hard substrate assemblage.

In a comparable study of the epifaunal and shallow infaunal level-bottom crustaceans in the vicinity of Lizard Island, Great Barrier Reef, Jones (1984) found that their distribution was surprisingly heterogeneous in terms of location and substrate parameters (i.e., high within-habitat endemism). Of the 91 species identified (mostly microscopic), 51 were present at only 1 of 11 closely spaced sampling locations; 35 species were represented by a single specimen and the same species pairs rarely occurred at more than 1 location. The crustacean component of the level-bottom community appears to vary continuously along a sediment grain size gradient, which in turn may account for the heterogeneity of the species distribution and high dissimilarity of faunas among the collecting locations (i.e., an example of a non-objective ecological boundary). These results are quite different from those of Thomassin (1974); he found that in the level-bottom between the reefs at Tulear, Indian Ocean, the distribution of the numerically dominant species was strongly affected by substrate grain size.

The marked taxonomic differences between parts of reef systems also extends to the foraminifera. At Bikini Atoll, Marshall Islands, nearly all of the 256 lagoonal species are benthic and most species are also present on the upper part of the seaward slope. Assemblages from the reef flat are strikingly different from the lagoon and deep water, being composed almost entirely of planktonics, are almost wholly different from all of the other environments (Cushman et al., 1954).

Among ancient reef and level-bottom communities, between-habitat endemism also appears to be very high. Although Wolfenden (1958) doesn't discuss the probability of postmortem transport of skeletons from reef to the adjacent reef flat and seaward slope ("shelf" and "fore-reef" of Wol-

TABLE 5.2. Simpson's and Jaccard's Similarity Coefficients from Comparison of Species/Genus Composition of Reef and Associated Fossil Assemblages, Early Carboniferous, Derbyshire, UK[a]

	Reef	Reef flat	Seaward slope
Reef		0.45 (32)	0.78 (78)
Reef flat	0.11 (113)		
Seaward slope	0.31 (199)		

Source: Data from Wolfenden, 1958, Table 3.

[a]Simpson, above diagonal line; Jaccard, below diagonal line. Simpson's $= C/N_1$ and Jaccard's $= C/N_1 + N_2 - C$ where $C =$ number of taxa common to both fossil assemblages and N_1 and $N_2 =$ number of taxa in assemblage of lower and higher diversity, respectively. Numbers in parentheses are values of N_1 and $N_1 + N_2 - C$.

fenden), taxonomic similarity among samples from these three environments is very low and suggests considerable original between-habitat endemism (Table 5.2). Furthermore, the degree of endemism among these assemblages is quite similar to that for reef and level-bottom Devonian communities in eastern North America (Fagerstrom, 1983).

In comparing the abundance and diversity of deep-water reef and level-bottom communities from the Jurassic of southwestern Germany, Gwinner (1976, Table 1) reported that: (1) in the level-bottom, 50% of the specimens consisted of ammonite cephalopods, while 40% were bivalves, belemnites, and brachiopods; (2) in the reef, nearly 40% of the specimens were serpulids, 20% brachiopods, 12% ammonites, 12% bryozoans, 7% siliceous sponges, and 2% calcareous sponges; (3) brachiopods are twice as diverse (genera) and four times as abundant in the reefs as in the level-bottom; and (4) about 90% of the specimens of the 5 level-bottom bivalve genera were partially sessile as juveniles or lived on drifting materials, whereas only 5% of the reef bivalves fit this mode of life.

ABUNDANCE, COMPOSITION, AND DIVERSITY

Compared with other Holocene benthic communities, reef communities are dominated by taxa of relatively simple biological complexity, such as algae (*sensu lato*), foraminifera, sponges, coelenterates, and bryozoans. Most of these taxa are colonial and/or encrusting. Furthermore, the species diversity (richness) of Holocene photic zone reef communities is incredibly large; in fact, diversity is so large that the biologic literature does not contain a single "complete" species list of even the skeletonized taxa of any reef system! Perhaps the closest approach to such a list could be compiled from the various taxonomic reports in *U.S. Geological Survey Professional Paper 260* on Bikini Atoll, but even these listings would be vastly incomplete. Although the diversity of most ancient reef communities is remarkably high, it pales when compared with similar Holocene reefs. High reef diversity (Holocene and ancient) is not confined to species; it is characteristic of reef taxa at all levels. In fact, virtually every higher marine taxon has representatives in reef communities, and in nearly every higher taxon, species diversity is higher in reef communities than in the adjacent level-bottom (Great Barrier Reef algae are a notable exception; Cribb, 1973, p. 73).

Selected Holocene Examples

Great Barrier Reef

At Batt Reef, in a 2-m^2 area between a lagoonal sand flat and sparce coral growth, Stephenson et al. (1931, p. 90) reported 70 coral colonies (9 genera), 42 stems of the brown alga *Turbinaria,* 69 tufts of *Amphiroa* (Rhodophyta), abundant other rhodophytes, 85 colonies of *Xenia* (Alcyonacea), abundant *Diplosoma* (Ascidiacea), and *Marginopora* (Foraminiferida), plus 1–2 species each of sponges, nudibranchs, bivalves, echinoids, and 1 polychaete.

At Heron Island (36 km^2) reef, Endean (1982, p. 223) reported 32 species of asteroids, 32 ophiuroids, 25 echinoids, 36 holothuroids, 27 crinoids, 107 corals, 31 conid gastropods, and *931* fish species. In a 90-m^2 quadrat at the reef crest, Grassle (1973, p. 259) identified 17 gastropod species, 1 of which included 53 individuals; 8 species were represented by only 1 individual.

Algae

In reef communities, algae are exceedingly diverse and the calcareous forms contribute much more to the diversity than the non-skeletal ones. Examples of total algal species diversity include (Cribb, 1973, p. 72): (1) Bunker and Capricorn Groups, Great Barrier Reef: 230; (2) total Great Barrier Reef: about 330 (for comparison, there are about 340 species of corals in the entire Great Barrier Reef province); (3) southern Marshall Islands: 146; northern Marshalls: 145 (excluding Cyanophyta) and Enewetak Atoll: 219; and (4) Maldive Islands: 320. In nearly all organic reef frameworks, regardless of their location, algae are somewhat less diverse than corals.

Hillis-Colinvaux (1980) reported that the highest diversity of *Halimeda* (Cordiacea) in the world was 14 species at Enewetak; at Flinders Reef, Great Barrier Reef, which is comparable in size to Enewetak, Drew (1983) found 11 *Halimeda* species.

Corals

The abundance and diversity of corals vary considerably among samples from different parts of the Heron Island Reef as well as among samples from the same part; in 1 m^2 at the crest, Grassle (1973) identified 13 species and 66 colonies, and in a 90-m^2 area of the reef flat, he found 24 species and 913 colonies.

Annelids
Hartman (1954) noted the presence of more than 100 species of annelids (based on "casual" collecting) in the northern Marshall Islands. Grassle (1973, p. 263) reported that a single branching coral colony at 5-m depth at Heron Island contained 1441 individual annelids belonging to 103 species! Other inhabitants of the same corallum included tanaids (Malacostraca), amphipods, isopods, sipunculids, oligochaetes, decapods, and ophiuroids.

Fish
Among the atolls in the Tuamotu Archipelago, French Polynesia, fish diversity varies from 33 to about 400 species (Raroia); diversity is even higher at Kapingamarangi in the Carolines (Wiens, 1962, p. 231), and as high as 650 species at St. Croix, U.S. Virgin Islands. Schooling is a common behavioral characteristic of numerous species of small fish (safety in numbers, perhaps) and produces incredibly high local and shifting (moving target for predators) herbivore biomass.

Why So Many Species?

In addition to the enormously important interspecies relations involving symbiosis (Chap. 2) and competition (Chap. 3), the organization of Holocene reef communities is also characterized by various "special or cooperative" species associations (e.g., endoecism, inquilinism, epizoism, mutualism, and commensalism) that appear to enhace the overall diversity of reefs. Many of these or similar associations are also present in nonreef communities (e.g., Cloud et al, 1962, p. 32) but the level of incidence and degree of interspecies intimacy are generally higher in reef communities. Some of the associations involve sharing of shelter, living space, or other protection; others involve sharing food and still others elaborate behavioral responses (e.g., cleaning of external and internal parasites). Some associations are beneficial to both species, whereas in others, the benefit seems one-sided.

These associations are generally believed to begin as neutral or mutually beneficial relationships, perhaps to reduce the intensity of competition for space on the substrate. The species then co-evolve toward increasing intimacy, one-sided benefit, and end in parasitism. In reef communities, the number of parasitic individuals and species exceeds the number of free-living or host individuals and species.

Selected Holocene Examples
Reef corals are involved in a great many different associations with a large number of individuals (up to 25 damselfish in 1 branching corallum)

and species (Patton, 1976). (Dead coralla are even more attractive to other animals than living corals, but the associations considered here involve only living partners.) In most of these associations, the coral is clearly the host and may provide the "guests" with either food, shelter, or a firm substrate; some of the "guests" may help the coral by repelling polyp predators, whereas for others, the coral branches represent excellent refuge from predators.

At Heron Island, Great Barrier Reef, Patton (in Levinton, 1982, p. 420) recognized 16 guest species, including crabs, shrimp, and fish, among the branches of the common coral *Pocillopora damicornis*. Other common coral guests include barnacles, annelids, and molluscs. In some cases, these external guest species (epibionts) are good examples of exceedingly fine niche and habitat partitioning (e.g., they may include suspension and deposit feeders, herbivores, and carnivores located at particular sites along the branches from the basal colony attachment to the crotches between the branches to the branch tips). Endobionts include both borers and species that attach as larvae to the corallum surface and are later overgrown by the coral.

Other similar associations revolve around the abundant and diverse crinoids in reef communities. The dense network of crinoid arms harbors a greater abundance and diversity of associated epibionts (i.e., small fish, shrimp, crabs, copepods, isopods, annelids, and ophiuoids) than any of the other echinoderm classes (Macurda and Meyer, 1983). Most of the guests are communsals that remove food passing down the arms toward the crinoid's mouth.

Reef sponges contain abundant epibionts and endobionts in the canals and spongocoel; Hartman (1984) has reviewed the associates (including borers) of the reef-dwelling species of the Class Sclerospongiae.

Selected Ancient Examples

The most difficult aspect of determining and interpreting the significance of potential animal associations in ancient communities commonly involves proving that both of the species were alive at the same time. Thus, borings into dead coralla or the occupation of empty tubes, shells, or burrows are not considered here. Evidence for living associations of ancient corals and tube-dwelling metazoans includes walled tubes (borers do not produce walls); if the tube-dweller died before the coral, the tube should be spar-filled rather than sediment-filled because adjacent polyps would presumably grow over the tube opening and prevent sediments from entering the tube. If the coral died first, the empty tube should be filled by bedded sediment (concave upward if compaction preceded cementation).

Oliver (1983) has reviewed the nature and incidence of coral (both reef and non-reef) associations with other invertebrates (chiefly Devonian); he concluded that intracorallum tubes are much more common in tabulate than in rugose corals and that in most cases, the tube walls are formed by the coral polyp to protect itself from the borer. In some Devonian rugosans, the walled tubes located near the corallite axis almost surely penetrated the basal disk of the polyp and the "tube-dweller" ("worm"?) may have fed commensally on the contents of the enteron or competed with the tentacles for planktonic food.

Long, straight, subcylindrical, open or internally tabulate, walled tubes 0.5–2 mm in diameter and oriented perpendicular to the laminae are present in many species of Silurian and Devonian stromatoporoids (called *Caunopora, Diapora,* or caunopores by numerous previous authors; Mistiaen, 1984a). These tubes have been interpreted as an example of some type of "special" interspecies association. In the vast majority of the tubes, the filling is sparry calcite, essentially the same as the gallery filling of the stromatoporoid coenosteum, which strongly suggests that the organisms lived simultaneously. Only rarely does the stromatoporoid seal off the upper end of the tube so that growth rates of the organisms were approximately the same. Stromatoporoid coenostea generally surround the tubes, suggesting that their occupants received some protection from predators by the association. Nicholson (1886–1892) regarded the tubes as either another species of stromatoporoid or as specialized (reproductive?) structures of the so-called host species, in which case there is no interspecific association involved. Nearly all subsequent authors have rejected this interpretation. The open tubes are suggestive of small gregarious polychaetes or other "worms" and are similar to the tubes in tabulate and rugose corals noted above.

However, evidence for special associations in ancient reef communities, even in the Cenozoic, is surprisingly meager in comparison to their tremendous importance in Holocene reefs. Part of the reason for this difference, especially when comparing Holocene and Pleistocene reefs, lies in the selective preservation of organisms involved in the associations (see Chap. 6). However, the discrepancy is almost surely real. Taxonomic diversity, and hence interspecific competition for space in reefs, has increased during the Phanerozoic; it surely was accompanied by increasingly diverse types of cooperative associations to alleviate such competition. The fossil record simply does not show this relationship. However, there is good evidence of the progressive importance of borers (Kobluk et al., 1978) and other bioeroders through geologic history (Steneck, 1983).

Ancient Cenozoic Photic Zone Reefs

Paleogene

Corals. Of the 14 living families of reef-inhabiting (and therefore presumably containing primarily zooxanthellate species) scleractinians, 10 were also present in the Mesozoic (Wells, 1956, pp. F363–F368; Newell, 1971, Fig. 2; the Caryophyllidae are here regarded as primarily non-zooxanthellate; the Merculinidae have no fossil representatives). Of the 16 families that survived the end of the Cretaceous extinction event, only 6 became extinct prior to the Pliocene. At the generic level not a single new hermatypic coral appeared during the Paleocene. There are, however, representatives of many important Holocene reef-constructors (e.g., *Porites, Goniopora, Acropora, Astrocoenia, Siderastrea, Montastraea*) in reefs as old as Middle–Late Eocene. Thus, at the family and genus levels, the Eocene was a time of major diversification (Newell, 1971, pp. 14–15). Oligocene and younger reef corals have a distinctly modern familial–generic composition. Paleocene and Early Eocene photic zone reefs are exceedingly rare; in fact, there are very few coralla of reef-constructing sizes present in rocks of this age. The Middle–Late Eocene was an interval of rapid coral diversification and increasing abundance, geographic distribution, and size of reefs that reached its Paleogene climax during the Oligocene.

The families and genera of Paleogene reef corals are also almost worldwide in their distribution, but the data of Frost (1977a, Table 1) indicate considerable species-level endemism (cf. Frost, 1977b, p. 103). Middle Eocene Caribbean reefs are composed of about 10 genera and 15 species of frame-building corals (chiefly *Goniopora, Astrocoenia, Astreopora, Haimeastraea, Siderastrea,* and *Montastraea;* of these, only *Haimeastraea* is not still present in Caribbean reefs). By the Late Eocene, virtually all of the large, frame-constructing genera of Neogene Caribbean reefs had evolved. At the end of the Eocene, four families of archaic reef-constructing corals (some of the Calamophylliidae may have been non-zooxanthellate) became extinct; each of these families had its greatest generic diversity during the Mesozoic (Newell, 1971, Fig. 2).

The Oligocene was marked by a global decrease in familial and generic coral diversity (Newell, 1971, Figs. 2, 5), but in the Caribbean, this period was the acme of Paleogene fringing and patch reef growth. The corals included about 40 cosmopolitan genera and 65–70 species, 25 of which were massive frame-constructors. About half of these genera became extinct in the Caribbean during the Miocene and Pliocene, although they still survive in Indo-Pacific reefs.

Other Higher Taxa. There is also a distinctly modern aspect to nearly all the families and genera of the calcareous algae, smaller foraminifera, and molluscs in Paleogene reef communities. Kazmer (1982) listed the major taxa in Late Eocene reefs near Budapest dominated by encrusting red algae (10 genera including *Lithophyllum, Lithoporella,* and *Ethelia*). These communities also include foraminifera (15 genera, including encrusters), corals (mostly fragmented branching coralla), bivalves, gastropods, "worms," bryozoans, echinoderms, and calcispheres.

The greatest taxonomic difference between Paleogene–Miocene and Holocene reef communities is the great abundance and considerable diversity of the orbitoid, nummulitic, and other "larger" foraminifera in the former. They were not attached to the substrate and occur in both the reef and adjacent reef flat communities, commonly as different species or even genera. Several larger foram species and genera seem to have been quite restricted in their ecological tolerances and so have been used to delineate various laterally adjacent geomorphic zones and subcommunities across Eocene–Miocene reef systems. The level of Paleogene cosmopolitanism of the larger foraminifera is not as high as for the corals; there are distinct differences between the larger foraminifera of the Caribbean and the Mediterranean. The orbitoids are especially important in Eocene and Oligocene reefs; *Lepidocyclina (Eulepidina)* reaches diameters up to 5 cm and locally occurs in rock-forming abundance in Oligocene seaward slope deposits.

Neogene

Corals. The Miocene marked the beginning of the development of the Atlantic Province. As noted above, the chief differences between the Atlantic and Indo-Pacific Provinces are the much lower coral diversity (both genera and species) and species-level endemism of the Atlantic Province from the Middle Miocene to the present (Newell, 1971, pp. 18–21). At the family level, there is almost no difference between Oligocene and Miocene corals. Along with increasing Neogene provincialism, there has also been a progressive decrease in the width of the tropical reef belt due to the onset of declining world temperature. During the Pliocene, the width of the photic zone reef belt reached the latitudinal limits it has today (cf. Newell, 1971, Fig. 8, and Fig. 2.2 herein).

There are no large Early Miocene reefs in the Caribbean, and coral generic diversity dropped from about 40 in the Oligocene to about 25 in the small Early Miocene reefs that are present (Frost, 1977b). Of these 25 genera, all are still present in the Indo-Pacific, but about half subsequently became extinct in the Caribbean. From drill cores at Bikini Atoll, Marshall Islands, Wells (1954b) described a poorly preserved Middle Miocene reef coral assemblage consisting of about 13 genera and 22 species. By the Late Miocene, Caribbean reefs were again well-developed and the corals are very modern; about 20–25 of the common Holocene *species* have fossil records dating to the Late Miocene. Conversely, in the Mediterranean, the Neogene coral diversity maximum came in the Early Miocene (Burdigalian) with progressive reduction during the Middle Miocene and virtual extinction by the end of the Miocene (Messinian) due to hypersalinity (Esteban, 1979, p. 183).

Other Higher Taxa. The Miocene and Pliocene mark the gradual decline in importance of the larger foraminifera. The genera *Lepidocyclina* and *Miogypsina* extend through the Middle Miocene and *Operculinoides* occurs in the Pliocene in the Caribbean. Nearly all forams are less abundant and diverse than in the Paleogene, but a few relatively large forms persist in Holocene reef communities (e.g., the abundant encrusting *Homotrema rubrum* in the western Atlantic and *Marginopora vertebralis* in the Great Barrier Reef). The smaller foraminifera from the Neogene of the Bikini Atoll cores consist predominantly of extant genera; the benthics indicate rather uniform and continuous shallow, tropical environments and the planktonic forms indicate access to open ocean (Todd and Post, 1954).

Pleistocene. The overall composition of the preserved fauna of Pleistocene reef and level-bottom communities is strikingly similar, even to the species level, with their Holocene counterparts. The most important differences between Quaternary and pre-Quaternary reefs involve light-weight, rapidly growing dendroid coralla (e.g., *Acropora, Porites, Pocillopora, Seriatopora,* etc.) that dominate the crests of most Quaternary reefs. During the Pleistocene, these forms rapidly increased in relative importance and also underwent rapid diversification in the Indo-Pacific; in the Atlantic, however, this increased significance involved only a few species. In Caribbean reefs, extinction of *Stylophora* and *Goniopora* occurred at or about the beginning of the Pleistocene and that of *Pocillopora* only about 60,000 years ago (Frost, 1977b, p. 95; Geister, 1984a, p. 3.20).

Except for these corals, Quaternary evolution and extinction rates were generally slow in reef communities; dating is done by radiometric methods or by positions of reefs relative to present sea level rather than by faunal composition. Pleistocene glaciation had only limited effect on the evolution of reef organisms (Wise and Schopf, 1981) because tropical surface water temperatures were relatively uniform (Newell, 1971, p. 21; CLIMAP, 1976).

Aphotic Zone Reefs

Holocene

Compared with photic zone reefs, the diversity of Holocene aphotic zone reefs is *much* lower; in some aphotic zone reefs, the framework constructors consist of just 1–3 genera (Squires, 1964), most of which are monospecific. The lower diversity of aphotic zone reefs is also partly due to different (dredging, trawling, photographing, etc.) and far less complete collecting techniques. But like the photic zone, diversity of aphotic zone reefs is much higher than in the adjacent level-bottom communities (Stetson et al., 1962, p. 3). Unfortunately, none of the discussions of faunas of aphotic zone reefs includes any direct comparative data on faunas of the adjacent level-bottoms (e.g., Teichert, 1958, pp. 1066–1067; Neumann et al., 1977; Reed, 1980; Mullins et al., 1981; Cairns and Stanley, 1981).

Squires (1964, Table 1) summarized the distribution of species in eastern Atlantic aphotic zone reefs among the various higher taxa. In one of the Norwegian fiord reefs, there are 300 species of which only 18 are confined to the reef. In another near-by reef containing 198 species, 50 are confined to the reef.

In aphotic zone reefs of the Blake Plateau, western Atlantic, Stetson et al. (1962) reported 5 species of corals (only 2 are frame constructors), 3 of which are also present in greater abundance in the adjacent level-bottom. Other elements of the reef fauna include abundant Hydrozoa and Alcyonaria, echinoids, Actiniaria, ophiuroids, and some rare molluscs.

The fauna from reefs north of Little Bahama Bank seems considerably more diverse (better sampling?) than from the Blake Plateau. Mullins et al. (1981, p. 1004) identified a rich coelenterate assemblage, including gorgonians, alcyonarians, antipatharians, hydroids, and scleractinians. The latter consist of 16 species in 11 genera, but only 2 of the species (one branched, the other solitary) are abundant. Elsewhere in the north Atlantic, the dominant coral genera are *Lophelia, Dendrophyllia,* and *Enallopsammia,* but in the Little Bahama Bank reefs, only the latter is present. Furthermore, small, solitary coralla are more common than large, frame-constructing colonial coralla. Sessile invertebrates attached to dead gorgonians and scleractinians include calcareous and siliceous sponges, bryozoans, serpulids, and perhaps also barnacles. Other elements of the fauna consist of crinoids, gastropods, a bivalve, ophiuroids, and crabs.

Miocene–Pliocene

Squires (1964) has described the fauna of a large (40-m long; 3–4-m thick) Late Miocene reef and a small (9 × 0.5 m) Pliocene reef in New Zealand. In both faunas, the most important constructing coral is a dendroid, non-zooxanthellate species of *Lophelia* (also the most common constructor of Holocene aphotic zone reefs). Squires estimated the depth for the Miocene reef at 1500–2000 m based on the foraminiferal component of the fauna and 400–600 m based on the molluscs; depth estimates for the Pliocene reef are much shallower (150–300 m).

In both reefs and their enclosing mudstones, the most abundant and diverse non-coral macrofossils are molluscs; they are *much* more abundant in the reef than in the mudstones (Vella, 1964, p. 925). In the more diverse Pliocene reef, there are 9 bivalve species, of which 4 are confined to the reef and 3 to the adjacent level-bottom. Of the total of 16 gastropods, only 1 is confined to the reef; 12 are confined to the level-bottom. There is also 1 ubiquitous scaphopod and 1 brachiopod found only in the reef.

Foraminifera are much more diverse in the Miocene reef and adjacent mudstones (94 spp.) than in the Pliocene (44 spp.). In the Miocene case, pelagic species comprise about 90% of tests in both reef and level-bottom. Of the benthics (72 spp.), 47% occur in both the reef and level-bottom, 42% are confined to the reef, and only 11% are absent from the reef.

Frost (1977b, p. 96) noted that there were approximately 12 species of non-zooxanthellate corals during the Miocene–Pliocene in the Caribbean, in contrast to only 2 species living there now.

Paleocene

In the Lower Paleocene (Danian) rocks of Denmark and southern Sweden, there are two very different types of reeflike structures. Teichert (1958, p. 1078) briefly described the fauna from one type, which he estimated to have lived in at least 100 m of water. The constructors consisted of two scleractinian species, *Dendrophyllia candelabrum,* a non-zooxanthellate, and *Calamophyllium faxense,* an extinct genus, which therefore is questionably non-zooxanthellate (Wells, 1967, Table 1). The accompanying fauna includes hydrozoans, gorgonians, brachiopods, bivalves, gastropods, cephalopods, crustaceans, echinoids, fish, and planktonic foraminifera and coccoliths.

Thomson (1983) has carefully described numerous bryozoan-dominated mound-shaped structures of probable reef origin. They are larger and biologically *much* more diverse than the Holocene bryozoan-dominated reefs described in Chapter 1; although most of the delicate zoaria are fragmented, their non-random distribution and excellent preservation clearly show that preburial transportation was negligible (i.e., the structures are not "shell heaps"). The absence of calcareous algae suggests that the structures lived below the photic zone; Thomsen estimated depth at 80–150 m.

The skeletal debris from *91* bryozoan species comprises about 90% of the benthic fauna and about 30% of the volume of the reef rocks. All other benthic macrofossils comprise only about 5–10% of the volume and include echinoderms, brachiopods, molluscs, and alcyonarians. The microfossils are chiefly planktonic foraminifera, coccoliths, and a few siliceous sponge spicules.

DOMINANCE: SUBCOMMUNITIES

Zonation is the most visible of all manifestations of pattern in the distribution and abundance of organisms . . . it results from a grand natural experiment in which the dose rate of virtually all ecological factors . . . are varied in space and time.

(Done, 1983, pp. 139–140)

Even casual investigation of nearly all photic zone reef systems quickly establishes that the species are not randomly or uniformly distributed. In other words, the system is ecologicaly and taxonomically zoned; these biological zonations commonly bear close correspondence to the geomorphic zonation (seaward slope, reef crest, reef flat, lagoon) described in Chapter 3. In some reef systems, the biological zonations represent distinctly different responses to what may appear to be subtle variations in the physical or geomorphic factors. Thus, reef flats commonly contain several well-defined lateral biological zones (see Tracey et al., 1948, Pls. 6, 7, and Wells, 1957a, Pls. 1–4, for excellent photographs of examples of geomorphic/biologic zonations of Pacific reefs). The reef crest and seaward slope are bathymetrically zoned.

Wells (1954a, p. 396) described a reef ecological zone as "an area where local ecological differences are reflected in the species association and signalized by *one or more dominant species*" (italics added for emphasis); in Wells' case, the dominant species were corals, but other authors have recognized zonal distributions of other taxa. Some geological studies that recognize this same type of lateral or vertical variation in fossil assemblages (associations) refer to the zones as *biofacies* (or facies). However, in this book, the term *zone* is reserved for the geomorphic subdivisions of reef systems, and the areally segregated biological subdivisions are called *subcommunities*.

Some communities (including a few reefs) have equitable distributions of individuals and species and so are unzoned and lack subcommunities. But in typical reef systems, distributions of individuals and species are not equitable and various subcommunities are recognized by a few dominant species. Subcommunity boundaries on reef crests and flats are generally well-defined and easily mapped. In windward reefs exposed to high turbulence, subcommunities are arranged in belts roughly parallel to the reef margin; in protected locations, subcommunities on smaller, subcircular reefs may be arranged in concentric belts (Pichon, 1981, p. 587). Because of lower diversity, Atlantic Province reefs generally have fewer subcommunity dominants than exist in Indo-Pacific reefs.

Lateral (horizontal) subcommunities across lagoons, reef flats and crests, and bathymetric subcommunities down seaward slopes have been described in varying detail for particular reefs, reef systems or parts of reef systems (e.g., windward vs. leeward sides), and biogeographic provinces (Tables 5.3 and 5.4). These descriptions have been based on a single higher taxon or on several. The degrees of fidelity of particular taxa to particular geomorphic zones or particular subcommunities are highly variable (e.g., Done, 1983, Table 1) and reflect their differing degrees of eurytopism.

Is There a "Universal" Pattern?

Several previous authors attempted syntheses of subcommunity compositions and distributions at scales from a single reef system or province to global (a few are listed in Tables 5.3 and 5.4; see also Pichon, 1981, and Stearn, 1982a, for summaries). However, comparison of several of these schemes quickly indicates that almost none of them agree. For example, despite the fact that all genera in Rosen's (1975) scheme of lateral subcommunities are present in the Great Barrier Reef, Done (1982) found that they do not occupy exactly analogous locations (cf. Geister, 1977, p. 29). It appears as if almost each reef system, regardless of size, has its own subcommunity distribution pattern and its own succession of dom-

TABLE 5.3. Locations and Taxonomic Basis for Selected Subcommunity Descriptions Emphasizing Lateral Distribution in Holocene Reef Systems

Atlantic Province		Indo-Pacific Province	
Location; General/Taxon	Ref.	Location; General/Taxon	Ref.
1. Abaco Island, Bahamas		1. Great Barrier Reef	
General	Storr, 1964[a]	General	Maxwell, 1968
2. Jamaica		Corals	Done, 1983
General	Goreau and Goreau, 1973[a]	2. Marshall Islands	
	Pang, 1973		
Sponges		Corals	Wells, 1954
Corals	Goreau, 1959	Bryozoans	Cuffey, 1973
Gorgonians	Kinzie, 1973[a]	3. Syntheses	
3. Anegada, British Virgin Islands		Corals	Ladd et al., 1950; Wells, 1957; Rosen, 1975
Corals	Brown and Dunne, 1980	General	Wiens, 1962
4. Carrie Bow, Belize			
Corals	Rützler and Macintyre, 1982[a]		
5. Caribbean			
Corals	Geister, 1977		

[a]See Table 5.4.

TABLE 5.4. Locations and Taxonomic Basis for Selected Subcommunity Descriptions Emphasizing Bathymetric Distribution in Holocene Reef Systems

Atlantic Province		Indo-Pacific Province	
Location; General/Taxon	Ref.	Location; General/Taxon	Ref.
1. Abaco Island, Bahamas		1. Great Barrier Reef	
General	Storr, 1964	Corals	Done, 1983
2. Yucatan		2. Bikini Atoll	
General	Logan et al., 1969	Corals	Wells, 1954[a]
		Fish	Wiens, 1962
3. Florida		3. Synthesis	
"Corals"	Jaap, 1983	Corals	Wells, 1957
4. St. Croix, U.S. Virgin Is.			
Algae	Adey and Vassar, 1975; Steneck and Adey, 1976		
5. Jamaica			
General	Goreau and Goreau, 1973; Lang, 1974[a]		
Sponges	Hartman, 1977; Lang et al., 1975; Pang, 1973		
Gorgonians	Kinzie, 1973[a]		

[a]See Table 5.3.

inant taxa (Tables 5.5 and 5.6). Furthermore, distributions based on different higher taxa are wholly different and serve to illustrate that communities and subcommunities are synthetic ecological units and so require a synthetic, multitaxa approach to their characterization.

Why Not?

There are many reasons for the absence of "universality," even within the same province, mostly stemming from the fact that reefs and reef systems represent the epitome of lateral and vertical variation in numerous controlling factors (Chap. 3). These factors in turn influence the simultaneous operation of numerous processes (Chap. 4). The complex interactions of factors and processes are biologically expressed as communities and subcommunities. Because these interactions vary from place

TABLE 5.5. Lateral Geomorphic Zonation of Selected Western Atlantic Reefs and Accompanying Ecologic Subcommunities

Geomorphic Zones	Jamaica (After Goreau and Goreau, 1973)	Carrie Bow Cay (After Rützler and Macintyre, 1982)	Abaco Island (After Store, 1964)
Lagoon	*Thalassia*	*Thalassia;* algal felts	echinoid; *Porites astreoides*
Reef flat	*Zooanthus*	*Montastraea–Diploria Siderastrea–Porites*	*Acropora palmata*
Reef crest	*Acropora palmata*	*Acropora–Agaricia; Acropora–Millepora; Corallines–Millepora*	Sea fan *(Gorgonia flabellum)*
Seaward slope (0–20 m)	*A. palmata; A. cervicornis; Montastraea annularis*	*Millepora; Acropora; Agaricia; Montastrea; Gorgonacea; Diploria*	*Montastraea annularis; A. palmata*

to place and reef to reef, no two reefs should be expected to have precisely the same subcommunities arranged in precisely the same pattern. A few selected examples may help to understand the complexity of these interrelations.

Depth/Turbulence Controls. Several authors (e.g., Rosen, 1975; Geister, 1977; Pichon, 1981; Done, 1983) have stressed the considerable influence that various levels of turbulence exert on the lateral distribution of reef subcommunities; they have suggested subcommunity distribution models based primarily on the interrelations between depth and turbulence, especially by waves. These models reflect different sets of biological/taxonomic responses to a gradient of decreasing turbulence from reef crest across the flat and lagoon; they seem to explain the beltlike arrangement of subcommunities parallel to the crest. However, this decreasing turbulence is not uniform across these subcommunities and varies with differences in depth and geomorphic configuration of the reef system. On the more protected leeward sides of reef systems where there is less wave turbulence, the succession of subcommunities is typically less well-developed than on the windward sides of the same reef system (Wells, 1957a).

The geomorphic zonation and distribution of subcommunities at West Reef, Discovery Bay, Jamaica (summarized by Graus et al., 1984, pp. 61–63) appear quite stable and are believed to reflect the primary control exerted by depth and bottom current velocity (Graus et al., 1984, Fig. 4). The West Reef subcommunities are also distributed in very close agreement with the depth/turbulence control model of Geister (1977; Fig. 5.1 herein, i.e., from the reef crest algal ridge down the seaward slope, the

TABLE 5.6. Bathymetric Zonation of Seaward Slope of Selected Reefs and Accompanying Ecologic Subcommunities

| Depth (m) | Bikini Atoll (After Wells, 1954) | Jamaica | |
		After Lang, 1974	After Kinzie, 1973
20			*Acropora cervicornis*

40			*Montastraea annularis, Pseudopterogorgia* spp., *Eunicea clavigera, Muricea laxa, Ellisella*[a]
60	*Echinophyllia*		----------------------------
80		Sclerospongiae[a]: *Ceratoporella, Stromatospongia*	*Agarica* spp., *Nicella*[a], *Lingella*[a], *Hypnogorgia*[a], *Iciligorgia*[a], *Thesia*[a]
100	----------------------------		
120	*Leptoseris* spp.	Scleractinia[a], Sclerospongiae[a], Demospongia[a]	
140			
160		Porifera[a] Scleractinia[a]	
180	*Sclerhelia*[a]– *Dendrophyllia*[a]		

[a]Denotes non-zooxanthellate taxa.

Figure 5.1. Idealized distribution of six basic geomorphic zones of Caribbean reefs and their accompanying subcommunities. The composition and distribution of each subcommunity is controlled primarily by the interrelations between water depth and turbulence (degree of wave turbulence indicated by thickness of arrows). In the terminology of this book, "rear wave zones" are equivalent to the reef flat and lagoon, the "breaker zone" is the reef crest, and the "front wave zones" are equivalent to the upper seaward slope. See text for discussion of the significance of the vertical and lateral arrangements of the subcommunities. Melobesieae = heavy encrustations by coralline algae (algal ridge); *strigosa–palmata* = *Diploria strigosa–Acropora palmata; cervicornis* = *Acropora cervicornis; porites* = *Porites porites; annularis* = *Montastraea annularis;* see Geister, 1977, p. 25, for general characterization of each zone and subcommunity. (After Geister, 1977.).

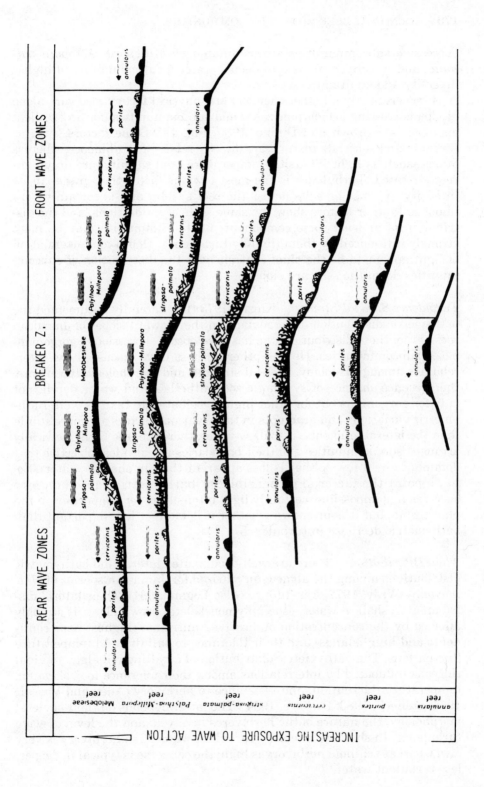

successive subcommunities are dominated by *Millepora, Acropora palmata,* and *A. cervicornis* and in deeper water a subcommunity of higher diversity and equitability).

However, nearly all other chemical and physical factors also vary along gradients crossing geomorphic zones and subcommunities (for an excellent example, see Brown and Dunne, 1980, Fig. 14). Some factors, such as turbidity and substrate texture, are directly related to turbulence, whereas others, such as light intensity, temperature, and salinity, are only indirectly related. Turbulence is the most obvious factor that grades in its intensity in zones or belts across the reef system and is certainly very important; other factors show the same sorts of gradiations, and the distribution of at least some components of the community may be more strongly influenced by them than by turbulence. Depth and attenuation of light appear to be the chief controls over the distribution of subcommunities down the seaward slope.

Turbulence/Skeletal Strength. Kinzie (1973) has carefully documented the bathymetric distribution of gorgonians on the seaward slopes of Jamaican reefs. From these distributions, he has developed a succession of gorgonian-based subcommunities. He and other authors have discussed the interrelations among taxonomy, skeletal strength and morphology, turbulence, the presence/absence of symbiotic zooxanthellae, and water depth, not only for gorgonians but for other higher coelenterate taxa as well. Bathymetric variations and gradients in these various factors are more subtle than the lateral gradients in shallow water; therefore, the bathymetrically arranged subcommunities and their boundaries are also less objective (i.e., dominance by a few species is less apparent than in shallow water). So, to pinpoint the factor(s) responsible for bathymetric subcommunity succession is impossible; certainly light intensity is *very* important in the photic zone, but it is unknown whether it is more or less important than bathymetric decrease in turbulence.

Algal Distributions. There are well-documented lateral and bathymetric distributions among the algae (summarized for Jamaican species of *Halimeda* by Wray, 1977, Fig. 146; see also Logan, 1981). Their lateral distribution in shallow water, especially nonskeletal brown algae, is strongly affected by the concentration of dissolved nutrients (highest near continents and high islands) and their tolerance to salinity and temperature fluctuations. The bathymetric distribution of coralline red algae in algal ridges is influenced by interrelations among their tolerance to desiccation, temperature fluctuation, and resistance to herbivory (Adey and Vassar, 1975; Steneck, 1983; Bosence, 1984). The latter depends on their skeletal morphology, the nature of the herbivores involved, and the level of wave turbulence. In shallow, intensely turbulent water, fish herbivory is very low, whereas echinoid herbivory is high; the converse is typical in deeper, less turbulent water.

Well-developed lateral zonations of stromatolitic algal reefs have been described from Precambrian and Paleozoic rocks (Hoffman, 1974; Goldring, 1938; Fagerstrom and Burchett, 1972).

Coral Distributions. Rogers et al. (1984) have reviewed the importance of such purely biological factors as larval recruitment, polyp mortality/survivorship, growth, reproduction, and aggressive behavior on the abundance and distribution of reef corals. They suggested that at St. Croix, U.S. Virgin Islands, recruitment success and survival depend primarily on the interaction between space competition and disturbance by grazers; grazers play a major role in determining the structure of both algal- and coral-dominated communities.

Sheppard (1982) has reviewed the factors influencing the bathymetric distribution of corals on seaward slopes, and Wellington (1982) and Hixon (1983) have described their zonation in Panamanian reefs. Here, there is excellent evidence that the interrelations among coral morphology and intensity of grazing by damselfish and pufferfish are responsible for the bathymetric distributions of dominant taxa in the upper 10 m. In 0–6 m, the damselfish intensely graze the surficial polyps of the less abundant massive corals (e.g., *Pavona*) but are excluded from grazing among the tightly spaced branches of the dominant *Pocillopora*. At 6–10 m, coral density is lower, so damselfish have less cover and are replaced in dominance by pufferfish. The puffers selectively graze and break the branched corals, leaving the massive forms to dominate.

Reefs Lacking Subcommunities. Not all photic zone reefs appear to be divided into subcommunities; in most such cases, the reefs are small and located in areas of weak lateral environmental gradients (especially turbulence) such as lagoons, wide shelves, (i.e., mid-shelf reefs of the Great Barrier Reef), and open ocean platforms (Braithwaite, 1973, p. 1103; James, 1983, p. 352). At Lord Howe Island, Great Barrier Reef, Veron and Done (1979; also reported in Done, 1983, p. 124, Fig. 13) found that coral distribution among 66 collecting sites was homogeneous within each major geomorphic zone (reef flat, lagoon, etc.) but that the sites within each such zone were widely dispersed around the island rather than geographically clustered into subcommunities. They reasoned that because of the complex morphology of the reef system, it was impossible to relate taxonomically similar sites to a generalized reef profile. Furthermore, coral species showed no predictable distribution pattern among the sites which could then be arranged in a succession of subcommunities across the reef system.

As reefs increase in size and topographic relief, they also begin to modify the formerly more uniform environment and create their own local environment in a feedback relationship that leads to development of progressively strengthening environmental gradients. This feedback relationship also leads to development of geomorphic zonations which are accompanied and accentuated by their associated subcommunities. Thus, it might be argued that unzoned or poorly zoned reefs (in both geomorphic and ecological senses) have not grown large enough to be "true" reefs. This lack of zonation could then be the basis for establishing a threshold of minimum size. Such a criterion would exclude a very large number of varied structures that have long been regarded as reefs. These structures include:

a.   Holocene atoll lagoon, mid-shelf, and open ocean platform photic zone reefs.

b.   Most aphotic zone reefs. Evidence of subcommunities on Holocene aphotic zone reefs is generally poor (Neumann et al., 1977; Lang and Neumann, 1980; Wilson, 1979) or they have simply not been recognized in the samples (an artifact of incomplete sampling?). Furthermore, several aphotic zone reefs are as large or larger than photic zone reefs that do contain well-developed subcommunities. The apparent lack of subcommunities on large aphotic zone reefs may be real, rather than the result of sampling bias, and simply reflect a lack of strong environmental gradients across these reefs. However, in Paleocene deep-water reefs in Denmark, Thomsen (1983) recognized both lateral and vertical subcommunities.

c.   Ancient small reefs located in the interior regions of continents, especially the margins of cratonic basins. For many such reefs, mid-shelf locations on very wide continental shelves would be the closest Holocene analogue. In terms of absolute numbers of structures, there are probably more small unzoned or poorly zoned reefs in the ancient rock record than there are large, well-zoned reefs. For example, within the extensive Devonian reef system marginal to the Canning Basin in Western Australia, there are three small, stromatolitic reefs near Elimberrie Spring that have neither lateral nor vertical subcommunities (Playford et al., 1976; also see discussion in Chap. 12). Similarly small, poorly zoned rudist reefs in the Cretaceous of Texas were described by Roberson (1972). Each of these reefs is composed of a massive core constructed by caprinids and monopleurids surrounded by a succession of uniform concentric rings (up to 15) containing abundant radiolitids in approximate growth positions. There are no subcommunities of radiolitids either across the reef or from ring to ring on any one side indicative of environmental gradients as the reefs grew. This succession of concentric "rings" seems quite similar to the growth pattern of some aphotic zone reefs that also lack subcommunities (Wilson, 1979).

Stochastic Events. The objectivity by which reef subcommunities are determined and then mapped may be diminished by two important stochastic events: major storms and larval recruitment/infant survivorship.

The importance of destruction of colonial reef organisms (including corals and sponges) and transport of living fragments (propagules) to other locations is a matter of dispute. In their study of composition and distribution of subcommunities at a Jamaican reef system, Graus et al. (1984) concluded that despite the destructive impact of some hurricanes, the relatively long interval between them allowed reef subcommunities to recover and return to the "normal," stable, trade-wind-controlled distributions in existence prior to the hurricane. In other cases, the short-term effects of more closely spaced intense storms and the differential survival of propagules of the more hardy and eurytopic species tend to break down the level of dominance in reef subcommunities and thus increase equitability (e.g., survival rates of sponges are relatively higher than for other reef organisms, and they are higher for branching corals than for other coral growth forms).

Settlement of planktonic larvae is not random because numerous mechanisms (e.g., toxins to repel larvae; larval substrate selection, etc.) operate to enhance clumping of conspecific individuals (Yonge, 1973, p. 10). Larval dispersal by currents is locally important in establishing individuals in newly occupied habitats (cf. Rogers et al., 1984, and Done, 1982, p. 105). Random environmental fluctuations and unpredictable predation then determine their postsettlement survival. The net result of differential dispersal and survival is to produce more random and equitable species distributions.

Subcommunities in Ancient Cenozoic Reefs

Death of a reef intensifies the effects of destructive processes already operating when the reef was alive and growing; important new processes are initiated, especially if the cause of death is subaerial exposure. The alteration of former photic zone reefs by erosion following subaerial exposure has been particularly significant in the history of Pleistocene reefs.

Subaerial erosion has commonly altered or destroyed the original geomorphic zonation of these reefs. But because of the close correlation of geomorphic zones and subcommunities, the distribution of the *in situ* fossils can often be used with confidence to determine location of the original reef crest as well as the source of transported skeletal fragments in the rocks of original reef flat and seaward slope environments. Erosion and transportation alter the composition and lateral distribution of shallow-water subcommunities to a greater degree than those of the deeper-water seaward slope, and because of successional changes in sea level, older Pleistocene reefs are more altered than young ones.

Subfossil and Pleistocene

Geister (1977; 1980) presented a generalized model for Caribbean Holocene reef subcommunities and in 1984 he applied this model to the analysis of similar Pleistocene reefs exposed in near-shore terraces. The model

(Fig. 5.1) is based on Geister's belief that composition and distribution of subcommunities are primarily controlled by the interrelations between depth and turbulence (i.e., the shallower the water, the higher the turbulence or "wave action" of Geister). Other factors (chemical, physical, etc.) and processes were regarded by Geister as much less important. Depth/turbulence controlled the lateral and bathymetric occurrence of subcommunities and also the history of ecological succession of the six subcommunities recognized by Geister and shown in Fig. 5.1. Thus, the establishment of the reef in deeper, less turbulent water was by a pioneer community dominated by *Montastraea annularis;* as the structure grew into progressively shallower water, the reef crest ("breaker zone" of Geister) was occupied by a succession of subcommunities adapted to progressively higher levels of turbulence. As the succession proceeded, each subcommunity that had formerly occupied the crest was ecologically displaced to shallow seaward slope ("front wave zones") and reef flat ("rear wave zones") locations where it could maintain its proper or optimal depth/turbulence regime.

Geister noted that the model is idealized and that in any particular Holocene reef, one or more of the subcommunities (his zones) is commonly missing due to differences in substrate topography, composition or grain size, or selective destruction of coralla by storm waves.

In many Caribbean Pleistocene reefs, the original geomorphic zonation, including the reef crest, is preserved and there is evidence of *in situ* coralla in the adjacent reef flat and upper seaward slope. Transported fragments of broken coralla are present in deeper-water areas. Geister (1980; 1984a) used his Holocene Caribbean model to recognize the same general spectrum of depth/turbulence-controlled subcommunities in several Caribbean Pleistocene reefs (Fig. 5.2) and interpret their relative levels of turbulence and the direction of Pleistocene winds. The chief difference is that coenostea of the abundant and widely distributed Holocene *Millepora* appear to be absent from all of his Pleistocene examples. Otherwise, the analogues are very direct, even to the species level. Cores from the coralline algal ridge near St. Croix, U.S. Virgin Islands (Bosence, 1984, p. 564), indicate that with rising Holocene sea level the algae overgrew *in situ* coralla of *Acropora palmata* and *Millepora,* as would be predicted by the Geister model. Similarly, two of the Geister model subcommunities in "proper" lateral and bathymetric arrangement are present in sub-Holocene reefs in the Dominican Republic (Mann et al., 1984, Fig. 6).

Klovan (1974, pp. 795–797) used a bathymetric succession of Holocene coral-dominated subcommunities to estimate water depths for a vertical succession of coral- and stromatoporoid-dominated subcommunities in Devonian reefs in western Canada (Fig. 5.3). Although the applicability of the Holocene–Devonian analogy is debatable, Klovan's method of interpretation is essentially the same as in Geister's model (Fig. 5.1).

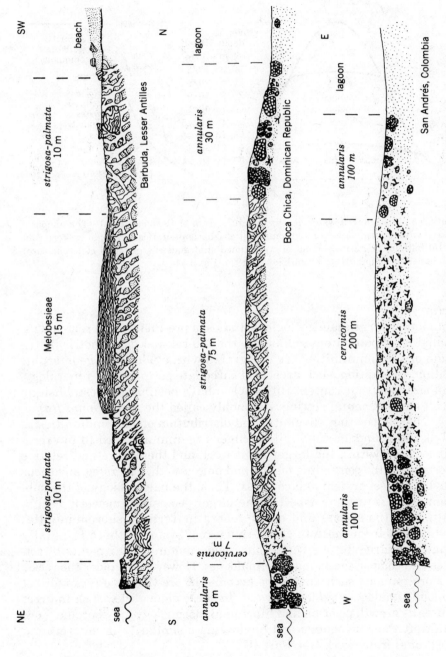

Figure 5.2. Lateral distribution of Caribbean shallow-water Pleistocene reef subcommunities arranged as predicted by the model shown in Figure 5.1. (Modified from Geister, 1980, 1984a.)

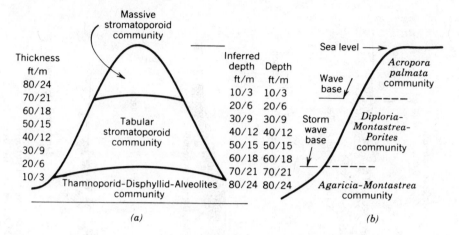

Figure 5.3. (a) Inferred water depths of a succession of Devonian coral- (Thamnoporid, etc.) and stromatoporoid-dominated communities (subcommunities herein) in western Canada. (b) Bathymetric arrangement of a presumed analogous succession of Holocene coral-dominated subcommunities. (From Klovan, 1974, Fig. 14.)

Tertiary

In numerous large-scale geological studies of pre-Pleistocene reef and associated level-bottom environments, the lateral and bathymetric distribution of subcommunities are integrated with evidence of geomorphic zonation. In addition, such aspects of carbonate petrology as mineralogy, grain size, and spar content (lithofacies) have been used to establish an overall environmental setting, commonly called the *depositional framework*. The composition, diversity, and distribution of subcommunities as well as the abundance of fossil specimens therein are used to interpret their location within the larger framework and the nature and relative importance of the controlling factors and processes that operated in various parts of the reef system and complex. Thus, the paleoecology of the subcommunities is just one aspect of the larger geologic framework.

Although the species and many genera in Tertiary subcommunities are different from those in Quaternary reef systems, there is usually enough similarity to use Quaternary subcommunities as points of reference and comparison in making analogues. However, the older the rocks, the more tenuous such analogues become; in pre-Cenozoic rocks, direct taxonomic analogues no longer exist. In these older rocks, such indirect features as growth position and functional morphology may become more significant than taxonomic and phylogenetic similarity in determining depositional framework (see Part III).

Selected Example. In the Oligocene rocks of the Caribbean, Frost (1977a) made a distinction between "coral banks" and "climax reefs." The former are smaller structures, lack subcommunities, and have a less diverse fauna dominated by scleractinians (*Porites, Goniopora, Acropora, Alveopora*, Actinacis**, and *Astrocoenia**; extinct genera indicated by asterisk). The "climax reefs" include both barrier and fringing types with geomorphic zonations and laterally arranged subcommunities (Table 5.7). The "lagoonal patch reefs" are 1–2 m thick and, in addition to corals, also contain abundant algae, foraminifera, and molluscs. The "leeward coral thickets" are only 10–20 cm thick. The diverse coral fauna of the "crest and upper buttress zones" consist of 10–15 coral species (massive and encrusting coralla) and large masses of coralline algae. The "lower buttress and upper fore-reef slope" assemblage is similar to the seaward slope of Holocene Indo-Pacific reefs according to Frost.

TABLE 5.7. Geomorphic Zones and Dominant Coral Genera in Caribbean Oligocene "Climax" Barrier and Fringing Reef Subcommunities

Genus	Lagoon Patch Reefs	Leeward Coral Thickets	Reef Crest and Upper Buttress	Lower Buttress; Upper Fore-reef Slope	Lower Fore-reef Slope
Goniastrea	x		x		
Goniopora	x		x		
Siderastrea	x				
Agathiphyllia[a]	x		x		
Antiguastrea[a]	x		x		
Porites	x	x (Branching)	x		
Diploastrea	x		x		
Diploria			x		
Colpophyllia			x		
Stephenocoen-ia			x		
Favites			x		
Pavona (P.)				x (Foliaceous)	
Fungophyllia[a]				x	
Leptoseris				x	
Trachyphyllia					x
Indophyllia[a](?)					x
Placocyathus					?
Stylophora					?
Actinacis[a]				?	
Parasmilia[b]					x
Balanophyllia[b]					x
Archohelia[b]					x
Flabellum[b]					x

Source: After Frost, 1977.
[a]Extinct.
[b]Non-zooxanthellate.

Problems of Transgression and Regression

Sea-level changes caused by waxing and waning glaciers, isostatic subsidence, or tectonism, theoretically should produce marked changes in lateral and bathymetric arrangements of reef and level-bottom sub-communities. However, few authors have recognized these shifting arrangements and specifically attributed them to sea-level, isostatic, or tectonic changes (exceptions include Hopley, 1982, and Davies, 1983, pp. 82–95).

If the Geister (1977; 1980; 1984a) and Rosen (1975) models, based primarily on water depth/turbulence interrelations, are correct, lateral shifts in the locations of shallow-water reef subcommunities should have been considerable, especially on gently sloping continental shelves.

The vertical succession of the six depth/turbulence-controlled "breaker zone" reef subcommunities shown in Figure 5.1 could be caused by either upward growth of the reef crest into progressively shallower water or by a drop in sea level (regression) accompanied by lateral shift of the "rear wave" or "front wave zones" and their subcommunities to the shallowing water of the reef crest. In this manner, the vertical succession of *annularis* to Melobesieae could represent successive shifts of depth/turbulence-controlled subcommunities that live together in laterally adjacent positions to a vertically stacked arrangement during the time of falling sea levels (i.e., the deep-water/low turbulence *annularis* subcommunity is successively overlaid by the *porites, cervicornis*, etc., subcommunities).

Furthermore, these lateral and vertical arrangements can occur throughout the reef system, on the reef crest, flat (or "rear wave zones"), and upper seaward slope (or "front wave zones"). The vertical succession of subcommunities in Figure 5.1 would be reversed in case of rising sea level (trangression; Melobesieae successively overlaid by *Polythoa–Millepora, strigosa–palmata;* etc.) if the rate of sea-level rise were to exceed the rate of upward accretion of the reef. Both regression and transgression are excellent examples of Walther's Law of Succession of Facies and Faunas (Middleton, 1973).

If rates of transgression and regression are rapid and the processes repetitive, as was true during the Pleistocene, the resulting patterns of vertical and horizontal shift in the distribution of both reef and level-bottom communities and subcommunities lose the symmetry shown in Figures 5.1 and 5.2.

Conversely, lateral shifts of bathymetric subcommunities on steep seaward slopes of volcanic island reefs should be relatively minor; instead, the vertical stacking of successive deep-water subcommunities marking their upslope or downslope migration should be simple. However, the subtle distinctions between adjacent bathymetric subcommunities make them more difficult to recognize and interpret as indicators of absolute depth.

Cryptic Subcommunities

Below the exposed upper surface of Holocene photic zone reefs, there is a wholly different environment consisting of pores or voids that contain assemblages of organisms quite different in composition and abundance from those described thus far. These are cryptic subcommunities and, despite the relatively small *in situ* skeletal volume of individual members, they are remarkably diverse. In addition to being called cryptic, these organisms have been named "coelobites" (Ginsburg and Schroeder, 1973), "sciaphiles" (Laborel, 1960), "secondary" frame-builders (Bosence, 1984), or "cryptofauna" (Jackson, 1977).

Cryptic habitats within the organic framework of Holocene reefs that contain macroorganisms consist of (for a more detailed classification, see Ginsburg, 1983, p. 148):

a. Small spaces below overhanging individual *in situ* foliaceous, sheetlike (Pl. 21a) or arching coral or crustose calcareous algal skeletons.

b. Larger caves, tunnels, and crevices formed by erosion or by "roofing-over" growth by numerous *in situ* corals and crustose algae.

c. Spaces within piles of transported skeletal rubble.

Volumetrically, the caves, tunnels, and crevices are the most important; estimates of the volume of cryptic habitats range from 30 to 70% of the framework, depending upon location and the amount of internal sediment they contain (Garrett et al., 1971; Froelich, 1983; Bosence, 1984). Total surface area of cryptic habitats commonly exceeds the exposed upper surface area of the reef by 2–3 times (Buss and Jackson, 1979, p. 224; Ginsburg and Schroeder, 1973, p. 611; Logan et al., 1984).

Although cryptic faunas are known from rocks as old as Lower Cambrian (Kobluk and James, 1979), ecologists have just begun to appreciate their importance in Holocene reef communities. However, the relatively poor preservation potential of cryptic organisms may seriously hamper progress in their recognition and interpretation in ancient reef communities (cf. Kobluk, 1980; Kobluk and James, 1979; Rasmussen and Brett, 1985). In both Holocene and ancient reefs, internal cavities have considerable geological significance as sediment traps, and skeletons of cryptic fauna may comprise a good proportion of the internal sediment. Furthermore, the internal voids act as preferred sites of early cementation in the inorganic framework of the reef (Macintrye, 1984; Mazullo and Cys, 1978).

Abundance, Composition, and Diversity

Holocene cryptic subcommunities are dominated by colonial, encrusting invertebrates, especially cheilostome bryozoans (Cuffey, 1972; Cuffey and

Fonda, 1979; Logan et al., 1984), sponges (Hartman, 1977), and both zooxanthellate and non-zooxanthellate corals. Locally, such other higher taxa as coralline algae (St. Croix; Bosence, 1984) and encrusting foraminifera (Bermuda; Ginsburg and Schroeder, 1973) are of major importance. Accessory species include brachiopods (Jackson et al., 1971), bivalves, vermetids, serpulids, barnacles, crinoids, and colonial ascidians (Ginsburg, 1983, p. 150).

Buss and Jackson (1979, p. 224) estimated the total species diversity of Caribbean seaward slope cryptic subcommunities at about 300; at Bermuda, Logan et al. (1984) identified 93 species, 35 of which are bryozoans. In the area of the Florida Keys, Choi and Ginsburg (1983) identified 80 cryptic species, of which bryozoans (at least 29 species) are by far the most abundant and diverse; 20% of the remaining fauna are *boring* sponges, molluscs, sipunculids, and polychaetes, and 80% are *encrusting* foraminifera, sponges, serpulids, molluscs, etc. The highest diversity is at 20–30 m deep.

Comparison With Exposed Surface Communities

Environmental Factors. Cryptic habitats differ from surface environments in providing greater stability and less stress to organisms from fluctuations in chemical and physical factors. They are characterized by lower light intensities, the near-absence of ultra-violet radiation (Jokiel, 1980), and total darkness in large or deep cavities. This allows the shade-loving surface epifauna in deep water to live in shallower-water cryptic habitats. In addition, there is less turbulence, higher turbidity, and more rapid sediment deposition in reef cavities than at the surface, enabling taxa with fragile skeletons such as bryozoans and sponges to dominate cryptic subcommunities. Hutchings (1983, p. 204) cited evidence that deposit feeding is more important in cryptic subcommunities than on the exposed reef surface; this may be due to higher turbidity and depositional rates in the cavities.

Because of lower light intensity, algae and zooxanthellate corals are restricted to entrances of cryptic habitats; here, their growth rates and skeletal volumes are less than for conspecific individuals at the exposed reef surface. In cryptic habitats, the energy sources available to organisms are less abundant and varied, but the competition for space is as intense as at the surface. The result is that cryptic organisms are generally small and competitive networks are more common than competitive hierarchies (Buss and Jackson, 1979); space acquisition and dominance proceed much more slowly than at the exposed surface.

For many epifaunal invertebrates, cryptic habitats offer refuge from predation, although numerous fish live within cavities and others regularly visit them. Levinton (1982, pp. 423–424) has argued that because slow-growing bryozoans, sponges, and ascidians are so important in cryptic subcommunities, escape from predation is not an adequate explanation for their high species diversity. The small sizes of individuals and of their habitats and the protection afforded by low light intensity may reduce predation so that its influence over diversity is minimal. In contrast, predation by an enormous number of vagrant nektic and benthic forms is so intense at the exposed reef surface that the prey have adapted various means of escape and survival (boring, chemical repellents, rapid regeneration/recolonization, etc.). High cryptic diversity may instead be the result of the well-devloped competitive networks rather than hierarchies.

Zonations. Distributions of cryptic organisms are as distinctly zoned as distributions of exposed reef organisms, but the degree of dominance by a few large species is less clear. Cryptic zonations have been described on scales from a large reef system to individual large cavities to the undersurface of a single corallum or rubble boulder.

In coral rubble toward the north end of the Florida Keys reef complex, Choi and Ginsburg (1983) recognized both lateral (in shallow water from the reef crest, across the reef flat to the shore) and bathymetric (down the seaward slope to 40 m) zonations. Cryptic species are most abundant and diverse near the reef crest (1–3 m deep); they are least important in the near-shore lagoon and elsewhere from 3 to 20 m. The authors attributed these large-scale zonations to differences in productivity, depositional rates of internal sediment, and environmental stability.

In seaward slope cryptic subcommunities at Jamaica, Jackson and Winston (1982) found that abundance of sponges increased from 10 to 20 m, but abundance of cheilostomes was inversely related to depth; these same general abundance patterns also exist in Florida. In contrast, Reiswig (1973) found that in Jamaica, the greatest abundance of sponges on *exposed* reef surfaces is at 30–50 m.

Garrett (1969) and Garrett et al. (1971) subdivided large cavities in some Bermudan reefs and their cryptic subcommunities into three intergrading units based on intensity of penetrating light:

a. Open light; intensity 6–50% of surface intensity.
b. Gloomy; very low light intensity.
c. Dark; essentially no light.

Several subsequent authors have used this general scheme to subdivide cryptic subcommunities in other reefs (Table 5.8). The investigations of Logan (1981) and Logan et al. (1984) are the most detailed undertaken so far. These authors agree that light intensity confines algae and zooxanthellate corals to cavity openings but that the other higher taxa (e.g., bryozoans, sponges, foraminifera, brachiopods, and serpulids) are widely distributed. In some cases, cryptic species strongly reflect the composition

TABLE 5.8. Subdivisions of Selected Cryptic Subcommunities in Large Internal Cavities in Holocene Photic Zone Reefs

Location; Depth; Ref.	Subdivisions; Fauna		
	Open	Gloomy	Dark
I. A. Bermuda; <10 m; James, 1983, p. 351; Garrett, 1969	*Spondylus, Spengleria,* coralline algae, bryozoans; serpulids, *Homotrema rubrum*	Algae, sponges, bryozoans	Bryozoans, sponges, *H. rubrum,* serpulids
B. Bermuda; 2–15 m; Logan et al., 1984	Coralline algae, ascidians, demosponges, bryozoans, foraminifera, coelenterates	Encrusting sponges, foraminifera, bryozoans; few ascidians	
II. St., Croix; algal ridges; Adey and Vassar, 1975; Bosence 1984	*Lithothamnion ruptile, Mesophyllum syntropicum, Neogoniolithon, Lithophyllum congestum, Tenarea*		
III. Florida, 0–17 m; Jamaica, < 40 m; Bonem, 1977	Coralline algae, sponges, bryozoans, *Agaricia fragilis,* antipatharians, crinoids	Coralline algae, sponges, bryozoans, *H. rubrum,* serpulids, non-zooxanthellate corals, *A. fragilis,* crinoids, antipatharians, *Spondylus, Chama, Pseudochama*	
IV. Grand Cayman; 2–11 m; Logan, 1981	Coralline algae, especially *Peyssonnelia,* zooxanthellate corals, demosponges, ascidians, bryozoans, bivalves	Demosponges, bryozoans, *H. rubrum,* etc.	Sclerosponges, cemented brachiopods, sponges, bryozoans, bivalves
V. General; Ginsburg, 1983	Chlorophyta, zooxanthellate corals, bivalves, coralline algae	Coralline algae, bivalves	Bryozoans, serpulids, foraminifera, sponges

of the exposed surface biota and in others there is considerable endemism among cryptic species (Adey and Vassar, 1975; Bosence, 1984).

Because most cryptic invertebrates are deposit feeders and depend upon a supply of sediment for their food, biomass and diversity in these cavities progressively decreases from base to ceiling and from entrances to the deep recesses. Non-encrusting, sessile suspension feeders are most abundant on and near cavity ceilings.

Finally, Choi and Ginsburg (1983, pp. 168–169) recognized "microzonations" on undersurfaces of individual rubble clasts of cobble–boulder size collected from near shore to depths up to 40 m in the Florida Keys. The distribution of these cryptic organisms also is light-controlled and generally similar to the large cavity subdivisions of Garrett (1969; i.e., open, gloomy, dark). These organisms are most abundant, diverse, and algal-dominated near the clast periphery, grading toward the clast center to a lower diversity, foraminifera-dominated assemblage; sponges and bryozoans dominate the intermediate areas.

Death comes to cryptic subcommunities by restriction of the entrance. Such restriction results in inadequate flushing of wastes, no renewal of nutrients from the open ocean, and cavity filling with sediment (Kobluk and James, 1979, p. 213).

TROPHIC STRUCTURE

Because of the relatively passive modes of life and means of reproduction of most organisms in benthic marine communities, there are only two important environmental resources for which competition is intense: space and energy/nutrition (Table 5.9). (The latter is the subject of this section; forms of chemical, physical, and biological energy in reef ecosystems were discussed in Chap. 3; the structure of benthic communities with respect to space is considered in the next section.)

Because of the geomorphic and biologic complexity of reef communities, especially high taxonomic diversity, their organization with regard to nutrition of individuals and species populations is also exceedingly complex. The general subject of the nutrition of particular taxa has been discussed in several places in the preceding chapters (e.g., symbiosis, commensalism, competition, herbivory, etc.); therefore, only a summary of basic concepts and community-wide nutrition is presented here.

The Traditional View

In simple, low diversity ecosystems typical of high latitudes, nutritional relationships are commonly described in terms of production and degradation "chains." Most organisms in the production "chain" can be rather definitively assigned to one of three "links": producer, herbivore, or car-

TABLE 5.9. Chief Environmental Resources of Marine Communities and Structures for Their Utilization

	Energy	Space
I. Resources		
II. Structures	A. Trophic structure (nutritional relationships; see Table 5.10)	A. Guild structure (see Table 5.11) and Fig. 5.4)
III. Relative importance	1. Generally the major control in *pelagic* and *level-bottom* communities	1. Generally the major control in *reef* and other hard substrate communities
IV. Colonial/solitary animals	2. Predominantly solitary	2. Predominantly colonial
V. Competitive aspects	a. Competition alleviated by niche partitioning	a. Competition alleviated by habitat partitioning, directional growth, tiering, etc.
VI. Interrelations between niche and guild structures	a. Tiering may subdivide both energy and space resources	
	b. Many nekton (especially fish) live above substrate but get energy on substrate	

nivore. Because of the relatively low efficiency of energy production and transfer (governed by the laws of thermodynamics) from link to link, these three links became quite firmly emplaced in ecologic theory as the basic trophic levels by which all ecosystems operate. In a few cases, a fourth level (top carnivore) was recognized with the understanding that such animals and ecosystems were relatively uncommon and operating near the upper limit of ecologic/thermodynamic efficiency.

In lower latitudes, ecosystems and communities are more complex; nutritional "chains" become "webs," and it becomes much more difficult to assign organisms and species to just one trophic level. The "chain" sequence of energy transfer from primary production to herbivore to carnivore fails for two reasons. First, it does not account for feedback from complex energy shifts among various animal "feeding groups" and "special" trophic relations; second, it does not consider energy input and loss in the ecosystem from sources outside its biotic components (Dawes, 1981, pp. 353–354).

Reef Communities

Photic zone reef communities represent the highest degree of trophic complexity of all marine communities. This complexity is due to high diversity and the great importance of such "special" trophic relationships as symbiosis, commensalism, endoecism, inquilinism, mutualism, and parasitism (discussed in Chap. 3). For instance, in photic zone reefs the varied degrees of symbioses of corals, sponges, foraminifera, and molluscs with bacteria and zooxanthellae make determining their "average" levels of autotrophism and heterotrophism difficult. In a coral colony, some polyps may be more plant than animal; others are herbivores absorbing dissolved metabolites from their symbiotic zooxanthellae or dissolved organic materials in the water column. Still other polyps may be "lucky" captors of pelagic animals and some are even scavengers on organic detritus (Muscatine, 1973). Corals are a thermodynamic nightmare and yet clearly dominate the trophic structure of typical Holocene reefs.

In reef sponges studied by Wilkinson (1983), up to 83% of daily maintenance nutrition requirements could be provided by absorption of dissolved organics in the water column by their symbiotic bacteria. Most reef fish are carnivores, but many are algal grazers; a few are omnivores and several feed on or within the substrate (Endean, 1982, p. 214). Analyses of gut contents of larger reef animals indicate that many are remarkably omnivorous (Polovina, 1984, Table 1). To determine quantitatively the trophic relations of just the highly diverse fish in typical reef communities is incredibly difficult (Hiatt and Strasburg, 1960; Polovina, 1984).

There is considerable disagreement among previous authors regarding the synthesis of trophic relationships in reef communities, the relative significance of various organism components, and how they might be diagrammatically presented (Lewis, 1977, pp. 326–329). A few selected examples, in historical sequence, illustrate these different approaches:

a.   Odum and Odum (1955) presented the traditional 3-trophic level, biomass pyramid approach; they emphasized the algal producer aspect of coral–plant symbiosis in the area of the reef crest. In the reef flat, they subdivided herbivores into as many as 5 informal higher taxa. Of the 4 examples presented here, only this one seriously addresses the quantitative importance of the auto- and heterotrophic roles of corals.

b.   Frost (1977b, pp. 101–102; see also Biomass, Chap. 3) presented irregularly shaped "pyramids" with 7 "trophic categories" or "trophic levels" among which 40 higher taxa were arranged.

c.   Hiatt and Strasburg (1960) emphasized the role of fish and recognized 5 community trophic levels: algal producers, small–large herbivores, algal and detritus feeders, omnivores, and successive levels of carnivores (mostly fish). They constructed a food web consisting of 14 major feeding categories.

d.   In another study emphasizing reef fish, Polovina (1984) determined that within both the "heterotrophic benthos" (all the benthic invertebrates) and the "reef fishes" (primarily coral reef fish, excluding snappers, groupers, and carangids) trophic groups, there was "high internal predation."

He therefore subdivided each group into 2 groups, thus giving 6 trophic levels: producers, herbivores (especially zooplankton), 2 heterotrophic benthos levels, and 2 reef fish levels. The high proportion of "internal predation" within the same trophic level, together with the accompanying loss of energy, is apparently one reason why fish production in reef communities is low relative to primary production. For example, at French Frigate Shoals, Hawaii, the estimated net annual primary production is $2.73 \times 10^6/kg/km^2$, and for the top predators, only $462 \ kg/km^2$. According to Polovina, another reason for low fish production is that a large amount of the organic carbon produced by plants is lost from reef ecosystems by offshore transport.

There is little agreement among researchers studying photic zone reef community energistics regarding their structure, the number and relative importance of diverse trophic "groups," the taxa present in each, or the overall significance of "special" trophic relations involving symbioses, commensalism, etc. Table 5.10 summarizes some of the major trophic and taxonomic relationships; tables such as this one, as well as the trophic structure diagrams of the authors cited above, fail to show important temporal variations (both cyclic and successional) adequately.

By comparison, the energistics of aphotic zone organisms and reef communities must be simple (data comparable to those cited above for photic zone reefs are not available for deep water). They completely lack producers, and the proportion of planktic and nektic taxa to benthic is much higher. The chief local energy sources are organic detritus, zooplankton, and benthic invertebrates. Carnivores are less important than in photic zone reefs, but degradational energy sources are more significant. Thus, in addition to the important compositional differences noted earlier in this chapter, there are also major differences between trophic structures of photic and aphotic zone reefs. Although biomass and energy pyramids and other trophic diagrams for aphotic zone reefs have not as yet been prepared, they should show shapes that greatly differ from those noted above for photic zone reefs.

Trophic Levels; Extinct Organisms

For some extinct organisms, assignment to even one of the three major trophic levels (producer, herbivore, carnivore) may be uncertain, and if these organisms dominate the community, the construction of trophic pyramids and diagrams becomes speculative. Perhaps the best example of this problem is the Paleozoic Stromatoporoidea.

Kaźmierczak (1976, 1980, 1981; Kaźmierczak and Krumbein, 1983) has argued that the stromatoporoids were coccoid Cyanophyta and would therefore have been autotrophs. Stearn (1972, 1975, 1984) believes that they were sponges and so would have been suspension-feeding herbivores; Mori (1982, 1984) has stressed their coelenterate affinities, perhaps making them partial carnivores. The sponge versus coelenterate affinities are not easily clarified from fossil skeletons alone and so are neither the suspension-versus-polyp-feeding nor the herbivore-versus-carnivore trophic levels. Thus, the trophic structure of numerous mid-Paleozoic reefs dominated by stromatoporoids is uncertain (Kapp, 1975, Fig. 5), but the laws of thermodynamics strongly suggest that such reefs could not have been dominated by carnivorous coelenterates.

GUILD STRUCTURE

A guild is defined as a *group of species* that exploit the same *class of environmental resources* in a similar way . . . without regard to taxonomic position . . . (and) overlap significantly in their niche requirements . . . The limits that circumscribe the membership of any guild must be somewhat arbitrary . . . A species may be a member of more than one guild . . . the guild concept focuses attention on *all sympatric species* involved in a *competitive interaction,* regardless of their taxonomic relationship. (Italics added for emphasis.)

(Root, 1967, p. 335)

The Reef Guild Concept

There are five essential components to Root's definition:

a. Each guild consists of several sympatric species.
b. There is interspecific competition for the same "class of environmental resources."
c. "Class of environmental resources" is undefined.
d. There may be niche overlap among species in the same guild.
e. There may be overlap in the species composition of different guilds (i.e., the same species may belong to more than one guild; guild overlap).

In reef communities where living space is usually the chief limiting environmental resource, and the one for which competition is most intense, the irregular surface of the hard organic (skeletal) substrate provides an ecological opportunity to subdivide this resource in ways to alleviate competition among the highly diverse members of the community. This spatial subdivision (into "classes" of Root) of the community, based on the location and orientation of benthic organisms with respect to the substrate surface (Table 5.11), produces major functional units (guilds; Fig. 5.4) in which intraguild spatial competition is presumably more intense than interguild competition. In addition, there is greater intraguild gross morphological similarity than interguild similarity, so that each guild performs a separate function in the successful operation of the reef community.

TABLE 5.10. Generalized Trophic Structure of Holocene Photic Zone Reef Communities Emphasizing Major Energy Sources and Location of Energy Consumption[a]

Producers	Herbivores	Carnivores
I. Planktic 　A. Dinoflagellates 　B. Diatoms	I. Planktic 　A. Tintinnids 　B. Copepods 　C. "Larvae"[b] 　D. Foraminifera	I. Necktic 　A. Squid[c] 　B. Lobsters/ 　　　crabs 　C. Small fish[b] 　D. Sharks 　E. Large fish[b] 　F. Mammals[c]
II. Benthic 　A. Skeletal Algae[b] 　　1. Chlorophytes 　　2. Rhodophytes 　B. Non-skeletal algae[b] 　　1. Filamentous 　　2. "Fleshy" 　　3. Zooxanthellae 　C. Bacteria[c] 　D. Grasses[c]	II. Benthic 　A. Suspension feeders 　　1. "Pumpers" 　　　a. Sponges[d] 　　　b. Bivalves 　　　c. Annelids 　　　d. Brachiopods 　　　e. Tunicates 　　2. "Strainers"[a] 　　　a. Bryozoans 　　　b. Annelids 　　　c. Crinoids 　　　d. Barnacles[c] 　　3. "Absorbers" 　　　a. Corals[d] 　　　b. Foraminifera[a]	II. Benthic 　A. Corals[d] 　B. Active fish[b] 　C. Morays, 　　　etc.[c]

B. Grazers/predators, etc.
   1. Gastropods
   2. Small crustaceans
   3. Annelids
   4. Echinoids
   5. Starfish[b]
   6. Fish[b]
   7. Turtles[c]

Source: Modified from Odum and Odum (1955), Frost (1977b), and Polovina (1984).

[a]Excluding level-bottom deposit feeders, degraders, birds.
[b]*Sensu lato.*
[c]Of local importance only.
[d]Important omnivores.

TABLE 5.11. Spatial Classes and Guild Structure of Reef Communities

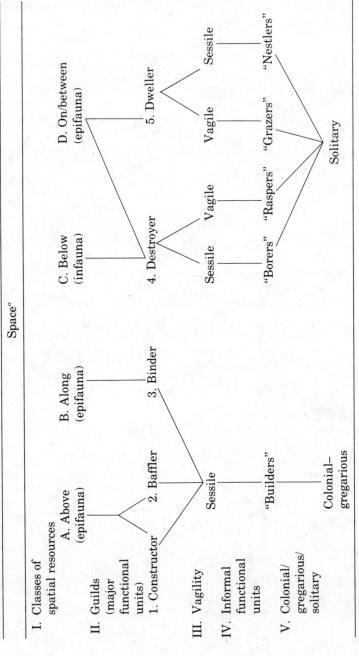

I. Classes of spatial resources
   A. Above (epifauna)   B. Along (epifauna)   C. Below (infauna)   D. On/between (epifauna)

II. Guilds (major functional units)
   1. Constructor   2. Baffler   3. Binder   4. Destroyer   5. Dweller

III. Vagility
   Sessile   Sessile   Vagile   Vagile   Sessile

IV. Informal functional units
   "Builders"   "Borers"   "Raspers"   "Grazers"   "Nestlers"

V. Colonial/gregarious/solitary
   Colonial–gregarious   Solitary

Space[a]

[a]In relation to substrate surface.

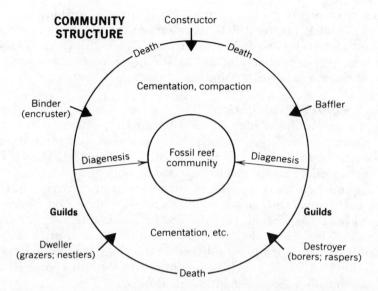

Figure 5.4. The five major functional units (guilds) of typical Holocene reef communities (outer circle). The combined activities of the constructor, baffler, and binder guilds ("reef-builders" of numerous previous authors) produce the organic framework of the reef. The upward growth of the constructors provides most of the skeletal volume, the bafflers slow down the velocities of currents crossing the reef surface, and the lateral growth of the binders unifies and consolidates the framework and the internal sediment. The members of the destroyer guild break down the framework, and the dwellers are passive (neither build nor destroy the framework) members of the reef community; see text for complete discussion. Upon death, the skeletal organisms of the guilds undergo various types of diagenetic alteration (e.g. cementation, compaction) to form a fossil reef community (*sensu* Fagerstrom, 1964).

Spatial Resource Exploitation

The benthic reef and other "hard substrate" organisms may be easily subdivided into the following four spatial classes based on their growth form and growth direction with respect to substrate surface:

A. Growth is primarily upward from the surface so that organisms extend *above* the surface into the water column.

B. Growth is primarily lateral *along* the surface; extension into the water column is minimal.

C. Growth and/or extension of habitat is *below* the surface.

D. Growth is relatively equidimensional (lacks a single pronounced vector with respect to substrate); organisms occupy space between or on members of Classes A–C.

These spatial classes are also present in level-bottom communities; in these, however, the intensity of competition for energy or nutritional sources is commonly greater than for space. Among benthic communities, Classes C and D are relatively more critical to the success of those on level-bottoms; on non-reef hard substrates, Classes B, C, and D are most important; reefs are characterized by the greater importance of Classes A and B than in other communities.

Other Resource Exploitation

The guild concept may also be used to subdivide utilization of energy resources in communities; in fact, this use was the original application of the concept by Root (1967). For instance, in such a subdivision of benthic communities, the "classes" might be based on energy source (e.g., producer and consumer guilds or producer, herbivore, and carnivore guilds) or, among herbivores, the classes might be based on how and where food is gathered (e.g., suspension, deposit, and predator guilds or infaunal and epifaunal guilds). However, these aspects of energy utilization in marine communities are so firmly established in the concept of trophic structure that in this book guild structure is confined to the ways space is utilized and subdivided (cf. Bambach, 1983, p. 728–740).

The guild concept apparently has not yet been applied directly to purely pelagic communities. In the ensuing discussion, attention to the pelagic component of reef communities is quite minimal; however, most of the fish belong to the *destroyer* and *dweller* guilds (Table 5.10).

Reef Guilds and Functional Morphology

Benthic reef organisms are morphologically adapted for living in one, or rarely more than one, of the spatial resource classes (A–D) described above. Because of these adaptations, the assignment of individuals and species to membership in a particular guild is generally not difficult. There are three important advantages for applying the guild concept to reef communities:

a.   Determination of guild membership and overall community guild structure is far more objective than determination of trophic structure or most other community characteristics and attributes listed in Table 5.1. In fact, guild structure of reef communities may be less arbitrary than for most other marine communities.

b.   From the close interrelationships among functional morphological adaptations of species populations and their guild membership, it is possible to determine functional roles of individuals, populations, and guilds in the overall success of the reef community. Furthermore, paradigms or models based on functional morphology are applicable to reef communities regardless of their geologic age; thus, there are particular functional homeomorphs by which phylogenetically unrelated taxa may be assigned to guilds regardless of their geologic age. According to Ginsburg and Schroeder (1973, p. 605), the idea of subdividing reef communities into major functional units (e.g., frame-builders, sediment producers, etc.) can be traced to Walther (1888), if not earlier. Numerous subsequent authors have added to or modified these units in various ways to synthesize and simplify the overwhelming complexity of reef communities (the scheme of Kornicker and Boyd, 1962, also in Orme, 1977b, p. 174, is an excellent example).

    c.   The guild concept and its application to reef communities are as valid and objective for ancient reefs as for the Holocene (discussed below). Part III of this book is largely devoted to tracing the geological history and evolution of the composition and guild structures of pre-Cenozoic reef communities.

Constructor Guild

Comparison With Baffler Guild

In reef communities, there are two guilds that efficiently utilize the water column directly *above* the general reef surface for both living space and for energy requirements (Class A, above). These are the constructor and baffler guilds (Table 5.11); the member taxa of both these guilds have their most rapid growth vector (direction) upward (they generally include, among others, the "mound" and "tree" growth forms of Jackson, 1979). In successful reef communities, such taxa live in densely packed associations and are therefore presumed to compete for space and for energy *in* the water column. In situations where the constructors are particularly large, their skeletal surface may be regarded as the substrate itself so that the living tissues extend only slightly into the water column. Nonetheless, they generally feed on material suspended in the water. Some of the organisms in both guilds are zooxanthellate and therefore involved in primary production, but for most members suspension feeding is the chief energy source.

From the viewpoint of gross functional morphology and importance to the success of reef communities, there is considerable overlap between the constructor and baffler guilds. By virtue of their vertical or erect growth habit and dense association, members of both guilds function in two similar and interrelated ways: (1) they impede (baffle) water flow across the reef surface and thereby protect it from physical destruction; and (2) by reducing current velocity, they enhance the process of deposition of internal and external reef sediments.

However, from the viewpoints of skeletonization, skeletal size, and taxonomy, the two guilds are quite different. Members of the constructor guild are well-skeletonized and either colonial or gregarious. Current baffling is their secondary functional role in the success of the reef community. Their *primary* role is to construct the organic reef framework. By contrast, members of the baffler guild are poorly skeletonized or non-

TABLE 5.12. Major Growth Forms and Selected Examples of Important Members of the Constructor Guild During Geologic History

Growth Forms (Erect)	Taxa (Rigid Skeletons)	Geologic Age
I. Massive; domal– hemispherical; skeletal elements tightly packed	A. Milleporina	Eocene–Holocene
	B. Scleractinia	Mesozoic–Cenozoic
	C. Sclerospongiae	Triassic; Holocene
	D. Chaetetida	Carboniferous; Jurassic
	E. Stromatoporoidea	Middle Paleozoic; Jurassic–Cretaceous
	F. Rugosa; Tabulata	Ordovician–Early Carboniferous
	G. Filamentous algae; stromatolites (non-rigid)	Precambrian
II. Upward branching; digitate, sticklike, bouquets; branches loosely packed	A. Milleporina; Stylasterina	Eocene–Holocene
	B. Scleractinia	Late Cenozoic
	C. Bivalvia: Monopleuridae	Cretaceous
	D. Sphinctozoa	Carboniferous–Triassic
	E. Rugosa; Tabulata	Ordovician–Early Carboniferous
	F. Archaeocyatha	Early Cambrian
	G. Filamentous algae; stromatolites (non-rigid)	Precambrian
III. Upward flaring cups and bowls	A. Bivalvia: Caprinidae; Radiolitidae, Hippuritidae	Cretaceous
	B. Brachiopoda: Richthofeniacea	Permian
	C. Sphinctozoa: Guadalupiidae	Permian
	D. Archaeocyatha	Early Cambrian
IV. Columnar–bladed	A. Milleporina	Eocene–Holocene
	B. Chaetetida	Carboniferous
	C. Stromatoporoidea	Middle Paleozic
	D. Filamentous algae; stromatolites (non-rigid)	Precambrian

skeletal and many are non-colonial; while alive, their *primary* role is to baffle the currents.

Functional Morphology

There are several major morphological characteristics shared by most members of the constructor guild. In addition to being well-skeletonized and colonial–gregarious, they also have the following features:

a. Skeletons are large, strong, and heavy; skeletal size makes these organisms the most important volumetric contributors to the organic framework of Cenozoic reefs (Pl. 21*b*). Their strength and mass provide rigidity and resistance to turbulence.

b. The upward growth direction of skeletons exceeds the lateral growth direction; this provides constructors with access to both energy and living space in the water column.

c. Skeletal growth is rapid and skeletal mineralogy almost universally calcareous. Such growth provides topographic relief to the reef surface plus a large potential volume of calcareous skeletal debris to the internal sediment and the adjacent level-bottom.

Despite the apparently endless variety and unbroken gradations in the morphology of constructor guild members (consult excellent discussion of functional morphology in sessile animals by Jackson, 1979, pp. 507–533), it is possible to establish a reasonably restricted set of major growth forms (Table 5.12). Furthermore, each major growth form has been adopted by several different higher taxa and at several different times during geologic history. The variety of growth forms and the diversity of higher taxa represented in the constructor guild in post-Cambrian reefs are considerably greater than in older reefs. There is also a higher level of biologic complexity of constructor taxa in post-Cambrian reefs. Precambrian reefs were constructed by non-skeletal algae alone; Cambrian reefs were formed by more varied algae and primitive sponges. The Middle Ordovician marked the first appearance of *several* constructor guild metazoan taxa having growth forms convergent on those of their predecessors (especially the stromatolites).

Skeletal Arrangement

The success of the constructor guild also strongly depends on the arrangement (erect growth; packing density) of individual skeletons, both before and after death of its members. Prior to death, skeletons are densely packed to provide mutual support and protection from high turbulence.

Following death of the reef, destruction and cementation replace construction as the dominant processes. The volume of sediment of skeletal origin may increase dramatically in both the reef interior and on the level-bottom; therefore, in many ancient reefs the volume of *in situ* skeletons of the constructor guild seems surprisingly small. Even so, in ancient reefs the volume of *in situ* constructor skeletons commonly exceeds the volume of *in situ* skeletons of members of any of the other guilds.

Guild Membership and Overlap

In typical Holocene photic zone tropical reefs, the constructor guild is dominated in every way (by volume, diversity, growth rate, packing density, etc.) by scleractinian corals; Milleporina are a distant second in importance (for other *potential* constructors, see "mounds/plates" of Jackson, 1979, pp. 501, 515; some other authors also include Stolonifera and Coenothecalia). All other erect-growing well-skeletonized animals lack either sufficient skeletal volume or packing density to be included in this guild (i.e., without scleractinians and millepores, they could not construct the organic framework of a reef). Another way of determining which erect-growing organisms constitute the constructor guild is to ask: "If Species A, B . . . N (listed in order of decreasing *in situ* skeletal volume) were removed, would the remaining organisms still be a reef community?" When the community can no longer be considered a reef, those remaining organisms are not members of the constructor guild.

However, in many reef systems there is considerable overlap or amalgamation of function between the constructor and binder guilds. For example, in algal ridges skeletal volume and density of members of the binder guild (especially crustose corallines) commonly exceed those of all other guilds combined, so that constructor and binder guilds are not easily separable (Pls. 24, 36*a*). Even where algal ridges are absent, the reef crest scleractinians (Pl. 6*a*) and millepores may have sheetlike morphologies for binding and encrusting; such organisms thus partly fulfill the binder guild function (Storr, 1964, p. 39). It is uncommon for scleractinians and coralline algae to live together in equal abundance (for an exception, see Stearn et al., 1977, Table 1) because when algal spores settle on submerged coral surfaces, they commonly are consumed by the polyps. However, encrusting corallines quickly colonize the surface of dead corals. Thus, scleractinians and coralline algae may overlap the constructor and binder guilds, depending on their skeletal volumes in the reef framework (Pl. 23).

In the Bermudan algal cup reefs described by Ginsburg and Schroeder (1973), construction and binding functions are combined and shared by lamellar encrusting corallines (Bosence, 1983; 1984, p. 572) and millepores growing in sheetlike coenostea; this is also an excellent example of niche overlap (to be discussed at the end of this chapter). Somewhat similar subfossil, algal-bryozoan reefs in which the constructor and binder guilds were combined have been described from the present aphotic zone in the Gulf of Mexico (Ludwick and Walton, 1957).

Membership in the constructor guild may change laterally across reef systems and down the seaward slope (Fig. 5.1). For example, at Jamaica, the shallower-water (0–70 m) scleractinian-dominated constructor guild (Goreau, 1959; Liddell et al., 1984) is replaced downslope by a sclerosponge-dominated constructor guild (70–105 m; Lang, 1974; Lang et al., 1975; Fagerstrom, 1984). In typical aphotic zone reefs, the delicately branched scleractinian coralla play the roles of both the constructor and baffler guilds.

Summary and Conclusions
The above discussion of the constructor guild introduces several points that need reemphasis before proceeding to other guilds:

a.   The constructor guild is the most important functional unit in Holocene reef communities; without its vigorous expression, the community is not a reef !

b.   The constructor guild commonly overlaps or even replaces the baffler guild and may also overlap the binder guild. In such cases, the same organisms perform two functions. Thus, the constructor function is a matter of gross morphology (size and shape), skeletonization/skeletal volume, and skeletal arrangement (packing density).

c.   Constructor and baffler guilds share the same spatial resource and, if both are animals, share the same energy resource (suspended food).

d.   Despite these overlaps in function, space, and food members of the constructor, baffler, and binder guilds are morphologically (degree of skeletonization; skeletal volume; skeletal arrangement), taxonomically and structurally quite distinct (guild and niche segregation).

e.   Taxa at almost all levels may belong to more than one guild (see also Morphological Plasticity below), but such overlap is less common at lower levels (i.e., niche overlap is uncommon).

f.   There is a reasonably restricted set of growth forms that can be assigned with confidence to the constructor guild (Table 5.12); constructors must also attain large skeletal volume and dense packing. The same aspects of skeletal volume, functional morphology, and skeletal arrangement (packing) used to determine membership in the constructor guild in Holocene reef communities can be used with equal confidence to assign analogous organisms to this guild in ancient reef communities.

g.   Furthermore, this general principle of analogous skeletal volume, morphology, and arrangement also can be used to determine membership in the other guilds in ancient reef communities. (The gradual transition from emphasis on Holocene to ancient reefs has now begun!)

Baffler Guild

The effectiveness of the baffler guild in reducing current velocity in the reef environment depends on the size, shape, orientation, and closeness of spacing of its members as well as on the physical and geological factors influencing current velocity (Chap. 3).

Functional Morphology

Members of the baffler guild are characterized by firm attachment to the substrate and a dominant upward growth direction, as in the constructor guild. They differ from members of other reef guilds in the following ways:

a.   Although baffler guild organisms vary considerably in size and degree of skeletonization, none of the members has large, strong, and heavy skeletons.

b.   Some members have thin, easily broken, but nonetheless rigid skeletons composed of either $CaCO_3$ or SiO_2 (Pls. 22b, 29a, 31b).

c.   Other members of the guild are flexible and sway with the currents (Pl. 22a). They may have partly mineralized or organic skeletons, but the skeletal elements are not rigidly united.

d.   Still other members are non-skeletal (Pl. 23a). These organisms are also flexible and locally important in Holocene reef communities but have no fossil record.

e.   Most members are colonial, but many are solitary (e.g., sponges, "pelmatozoans").

There is some overlap of external morphology among members of constructor and baffler guilds, but skeletons of the latter are typically smaller and more delicate. Although the growth forms represented in the baffler guild are highly varied, they are amenable to subdivision into a few major shapes (Table 5.13). Each major growth form has been adopted by quite different higher taxa at different times during geologic history; because of small size and poor skeletonization, however, their fossil record is less complete than for the other guilds.

Skeletal Arrangement

In Holocene reef communities, the living blade and fan-shaped bafflers are usually oriented with the broad surface perpendicular to the prevailing current direction (Kinzie, 1973, p. 148; Stearn and Riding, 1973, pp. 195–198; Done, 1983, pp. 130–131). This orientation maximizes effectiveness in baffling and exposure to suspended food. Recognition of the presence of an effective baffler guild and estimation of its diversity and abundance in many ancient reef communities must often be inferred from the composition and volume of its skeletal debris and the internal sediment that has been baffled and deposited. Only rarely are fossil members of this guild preserved in growth position (cf. Pl. 29a).

Estimating the importance of bafflers becomes quite difficult when baffling is so ineffective that a great deal of skeletal debris is transported to the adjacent level-bottom substrate (Pray, 1958; Lane, 1971, pp. 1438–

1442). Susceptibility of the poorly skeletonized bafflers to fragmentation and transport is high; it depends on many factors, including size, degree of skeletonization, shapes of the whole organism and its parts, level of turbulence, and rate of reef accretion or level-bottom deposition.

Guild Membership and Overlap

The baffler guild is more prominently developed in Holocene Atlantic Province photic zone reefs than in the Indo-Pacific due to the much greater importance of Gorgonacea and Antipatharia. The bladed and branched Milleporina are of similar importance in both provinces; crinoids are more important in the Indo-Pacific. Although erect Bryozoa are varied in form and widely distributed in Holocene reefs, the sizes of their zooaria are too small to make them either important bafflers while alive or contributors to internal sediments.

However, in numerous Paleozoic (especially Middle Ordovician–Devonian) reefs, both pelmatozoans (Lane, 1971) and the erect (fans, branches, cups) Bryozoa were the dominant bafflers; in some reefs, their fragments constitute most of the internal sediment. During the Late Paleozoic, the baffling pelmatozoans and bryozoans were important members of reef communities and also formed large, mud mounds of baffled sediment (Pray, 1958). There is a continuous spectrum of mound-shaped structures in the stratigraphic record. The range of this spectrum runs from structures composed predominantly of *in situ* constructors ("pure" or "true" reefs) to those containing large volumes of fragmented but nontransported skeletal bafflers to non-reefs composed almost entirely of baffled and trapped sediment (mud mounds). The reef-versus-non-reef status of those structures near the center of the spectrum depends on two subjective judgments:

a.   Rigidity of the organic framework. In the context of Holocene reefs and of this book, rigidity is given prime consideration in the recognition of reefs (Table 1.2).

b.   The relative importances of constructor-versus-baffler guilds and the degree of guild overlap between them. This factor may be impossible to determine if the main bafflers were very poorly skeletonized or nonskeletal (e.g., the Antipatharia, Gorgonacea, "grasses," etc.) and therefore not represented in the fossil record.

The problem of the reef-versus-non-reef distinction may also hinge on the presence and importance of the binder guild, which is considered next.

Binder Guild

The concept of binding in Holocene reef communities is generally taken in the broad sense of uniting (tying, knitting, holding together) all the various organic and inorganic elements of the reef, including both frame-

TABLE 5.13. Major Growth Forms and Selected Examples of Important Members of the Baffler Guild During Geologic History^a

Growth Forms (Erect)	Taxa			Geologic Age
	Flexible	Semirigid	Rigid	
I. Cylinders, vases, stalks, branches, stems, whips	A. Antipatharia			Late Cenozoic
	B. Gorgonacae			Late Cenozoic
			C. Stylasterina	Eocene–Holocene
			D. Milleporina	Eocene–Holocene
		E. Demospongiae		Ordovician; Silurian; Permian; Jurassic; Holocene
			F. Bryozoa (dendroid)	Ordovician–Silurian; Paleocene
			G. Sphinctozoa; Inozoa	Late Carboniferous–Jurassic
		H. Dasycladacea		Permian
		I. "Pelmatozoans" (especially Crinoidea)		Ordovician–Permian
		J. Archaeocyatha		
	K. "Filamentous algae"; stromatolites			Early Cambrian
				Precambrian

Taxa	Range
II. Blades, fans, box-works	
1. Non-porous	
A. "Frondescent algae"	Holocene
B. Codiacae ("phylloid")	Late Paleozoic
C. Bryozoa (frondescent)	Ordovician–Silurian
D. Milleporina	Eocene-Holocene
2. Porous	
A. Gorgonacea	Late Cenozoic
B. Bryozoa (fenestrate; reteporiform)	Devonian–Permian
III. Upward flaring "cups and bowls"	
A. Bryozoa (reteporiform)	Holocene
B. Demospongiae	Holocene
C. Codiacea: Anchicodium	Jurassic; Holocene
	Late Paleozoic
D. Archaeocyatha	Early Cambrian

"Columns under Taxa are arranged by degree of skeletonization: flexible–rigid.

207

work and internal sediments. The binding process is very comprehensive and occurs on both hard and sedimentary substrates located on the outer surface of the reef as well as the surfaces of internal caves, caverns, and pores. Part of the binding process includes precipitation of cement in the reef pores (Chap. 4), but, quantitatively, the most important aspect of this process involves the organisms of the binder guild (Buss, 1979, Table 1 lists Holocene taxa of actual/potential importance in the binder guild). By means of this uniting function, the binders give strength, rigidity, and cohesion to the entire reef structure; they firmly join the separate elements of the constructor, baffler, and other guilds as well as the loose internal sediment. In this way, the binders transform the growing reef from a loose to a semirigid mass of disparate elements to a progressively more dense, firm, and rigid structure. Such a structure has increased resistance to destruction and potential to become part of the stratigraphic record as a reef limestone.

The rate of binding may be remarkably fast. Wulff (1984) found that in just a few days sponges had begun to bind piles of dead coral rubble; by seven weeks, coralline algae had begun to encrust the piles, and by seven months the rubble was firmly bound with a thick crust of coralline algae.

Functional Morphology

Members of the binder guild are highly varied in both morphology and taxonomy (Table 5.14). Their chief unifying feature is the greater development of their lateral growth direction relative to the vertical (Pls. 20b, 21a, 24b, 25a). Many binders increase in width at several times the rate at which they increase in thickness. Thus, binders compete with constructors and bafflers for attachment space on the substrate. Their more rapid lateral growth, however, often allows them to overgrow a wide variety of sessile benthic organisms. The energy required by binders must reach the substrate, so they are relatively poor competitors for energy. The algal and zooxanthellate animal binders are commonly deprived of radiant energy by shading from the constructor and baffler guilds and except, for the sponges, non-zooxanthellate animal binders are poor competitors for suspended food. Locally, however, deposit-feeding bryozoans and some foraminifera are very successful.

Determination of growth directions among the highly diverse binders may be difficult because their lateral growth usually conforms to the orientation and configuration of the irregular substrate over which they are growing. Thus, rapid lateral growth produces relatively thin skeletons, broadly expanded parallel to the substrate which may not be horizontal. The substrate includes the erect attachment areas of the constructors and bafflers, broken shells or skeletons, walls of internal caves and caverns, or the irregular surface of sediment awaiting binding.

Other important characteristics of binders are listed below:

TABLE 5.14. Major Growth Forms and Selected Examples of Important Members of the Binder Guild During Geologic History[a]

Growth forms (Lateral/Reptant)	Taxa		Geologic Age
	Non-skeletal	Skeletal	
I. Sheets, mats, lenses (on substrate)	A. "Filamentous algae"; stromatolites		Precambrian–Holocene
		B. Melobesoideae	Eocene–Holocene
		C. Milleporina	Eocene–Holocene
		D. Scleractinia	Triassic–Holocene
		E. Demospongiae	Permian–Holocene
		F. Chaetetida	Late Paleozoic
		G. *Tubiphytes* (alga?)	Carboniferous–Jurassic
		H. Sphinctozoa: Guadalupiidae	Permian
		I. Stromatoporoidea	Middle Paleozoic
		J. Bryozoa	Ordovician–Silurian; Cenozoic
		K. *Renalcis; Epiphyton* (algae?)	Cambrian–Devonian
II. Runners, webs (on substrate)	A. Stolonifera		Holocene
III. Plates; foliaceous (above substrate)		B. Bryozoa: Cheilostomata	Cenozoic
		C. Tabulata	Middle Paleozoic
		A. Scleractinia	Eocene–Holocene
		B. Demospongiae	Holocene
IV. Arches, bridges, umbrellas (above substrate)		A. Peyssonneliacea ("phylloid")	Late Paleozoic; late Cenozoic
		B. *Archaeolithoporella* (alga?)	Permian

[a]Column under Taxa arranged by degree of skeletonization.

a.   They may be skeletal or non-skeletal. If they are skeletal and the skeleton is cemented to a hard substrate, they are called *encrusters*. Large encrusters are of local importance in supporting or reinforcing the bases of attachment of erect constructors and bafflers. Wulff and Buss (1979) reported that foliaceous corals in deep water that lacked surficial (binding) sponges were 10 times as susceptible to breakage as similar corals with well-developed surficial sponges. Degrees of skeletonization vary from very firm (e.g., coralline algae) to poor (e.g., demosponges).

b.   The non-skeletal binders are mostly "filamentous algae" with sticky mucilagenous sheaths (see Cyanophyta, Chap. 7); they also include organisms with stolons and holdfasts. Some non-skeletal binders have "soft parts" (e.g., ectoplasm or pseudopods of sarcodinans) that bind grains and firmly hold the animal to the substrate.

c.   A few binders do not conform to the substrate but instead form "arches, bridges, and umbrellas" that span the gap between depressions on the substrate, leaving water- and sediment-filled voids beneath them.

Skeletal Arrangement

Because of their generally low profile and broad base of attachment to the substrate, members of the binder guild are the most likely to resist current transport and to be preserved in growth position. This is especially true of the skeletal encrusters, which resist all but the most intense storms. Except for stromatolites and "algal crusts," the fossil record of non-skeletal binders is poor; in most stromatolites, crusts, and algal ridges, the binder guild is the only guild present.

The volume of skeletal debris in a reef complex derived from the destruction of constructors and bafflers is usually greater than the volume of unbroken skeletons by a factor of 2–10 times or more. In addition, the volume of internal voids between unbroken skeletons of *in situ* constructors also exceeds the volume of the organic reef framework. Therefore, one of the most important *physical* reef processes is the transport and deposition of this skeletal debris within these voids. One of the most important *biological* processes is the binding of these internal grains to the reef framework. Each bound layer of internal sediment is of sand-granule size and may have poorly developed grading from coarse texture at the base to finer at the top.

Among reefs in which the efficiency of the binding guild is low, breakage, transport, and deposition of skeletal grains outside the reef system are high. This means that the reef framework is less cohesive, less able to resist destruction processes, and less likely to become part of the stratigraphic record. However, if the binder guild is efficient, it performs an important function in retaining those surficial grains within reef voids.

Binding by *in situ* crustose coralline algae is most important in reef areas exposed to the highest surf and high light intensity (algal ridges and reef crests). In near-shore rubble ramparts, binding by mat-forming cyanophytes is most important. In areas of the ridges and crests, rapid lateral growth of corallines quickly binds the relatively low volume of surficial sediment; the densely overlapping sheets of these organisms effectively resist and break the force of incoming waves to protect the reefs in lagoons and flats from physical destruction (Pl. 14). There is usually such a marked reduction in turbulence across the relatively narrow algal ridge that its leeward, lagoon-facing slope contains a higher amount of coral cover than algae.

Conversely, the binding algae are least important in deeper and darker areas below overhangs on the reef surface and inside caverns and caves; they are locally important binders to depths as great as 80 m. Below about 30–40 m, algae are usually less important than binding sponges (Hartman, 1977; Suchanek et al., 1983).

Guild Membership and Overlap

Algae. In Holocene communities, the chief function of algae, both skeletal and non-skeletal, is to bind; they are abundant and widely distributed in photic zone reefs and are commonly the most important members of the binder guild. The binding role of non-skeletal algae has been described by Ginsburg (1960) and Kobluk and Risk (1977; see also Chap. 7).

Goreau and Goreau (1973, p. 451) divided calcareous algae into two categories based on their method of binding: (1) *psammophytes:* algae that live on sedimentary substrates (typically sand or mud) and are attached to the substrate by holdfasts that extend down into the sediment; and (2) *lithophytes:* algae attached to hard substrates such as rocks, dead corals, and rubble. A third category, not recognized by the Goreaus but of considerable significance in many Late Paleozoic reefs, consists of those skeletal algae that build "arches, bridges, and umbrellas" (Table 5.14) between discontinuous hard substrates (see Chaps. 7 and 13).

A typical representative of the first category is the common Cenozoic codiacean *Halimeda.* Other psammophytes include both codiaceans and dasycladaceans. However, some species of *Halimeda* are lithophytes, but the binding ability of their holdfasts is volumetrically quite minor.

The chief Cenozoic lithophytes are the crustose coralline algae (Rhodophyta: Melobesoideae; especially important are *Porolithon, Neogoniolithon,* and *Lithophyllum*) These taxa have two characteristics that make them particularly well-suited for membership in the binder guild: they have heavily calcified (high-Mg calcite) cell walls to resist turbulence and very rapid lateral growth rates (Skeletal Growth, Chapt. 3). The Paleozoic and Mesozoic Solenoporacea were important binders but were neither as large nor as well-calcified as the Melobesoideae.

In both Holocene and ancient reefs, the well-skeletonized, thick, and

densely packed algal members of the binder guild overlap with the constructor guild; in algal ridges, they become the constructor (see discussion
above under Constructor Guild). Numerous members of Melobesoideae
also extend upward from the substrate as short (up to 5 cm) branches,
pustules, or plates and thus overlap with members of the baffler guild.

Several previous authors have documented the considerable importance
of calcareous algae in ancient reefs and have ascribed to them the role
of "secondary frame-builders." In most of these cases, the distinction between primary and secondary has been based on a skeletal volumetric
distinction rather than on differences in growth form and function. Furthermore, in many pre-Cenozoic reefs the growth form and guild membership of some presumed algal taxa involved are uncertain or very difficult to determine (e.g., *Renalcis* and *Epiphyton* in Paleozoic reefs; Riding
and Toomey, 1972).

By definition, all algae are absent from aphotic zone reefs; their dis-
appearance down seaward slopes is staggered over a considerable bathymetric range and depends on several physical and biological factors.
However, rarely are they sufficiently abundant below about 80 m to contribute substantially to the binding guild (cf. Hillis-Colinvaux, 1984).

Sponges. Like algae, the chief function of most demosponges in Holocene
reef communities is to bind, but unlike the calcareous algae, these sponges
are poorly skeletonized and so cannot withstand high turbulence and are
much less effective in providing cohesion and rigidity to the framework.
(Although the Hexactinellida and Calcarea are present in Holocene reef
communities, they are so rare that their contribution to reef-building is
inconsequential; the Sclerospongiae in deeper water belong to the constructor guild.)

The erect and laterally expanded demosponges are quite easily broken
by strong currents into viable propagules and rolled to new habitats, where
they begin again their baffling and binding function. Laterally expanded
encrusters are the most permanent and effective sponge binders; those
with high proportions of spongin fibers are best able to withstand fragmentation in strong currents. All these aspects of demosponge morphology,
plus their general lack of symbiotic algae and bacteria, contribute to their
better adaptation and relatively higher biomass and diversity in water
deeper than about 10–20 m.

Sponges of all types are exceedingly rare in pre-Holocene Cenozoic reef
communities (Rigby, 1971), but the poorly skeletonized demosponges and
hexactinellids are extremely important in the baffler/binder guilds of Late
Paleozoic and Mesozoic reefs (see Chap. 8).

Foraminifera. There are relatively few encrusting foraminifera that are
sufficiently large and abundant in Holocene reef communities to make

substantial contributions to the binder guild. However, Emiliani (1951, Fig. 1) and C. S. Ross (1972) noted the characteristic general association of large foraminifera and reefs. By far the best known and most important species is the common Atlantic Province encruster *Homotrema rubrum* (excellent photographs in Kobluk and James, 1979). Other large binders include *Gypsina plana* and *Alveolina* sp. (both encrusters) and *Marginopora vertebralis*.

Although the maximum test diameter of *H. rubrum* is only 4–8 mm, Glynn (1973, Table 2) reported such dense concentrations in Panamanian reefs, especially on undersurfaces of corals and in relatively small internal reef voids, that they are major contributors to both the total community biomass and overlap constructor and binder guilds. They seem to be more common in cryptic habitats where they find some relief from the more intense fish predation on exposed surfaces (Emiliani, 1951; Lipps, 1984, personal communication). The packing density of *H. rubrum* is so high in the Bermudan algal cup reefs that Ginsburg and Schroeder (1973) regarded it as an important frame-builder.

In the deeper part of the steep seaward slopes of photic zone reefs on the Yucatan Shelf, Logan et al. (1969) described *Gypsina plana* as the most important member of the binder guild in some areas. Enormous individuals (up to 4 cm in diameter) of *G. plana* and other encrusters such as coralline algae, bryozoans, *H. rubrum,* sponges, and calcareous annelid tubes have built crusts on the outer reef surface up to 2 cm thick. Goreau and Goreau (1973, p. 439) reported that *Gypsina* sp. also is an important binder in the upper part of the seaward slope in Jamaican reefs.

The very large (diameter: 30+ mm) foraminifer *Marginopora vertebralis* is abundant and widely distributed in the Great Barrier Reef and elsewhere in the Indo-Pacific Province (C. S. Ross, 1972). It is a characteristic binder of level-bottom substrates, where it is firmly attached by the ectoplasm. Ross also reported rapid lateral growth rates (up to 0.2-mm increase in 2 wk for juveniles).

Guilds and Morphological Plasticity

There is considerable variation in both gross external morphology (growth form) and in the more detailed internal morphology of sessile, benthic colonial organisms, including most members of constructor, baffler, and binder reef guilds (reviewed by Lang, 1984, pp. 18–19). These organisms include some of the best examples of high intraspecific variation in the animal kingdom. However, the causes of such variation, especially the relative importance of genetic and environmental factors, have been the subject of considerable debate. Different morphological forms in colonial organisms occur at three levels of integration, increasing levels of genetic difference and levels of expected morphologic variation:

a. *Intracolonial:* genetic variation is minimal (clones).

b. *Intercolonial:* colonies of the same species living in the same habitat.

c. *Interpopulation:* colonies of the same species living in different habitats (see examples in Borel Best et al., 1984, pp. 70–73).

Intraspecific morphological variants that are presumed to be the result of external environmental variation (called ecophenotypes, ecomorphs, etc.) have been recognized in a great number of important reef organisms. The most intense effort, however, has been directed toward the corals. In earlier studies, the rationale was that internal morphology is largely genetically controlled and is therefore more conservative and "fundamental," and that intraspecific variation in external morphology is caused by the environment (i.e., coral identification was largely based on internal morphology, whereas external morphology was used to interpret the influence of such environmental factors as depth, turbulence, etc.). These assumptions have been tested and compared in three ways:

a.   Transplantation experiments in which an ecomorph typical of a particular habitat was moved to a different habitat and assumed a new growth form characteristic of the new habitat (Yonge, 1973; Foster, 1979).

b.   Recognition that intracolony variation, caused by environmental factors, exceeds intercolony and interpopulation variation in some species; this suggests that the environmental factors influence morphological variation more than genetic factors (Foster, 1980).

c.   Comparison of intraspecific morphological variation among suites of characters from different habitats (Foster, 1980); these comparisons indicate that morphological variation in internal features is also environmentally induced and not clearly related to colony shape (Foster, 1983).

Thus, there is good evidence that the environment significantly controls both internal and external morphology and that genetic factors establish an overall architectural pattern and range of intraspecific variation upon which the environment operates. This range or degree of plasticity must be determined for each species with similar consideration given to all morphological features.

Factors

In highly plastic taxa, the interrelations among various ecophenotypes and the numerous physical, chemical, geological, and biological factors are exceedingly complex. Ideally, the morphological response to each such factor is amenable to controlled laboratory testing on a species-by-species basis (e.g., Winston, 1976, found that food type and abundance influenced zoarial shape in a bryozoan species). Factor-by-factor testing creates quite difficult problems, because in nature many factors are interrelated in complex ways (e.g., light intensity/depth or feeding method/turbidity). Interspecific variation is not amenable to such testing because much of the morphologic variation is under genetic control and cannot be separated from environmental controls. Yet, evolutionary trends of convergence of widely differing higher taxa to produce similar adaptations to similar environments demonstrate the overall importance of environmental, individual, and species selection in determining genotype.

Jackson (1979, p. 533) has suggested that external morphology in sessile colonial animals represents a strategy for survival. The more plastic the morphology, the better the chances of survival in different or changing environments. Similarly, in cases of short-term environmental change, morphologically plastic species can change growth form to one that is better adapted to the new environment (Foster, 1979; 1983, p. 24).

Largely Genetic Factors. In her research on plasticity in massive Caribbean corals, Foster (1979, 1980, 1983) has repeatedly stressed that each morphologic character (external and internal) for each species represents a unique response to the local habitat. Some species (e.g., *Montastraea annularis*) are far more plastic than others; however, Barnes (1973, p. 295) noted that coralla of *Dendrogyra cylindrus* from different environments have similar growth forms and reasoned that, in this species, genetic factors control form.

Barnes (1973) presented evidence of the interrelations between corallum shape and such aspects of polyps as their manner of division during asexual reproduction, their size and degree of crowding, and the number of mouths per polyp and per calyx. He noted that large polyps and calyxes have relatively more mouths than small ones and are characteristic of hemispherical–spherical coralla; small polyps are typical of flattened coralla. Wells (1967, p. 351) regarded rounded coralla as indicative of horizontal, evenly lighted substrates, whereas flattened coralla of the same species seemed indicative of steep, shaded substrates. Foster (1979) found that the nature of food and the way it is gathered by the polyps strongly influences interspecific differences in skeletal morphology. Some of these relationships are based on genetic factors which control the overall growth mechanism; others are based on depth (plus light intensity and skeletal growth rate).

Largely Environmental Factors. The growth and division of zooxanthellate coral polyps are functions of tissue productivity, which in turn depends on availability of food and/or light. Thus, the more rapid the polyp growth and division, the less closely spaced the corallites in colonial species (Barnes, 1973, pp. 284–295). In shallow water, where polyp growth and calcification are most rapid, repeated complete division of polyps results in convex tissue and skeletal surfaces; irregular surfaces (lobate-branched) increase the feeding area/skeletal mass ratio and potential growth rate. On the other hand, colony shape also depends on location patterns of live-versus-dead individual polyps which may be related either to very local environmental differences (e.g., sediment deposition) or to stochastic events such as predation.

In some coral species, light intensity exerts a major control over calcification rate, corallum shape, and thickness of the vertical corallite structures (Foster, 1983). Increased calcification and stronger skeletons may be viewed as adaptations to generally higher turbulence in shallow water. Similarly, low profile, streamlined coralla may also be viewed as adaptations to high turbulence (Done, 1983, p. 112). However, Foster (1979, 1980, 1983) has carefully documented that numerous other factors, both environmental and genetic, exert much more control over corallum form than does turbulence.

Kershaw (1981, p. 1293) suggested that the degree of crowding of intraspecific coralla on the substrate increases their competition for space and therefore affects their external morphology. Each different growth form simply represents a different solution to crowding problems; forms that increase the surface area/volume ratio also increase exposure of the polyps and zooxanthellae to sunlight and food while decreasing their area of attachment and stability on the substrate.

Chappell (1980, pp. 249–250) has summarized the theoretical interrelations among corallum growth form and light intensity, turbulence, sediment deposition, and degree of subaerial exposure. Because each of these environmental factors and the species composition (genetic factors) varies across individual reefs and reef systems, the assemblages of morphologies at any one place are also highly varied (i.e., the same growth form may be present at more than one location and in more than one species). The complexity of the interrelations among numerous factors that influence corallum morphology in colonial corals makes it very difficult to use morphology to predict or interpret either the factors responsible for a particular morphology or where that morphology will occur on the reef.

Selected Holocene Examples

Scleractinia. The common shallow-water Caribbean coral *Montastraea annularis* is among the most plastic species known (Hoffmeister and Multer, 1964; Levinton, 1982, p. 411; Foster, 1979, 1980; Graus and Macintyre, 1982). Barnes (1973, pp. 281–283, 296) reported that at 10–15 m depth at Discovery Bay, Jamaica, there are about 5 different growth forms living side by side.

Except for this last case, most previous authors agree that there is a relation between corallum form and water depth: (1) in shallow water (<10 m), most coralla are massive and hemispherical; (2) at intermediate depths (10–15 m) they are broad, flat, or foliaceous. These bathymetric variations are presumably adaptations to progressively lower levels of light intensity. Deeper-water growth forms provide increasing areal exposure of the zooxanthellate polyps but reduce the ratio of skeleton/living tissue and hence the calcification rate.

Although corallum morphology in branching forms also changes with water depth, the causative factor in these cases is believed to be variation in wave turbulence rather than light intensity (cf. Barnes, 1973, p. 286; Stearn, 1982a, p. 231). Morphological adaptations of branched forms to variations in turbulence include (Graus et al., 1977; Schuhmacher and Plewka, 1981b): (1) branch elongation, orientation, shape, and size; and (2) skeletal porosity, compressive and bending strength, elastic modulus, and resistance to abrasion. These latter skeletal properties seem less important for resisting breakage than growth form and orientation. Therefore, in high turbulence locations, branched coralla have the following features: (1) they have rounder, shorter, and fewer branches; (2) individual branches point into the currents; but (3) the entire corallum elongates parallel to current direction. In currents of moderate strength, branches point in the same direction as the current; in weak currents, they show no preferred orientation.

Brakel (1983) found poor correlation among corallum form (especially height) and water depth, light intensity, and turbulence in *Porites astreoides* at Discovery Bay, Jamaica. He discovered that: (1) in bright light, all heights coexist, but in low light, most coralla are flattened; and (2) in low turbulence, all shapes coexist, but in high turbulence, there are only flattened forms.

Other reported examples of ecophenotypic variation in corallum form include *Madracis pharensis pharensis* in Jamaican cryptic habitats (Jackson, 1979, p. 545), *Oculina varicosa* in water 6–80 m deep in east-central Florida (Reed, 1980, 1981, 1983), and *Caryophyllia smithi* in aphotic zone reefs where current velocity apparently controls growth form (J. B. Wilson, 1975).

The upper limit to scleractinian growth is near the base of the intertidal zone. When upward growth of the corallum reaches this level, the polyps on the upper surface die of subaerial exposure; those on the sides, however, continue to grow laterally to form *microatolls* (Pl. 17b). This growth form typifies most large, massive intertidal coralla (in the northern part of the Great Barrier Reef, Scoffin and Stoddart, 1978, reported that at least 43 species form microatolls) and is not related to true ecophenotypic variation.

Millepora spp. The abundant, shallow-water calcareous hydrozoan *Millepora* occurs in highly varied growth forms and thus belongs in more than one guild (guild overlap). These forms and guilds include (Stearn and Riding, 1973):

a. *Binder:* sheets less than 1 cm thick that take the form of the substrate; they may give rise to bladed or branched forms (baffler guild).

b. *Boxwork/baffler:* undulating blades usually joined along edges to form subangular cavities.

c. *Bladed/baffler:* gently folded, erect blades or curtains up to 50 cm high (Pl. 22*b*).

d. *Branching/baffler:* erect branches up to 20 cm high and 2 cm in diameter.

e. *Massive/constructor* (Endean, 1982, p. 86): large colonies covering 1 + m².

Much variation exists within each of these main forms; some variation is ecophenotypic, but Stearn and Riding (1973) recognized three morphologically distinct sympatric species on the reef flat at Bellairs, Barbados. For instance, among the boxwork forms *(M. squarrosa)* in shallow water, the coenostea tend to be low, compact, and encrusting, whereas in deeper water, they are taller and of simpler shapes. Basal attachments of all three species are encrusting sheets from which boxworks, blades, and branches arise.

Lithophyllum congestum. This crustose coralline alga grows laterally in thin, binding sheets covering the algal ridges of Caribbean reefs (Steneck and Adey, 1976). Where adjacent sheets meet, their margins tend to grow rapidly upward into erect, anastomosing branches (baffles) about 10 mm high and up to 20 mm in diameter. The ecophenotypic variation in branch form is influenced by turbulence, light, and grazing by parrot fish; because of the considerable sensitivity of this species to microenvironmental changes, many different growth forms are present in close association.

Porifera. Although sponges are not truly colonial (Fry, 1979), they exhibit both intra- and interspecific variation in ways that are very similiar to the variations described above. Finks (1960, pp. 35–37) has reviewed some environmental factors (chiefly turbulence) that influence variation among living sponges and analyzed and interpreted similar variations in large samples of Late Paleozoic sponges. Finks' examples include both interspecific ("ecophenotypes") variation among adults and "ontogenetic" variation among taxa that are herein regarded as members of the constructor, baffler, and binder guilds.

Bryozoa. Morphological plasticity among bryozoans is just as prevalent as in the higher taxa discussed above (Boardman, 1983; Lidgard, 1985; cf. Cuffey and Foerster, 1975, p. 365). Because bryozoans are much less important as reef builders than corals and sponges, their plasticity is not considered here.

Relations of Growth Forms to Geomorphic Reef Zones

The observation that growth forms of corals show a clearer zonation than do species distributions is longstanding . . .

(Done, 1983, p. 107)

No general pattern of shape distribution that is applicable to the great variety of reefs in modern oceans has been found. The shapes of reef animals are not specific guides to environments of modern reefs and should not be expected to be in ancient ones.

(Stearn, 1982a, p. 238)

In the discussion under Dominance: Subcommunities, it was concluded that in most Holocene photic zone reef systems, there are distinct lateral and bathymetric species zonations but that various province-wide or "universal" species zonation patterns are contradictory and therefore of limited value.

Numerous authors (summarized by Done, 1983, pp. 110–122; Stearn, 1982a, pp. 228–234) have also attempted to establish lateral and bathymetric zonations of reef systems based primarily on the growth forms of the most abundant taxa. Because most of these zonations are tied to water depth, a cause-and-effect relationship was presumed to exist between growth form and such depth-related environmental factors as turbulence, light intensity, and turbidity. Furthermore, because depth is related to location within the geomorphic zonation of the reef system, it seemed reasonable to presume that growth form zonations conform in some degree to geomorphic zonations.

There are three major problems to be considered in determining the validity of these growth form/geomorphic zonation schemes:

a. Is the growth form zonation ecophenotypic/intraspecific or interspecific? Many interspecific differences in growth form occur in adjacent reefal environments and their form differences are usually more controlled by genetics than environment (e.g., in Fig. 5.1, the variation in growth/form is unrelated to ecophenotypic variation). Therefore, taxonomic identifications must precede simple analyses of growth form distributions.

b. If variation is indeed ecophenotypic, which environmental factor(s) exert the greatest effect over growth form? The data of Stearn (1982a) suggest that growth form and depth per se are poorly correlated; however, several physical and biological factors are depth-related and may exert control over growth form. To isolate the effects of potential individual factors requires very difficult controlled laboratory experiments.

c. If there is indeed a growth form–environmental factor(s) relation, what is the relationship between the factor(s) and the geomorphic zonation of the reef? Are some environmental factors and their potential influence on growth form uniformly distributed within reef systems, thus bearing no relation to either depth or geomorphic zonation?

Holocene Corals. In addition to the data-based examples cited by Stearn (1982a, pp. 228–234) of growth form zonations, the literature also contains two theoretical and more "universal" zonation schemes (Pichon, 1978, reproduced by Done, 1983, Fig. 6; Chappell, 1980, Fig. 2). Although the terminology is different and the Chappell zonation scheme more detailed, these schemes are comparable.

First, because both are theoretical and therefore not based on eco-phenotypic variation, it is not possible to isolate the causative environmental factor(s) that produce the zonation; Pichon regarded turbulence as the primary control, whereas Chappell ascribed variation to complex interrelations among four factors.

Second, in both schemes, two different growth forms occur in all parts of the reef (seaward slope, reef flat, and back-reef/lagoonal); each of Chappell's 10 generalized growth forms occurs in at least 2 of his 3 geomorphic zones.

Third, in Pichon's scheme, encrusters are confined to the upper part of the seaward slope; in Chappell's scheme, they also occur near the reef flat–back-reef boundary. Each of Chappell's geomorphic zones contains various growth forms and so it is the assemblage, rather than a particular growth form, that characterizes each zone.

Paleozoic Stromatoporoids. Using the doubtfully valid assumption that there is a generalized scheme of coral growth forms in Holocene reef systems that is directly correlated to their geomorphic zonation, paleoecologists sought to establish similar growth form zonations in large Devonian reef systems based on the extinct stromatoporoids (Porifera?). In some cases, linkage of growth form to geomorphic zone was direct and unequivocal (Cockbain, 1984, pp. 8–10); in other situations (poor exposure or subsurface), growth form was used to infer both location in the geomorphic zonation and bathymetry. (It is important to understand that at the time many of these growth form/geomorphic zonation inferences were made, it was generally agreed among paleobiologists that stromatoporoids were coelenterates; thus, taxonomic analogy with scleractinians seemed less doubtful than it is today.)

Like corals, the stromatoporoid skeletons (coenostea) occur in several growth forms. On the basis of uniformitarian principles, paleoecologists reasoned that the same stromatoporoid shapes would occur in the same geomorphic locations as the most closely analogous coral shapes. Like coral workers, paleoecologists differed on which environmental factor(s) exerted the major influence over stromatoporoid shape (Stearn, 1982a, pp. 234–238). In some cases, no attempt was made to identify the stromatoporoid taxa involved in growth form zonations or to determine whether the zonation was ecophenotypic. Instead, the questionable assumption was made that environmental factors exerted the *only* influence over coenosteal shape.

The probable fallacy of this assumption was recognized by Kershaw (1981); he described a variety of different growth forms mostly in or near their original growth positions and closely packed together on the same bedding surface. Kershaw assumed that in this situation, lateral environmental gradients were weak; when he determined that the same species (based on internal skeletal features) occurred in several different growth forms, he realized that form was more strongly influenced by genetics than by environmental factors (see especially his Figs. 4 and 6). Furthermore, among coenostea of the three most common species, there was virtually no morphologic overlap.

Paleozoic Tabulate Corals. Pandolfi (1984) compared corallum shapes in two samples of Devonian tabulates in New York. Each sample contained specimens of the genera *Favosites, Alveolites,* and *Pleurodictyum;* no species-level taxonomy was undertaken. The author assumed that most of the variation was environmentally induced. In the sample from rocks with more carbonate, most of the corals are sheets (63%) and low domes (37%); corallite walls are less broadly flaring and were interpreted by Pandolfi to be better adapted for suspension feeding in clear water. By contrast, the sample from a shale was interpreted to indicate higher turbidity (rapid sedimentation); it contained 88% high domes and hemispheres and 12% sheets–low domes with more broadly flared corallite walls. These latter adaptations successfully kept the polyps above the substrate surface as sediment enclosed the basal parts of the upward growing corallum.

Abbott (1976, pp. 2120–2121) studied the distribution of several growth forms in three genera of tabulate corals in the Silurian (Wenlockian) reefs in Shropshire, UK. Two of the genera included forms ranging in shape from lamellar to hemispherical to conical; the other contained only tabular coralla. Abbott regarded the depth/turbulence relationship as the dominant control over corallum shape.

Paleocene Bryozoans. The mound-shaped Paleocene reefs in Denmark and southern Sweden are dominated by a highly diverse (taxonomic and morphologic) assemblage of cheilostome bryozoans. The bryozoans exhibit both ecophenotypic and interspecific variation in growth form (Thomsen, 1977, 1983).

In several species with erect, arborescent zoaria, there is a progressive change in mean branch diameter across the reefs from smaller forms on the level-bottom and low on the flanks to largest on the summit (variation in branch diameter and width is mainly controlled by the geometric arrangement of the zoecia). Thomsen interpreted this change as an adaptation to higher current velocities on the reef summit and the side facing the current than on the level-bottom and leeward side. Furthermore, the most plastic species, especially with regard to branch width, were the most abundant and widely distributed across the reef and were presumably adapted to the greatest variation in the environment. Lightly constructed zoaria with slender branches and stems and thin zoecial walls were most abundant on the level-bottom and low on the reef flanks.

Thomsen assumed a direct correlation among the morphology of zoaria and zoecia, their occurrence on the reef, and current velocity; he used this correlation to interpret current velocities and directions in relation to the overall shape of the reefs. No other environmental factors were given serious consideration.

Summary and Conclusions

1. In all marine organisms, morphologic plasticity is highest among those that are benthic, colonial, and sessile. These organisms are abundant in Holocene and ancient, photic, and aphotic zone reef communities, especially in the contructor, baffler, and binder guilds.

2. Plasticity, in its varying degrees, crosses taxonomic boundaries indiscriminantly; because of it, homeomorphism is particularly high in the constructor, baffler, and binder guilds and may lead to considerable guild overlap among individuals of the same species and species of the same genus (e.g., *Millepora* spp.). Plasticity exists among corals, coralline algae, bryozoans, and perhaps also among the extinct stromatoporoids.

3. Plasticity may be caused by genetic (interspecific variation) factors and numerous environmental factors (ecophenotypic variation). Gradational growth forms, mostly due to genetic differences, exist in Holocene *Millepora* spp. and branching corals and the extinct stromatoporoids. Ecophenotypes exist in numerous reef coral species and at least one species of coralline algae.

4. The potential causes of plasticity are so numerous that it is difficult to determine their relative importance in each particular case. Zonations of reef systems based purely on growth form are of uncertain validity and the correlation between growth form zonations and geomorphic zonations is weak.

5. Plasticity leads to considerable niche and guild overlap. Thus, some highly ecophenotypic species may include individuals in more than one guild, and genera with great variation in the growth forms of its sympatric species may contain species in more than one guild ("A species may be a member of more than one guild . . . species overlap significantly in their niche requirements," Root, 1967, p. 335).

6. Problems of determining guild membership and overlap are exemplified by the common Holocene Caribbean photic zone coral *Montastraea annularis*. In very shallow water, the dominant upward growth pro-

duces domal/hemispherical coralla (Barnes, 1973, Fig. 1; Levinton, 1982, Fig. 20.10), which are the chief constructors of many reefs. In water near the lower bathymetric limit for this species, the lateral growth rate exceeds the upward growth rate so that coralla are platelike and foliaceous (Barnes, 1973, Fig. 3; Levinton, 1982, Fig. 20.1). On steep seaward slopes, foliaceous corals of this and other species play an important role in lateral accretion of reefs and are also constructors. Their relatively small areas of attachment make them atypical binders, but their locally high packing density enables them to perform both constructor and binder functions. Thus, foliaceous corals represent difficult cases of guild overlap and demonstrate that both growth form and packing density are important considerations for assignment of guild membership.

7.   Despite problems with the nature and causes of plasticity, they in no way alter the general concept of reef guilds presented above. Guilds are the *major* functional units of reef communities. Guild membership is determined partly on the basis of functional morphology; plasticity may blur the boundaries between guilds, but the conceptual distinctions between guilds remain. ("The limits that circumscribe the membership of any guild must be somewhat arbitrary," Root, 1967, p. 335).

Who are the Reef-Builders?

Reef accretion takes place when the processes of construction exceed the processes of destruction. Guilds involved in construction are the constructor, baffler, and binder guilds. Different reefs in different places and at different times in geologic history vary considerably in the relative importance of these guilds.

In ancient reefs, the relative significance of the baffler guild is especially difficult to determine because its members are most susceptible to postmortem destruction and transportation. In the extreme case, all members of the guild might be soft-bodied and yet produce a mound-shaped nonreef structure lacking an organic framework (e.g., a mud mound).

All members of constructor, baffler, and binder guilds are potential reef-builders or frame-builders (Table 5.11). In ancient reefs, the *in situ* skeletons of constructors and binders are generally of greatest volumetric importance; however, the role of bafflers in sediment production and deposition may be essential to the construction process. Interrelations among the three reef-building guilds and their differing functions distinguish one reef community from another and distinguish reef communities from non-reef communities. A shared characteristic of nearly all members of reef-building guilds, especially constructors and binders, is coloniality/gregariousness (Table 5.11). Because of intense competition for space in reef communities and because solitary animals are poor space competitors (Jackson, 1977, p. 759) compared with colonial organisms (including algae), most successful builders are colonial. Conversely, solitary animals dominate the destroyer and dweller guilds.

The two remaining reef community guilds (destroyer; dweller) are neither unique to reef communities nor important in distinguishing reef from non-reef communities. Their members are generally solitary, morphologically less plastic than reef builders (ecophenotypic variation and guild overlap are minimal), and therefore more easily assigned to their appropriate guild.

Destroyer Guild

The organisms of the reef community that destroy its framework belong to the destroyer guild. In Holocene reefs, their activities may be relatively overt and rapid with very obvious effects or they may work covertly and slowly with disguised effects. In either case, members of the destroyer guild are relentless in their actions to remove, weaken, and destroy the rigid reef framework.

Although the relative importance of physical and biological destruction varies widely in time and space, the local significance of the destroyer guild in Holocene reefs may be very impressive. MacGeachy and Stearn (1976) investigated the extent of destruction of coralla of *Montastraea annularis* by borers in a fringing reef at Barbados; they found that almost 4% of the annual calcification was removed by borers. The bored volume of individual coralla varied from 3 to 60% and was directly related to water depth. The borers included (at species level) 16 sponges, 5 bivalves, 7 sipunculids, 6 polychaetes, and 2 barnacles; sponges accounted for more than 90% of the boring. Hein and Risk (1975) found that boring volume due to sponges and polychaetes was 7–69%.

At Senora Islet, Panama, reefs are dominated by *Pocillopora* spp. Glynn and Stewart (1972, pp. 512–513) estimated their skeletal mass at about 105 metric tons/hectare and their tissues at another 8.8 metric tons/hectare (dry weight). The 4 main destroyers (1 gastropod, 2 crustaceans, 1 fish) remove and ingest about 6.4% of the skeletal matter and about 3.6% of the organic matter per year; they excrete about 6 metric tons/hectare/yr (about 30% of annual growth) of sand-, granule-, and pebble-sized *Pocillopora* skeletal sediment. At depths of 1.5 m on the algal ridges near St. Croix, U.S. Virgin Islands, Adey and Vassar (1975, p. 61) noted that algal destroyers annually removed a surface layer of coralline algal skeletal material nearly 3 cm thick.

Members of the destroyer guild are remarkably varied taxonomically, morphologically, and in their mode of life (Table 5.15); however, unlike the almost exclusively colonial reef builders, nearly all members of the destroyer guild are solitary. Some destroyers (e.g., fish) live above the substrate (nektic) but, because of their vagility, do not compete directly for space with constructors or bafflers; many species use the erect growing

TABLE 5.15. Selected Examples of Important Members of the Destroyer Guild in Holocene Reef Communities

Mode of Life	Taxa	Ref.
I. Nektic; vagile; "biters"		
	A. Fish (Scaridae; Acanthuridae; Labridae; Monacanthidae; Tetraodentidae; Balistidae)	Endean, 1982, pp. 72–73; Ogden, 1977; Frydl and Stearn, 1978; Glynn and Stewart, 1972; Davies, 1983; Rogers et al., 1984; Steneck, 1983, p. 53
II. Epifaunal; vagile; "raspers"		
	B. Mollusca ("limpets, chitons")	Glynn and Stewart, 1972; Steneck, 1983, pp. 47–52
	C. Echinodea	Levinton, 1982, p. 433; Steneck, 1983, pp. 52–53
III. Epifaunal–infaunal; vagile–sessile; "borers"		
	D. Echinoidea	James, 1983, p. 350; Warme, 1977, p. 271; Ogden, 1977, pp. 284–286; Trudgill, 1976; Adey and Vassar, 1975; Bosence, 1984
IV. Infaunal; sessile; "borers"		
	E. endolithic "filamentous algae" (Cyanophyta; Chlorophyta), bacteria, fungi	Stetson et al., 1962, p. 31; Endean, 1982, p. 64; Cribb, 1973, pp. 65–70; Hopley, 1982, p. 90; Bosence, 1984; Kobluk and Risk, 1977; Kobluk, 1977; Kobluk et al., 1978
	F. Porifera (*Cliona, Anthosigmella, Spheciospongia, Siphonodictyon*)	Pang, 1973; Warme, 1977, p. 264; Hartman, 1977; Davies, 1983, p. 73; Wilkinson, 1983; Bosence, 1984.

TABLE 5.15. *(Continued)*

Mode of Life	Taxa	Ref.
	G. Bivalvia *(Tridacna, Lithophaga, Nigra, Gastrochaena)*	James, 1983, p. 350; Hopley, 1982, p. 92
	H. Sipunculida	Patton, 1976, p. 6; Warme, 1977, p. 270; Bosence, 1984
	I. Polychaeta (Eunicidae; Sabellidae	Hartman, 1954; Warme, 1977, p. 270
	J. Cirripedia *(Lithotrypa)*	Ahr and Stanton, 1973; Bosence, 1984

forms for refuge. Furthermore, many nektic destroyers feed on the substrate binders and so do not compete for food with constructors and bafflers; still others feed directly on the constructors and bafflers.

Other destroyers are vagile, epifaunal, and relatively small; they occupy space and feed on or just above the substrate and thus do not compete directly with constructors or bafflers. They commonly feed directly on the binders, constructors, or bafflers.

Organisms that feed at the reef surface may be subdivided into two *overlapping* categories: (1) those that ingest only soft tissues while leaving the framework intact and (2) those that ingest both tissues and framework. The former organisms are "grazers" and belong to the dweller guild; they inhibit skeletal growth rate and reef accretion but do not remove or destroy the framework. The latter organisms are "biters" and "raspers" and true members of the destroyer guild; much rasping is merely an accidental aspect of grazing. Some fish delicately graze the polyps from their calyxes, whereas others clumsily bite off pieces of corallum (destroyers) as they remove the polyps.

Finally, the smallest destroyers find refuge from predators within the framework itself as sessile, infaunal borers, where they have almost no competition for space. However, there is considerable competition for food among grazers and raspers.

Skeletal Arrangement
In reef communities, the skeletal fossil record of the nektic destroyers, especially fish, is generally poor. Some nektic and benthic raspers record their presence by leaving highly characteristic marks on the hard sub-

strate (Pl. 19) from which they have indiscriminantly removed both tissue and skeletal fragments of their prey (Steneck, 1983, Fig. 2).

The skeletal epifaunal, vagile raspers are abundant and diverse in Holocene reefs; upon death, their shells are commonly broken and the fragments are generally transported either to the internal sediment or level-bottom. The chief difficulty for the paleocologist is to distinguish the rasper/destroyers from similar grazer taxa in the dweller guild. In Paleozoic reefs, Polyplacophora ("chitons") were the only raspers present; they were neither abundant nor diverse, whereas grazers, especially non-limpet gastropods, were abundant and diverse (Steneck, 1983).

Although a few borers penetrate living tissues covering the underlying substrate, the vast majority are repelled while the frame-builder is alive and so they begin to bore only after its death. In the former situation, the borer is usually entombed for life in the reef framework. In the latter case, there is commonly a very short-term succession, first involving en-crusting by sponges and algae and then boring. Some skeletal encrusters (e.g., corals, hydrozoans, bryozoans) protect the underlying skeleton from borers; others (e.g., calcareous algae) have no effect on boring activities (MacGeachy and Stearn, 1976, p. 740). Because basal attachment areas of upwardly branching coralla commonly lack repelling polyps, they are often sites of the most intense encrusting and boring. The borers slowly weaken entire coralla so that they simply topple from their own weight. Borers may occupy almost precisely the same habitat for two or more "generations" (borers followed by reborers; Ginsburg and Schroeder, 1973, Fig. 13).

The fossil record of borers consists of sediment- and cement-filled pores and calcareous tubular linings of pores of highly varied sizes and shapes. In Cenozoic reefs, such pores and pore linings occur in quite characteristic forms that can be ascribed with considerable confidence to particular "makers" (Warme, 1977, pp. 268–273; Ward and Risk, 1977); in other situations, especially in the pre-Cenozoic, origin of pores is uncertain (Kobluk et al., 1978). In these latter cases, taxonomic, niche, and behav-ioral overlap are high but guild overlap low (i.e., all borers belong to the destroyer guild).

Guild Membership

The process of boring into hard substrates is accomplished by chemical and mechanical methods, depending on the boring organism and the na-ture of the hard substrate; boring (endolithic) algae also penetrate in-organic substrates to obtain nutrients. Chemical boring by secretion of acids and enzymes is particularly effective in reef carbonate substrates and has been adapted by biologically simple organisms, especially "algae" and sponges. The more complex higher taxa, such as barnacles, some biv-alves, and polychaetes, bore mechanically by scraping their shells against the substrate; other polychaetes and bivalves combine chemical and mechanical methods.

In photic zone reefs, some damage by borers is "healed" by the rapidly growing algal (Pl. 24b) and zooxanthellate members of the frame-building guilds (Wilkinson, 1983). Warme (1977, p. 264) suggested that boring diversity and intensity are inversely related to water depth and that only sponges are important below about 70 m. Conversely, MacGeachy and Stearn (1976) found that boring of the coralla of *Montastraea annularis* is directly related to depth and that there is no relation between borer diversity and depth.

The epifaunal members of the destroyer guild are particularly vulnerable to predation by the nektic component of the reef community. Most of these epifaunal members are protected by spines, large attachment areas, heavy shells, or chemical repellents. Some members also bore shallow depressions in the hard substrate for better anchorage and to present a lower profile to the currents. Deep borings afford even better protection from predators and current transport.

The chief borers in the aphotic zone reefs examined by Neumann et al. (1977) are sponges and fungi; the intensity of boring appears to rival photic zone reefs. J. B. Wilson (1975) noted intense boring by sponges near the bases of the branches of the non-zooxanthellate coral *Lophelia pertusa;* he postulated that the destruction and transport of branch propagules were important aspects of accretion and recolonization of aphotic zone reefs.

Geologic History of Herbivorous Grazers and Raspers

Steneck (1983, pp. 45–54) has reviewed the nature and geologic occurrence of herbivorous grazers ("non-excavators" of Steneck) and raspers/biters (excavators) on calcareous algal crusts. The grazers include fish, echinoids, molluscs, arthropods, and annelids. His data clearly show that:

a.   Grazers (non-excavators) of calcareous substrates have been more diverse throughout the Phanerozoic and appeared earlier in the fossil record than raspers. (Grazers are here considered members of the dweller guild and raspers members of the destroyer guild.)

b.   Diversity of raspers is closely correlated with diversity of crustose coralline algae. (The diversity of crustose coralline algae is in turn correlated with the progressive rise in importance of reefs during the Middle Triassic–Cretaceous and Middle Eocene–Holocene.)

c.   The earliest "limpet" (Gastropoda) raspers appeared in the Middle Triassic, the earliest biting fish in the Eocene, and the earliest rasping echinoids in the Jurassic. Diversity of rasping molluscs (chitons and limpets) has remained virtually unchanged since their appearance. Echinoid raspers underwent an expansion in diversity during the Cretaceous (Bromley, 1975); since then, they have been more diverse (at higher taxonomic levels) than fish and molluscs combined. None of the annelids rasp crustose coralline algae.

d. There is a succession of discrete "destroyer groups" based on the depth of their bites and rasp tracks into crustose corallines. Mollusc rasps are the shallowest, echinoids intermediate, and fish bites are deepest and potentially most damaging.

Because the fossil record of boring members of the destroyer guild is much more complete than for raspers and grazers, their geologic history is included in Part III.

Dweller Guild

The dweller guild represents the residue remaining after all other members of the reef community have been assigned to the constructor, baffler, binder, and destroyer guilds. In terms of either building or destroying the reef framework, the dwellers have a rather benign functional role in the success or failure of the community; dwellers neither build nor destroy. But from a trophic point of view, the dwellers are very important because they include producers, herbivores, carnivores, and decomposers.

Dwellers are epifaunal and include vagile herbivores ("grazers") and carnivores as well as sessile suspension and deposit feeders ("nestlers"). Dwellers occupy space between or on the members of all other guilds (Table 5.11), and, except for some bryozoans, are solitary. Dwellers compete for food and space with animal members of the binder and destroyer guilds and rarely for food with constructors and bafflers. A few dwellers are scavengers and, to make the reef community trophically complete, the dweller guild also includes decomposing microbes in and on the reef framework.

Species diversity of invertebrates in the dweller guild is usually higher than in the other guilds. At high taxonomic levels, members of the dweller guild and epifaunal members of adjacent level-bottom communities are quite similar. In Holocene reefs, the chief members of the dweller guild are the Foraminiferida, Mollusca, Arthropoda, Echinodermata, and "fishes." Taxonomic "censuses" of Holocene shallow-water reef dwellers may be found in Endean (1982) and Patton (1976).

Dwellers vary enormously in form and abundance, but unlike members of the frame-building guilds, dwellers lack a particularly characteristic main growth direction. Dwellers, especially the nestlers, tend to be roughly equidimensional. Finally, in local situations, dwellers may become major contributors to the substrate sediment.

Because of its relatively benign functional role in reef communities, the dweller guild is not emphasized in Parts II and III of this book. However, there are three higher taxa that are dwellers because of their comparatively small size and low biomass in Cenozoic reef communities, yet in Paleozoic reefs, they were very important members of one or more of the frame-builder guilds. These taxa, discussed in both Parts II and III, are: (1) Bryozoa (Cuffey, 1972, 1973): Paleozoic constructors, bafflers, and binders; (2) Brachiopoda (Cooper, 1954; Grant, 1971, p. 1444): Permian constructors and bafflers; and (3) Crinoidea (Macurda and Meyer, 1983; Lane, 1971): Paleozoic bafflers.

Cryptic Subcommunities

Although competition for space among members of the cryptic reef subcommunities is more intense than that for food (as in exposed reef communities and subcommunities), their guild structures are markedly dissimilar. The encrusting colonial organisms that cover cryptic hard substrates grow in sheets usually less than 1 cm thick; many of the dominant bryozoan sheets and runners are less than 2 mm thick. Jackson (1979, p. 528) suggested that the living system for these organisms is two-dimensional.

Logan (1981) reported that in the entrance area of large cavities at Grand Cayman, British West Indies, cryptic species, especially the coralline alga *Peyssonnelia,* completely cover the hard substrate; surface coverage remains at 100% for about 5 m into the caverns and drops to 80% only in the deepest recesses, 8 m from the entrance.

Guild Structure

Ginsburg (1983, p. 150) subdivided the sessile, benthic members that depend on the hard reef surface into three groups based on differences in their modes of life. Although the terminology differs, Ginsburg's groups correspond directly to the spatial resource classes (Table 5.11) upon which guild structure of exposed reef communities is based (i.e., Ginsburg's encrusting mode of life consists of organisms that utilize space along the hard substrate surface and belong to the binder guild, just like reef surface encrusters discussed above; his boring forms are members of the destroyer guild and his attached forms are dwellers). Ginsburg's vagile and nektic "groups" include members of the destroyer and dweller guilds, depending on whether they graze or rasp the substrate as they feed. His burrowing forms are dwellers, analogous to members of the burrowing guild of level-bottom communities.

The chief difference between cryptic reef subcommunities and exposed reef communities and subcommunities lies in the paucity or absence of the constructor and baffler guilds in the former. Cryptic subcommunities are characterized by the exaggerated importance of the binder guild. However, its members lack sufficient skeletal volume or rapid growth rates to become binder/constructors like the exposed crustose coralline algae in algal ridge subcommunities.

The cheilostome bryozoans are particularly abundant and diverse in cryptic subcommunities; they have been described in numerous publications by Cuffey (e.g., 1972, 1973, 1974, 1977, with McKinney, 1982). The role of Holocene cheilostomes (especially anascans, cribrimorphs, and ascophorans) in reef communities is confined to reinforcing the framework by encrusting it; their role in trapping and binding loose sediment is minimal. Because of their relatively slow growth rates, they are poor competitors for space on the exposed reef surface with corals or calcareous algae but are more successful in cryptic habitats against such other "slow growers" as serpulids, sponges, and foraminifera. Their small, fragile zoaria are volumetrically insignificant as frame-builders and are only locally important contributors to the volume of internal sediment.

CENOZOIC REEF GUILDS

Selected Examples

Holocene; Photic Zone

The discussion in Chapters 1 and 2 clearly demonstrates great variability in the taxonomic composition of photic zone reefs; most are coral-dominated, but some are algal-, bryozoan-, vermetid-, serpulid- or oyster-dominated. In Chapter 3, the distinct differences between coral-dominated reefs of the Atlantic Province and those of the Indo-Pacific Province were emphasized.

Even within the same province, there are distinct differences that depend on the location of reefs within the geomorphic zonation of the reef system to which they belong or on their bathymetric occurrence on the seaward slope (Chap. 5). Therefore, it is impossible to describe the guild structure of *the typical* photic zone reef or reef system. However, in Table 5.16A and B, the generalized guild membership and structure of Atlantic Province reefs (such as those on the north coast of Jamaica) and of Indo-Pacific atolls are presented. The main differences in these two shallow-water examples are: (1) the great importance of the Gorgonacea, and hence the baffler guild, in the Atlantic Province (Jamaica); and (2) the great significance of the Melobesoideae and the binder guild in Indo-Pacific atolls.

Table 5.16 lacks data on cryptic subcommunities and the term "importance" is deliberately left undefined. The table also exemplifies two important problems of interpretation:

a. Reef literature is fragmented and, because of their high taxonomic diversity and hence the need for specialized study, most attention has focused on the three frame-building guilds. Most uncertainty, especially with regard to "importance," is in the destroyer and dweller guilds.

TABLE 5.16. Selected Examples of Holocene Reef Guilds Showing Major Taxa in Presumed Order of Relative "Importance"

Constructor	Baffler	Binder	Destroyer	Dweller
A. Jamaica; depth 3–40 m (Zones 7–9 of Goreau and Goreau, 1973; also Kinzie, 1973; Pang, 1973); algal ridge absent				
1. Colonial Scleractinia; 25 spp. common or abundant	1. Gorgonacea; 8 genera, numerous species	1. Porifera; binder/constructor guilds overlap	1. Porifera; at least 9 spp.	1. Mollusca
2. *Millepora*	2. Antipatharia	2. Melobesoideae	2. Scaridae	2. Crustacea
	3. *Millepora*	3. Other algae	3. Echinoidea	
B. Generalized Indo-Pacific atoll algal ridges; depth 0–12 m (Wells, 1957a, p. 615)				
1. Melobesoideae; about 5 genera	1. *Millepora?*	(Binder/constructor guilds overlap)	1. Echinoidea	1. Gastropoda; *Turbo, Trochus*
2. Colonial Scleractinia; about 7 genera, 10 spp.	2. "Fleshy" algae *Turbinaria* *Sargassum*		2. Cirripedia	

C. Little Bahama Bank; depth 1000–1300 m (Mullins et al., 1981)

1. Colonial, non-zooxanthellate Scleractinia; about 2 spp.
2. Solitary non-zooxanthellate Scleractinia; about 14 spp.
3. Antipatharia

  1. Gorgonacea

    1. Porifera
    2. Bryozoa

      1. Porifera

        1. Mollusca
        2. Crustacea
        3. Echinodermata
        4. Serpulida

D. Blake Plateau: depth 750–850 m (Stetson et al., 1962)

1. Colonial, non-zooanthellate Scleractinia; 2 spp.
2. Other colonial Scleractinia; about 4–5 spp.

  1. Gorgonacea

    1. Polychaeta; *Eunicia*

      1. Echinoidea

        1. Actiniaria
        2. Ophiuroidea
        3. Mollusca

b.   Because of morphological plasticity among some members of the frame-building guilds, determining guild membership from taxonomic lists is difficult. Such lists generally do not include information on growth form and packing density, essential for determining guild membership among the various frame-building taxa.

Holocene; Aphotic Zone

The most recent discussion of the fauna in aphotic zone reefs (Mullins et al., 1981) describes the relatively diverse community of Little Bahama Bank (Table 5.16C). The lower diversity community from the nearby Blake Plateau is included for comparison (Table 5.16D). In both these examples, the binder and destroyer guilds are notable for their poor development and the constructor guild for its low diversity.

Late Miocene: Photic Zone

Esteban (1979) has described two intergrading reef types in the western Mediterranean. Type A reefs grew in shallow, warm water of normal marine salinity near tectonically active coasts, are closely associated with terrigenous sediments, and contain a relatively diverse fauna dominated by a variety of colonial corals (Table 5.17A). During the Late Tortonian–Early Messinian existence of Type A reefs, there was a gradual lowering of sea level by at least 200 m that led to progressively increased salinity and evaporite deposition during the Middle Messinian.

During the latest Miocene (Late Messinian), there were repeated sea-level oscillations of 200–400 m; 7 episodes of low sea level and high salinity are represented in the reef complex at Santa Pola, Spain (Table 5.17B) by well-developed stromatolites and associated evaporite minerals ($CaSO_4$ in the stromatolites grading southward to halite in the central Mediterranean basin; Hsu, 1972, pp. 385–392). The salinity-stressed Type B reefs such as those at Santa Pola and Nyar, Spain (Dabrio et al., 1981) are thicker than the Type A reefs but contain a community of very low diversity. Diversity at Nyar appears to be even lower than at Santa Pola. Esteban (1979, p. 184) has also suggested that periodic incursions of colder Atlantic water into the western Mediterranean stressed the latest Messinian Type B reefs and therefore also contributed to their low diversity and simplified guild structure.

Early Paleocene; Aphotic Zone

The earliest Paleocene (Danian) reefs of Denmark and southern Sweden (Table 5.17C) are remarkable for two reasons: (1) they are among the very few reefs of this age anywhere in the world; and (2) bryozoans completely dominate the frame-building guilds. Thomsen (1983) has subdivided the bryozoans into two major growth forms: erect/aborescent and encrusting. The former is more abundant (by zoarial weight) but less diverse and shows evidence of gross zooarial morphologic plasticity from

TABLE 5.17. Examples of Late Miocene and Paleocene Reef Guilds in the Western Mediterranean Showing Major Taxa in Presumed Order of Relative Importance

Constructor	Baffler	Binder	Destroyer	Dweller
A. Late Tortonian–Lower Messinian, normal marine (Type A of Esteban, 1979)				
1. Colonial Scleractinia; up to 15 spp. varied growth forms	1. (Baffler/constructor guilds may overlap) 2. Rhodophyta? 3. Serpulida	1. Bryozoa?	1. Echinoidea	1. Diverse; Bivalvia, Gastropoda, Cirripedia, "forams," *Halimeda*
B. Late Messinian salinity/temperature stressed, Santa Pola, Spain (Type B of Estaban, 1979)				
1. Colonial Scleractinia; 1 genus (*Porites*) "stick-like" coralla up to 4 m high; "sticks" 2–3 cm in diameter	1. (Baffler/constructor guilds overlap)	1. Stromatolites; "encrust" corals and in "heads" up to 5 m high 2. *Porites*; laminar/disk-like coralla; 1–3 cm thick	1. (Not represented)	1. Gastrododa: Cerithidae (an algal turf grazer)
C. Early Paleocene, Denmark; depth 80–150 m (Thomsen, 1983)				
1. Bryozoa; erect, arborescent zoaria; 20 spp.	1. (Baffler/constructor guilds overlap)	1. Bryozoa; encrusting zoaria; 51 spp.	1. (May include Porifera, Echinodermata, Mollusca)	1. Diverse; Echinodermata, Brachiopoda, Mollusca, Alcyonaria, "forams" (benthic), Porifera (SiO_2)

the flanks to the tops of the reefs. Those on the lateral flanks are rigid and arborescent and the branches are circular in cross section; the branched reef top zoaria are oval and the erect zoaria on the flank facing the currents were attached to the substrate by flexible fibers. (There was considerable postmortem zoarial breakage, but Thomsen regarded the effects of subsequent transport as minimal.)

COMMUNITY STRUCTURE: CONCLUSIONS

Guild Structure

The influence of guild structure in reef communities is pervasive! The differences among reefs, regardless of their geographic or bathymetric occurrence or geologic age, are the direct result of differences in their guild structure. Members of reef communities, regardless of their taxonomy, occurrence, or geologic age, can be assigned to the appropriate guild(s) on the basis of their size, growth form and direction, skeletonization, and packing density. The emphasis in Part III is on reconstructing and comparing guild structures of pre-Cenozoic reef communities and interpreting the causes for changes during earth history.

Paleoecologists studying ancient reef communities have three important advantages over those studying non-reef communities:

a.   Most of the crucial biological elements that influence the success or failure of reef communities are preserved in the well-skeletonized, *in situ* members of the constructor and binder guilds.

b.   Competition for space exerts a larger influence over structure of reef communities than that for energy. Because the guild structure of reef communities reflects competition for space and not energy, the major functional biological attributes of reef communities are more amenable to interpretation than in non-reef communities.

c.   In virtually all paleocommunities, the reconstruction and interpretation of their trophic structure are exceedingly subjective; however, in reef communities, trophic structure is less important than guild structure in understanding the overall success of the community.

Niche Structure

The concept of the niche in ecology is perhaps as vague and ill-defined as the concept of reef is in geology (see Glossary). Every ecologist uses the term and generally knows what is meant by it; most never define their meaning and usage. Regardless of these varied usages, it is agreed that niche concerns a *single species*. Therefore, the niche structure of a community consists of the total of the complex interrelations of *each* species in the community. In large, diverse, and complex Holocene communities, such as reefs and reef systems comprised of hundreds or thousands of species, determination of niches and niche structure is impossible. The concept of niche and niche structure is even more vague and impractical in the study of ancient communities due to selective preservation of only the skeletal organisms (discussed at length in Chap. 6).

The concept of guild and guild structure is a level of synthesis above niche and niche structure; it concerns *groups of species* and so is somewhat less precise and more abstract than niche. Nonetheless, this kind of synthesis is the best practical approach to the study of the complexities of very diverse communities such as reefs. Root (1967, p. 335) summarized some advantages of the study of guilds rather than niches as follows:

a.   The guild concept focuses on competitive interactions among all sympatric species (especially intraguild competition). The guild is an ecological category that has been molded by adaptation to the same class of resources by local intraspecific and interspecific competition. By contrast, the niche concept is more diffuse in its emphasis and so may lose sight of the functional role of the guild to which the species belongs.

b.   Guilds cross taxonomic boundaries and so are less limited in scope; species performing several different unrelated roles in the community are considered together.

c.   Because the same guild may be present in more than one community, guild structure may be used to compare communities with regard to species diversity, biomass, productivity, etc.

INTEGRATION OF SIMULTANEOUS PROCESSES AND GUILD STRUCTURE

In the coral reef environment the role of organisms is manifold.

(Orme, 1977b, p. 173)

Earlier it was emphasized that reefs and their environments are primarily biological phenomena and that the biological factors influencing the success or failure of reef communities are in turn affected by interrelations among numerous chemical, physical, and geological factors (Chap. 3). The processes of reef construction (biological construction; binding and early cementation; Fig. 4.1) are strongly modified by the simultaneous processes of destruction, transportation, and deposition of sediments (Chap. 4). Finally, building, destruction, and deposition are strongly influenced by the various reef guilds discussed above. Thus, the progressive synthesis of reef phenomena has now proceeded from factors to processes to guilds and, as noted in Chapter 1, there is continual modification ("feedback") during reef growth among factors, processes, and guilds. Most of this modification is the result of variation in the relative influence over reef growth by different guilds. Reefs are indeed biological phenomena, and the frame-building guilds steal the show!

The direct relationship between the construction process and the constructor guild is unique to reef communities; reefs are constructional features, and organisms of the constructor guild or that overlap the constructor guild are absolutely essential to the process. The destruction process is not unique to reef communities but, for long-term success and inclusion of reefs in the stratigraphic record, construction must exceed destruction. Otherwise, the skeletal debris from former reefs is simply included in the stratigraphic record of adjacent level-bottoms. Destruction includes both physical and biological aspects; their relative importance varies in time and space. Biological aspects are directly affected by the destroyer guild.

Deposition of largely autochthanous skeletal grains produced by destruction of the framework involves a two-step process: (1) reduction of the velocity of sediment-transporting currents (baffling) and (2) holding grains where they have been deposited to prevent their further transport (trapping/stabilization). The baffling aspect of deposition is under direct influence of the baffler guild. Trapping and stabilization are initial steps in consolidation of skeletal grains into the internal reef sediment and involve the binder guild.

Unification and solidification of the internal sediment and reef framework by the processes of binding/encrusting and early cementation are both biological and physical; however, the initial role of the binder guild is clearly paramount. The volume of cement that is precipitated while the adjacent exposed and cryptic surfaces of the reef are alive is generally minor compared with the volume of skeletons of members of the binder guild. During the long geologic history of ancient reef frameworks, there is a slow, progressive increase in volume of late diagenetic cement that transforms the reef and internal sediment into a reef limestone.

Only the process of transporting reef sediments by currents is predominantly abiotic. The continuous breaking, shifting, and sorting of sediment primarily involves physical and geologic factors. However, the configuration of the reef surface is partly determined by the interrelations between constructor and destroyer guilds; these in turn influence turbulence levels within reef systems. In addition, some vagile biters and raspers in the destroyer guild ingest pieces of framework at one location and defecate them elsewhere. However, sediment transportation is largely under control of turbulence and therefore not directly related to guild structure of the reef community.

SUMMARY

In Chapters 2–5 the emphasis has been to establish models for Cenozoic reefs that reinforce and exemplify the general characteristics described in Chapter 1. These characteristics (Table 1.2), regardless of geologic age, consist of (1) a rigid framework dominated by densely packed skeletons of colonial/gregarious organisms in growth position, (2) rapid growth to attain large, heavy skeletons that resist turbulence and provide reefs with positive topographic relief, and (3) high taxonomic diversity.

Some Cenozoic reefs lack one or more of these characteristics (also noted in Chapters 1–5) and thus differ from the typical photic zone model. However, the vast majority of living and fossil Cenozoic reefs display these features. Therefore, Cenozoic reefs provide various analogue models for comparison with pre-Cenozoic reefs (Chapter 6).

Part III focuses on the comparison of the higher taxonomic composition and guild structure of pre-Cenozoic reefs; species composition and niche structure are only rarely considered. However, first the major autecological aspects of important members of the building guilds are considered in Part II.

6

Ancient Reefs

ADEQUACY OF CENOZOIC MODELS

The great success of reefs during the Cenozoic (Eocene–Holocene) can be attributed to their efficient occupation and exploitation of environments controlled by a relatively restricted set of interrelated factors (Chap. 3). Reefs also are dynamic ecosystems characterized by the simultaneous operation of numerous biologic and sedimentologic processes (Chap. 4). These factors and processes influence the organization (composition and structure) of reef communities (Chap. 5).

Most of the non-biologic aspects of Cenozoic reef ecosystems appear to have operated in much the same manner in older ecosystems, whereas the biological aspects have undergone considerable change. These biological differences are due to organic evolution and have involved both the taxonomic composition and structure of reef communities. In fact, the biological differences between Cenozoic and pre-Cenozoic reef communities are so great that most aspects of the Cenozoic community models (Chap. 5) do not make good analogues for pre-Cenozoic reef communities.

In this chapter, emphasis is on the comparison of Cenozoic and pre-Cenozoic reefs and reef complexes with regard to the factors and processes that have influenced their physical properties (size, shape, occurrence, etc.). Comparisons of their biological properties (composition, structure, diversity, etc.) is emphasized in Part III.

Comparison of Factors

Chemical
Salinity is one factor that commonly exerts considerable influence over species diversity in both Holocene and ancient shallow-water reef com-

munities. Virtually all highly diverse Holocene reefs occur in water of normal marine salinity, whereas most examples of low diversity reefs occur in brackish, hypersaline or deep water. The most important builders of large, high diversity Cenozoic reefs (Scleractinia; crustose Corallinacea; Porifera) are remarkably stenohaline. Conversely, the builders of small, low diversity Cenozoic reefs (oysters; vermetids; annelids) are euryhaline and appear to be opportunistically exploiting an environment closed to stenohaline builders; Holocene bryozoans are mostly confined to normal marine water but locally may become builders of poorly skeletonized reefs in slightly brackish water.

Although the environmental factors that influence diversity in Holocene communities are controversial, the same general relationship between high diversity and normal salinity, indicated by abundant stenohaline organisms, appears to exist for ancient communities. Low diversity in ancient reefs may be correctly attributed to non-normal salinity, deep water, or other factors, but highly diverse ancient reefs almost surely are indicative of normal marine salinity. Examples of presumed euryhaline builders of pre-Cenozoic shallow-water reefs include Cyanophyta (builders of stromatolites and thrombolites since the late Precambrian) and some Hippuritacea (Bivalvia; builders of Late Cretaceous reefs).

The general abundance of various algae in most pre-Cenozoic reefs indicates both shallow-water origin and abundant dissolved oxygen and nutrients; abundant skeletal metazoans are also indicative of adequate supplies of dissolved oxygen. The absence of algae may be either the result of deep-water origin or the absence of skeletal algae in the original ancient shallow-water reef communities.

Physical

The association of shallow-water reefs and carbonate rocks is as well-established for the pre-Cenozoic as the Cenozoic. Numerous non-biological attributes of rocks deposited on level-bottoms adjacent to carbonate reefs clearly indicate their shallow-water origin. In the Holocene, the association results from their common origin in warm water and so has been used to infer tropical–subtropical settings for ancient reefs. However, Holocene low diversity reefs dominated by oysters, vermetids, bryozoans, and annelids are not as latitudinally restricted as those dominated by Scleractinia, Corallinacea, and Porifera because the former are somewhat more eurythermal. Temperate-water oyster, vermetid, bryozoan, and annelid reefs commonly occur on non-carbonate Cenozoic and pre-Cenozoic substrates. Conversely, those relatively uncommon high diversity reefs in non-carbonate matrices are mostly of deep-water origin or were transported (mostly by slumping) to deep water.

Rocks adjacent to shallow-water reefs also contain numerous non-biological features indicative of high turbulence. These features, regardless of geologic age or the composition and structure of the reef community, are commonly used by sedimentologists to recognize ancient reef complexes and subdivide them into their component parts (seaward slope, crest, flat/lagoon).

The interrelations among turbulence, turbidity, and water depth in reef complexes strongly influence both their biological and non-biological attributes. One of the major dynamic aspects of the reef environment is the variation in turbulence and turbidity as reefs grow. Their growth commonly enhances overall environmental quality in a "feedback" relationship that augments the growth rate of the whole reef complex. In both Holocene and ancient reef communities, the predominant metazoan builders are suspension feeders that require at least moderate turbulence. Many of them also require low turbidity for survival. These two interrelated influences over metazoan success in reef communities involve their location and efficient binding or early cementation of loose substrate grains.

Geological

Location. In contrast to the general similarity of the chemical and physical factors in Cenozoic and pre-Cenozoic reefs, there are distinct differences in some of the geological factors. In Holocene tropical seas, shallow-water reefs are abundant in both the open oceans, often in association with young volcanoes, and on continental shelves. Pre-Cenozoic oceanic reefs in association with volcanoes are very rare and many have presumably been destroyed by processes of prolonged subsidence into the crust, accretion of continental margins, and subduction at plate boundaries. However, in the Carboniferous Akiyoshi Limestone in southern Japan, there is a rather complete atoll located atop a slightly older oceanic volcanic cone (see Chap. 13); the atoll was then overturned by post-Carboniferous tectonism (Schwan and Ota, 1977).

Pre-Cenozoic continental intrashelf patch reefs and shelf margin barrier reefs are abundant. Ancient patch reefs are much more abundant than barrier reefs, but shelf margins have been preferred locations for the largest and best developed reef systems since the early Proterozoic (e.g., near Great Slave Lake, Northwest Territories, Canada, stromatolite shelf margin reefs in the Pethei Group are dated at about 1.8 billion years; Hoffman, 1974; see Chap. 7).

Ancient patch reefs, especially of Paleozoic age, are also abundant in continental interior locations (cratons). Cenozoic continents are relatively higher than Paleozoic continents, probably due to more active diastrophism; therefore, there were no extensive, shallow, tropical cratonic seas during the Cenozoic comparable to those of the Paleozoic. In North America, the building of cratonic patch reefs was extensive and remarkably continuous (Middle Ordovician–Late Carboniferous except for the Famennian–Early Carboniferous). Despite their interior location, cratonic patch reefs are similar in form to continental shelf patch reefs and were affected by similar chemical and physical factors (Vaughan, 1911).

Size. The Cenozoic Great Barrier Reef system and complex is the largest that has ever existed in the entire 1.8 billion-year history of reef-building. Erosion has reduced the size of all well-documented pre-Cenozoic shelf reefs and reef complexes, but the largest (Late Devonian, Canning Basin, Western Australia; Late Permian, Delaware Basin, western Texas–New Mexico) are less than half the size of the Great Barrier Reef and contain only a small percentage of the total number of individual reefs.

The geological duration (Miocene–Holocene; 15 + million years) of the Great Barrier Reef complex may also exceed the duration of pre-Cenozoic shelf complexes. The maximum thickness of both Cenozoic and older barrier reefs and atolls is related to several factors, but especially subsidence rates of their foundations. The thickest, nearly complete succession (Eocene–Holocene with at least three unconformities) of reef limestones appears to be in the 1400-m long core from Enewetak Atoll, Marshall Islands. For comparison, the total thickness of the exposed Akiyoshi Limestone atoll is about 700 m. The thickest continental shelf margin reef (about 1000 m) may be the Late Devonian Windjana Limestone of the Canning Basin (Playford, 1980). The reefs of the Permian Capitan Limestone marginal to the Delaware Basin are much broader than they are thick (only about 300–400 m; Newell et al., 1953, pp. 105–107) because most of the reef accretion was toward the seaward slope (rather than upward).

Although there are many exceptions, there has been a long-term trend toward increased reef size during geologic history that is partly related to increasing skeletonization of reef framework builders. Late Precambrian to Middle Ordovician reefs, among the smallest reefs known, were built by small, poorly skeletonized and non-skeletal algae (and archaeocyathids during the Early Cambrian). Thus, the concept of minimum size for these reefs is much different than for younger reefs built by larger, well-skeletonized metazoans (i.e., an Early Cambrian *reef* is commonly smaller than a single Cenozoic scleractinian *corallum*).

Typical Holocene aphotic zone reefs are much smaller (in area and thickness) than photic zone reefs. This inverse relation between reef size (and the corallum sizes of the frame-building corals) and water depth is largely due to the absence of symbiotic zooxanthellae in deep-water reefs. Smaller sizes are also characteristic of pre-Cenozoic deep-water reefs.

Shape. The shapes of pre-Cenozoic shallow-water continental shelf and craton reefs are probably as varied as those of Cenozoic shelves. Small, poorly zoned patch reefs are much more plentiful than either elongate barrier reefs and atolls; ancient fringing reefs are rare. The shapes of ancient shelf reefs were surely controlled by the same factors (foundation topography, diastrophism, eustasy, turbulence) as Quaternary reefs. However, glacially induced eustatic sea-level fluctuations were less important than diastrophically induced fluctuations over the long geologic history of reef-building, with the possible exception of the Late Ordovician and Late Paleozoic (see Chap. 15). In addition, the less well-skeletonized pre-Cenozoic reefs were much more easily eroded or destroyed than the unusually well-skeletonized Cenozoic photic zone reefs. From studies of reef terraces up to 20 m thick formed at the end of major Pleistocene transgressions, Geister (1984c) estimated that they could resist erosion for only about 0.5–1 million years during subsequent regressions.

Biological

In addition to the differences between Cenozoic reefs and older reefs due to organic evolution, there is an enormous difference between Holocene and ancient reefs due to the disparity between presence of numerous non-skeletal ("soft-bodied") organisms in the former and their virtual absence in the latter. This difference is frequently discussed as the "preservation potential" of Holocene organisms (see Bambach, 1977, pp. 154–155, and Staff et al., 1985, pp. 220–225, for subtidal level-bottom communities; Schopf, 1978, for intertidal faunas; Lasker, 1976, for effects on diversity measurement).

Preservation Potential. Of all the organisms that have ever built reefs, the soft-bodied cyanophyte- and chlorophyte-built stromatolites and thrombolites have the lowest preservation potential. Those shallow-water features are easily destroyed by physical erosion, herbivore grazing, or bioturbation unless they are strengthened by early cementation or quickly entombed in the sedimentary matrix (Park, 1977; Pratt, 1979; Dravis, 1983). Nonetheless, stromatolites, thrombolites, and other soft-bodied algal and problematical forms are locally of considerable importance in the binder guild of numerous reef communities from the Late Precambrian–Cenozoic. In these situations, the structures produced by these soft-bodied organisms may be preserved in protected reef cavities and by very early cementation in special diagenetic environments (e.g., rapid drying during low tide; high pH) related to their very shallow-water occurrence.

Frost (1977b, pp. 94, 101–102) estimated the percentage of biomass on the exposed surface of Holocene photic zone reefs that is potentially preservable in subsequent fossil reef communities. He found considerable selective preservability that is related to the trophic structure of reef communities. Thus, in Holocene reefs the preservation potential is lowest for producers and highest for well-skeletonized "filter-feeders" and "tentacle-feeders." The reverse approach was undertaken by Gaillard (1983, pp. 235–236). He attempted to reconstruct the original biomass pyramid of a Late Jurassic algal–sponge reef community on the basis of the skeletonized fossils and his estimate of the biomass of the non-skeletal mem-

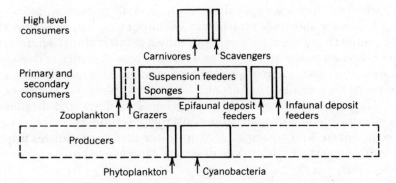

Figure 6.1. Reconstruction of biomass pyramid for Late Jurassic (Oxfordian) sponge–algal reef communities, Jura Mountains, France. Dashed rectangles = estimated biomass lost from original community by non-preservation in fossil community; lowest preservation potential in producer trophic level, highest in consumer levels. (From Gaillard, 1983.)

bers (Fig. 6.1). The greatest loss in biomass from the original to the fossil community was at the producer trophic level, especially the phytoplankton; there was minimal loss of herbivores and carnivores. These differences in preservation potential of members of different trophic levels are the chief factors that limit validity of interpretations of trophic structures of fossil reef communities. Conversely, the generally high preservation potential of members of the constructor and binder guilds, regardless of geologic age, makes interpretation of fossil reef guild structures much more satisfactory. By definition, members of the baffler guild have lower preservation potential than constructors and binders, and the overall preservability of destroyers and dwellers is intermediate (i.e., some are well-skeletonized; others are soft-bodied).

Rasmussen and Brett (1985) studied the preservation potential of Holocene cryptic reef subcommunities and determined that over 60% of the species were unlikely to become fossils. They also estimated that those organisms with high preservation potential, excluding coralline rhodophytes, covered (encrusted) only about 15% of the area occupied by the original subcommunity. If coralline rhodophytes are included, the areal coverage of the preservable subcommunity is over 50%. However, inclusion of the encrusting corallines produces some bias in the Holocene data for use in interpreting fossil cryptic subcommunities because corallines are very uncommon in pre-Cenozoic reefs. So, at least part of the explanation for the general dearth of cryptic subcommunities in ancient reefs may be their low preservation potential. Other explanations include the recent recognition of their importance in Holocene reefs and the lack of awareness by paleoecologists of their potential presence in ancient reefs.

Finally, the *in situ* preservation potential of skeletal organisms is also influenced by such factors as their shape, the efficiency of the destroyer guild, whether they are vagrant or sessile, and, for sessile organisms, the strength of their substrate attachment (Kobluk et al., 1977). Scoffin (1981, p. 501) noted that Paleozoic coralla are much smaller than Cenozoic, were poorly attached to the substrate, and contain less evidence of destruction by borers. Reconstruction of ancient reef communities largely depends on their resistance to destruction and transport by waves, currents, and gravity (Polan and Stearn, 1984). In general, bafflers and dwellers are more susceptible to transport than constructors, binders, and destroyers. The composition and structure of deep-water reef communities are more commonly preserved with fewer effects of transport than shallow-water communities.

Photic Zone–Aphotic Zone Communities. Although there is a continuous bathymetric range in distribution of Holocene reefs from intertidal to about 1500 m (Fig. 2.1), there is a rather distinct difference in both the reef-builders and the overall size of reefs that occurs near the base of the photic zone (about 100 m). Several higher taxa of photic zone reef communities contain symbiotic algae (see Chap. 2) and some authors have suggested that similar algal–metazoan symbioses also occurred at several times in geologic history (reviewed by Cowen, 1983, pp. 433–435; Vacelet, 1983, p. 22). The only symbiotic relationship to be considered here is the one between corals *(sensu lato)* and zooxanthellae. If algal–coral symbioses can be recognized in ancient reefs and the time of its establishment determined, paleoecologists could quantify the rather nebulous current distinction between "shallow" and "deep" into photic and aphotic zone reefs.

Cairns and Stanley (1981) reviewed the literature on scleractinian-built reefs and found only eight adequately documented deep-water examples ranging in age from Late Triassic to Pliocene. The reef size data of Coates and Kauffman (1973) suggest that some deep-water reefs are so small that they could be easily overlooked in the field, which may partly explain the disparity. Another important factor is the general paucity of outcrops of rocks of deep-water origin compared with the abundance of outcropping rocks of shallow-water origin. Continued drilling in the deep sea will undoubtedly increase the number of ancient deep-water reefs; the disparity, however, in the numbers of shallow-versus-deep-water reefs is surely real and not likely to change significantly.

Holocene Scleractinia have several morphological adaptions of both the tissues and the skeleton that appear designed to promote the physiological advantages of their symbiotic association with zooxanthellae. (Some of the skeletal adaptations can be rationalized equally well as advantageous for living in the warmer, more turbulent water of the photic zone.) The most direct approach for recognizing presumed fossil zooxanthellate corals is to determine that they are the phylogenetic ancestors of Holocene corals that are exclusively zooxanthellate. Unfortunately, such determinations are confined to Late Cenozoic species because some Holocene genera and species contain both zooxanthellate and non-zooxanthellate individuals.

Both photic and aphotic zone Holocene reefs are built primarily by colonial corals. Virtually all Holocene meandroid scleractinians are zooxanthellate. Both non-zooxanthellate and zooxanthellate species build
phaceloid and cerioid coralla; such coralla dominate deep-water reefs but
are also present in shallow-water reefs. Astreoid and aphroid rugose corals
are especially abundant in mid-Paleozoic reefs of presumed shallow-water
origin. These data on corallum morphology indicate that shallow-water
reef-building corals have had a long history of more highly integrated
polyps than deep-water colonial corals (Coates and Oliver, 1973), but this
does not prove that they were zooxanthellate.

There is other indirect evidence of fossil non-zooxanthellate scleractinians, such as the fact that most of the colonial forms are branching;
the branches are thin, elongate, cylindrical, and contain relatively large
corallites. The corallite walls and septa in several Holocene genera are
thickened by stereome, which may also fill the interseptal spaces (Mullins
et al., 1981, p. 1009). The coralla are commonly bored, and because the
depositional rate of the surrounding sediments is too slow to support the
branches, they are easily broken into rods that accumulate nearly in place
as small lenses and mounds (Scoffin, 1981; Squires, 1964, Pl. 148; Coates
and Kauffman, 1973). However, polyp and calyx size of both zooxanthellate
and non-zooxanthellate corals may be more closely related to size of food
items than to water depth or temperature (Yonge, 1973).

Solitary corals are less important as builders than colonial. Nonetheless,
if their coralla are large and abundant, they may significantly contribute
to the constructor guild. Holocene aphotic zone solitary coralla are small
and unimportant constructors, whereas zooxanthellate photic zone solitary
coralla are remarkably large (e.g., *Fungia, Scolymia/Mussa*) and locally
of some importance as builders. Solitary rugosans were relatively more
important as constructors of mid-Paleozoic reefs than solitary scleractinians in Mesozoic and Cenozoic reefs (Coates and Oliver, 1973).

The polyps of many colonial scleractinians are separated by coenosarc
tissue containing abundant zooxanthellae. The coenosarc secretes skeletal
material (coenosteum) which is absent in Paleozoic corals and very poorly
developed in deep-water and temperate zone scleractinians, but in many
tropical, photic zone zooxanthellate scleractinians, the polyps are remarkably far apart and connected by well-skeletonized coenosteum. The
degree of coenosteum development, therefore, is only useful for scleractinians; for these corals, it is inversely related to depth.

Using these features of corallum and corallite morphology, several authors have discussed the possible time of origin of the scleractinian–zooxanthellae symbiosis (e.g., Coates and Oliver, 1973, pp. 23–24; Rosen, 1977,
p. 513; Cairns and Stanley, 1981). In perhaps the most complete analysis
of the problem of its origin, Stanley (1981) proposed that it began near
the end of the Triassic.

The question of whether any Paleozoic corals were zooxanthellate is
far from settled. The very limited data on growth rates of all pre-Cenozoic

corals (Table 3.4) are more similar to growth rates of Holocene non-zoox-anthellates (Table 3.5) than to rates for Holocene zooxanthellate corals. This suggests that pre-Cenozoic corals were non-zooxanthellate. Furthermore, if these corals were zooxanthellate, the question remains as to when the symbiosis began. Page et al. (1984) suggested that it could have occurred as early as the Silurian!

Scleractinian species diversity is also inversely related to depth. In Holocene reefs less than 20 m deep, there are often 50–100 species, whereas in most aphotic zone reefs, there are only 1–5 species. (The 16 species recognized by Mullins et al., 1981, are many more than had been previously identified from a single area.) Similarly, the Miocene–Pliocene deep-water reefs in New Zealand contain only 1 coral species (Squires, 1964). However, the use of species diversity alone may be limited to the Cenozoic; most Mesozoic reefs of presumed shallow-water origin have fewer than 15 scleractinian species, while many mid-Paleozoic shallow-water reefs have more than 15 coral species.

Other reef organisms besides the corals may be useful depth indicators. For example, algae are clear indicators of the photic zone, but the absence of algae ("negative data") does not indicate either deep or shallow water. Again, numerous mid-Paleozoic reefs of presumed shallow-water origin lack both skeletal and non-skeletal algae. In post-Paleozoic reefs, an abundance of pelagic microorganisms in the internal sediment may clearly indicate deep-water origin; an abundance of benthic bioclasts of high taxonomic diversity usually indicates shallow-water origin.

Finally, there are many sedimentologic features in the rocks enclosing ancient reefs that are often as valuable as the biological features discussed above in determining water depths at the time of reef growth (see Cairns and Stanley, 1981; Shinn, 1983; Mullins et al., 1981). Because neither lateral nor bathymetric ecological zonations (subcommunities) are well developed in pre-Cenozoic reefs, several geologic features commonly have been used with more success to determine spatial and bathymetric relationships in ancient reef complexes (J.L. Wilson, 1975; Longman, 1981) than ecological zonations.

Comparison of Processes

Although the organic community influences to some extent virtually all processes operating simultaneously in reefs systems (Fagerstrom, 1985), these processes may be subdivided into those that are predominantly biological (construction, binding/encrusting, and organic destruction) and those that are predominantly non-biological (physical destruction, transportation, deposition, and early cementation; Fig. 4.1). The present discussion emphasizes those processes that are most similar among reefs regardless of age. Dissimilarities due largely to differences in composition and structure of ancient reef communities are emphasized in Part III.

Construction

The construction process is the most unique aspect of reefs and distinguishes them from level-bottoms and other hardgrounds. It has distinguished reefs throughout their history, despite the fact that the degree of rigidity and magnitude of relief have varied considerably since the earliest reefs were formed almost two billion years ago by non-skeletal cyanophytes. There is a continuous spectrum from small, low, non-skeletal or poorly skeletonized structures to large, well-skeletonized reefs of high relief (wall reefs of many authors) that has been the basis for an extended debate over what is and is not a reef. There is little similarity in the rigidity of organic frameworks of well-skeletonized Cenozoic reefs dominated by the constructor guild and the poorly skeletonized, baffler/binder-dominated Paleozoic and early Mesozoic reefs built by sponges, algae, some corals, brachiopods, and bryozoans.

Although the construction process is essential to reefs, the manner of construction, the organisms involved, and the final products have varied enormously in pre-Cenozoic reefs. Cenozoic reefs are poor models for most pre-Cenozoic reefs, and the construction processes involved are not easily compared. Most pre-Cenozoic reef builders grew more slowly and were less well-skeletonized and densely packed than their Cenozoic analogues.

Binding

The binding process was of relatively greater importance in pre-Cenozoic reefs and was generally performed by non-skeletal or poorly skeletonized organisms. Among Cenozoic reefs, the distinction between photic zone and aphotic zone reefs is closely correlated with the need for binding and the degree of development of the binder guild. One characteristic of Cenozoic aphotic zone reefs is the virtual absence of the binder guild compared with the usual tightly bound photic zone reefs. Conversely, some pre-Cenozoic shallow-water reefs are so completely dominated by the constructor guild that it has essentially excluded the binder guild.

The greater importance of binding and greater diversity of higher taxa in the binding guild in pre-Cenozoic reefs seems to have been more important in providing rigidity to the framework than in typical scleractinian-dominated Cenozoic reefs.

Destruction

As a consequence of these significant differences in size, degree of skeletonization, and importance of the construction and binding processes, there were also some major differences in the non-biological processes of pre-Cenozoic reef complexes. Physical destruction is closely related to turbulence, water depth, skeletonization of the builders and their packing density, and to biological destruction or weakening of the framework. Poorly skeletonized pre-Cenozoic shallow-water reefs in areas of high turbulence were more easily destroyed than analogous Cenozoic reefs; if they were exposed to subaerial erosion by diastrophism or eustasy, they were also more easily removed. Thus, the overall proportion of deeper-water reefs in pre-Cenozoic rocks may be higher than for the Cenozoic. However, the products of this destruction (grains; clasts) were subject to essentially the same non-biological processes of transportation and deposition.

Baffling

The significance of non-skeletal bafflers in pre-Holocene reefs is so poorly known that their overall importance in the baffling process can only be judged indirectly by the abundance of fine-grained internal sediment. Poorly skeletonized bafflers, such as some sponges and erect bryozoans, are more abundant in pre-Cenozoic than in fossil Cenozoic reefs. Although there are numerous exceptions, the mud content of the internal sediment in pre-Cenozoic reefs also is generally higher than in Cenozoic reefs. This suggests lower turbulence, which could be due either to efficient baffling by organisms or to living in deeper water.

Conversely, the interrelations among turbulence, turbidity, and water depth in reef complexes strongly affect both their biological and non-biological attributes. One of the most dynamic aspects of the general reef environment is the modification of turbulence and turbidity that occurs as the reefs grow vertically and laterally. Reef growth often enhances the environmental quality in a "feedback" system that augments its own success. In both Holocene and ancient reef communities, the predominant metazoan builders are suspension feeders that require moderate turbulence and low turbidity. These two factors are also related to reef location and to the efficiency of the baffling, binding, and cementation processes. In shallow-water environments, these same processes are important for distinguishing reefs from level-bottoms and such non-reef structures as mud mounds and shell heaps.

Transportation and Deposition

Because of the overall similarity of the predominantly non-biological processes that operate in reef complexes, J. L. Wilson (1975, pp. 24–29, 350–369), Longman (1981, pp. 22–25), and others have established models for the study of ancient carbonate rocks. The major units ("facies belts") of these models are based largely on sedimentologic rather than biologic features and so are unrelated to the geologic age of the reef complex. Sedimentologic features are most strongly influenced by physical, chemical, and geologic factors and the processes of destruction, transportation, and deposition. Lateral and bathymetric differences in turbulence are of major significance in the origin and distribution of facies belts; use of the models in exploration for natural resources in ancient reef complexes depends upon presumed analogous relations among these same factors and processes regardless of geologic age. The great success in these exploration efforts attests to the generality of Wilson's model (among others), the overall greater influence of dominantly non-biological aspects of reef environments in the origin of facies belts, and the constancy of non-biologic factors and processes during the last 2 billion years. Of Wilson's "nine standard facies belts," biological factors and processes outweigh the non-biological in only one (his belt Number 5: "Organic Build-up").

Summary

Abiotic Factors/Processes. The Cenozoic models presented above are far more adequate and useful for recognizing and interpreting the predominantly non-biological aspects of pre-Cenozoic reef complexes and carbonate level-bottom substrates than they are for reef communities. J. L. Wilson's (1975) sedimentologic model for interpreting depositional systems adjacent to reefs clearly demonstrates the adequacy of chemical, physical, and geological factors and the physical/mechanical processes of destruction, transportation, and deposition for establishing abiotic Cenozoic analogues for the interpretation of pre-Cenozoic rocks of level-bottom origin. Thus, sedimentologic models based on abiotic factors and processes include a level of generality that is much greater than biologic models based on Cenozoic communities.

Biotic Factors/Processes. Because reefs are predominantly biological phenomena and have evolved as the result of organic evolution and extinction in the marine biosphere, Cenozoic reef communities are clearly inadequate models for the interpretation of pre-Cenozoic communities. The greatest inadequacies involve comparisons of the taxonomic composition of reef communities through geologic time. However, because these communities have evolved and the influence of the biological factors and processes are so pervasive in reef ecosystems, there has also been a long history of changing environments within and immediately adjacent to reefs.

These aspects of reef community evolution chiefly involve changes in the degrees of skeletonization of the building taxa and the relative importance of each of the building guilds. Thus, Cenozoic reef communities are characterized by unusually well-skeletonized builders and domination of the building process by the constructor guild. By contrast, most builders of pre-Cenozoic reefs were less well-skeletonized and the binder and baffler guilds often overlapped with the constructor guild and played relatively greater roles in the building process. Consequently, Cenozoic reefs are typically larger, stronger, and more distinctly zoned than pre-Cenozoic reefs and have greater topographic relief. Cenozoic reef communities are more diverse and guild overlap is less common than in pre-Cenozoic communities.

The greatest similarities between Cenozoic and pre-Cenozoic reef communities concern their guild structures. Therefore, in Part III, the guild structure model for Cenozoic reef communities (Chap. 5) will provide the main basis for comparison of reef communities through geologic time.

TERMINOLOGY AND NOMENCLATURE

> . . . these bioherms at least have most of the sedimentologic/biologic attributes
> that characterize reefs throughout the geologic record . . . The reefs are typically
> biconvex bioherms (dilophoids) . . . sometimes forming reef complexes . . . Each
> bioherm is composed of many small loaf-shaped mounds (spherical calyptra)
> . . . and are best classified as 'stratigraphic reefs.'
>
> (James and Debrenne, 1980, p. 659)

Because of the various inadequacies of the Cenozoic model, attempts to
apply it directly to recognition and interpretation of pre-Cenozoic reefs
have been plagued with problems and controversies (e.g., Klovan, 1974;
Longman, 1981, p. 9). Unfortunately, the solution to these problems and
controversies has often been so elusive that is has led to an enormous
proliferation of terms that have been proposed, defined, revised, and re-
defined in numerous ways to fit particular cases and their interpretation.

Ancient reefs and similar features have been classified and reclassified
descriptively and genetically by numerous authors; there is still no broadly
accepted terminology or classification (see Nelson et al., 1962, Vogel, 1963,
Heckel, 1974, and Gaillard, 1983, pp. 115–123, 286–288 for extended discussions of terminology and classification). Some authors (e.g., J. L. Wilson, 1975, pp. 20–24) have defined their use of terms, a bewildering pro-
cedure for the non-specialist and certainly an impediment to scientific
understanding and progress. This "nomenclature hurdle" is particularly
difficult for Holocene reef ecologists who wish to compare Holocene and
ancient reef communities. The hurdle is readily apparent to anyone trying
to understand the quotation by two eminent geologists at the beginning
of this section.

In this book, a very broad view has been purposely taken regarding
the long-debated question of exactly what constitutes a reef (Chap. 1).
The spectrum from reef to non-reef is impossible to divide objectively, but
prime emphasis here has been on presumed rigidity, topographic relief,
abundant *in situ* builders, and minimum reef size; none of these attributes
can be objectively defined in ancient reefs because all have evolved during
geologic history.

In addition, considerable effort has been given to the consistent use of
a minimum number of essential terms; other terms and various synonyms
are included in the Glossary for completeness. In choosing which terms
are "essential," some consideration has also been given to priority among
synonymous terms. The following terms, and distinctions between them,
are here regarded as "essential"; they have been used in Part I, are included in the Glossary, and are used extensively in the remainder of this
book:

    a.   Reef, biostrome, and level-bottom: the distinction among them in-
        volves size, shape, rigidity, and topographic relief and so is crucial.

b.   Reef framework, internal sediment, and cement.

c.   Reef, reef system, and reef complex.

d.   Reef location and shape: fringing, barrier, patch, and atoll.

e.   Geomorphic zonation of reefs: seaward slope, reef crest, algal ridge, reef flat, and lagoon.

There is no need for separate sets of terms for Holocene and ancient reefs, photic and aphotic zone reefs (Teichert, 1958; Squires, 1964), "large" and "small" reefs (Kauffman and Sohl, 1974, pp. 429–443), "stratigraphic" and "ecologic" reefs (Dunham, 1970), coral reefs and algal reefs (Zhuravleva and Miagkova, 1977), "mature" and "immature" reefs (Longman, 1981), "true" reefs and "reefoid limestones," etc. Most of these distinctions merely skirt the fundamental issues, such as:

1.   Presence and size of framework and the adequacy of the framework to provide rigidity and topographic relief. These matters are interpretive and involve decisions regarding the adequacy of the Cenozoic model. There is indeed value in such descriptive terms as bioherm, buildup, etc., but their use merely postpones the fundamental question of whether the feature is a reef.

2.   If the feature is deemed a reef, numerous subsidiary questions may follow regarding its location (oceanic, continental shelf, craton), shape, biologic composition and structure, zonation, etc.

3.   Last are the interpretive questions regarding origin of the reef, various factors and processes operating during its history, the community guild structure, cause of death, etc.

CLASSIFICATION OF REEF LIMESTONES

There is a vast difference in the way that a biologist, a sedimentologist, and a carbonate petrologist view and classify a reef and a reef complex. To the biologist, a reef consists of the thin, living veneer on top of the framework, extending (in a broad sense) to the organisms immediately adjacent to the framework. To the sedimentologist, a reef is the framework and associated internal sediments (Fig. 6.2); a broader view may include the adjacent level-bottom sediments. To the carbonate petrologist, a reef consists of the reef rocks and all diagenetic processes involved in transforming the organisms to fossils and sediments to rocks. Very often the petrologist is even more interested in why the rocks contain or don't contain hydrocarbons or metallic minerals regardless of whether they are in the framework or the adjacent rocks of level-bottom origin. The following discussion is limited to the classification of the rocks transformed from the reef framework and the internal sediment; discussion of the classification of carbonate rocks formed from level-bottom sediments is found

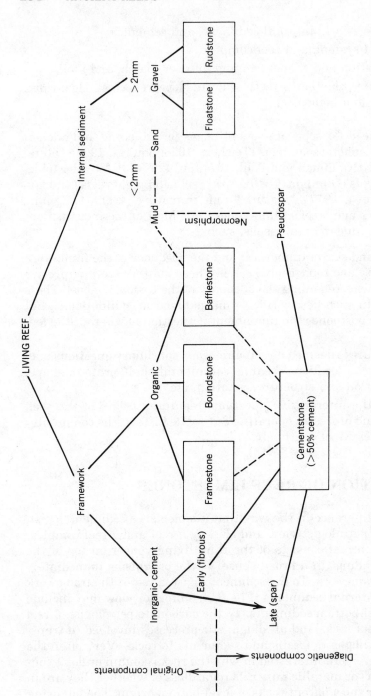

Figure 6.2. A descriptive/genetic classification of reef limestones incorporating biologic (the living reef; framework; internal sediment), and petrologic (original and diagenetic components) aspects. The major types of reef limestones are indicated by boxes. The terms framestone, bafflestone, floatstone, and rudstone were proposed by Embry and Klovan (1971) and boundstone by Dunham (1962). Grain sizes of internal sediment are influenced by nature of the skeletal organisms and level of turbulence. Floatstones and rudstones are also present in level-bottoms. Bafflestones of low skeletal volume may be mud mounds. Cementstones are composed of spar of three origins (solid lines). Mud-to-sand size sediments are present in varying amounts in all reef limestones and adjacent level-bottom limestones (see Folk, 1959, 1962 and Dunham, 1962 for their classification).

in Folk (1959; 1962) and Dunham (1962) and of "buildups" in Heckel (1974).

Because of the generally rapid vertical and lateral variations in lithology of reef limestones, their classification must be based on a much broader view than can be gained from a hand specimen and thin section. A typical reef contains several types of limestones that must be carefully sampled in order to determine the proportions of framework, internal sediment, each of the building guilds, and cement. Large, polished slabs such as those described by Nagai (1985, pp. 3–4, and Figs. 4, 5, 7, 8) are very useful for properly classifying reef limestones. Nearly all modern classifications are based on reefs of presumed shallow-water origin and are both descriptive and genetic. Some informal classifications emphasize the taxonomic composition of the framework (e.g., algal reefs, coralgal reefs, sponge mounds) and others emphasize the sizes and shapes of the builders.

Basic Components

Original
There are three basic components of reef limestones: framework, internal sediment, and cement. The framework and internal sediment are regarded as original, in the sense that they were added to the reef while it was alive, and in some reefs part of the early diagenetic cement was also formed at this time (Fig. 6.2); most of the cement was formed by diagenetic processes after the reef was dead.

Framework. The framework provides rigidity and topographic relief to the living reef; it resists compaction/destruction during diagenesis and produces the original dip of the flanking bedded deposits and draping of the overlying beds. It consists of two components:

a.   *Organic:* the *in situ* or nearly *in situ* skeletons of the reef-builders (members of the constructor, binder, and baffler guilds) when it was growing. If skeletons of closely spaced *in situ* builders are in contact, ideally they originally grew that way or were organically bound together (organic contact) while alive. During compaction, the well-skeletonized constructors resist breakage most effectively, the binders are intermediate, and the weak skeletons of the erect-growing bafflers are generally broken soon after death as well as by later compaction. Bafflers are rarely found in their original growth position (cf. Embry and Klovan, 1971, p. 737), and yet their skeletons may be abundant in the internal sediment and indicate that their role was important to the original frame-building process. The non-skeletal bafflers may also have been significant, but their former presence in ancient reef communities is almost entirely speculative.

b.   *Inorganic:* the early cement formed on the walls of pores that were filled with surging seawater at the time the reef was alive. This cement is almost always of much less volumetric importance than the organic framework; it does help, however, to stabilize loose internal sediment and support the organic framework.

Internal Sediment. Most internal sediment of a living reef consists of skeletal fragments (grains) derived from members of the reef community itself, transported into the internal pores of the reef framework, and deposited there. Only fortuitously are fragments oriented in growth position; instead, they are found in stable mechanical contact. The size, shape, degree of sorting, and arrangement of skeletal grains (graded, geopetal, bedded, etc.) of the internal sediment vary greatly from pore to pore in the framework and usually differ considerably from the adjacent level-bottom. In most living reefs, the total non-skeletal pore (caverns, caves, tunnels, etc.) volume exceeds the volume of the framework; few of the pores are completely filled with sediment and they may house an important cryptic subcommunity.

Classification of internal sediment is based on entirely different parameters (grain size, sorting, packing of grains, etc.) than classification of the framework. Mud- and sand-rich internal sediment is so similar to level-bottom sediment that their classification and terminology are the same (Folk, 1959, 1962; Dunham, 1962). Internal sediments rich in gravel (>10% of volume) are classified as floatstones if the gravel grains are not in contact or as rudstones if they are in contact (Fig. 6.2). These same terms are also used to classify such non-reef rocks as flanking beds, shell heaps (Pl. 4), and debris flows.

Diagenetic

Filling of pores by cement in both the organic framework and internal sediment may begin while the reef is still alive, but most cement is formed by precipitation of calcite spar from freshwater long after the reef is dead (reviewed in Schröder and Purser, 1986). Skeletal pore volumes vary greatly and depend on the mineral composition and structure of the original organisms and the degree of leaching prior to cementation. Cement may be precipitated rather continuously during a prolonged diagenetic "event" or in several stages ("generations").

The largest pores generally begin as open, interconnected cavities that are partially filled with internal sediment and seawater. During diagenesis, these pores are filled with calcite spar cement of various crystal sizes to varying degrees of completeness. However, in both the organic framework and the internal sediment, incomplete cementation is very common, leaving variably porous or vuggy reef limestones. These pores and vugs may in turn contain abundant hydrocarbons or become preferred sites of metallic mineralization.

Some reef cements are formed by the neomorphism (crystal growth) of original lime mud. Such cements generally consist of much smaller crystals (pseudospar) than the pore-filling cement crystals. When both these types of cement are abundant, their volume may locally exceed that of the framework or internal sediment and form a reef cementstone (Fig. 6.2; Pl. 3*b*). Cementstones are present in highly porous–cavernous and fractured (fissure fillings; neptunian dikes; Pl. 3*a*) reefs and are of local value in understanding the original nature of the reef community.

Classification of Organic Frameworks

The presence of an organic framework makes reefs unique and so it is the recognition, reconstruction, and classification of these frameworks that are most important in reef paleoecology and carbonate petrology. The most widely used system of terminology and classification of organic frameworks was proposed by Embry and Klovan (1971, pp. 733–737) as an expansion of the earlier carbonate rock classifications of Folk (1959, 1962) and Dunham (1962; see also Tsien, 1981, and James, 1983, p. 347). The organic frameworks are subdivided in the Embry and Klovan classification into intergradational units on the basis of the nature of the frame-building organisms of the original reef community (Fig. 6.2). These units correspond to the inferred relative importance of each frame-building guild (i.e., constructor, binder, and baffler guilds) described in Chapter 5.

Framestone
Framestones are organic reef frameworks dominated by the constructor guild. The *in situ* skeletons of the constructors support the reef framework and in life provide the structural base for vertical accretion of the reef (Pls. 2, 7). Before and after death, their skeletons are generally broken by destructive processes (Chap. 4) and may suffer additional minor breakage after burial by compaction of the framework. In such cases, the petrologist must restore the broken portion of the organic framework in his mind and assess the relative significance of the building guilds to classify the reef limestone correctly.

Boundstone
Boundstones (bindstones of some authors) are frameworks dominated by the binder guild. Skeletons of the binders partly support the organic framework (Pls. 20*b*, 24, 25*a*) and in life provide the structural base for much of the lateral accretion of the reef. Their skeletons are more commonly preserved *in situ* than members of any other frame-building guild because their laterally expanded growth form resists destruction during life, before burial, and by compaction after burial. Boundstones generally require less "mental restoration" by by the reef petrologist than any other organic framework. The chief difficulty is determining the frame-building roles of some volumetrically important extinct taxa discussed in Part II

(e.g., *Tubiphytes, Archaeolithophyllum, Renalcis;* Babcock, 1977; Toomey, 1979; Riding and Toomey, 1972).

Bafflestone

The ingredients for the recognition of a bafflestone are the presence of a large number of in situ stalk-shaped fossils, and a good imagination on the part of the geologist.

(Embry and Klovan, 1971, p. 737)

Bafflestones are organic frameworks dominated by the baffler guild. Bafflers include non-skeletal (flexible), poorly skeletonized (semirigid), and well-skeletonized (rigid; see Table 5.13) organisms whose chief function is to baffle (reduce) current velocities across the reef surface. Non-skeletal bafflers (e.g., Antipatharia, Gorgonacea, algae, "sea grass") may leave traces of their former presence (similar to biocementstone of Tsien, 1981), but much more often leave no record. Such organisms and sediments have no rigidity and so are not reefs, but they may have minor topographic relief and may have played a major role in the formation of some mud mounds (discussed in Chap. 1).

Of much greater concern to the petrologist is the establishment of the original functional importance of the numerous poorly skeletonized bafflers (e.g., pelmatozoans, sponges, some bryozoans, skeletal algae, etc.) that are easily broken after death and deposited as fragments in the internal sediment (Pl. 5b) and the adjacent level-bottom. Contrary to the strict original definition of bafflestone (Embry and Klovan, 1971), the poorly skeletonized bafflers are almost never preserved *in situ;* nonetheless, their role in life may have been critical to the success of the reef-building process.

As indicated by Embry and Klovan (see above quotation), the "mental" reconstruction of the role of the baffler guild may require considerable imagination. The recognition of most bafflers is based on the size and abundance of their fragments in the internal and adjacent level-bottom sediment (Pl. 4b). Even moderately rigid bafflers (e.g., short, broad, cylindrical-bladed bryozoans, stromatoporoids, sponges, algae; Table 5.13) are rarely preserved *in situ.* Most are broken soon after death; the others rarely survive compaction and therefore are not preserved in their original erect growth habit.

Bafflestones are indeed the most difficult frameworks to recognize and reconstruct. In the narrow definition of Embry and Klovan (requiring *in situ* preservation), they are almost unknown. In the more "imaginative" sense of their definition, the relative importance of the baffler guild can often be "mentally" reconstructed, but only rarely is it the dominant frame-building guild. In fact, if the bafflers are dominant (e.g., the late Paleozoic bioherms described by Pray, 1958), the matter of original rigidity of the structure must then be considered. Such structures are usually also mud-rich and thus may be more similar to mud mounds than to reefs. The distinction among non-skeletal and weakly skeletal mud mounds, shell heaps, and reefs is highly interpretive in the stratigraphic record.

In conclusion, "pure" (end-member) bafflestones are rare as organic frameworks of ancient reef limestones. The baffler guild, however, may have a very large role in the reef construction process. In the building of ancient reefs, the importance of the baffler guild must be interpreted (reconstructed) from the sedimentary debris within and adjacent to the organic framework dominated by the constructor and/or binder guilds. In most reef communities, the baffler guild is accessory to the constructor and binder guilds so far as the total building process is concerned.

Other Classifications (not included in Fig. 6.2)

In Tsien's (1981) classification of reef limestones, framestones and bafflestones as defined by Embry and Klovan (1971) are recognized and the roles of the organisms present in each of these units is discussed in detail. Tsien did not relate these limestones to reef guild structure but did subdivide boundstones (of Dunham, 1962, and herein; bindstones of Embry and Klovan, 1971) into those dominated by sediment-binding organisms (coverstones) and those dominated by encrusting organisms (bindstones). In Chapter 4, the distinction between binding and encrusting was discussed, but because the processes (Fig. 4.1) and the organisms involved are so similar, as well as the end result (a boundstone), the difference between coverstones and bindstones is not considered to be very significant.

Tsien (1984) also discussed the importance of several taxa in ancient (especially Devonian) reefs as indicators of various environmental factors but did not formally relate the organisms to reef processes. Therefore, Tsien's interpretation of the roles of various organisms in the overall construction process and the structure of reef communities is quite different from the views presented here. Hence, his classification differs substantially from the one presented in Figure 6.2.

Cuffey (1985) noted the greater diversity of colony growth forms among bryozoan reef-builders than among most other higher taxa of builders and proposed a classification of reef limestones to accommodate this diversity. His discussion expands the number of types of organic frameworks (and terms to denote them) to nine. For comparison, Folk (1959, 1962) and Dunham (1962) recognized one type of reef limestone, Embry and Klovan (1971) recognized three, and Tsien (1981) recognized five; Cuffey recognized four of Tsien's types and added five new ones. With the addition of each new type of organic framework, the distinctions among them have become more subjective. This is particularly true when distinctions are based on differences in growth forms of easily broken builders, such as bryozoans, that played accessory roles as bafflers in the reef construction process.

For example, both Tsien (1981) and Cuffey (1985) have discussed the

importance of branching forms; Tsien regards them as the most characteristic elements of bafflestones. Cuffey subdivides the former bafflestones
into two types of frameworks on the basis of the spacing (packing density)
of the skeletons:

  a. *Bafflestone:* the skeletons are more widely spaced and their chief
role is to baffle currents and enhance deposition of sediment; hence, during
life they are relatively deeply buried in trapped sediment (Cuffey, personal
communication, 1985). This is essentially the same usage as Tsien's and
that used here.

  b. *Branchstone:* the skeletons are more closely spaced and the space
between branches contains less sediment, and in some cases a cryptic
subcommunity, and when lithified are filled with a relatively greater volume of cement.

  This distinction is ecologically important and theoretically quite objective. However, because of the problems in recognizing members of the
baffler guild and estimating their overall importance in the construction
process, the practical petrologist cannot distinguish Cuffey's bafflestones
from branchstones in most reefs, except in those rare cases where the
baffler guild is preserved *in situ*. Branchstones (of Cuffey) supporting a
cryptic fauna were formed by well-skeletonized members of the constructor
guild and are here regarded as framestones. Cuffey (1985) includes
branchstones as a subdivision (?) of framestones, so the difference is largely
a matter of the relative emphasis to be given to branching skeletal organisms as constructors versus bafflers. This depends in turn on their
skeletonization, size, and packing density. Typical large branching corals
construct reefs, whereas small, fragile, branching bryozoans baffle currents. But in many early Paleozoic, Paleocene, and a few Holocene reefs,
bryozoans overlap among all three building guilds (constructor, binder,
and baffler) and their relative importance in each may be very difficult
to determine.

Example: Classification of the Capitan Limestone (Permian; Southwestern U.S.)

Is This a Reef ?

Numerous authors have participated in the 60-year long debate regarding
the reef-versus-non-reef origin of the Capitan Limestone of western Texas
and southeastern New Mexico (summarized by Toomey and Babcock, 1983,
pp. 237–250). The Capitan is very well-exposed along the summit and
steep south-facing escarpment of the Guadalupe Mountains (King, 1948,
Pls. 1, 4, 12; Harms, 1974, Fig. 1) for a distance of about 65 km; it can
be traced in the subsurface around nearly the entire margin of the Delaware Basin, making the total length nearly 600 km (Fig. 6.3).

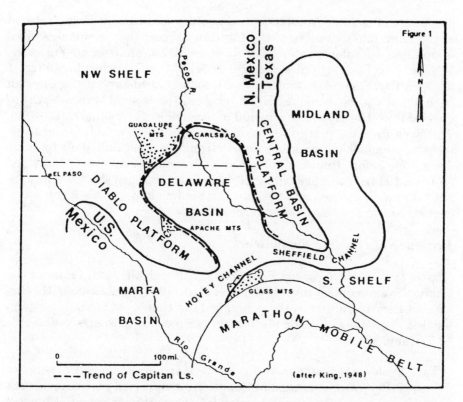

Figure 6.3. Distribution of major tectonic elements in the southwestern United States that influenced the location of Permian reefs. The major outcrop area of the Late Permian Capitan Limestone is in the Guadalupe Mountains (discussed here and in Example 13.7); that of Early Permian reefs (Example 13.6) is in the Glass Mountains. (After Babcock, 1977, modified from King, 1948.)

During deposition, the original framework and sediments of the Capitan occupied the margin between the intracratonic Delaware Basin and the adjacent shelf or platform that nearly surrounded the basin. Because of this shelf margin location, some authors have regarded the Capitan as a barrier reef complex, but this term is valid only to describe it as a barrier to the free interchange of water and sediment between the shelf and basin areas. It is not a barrier reef in the sense used for Holocene open ocean reefs or the Great Barrier Reef (see Chap. 3).

The answer to the question of whether the Capitan Limestone is an ancient reef complex will be examined by attempting to answer some subsidiary questions that were posed earlier in this chapter and that bear directly on the reef-versus-non-reef problem.

Presence of Topographic Relief
The width of the framework crest was relatively narrow (a few hundred meters) at the time of deposition of each chronostratigraphically equiv-

alent part of the Capitan. Some sedimentary and paleontologic features of the more massive parts of the Capitan suggest that it was deposited in shallow, turbulent water (Newell et al., 1953, pp. 8–9; cf. Yurewicz, 1977, p. 75). The original structural relief of the Delaware Basin (crest to basin floor) decreased during the depositional history of the Capitan from about 600 m to about 550 m, whereas the basinal water depth increased from 10–15 m to nearly 600 m (Newell et al., 1953, pp. 187–190). The slope from the margin to basin floor was steep enough for large allochthanous blocks and other debris from the crest and shelf to move downslope before final deposition in less steep, deeper-water locations (Harms, 1974). Water over the shelf (reef flat) remained shallow throughout Capitan deposition and periodically became hypersaline when interconnections to the basin became restricted.

Presence of Organic Framework

Higher taxa; Growth forms; Functions. Although the total fauna of the Capitan is exceedingly diverse (Newell et al., 1953, pp. 227–232), the discussion here is limited to those higher taxa that were potential framebuilders. These taxa include (for a more complete discussion, see Example 13.7, Chap. 13):

a. Problematic algae (*Archaeolithophyllum; Archaeolithoporella; Tubiphytes;* discussed in Chaps. 7, 13) of varied growth forms but predominantly laterally expanded sheets (Pl. 3); potential binders (Babcock, 1977).

b. Phylloid green algae (*Eugonophyllum,* etc.; discussed in Chaps. 7, 13) and the dasycladacean *Mizzia;* erect, leaflike, and cylindrical growth forms; potential bafflers.

c. Calcareous sponges (discussed in Chaps. 8, 13) of varied growth forms (and potential functions) from short, erect, cylindrical (bafflers) to sheetlike (binders).

d. Fenestrate bryozoans (discussed in Chap. 10); potential bafflers.

None of these taxa are well-skeletonized when compared with major Holocene frame-builders, so it has been argued that they could not form a wave- or current-resistant framework. The Capitan clearly is not a framestone. Furthermore, many of the potential builders (especially the erect calcareous algae and sponges) are not in their original growth positions and so may have been transported to their present locations in the Capitan. However, when their degree of skeletonization is compared with several other Paleozoic and early Mesozoic frame-building higher taxa, their potential to build reefs seems much greater. The abundance of organisms of the baffler guild suggests that it was of major importance in the building process. Large parts of the Capitan are bafflestones.

Packing Density. The Capitan contains a variable proportion of lime mud and sand. In the parts with abundant mud (>50%), the packing density of the above potential frame-builders may not have been sufficient to make a wave- or current-resistant structure. However, many other ancient reefs contain at least as much lime mud as the Capitan Limestone (discussed in Chaps. 1, 4, 11). In fact, the high mud content may demonstrate the overall effectiveness of the baffler and binder guilds.

Presence of Inorganic Framework
Beginning with Newell (1955; 1971, p. 6), numerous authors (e.g., Schmidt, 1977; Babcock, 1977; Yurewicz, 1977; Mazullo and Cys, 1978) have discussed the origin of reef cements and concluded that a significant portion of the Capitan Limestone cement is of early diagenetic submarine origin (Pl. 3*b*).

Conclusions
Evidence derived from study of the abundance, skeletonization, and growth forms of the most important skeletal organisms and the early diagenetic cement indicates that the Capitan had a rigid framework. The presence of numerous, large, steeply dipping fissures extending generally parallel to the shelf-basin margin and containing an encrusting cryptic subcommunity embedded in early cement (Pl. 3*a*) supports evidence of early rigidity. Coupled with evidence of considerable initial topographic relief, it helped Newell et al. (1953), Babcock (1977), and Yurewicz (1977) conclude that a very large part of the Capitan Limestone was indeed a reef! The original reef community contained important binder and baffler guilds; no organisms typical of the constructor guild were present.

As would be expected, this enormous reef and reef system were highly varied in space and time. The organic framework includes sponge–algal boundstones and bafflestones associated with early diagenetic reef cementstones of greater volumetric importance than perhaps any other reef system in the entire history of reef building. The Capitan also contains abundant non-reef rocks, so at least part of the continuing debate over its origin can only be resolved by determining the relative amounts of organic and inorganic frameworks and non-reef rocks. This is difficult for at least two reasons:

a. Sampling problems due to the great size of the Capitan outcrop region and problems in relating outcrop data to the subsurface.

b. Sampling problems due to the rapid lateral and vertical variation in biota and sedimentologic features (e.g., Toomey and Babcock, 1983, pp. 292–307).

Babcock (1977) and Yurewicz (1977) have shown that there is an increase in relative importance of organic and inorganic frameworks from the base to the top of the "massive" Capitan and from the basinward slope and shelf deposits to the former reef crest. Similarly detailed future investigations will provide data regarding the proportions of boundstones, bafflestones, and cementstones and the contributions of various higher taxa of builders, especially sponges, to the overall construction process.

Finally, the present discussion makes it clear that Holocene scleractinian–rhodophyte reef frameworks are very inadequate models for determining whether or not the Capitan Limestone is an ancient reef complex. In most aspects, except size, the Capitan reefs are much more similar (in taxonomy, guild structure, early cement content) to other late Paleozoic and Middle Triassic boundstone and bafflestone reefs than to Holocene framestone and boundstone reefs. Assessment of composition and structure of ancient reefs is much more valid and useful if comparisons are made with other reefs of comparable age, size, and geologic (tectonic) location and placed in a context of evolving reef communities (as opposed to comparisons with Cenozoic reefs). There are important constraints on the use of uniformitarianism/actualism (Gould, 1965, 1984), especially when biological phenomena such as reefs are involved!

PART II

AUTECOLOGY AND HISTORY OF MAJOR REEF-BUILDING TAXA (with emphasis on the pre-Cenozoic)

INTRODUCTION

Part II is a detailed review of the geologic history of the numerous and diverse organisms that have been important contributors to the building of pre-Cenozoic reef frameworks. The organic frameworks of Cenozoic reefs were discussed in Part I (Chap. 1; Construction Process, Chap. 4; and especially Constructor, Baffler, and Binder Guilds, Chap. 5).

One of the earliest syntheses of the geologic history of important reef-building organisms was by Twenhofel (1950). Subsequently, several other authors refined various aspects of this history for one or more taxa (e.g., Newell, 1972; Heckel, 1974, pp. 121–134; J. L. Wilson, 1975, pp. 374–375; Longman, 1981, Table 2; James, 1983, Fig. 61; Bambach, 1985). At the 1969 North American Paleontological Convention, an entire symposium session was devoted to "Reef Organisms Through Time" and speakers discussed the geologic history of algae, sponges, and crinoids (Wray, 1971; Rigby, 1971; Lane, 1971).

7

Algal Autecology and History

INTRODUCTION

Throughout reef history, the greatest abundance and diversity of algae has usually coincided with the abundance of photic zone reefs (Wray, 1969). Much of the major evolutionary history of algae has taken place in reef communities (Elliott, 1979; Chuvashov and Riding, 1984, pp. 493–494; the term *algae* is used here in the informal sense of plants lacking true roots, stems, and leaves). Although numerous ancient reefs lack any evidence of algae, such reefs are relatively uncommon; the fact that algae are the primary (or only) autotrophs (producers) in all marine communities implies that non-skeletal algae must have been abundant in reef communities that lack algal skeletons. The present discussion is restricted to non-skeletal and skeletal benthic algae that lived in or immediately adjacent to pre-Cenozoic reefs.

The classification of algae, both Holocene and ancient, has recently undergone several revisions; in contemporary biological literature, the term has largely been replaced by two major divisions (kingdoms of numerous authors, e.g., Margulis, 1982) called Monera (procaryotes) and Protista (eucaryotes). In the classification used here, the procaryotic forms in reef environments belong to the Cyanophyta; benthic reef skeletal eucaryotes belong to either the Chlorophyta (green) or Rhodophyta (red; Wray, 1977, pp. 28–31) or the non-skeletal Phaeophyta (brown).

Classifications of extinct algae and "algal-like" forms are tenuous because many are quite unlike Cenozoic algae. Also, the quality of their preservation, especially in the Paleozoic (Riding, 1977; Roux, 1985; Riding and Voronova, 1985), is frustratingly poor. Therefore, the same "forms" or "form-genera" have been shifted by both algal and non-algal taxonomists among numerous extant higher algal taxa, the foraminifera, and even sponges. These "problematic" forms are discussed below following the forms to which they presently appear to be most closely related (following Wray, 1977; Riding, 1977; and modifications of Chuvashov and Riding, 1984). Exceptions include some particularly enigmatic forms (*Tubiphytes*, etc.) that are discussed separately near the end of this chapter.

The calcareous skeleton (thallus) of reef algae provides support and protection for the plants' cells and tissues; at the same time, the skeleton may play varied and important functional roles in the success of the whole community. The external skeletal morphology of living benthic algae (Wray, 1977, pp. 13–16) includes relatively low-growing (encrusting) shapes, upright (erect) plants, or elongate strands of cells (filaments). By use of inferences based on functional morphology, most similarly shaped pre-Cenozoic taxa can be quite confidently placed in the guild structure of ancient reef communities. Such comparisons and inferences are less certain for the extinct, problematic taxa (especially Paleozoic); nonetheless, the functional roles of these taxa in the community structure are commonly better understood than their taxonomic classification. Influences of the major chemical and physical environmental factors on distribution of Holocene algae are reviewed in Wray (1977, pp. 19–22, 123–132) and Jamieson (1969, pp. 1306–1308); biological factors related to their success in Cenozoic reefs are discussed in Chapter 3.

Algae are important members of all the guilds discussed in Chapter 5; however, their role as dwellers is not included in the ensuing discussion. Their significance as constructors in most Cenozoic reefs has been volumetrically overshadowed by the Scleractinia, but in many Paleozoic and Mesozoic reefs, various algae were major constructors; during the Precambrian, algae were the only constructors. They have also been of great importance in the baffler and binder/encruster guilds virtually throughout their history. The destructive role of boring filamentous algae in reefs is well-documented for the Holocene (Golubic et al., 1975; Kobluk, 1977); the problems of extending this function with certainty to pre-Holocene algae are considerable, however. But the biological simplicity of the organisms involved and of the boring process suggests that membership of algae in the destroyer guild may have begun nearly as early as the appearance of the earliest skeletons to be bored (Early Cambrian; Tommotian?).

CYANOPHYTA
(Synonyms: Schizophyta, Cyanobacteria, Blue–green Algae/Bacteria)

Non-skeletal (Spongiostromata of many authors)

Although the common algal mats of tropical regions consist of numerous filamentous and coccoid species belonging to both the Cyanophyta and

Chlorophyta ("green algae"), the filamentous Cyanophyta are generally the most important (Fig. 7.1). Unless unusual chemical conditions exist within the mat, the filaments are not preserved in ancient rocks and their former existence must be based on indirect sedimentological evidence. The nature of this indirect evidence is highly varied and so has given rise to a specialized terminology (e.g., cryptalgal, thrombolite, oncolite, etc.). The only terms of relevance to reef communities are *stromatolite* and *thrombolite* (Pls. 25*b*, 26*a;* see Glossary and Chap. 1).

Stromatolites exemplify the overlap of the constructor, binder, and baffler guilds (Fig. 7.2); the former algal filaments dominated the original construction by their volumetric abundance and the mucilaginous sheaths surrounding the filaments (trichomes) provided sediment binding. The topographic relief of the stromatolites (domes, columns, etc.) permit them to act as baffles. In non-skeletal stromatolites, evidence of the destroyer guild consists of burrows rather than borings, and burrows are locally present in reefs as old as the Late Precambrian (Vendian). Most stromatolites lack evidence of an important dwelling guild, either because of their Precambrian age, or because they lived in stressful environments of inherently low taxonomic diversity. For such stromatolites, there is no discernible synecology; therefore, their overall pre-Cenozoic ecology and history are discussed here rather than in Part III. However, stromatolites are also commonly found in close association (e.g., "algal crusts") on or adjacent to skeletonized, diverse metazoans in Paleozoic and Mesozoic reefs; the synecology of these forms is discussed in Part III.

Previous authors (e.g., Logan 1961; Logan et al., 1969, 1974; Hoffman, 1976) have directed considerable attention to the value of stromatolites as indicators of shallow-water depositional environments. However, Playford and Cockbain (1969) and Playford et al. (1976) clearly demonstrated that, during the Devonian, they lived to depths as great as 45–100+ m. Numerous Russian stratigraphers have described the utility of stromatolite shapes for Precambrian correlation (summarized in Cloud and Semikhatov, 1969). The problem of relative importance of environment-versus-genetics/phylogeny in determination of stromatolite shape is still uncertain.

The Precambrian was the unbridled heyday of stromatolite reefs; they are large (Hoffman, 1967), abundant, and widely distributed in Precambrian sedimentary rocks of moderately shallow-water origin. They have been most intensely studied in the Canadian and Siberian Shields and almost never exist in isolation. Large columnar, club, and domal shapes are commonly so closely spaced (Hoffman, 1974, Figs. 6–8; James, 1983, Figs. 63, 67, 68, 71) that they formed what were surely mutually supportive wave- and current-resistant reefs (Pl. 27). In addition, the stromatolites that dominate a 24–32-m thick unit of the Precambrian Siyeh Formation, Glacier National Park, Montana, are believed to have achieved some rigidity by early carbonate precipitation (Horodyski, 1983).

Estimates of stromatolite growth rates are highly varied. Some of the

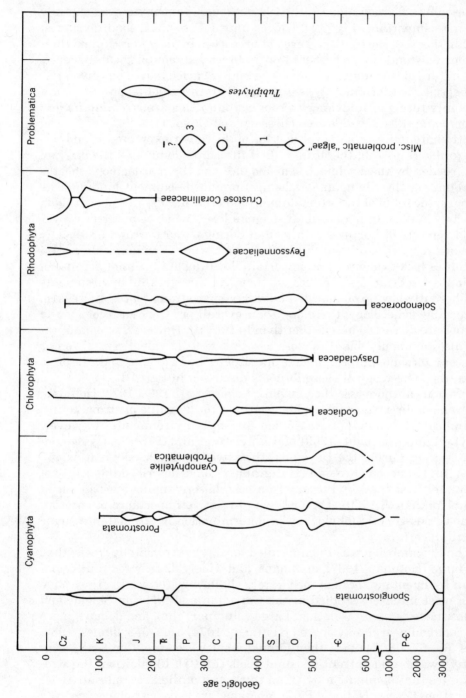

Figure 7.1. Summary of the relative stratigraphic importance of various algal and "algal-like" major taxa typical of, but not confined to, reef and reef-associated limestones. 1 = *Wetheredella* "group" and 2 = *Ungarella–Stacheia + Kamaena–Donzella* "groups" of Chuvashov and Riding, 1984. 3 = *Archaeolithoporella*. Absolute age in million years; note change of scale. Symbols for geologic periods conventional; C = Carboniferous, Cz = Cenozoic.

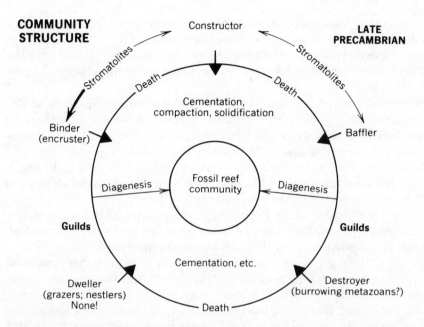

COMMUNITY STRUCTURE

LATE PRECAMBRIAN

Constructor

Stromatolites

Stromatolites

Death

Death

Cementation, compaction, solidification

Binder (encruster)

Baffler

Diagenesis

Fossil reef community

Diagenesis

Guilds

Guilds

Cementation, etc.

Dweller (grazers; nestlers) None!

Destroyer (burrowing metazoans?)

Death

Figure 7.2. Guild structure of Late Precambrian (Vendian) reef communities composed of stromatolites and probable metazoan burrowers. Stromatolitic algae were primarily binders (indicated by thick arrow around circle) but because of their large sizes, domal–columnar shape, and dense packing, also functioned as bafflers and constructors (examples of guild overlap indicated by thin arrows around circle). There was no skeletal dwelling guild.

internal laminations (Pl. 26a) may be related to semidiurnal tides; others may represent daily growth increments or even longer and irregularly spaced events (Monty, 1967; Gebelein, 1969; Park, 1976). Zhang and Li (1984) reported evidence of *daily* increments in 1.4–1.5-billion year old stromatolitic chert in northern China; increments are up to 600–700 μm thick. Playford et al. (1976) suggested, however, that *annual* growth of deep-water stromatolites in Devonian reefs of Canning Basin, Western Australia, was only a few microns.

Perhaps the most spectacular development of Precambrian stromatolites in North America occurs in the approximately 1.8-billion year old Pethei Group just east of Great Slave Lake, Northwest Territories, Canada (Hoffman, 1967, 1974). The stromatolites are abundant in varied environmental settings from current-dominated peritidal shoals to the seafloor of an adjacent subsiding basin with water depths of "at least tens of feet" and below wave base (7?–30? m; Hoffman, 1974, p. 862). Across this current- and depth-related environmental transition, there is also a regular transition in the forms of the stromatolites. In the shoal waters, there were near-shore biostromes characterized by laminar stromatolites which graded offshore into very large columnar stromatolites at the platform margin; these in turn graded abruptly down the basin slope and onto the basin floor into much smaller, poorly laminated columnar shapes (James, 1983, Fig. 72).

Hoffman (1974, pp. 865–866) regarded the abrupt transition at the platform margin and the large columnar stromatolites growing there as "morphologically analogous to Phanerozoic reefs" (Fig. 7.2). These stromatolites are mound-shaped, up to 20 m thick (James, 1983, Figs. 69–71); when they were alive, their tops were only about 3 m above the channel floors between the mounds. Mounds show a striking parallel elongation which, by analogy with Holocene stromatolies (Logan et al., 1974), is presumably perpendicular to the Precambrian shoreline. As the stromatolite columns grew upward, they became wider, more closely spaced, branched, and with progressively less relief above the channel floors.

Because of their great age, no Precambrian stromatolites are associated with any animal body fossils (possible "burrows" and "fecal" pellets from presumed soft-bodied forms have been described from very Late Precambrian stromatolitic rocks by Cloud et al., 1974; Walter, 1972). Metazoans also are absent from a great many Phanerozoic intertidal–supratidal stromatolites (e.g., Fagerstrom and Burchett, 1972). Furthermore, the absence of metazoans in association with other Phanerozoic stromatolites can be directly attributed to the survival of stromatolite-building cyanophytes in hypersaline or brackish water from which typical stenohaline metazoans have been ecologically excluded.

During the Cambrian and Early Ordovician, stromatolites were nearly as important as they were during the Proterozoic; thereafter, they declined considerably (Wray, 1977, p. 120; cf. Pratt, 1982). This decline in diversity and abundance of stromatolites has been attributed to the rise in importance of algal grazers and burrowers (e.g., gastropods, monoplacophorans; Garrett, 1970; Awramik, 1971) or other factors (Pratt, 1982). Regardless of the causes for their decline, there is little doubt that the Proterozoic marked the period of the largest and most diverse stromatolites.

Skeletal (Porostromata of several authors)

Several authors have suggested that some Precambrian stromatolites had a calcareous framework (e.g., Hoffman, 1974, p. 862; Horodyski, 1983) that may have included traces of weakly calcified cyanophyte sheaths. However, the oldest well-calcified filament sheaths capable of building an organic framework appear to be from latest Proterozoic or earliest Cambrian rocks (approx. 580-million years old) in Siberia (Riding and Voronova, 1982). Riding (1982) believes that the ability to produce a calcified skeleton by the cyanophytes is strongly influenced by the chemistry of the seawater (in particular, Mg^{+2}/Ca^{+2} ratio); therefore, the nature of the fossil record of calcified cyanophytes depends on both chemical and biological factors. *Plectonema* sp. appears to be the only Holocene filamentous cyanophyte having a calcareous sheath and it does not occur in marine water.

Throughout the Paleozoic, calcareous stromatolites are much less common than small nodules and laminar sheets formed by calcified cyanophytes of the *Hedstroemia–Ortonella* and *Girvanella* "groups" (Chuvashov and Riding, 1984); however, only during the Devonian (e.g., *Sphaerocodium;* Pl. 26b) and Early Carboniferous did they participate in building of organic frameworks in stromatolites.

Cyanophytelike Problematica

Living cyanophytes include both filamentous (discussed above) and coccoid forms. Holocene marine coccoid species that calcify their cell walls are unknown, but several enigmatic fossil forms (e.g., the *Renalcis–Shugaria,* Epiphytales–Cambrinales, and *Rothpletzella* "groups" of Chuvashov and Riding (1984) have been regarded as coccoid Cyanophyta, Chlorophyta, Rhodophyta, or foraminifera by previous authors (summarized in part by Riding and Brasier, 1975; Kobluk and James, 1979; Pratt, 1984).

Distribution of these early and middle Paleozoic problematic taxa is nearly confined to reefs. Forms in the *Renalcis–Shugaria* (Pl. 28a) and Epiphytales–Cambrinales "groups" are small and locally very abundant; because of their abundance, they may be the major constructors in many reefs. They are especially important in Early Cambrian–Early Ordovician reef communities, are nearly absent from Middle Ordovician and Silurian reefs, and then reappear in the Devonian (especially Late Devonian; Wray, 1977, p. 151; Chuvashov and Riding, 1984, p. 493). *Renalcis* and *Rothpletzella* encrust larger metazoan skeletons in Ordovician–Devonian reefs (Pl. 28b; Riding and Toomey, 1972; Riding and Watts, 1983; Chuvashov and Riding, 1984).

CHLOROPHYTA

Marine calcareous chlorophytes belong to two families, Codiacea and Dasycladacea, both of which are abundant and diverse in Holocene and ancient tropical reef environments. Chlorophytes generally have an erect growth habit; the degree of calcification is quite varied, but, even in heavily calcified forms (e.g., *Halimeda*), the thallus easily breaks into fragments that become part of the sedimentary substrate (Chuvashov and Riding, 1984, pp. 495–496).

Codiacea

Although Holocene codiaceans include species that live attached by rhizoidal holdfasts to both sedimentary substrates and hard surfaces such as rocks, dead corals, and coralline algae, all pre-Cenozoic forms apparently were of the former type and belonged to the baffler guild.

Pray and Wray (1963, p. 209) introduced the term *phylloid* for a taxonomically heterogeneous group of rather lightly calcified and fragile algal genera that are abundant in many Late Paleozoic reefs and biostromes (Fig. 7.1). The thallus is thin and leaflike, and because phylloid algae apparently lived in shallow, turbulent water, it is rarely found in growth position. Pray and Wray did not intend the term phylloid to have any taxonomic validity (such algae belong to both the Chlorophyta, discussed here, and Rhodophyta, see below); they emphasized instead the sedimentological and ecological importance of these algae.

Some phylloid algae have microstructures within the leaflike sheets that quite clearly indicate that they are codiaceans. The most common of these genera are *Eugonophyllum, Ivanovia,* and *Anchicodium;* each genus appears to have had an upright growth habit (Wray, 1977, pp. 83–84; Toomey, 1976, Figs. 4, 5E, 6Y) and so would have been effective bafflers in water of low-to-moderate turbulence (Pl. 29a). However, during episodes of high turbulence, their erect thalli were easily broken, transported, and deposited with thallus fragments (Pl. 4b) in varied orientations (Wray, 1968, Figs. 3–5, 8) to form biostromes (e.g., Bed 13 of Toomey, 1976) or skeletal "leaf piles" ("banks" of some authors). Thus, *in situ* chlorophyte algal bafflestones are quite rare; only a few meet the minimum size requirement and have sufficient topographic relief to be regarded as reefs (cf. Chuvashov and Riding, 1984, p. 494). The "bioherms" (Elias, 1963), "sparry algal *(Ivanovia)* facies" (Pray and Wray, 1963), or "reef-mounds" (Choquette, 1983) of the Paradox Formation (Late Carboniferous), southwestern United States, had a two-stage history:

a.   Growth of a current baffling community dominated by erect, poorly calcified phylloid codiaceans *(Ivanovia)* and fenestrate bryozoans. Baffled and trapped carbonate sediment probably accumulated around the bases of these organisms.

b.   Death of the baffling organisms, destruction of the original community by currents, transport of skeletal fragments, and deposition of fragments in a mud-rich matrix. Differing arrangements and packing densities of the skeletal fragments produced such varied rocks as rudstones and floatstones with extensive fragmentation and bafflestones. Recognition of the latter requires imaginative reconstruction of the living community, determination of the degree of postmortem community destruction and fragment transport, and estimating the importance of the deposited "leaf pile" (Toomey and Babcock, 1983, Figs. 5–8) in baffling currents and trapping sediment among the broken thalli (Choquette, 1983, Fig. 7).

Ball et al. (1977, pp. 251, 256) studied phylloid algal limestones in the Late Carboniferous of the south-central United States and doubted the erect growth habit of *Eugonophyllum, Anchicodium,* and *Ivanovia* and hence their ability to act as current baffles and sediment traps. The virtual absence of phylloid algae preserved in erect positions makes it difficult to prove that this was indeed their growth habit. However, it is clear that at least *Anchicodium* grew in an erect position (Pl. 29*a*), acted as a current baffle and sediment trap, and was easily broken into irregularly shaped leaves and chips (Pl. 4*b*). The discovery of other codiaceans in growth position, either dead Holocene or fossil, is rare, but because nearly all living codiaceans are erect, it is plausible to attribute this same original growth habit to their delicate thallus fragments in ancient limestones.

Badly recrystallized phylloid algae (*Eugonophyllum?;* Toomey and Babcock, 1983, pp. 277–282) are also abundant in parts of the Late Permian reefs of the Guadalupe Mountains, southwestern United States, but whether their chief role was baffling (Pl. 46*a*) or binding is uncertain.

Dasycladacea

Although the generic diversity of fossil dasycladaceans is nearly three times the diversity of any other major group of marine calcareous algae, only a very few are important in reef and reef-associated rocks (Wray, 1977, Fig. 11; Chuvashov and Riding, 1984; Klement, 1968; Elliott, 1979), regardless of their geologic age.

Rocks deposited in reef flat and lagoonal areas behind the crest of the Late Permian reefs of the Guadalupe Mountains, southwestern United States, contain abundant thallus fragments of the dasycladacean genera *Mizzia* and *Macroporella* (Klement, 1968). These erect-growing, fragile forms presumably grew in such close association that they acted as effective baffles to waters of low-to-moderate turbulence; in high turbulence environments, such as the reef crest, their thalli were quickly broken into fragments and transported to protected flats and lagoons. Bafflestones composed of abundant dasycladaceans in growth position are virtually unknown, and even broken thalli are quite scarce in rocks of reef crest origin.

Conclusions

Pre-Cenozoic Chlorophyta appear to have inhabited environments similar to their analogous Holocene representatives. The erect phylloidal forms are the chief exception (they have no Holocene analogue) and most of these forms seem to have performed the same ecological functions as other chlorophytes (i.e., current baffles and sediment producers). They are characteristic of tropical marine level-bottom communities, some of which were located adjacent to reefs. Locally, their skeletons may be so densely packed that they may have had some topographic relief and formed reef bafflestones.

RHODOPHYTA

Solenoporaceae

The solenoporaceans have had a very long and locally important association with reef environments. Their greatest relative importance seems to have been during the Middle Ordovician, when they comprised up to about 25% of the framework (Pitcher, 1971), and in the Triassic–Jurassic. At other times, they were not important in reefs or were confined to level-bottoms.

Solenoporacean thalli vary considerably in size and shape from small, rounded nodules to irregularly hemispherical masses several cm in diameter to thin crusts. In some small reefs of the lower Crown Point Formation, Isle LaMotte, Vermont, "*Solenopora* is the principal contributor" to the framework (Pitcher, 1971, pp. 1348–1352; i.e., constructor guild). "*Solenopora texana*," a questionable alga (Babcock, 1977, pp. 19–20) is also locally important in the Late Permian reefs of the Guadalupe Mountains, southwestern United States (Rigby, 1957; Klement, 1968; cf. Achauer, 1969).

Peyssonneliacae (Squamariacaea of some authors)

The peyssonneliaceans include another type of "phylloid" alga of Pray and Wray (1963) belonging to the late Paleozoic genera *Archaeolithophyllum* and *Cuneiphycus,* and perhaps also *Archaeolithoporella* and the Cretaceous–Holocene *Peyssonnelia* and *Ethelia* (James et al., 1984). The rhodophyte affinities of the Late Paleozoic genera are based on the presence of differentiated cell layers and sizes arranged in essentially the same manner as Mesozoic–Cenozoic coralline algae (Steneck, 1983, p. 55). These forms differ from codiacean phylloid algae (discussed above) in having a low growing (prostrate–arched), encrusting or binding growth habit; in reef communities, they belong to the binder guild.

Wray (1964) described two species of *Archaeolithophyllum* having somewhat different growth habits:

a.   "*A. lamellosum* had an encrusting form that developed multilayered masses several centimeters thick and extended along bedding surfaces for at least 15 cm . . . this alga locally forms a boundstone . . . encrusts trepostome and fenestrate bryozoans, shells, and fine-grained sedimentary particles . . . is presumed to have had potential wave-resistant qualities" (Pl. 30*a;* cf. Ball et al., 1977, p. 256).

  b. *A. missouriense* "developed as free or locally attached crusts . . . able to exist on both carbonate mud bottoms and those characterized by coarser sediment" (Pl. 30*b;* Wray, 1964, Pl. 2, Figs. 1, 4, Pl. 1, Figs. 1, 2, and Fig. 4; Toomey, 1979, pp. 848–850).

  Kotila (in Wray, 1977, p. 135) suggested that *A. lamellosum* lived in shallower, more turbulent water than *A. missouriense* and that there was a well-developed lateral zonation of these and other algae across the presumed algal-built structures that he studied.

Crustose Corallinaceae

The crustose corallines include three subfamilies (Melobesioideae, Lithophylloideae, Mastophoroideae) and each has representatives at least as old as the Middle Jurassic (Adey and Macintyre, 1973); Zankl (1969) and Elliott (1979) have recognized one species of encrusting coralline as a minor constituent in an Upper Triassic reef in the northern Alps (cf. Steneck, 1983). During the interval from the Late Jurassic or Early Cretaceous to Holocene, crustose corallines increased in importance in reef communities so that by the Late Cretaceous–Miocene, they had become the dominant element in the binder/encruster guild. A great deal of the Cretaceous–Holocene diversification of crustose corallines at the genus level (Adey and Macintyre, 1973) is related to their success in entering and dominating this guild in reef communities (Elliott, 1979). At least part of this success is due to differentiation of the cellular skeleton and by the addition of fusion cells and conceptacles (see Bosence, 1983b, for excellent illustrations). In addition, the firm attachment of crustose corallines to hard substrates (Pl. 24*b*) represents a significant increase in stability in highly turbulent reef environments (Bosence, 1983) compared with the loose attachment of the Late Paleozoic peyssonneliaceans to sedimentary substrates.

  Steneck (1983; 1985) has described and charted the interrelations among evolutionary histories of solenopores and crustose corallines during the mid-Mesozoic to early Cenozoic interval and the concomitant increase in intensity of herbivore grazing. He concluded that the more primitive arrangement and non-specialized cells of solenopores left them vulnerable to herbivore attack and that their extinction in the Eocene may have been due to increased herbivory. This extinction broadly coincides with a major expansion in diversity of crustose coralline algae (Fig. 7.1); Steneck suggested that coralline expansion was a result of their more complex cellular and skeletal structure and provided a much better defense against herbivore grazing and contributed to their considerable success in post-Eocene hard substrate communities such as reefs.

PROBLEMATIC ALGAE

Included here are a variety of enigmatic Paleozoic and Triassic–Jurassic forms that most workers regard as algae but are uncertain as to which major taxon they belong and that *locally* have importance in reef communities. They belong to: (1) the *Wetheredella, Kamaena–Donezella,* and *Ungdarella–Stacheia* "groups" of Chuvashov and Riding (1984, pp. 493–494); and (2) the genera *Archaeolithoporella* and *Tubiphytes* (Fig. 7.1). The former "groups" are present in reef communities, usually as crusts on metazoan skeletons. However, only locally do they become volumetrically important enough to be regarded as members of the binder guild. Copper (1976) described thick *Wetheredella* crusts that bound coral colonies in Late Ordovician (Ashgillian) reefs in eastern Canada. *Donezella, Ungdarella,* and *Komia* are important in Carboniferous reefs in the western United States, Spain, and central Texas (Chuvashov and Riding, 1984).

Archaeolithoporella is of major importance in Permian reef communities (Pl. 29*b*). The thallus consists of alternating light and dark, very thin (10–30 µm), non-cellular calcite laminae of presumed skeletal origin (Babcock, 1977, pp. 14–17; Mazullo and Cys, 1978) that form crusts up to several millimeters thick. In the Late Permian reefs of the Guadalupe Mountains, southwestern United States, *Archaeolithoporella* is one of the dominant members of the binder guild; it is exceedingly abundant in rocks of reef crest origin where it coats and binds skeletal grains of sponges, bryozoans, other calcareous algae, and the enigmatic microfossil *Tubiphytes* (discussed below). *Archaeolithoporella* also lines the walls of seaward slope fissures as an important member of the cryptic subcommunity (Pl. 1*b*).

Tubiphytes is a tubular (cylindrical–ovoidal) microfossil with a rather thick, dense outer wall and variously shaped, thinner internal partitions; tube diameters range from about 0.7 to 2 mm. *Tubiphytes* is most abundant in Late Carboniferous–Jurassic reefs and very commonly it is one of the major members of the binder guild. It forms remarkably thick (up to several centimeters) encrustations on various skeletal grains, such as sponges, bryozoans, and corals, and may also occur abundantly between grains or in rocks of lagoonal/reef flat origin.

One of the strongest arguments in favor of the algal affinity of *Archaeolithoporella* and *Tubiphytes* is their virtual restriction to rocks of shallow-water environmental settings, especially reef crest or near-crest locations.

SUMMARY AND CONCLUSIONS

Figure 7.1 summarizes the geologic importance of the various algal taxa discussed above. Previous authors (e.g., Wray, 1971; Elliott, 1979; Adey and Macintyre, 1973; Chuvashov and Riding, 1984) have discussed the close relation between the abundance, diversity, and major evolutionary events in the history of these algae and the abundance of reefs.

There are six stratigraphically distinct non-skeletal–calcareous algal reef floras that are rather clearly indicated in Figure 7.1:

a. A Precambrian stromatolite-building spongiostromate flora; it is abundant, widely distributed, and of high gross morphologic diversity (Cloud and Semikhatov, 1969).

b. A Cambrian–Early Ordovician flora of moderate diversity consisting of spongiostromate/porostromate stromatolites and the sudden appearance of several problematic taxa with well-calcified skeletons (Chuvashov and Riding, 1984, pp. 496–497).

c. An Ordovician–Devonian flora of still greater diversity and dominated by solenoporaceans, porostromate stromatolites, and problematic taxa.

d. A very diverse Late Carboniferous–Permian flora dominated by phylloid algae, *Archaeolithoporella,* and *Tubiphytes.*

e. A Middle Triassic–Cretaceous flora of much lower diversity dominated by solenoporaceans, *Tubiphytes,* and archaic, long-ranging crustose Corallinaceae of progressively increasing importance.

f. An Eocene–Holocene flora dominated by essentially modern genera of crustose corallines (Adey and Macintyre, 1973) and associated codiaceans.

The significance of reef environments to the evolution of calcareous benthic algae becomes especially apparent when it is realized that intervals between these floras (e.g., Early Carboniferous, Early Triassic, and early Cenozoic) were times of no reef development or of relatively small, local reefs (discussed in Part III).

Steneck (1983) described the possible cause-and-effect relation between herbivore grazing on crustose coralline algae and their evolutionary success. He regarded the late Paleozoic *Archaeolithophyllum* as the earliest "coralline" with cellular differentiation; noting that onset of intense herbivory followed this earliest form by over 100 million years, he concluded that herbivory (cause) and cell specialization (effect) were unrelated.

8

Poriferan Autecology and History

ECOLOGY

Like the calcareous algae, whose evolutionary history is intimately tied to the geologic history of reef communities (Chap. 7), most of the evolutionary history of pre-Cretaceous sponges is also related to reefs. The Late Triassic–Cretaceous were times of declining importance in reef-building sponges, and Tertiary reef sponges are very rare indeed. From the very base of the Cambrian (Tommotian Stage), almost continuously to the end of the Jurassic, various higher taxa of sponges have either dominated or played a major role in reef-building (Fig. 8.1).

Locally, sponges may be second only to corals in their contribution to the biomass of Holocene reef communities. However, most of these sponges are demosponges with loosely spiculated siliceous and spongin fiber skeletons that lack rigidity and therefore belong to the baffler guild. A possible exception to this generalization are the "sponge reefs" located north of Andros Island in the Bahamas (discussed in Chap. 2). In addition, the framework of the deep-water (70–105-m) parts of several Jamaican reefs is dominated by large, massive skeletons of sclerosponges (Fagerstrom, 1984b; also discussed in Chap. 2); in shallow-water cryptic subcommunities in Jamaica, and in the Indo-Pacific, sclerosponges are sufficiently abundant to be included in the binder guild (Fagerstrom, 1984b, pp. 373–374). Vacelet (1983, p. 15) also reported tropical calcareous sponges up to 1 m high as reef constructors.

The chief role of sponges (especially the clionids) in most Holocene reefs, regardless of water depth, is as borers (destroyer guild). The fossil record of undoubted sponge borings is difficult to determine. Although numerous

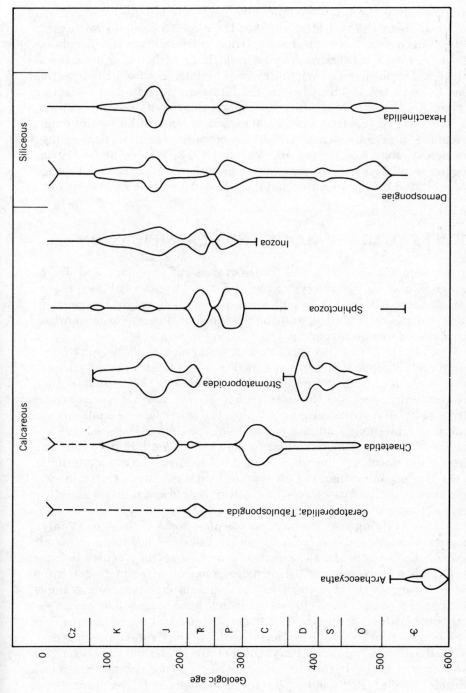

Figure 8.1. Summary of the relative stratigraphic importance of various major taxa in the Phylum Porifera in the building guilds of Phanerozoic reef communities. Absolute age in million years. Symbols for geologic periods conventional; C = Carboniferous, Cz = Cenozoic.

examples from the late Paleozoic have been attributed to sponges, it is not until about the mid-Mesozoic that their record becomes important.

In modern seas, there is a sharp contrast in the bathymetric distribution of sponges with calcareous spicules and those with hexactine siliceous spicules. The former are most numerous and diverse from the intertidal zone to less than 100 m, whereas the latter are rare in depth less than 200 m (Reid, 1968). Most sclerosponges (calcareous skeleton; siliceous spicules) live at less than about 130 m, but at least three species extend to about 175 m (Fagerstrom, 1984b). By contrast, Holocene demosponges are nearly ubiquitous (Sarà and Vacelet, 1973; Wiedenmayer, 1980b). Regardless of their skeletal composition or bathymetric optima, all sponges are inhibited by turbid water and most live attached to hard substrates.

SKELETAL MINERALOGY AND CLASSIFICATION

As a result of discoveries and "rediscoveries" of abundant and diverse sponge faunas mostly in cryptic reef habitats (reviewed by Fagerstrom, 1984a), there has been a serious reevaluation of the significance of spicules, spicule mineralogy, and the presence or absence of mineralized skeletons in sponge taxonomy.

Vacelet (1985, p. 11) regards calcareous skeletons as polyphyletic in origin and as relict structures retained in a few Holocene sponges as an inheritance from ancestors with massive skeletons. For example, there are two living species of the sclerosponge *Merlia:* one has a massive calcareous skeleton with siliceous spicules; the other has siliceous spicules typical of demosponge but lacks a calcareous skeleton. The tissues of both species of *Merlia* are more similar to the Demospongia than to Calcarea. Tissues and spicules of the other living sclerosponges also are more similar to the Demospongia than to Calcarea, but their massive calcareous skeletons suggest that they have their affinities closest to several extinct higher taxa with massive skeletons.

Numerous living sponges have no spicules; some of these have only a spongin skeleton, and one sphinctozoan genus *(Vaceletia)* has a calcareous skeleton but no spicules. The presence or absence of spicules becomes considerably more complex when paleobiologists attempt to determine the affinities of extinct sponges with calcareous skeletons. For example, living sclerosponges have siliceous spicules, but the only fossil examples with spicules (and these are pseudomorphs) are in rare specimens from the Cretaceous of Poland (Kaźmierczak, 1974), the Crimea (Kaźmierczak, 1979), the Upper Triassic of Italy (Dieci et al., 1977), and the Lower Carboniferous of Wales (Gray, 1980). Conversely, living sphinctozoans lack spicules (Vacelet, 1979), but a very few fossil representatives have spicule pseudomorphs (Ott, 1967; Reitner and Engeser, 1985).

The absence of spicules in the vast majority of fossil sclerosponges and other extinct sponges with massive calcareous skeletons may be due to:

a. The mineralogic instability of SiO_2 in carbonate environments (Friedman et al., 1976; Land, 1976; Rützler and Macintyre, 1978). This also explains the rarity of spicules in fossil demosponges from reef limestones.

b. The spicules in extinct sponges with massive calcareous skeletons were confined to soft tissues, so that their former presence was not recorded (pits or holes) in their skeletons.

c. The extinct sponges with massive calcareous skeletons completely lacked spicules and were thus similar to other living and fossil Demospongia and Calcarea that lack spicules.

The mineralogy and microstructure of non-spicular calcareous skeletons are also highly varied among several higher taxa and have been used with varied success in establishing biological affinities (Wendt, 1979, 1984; Sandberg, 1984). For example, some Holocene sclerosponges have aragonite and others have high-Mg calcite skeletons. Some sclerosponges of the genus *Merlia* are calcitic and others are aragonitic (Cuif et al., 1979); furthermore, the original skeletal mineralogy and microstructure may undergo considerable alteration during diagenesis (cf. Wendt, 1975). Such differences and alterations make interpretation of the original mineralogy and microstructure very difficult and of uncertain significance in classifications of extinct taxa.

These important and unresolved problems are crucial to the reconstruction of poriferan phylogeny but not to interpretation of their reef guild membership. In the following discussion, a very broad view is taken of the poriferan affinities of several extinct higher taxa with abundant fossil records in Paleozoic and Mesozoic reef communities (i.e., archaeocyathids, chaetetids, and stromatoporoids; for discussion of sponge affinities of these taxa, see Debrenne and Vacelet, 1984; Hartman and Goreau, 1966, 1970, 1972; Gray, 1980; West and Clark, 1984; Stearn, 1972, 1975, 1984). Many of these Paleozoic and Mesozoic taxa had skeletons that were more compact (harder; stronger) than those of scleractinians (Schuhmacher and Plewka, 1981a) and therefore built very rigid reefs.

Recent summaries of the general paleobiology of pre-Cenozoic sponges may be found in Hartman et al. (1980), Rigby and Stearn (1983), and *Paleontographica Americana No. 54* (Sect. 5, pp. 303–381). The history of typical spicular sponges in reef communities was last reviewed by Rigby (1971). The present review is arranged on the basis of mineralogy of the skeleton (massive forms) or the spicules and includes only those taxa important in frame-building guilds of pre-Cenozoic reef communities.

CALCAREOUS PORIFERA

Archaeocyatha

Although a few archaeocyathids are present in Middle and Upper Cambrian rocks (Debrenne et al., 1984), their acme in both diversity and abundance was during the Early Cambrian (James and Debrenne, 1980, pp. 656–657), and, in particular, the Botomian Stage in the Siberian Platform (Fig. 8.1). The base of the Cambrian is determined by the simultaneous appearance of about 5 archaeocyathid species at the base of the Tommotian Stage in Siberia (Rozanov and Debrenne, 1974).

In the region of the Siberian Platform and the Altai–Sajan fold belt, especially along the middle reaches of the Lena River and along the Aldan River, the Lower Cambrian rocks have been subdivided into 4 stages (Tommotian, Atdabanian, Botomian, Elankian from base to top) and 14 zones on the basis of the distribution of over 200 archaeocyathid genera (Hill, 1972, p. 30; Rozanov and Debrenne, 1974; Debrenne and Rozanov, 1983).

Archaeocyathids are nearly confined to carbonate substrates, both level-bottom and reef. They were more common on hard substrates and most were attached by calcareous outgrowths (the sole) from the base of the outer wall of the cup. Optimum water depths for most species were 25–50 m and the depth range was about 0–100 m (Hill, 1972). Evidence for the shallow optima for most archaeocyathids is their common association with such sedimentologic features as oolites, ripple marks, cross-beds, and flat-pebble breccias and biologic features such as stromatolites, oncolites, and other probable algae (Gangloff, 1983, p. 192).

The earliest archaeocyathids in Siberia were inhabitants of small reefs and level-bottoms *(Dokidocyathus regularis, D. lenaicus, Aldanocyathus sunnaginicus);* Riding (1983; *Reef Newsletter* **9,** p. 43) reported that the oldest algal–archaeocyathid reef occurs only 0.75 m above the base of the Tommotian along the Aldan River. The association of archaeocyathids and reefs became more firmly established in the second archaeocyathid zone of the Tommotian and progressively increased in importance to the middle of the Botomian Stage.

The Archaeocyathida are subdivided into two major categories (Regulares; Irregulares) on the basis of features formed very early in their ontogeny and found at the tip of the cup (Hill, 1972; Debrenne, 1983). The Regulares are more abundant and diverse and include both single-walled (Monocyathida) and double-walled (Ajacicyathida) cups; the earliest archaeocyathids included both types.

Evolutionary History

During the Tommotian, the cup pores, outer wall, and intervallum structures were simple but subsequently became progressively more complex.

From the Late Tommotian through the Botomian, the evolution of archaeocyathids consisted of a succession of steps based on varied combinations of outer wall and intervallum features (Rozanov and Debrenne, 1974, pp. 835, 839) followed by severe reduction in morphologic diversity at the beginning of the Elankian. Temporally repeated occurrence of the same morphological features, but in different combinations, suggests that many suborders or families may have had polyphyletic origins.

Most archaeocyathids were solitary, with slender conical (ceratoid) cups in their early growth stages, becoming cylindrical as adults; others had growth forms of large, open, rapidly expanding cups. The cones, cylinders, and cups commonly had various supporting structures outside the outer wall near the sole, as well as structures on the outer wall and in the intervallum and central cavity, to provide increased strength and stability in their upright living position (Hill, 1972, Fig. 4). Still others were in the form of flat discoids (saucers) or globular-hemispherical bulbs lying freely on level-bottom substrates. Colonial archaeocyathids were rare, but they included cateniform and dendroid growth forms; in others, the cups were linked together by exothecal (exocyathid) tissue to make small, massive colonies (Hill, 1972, Fig. 5; Cooper, 1974, Fig. 4).

In Early Cambrian reefs, the cones, cylinders, cups, and colonies overlapped the constructor and baffler guilds (Pl. 31). Compared with the builders of younger reefs, archaeocyathid skeletons were relatively small (average sizes: 10–25 mm dia, 80–150 mm high) and fragile and so the rigidity of the reefs they built was less than in most younger reefs. However, the largest specimens (up to 250–300 mm high) and their most dense packing are found in reefs (up to 70% of rock volume; Gangloff, 1983, p. 194).

During the Tommotian–Botomian interval, both archaeocyathids and the reefs they built increased in size. In the Atdabanian (Gangloff, 1983), there was a significant increase in diversity of growth forms, including the first colonies with cups joined by budded branches (Rowland, 1984) as well as abundant dissepiments in the intervallum.

The Archaeocyatha attained their maximum generic diversity during the Botomian; of the 228 genera of Regulares listed by Debrenne and Rozanov (1983), about 208 are present in the Botomian. There are only 7–8 regular genera in the Early Elankian, and, by the Late Elankian, only about 6 genera. Elankian archaeocyathid-built reefs are much less common than earlier in the Cambrian; the diversity of archaeocyathid growth forms is much lower and post-Elankian archaeocyathid-built reefs are unknown.

Homologous Growth Forms

Some excellent examples of homologous growth forms occur among calcareous poriferans with solid, massive skeletons such as sclerosponges and stromatoporoids. The most detailed studies of growth form have been based on Paleozoic stromatoporoids and from these, a complex and partially conflicting array of terms to describe external skeletal growth forms has developed (Galloway, 1957; Abbott, 1973; St. Jean, 1971, pp. 1402–1415).

More recently, Kershaw and Riding (1978, 1980) presented a graphical scheme for characterizing shapes of stromatoporoid coenostea and a simplified set of terms describing them. This same scheme is applicable to most other massive calcareous sponges such as sclerosponges and chaetetids but has received rather limited usage. The problems of coenosteal shapes as indicators of such environmental factors as turbulence and depth were discussed above (Guilds and Morphological Plasticity, Chap. 5). However, in the following discussion of Sclerospongiae and Stromatoporoidea, the guild membership of various taxa is based on their growth form.

Sclerospongiae

Although pre-Cenozoic sclerosponges (*sensu stricto;* Ceratoporellida, Tabulospongida in Fig. 8.1) are quite rare, there seems a strong association between their occurrence and the occurrence of reefs, especially in the Middle and Upper Triassic of northern Italy. Fürsich and Wendt (1977, p. 265) reported 32 sclerosponge species from the Cassian back-reef (flat/lagoon) beds and patch reefs. They indicated that the chief function of sclerosponges was in the binder/encruster guild, especially in the later stages of reef growth. Cuif (1974, p. 152) noted that sclerosponges were also abundant in peripheral parts of other contemporaneous reefs.

Order Chaetetida
Chaetetids have had a long geologic history (Late Ordovician–Holocene with lengthy gaps) in both reef and shallow-water, carbonate level-bottom communities, but it was only during the Carboniferous and Late Jurassic that they were significant as members of the building guilds (Fig. 8.1).

In Late Carboniferous reefs in the south-central United States, the packing density is so great that there is very little space between colonies for other organisms (Pl. 7b; West and Clark, 1984; Sutherland, 1984); in contemporaneous Japanese reefs described by Ota (1968), community diversity is much higher and chaetetids shared the building role with members of several higher taxa.

Chaetetid growth forms are highly varied and range from flat, binding–encrusting sheets (Pl. 25a) to domes of varying degrees of convexity (Pls. 32a, 33a), spheres and hemispheres, to erect clubs, columns, and cylinders (Pl. 7b) with a pronounced upward growth direction (West and Clark, 1984, pp. 338–340; Sutherland, 1984; Fischer, 1970). The largest skeletons are high domes and columns up to 3 m tall and 0.8 m in diameter. West and Clark (1984) stressed the importance of hardgrounds, especially shells, lithic fragments (Pls. 32a, 33a), and oncolites, as basal attachments for hemispherical and columnar chaetetids. Such attachments probably were selectively favored because they brought the filter-feeding (?) chaetetids above the turbid substrate. During the Late Carboniferous, chaetetids were important members of both constructor and binder guilds, whereas in the Early Carboniferous and older reefs, most chaetetids were binders/encrusters (Wolfenden, 1958).

Stromatoporoidea

In both variety of growth forms and general arrangement of their major internal structures, the Paleozoic and Mesozoic stromatoporoids are very similar. However, the microstructure of internal structures is generally quite different in many lower taxa when viewed with the light microscope (Turnšek, 1970, pp. 181–185; cf. Wendt, 1984). The nature of these microstructures and interpretation of their mineralogic and taxonomic significance are perhaps more uncertain than for any of the other groups of extinct calcareous poriferans. The considerable stratigraphic gap between the youngest Paleozoic and the oldest Mesozoic stromatoporoids (Fig. 8.1) strongly suggests that the two groups are not phylogenetically related in a direct ancestor–descendant lineage and that their similarities are homoplastic. During both the Paleozoic and Mesozoic, there was a distinct decrease in importance of stromatoporoids (Early Devonian, Stearn, 1982b, Fig. 1; Early–Middle Jurassic, Flügel, 1975, Fig. 2) which corresponds with an overall reduction in the global importance of reef communities.

Assignment of at least the Mesozoic stromatoporoids to the Porifera, and probably to the Class Sclerospongiae or Demospongiae, has been strengthened by the discovery of spicule pseudomorphs (Wood and Reitner, 1986). However, neither *in situ* spicules, pseudomorphs, nor pits in which former spicules were presumably located have been described from Paleozoic stromatoporoids.

Coenesteal Form; Guild Membership

Size; Growth Rates. Individual stromatoporoid coenostea attain remarkably large sizes. The Middle Ordovician rocks of Vermont contain the oldest stromatoporoids and Stearn (1984, p. 318) reported individuals up to 4–5 m across. Paleozoic coenostea generally are much larger than those of Mesozoic stromatoporoids.

Meyer (1981) determined that the lateral growth rates of some Devonian stromatoporoids exceeded their vertical growth rates by nearly 10 times, and detailed sedimentologic relations between some tabular/laminar coenostea and the internal sediment confirm their rapid lateral growth rates (Pl. 35a).

Shape; Guild Membership. Because of their excellent skeletonization and considerable variation in coenosteal shapes (St. Jean, 1971, pp. 1402–1415), stromatoporoids can be assigned to membership in either the constructor or binder guilds. In cases of very densely packed coenostea (Pl. 20*b*), the stromatoporoids were both constructors and binders (guild overlap; Pl. 36*a*).

Relatively thin, tabular/laminar stromatoporoid coenostea are excellent homologues of the Holocene crustose coralline red algae; both taxa perform the functional role of binders/encrusters. Large, domal–bulbous–columnar coenostea (e.g., Kershaw, 1981, Text-Figs. 3, 7) are members of the constructor guild and are analogous to similarly shaped stromatolites or chaetetids. Such coenostea are commonly so closely spaced that they are also mutually supporting, effective current baffles, but their well-mineralized, massive skeletons exclude them from the baffler guild as defined in Chapter 5.

Sphinctozoa (*sensu lato;* cf. Reitner and Engeser, 1985)

The classification and phylogeny of "sphinctozoan sponges" (in the sense of those forms with repetitous bulbous chambers having calcified walls and variable development of chamber wall pores and internal structures; Finks, 1983, pp. 55–58; Dieci et al., 1968, pp. 102–103, Figs. 3–7) are currently in considerable turmoil as the result of varying interpretations of the presence/absence and significance of spicules and of the original mineralogy and microstructure of the main calcareous skeleton.

The fossil record of Sphinctozoa is longer than any other calcareous sponges (Fig. 8.1), but they were only important as reef builders during the mid–Late Permian and mid–Late Triassic (Fagerstrom, 1984b; Flügel and Stanley, 1984).

Sphinctozoans may be divided into two major groups on the basis of pores in the calcareous wall of the chambers (Seilacher, 1962): (1) the Aporata, which lack wall pores or have a few relatively large spoutlike pores; and (2) the Porata, which have numerous, small wall pores. For purposes of determining their guild placement, both the Aporata and the Porata may be subdivided informally into those with chambers lacking internal structures and those with internal chamber structures (pillars, vesicles, diaphragms). The late Paleozoic and Mesozoic occurrences of these subdivisions and some of the characteristic genera in each are shown in Finks (1970, p. 15) and Wendt (1980a, p. 176).

The Early Permian (Sakmarian?) marked the appearance of the first sphinctozoans (mostly Porata) with internal chamber structures; through the later Permian and mid–Late Triassic, these forms increased in importance in both the Aporata and Porata (Ott, 1967, Fig. 6; Dieci et al., 1968). There are almost no Early Triassic sphinctozoans and many mid–

Late Permian genera "reappear" in the Middle Triassic (Finks, 1960, p. 10 [Thalamida]; Finks, 1983, p. 58). At the end of the Triassic, the Aporata became extinct, and the surviving Porata of the Jurassic and Cretaceous have simple internal morphologies similar to their Carboniferous ancestors.

Growth Form; Guild Membership

Sphinctozoan skeletons were neither as large nor as well calcified (rigid) as the more densely built skeletons of the Sclerospongiae and Stromatoporoidea. In both size and degree of calcification of their skeletons, the Sphinctozoa and Archaeocyathida seem to have been quite similar.

There is considerable morphologic variation among the sphinctozoans (for examples of variation in *Guadalupia*, see Finks, 1960, p. 36). Much like the archaeocyathids, most sphinctozoans grew upward from a relatively small attachment to the substrate (cateniform). New sphinctozoan chambers were added in a linear series up to 15 cm long (Pl. 33*b;* Finks, 1983); "daughter chambers" form by budding to produce clusters of stems and branches (Pl. 34*a*) up to 20–25 cm across.

Poorly calcified, thin-walled cateniform and dendroid forms that lacked internal strengthening structures were members of the baffler guild; stems and branches are rarely in growth position in the reef framework but are frequently very abundant in the internal sediment and reef flat beds adjacent to reefs. Similarly shaped but internally strengthened forms that characterized Middle–Late Triassic reefs are assigned to the constructor guild (Fagerstrom, 1984b, pp. 375–377).

Other sphinctozoans produced open, cup-shaped skeletons ("cyathiform" of Finks, 1983) that morphically intergrade with the cateniform shapes. The cup-shaped skeletons may be assigned to either the constructor or baffler guilds, depending on their skeletal strength and packing density. Finally, a few sphinctozoans grew in well-calcified sheets, with and without internal chamber structure, parallel to the substrate ("stratiform" of Finks, 1983) and include members of the mid–Late Permian Family Guadalupiidae (Pls. 32*b*, 34*b*) and the Middle–Late Triassic genus *Ascosymplegma* (Dieci et al., 1968, Pl. 31). These sheetlike forms were members of the binder guild (Fagerstrom, 1984b, pp. 375–378) or, if they are densely packed (e.g., Dieci et al., 1968, Pl. 32), they may overlap as constructors.

Inozoa

... the entire group of aspicular, aragonitic, spherulitic sponges from the Late Paleozoic and Triassic, inozoan as well as sphinctozoan, form an intergrading assemblage that could well belong to a single higher category.

(Finks, 1983, p. 66)

Finks (1983, pp. 59–68) has reviewed the general nature and evolutionary history of the Inozoa, including numerous "problem genera," and the generally unsettled classification of this important reef-building group of calcareous sponges. Most problems involving the taxonomic and phylogenetic importance of spicules, skeletal mineralogy, and microstructure noted at the beginning of this chapter are particularly difficult to interpret in the Inozoa. The future will undoubtedly see considerable taxonomic reorganization of these sponges at higher levels and the shifting of genera among them. Nonetheless, Inozoa are particularly abundant in the Mesozoic reefs of western Europe (Fig. 8.1).

Growth Form; Guild Membership

During the late Paleozoic and Triassic, the reef-building sphinctozoans and inozoans commonly occur together, although sphinctozoans are typically more abundant and more diverse. They are also of similar external morphology; most reef-building Inozoa are similar in size and shape (cateniform, dendroid, cyathiform) to the Sphinctozoa. Internally, typical inozoans are much better calcified than sphinctozoans (cf. Dieci et al., 1968, Figs. 2, 3, 6, 7; Wendt, 1980a). This difference, however, does not become clearly evident until the Jurassic and Cretaceous, when inozoans become more abundant and diverse than sphinctozoans in reef communities.

Because they are relatively well-calcified and hence rigid, most erect inozoans were members of the constructor guild in Mesozoic reefs (e.g., Dieci et al., 1968, Pl. 26). Inozoans are much less common than sphinctozoans in the baffler and binder guilds.

SILICEOUS PORIFERA

The siliceous spicules of both demosponges and hexactinellids are quite uncommon in typical carbonate rocks of most ancient reefs. Therefore, these sponges are recognized on the basis of pseudomorphs of the original spicules (mostly desmas and hexactines), the nature of the canal systems, and general external form of individual sponges. In typical siliceous sponges, the spicular skeleton comprises a loosely formed support for the tissues, and, in many Holocene demosponges, this is reinforced by a spongin supporting framework. This latter group, plus demosponges with firmly united desmas (Lithistida), is the most common siliceous sponge in Holocene and ancient shallow-water reef communities.

Most Hexactinellida live in deep (>200 m), cold, non-turbulent water, where their thin, fragile, spicular skeletons and isolated spicular fragments may be preserved in non-carbonate level-bottom sediments and rocks. Other factors that account for the general scarcity of siliceous sponges in reef communities are their weak attachment to the substrate (relatively few pre-Cenozoic siliceous sponges were binders or encrusters) and their lack of skeletal rigidity and strength to resist fragmentation during current transport.

The geologic histories of demosponges and hexactinellids in pre-Cenozoic reef communities are very similar (Fig. 8.1). The most important aspects of these patterns include:

a. Demosponges have generally been more important in reef communities than hexactinellids. Except for numerous, small reefs in the Permian (Finks, 1960), Middle (Palmer and Fürsich, 1981), and Late Jurassic (Pl. 36b; Gaillard, 1983; Gwinner, 1976), neither was a major contributor to the framework. This may be as much a reflection of the general paucity of deeper-water reefs in the stratigraphic record as it is of the ability of siliceous sponges to become major participants in the reef-construction process.

b. Demosponges played important roles in the baffler and constructor guilds in Ordovician–Silurian (Rigby, 1971, pp. 1374–1378; Narbonne and Dixon, 1984) patch reefs; only rarely were they important as binders (Finks, 1960, p. 27, Pl. 8, Figs. 2–4). (Fig. 8.1 does not include boring demosponges in the destroyer guild.)

SUMMARY AND CONCLUSIONS

From the data presented in Figure 8.1, it is obvious that several poriferan higher taxa, especially those with massive calcareous skeletons, have been of major significance in the building guilds of pre-Cenozoic reef communities. Due to the discovery and "rediscovery" of several species of so-called living fossils and because of uncertainties resulting from differential preservation and diagenetic alteration of spicules and skeletal microstructures, the phylogeny and classification of calcareous poriferans have been in turmoil since 1966, when Hartman and Goreau suggested that sclerosponges and stromatoporoids might be phylogenetically related.

Poriferans dominated reef-building guilds during the Early Cambrian (Archaeocyatha), Late Carboniferous (Chaetetida), Permian, and Middle Triassic (Sphinctozoa). They were of major importance during the mid-Paleozoic (Demospongiae; Stromatoporoidae) and Late Jurassic. Figure 8.1 shows five episodes in which sponges were not important builders of reefs (Middle–Late Cambrian, latest Devonian, Early Triassic, Early Jurassic, and Late Cretaceous through Pliocene). Each of these corresponds with a global extinction event followed by a general dearth of well-developed skeletal framework reefs.

Finks (1960, pp. 9–10; 1983, p. 58) and Wendt (1980a, ppp. 170–177) reviewed the stratigraphic distribution of late Paleozoic–early Mesozoic sponges and concluded that, except for their sharp decline during the Early Triassic, there is a extraordinary continuity at the family and genus levels through this time interval. This is quite remarkable because numerous non-sponge higher taxa that literally lived on top of these surviving sponges became extinct at the end of the Permian (e.g., productid brachiopods, cryptostome bryozoans, and rugose corals). Locally, especially in western Europe, a wide variety of sponges were major contributors to the building of numerous reefs during the Late Jurassic; post-Jurassic reef-building guilds have a sharply reduced input from sponges.

Vacelet (1985) and Fagerstrom (1984) suggested that post-Jurassic sponges are slow-growing relics that have been forced into protected or cryptic habitats by better space competitors such as the scleractinians and crustose coralline algae. The slow turnabout in relative importance of sponges and corals during the Middle Triassic–Late Jurassic interval may be related to the development of a symbiotic relationship with the zooxanthellae by more rapidly growing corals and a lack of such a relationship by the calcareous sponges.

9

Coelenterate Autecology and History

The reef-building coelenterates include the traditional corals (Tabulata; Rugosa; Scleractinia) as well as the lesser-known calcareous hydrozoans (Milleporina; Stylasterina), spicular alcyonarians (Stolonifera; Gorgonacea; Coenothecalia), the non-calcareous antipatharians, and the extinct "hydrozoans(?)" called Spongiomorphida. Of these taxa, all but the Tabulata, Rugosa, Scleractinia, and Spongiomorphida are insignificant in pre-Cenozoic reefs and so are not discussed here; Milleporina, Antipatharia, and Gorgonacea were considered in Part I.

Comparison of Figures 7.1, 8.1, and 9.1 rather clearly indicates that, except for the Middle Paleozoic, and locally in the Late Triassic–Early Cretaceous interval, corals were relatively unimportant as builders of pre-Eocene reefs. During the early and late Paleozoic, Middle Triassic, and Late Jurassic, algae and sponges were more important in the reef-building guilds, especially as bafflers and binders, than corals. However, due to their better skeletonization, corals have generally been better constructors than algae and sponges. Not only is the absolute domination of reef-building by corals a geologically young phenomenon, the abundance of branching scleractinian growth forms that characterizes most shallow-water (<20-m) Holocene reefs (Pl. 21b) is a late Cenozoic phenomenon. However, branching tabulate and rugose corals were also significant growth forms in middle Paleozoic constructor guilds. From a geological perspective, Precambrian, early Paleozoic, and Late Carboniferous reefs are most properly called "algal reefs"; most middle Paleozoic, Late Permian, and Middle Triassic–Late Jurassic reefs are "sponge reefs." The term "coral reefs" applies locally only to mid-Paleozoic, Middle Jurassic–Early Cretaceous, and mid–late Cenozoic reefs. Even during the late Cenozoic, there are numerous cases of reefs built primarily by algae, bryozoans, molluscs, and annelids (see Chap. 1).

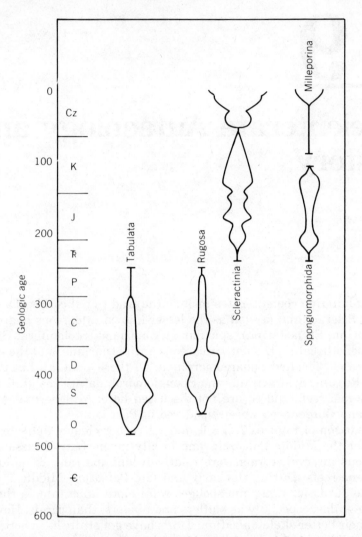

Figure 9.1. Summary of relative stratigraphic importance of Coelenterata in building guilds of Phanerozoic reef communities. Absolute age in million years. Symbols for geologic periods conventional; C = Carboniferous, Cz = Cenozoic.

CORAL COLONIALITY

Of all higher animal taxa that have been major builders of reefs, corals (both Paleozoic and Mesozoic–Cenozoic) are the only ones that contain both solitary and truly colonial forms. Tabulate corals and Bryozoa are exclusively colonial; Brachiopoda, Mollusca, and Annelida are exclusively solitary, as are most Porifera, but rugose and scleractinian corals include numerous solitary and colonial lower taxa.

The general importance of coloniality and particularly coral coloniality, to the success of Cenozoic reefs, was reviewed in Chapter 3; the significance of gregariousness (dense packing) of some brachiopods and bivalves is discussed in Chapter 10. Gregariousness in oyster-, vermetid-, and ser-pulid-built reefs was noted in Chapter 1. Although living sponges are individuals (Fry, 1979), the calcareous skeletons of some extinct sponges (i.e., Archaeocyatha, Chaetetida, and Stromatoporoidea) and Sclerospon-giae are so large and internally continuous that they suggest a higher level of integration (quasi-colonial?) than for the sponges discussed by Fry (1979).

Coates and Oliver (1973, pp. 5–7) have reviewed the relative generic diversity of all corals during geologic history and suggested that there was an significant correlation between the diversity of colonial corals and the importance of reef-building. The earliest reef-building corals were the colonial tabulates in the Middle Ordovician (Fig. 9.1), but most of the earliest rugose corals were solitary. Colonial rugosans did not participate in reef-building (as constructors) until the Late Ordovician. Solitary and colonial scleractinians appear simultaneously as minor components in sponge-built Middle Triassic reefs. Total coral diversity was at a Pha-nerozoic minimum during the Triassic, with neither corals nor reefs of any kind during the Early Triassic.

Coates and Oliver (1973), however, failed to stress that during the middle Paleozoic (Middle Ordovician–Devonian) there is an equally good cor-relation among the size, abundance, and diversity of stromatoporoids and reef-building. In a great many reefs of this age, the volumetric importance of colonial corals is exceeded by algae, stromatoporoids, and/or bryozoans. Although the contributions of colonial corals to late Paleozoic, Middle Triassic, and of some Late Jurassic and Late Cretaceous reefs were minor, the process of reef-building by other organisms continued with vigor.

Thus, coral coloniality was important in the building of Silurian–De-vonian (and locally, Late Ordovician and Early Carboniferous), Jurassic, Early Cretaceous, and especially Eocene–Holocene reefs (Fig. 9.1). On the other hand, the gregariousness of various other animals at other times was a factor at least as important to successful reef-building (see Part III).

POLYP/COLONY INTEGRATION

Among colonial corals, there are differing degrees of integration among the polyps in performing essential functions for the success of the entire colony. Some aspects of integration are reflected in the corallum and corallites and so can be used to infer degrees of integration in extinct corals. In this manner, Coates and Oliver (1973, pp. 7–8) established 17 stages of progressively increasing integration that they then applied to the study of all corals (Tabulata; Rugosa; Scleractinia). These stages were described in part using the "standard" terminology for corallite/corallum morphology (see Table 9.1 and Glossary). Their data and discussion indicate that:

a. Loosely integrated colonies (*cerioid* and phaceloid) dominated the entire Paleozoic and Triassic. The highly integrated coenenchymal Heliotilidae of the Ordovician–Devonian had very limited success, especially in reef communities, compared with other tabulates (especially Favositidae) and the Rugosa.

b. The polyps of the Tabulata were more highly integrated than those of the Rugosa, unless perhaps the cerioid rugosan polyps were integrated above the corallum surface. This may account for the greater corallum sizes and abundance of the tabulates in most Silurian, many Devonian, and a few Carboniferous reef communities. Only locally during the Devonian and Early Carboniferous were Rugosa of greater volumetric importance as reef constructors than Tabulata.

c. Post-Triassic polyps and coralla were much more highly integrated than in earlier corals. Coenenchymal and meandroid scleractinians greatly increased in importance during the Jurassic–early Cenozoic interval relative to poorly integrated types (i.e., phaceloid, cerioid). This may partly explain the great success of scleractinians in Eocene–Holocene reefs; however, their successful domination came long (40 million years) after the major rise in the relative importance of highly integrated coralla during the Middle Triassic through Early Cretaceous.

d. Except for the Triassic minimum, Phanerozoic coral faunas, especially middle Paleozoic and Jurassic–Cenozoic reef communities, have been taxonomically diverse and include a variety of differing integration levels. (However, the success of corals in reef communities has depended on much more than just their degree of intracorallum integration.)

Competition for space based on relative growth rates of numerous potential reef-building taxa seems to have been of greater influence in determining the guild structure of pre-Cenozoic reef communities than the degree of polyp/corallum integration. Therefore, despite the metabolic advantages of polyp/corallum integration, colonial corals were relatively poor space competitors through most of their pre-Eocene history. From this, it might be inferred that there is little relation between polyp integration, growth rate, and success in competition for space in any higher coral taxa regardless of geologic age (cf. Coates and Oliver, 1973, pp. 23–24). (For a discussion of factors affecting Holocene scleractinian growth rates, see Chap. 3.)

TABLE 9.1. Terminology for Corallum Morphology of Colonial Tabulata (T), Rugosa (R), and Scleractinia (S) Based on the Arrangement of Corallites and Associated Structures

I. Massive
Corallites erect–suberect, in close contact, cylindrical–polygonal. Walls of adjacent corallites united (T; R; S)
  A. Cerioid
     Walls of adjacent corallites united (T; R; S)
  B. Meandroid
     Corallites form linear or flabellate series or meandering rows of confluent corallites with walls only between rows or absent (S)
  C. Astreoid
     Corallite walls absent; septa of each corallite fully developed; septa of adjacent corallites alternate in position (R)
  D. Plocoid
     Corallite walls separated, distinct; adjacent corallites united by costae, dissepiments, or coenosteum (S; used differently in R)
  E. Hydnoporoid
     Corallite centers arranged around protuberant ridges between corallites (S)
  F. Thamnasterioid
     Corallites lack walls; septa confluent between adjacent corallites (R; S)
  G. Aphroid
     Septa of each corallite shortened peripherally; walls between adjacent corallites replaced by dissepimental zone (R; S)
  H. Coenenchymal (coenosteoid of some authors)
     Corallites separated but united by common (shared) skeletal tissue (T; S)
II. Fasciculate
Corallites erect–horizontal, not in close contact; subcylindrical (T; R; S)
  A. Phaceloid
     Corallites erect, parallel–subparallel (R; S; T)
  B. Cateniform
     Corallites erect, united laterally as palisades which appear chainlike in cross section; palisades commonly form network or boxwork (T; R)
  C. Dendroid (branching or ramose of some authors)
     Coralla erect, irregularly branching (R; S; includes zigzag, umbelliferous in T)
  D. Reptant (reptoid of some authors)
     Corallites have horizontal, creeping growth form; coralla attached to substrate as sheets or webs (T; R; S)

Source: Hill et al. (1956); Hill (1981); Coates and Oliver (1973); Barnes (1973).

CORALLUM GROWTH FORMS; GUILD MEMBERSHIP

To the non-coral specialist, the interrelations between the terminology for describing corallum/corallite morphology (Table 9.1 and Glossary) and growth form/habit (corallum shape, growth direction, and orientation) may appear confusing and contradictory, especially when compared with terminology for reef-building skeletons of other higher taxa. For example, in corals, the term "massive" has a specialized meaning with regard to the arrangement of corallites in the corallum; the term is also often used as a synonym of domal or hemispherical (Wells, 1956, p. F352) and as an antonym of branching or encrusting. "Massive" is also often used to describe the domal–hemispherical growth form of numerous non-coral taxa (Table 5.12) in the constructor guild.

Because of varied sizes, growth forms, and degrees of skeletonization of colonial forms, corals have been members of all reef-building guilds (constructor, baffler, binder; Table 9.2) almost continuously during their geologic history. The variation in scleractinian coralla is greater than for tabulates or rugosans and so they have had somewhat greater guild overlap. Because of the generally high degree of skeletonization of virtually all corals, the erect, branching forms belong primarily in the constructor guild. The more delicate, dendroid, phaceloid, and cateniform coralla were mainly constructors but also locally important as bafflers.

Foliaceous coralla (see Glossary) are most common in Cenozoic scler-

TABLE 9.2 Interrelations Among Corallum Growth Form/Habit, Corallum Morphology, and Guild Membership of Colonial Reef-building Tabulata (T), Rugosa (R), and Scleractinia (S)

Growth Form/Habit (Corallum Shape; Growth Direction)	Corallum Morphology[a]	Guild Membership (Primary/Secondary)
I. Massive (domal–hemispherical)	1–6 T; R; S	Constructor
II. Branching; bladed (erect growth)	1, 2, 4, 6–9 T; R; S	Constructor/baffler
III. Encrusting; flattened (lenses, sheets, webs; horizontal growth)	1–5, 6?, 10 T; R; S	Binder/dweller?
IV. Foliaceous (plates; horizontal growth)	1, 2, 4 T; S	Binder

[a]Key: (see Table 9.1)
1 = cerioid   5 = aphroid   8 = cateniform
2 = meandroid   6 = coenenchymal   9 = dendroid
3 = astreoid   7 = phaceloid   10 = reptant
4 = plocoid

actinians but also present in a few Paleozoic tabulates. They present a special problem in determining their guild membership. Their main growth direction is lateral (Pl. 21*a*), as is true of binders (see Chap. 5), but the undersurface is commonly not in direct contact with the substrate. Foliaceous coralla are usually large, well-skeletonized, and densely packed; in such situations, they may overlap the constructor guild and become especially important in the lateral growth of the reef framework.

Large, well-skeletonized solitary corals also present problems in guild assignment, particularly in middle Paleozoic and late Mesozoic–Cenozoic deep-water reefs, where they may be volumetrically important. Most solitary coralla are unstable in their erect living position and large specimens are very rare in this position in the fossil record. Their erect growth habit and upward growth direction suggest that they were unstable above the substrate and therefore ineffective as long-term baffles.

From the fossil and stratigraphic records, it is usually impossible to determine whether toppling of erect solitary coralla preceded or followed death of the polyp and whether it was due to currents, the activities of vagile benthic organisms, or processes involved in the compaction of the enclosing sedimentary matrix. However, parallel alignment of the corallite axes of numerous solitary coralla strongly suggests that currents were the cause of toppling and, in such cases, that toppling was the cause of death. Regardless of the cause or time of polyp death, the conclusion is that large, densely packed, erect solitary coralla were constructors, whereas small, loosely packed, toppled coralla were dwellers. In intermediate cases (so common in the middle Paleozoic), solitary corals overlapped the constructor and dweller guilds. Guild membership of solitary scleractinians, especially in the Cenozoic, is less of a problem because their coralla are much smaller, less abundant, and less well-skeletonized than Paleozoic solitary rugosans; in nearly all cases, solitary scleractinians were dwellers.

Summary

The assignment of pre-Cenozoic corals to one or more of the reef guilds depends on the same factors that were described in Chapter 5 for Holocene corals, namely their dominant growth direction, packing density, skeletal volume, and degree of skeletonization. Virtually all reef corals, regardless of geologic age, are well-skeletonized and thereby excluded from the baffler guild; exceptions include *some* middle Paleozoic dendroid tabulates, phaceloid rugosans and non-zooxanthellate Cenozoic scleractinians (discussed in Chap. 5).

Because most domal–hemispherical coralla are large, they belong to the constructor guild if they are densely packed. Branching Cenozoic scleractinians and massive, branching Paleozoic tabulates are also constructors. The erect phaceloid and cateniform coralla were primarily constructors with some overlap with the baffler guild (depending on corallum volume and packing density). Foliaceous scleractinians overlap constructor and binder guilds, while solitary coralla overlap constructor and dweller guilds.

Laterally expanded sheets and webs are of minor importance in most pre-Cenozoic reefs (i.e., they are dwellers) compared with analogous Cenozoic scleractinians. Where they are volumetrically significant, they belong to the binder guild. Lenticular coralla are common among middle Paleozoic cerioid, astreoid, and aphroid rugosans and may reach a diameter of nearly 1 m and a height of 30 cm. Such forms overlap the binder (relatively thin coralla) and constructor (relatively thick, domal coralla) guilds.

The degree of guild overlap among pre-Cenozoic corals is generally greater than for Cenozoic scleractinians for two important reasons:

a.   Their skeletons are smaller and they therefore are volumetrically less important than the scleractinian constructors of Holocene reefs.

b.   They are less densely packed and therefore the role of corals in the reef-building process is less important than in Cenozoic reefs.

TABULATA

The long-extinct tabulate corals (excluding Chaetetida but including Heliolitidae and Tetraiida) are a morphologically diverse and biologically enigmatic fossil group; the taxonomic status of the abundant and widespread Favositidae has been especially controversial (Hartman and Goreau, 1970; Flügel, 1976; Oliver, 1979; Kaźmierczak, 1984; Copper, 1985).

With the possible exception of *Cothonion sympomatum* from the Middle Cambrian of Australia, the earliest fossil corals (but not the earliest coelenterates; Jenkins, 1984; Jell, 1984) of any kind were tabulates of the genus *Lichenaria* from Early Ordovician (Tremadocian) reefs in eastern Canada (Pratt and James, 1982). In these reefs, they were sufficiently abundant to be the first members of any taxon in any reef community with the sole function (no guild overlap) of reef construction (Fig. 11.4). Furthermore, tabulates were generally more abundant and diverse in reef communities than in level-bottom communities from their Ordovician origin through the Middle Devonian and locally to the Early Carboniferous.

The earliest *Lichenaria* are morphologically simple, lacking septal ridges, mural pores, and generally also tabulae (Scrutton, 1984). By Arenigian time, there were at least two *Lichenaria* species and by the early Middle Ordovician (Llanvirnian), there were at least three tabulate genera. Through the Arenigian–Middle Ordovician interval, tabulates were relatively minor members of the reef dweller guild.

During the late Middle and early Late Ordovician (Llandeilan–Caradocian), there was a dramatic increase in diversity and abundance of tabulates (including numerous taxa with well-developed tabulae and mural pores) in reef communities. Most notable were the appearances of heliolitids and favositids; the former rose rapidly in importance in many Late Ordovician reefs, and the latter became the dominant tabulates in Silurian and Devonian reefs. The largest reef-building tabulates were massive, domal favositids up to 2 m in diameter from the Middle Silurian in Gotland and Middle Devonian in North America. Branching cerioid tabulates were also very important in the constructor guild by virtue of their large coralla; the largest mid-Paleozoic favositids had individual branches up to 60 cm long (more commonly, 10–20 cm).

The earliest cateniform constructors/bafflers (Halysitiida) were Caradocian and they rapidly assumed considerable importance in many Late Ordovician and Silurian reefs. Finally, the earliest reptant tabulates (*Aulopora*) were also Caradocian, but they rarely assumed importance as reef binders/encrusters.

Thus, by the end of the Caradocian, tabulate corals were clearly established as diverse, well-skeletonized, and locally important members of the constructor guild; they also occupied positions of varying degrees of importance in the baffler and binder guilds.

The relative importance of tabulates, particularly the favositids, continued to increase during the Silurian through Middle Devonian interval, and at least in North America, they reached their greatest importance in Middle Silurian and Middle Devonian cratonic patch reefs. In these reefs, the varied favositid coralla (domal, hemispherical, branching, encrusting) make them excellent examples of overlap among the constructor, baffler, and binder/encruster guilds. The Late Devonian marked the beginning of a long (130 million years), slow decline in importance of tabulates, especially favositids, in reef communities. Both reefs and tabulates were quite rare during the Early Carboniferous, and when reef-building revived during the Late Carboniferous and Permian, tabulates played only minor roles in all building guilds, with the local exception of phaceloid species of *Syringopora* as constructors/bafflers. The extinction of the Tabulata at the end of the Permian completed their prolonged declining importance; by this time, they were insignificant members of both reef and level-bottom communities.

RUGOSA

Although the Tabulata appear in the fossil record (Tremadocian) much earlier than Rugosa (appeared in early Caradocian; Fig. 9.1), there is some uncertainty as to whether the Tabulata were the phylogenetic ancestors of Rugosa. The Rugosa appeared almost simultaneously in Australia *(Hillophyllum)*, Estonia–Russia *(Primitophyllum)*, and North America *(Lambeophyllum)* (Neuman, 1984) and included both solitary and colonial forms. Throughout the history of the rugosans, solitary forms were generically more diverse than colonial (Fig. 3.11); in most reef communities, however, colonies were of greater volumetric importance (Hill, 1981, p. F48) and commonly more diverse. The coralla of all Early and Middle Caradocian rugosans were relatively small and rare members of level-bottom communities, but by the Late Caradocian, they had assumed membership in the constructor guild. During the interval from the Late Caradocian to the Middle Devonian, the Rugosa increased in abundance, corallum size, taxonomic diversity, and overall importance in the reef-building guilds. Their significance as builders was sharply reduced during the Famennian, rose briefly during the Visean, and then again declined during the Late Carboniferous and Permian. Rugosans and tabulates became extinct almost simultaneously near the end of the Permian.

Because of their well-skeletonized coralla, most rugose corals were confined to the constructor guild of middle Paleozoic (Late Caradocian–Frasnian) reefs; a few were binders and fewer still were bafflers. They seldom attained the overall importance as reef-builders of either the Tabulata or Scleractinia. There appear to be two reasons for this:

    a.   Rugosan coralla are generally smaller. Domal–hemispherical coralla seldom exceed 15–20 cm in diameter and 10–15 cm in height. Lenticular astreoid coralla attain sizes of 0.7–1-m diameter and 25–30 cm high. The largest rugosan colonies are fasciculate (mostly phaceloid) and these are nearly 1.25 m in diameter and up to 1 m high.

    b.   Rugosans had limited success in attaching to and encrusting hard substrates such as stromatoporoids and other corals. This may have prevented their occupation of geomorphic zones of high turbulence such as the reef crest. They reached their greatest importance in cratonic patch reefs and are replaced (or displaced?) by other metazoans and algae of the binder guild in environments of highest turbulence. Flattened and laterally expanded rugosan coralla generally covered sedimentary substrates (as binders) where they were less likely to be overturned or transported by currents. Conversely, rugosans are themselves commonly overgrown and encrusted by stromatoporoids and tabulate corals; whether the overgrowth occurred before or after death of the rugosan is difficult to determine. Nonetheless, Rugosa were apparently less successful space competitors during their mid-Paleozoic heyday than most other framebuilders. However, the rather meager data available on *solitary* rugosan growth rates (Chap. 3) suggest that they were similar to many tabulates and scleractinians. Thus, the less successful space competition by rugosans may have been due to factors other than growth rate.

SCLERACTINIA

Oliver (1980) has critically reviewed evidence regarding ancestry of the scleractinian corals. He concluded that they were not direct descendants of the Rugosa but instead were of wholly independent origin by skeletonization of one or more of the presumably numerous and diverse late Paleozoic anemones. In terms of degree of colony integration, the Mesozoic–Cenozoic scleractinians are not particularly more advanced than Paleozoic tabulates and rugosans. However, more scleractinian genera than Paleozoic corals are highly integrated (i.e., weakly integrated cerioid and phaceloid genera dominate the Paleozoic, whereas highly integrated coenenchymal and meandroid taxa dominate the Jurassic–Holocene; Coates and Oliver, 1973, pp. 7–12). Nevertheless, about 30% of Jurassic–Holocene colonial genera were poorly integrated (either cerioid or phaceloid).

Flügel and Stanley (1984) have reviewed the earliest (Middle–Late Triassic) scleractinian fossil record, mostly in Europe, and Qi (1984) has described the most diverse assemblage of the earliest scleractinians presently known. Of the 5 suborders known from the entire history of Scleractinia, 3 are represented in the South China fauna (cf. Wells, 1956, Fig. 259); it also contains 5 families, 6 genera, and 14 species (Qi, 1984, Table 1). The two missing suborders (Caryophylliina; Dendrophylliina) contain most of the dominant Holocene non-zooxanthellate genera; it appears, then, as if all the suborders that dominated Mesozoic and Cenozoic photic zone reefs appeared synchronously (Fig. 9.1).

Throughout the entire evolutionary history of Scleractinia, colonial genera have outnumbered solitary (in the Mesozoic by 2–3 times; Fig. 3.10). The earliest scleractinian (Middle Triassic [Anisian]) colonial forms included both fasciculate (e.g., *"Thecosmilia"*) and thamnasteroid taxa in well-skeletonized branching and massive growth forms (potential but not actual frame-builders).

By the succeeding Ladinian Stage, scleractinians were somewhat larger and more diverse; they produced small, coral-rich thickets and biostromes but remained in the dweller guild of reef communities. It was not until the latest Triassic (Norian Stage; Rhaetian in Europe) that the scleractinians, especially *"Thecosmilia,"* assumed major volumetric importance in the constructor guild for the first time (Fig. 9.1; Stanley, 1981, p. 509; Flügel and Stanley, 1984).

Of the approximately 50 genera of Triassic scleractinians, only 11 span the Triassic–Jurassic boundary and none extend beyond the Early Jurassic (Beauvais, 1984). During the Jurassic, the Scleractinia underwent their first major increase in generic diversity (Stanley, 1981, Fig. 2), especially those with coenenchymal and meandroid coralla (Coates and Oliver, 1973, p. 12) and trabecular septa (Beauvais, 1984, p. 219). The Jurassic generic diversity increase (60 genera in Early Jurassic, nearly 100 in Middle, and over 130 in Late Jurassic) produced a biostratigraphically unique assemblage because only 40 genera span the Jurassic–Cretaceous boundary.

Despite the dramatic, progressive increase in coral diversity during the Jurassic, no uniformly progressive increase in size and abundance of reefs or in the importance of corals in reef-building guilds accompanied it (Fig. 9.1). Reefs are less common in the Early Jurassic than in either the Late Triassic or Middle Jurassic (especially the Bajocian and Bathonian; Beauvais, 1984). After a brief time of reduced vigor near the Middle–Upper Jurassic boundary, reef building increased again in importance during the middle Late Jurassic (Late Oxfordian–Kimmeridgian); only in photic zone reefs (e.g., central England), were corals of major volumetric importance.

From the Middle Jurassic to the end of the Cretaceous, scleractinian familial and generic diversities underwent their greatest expansion (Wells, 1956, pp. F362–F368; Stanley, 1981, Fig. 2). No families became extinct at the end of the Jurassic, but most Late Cretaceous familial extinctions involved those that had appeared during the Jurassic rather than during the Cretaceous (Beauvais, 1984).

The characteristic Holocene deep-water, non-zooxanthellate families (Caryophylliidae and Dendrophylliidae) appeared during the Middle Jurassic and Late Cretaceous, respectively; however, neither diversified at the species level to the same degree as most shallow-water, zooxanthellate families.

In the higher scleractinian taxa, there is almost no predictable relationship among taxonomy and corallum morphology (Table 9.1), guild membership (Table 9.2), whether they are solitary or colonial, or among the colonial forms, their degree of colony integration. At the suborder level, none of these features is critical for identification (Wells, 1956, pp. F369–F370). At the family level, the distinction between solitary and colonial is usually important, but corallum morphology is of variable importance; growth form differences become important only at the genus/species levels. Thus, among Scleractinia, the potential for guild overlap and morphologic plasticity is higher than for the Tabulata and Rugosa. Ideally, each scleractinian specimen should be individually assigned to its proper guild. More realistically, however, because they are generally well-skeletonized, large, and densely packed in *most* post-Triassic reefs, *most* scleractinians belong to the constructor guild (Tables 5.12, 9.2). In all Middle Triassic and in many Late Triassic, Early Jurassic, and Late Cretaceous reefs, corals are neither large enough nor abundant enough to be constructors and, regardless of their growth form, are assigned to the dweller guild.

Two of the major differences between Paleozoic tabulate and colonial rugosan corals and Mesozoic–Cenozoic scleractinian corals are the more rapid growth rates (discussed in Chap. 3) and the successful development and utilization of the polyp edge zone in the latter (discussed by Wells,

1956, p. F335). The edge zone was one important aspect of the coenenchymal level of colony integration and attendant metabolic efficiency that was widely exploited during the Mesozoic by the Scleractinia but apparently only of limited value to Paleozoic corals (Coates and Oliver, 1973, Fig. 4A). Wells (1957b, p. 773) and Coates and Oliver (1973, p. 23) suggested that one reason that Paleozoic reefs are generally small is that the predominant corals were phaceloid and ceroid; they therefore lacked an edge zone to help them maintain a firm attachment to the substrate and an efficient system for removal of metabolic wastes from the colony.

Development of the edge zone and increased separation of the polyps were accompanied by increased lateral expansion of zooxanthellae-bearing tissue, chiefly coenosarc. The progressive increase in exposure of coenosarc zooxanthellae to sunlight may have led to increased calcification, skeletal strengthening, and growth rates, all of which would have been advantageous to the domination of reef-building guilds by scleractinians.

SPONGIOMORPHIDA

The Spongiomorphida (Spongiomorphoidea of some authors) are an enigmatic group of hydrozoanlike fossils of considerable local importance in Late Triassic and Early Cretaceous reefs (Fig. 9.1) of the Alpine region (Flügel, 1981, p. 307). They also occur in considerable abundance locally, in Jurassic reefs in Europe and Japan. The morphology and biological affinities of the spongiomorphids were described by Hill and Wells (1956, pp. F87–F88) and Turnšek (1968, p. 374), who concluded that they were very unusual hydrozoans. However, with future restudy and reevaluation of Mesozoic sclerosponges, stromatoporoids, and spongiomorphids, both latter forms will probably be regarded as calcareous sponges (Flügel, 1981, p. 307).

Spongiostromatids are well-skeletonized, occur in upwardly branching growth forms, and are locally of sufficient abundance to belong to the constructor guild. Only rarely do they bind or encrust the substrate.

10

Autecology and History of Bryozoa, Brachipoda, Bivalvia, and Crinoidea

BRYOZOA: ECTOPROCTA

Skeletal bryozoans appear in the fossil record in Late Cambrian level-bottom communities but by the Middle Ordovician (Fig. 10.1) had become very important members of reef communities (Ross, 1964; Pitcher, 1971). The abundance of zoarial fragments in both internal and external reef sediments (Rhomboporoids and bifoliates in the Paleozoic; cyclostomes in the Mesozoic–Cenozoic) indicates the long history of Bryozoa as members of the dweller guild. In fact, all major bryozoan taxa have been dwellers at one time or another during geologic history (Cuffey, 1974, 1985). Bryozoan importance and involvement in reef communities have also varied considerably and have included (Cuffey, 1972, 1974, 1977):

a.   Small, bryozoan-dominated (binder/constructor guild), quiet-water Ordovician (Pl. 40) and Holocene (Chap. 2) patch reefs. Bryozoans have generally been more important in patch reefs and banks (biostromes) than in other forms of ancient reefs.

b.   Bryozoan-dominated veneers (binder guild) on the surface of Paleozoic and Holocene reefs constructed by other major taxa and as encrusters and fillers of cryptic habitats in late Cenozoic reefs.

Only three major bryozoan groups have contributed extensively to reef-building: (1) massive, encrusting, and branching trepostomes and cystoporates during the Ordovician–Devonian; (2) delicately branching and lacy fenestrates and acanthoclads (Cryptostomata) during the late Paleozoic; and (3) encrusting and massive cheilostomes during the late Cenozoic. Bryozoans were generally insignificant in the building of Mesozoic reefs, except locally as binders/encrusters in the Late Triassic reefs of the

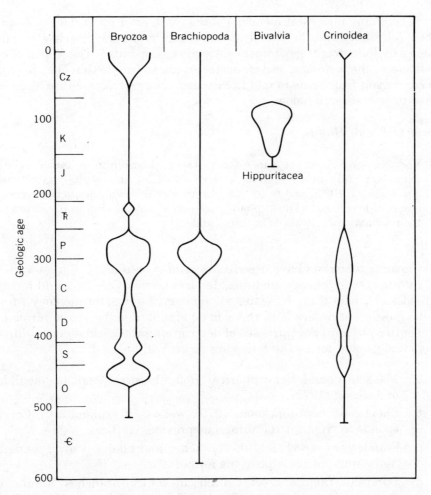

Figure 10.1. Summary of the relative stratigraphic importance of the Bryozoa, Brachiopoda, Bivalvia, and Crinoidea in the reef-building guilds of Phanerozoic reef communities. Absolute age in million years. Symbols for geologic periods conventional; C = Carboniferous, Cz = Cenozoic.

northern Alpine region (Flügel, 1981, p. 307, 309). The roles of bryozoans in the formation of mud mounds was discussed by Pray (1958).

Evolutionary History
The morphology, classification, phylogeny, and general ecology and paleoecology of bryozoans are discussed at length in Ryland (1970) and Boardman et al. (1983); the history of their roles in reef communities is covered by Cuffey (1974, 1977, 1985). The fact that throughout their history the zoecia and zoaria have remained small has prevented bryozoans

from becoming important members of the constructor guild. This is despite their coloniality and the heavily calcified zoaria of many forms, especially the early Paleozoic trepostomes and some cystoporates. The zoaria of cyclostomes, cheilostomes, and ctenostomes are so fragile that they usually occur only as fragments in reef limestones; the cryptostomes are a special case to be discussed below.

Growth Forms/Habits.

> Variations in form and texture (of zoaria) seem almost infinite, and are related to fundamental differences in the pattern of budding and resultant growth (*see also Lidgard, 1985*), and to certain characteristics pertaining to the different orders of bryozoa . . . Thus, colonies are almost bewildering in the variety of their formations . . . (words in italics added).
>
> (Ryland, 1970, p. 22)

Bryozoan taxonomists have described zoarial shapes using a great variety of informal (e.g., sheets, nodules, dendroid, sticklike, etc.) and formal (frondescent, fenestrate, bifoliate, trifoliate, etc.) terms; terminology varies among different orders, and there is no standard set of shape terms for the entire phylum. For purposes of determining the guild membership of taxa and growth forms the following terms will be used:

a. Massive: domal–hemispherical. Roughly corresponds to "mounds" of Jackson (1979).

b. Sheets, runners (Jackson, 1979), webs (self-explanatory). Corresponds to "reptant" of numerous previous authors.

c. Frondescent: erect, leaflike branches and blades. Corresponds to "foliaceous" of some previous authors.

d. Dendroid, ramose: erect, cylindrical–conical branches. Similar to "trees" of Jackson (1979). May be bifoliate, trifoliate, or multifoliate (see Boardman, et al., 1983, pp. 350–355).

e. Fenestrate: erect with branches forming a reticulate network. Corresponds to "reteporiform" of Stach (1936).

Homeomorphism of zoarial shapes is rampant among bryozoan higher taxa and has suggested to some previous authors that they have played analogous functional roles in reefs of widely discrepant ages. For example, Cuffey (1972, p. 548) and Soroka and Cuffey (1979) suggested that encrusting lichenoporoid cyclostomes (Holocene) and certain fistuliporoid cystoporates (mid-Paleozoic) might be analogues. Conversely, the deeper (23–34-m), quiet-water reef-dwelling Holocene reteporoid cheilostomes may occupy quite different environments from the mid- to late Paleozoic reef- and mound-building fenestrate cryptostomes (usually regarded to have been shallow, turbulent water; Cuffey and McKinney, 1982).

Guild Membership. Cuffey (1974, 1977) has developed a detailed scheme for describing the functional roles of bryozoans in reef communities that is somewhat different from the one used here. Nonetheless, his scheme is amenable to modification in ways that make the bryozoan functional roles comparable to other reef-building higher taxa (Table 10.1).

No bryozoan zoaria have been sufficiently large to be included in the

TABLE 10.1. Comparative Terminology and Assignment of Bryozoan Growth Forms to Reef Guilds and their Functional Roles in Reef Communities

Growth Forms (Zoarial Shapes)	Guild Membership (As Described in Chap. 5)	Roles (After Cuffey, 1974, 1977)
	I. Constructor guild (no bryozoans; may overlap with binder guild)	I. Principal frame-builders (examples from Holocene, Chap. 2 herein and Ordovician, Chap. 11 herein)
Frondescent; dendroid; fenestrate	II. Baffler guild (rarely in growth position)	II. Sediment-movement inhibitors A. Sediment stabilizers/trappers
Sheets; runners; webs	III. Binder guild A. Binders B. Encrusters (commonly in growth position)	IIIa. Sediment-movement inhibitors B. Sediment binders IIIb. Accessory frame-encrusters C. Dead-reef veneerers (open habitats) D. Hidden encrusters (cryptic habitats)
Massive plus all others	IV. Dweller guild	IV. Accessory frame-encrusters E. Cavity dwellers/fillers
All forms	V. All guilds	V. Sediment formers

constructor guild. However, in some Holocene (discussed in Chap. 2) and Middle Ordovician reefs, erect to sheetlike zoaria are so densely packed that the binder guild has assumed the role of the constructor guild (guild overlap) in a manner comparable to the crustose coralline algae of Holocene algal ridges. However, bryozoans never achieved the same importance as either constructors or binders that algae *(sensu lato)*, sponges, or corals did during their varied acmes of importance. Bryozoa functioned primarily as bafflers, binders, and dwellers; no bryozoans ever belonged to the destroyer guild.

Ordovician Guilds. Trepostomes and cystoporates, especially ceramoporids, were the dominant bryozoans in Middle and Late Ordovician reefs. Locally in Vermont, the constructor and binder guilds overlapped to produce small reefs with dendroid forms providing some baffling, but they were of lesser importance to the building of the framework than to the construction and binding processes. Massive zoaria, chiefly trepostomes, were too small to contribute to any of the building guilds and there is some evidence of a low diversity bryozoan cryptic assemblage (encrusters; cavity dwellers).

Silurian Guilds. By the Middle–Late Silurian, bryozoan species diversity of the trepostomes and ceramoporids had increased considerably and reef communities also included encrusting and foliaceous fistuliporids. The chief importance of bryozoans was as encrusters and secondarily as bafflers.

Late Carboniferous–Permian Guilds. Large cryptostomes ("fenestellids" and "acanthoclads") reached their acme during the late Paleozoic; they were very significant in Late Carboniferous and Permian (Zimmerman and Cuffey, 1985) reef communities and were present, but of lesser importance, in Devonian reefs. Their zoaria are usually highly fragmented, either from high turbulence during life or from postburial compaction (relative effects are difficult to determine). Nevertheless, the abundance of zoarial fragments clearly indicates their considerable importance as members of the baffler guild; in fact, the fenestellids are the epitome of poorly skeletonized Paleozoic bafflers.

BRACHIOPODA

Throughout their long (Early Cambrian: Atdabanian–Holocene) geological history, articulate brachiopods have been very successful members of the dweller guild in most reef communities. The slow replacement of sponges as the dominant reef-builders by the scleractinians during the Late Triassic–Late Jurassic was accompanied by a progressive decrease in abundance of reef-dwelling brachiopods. In post-Jurassic reefs, brachiopods are relatively small and abundant only in local situations such as cryptic habitats (Jackson et al., 1971). Elliott (1950) has suggested that the Mesozoic decline in the importance of brachiopods was due to the much higher mortality rates of their larvae by carnivorous coral polyps than by passive, microfilter-feeding sponges that dominated most pre-Cretaceous reefs. Throughout most of the Paleozoic, the abundance and diversity of the articulates were much higher in reef communities than in adjacent level-bottoms (except for the unattached forms). This fact suggests that a significant portion of brachiopod evolution may have occurred in reef communities (Fagerstrom, 1983).

During the Late Carboniferous–Permian in reefs marginal to the Delaware Basin in western Texas, brachiopod evolution produced four highly specialized (aberrant; bizarre) higher taxa that became important members of the reef-building guilds (Fig. 10.1; Scacchinellidae; Richthofeniacea; Streptorhynchinae; Lyttoniidae; see Rudwick, 1965, pp. H199–214; 1970, pp. 160–173). Grant (1971, pp. 1450–1456) has reviewed the occurrence of these and other higher brachiopod taxa in the most carefully studied Early Permian reef and level-bottom communities in the area of the Glass Mountains, Texas (Fig. 6.3).

Functional Morphology; Guild Membership. The aberrant morphological adaptations of the reef-building brachiopods included:

a. A deeply conical, upwardly expanding pedicle (ventral) valve (coralliform of Grant, 1971); the mantle cavity and "soft parts" were protected by an operculumlike brachial (dorsal) valve, with sievelike holes in some taxa, and internal spines. Rudwick (1961) has described the feeding mechanism of two such species.

b. Elongate rhizoid spines on the exterior of the valves. In the Richthofeniacea, the spines on the pedicle valve acted as struts or braces to hold the conical valve in an upright position. In dense clusters of such shells, the spines of neighbors commonly were entangled among several individuals to form mutually supporting clusters (Pl. 43b). Spines of the brachial valve and those around the aperture of the pedicle valve functioned to prevent large suspended particles from entering the mantle cavity.

c. Cementation of the apex of the pedicle valve in conical forms, or the area of the umbo in others, to hard substrates such as other brachiopods, sphinctozoans, bryozoans, or calcareous algae. These well-cemented shells provided considerable rigidity to the reefs that they built.

d. Although brachiopods are wholly solitary animals, the dense clustering of individuals indicates a highly gregarious mode of life for the Permian reef-builders that was probably achieved by a high level of larval habitat selection. Numerous non-reef brachiopods are able to cement or attach their shells together, but the degree of gregariousness by reef-builders is generally much higher than for non-reef taxa. The combination of good skeletonization, upright growth position and direction, dense clustering, and mutual support makes most of these aberrant brachiopods members of the constructor guild. However, some poorly skeletonized forms were members of the baffler guild; yet others grew generally parallel to the substrate as binders.

The Richthofeniacea were perhaps the most varied and successful of all aberrant higher taxa (Grant, 1971, p. 1450). Among various richthofenids, all four of the above morphological adaptations for reef-building were present, and during the Early Permian they were major constructors of reef frameworks. The Lyttoniidae ("leptodids") were the most peculiar members of the order Strophomenida with ladderlike "slots and rungs" on the brachial valve; they were able to cement their shells together (binders) to form clusters and mounds somewhat similar to those made by cemented Holocene oysters (Rudwick and Cowen, 1968; Grant, 1971, p. 1455). Cowen (1970; 1983) has suggested that in both richthofenids and leptodids, large areas of mantle were exposed to sunlight and contained symbiotic zooxanthellae. If true, this would probably have increased the skeletal growth rates of these forms to bring feeding structures above the more turbid substrate. Rapid skeletal growth and calcification and efficient suspension feeding were shown in Part I to be important attributes of successful Holocene reef-builders and, by analogy, should have contributed to the success of the Early Permian reefs of western Texas.

The oldest (Carboniferous–Early Permian) reef-building brachiopods in the Glass Mountains were conical scacchinellids and cemented streptorhynchids. These reefs were small and of relatively low diversity. Later in the Early Permian, the richthofenids, and to a lesser degree the leptodids, became the chief constructors of somewhat larger reefs of much higher diversity. The largest reefs in western Texas are Late Permian (Guadalupian in local usage) and are well exposed in the Guadalupe Mountains. In these extensive "barrier" reefs, the constructing brachiopods described above were rather insignificant members of the dweller guild.

The end of the Permian brought massive extinction, or near extinction, to numerous higher brachiopod taxa with long and important Paleozoic histories (e.g., Strophomenida, including all reef-builders, Orthida, Pentamerida, and most Spiriferida). Early Triassic brachiopods are exceedingly rare, but as reef dwellers, brachiopods progressively increased in abundance, but not diversity, through the Middle Jurassic.

BIVALVIA: HIPPURITACEA (RUDISTS)

Although fossil bivalves extend back to the Early Cambrian, they appear to be largely confined to level-bottom communities until the Middle Ordovician. From then until the Early Cretaceous, they were present as relatively unimportant members of the dweller guild (overshadowed by bryozoans, brachiopods, and gastropods). However, during the Cretaceous, there was a remarkable change in the functional role of bivalves in reef communities from one of dweller to constructor (Fig. 10.1).

The hippuritaceans, commonly called "rudists" or "rudistids," are aberrant or bizarre bivalves that differ from more typical forms in being highly inequivalve, with the large valve usually conical (Fig. 10.2), cylindrical, or coiled and cemented to the substrate by the apex or side of the shell (Fig. 10.3). The free valve is smaller, flatter, loosely coiled or uncoiled, and acted as a lid or operculum closing the aperture of the larger attached valve. Paired internal muscle scars (adductors and protractors) indicate that rudists could open and close the valves to allow water and food to enter the mantle cavity and to expel sediment and wastes. In the attached valve, the body cavity was very large unless divided by transverse–vertical tabulae (Pls. 35*b*, 38*a*) which confined the tissues to the apertural region (Skelton, 1976, Fig. 1). Infoldings (pillars), grooves for for the siphons, large teeth, and accessory cavities further subdivided the

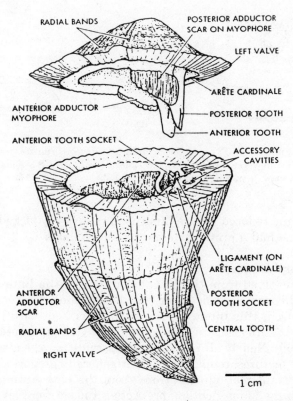

Figure 10.2. Morphology of a typical erect, conical shell of *Radiolites* sp. (Bivalvia: Hippuritacea) in posterior aspect (From Skelton, 1979a, © 1979 The Paleontological Society.)

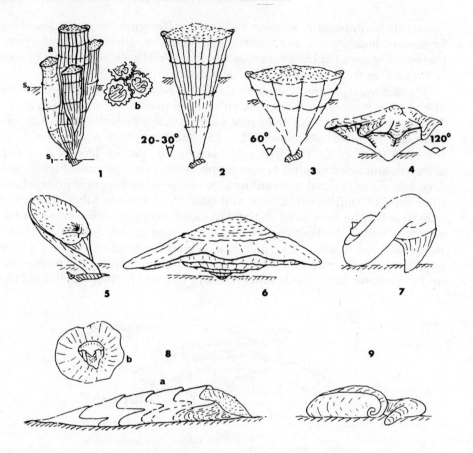

Figure 10.3.   Fundamental growth forms of Late Cretaceous rudists. 1 = cylindrical; (*a*) lateral view, (*b*) transverse section. 2–7 = various conical forms. 8 = foliaceous; (*a*) lateral view, (*b*) dorsal view. 9 = coiled. (From Philip, 1972.)

body cavity and reduced its size. Rudists almost surely lacked a protrusible foot, but some had a protrusive mantle and siphons.

Evolutionary History

The rudists evolved from the Megalodontidae in the Late Jurassic (Oxfordian) and became extinct near the close of the Cretaceous. Well over 100 genera from this interval have been described, with the main evolutionary diversification in the Albian and Campanian–Maastrichtian (Coogan, 1969). Nearly all Late Cretaceous rudists were large, with thick shells. These features, coupled with their generally gregarious habit, made rudists important reef-builders from about the Late Aptian or Early Albian through the Maastrichtian; pre-Aptian rudists were level-bottom and reef dwellers. The reef-building forms characteristically grew upward in erect clusters (Pl. 37), which brought the feeding margins up into the

water column for enhanced suspension-feeding efficiency (feeding in erect
rudists has been discussed at length by Skelton, 1976, 1978, 1979a, 1979b;
Kauffman and Sohl, 1974) and escape from sediment clogging.

Diversification. The Hippuritacea have been divided into either seven
(e.g., Dechaseaux, 1969) or nine (Skelton, 1978, pp. 315–318) families.
Four of these families (Diceratidae, Requieniidae, Caprotinidae, Mono-
pleuridae) were evolutionary "conservatives" (Coogan, 1969, Fig. E234).
The earliest and most primitive rudists were diceratids and monopleurids;
in their early growth stages, they may have been infaunal to semi-infaunal
(Bein, 1976, p. 268; Skelton, 1978, pp. 305–311); as adults, they had tur-
binate–helicospiral shells to bring the commissure and feeding structures
well above the substrate (cf. Kauffman and Sohl, 1974). These forms, plus
the requeienids, were most abundant and diverse as dwellers in Late Jurassic and Early Cretaceous shallow-water reef flat and lagoonal environments; despite moderately large shells (15–20 cm long), they rarely built
reefs. In many situations, these early rudist communities were dominated
by variously coiled, curved, and straight shells that were recumbent to
semirecumbent on the substrate.

During the Kimmeridgian, the first reef-building families (Caprotinidae
sensu Dechaseaux, 1969) evolved from the Diceratidae (Skelton, 1978,
Fig. 17). The Caprotinidae were not as important as reef-builders as the
three (or 6; Skelton, 1978) families that descended from them during the
mid-Cretaceous. The frame-building families (Caprotinidae; Caprinidae
sensu lato; Radiolitidae; Hippuritidae) diversified rapidly during the Late
Cretaceous and attained several advanced evolutionary traits lacking in
their more conservative megalodont or rudist ancestors. These advance-
ments included (Coogan, 1977, p. 37; Kauffman and Johnson, 1984):

   a.   Cementation of the attached valve to the substrate. One common
problem in understanding the mode of life of rudists is determining their
growth direction with respect to the substrate surface. More primitive
recumbent forms were broadly attached by the base and side of the valve.
The area of attachment to the substrate in erect forms was generally
small in proportion to the generally large size of the shell (Fig. 10.3, 1–
3); therefore, these shells were apparently unstable, particularly in high
turbulence. Rudists lived on a variety of substrates, including muds and
skeletal sands. On soft muds, the juvenile spirogyrate shells were partially
embedded by the heavy umbonal area to provide stability to the uncoiled,
erect adult shells (Fig. 10.3, 4–7; for examples of shell/substrate relations,
see Skelton, 1978, Fig. 16; Skelton, 1979b, Figs. 2, 3). On sands and
hardgrounds (including other rudists), attachment was by cementation
of special shell layers to support and maintain erect adult growth.

   b.   Uncoiling of the valves, especially the attached valve, to allow erect
growth and to put the feeding margin above the substrate (Fig. 10.2) and
conical–cylindrical shapes in the attached valve. This pattern resulted

in progressive reduction in ligament size and internalization of the ligament; it also allowed increased packing density of shells. The ligament changes led to a narrowing of the gape, which reduced problems related to sediment and predators entering the mantle cavity (Skelton, 1976, pp. 95–96).

c.   Lowering of the center of gravity in erect forms for increased stability. Such lowering was accomplished by reduction in size and weight of the free valve; in the early caprotinids and caprinids and later in the radiolitids and some hippuritids, the adjustment was made by development of liquid-filled pores, cellules, and canals in the attached valve (Pl. 38*a;* Kauffman and Sohl, 1974, p. 404; Skelton, 1979b, p. 263; Coogan, 1977).

d.   Increasing gregariousness and packing density of individual rudists into tightly knit, self-reinforcing, and self-supporting clusters (Pl. 37). In addition, in several erect forms, enhanced stability was achieved by the attached valves of adjacent individuals becoming intertwined, partially cemented together, or interlocked by external ornamentation (Pl. 35*b*) such as flanges, ribs, flutes, etc. (Skelton, 1979b, pp. 273–277; Philip, 1972, Fig. 2).

Extinction. Of the seven hippuritacean families recognized by Coogan (1969, Fig. E234), all but the Diceratidae and the Caprotinidae were present near the end of the Cretaceous (Maastrichtian); of the nine families recognized by Skelton (1978), six were present during the Maastrichtian. In fact, the Campanian–Maastrichtian was an interval of major diversity increase in the three reef-building families (Caprinidae, Radiolitidae, Hippuritidae). During the Maastrichtian, reefs composed chiefly of radiolitids and hippuritids were at their acme of abundance and diversity; they appear to have adapted to a greater variety of habitats than at any time during the nearly 100 million years of rudist history. Their extinction near the end of the Maastrichtian was very abrupt but not catastrophic, and approximately coincided with the final decline in ammonite diversity and led to a complete reorganization of reef ecosystems during the early Cenozoic (see Chap. 15).

Guild Membership

Size; Growth Rate. The aspects of rudist morphology and distribution that most strongly influenced their guild membership were the size and shape of individuals and their packing density (gregariousness) in the reef framework.

Adult rudists were the largest (by volume) bivalves that ever lived; the largest individuals were up to 2 m long and 60 cm in diameter (exterior dimensions). Furthermore, their shell walls were thick (Pl. 36*b;* up to 15 cm); so, despite the high porosity of some valves (30–70%), they were not easily transported as whole shells.

Several aspects of rudist shell morphology suggest that their growth rates were high and life spans short. In taxa with porous, cellular, or canaliculate shell walls, large sizes were attained without the extraordinary expenditure of metabolic energy that would have been required for solid shells. The presence of wall cells and thickened struts in the wall structure still provided adequate strength without unnecessary weight (Pl. 38a; Kauffman and Sohl, 1979, p. 725).

The thick walls of valves in the apertural area, especially in erect radiolitids and some hippuritids, were probably covered by marginally expanded and continuously exposed mantle lobes used for suspension feeding (Kauffman and Sohl, 1974; Skelton, 1976, 1978, 1979a). Kauffman (1969) and several subsequent authors (summarized by Cowen, 1983, pp. 456–460) suggested that the lobes may have contained endosymbiotic zooxanthellae to enhance the efficiency of precipitation of $CaCO_3$ in the valves, much as they do in Holocene corals and the bivalve *Tridacna* (discussed in Chap. 2). Vogel (1974) attempted to test this suggestion by comparing shell structures of the radiolitid *Osculigera* and the zooxanthellate Holocene bivalve *Colculum cardissa*. He concluded that they were sufficiently similar to support Kauffman's hypothesis, at least for *Osculigera*. Additional study is needed before the probable *Osculigera*–zooxanthellae symbiosis and its advantages of efficient calcium metabolism and rapid skeletal growth rates can be extended to other large rudists.

Growth Forms. In the Upper Cretaceous rocks of southeastern France, Philip (1972, pp. 212–215) recognized four fundamental rudist growth forms: cylindrical, conical (with six variants), foliaceous, and coiled (Fig. 10.3). There is considerable taxonomic and guild overlap among these forms, but the cylindrical, coiled, and long conical forms are characteristic of reef and biostromal communities. Skelton (1978, pp. 313–314) recognized three basic growth forms: (1) elevators (similar to cylindrical and long–large conical of Philip); (2) encrusters, with two variants (similar to dilate–flat conical and foliaceous of Philip); and (3) recumbents, with two variants (similar to inclined–spiral conical and coiled of Philip). The inclined–erect conical forms are mostly monopleurids and the coiled are mostly requienids. Cylindrical forms include both radiolitids and hippuritids; radiolitids occur in nearly all fundamental and variant forms. Other authors have used such descriptive terms as stubby, barrel or keg-like, and slender (pencil-like).

Gregariousness. Rudists varied in their degree of gregariousness during life from isolated to loosely packed groups of unattached individuals to densely packed pseudocolonies (Philip, 1972, pp. 215–216; Kauffman and Sohl, 1974, pp. 429–443, Figs. 10–21). The isolated mode of life was characteristic of most caprotinids and some requienids and caprinids; isolates included recumbent and semi-infaunal ("pivotantes" of Philip) growth forms. Many advanced recumbents were flattened ventrally with cemented sides or external ribs to increase their area of contact with the substrate. Higher packing densities were found in oysterlike, cemented recumbents and flat conical–foliaceous growth forms.

Progressively higher degrees of gregariousness are found in: (1) clusters of individual shells from loosely attached, moderately well-cemented "bouquets" 1–3 m high (Pl. 37a) and "bushes" (Philip, 1972, Fig. 3; Perkins, 1974, Text-Figs. 7, 8, 18, 19); and (2) "fan-like clusters morphologically similar to coral heads" (Bein, 1976, p. 261, Figs. 4, 5) typical of many monopleurids and tightly packed, well-cemented, interlocking hippuritid and radiolitid reefs and biostromes (Skelton, 1979b, Fig. 4).

Conclusions

The great variety of rudists (i.e., in individual sizes, growth forms, and packing densities) resulted in great differences in their overall paleoecological optima. These differences included adaptations to variation in numerous environmental factors such as salinity, depth, turbulence, temperature, etc., their occurrence in both reef and non-reef communities, and their guild membership.

Isolated to loosely packed, recumbent, coiled, and semi-infaunal forms belonged to level-bottom and biostromal communities. Moderately well-cemented and densely packed recumbent, broadly conical, flat, or foliaceous forms built low diversity reefs; these associations were commonly dominated by such non-rudist members of the constructor and binder/encruster guilds as corals or serpulids. Finally, reefs composed of erect, cylindrical, to long–large conical forms in densely packed bouquets and clusters of cemented, intertwined or interlocked arrangements were built by members of the constructor guild. Despite the fact that nearly all rudists extended above the substrate surface and thus impeded currents at the substrate surface, none were members of the baffler guild because of their very well-calcified shells.

Succession. Many Late Cretaceous reefs have an internal ecologic succession, or at least a vertical sequence of rudist taxa and growth forms, that appears related to progradation of reef complexes across shallow shelves (Kauffman and Sohl, 1974, pp. 449–464; note that the progression illustrated in Text-Fig. 10 can be achieved by the lateral migration of various rudist assemblages in the Text-Fig. 27 as in Fig. 5.1 herein). Such vertical sequences typically begin with solitary recumbent requienid, caprinid, or caprotined colonizers (pioneer community) of coarse-textured level-bottom substrates. This is succeeded by upright/erect, weakly cemented, moderately gregarious monopleurids, caprinids, and radiolitids in scattered clusters (intermediate community). The climax community consists of erect, highly gregarious (bouquets, bushes, fans, tight clusters), taxonomically diverse caprinids in the Early Cretaceous and radiolitids and hippuritids in the Late Cretaceous.

Evolution. In addition, there was a long-term (Late Jurassic–Late Cretaceous) evolution of rudist-dominated level-bottom and reef communities. The timing of the major evolutionary events depended on the geographic and geologic/tectonic locations of particular areas, but the general evolution of the communities can be subdivided into four units:

a. *Late Jurassic* During the Oxfordian, the only rudists were level-bottom and coral reef flat dwelling diceratids; during the Tithonian, these were locally joined by the earliest requienids, monopleurids, and caprotinids. Representatives of all four families continued into Early Cretaceous as important members of level-bottom and coral reef communities.

b. *Berriasian–Hauterivian (Early Cretaceous)* Monopleurids, requienids, and caprotinids replaced the diceratids as the dominant rudists of carbonate shelf (or platform) level-bottom communities. The earliest erect, cemented, and encrusting growth forms produced poorly constructed biostromal frameworks.

c. *Barremian–Cenomanian (mid-Cretaceous)* This interval marked the climax of the reef-building caprinids *(sensu lato)* and the appearance of radiolitids and their expanding importance in reef communities. During the Albian and Cenomanian, caprinid/radiolitid-built reefs were of high diversity (both taxonomic and growth form), with closely packed and well-cemented shells. These reefs were located at shelf margins and upper seaward slopes, reef flats, and lagoons. Requienids, monopleurids, and caprotinids continued to form loosely constructed lagoonal biostromes. In central Texas and New Mexico, caprinid/caprotinid-built reefs were most abundant near the shelf margin with low diversity monopleurid, requienid, and oyster biostromes in reef flat–lagoonal environments (Perkins, 1974; J. L. Wilson, 1975, pp. 319–325).

d. *Turonian–Maastrichtian (Late Cretaceous)* Reefs of this age are very well-constructed and are dominated by radiolitids and hippuritids; the former were especially important after the Coniacian and the latter after the Santonian. During this interval, particularly in the Maastrichtian, rudist diversity at the genus and species levels reached its maximum. The largest rudist reefs are shelf margin barrier reefs in western Europe and the Greater Antilles; smaller reefs, however, were also present in reef flat and lagoonal locations.

J. L. Wilson (1975, pp. 324–325) has compared the reef and biostrome-building rudists with some of the other reef-building taxa discussed in Part II. Some of the most significant differences include:

a. Many rudists seem to have been more euryhaline and tolerant to geologic settings of restricted seawater circulation.

b. Many rudists are associated with unconformities (diastems) suggesting that they lived in very shallow water and may even have tolerated periodic emergence.

c.   Many rudists in climax communities occur in carbonate rocks with high mud content matrices, suggesting that they were adapted to more turbid water than the Porifera and many Coelenterata.

d.   (not discussed by Wilson) The large, heavy, erect rudist shells lack external supports such as spines, struts, and large apical holdfasts and are commonly not in their presumed growth position. Some rudists compensated for this lack of upright stability by their dense packing, development of external flanges, and cocementation. Nonetheless, their common toppled position suggests that they were far less stable than most other major reef-constructing higher taxa. For this and other reasons, numerous previous authors have debated if any rudist-dominated structures can be properly regarded as reefs. Furthermore, most of these structures lack evidence of important members of either the baffler or binder guilds (Kauffman and Sohl, 1974). Encrusting/binding rudists were largely confined to level-bottom communities and were minimally involved in reef building. The view expressed here is that rudist-dominated structures span the full range from level-bottom non-reefs and loosely constructed biostromes to reefs. Each structure must be evaluated individually, using the criteria discussed in Chapter 1, in order to determine whether or not it is a reef and whether or not it was built by rudist members of the constructor guild.

CRINOIDEA

Although the fossil record of crinoids is very long (Late Cambrian–Holocene) and specimens are both abundant and taxonomically diverse, their importance as reef-builders is confined to the Paleozoic and in particular to the Middle Silurian, Middle Devonian, and Late Carboniferous to Permian (Fig. 10.1). During the Early Carboniferous (Tournaisian–Visean), crinoids were also important in the formation of non-reef mud mounds. Thus, crinoids were generally more characteristic of level-bottom than reef communities and, unlike algae, sponges, and corals, much of their evolutionary diversification took place in level-bottom locations.

The Paleozoic associations of crinoids and reefs are from the Middle Ordovician (e.g., Vermont; Pitcher, 1971), Middle Silurian (e.g., Illinois Basin/Gotland, Lane, 1971; and western England, Abbott, 1976), and Middle Devonian. The Middle Ordovician reefs contain abundant early inadunates and camerates, but the former were less well-adapted to the high turbulence of reef environments than the latter.

In contrast, Middle Silurian camerates were very well-adapted to reefs of high turbulence. Their special adaptation included (Lane, 1971):

a.   Strong, boxlike thecae.

b.   Short, stout arms arranged in an expansive net with small spaces between the brachial plates and pinnules for efficient suspension feeding.

c. Stout stems with massive holdfasts for secure substrate attachment.

d. Location of the anus below the bases of the arms to minimize self-fouling of the ambulacral system.

Guild Membership

At no time were crinoids of major importance as reef-builders. However, the abundance of columnals and other fragments in internal reef sediment (Pl. 5*b*) and reef flanking beds clearly indicates that they were significant members of nearly all Paleozoic reef communities.

Crinoids with the best adaptations for high reef crest turbulence (strong thecae, short stems and arms) belonged to the baffler guild. However, in more protected and less turbulent situations (pioneer or cryptic sub-communities), crinoids may have had longer stems and arms and so would have been much more effective bafflers. Paleozoic crinoids must have played roles as bafflers comparable to baffling by the Antipatharia and some Gorgonacea in Holocene reef communities. After death, the poorly constructed crinoid skeletons were easily broken; porous fragments were dispersed by currents to various reef cavities and adjacent level-bottom substrates. Because of the considerable discrepancy between the abundance of columnals and paucity of thecal plates in reef sediments, it is very difficult to estimate either the biomass or diversity of crinoids based on their skeletal debris.

Furthermore, other pelmatozoans were also potentially important contributors of skeletal debris in reef sediments; their columnals are almost impossible to distinguish from crinoid columnals. However, the extinct non-crinoid pelmatozoans apparently were more abundant in level-bottom than in reef communities.

PART III

SYNECOLOGY AND HISTORY OF PRE-CENOZOIC REEF COMMUNITIES

INTRODUCTION

Despite numerous inadequacies of Cenozoic reef communities as models for older communities (see Chap. 6), the guild concept (established in Chap. 5) is an effective method for describing and comparing reef communities through geologic history. The guild concept was used previously (Chap. 7) to describe the structure and function of Precambrian algal reefs and in Part III (Chaps. 11–14) will be the basis for describing and comparing Paleozoic and Mesozoic algal/metazoan reefs. Although all five guilds will be discussed, emphasis is on the reef-building guilds (constructor, baffler, binder). Selected examples of the guild structure of reef communities are presented, on almost a stage-by-stage basis. Most of the examples typify the particular geologic stage they represent. However, for some stages where essentially contemporaneous communities have distinctly different compositions and guild structures, more than one example is presented. Thus, ancient reef communities were as variable as Holocene communities (see Chap. 1). Chapter 15 is a general summary and overview of the entire history of reef communities and the numerous factors and events that have affected their composition and structure.

Part III is the first attempt to organize and analyze coherently the complete history of any type of benthic marine community. Reef communities are particularly appropriate for such an analysis because their unique properties (e.g., composition, structure, distribution) make them one of the most objective ecological evolutionary units in the history of the world biota.

In Parts I and II, it was stressed that *reefs are biological phenomena.* As such, their biological attributes are of greatest interest since they have undergone much more change than their non-biological attributes. It is these biological attributes that are the focus of the present volume and Part III is the culmination of "The Evolution of Reef Communities."

11
Early Paleozoic Reef Communities

CAMBRIAN AND EARLY ORDOVICIAN

The beginning of the Cambrian marked a major event in the evolution of reef communities: the transition from non-skeletal stromatolites (discussed in Chap. 7) to weakly skeletonized algae and metazoans. During the Late Precambrian and Early Cambrian, the non-skeletal stromatolitic algae underwent their first decline in importance; another came in the Early–Middle Ordovician (discussed below; Fig. 7.1). However, despite these declines, stromatolites and stromatolitic crusts as well as such weakly skeletonized Cyanophyta: Porostromata as *Girvanella* continued to be locally important as binders in Cambrian–Early Ordovician reefs.

Of far greater importance to the evolutionary history of reef communities is the almost simultaneous appearance of a remarkably diverse assemblage of the very first skeletonized organisms during the latest Precambrian (?) and earliest Cambrian. These include various enigmatic and problematic cyanophytelike "algae" (discussed in Chap. 7), including such well-known forms as *Renalcis, Epiphyton,* and *Ortonella* ("Cambrian Flora" of Chuvashov and Riding, 1984), and the earliest skeletal metazoans (Archaeocyatha, discussed in Chap. 8) and small, enigmatic shells and tubes. These varied algal forms were the dominant reef-builders throughout the earliest Cambrian through Early Ordovician interval. The Archaeocyatha are present in most Early Cambrian reefs and biostromes but are of major importance as builders only during the middle Early Cambrian (Late Atdabanian–Early Elankian Stages). The Early Cambrian stage names adopted for this discussion are those from the Siberian Platform; from base to top, they are: Tommotian, Atdabanian, Botomian, and Elankian.

Most early Paleozoic reefs are small and all of them lack large, well-skeletonized organisms of the constructor guild that characterized Middle Ordovician–Devonian reefs. Therefore, distinction between reefs and biostromes is often very difficult. In the following discussion, emphasis is on mound-shaped structures believed to have had some original topographic relief rather than on biostromes.

Early Cambrian

Guild Structure. Skeletal problematic algae clearly dominate all earliest Cambrian (Tommotian) reefs; archaeocyathids are present but of minor volumetric importance. The compositional and structural complexity of these first skeletal reefs is indeed low. They were built by algae of the binder guild (constructor–binder guild overlap); the small, erect, weakly skeletonized archaeocyathids functioned as bafflers. There is no apparent record of destroyers; dwellers consisting of enigmatic, small, phosphatic and calcareous shells are very rare in or absent from most Tommotian reefs.

During the Atdabanian–Botomian interval, reefs increased in size (Handfield, 1971, reported one in the Yukon, Canada, 100 m thick; see also Read, 1980) and biological complexity (James and Debrenne, 1980, pp. 656–657). The relative importance of archaeocyathids also increased, but in most of these reefs, algae remained volumetrically dominant. There are apparently two reasons for the increased size of reefs during this time: (1) a general increase in skeletal sizes of archaeocyathids and (2) increasing archaeocyathid colonialism (fusion of the walls by exothecal tissue; dendroid–catenulate growth forms, Copper, 1974, pp. 370–373). The earliest dwellers, especially trilobites, occur in Atdabanian reefs (James and Debrenne, 1980) and the oldest reef destroyers *(Trypanites)* in the latest Early Cambrian (Elankian; James et al., 1977). Other members of the dweller guild include brachiopods (especially inarticulates), sponges (especially chancellorids), and enigmatic helcionellids, hyolithids, and rare helicoplacoids.

Elankian reefs are smaller and less widely distributed than Botomian reefs and archaeocyathids are much less diverse (James and Debrenne, 1980). Thus, overall reef size, abundance, and geographic distribution during the Early Cambrian appear much more closely related to size, diversity, and distribution of archaeocyathids than to the volumetrically predominant algae. This suggests that an important functional role of archaeocyathids was to create voids and hard surfaces for growth of the binding/encrusting algae. *Renalcis* is especially common on both inner and outer walls of cup-shaped archaeocyathids.

Example 11.1: Tommotian; Siberian Platform. In the Lower Cambrian rocks of the Siberian Platform along the Lena and Aldan rivers, Russian geologists have recognized two forms of reefs: (1) monolophoids: plano–convex structures 1.5–3 m high and up to 12 m in diameter, separated from each other laterally and vertically by 1–5 m of bedded, interreef limestone; and (2) dilophoids: irregularly shaped (biconvex, funnel, diamond, etc.) structures 1–2 m high and 2–3 m in diameter (James and Debrenne, 1980, Figs. 2–4).

Most Tommotian reefs are dilophoids and had an original topographic relief of only about 20 cm. The organic framework is dominated by *Renalcis* (35% of rock volume; Fig. 11.1); archaeocyathids comprise only about 5% of the volume with lime mud (and cement?) about 60% (James and Debrenne, 1980, pp. 661–663). Rozanov and Debrenne (1974, Fig. 5A) recognized 26 archaeocyathid species from the Tommotian but did not distinguish between those confined to reefs and those confined to level-bottom substrates.

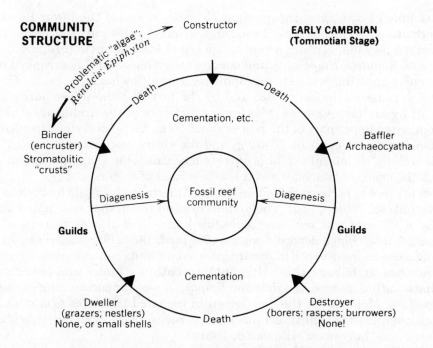

Figure 11.1. Guild structure of early Early Cambrian (Tommotian Stage) reef communities in the area of the Siberian Platform along the Lena and Aldan Rivers. *Renalcis* comprises about 35% of the rock volume. Although the archaeocyathids are diverse (>20 species), their skeletons are rather small, poorly calcified, noncolonial, and comprise only about 5% of the volume. Lime mud (and cement?) constitute the remaining 60%. There are no known members of these communities in the destroyer guild, and dwellers are exceedingly rare (small shells and tubes). Main guild membership indicated by thick arrow and guild overlap by thin arrow (around circle).

Example 11.2: Upper Atdabanian–Lower Botomian?; Sardinia. In the area of the Matoppe Valley, reefs were built primarily by *Epiphyton,* stromatolitic (cryptalgal) crusts, *Girvanella,* and archaeocyathids (Gandin and Debrenne, 1984). In one of the reefs, these authors recognized 22 archaeocyathid morphotypes in 11 genera. The most abundant archaeocyathids are branching colonies ("stick-shaped") of taxa with either a small central cavity or no central cavity and small, cylindrical forms of *Bicyathus* and *Agastrocyathus;* "saucer" and "bowl" growth forms are present but much less common.

The algae are all members of the binder/encruster guild and the archaeocyathids belong to the baffler guild; however, the packing density in both guilds appears sufficient for them to overlap with the constructor guild. Dwellers include trilobites, brachipods (linguloids and articulates), echinoderms, sponges (spicules only), and questionable Bivalvia. The internal sediment has been burrowed, but boring of archaeocyathid walls was minimal.

Example 11.3: Upper Atdabanian; Nevada. Rocks of the lower Poleta Formation (*Nevadella* Zone; based on trilobites) at Stewart's Mill, southeastern Nevada, contain a reef composed of stromatolitic/thrombolitic crusts, *Renalcis, Epiphyton,* and dendroidal archaeocyathids arranged in complex, interfingering stratigraphic relations (Rowland, 1981a, b). This reef is remarkable for its size and by the fact that the upper part was built by archaeocyathids. Maximum thickness of the archaeocyathid-dominated upper part of the reef is about 20 m; the underlying *Renalcis*-dominated part is about 20–30 m and the entire reef complex is nearly 70 m thick. Its lateral extent is uncertain because of incomplete exposure, but the original diameter was a few hundreds of meters.

This reef is perhaps the oldest North American reef built by archaeocyathids (cf. Read, 1980). The archaeocyathid fauna that dominated the top of the reef was not diverse; builders consisted of only two densely packed, intertwined dendroid species (Rowland, 1984). The subjacent rocks contain a more diverse fauna (pioneer community?) dominated by unbranched archaeocyathids (Pl. 38*b*). In both the upper and lower archaeocyathid faunas, *Renalcis* and *Epiphyton* were important binders/encrusters. Members of the dweller guild included trilobites *(Judomia),* helcionellids, hyolithids, echinoderms (ossicles only), sponges (spicules only), and "burrowers" (Rowland, 1981a).

In the area of the Ketza River, Pelly Mountains, in central Yukon, Canada, Read (1980) reported large archaeocyathid-dominated reefs of approximately the same age as those of the lower Poleta. Dominant archaeocyathids consist of two irregular genera (*Pychnoidocyathus,* represented by two species, and *Protopharetra sp.*) and one regular (*Coscinocyathus?*). *Pychnoidocyathus* and *Protopharetra* are weakly colonial, forming small catenulate thickets; the latter genus also produces dendroid colonies. These dominant, moderately well-skeletonized/colonial forms belonged to the constructor and baffler guilds (overlap). Other archaeocyathids (e.g., *Bicyathus?, Ajacicyathus, Cordilleracyathus?*) have small, poorly skeletonized, non-colonial cups and belonged to the baffler guild. *Renalcis* dominated the binder guild and the dwellers included trilobites (3 genera), echinoderms, and inarticulate brachiopods.

The Pelly Mountains reefs also contain a few specimens of the enigmatic form called *Altaicyathus?* (Read, 1980, p. 11). They include various growth forms (domes up to 6 cm in diameter; columnar and tabular) that occur in localized clusters and were minor contributors to the building guilds. Some authors have suggested that *Altaicyathus* was the earliest reef-building stromatoporoid, but the scarcity or complete absence of any stromatoporoids, reef or level-bottom, until the Middle Ordovician, casts doubt on stromatoporoid affinities of this problematic genus.

Example 11.4: Elankian; Eastern Canada. The reefs in the Forteau Formation (Elankian; *Bonnia–Olenellus* Zone) of Labrador and Newfoundland are among the most intensely studied and well-documented Early Cambrian reefs in the world. They are numerous, closely spaced, and with the associated biostromes, form carbonate–shale complexes up to 20 m thick and 200 m in diameter (James and Kobluk, 1978); individual reefs are pillow-shaped, 0.2–1.0 m high, and 1–2 m in diameter.

Although there are only 6 species of archaeocyathids in the reefs, their skeletons comprise 20–60% of the rock volume (Debrenne and James, 1981). One of the species *(Metaldetes profundus)* completely dominates the fauna (80–90% of the individuals); it grew as cylinders (about 10 mm in diameter and 190 mm long), cones (80 mm in diameter and 190 mm tall), cups, and bowls. All the other 5 archaeocyathid species included cylindrical ("stick-shaped") growth forms with fragments commonly larger than *M. profundus;* one of these *(Retalamina amourensis)* is most common as thin, sheetlike, or caplike (overturned bowls?) forms up to 3 cm high with *Renalcis* and *Epiphyton* encrusting the central cavity. Colonial forms were present (Cooper, 1974, Fig. 4.4), but not in sufficient numbers to be important builders.

The erect, cylindrical, conical, and cup-to-bowl-shaped archaeocyathids comprise the baffler build, whereas those with sheet-to-cap-shaped skeletons belong to the binder guild (Fig. 11.2). The degree of guild overlap among archaeocyathids in these reefs is greater than in the previous examples; most individuals were bafflers, a few were encrusters, and, because of their high packing density, both guilds overlap the constructor guild. The other binders/encrusters consisted of *Renalcis* and *Epiphyton* (Copper, 1974, Figs. 4.1, 4.3). Dwellers on the exposed reef surface included trilobites, hyolithids, brachiopods, echinoderms (plates only), and sponges (e.g., *Chancelloria*). Copper (1974, pp. 373–374) has sketched his interpretation of the appearance of the living community and discussed its

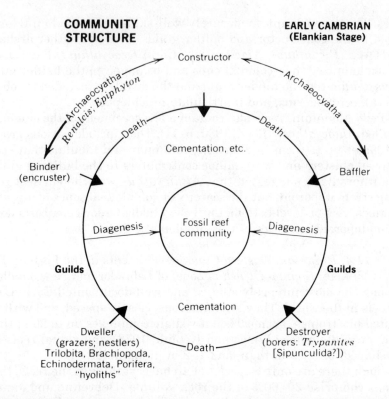

Figure 11.2.   Guild structure of reef surface community of reefs in the Forteau Formation, eastern Canada (late Early Cambrian; Elankian Stage). Archaeocyathid diversity is low (6 species) because these reefs were formed during the time of major taxonomic decline in these sponges; their erect skeletons are sufficiently large, colonial, and densely packed to have overlapped the baffler and constructor guilds. Sheetlike archeocyathids and encrusting *Renalcis* and *Epiphyton* were primarily binders but were abundant enough to have also participated in the construction process. Main guild membership indicated by thick arrows, and guild overlap by thin arrows (around circle).

presumed trophic structure; Kobluk and James (1979, pp. 209–212) discussed the role of possible fungi in the saprophytic system of the community.

The reefs of the Forteau Formation appear to contain the oldest record of the destroyer guild (James et al., 1977). Older Cambrian reef communities may have included filamentous algal microborers, but their presence has not yet been documented. The Forteau Formation boreholes belong to the form genus *Trypanites* (perhaps made by a sipunculid); they are about 1.3–2.5 cm long, cylindrical, straight, and approximately perpendicular to the original hard surface, which consisted of archaeocyathid skeletons and early cemented hardgrounds (Kobluk et al., 1978, pp. 167–168).

Kobluk and James (1979) have also detailed the composition and structure of a surprisingly diverse and complex cryptic subcommunity in these same reefs; it is similar to Holocene cryptic subcommitties in some ways. Their chief similarity is the absolute domination by encrusters; the major difference is the apparent absence of cryptic borers in the Cambrian.

The cryptic subcommunity within the Forteau Formation reefs occupied small cavities formed below skeletons of the dominant surficial archaeocyathids, especially *Metaldetes profundus* and *Retalamina amourensis,* and skeletal algae *(Renalcis; Epiphyton).* Archaeocyathids formed hard "roofs" to which were attached various encrusters and pendent forms consisting (in order of decreasing abundance) of:

a.   Pendent "Renalcis-like" organisms.

b.   *Renalcis* and *Epiphyton* so abundant that they encrusted/constructed layers up to 15 cm thick and hung from archaeocyathid roofs as pendent clusters.

c.   *Archaeotrypa* and *Bija* (biological affinity uncertain); encrusters.

d.   *Wetheredella* (chlorophyte or foraminifera); encrusted roofs and lived within pendent algal clusters.

e.   *Girvanella* (Cyanophyta: Porostromata); encruster.

f.   *Serligia gracilis;* possibly an encrusting rhodophyte.

g.   Fungi, which grew on cavity ceilings along with algae.

Kobluk and James (1979, p. 211) found that there was an orderly succession of "pioneering" encrusters that began with the "Renalcis-like" organism, followed by *Renalcis* and then *Epiphyton;* the other taxa were not divisible into intermediate or climax successional stages.

Skeletal fragments in the internal cavity fillings include trilobites, brachiopods *(Obolella?),* and ostracods. It is virtually impossible to determine whether these organisms lived in the cavities or whether their fragmented skeletons were transported there by currents. The internal sediments were also burrowed and pelleted by a "soft-bodied" deposit feeder and were believed by Kobluk and James to contain evidence of fungi. Thus, these cryptic subcommunities seem to have been essentially complete ecosystems with autotrophic algae of several higher taxa, consumers (mostly deposit feeders and scavengers), and presumed saprophytes (bacteria and fungi).

Paleobiogeography. Archaeocyathids were not confined to reefs, but were so very characteristic of reef communities during the Early Cambrian that a map of their distribution (Rozanov and Debrenne, 1974, Fig. 1) very closely approximates the distribution of reefs. However, their concentration in the northern hemisphere is certainly a reflection of the concentration of Cambrian research in the northern hemisphere.

Zhuravleva (reported in Hill, 1972, p. 33) recognized two archaeocyathid biogeographic subprovinces in the Tommotian of Russia (the presumed locus of origin of archaeocyathids and their dispersal center). By the end of the Atdabanian, there were perhaps as many as three "regions" (Afro-European, Siberian, Australian) and during the Botomian archaeocyathid acme, Zhuravleva recognized six provinces, three subregions, and two regions.

Primarily on the basis of trilobites, Cambrian workers currently recognize four global shallow-water provinces (American, Siberian, European, Hwangho; Ziegler et al., 1981). During the Tommotian, there was only the Siberian and it was confined to the Siberian Platform; with the advent of more cosmopolitan trilobites in the Atdabanian, the other three provinces came into existence. Because of the generally greater endemism of archaeocyathids (due to their greater stenotopism?) and perhaps also to slower migration rates, paleobiogeographic reconstructions based on archaeocyathids are quite different from those based on trilobites.

Using only genera of regular Archaeocyatha, Debrenne and Rozanov (1983) recognized 11 provinces. Of the total 228 genera, only 23 (10%) are present in 6 or more provinces, 2 (*Aldanocyathus; Coscinocyathus*) are present in 10 provinces, and 120 (53%) are confined to a single province. The lowest generic diversity is in the North American province and 6 of the 7 genera present there (86%) are endemics; the next highest endemism is in the Australia–Antarctica province. The Baikal–Mongolia–Tuva province contains the fewest endemics.

Archaeocyathid Decline and Extinction. The acme of archaeocyathid diversity and geographic range was in the Botomian (James and Debrenne, 1980; Debrenne and Rozanov, 1983). The beginning of the most rapid increase in archaeocyathid diversity (Atdabanian) approximately coincides with the rapid rise in importance of olenellid trilobites (Rozanov and Debrenne, 1974). Thus, for a period of about 10–15 million years (Late Atdabanian–Botomian), archaeocyathids were the dominant–subdominant members of nearly all reef communities, and olenellids dominated the level-bottoms.

The abrupt decline in diversity and range of archaeocyathids and of reefs coincides with the beginning of the *Elankian (Bonnia–Olenellus* Zone; Trilobita). The generic diversity of regular archaeocyathids declined from over 200 in the Botomian to 7 or 8 in the Early Elankian, to about 6 in the Late Elankian (the last of the archaeocyathid-built reefs), and to about 1–2 genera in the Middle and Late Cambrian (James and Debrenne, 1980; Debrenne and Rozanov, 1983; Debrenne et al., 1984). The post-Botomian decline and extinction of archaeocyathids took 30–35 million years, or approximately 3 times the duration of their heydey as reef-builders (Fig. 8.1).

Summary. The Early Cambrian was a time of great importance in the evolution of reef communities. It was marked by the appearance of the first *skeletal* reef-building organisms, including both problematical "algae" and metazoans. The earliest reefs were small and the building guilds dominated by skeletal *(Renalcis; Epiphyton)* and non-skeletal (stromatolitic "crusts") algae. Later, in the Early Cambrian (Late Tommotian–Atdabanian), reef size increased dramatically as did taxonomic diversity and guild complexity of reef communities.

During the Late Atdabanian and Botomian, the relative importance of algae and archaeocyathids underwent a reversal; the building guilds of most reefs of this age were dominated by large, weakly skeletonized, colonial, and densely packed individual archaeocyathids. There was considerable guild overlap by both algae and archaeocyathids. The great evolutionary diversification of archaeocyathids during this interval took place in reef environments rather than on level-bottoms.

Throughout the Early Cambrian, there was a gradual increase in the geographic distribution of reefs and in archaeocyathid endemism. Tommotian reefs were confined to the Siberian Platform and Altai–Sajan areas of Russia but expanded in size and range through the Atdabanian and Botomian to produce 11 archaeocyathid-based paleobiogeographic provinces, all of which were dominated by endemic genera.

The peak of Early Cambrian guild complexity came in the Elankian with the simultaneous appearance of the first macroscopic members of the destroyer guild *(Trypanites)* and the first cryptic subcommunity. This subcommunity is only known from eastern Canada, where it is surprisingly diverse. The cryptic habitats were created by archaeocyathid-built roofs; the subcommunity was dominated by microscopic, encrusting skeletal algae and other encrusters of uncertain biological affinities. There is almost no evidence that any of these early cryptic organisms later migrated to the reef surface to become important members of any major reef-building guilds. Both surficial and cryptic ecosystems during the Elankian apparently were trophically complete with producers, consumers (suspension and deposit feeders; scavengers), and saprophytes.

Tommotian reef dwellers consisted of rare, enigmatic, small shells and tubes of both phosphatic and calcareous compositions. During the Atdabanian–Elankian interval, trilobites and brachiopods increasingly dominated the dweller guild.

The rate of increasing importance of archaeocyathids in Tommotian–Early Atdabanian reef communities was very slow and their domination of Late Atdabanian and Botomian reef building guilds short (about 10–15 million years). The initial decline in diversity of archaeocyathids, and in size and geographic distribution of reefs during the Elankian, was very abrupt, but they continued to live in local level-bottom communities until the Late Cambrian (another 30 million years).

Middle and Late Cambrian

The decline of archaeocyathids and reefs during the Elankian was followed in the Middle Cambrian by the first of five extended Phanerozoic intervals characterized by a dearth of metazoan skeletal reef frameworks. Non-skeletal and skeletal algae were present and locally abundant enough to build a few small reefs during the Middle Cambrian–Early Ordovician interval, but most had a very poorly constructed skeletal framework. Instead, they typically contained stromatolitic "crusts" and such a high content of lime mud that many are better described as biostromes or mud mounds than as reefs.

Example 11.5: Late Cambrian; Central Texas. The rocks of the Wilberns Formation in the region of the Llano uplift, central Texas, contain a large number of biostromes and reefs built by varied assemblages of skeletal and non-skeletal algae and problematical "algae." Each of these algal reefs is generally composed of several types of macrostructures and form discrete mound-shaped structures up to 16 m high and 30 m in diameter (Pl. 9*b*).

Ahr (1971) recognized four main types of macrostructures arranged in ascending order (ecological succession?):

a. Mottled thrombolites (Pl. 39*a*). Interpreted by Ahr to have formed in a sublittoral, low turbulence environment.

b. Cryptalgal sheets or stromatolitic crusts up to 15 cm thick. Successive cryptalgal sheets form reefs up to 1.6 m high and 7 m in diameter.

c. Interlayered cryptalgal sheets and stromatolites that locally may form large cryptalgal domes or "giant stromatolites" (Pl. 39*b*).

d. Stromatolites 0.6–1 m high and wide. These never occur without at least one other macrostructural type and commonly form surficial "caps" or "crusts" up to 15 cm thick. They were interpreted by Ahr to have formed in high turbulence near the lower limit of the littoral zone.

Girvanella (Cyanophyta: Porostromata) dominates the skeletal algae and was the chief reef builder (Fig. 11.3); *Renalcis* was present in some cryptalgal–stromatolitic macrostructures but so rarely that it cannot be regarded as a builder. The *Girvanella* tubules are arranged in erect, dendritic "bushes" up to 5 cm tall and belonged to the baffler guild (Fig. 11.3). *Girvanella* tubules are also arranged in long, subhorizontal "fingerlike" strands with several strands stacked vertically with intervening sediment lenses to indicate their involvement in the binder guild. The clotted microfabric of some thrombolites also contains dendritic and tangled *Girvanella* "bushes." *Renalcis, Epiphyton,* detrital fragments of the tubular skeletons of problematical (alga?) *Nuia* (Toomey and Klement, 1966), and lithistid sponges (Rigby, 1971, p. 1374) are the only record of the dweller guild. Trilobites, brachiopods, and other metazoans were abundant on the adjacent level-bottoms but not on the algal reefs.

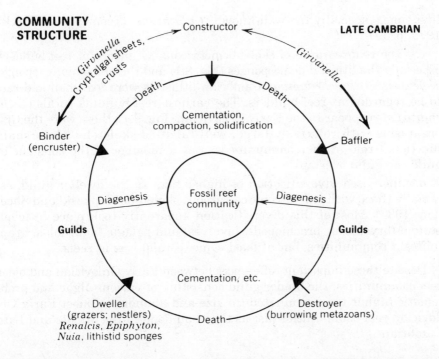

Figure 11.3. Guild structure of Late Cambrian algal reefs in the Wilberns Formation, central Texas. *Girvanella* tubules in erect, dendritic "bushes" were major bafflers, whereas tubules in subhorizontal "fingerlike" arrangements were important binders. The chief difference between these reefs and the late Precambrian stromatolite reefs (Fig. 7.2) is the abundance of weakly skeletonized (Porostromata: *Girvanella*) cyanophytes in the Cambrian and their absence in the Precambrian. Main guild membership indicated by thick arrows, and guild overlap by thin arrows (around circle).

Early Ordovician

The Early Ordovician was an important time of transition and reorganization of reef communities. Those of the Middle and Late Cambrian were completely dominated by cyanophytic algae, whereas those of the Middle Ordovician were dominated by a variety of higher taxa characterized by much larger, well-calcified skeletons. The major features of Early Ordovician reefs are:

a.   The decline in overall importance of major algal higher taxa that were the sole contributors to Precambrian and Middle–Late Cambrian building guilds (Fig. 7.1: Spongiostromata; Porostromata, especially *Renalcis* and *Epiphyton*). Early Ordovician reef-building algal higher taxa are more diverse than those during the Cambrian, and single genera no longer exert as dominant a role.

b.   The "Receptaculites Group" of "problematic" algae (Chuvashov and Riding, 1984, pp. 488, 490, Fig. 3) become important reef-builders for the first time, especially the well-known *"Calathium"* (Toomey and Nitecki, 1979, p. 17).

   c.   The reappearance of skeletal metazoans as important reef-builders, especially the lithistid demosponges (Fig. 8.1) and the problematic (sponge/coelenterate?) *Pulchrilamina*. Cambrian lithistids were too small and rare to be regarded as reef-builders. The earliest reef-building corals *(Lichenaria)* also appear in the Early Ordovician (Fig. 9.1); these were the first organisms with relatively large, well-calcified skeletons whose main functional role in the community was as a member of the constructor guild (no guild overlap).

   d.   Increased diversification of higher taxa in the dweller guild, especially those with macroscopic calcareous skeletons (Sepkoski and Sheehan, 1983). Most of this diversification apparently took place in level-bottom (bryozoans, brachiopods, bivalves) and pelagic (nautiloids, graptolites)) communities, but at least some (corals) was in reefs.

   Despite these important differences between Early Ordovician and older reef communities, the binder guild consisting of various algae and problematic higher taxa dominated (in size and abundance) most Early Ordovician reef communities just as they had done in the Middle and Late Cambrian.

Example 11.6: Tremadocian; Eastern Canada.   The rocks of the Isthmus Bay Formation, St. George Group, Newfoundland, contain a variety of cyanophyte–Problematica–coral-built reefs and biostromes (Fig. 11.4) that were described in detail by Pratt and James (1982). In virtually all of these structures, the chief organic components are thrombolites and stromatolites, in hemispherical–digitate/columnar growth forms which by themselves form reefs up to 1 m thick and 2 m in diameter. Pratt and James (1982, p. 564) estimated that individual shallow subtidal thrombolite structures had an original relief of nearly 20 cm above the floors of subjacent cavities. Other reefs contain associated sponges and corals. The sponges are archaeoscyphid lithistids which range from shallow, wide-mouthed "baskets" to long (0.5-m) cylinders; some are in growth position, but, because they are so rare, they were dwellers rather than builders. Similarly, the receptaculitid *"Calathium"* (up to 10 cm in diameter) occurs as individuals in growth position but also is too uncommon to have been builders.

   In most complex reefs (up to 12 m thick; original topographic relief 1 m), the organic framework consists of intergrown thrombolites, *Renalcis* clusters, and the tabulate coral *Lichenaria*. The thrombolites occur as irregular clots, columns that form hemispherical "heads," and roofs over varied cavities, and tunnels containing skeletal internal sediment. The *Lichenaria* coralla are less than 10 cm in diameter and occur in clumps growing on thrombolite "heads" or other *Lichenaria* coralla. *Renalcis* forms

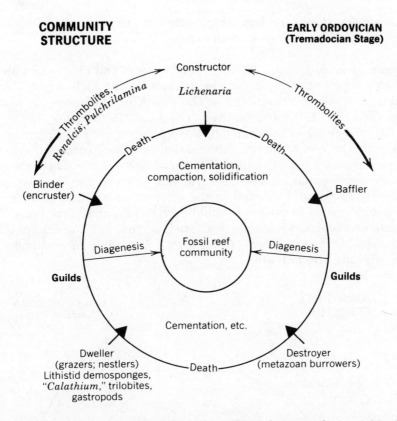

Figure 11.4. Guild structure of Early Ordovician (Tremadocian) reef communities in the Isthmus Bay Formation, St. George Group, Newfoundland. Thrombolites of various sizes and shapes were the chief frame-building organisms, but such problematical skeletal forms as *Renalcis* and *Pulchrilamina* were important binder/constructors. Small coralla of the tabulate coral *Lichenaria* appear to be the earliest well-skeletonized members of the constructor guild in the entire history of reef communities. Main guild membership indicated by thick arrows, and guild overlap by thin arrows (around circle).

mosslike clusters that encrust and drape from the undersides of corals or upper surfaces of thrombolites. The problematical (sponge/coelenterate?) *Pulchrilamina* is also an encruster; it is much less abundant than *Renalcis*, most commonly associated with thrombolites rather than *Renalcis* or *Lichenaria*, and grows as "plates" up to 5 cm in diameter and local "heads" of coalesced plates up to 60 cm thick (Pratt and James, 1982, Fig. 17B; for schematic reconstruction of the Isthmus Bay Formation reefs, see Figs. 28, 29; for discussion of trophic structure, see Copper, 1974, p. 376).

The cryptic subcommunity consists of encrusting cryptalgal laminae and *Renalcis* on the cavity walls and such unattached/uncemented invertebrates as gastropods (whole shells), articulate brachiopods, and pelmatozoan fragments (perhaps transported?). The internal sediment has been burrowed by unknown metazoans.

Example 11.7: Arenigian; Western Texas. Reefs and biostromes up to 6 m thick and 15 m in diameter are common in the McKelligon Canyon Formation at the southern end of the Franklin Mountains in western Texas (Toomey, 1970; Toomey and Nitecki, 1979; Toomey, 1981). The skeletal framework is dominated by the problematical *Pulchrilamina* (especially on the reef tops), the lithistid demosponge *Archaeoscyphia,* and the erect-growing receptaculitid *"Calathium"* (Fig. 11.5). The former two taxa are represented by whole individuals, often in growth position, as well as by spines and spicules in the internal sediment; the latter two are most abundant in the lower–middle mud-rich parts of the reefs. Reef-building was typically begun by scattered, current baffling clumps of pelmatozoans, *Archaeoscyphia, "Calathium,"* articulate brachiopods, and small, digitate stromatolites.

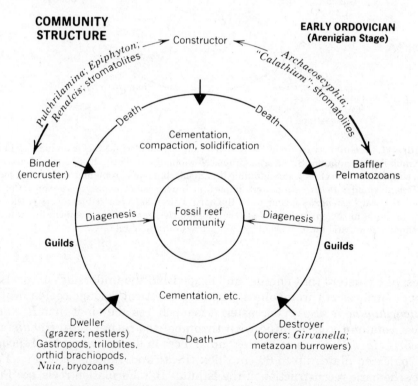

Figure 11.5. Guild structure of Early Ordovician (Arenigian) reef communities in Texas, Oklahoma, and Utah. The frame-building guilds were dominated by various combinations and proportions of lithistid demosponges (*Archaeoscyphia*), problematical "algae" (*Renalcis, Epiphyton, "Calathium"*), stromatolites, and the problematic *Pulchrilamina*. Main guild membership indicated by thick arrows, and guild overlap by thin arrows (around circle).

Pulchrilamina spinosa grew in massive, internally laminated colonies up to 50 cm thick and 25 cm wide and was a very effective sediment binder. Individual specimens of *Archaeoscyphia annulatum* are up to 25 cm long and 13 cm wide, and individuals of *"Calathium"* up to 13 cm long and 8 cm wide. The erect growth form and weak skeletonization of *Archaeoscyphia* and *"Calathium"* place them in the baffler guild; however, they may be locally abundant to overlap the constructor guild.

Lime mud predominates (60–75%) in most of the reefs/mud mounds, but local areas contain up to 60% skeletal grains dominated by bafflers and dwellers. These included pelmatozoans (crinoids, "cystoids"), large gastropods (also common as whole shells), orthid brachiopods, trilobites, and the problematical *Nuia* (alga?). The internal sediment has been burrowed and pelleted and many skeletal grains have been bored, presumably by *Girvanella*.

Example 11.8: Other North American Examples. Toomey and Nitecki (1979) and Toomey (1981) have described numerous other similarly mud-rich, small (up to 7 m thick) reefs in Texas and Oklahoma. They were built by various combinations and levels of relative importance of *Pulchrilamina, Archaeoscyphia, "Calathium,"* encrusting *Renalcis* (curiously inconspicuous in reefs of the McKelligon Canyon Formation in Example 11.7 but included in Fig. 11.5), *Epiphyton* (Riding and Toomey, 1972), the erect cyclostome bryozoan *Ceramopora unapensis* (baffler guild), and stromatolites.

Finally, similar small reefs with essentially the same fauna occur in the Late Arenigian Fillmore Formation (Pogonip Group), Utah (Church, 1974). Rigby (1971) suggested that diversity of sponges in the Fillmore may be somewhat higher than for the other Early Ordovician reefs described above; nevertheless, the main builders were stromatolites.

Conclusions

The early Paleozoic was a pivotal interval in the history of marine communities, both reef and level-bottom. It marked the appearance and great diversification of several higher taxa of skeletal organisms, including algae, various problematic taxa, and the earliest metazoa. During the Early Cambrian, much of this diversification involved reef-building taxa, but during the Middle Cambrian through Early Ordovician, most diversification occurred in level-bottom communities. Furthermore, Early Cambrian metazoans (archaeocyathids) began their involvement in reef-building almost simultaneously with their appearance in level-bottom communities.

Despite these major advances, early Paleozoic taxonomic diversity at all levels is very low when compared with later periods, and differences in species diversity between reef and level-bottom communities are less

pronounced than later. In addition, early Paleozoic reefs are characteristically small and commonly lack a well-defined skeletal framework (or
core) and dipping flank beds. They generally contain a higher volume of
mud than most younger reefs. Thus, distinctions among reefs, biostromes,
mud mounds, level-bottom communities presented in Part I were much
more subtle during the early Paleozoic and so the "Criteria for Recognition" (Chap. 1) of early Paleozoic reefs must be used with tempered
discretion.

Reef Size, Shape, Mud Content

The Early Cambrian reefs are only 1–2 m thick and 2–5 m in diameter.
Many individual Holocene scleractinian coralla exceed these dimensions
by a factor of 5 or more times. The margins of the early Paleozoic reefs
are commonly gradational with the adjacent bedded limestones, and their
mud content (up to 60–75% of rock volume) may be only slightly less than
that of adjacent rocks. Their mound-shaped form also may be difficult to
distinguish from adjacent biostromes; estimates of the original topographic
relief are usually only a few tens of centimeters.

The chief reef-building organisms are poorly skeletonized; many are
microscopic and difficult to recognize in the field or in hand specimens.
Early Paleozoic reefs commonly lack "aprons" or "halos" of transported
skeletal debris spread marginally from the reef core. True carbonate mud
mounds are also present in early Paleozoic rocks, especially Early Ordovician, and are commonly more difficult to distinguish from true reefs
in younger rocks because the skeletal content of both reefs and mud
mounds is so low. Additionally, some reefs have a core like a mud mound
and a "cap" or "crust" of abundant reef builders (a quasi-mud mound?).

However, during the early Paleozoic, the size and objectivity of reefs
increased due to several factors, including increased colonialism, packing
density, and skeletonization of the building organisms. Compound reef
systems and complexes in the Early Ordovician reached thicknesses of
10–12 m and diameters of several tens of meters. Increased colonialism,
packing density, and skeletonization led to increased rigidity, relief, and
shedding of skeletal debris to both internal and external parts of reefs
and reef complexes.

Community Composition and Structure

Early Paleozoic reef communities are dominated by a variety of problematic skeletal taxa that are geographically widespread, stratigraphically
long-ranging, and known mostly by their generic names. These include
Renalcis, Epiphyton, "*Calithium*" (probable "algae"?), *Pulchrilamina*
(sponges; coelenterate?), and *Nuia*. The non-skeletal (stromatolites,
thrombolites) and skeletal *(Girvanella)* cyanophytes that dominated Precambrian reefs were also of vital importance during the Early Paleozoic.
The diversity of higher metazoan taxa in reef and level-bottom com-

munities increased sharply during the Early Ordovician. Despite the fact that much of this diversification took place on level-bottoms, many new taxa also became dwellers on and in reefs. Others, such as lithistid demosponges, corals, and bryozoans arose on level-bottoms during the Cambrian, became members of varied importance in reef dweller guilds during the Early Ordovician, and then were major builders of many Middle Ordovician–Devonian reefs (see Chap. 12).

Guild Structure. Comparison of Figures 11.1 through 11.5 rather clearly indicates that:

a. All early Paleozoic reefs were dominated by the binder guild, and *Renalcis* was of continuing major importance during nearly the entire 100-million year interval. Thus, all early Paleozoic reefs are classified as boundstones. By comparison, episodes of domination or near domination of building guilds by the Archaeocyatha (10–15 million years) or *Pulchrilamina* (20–25 million years) were brief.

b. Non-skeletal algae (stromatolites, thrombolites) of various forms were second in importance. Their dominant role in reef-building during the Precambrian was taken over by weakly skeletonized, problematic taxa during the early Paleozoic.

c. Guild overlap among the major reef builders is considerable. Functional relationships and guild membership in early Paleozoic reef communities were *much* less clearly defined than in Holocene reefs. Reef-building by binders and bafflers overlapped with the constructor function except during the Tommotian.

d. Except for the early (Tremadocian) tabulate coral *Lichenaria*, none of the early Paleozoic reef-builders was adequately skeletonized for non-overlapping membership in the constructor guild.

e. There was a progressive increase in complexity of reef guild structure during the early Paleozoic. The earliest skeletal reefs (Tommotian) lacked a destroyer guild and possibly a dweller guild. However, by the middle Early Cambrian (Atdabanian), trilobites occupied the dweller guild, and by latest Early Cambrian (Elankian), they were joined by the earliest destroyers and by members of well-developed cryptic subcommunities. None of the early Paleozoic reefs were large enough to have sufficiently steep environmental gradients for development of either lateral or bathymetric subcommunities.

f. A progressive increase in diversity and biologic complexity of the dweller guild during the early Paleozoic reflects this same trend in level-bottom communities. There is very little taxonomic difference between members of level-bottom communities and the dweller guild of reef communities.

g. Because most early Paleozoic reef-builders were poorly skeletonized, the typical boring and rasping members of the destroyer guild are uncommon; the chief exception are skeletal microborers such as *Girvanella*. Instead, at least some of the biological aspects of reef destruction were due to burrowers in internal reef sediments.

Although some authors have recognized and described ecologic successional subcommunities in early Paleozoic reefs, the successions are poorly developed. There seem to be two main reasons for this:

a.   The reefs are too small to have caused much modification of their local environment as they grew.

b.   The taxonomic diversity of the reef community was so low that most organisms were environmental "generalists" (high guild overlap) and thus not specialized enough to occupy only a particular place in a successional sequence.

12

Middle Paleozoic Reef Communities

MIDDLE ORDOVICIAN–LATE DEVONIAN

The contrast in composition between Early and Middle Ordovician reef-building guilds represents one of the most profound changes in the entire geologic history of reef communities. With the exception of the relatively brief interval (10–15 million years) during the Early Cambrian, when archaeocyathids dominated the reef building processes (Botomian–Elankian Stages), non-skeletal and skeletal algae were the dominant reef-builders for well over 1500 million years (i.e., Late Precambrian through Early Ordovician). In the brief time (10 millions years) of the early Middle Ordovician (Llanvirnian Stage), algae were displaced by a variety of larger and better-skeletonized metazoan higher taxa; although algae persisted, they generally assumed functional roles in the construction process (chiefly as binders) of accessory importance.

The Llanvirnian reorganization of reef-building guilds involved the following major changes:

a. "First appearances": the Stromatoporoidea and the "*Rothpletzella* Group" of Chuvashov and Riding (1984).

b. Major increases in importance of preexisting taxa: the Solenoporacea (Rhodophyta), Bryozoa, and tabulate corals. Rare, poorly preserved level-bottom bryozoans were present since the Late Cambrian, but at the beginning of the Middle Ordovician, there was a veritable burst in their abundance, quality of preservation (skeletonization), and diversity. In the earliest Middle Ordovician Chazy Group in eastern North America, Ross (1964, Fig. 1) recognized 12 higher taxa (families/subfamilies), 10 of which were essentially "new" (5 trepostomes, 5 cryptostomes).

c. "Holdovers" that were still important but relatively less so: *Girvanella* and stromatolites.

Although the *Rothpletzella* and *Girvanella* groups and the Solenoporacea were locally important in the binder guild throughout the Middle Ordovician, they were volumetrically overwhelmed, first by the better-skeletonized bryozoans during the Early Llanvirnian and later (Middle–Late Llanvirnian) by the Stromatoporoidea.

Middle Ordovician

Guild Structure. In Middle Ordovician bryozoan-dominated reefs, the binder/encruster guild continued to be the most important. However, in many reefs dominated by stromatoporoids, importance of the constructor guild progressively increased. By the Late Ordovician, corals had replaced bryozoans as major reef-builders and, along with stromatoporoids, dominated the binder and constructor guilds until the latest Devonian, when algae again assumed a major role in the reef-building process.

The Middle Ordovician also marks the time of the first major expansion in importance of the destroyer guild (Kobluk et al., 1978) in reef communities. The relatively high mud content of pre–Middle Ordovician reefs and poor skeletonization of their builders severely limited the opportunities for various boring taxa. Although reef borers were present since the Early Cambrian (Elankian Stage), there was a dramatic rise in their abundance and diversity from one form of genus in pre–Middle Ordovician to four in the Middle Ordovician (Kobluk et al., 1978, Fig. 1). That rise coincided with the increase in size of reefs, better skeletonization and increased taxonomic diversity of their builders, and the reduced proportion of mud in the internal reef sediment. Because of these factors, the abundance and diversity of macroborers in middle Paleozoic reef communities have generally exceeded their importance in level-bottom communities.

The major expansion of the "Paleozoic Fauna" of Sepkoski and Sheehan (1983) that was begun in the Early Ordovician continued unabated during the Middle and Late Ordovician. Although the data presented by these authors was based almost entirely on level-bottom communities, the Ordovician rise in taxonomic diversity of level-bottoms was also reflected in reef communities. The greatest similarity between level-bottom and reef communities during the Ordovician was between level-bottoms and the dweller guild (especially bryozoans, trilobites, and brachiopods; J. P. Ross, 1972, 1981).

Example 12.1: Llanvirnian; Chazy Group, Eastern North America. During the Ordovician (Llanvirnian–Late Caradocian), there was a major reef complex (province) that extended from northern Alabama to Quebec (Pitcher, 1964; Walker and Ferrigno, 1973; Alberstadt et al., 1974; Read,

1982b, pp. 193–199). The rocks and faunas in the area of Lake Champlain, New York and Vermont, have been studied in considerable detail since the 1880s and are better known (taxonomically, biostratigraphically, and paleoecologically) than elsewhere in eastern North America. However, there seems an overall compositional and structural similarity in these communities throughout the reef complex so that many of the data presented below can be extended to other reefs of similar age in the Appalachian region.

The oldest Chazyan reefs in the Lake Champlain area occur in the Day Point Formation on Isle LaMotte and have been described by Pitcher (1971), Toomey and Nitecki (1979, pp. 159–163), and Ross (1981). These reefs are quite small (about 1–2 m high and 1–3 m in diameter) and absolutely dominated by bryozoans of the binder guild (Fig. 12.1), mostly in growth position. These same rocks also contain larger mud mounds and shell heaps with abundant, highly fragmented, transported shells (grainstones/packstones; calcarenites; (Pitcher, 1971, Fig. 5; Toomey and Nitecki, 1979, Fig. 78b).

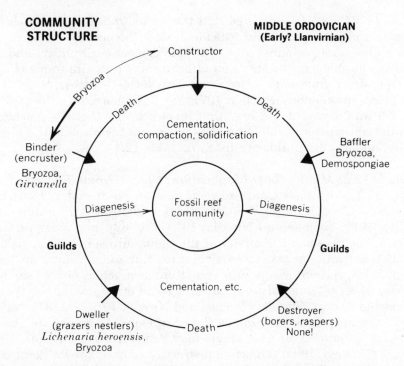

Figure 12.1. Guild structure of Middle Ordovician (Early? Llanvirnian) bryozoan reefs, Day Point Formation, eastern North America. Trepostome and cyclostome bryozoans were the main binder–constructors but also played important roles as bafflers and dwellers (cf. Table 12.1). Main guild membership indicated by thick arrow, and guild overlap by thin arrow (around circle).

TABLE 12.1. Taxonomic Composition and Guild Structure of Early Llanvirnian Reefs in the Lower Chazy Group (Day Point Formation) in the Vicinity of Lake Champlain, New York and Vermont[a]

Binder Guild	Baffler Guild	Dweller Guild
Bryozoa	Bryozoa	Tabulata
Batostoma chazyensis[b]	*Phylloporina*	*Lichenaria heroensis*
Cheiloporella sp.[b]	*Batostoma chazyensis*	Bryozoa
Champlainopora	*Atactoechus chazyensis*	*Champlainopora chazyensis*
Eopachydictya gregaria		
Porostromata	Demospongiae	Trilobita: 12 spp.
Girvanella	*Zittelella*	

Source: After Pitcher (1971) and Ross (1981).
[a]Minimum species diversity: 25.
[b]Dominants.

Ross (1964, p. 946) suggested that the ceramorphoid cyclostomes *Anolotichia* and *Cheiloporella* attached to, bound (Pitcher, 1971, Fig. 6), and built up level-bottom substrates (a simple pioneer community) and provided an elevated hard substrate for attachment of the main frame-builder, the trepostome *Batostoma chazyensis*. This latter bryozoan bound both lime mud and skeletons (Pitcher, 1971, Fig. 3; Toomey and Nitecki, 1979, Fig. 79) into a very dense organic framework and thereby overlapped with the constructor guild. Other less important members of the binder, baffler, and dweller guilds are listed in Table 12.1.

Example 12.2: Middle–Late Llanvirnian; Chazy Group, Eastern North America. The younger Chazyan reefs (Crown Point and Valcour Formations) are much larger (0.6–9 m thick and 50–150 m in diameter; Pitcher, 1971; Toomey and Nitecki, 1979, Fig. 82) than older reefs. In addition, the taxonomic diversity of the communities increases, as does variation in dominant taxa in particular reefs. In some reefs in the lower Crown Point, *Solenopora* sp. may constitute as much as 50% of the rock volume, whereas in middle and upper Crown Point reefs, either the anthaspidellid sponge *Zittelella* (Toomey and Nitecki, 1979, Fig. 84), various stromatoporoids, or the bryozoans *Batostoma* spp., *Pachydictyon sheldonensis,* or *Chazydictyon chazyensis* may be dominants (Pitcher, 1971; Kapp, 1975; Ross, 1981). The chief distinction of most Crown Point reefs is the sudden influx of numerous, large (up to 3 m in diameter), well-skeletonized, and diverse stromatoporoids which are generally regarded as the oldest in the world (Kapp and Stearn, 1975). The largest massive stromatoporoids belong to the constructor guild, while the smaller, thinner growth forms are binder/encrusters (Table 12.2; Fig. 12.2).

The destroyer guild is represented by unidentified borings. Many taxa

TABLE 12.2. Taxonomic Composition and Guild Structure of Reefs in the Middle Chazy Group (Crown Point Formation) in the Vicinity of Lake Champlain, New York and Vermont[a]

Constructor Guild	Binder Guild	Baffler Guild	Dweller Guild
Alga[b]	Algae	Demospongiae	Bryozoa
Solenopora	*Girvanella*	*Zittelella var-*	Trepos-
Stromatoporoidea[b]	*Solenopora em-*	*ians*[b]	tomes,
Pachystroma vallum	*brunensis*	*Anthaspidella*	cyclos-
P. goodsellense	*Rothpletzella*	2 other spp.	tomes,
Labechia eatoni	*Sphaerocodium*	Bryozoa	cystopor-
L. prima	Stromatoporoidea[b]	*Batostoma*	ates: 5 +
L. cf. *pustulosa*	*Pseudostylodictyon*	(ramose)	spp.
	lamottense	*Phylloporina*	
	Pachystroma polli-	"Pelmatozoans"	Brachiopoda:
	cellum		"orthids"
	Labechia valcour-		Gastropoda
	ensis		*Maclurites*
	Bryozoa		*magnus*
	Batostoma[b] (2		Cephalopoda:
	spp.)		13 genera
	Pachydictya shel-		Trilobita: 9
	donensis[b]		spp.
	Chazydictya cha-		
	zyensis[b]		
	Eopachydictya		Ostracoda:?
	gregaria[b]		spp.
	Tabulata		Problematica
	Billingsaria par-		*Nuia*
	va[b]		
	Eofletcheria sp.		

Source: After Pitcher, 1971; Kapp, 1975; Ross, 1964, 1972, 1981; Toomey and Nitecki, 1979, pp. 161–169.
[a]Minimum species diversity: 60.
[b]Local dominants.

in the dweller guild are present in the internal reef sediment; it is uncertain whether they were truly reef dwellers or members of adjacent level-bottom or pelagic communities whose dead shells were swept by currents into the reef or interreef channels (Pitcher, 1971, Fig. 16; Kapp, 1975, Fig. 4; Toomey and Nitecki, 1979, Fig. 85).

Late Ordovician–Late Devonian

Guild Structure. The Llanvirnian bryozoan-dominated reef communities continued into the Middle–Late Ordovician (early Caradocian) of the southern Appalachians (Walker and Ferrigno, 1973; Alberstadt et al.,

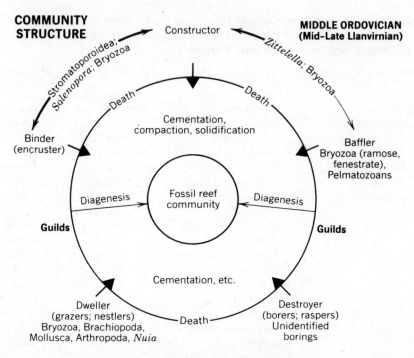

Figure 12.2. Guild structure of Middle Ordovician (mid–Late Llanvernian) reefs Crown Point Formation, eastern North America. The main builders included several species of stromatoporoids, bryozoans, the alga *Solenopora,* and the anthaspidellid sponge *Zittelella.* Various bryozoans also contributed to the baffler and dweller guilds (cf. Table 12.2). Main guild membership indicated by thick arrows, and guild overlap by thin arrow (around circle).

1974; Ruppel and Walker, 1984) and into the Ashgillian of Kentucky (P1. 40; Cuffey and Kamandulis, 1985). Bryozoan generic diversity appears higher in the younger reefs of the Appalachians by a factor of at least two (cf. Table 12.2 and Walker and Ferrigno, 1973, Tables 2, 3), but they lack other important frame-builders such as algae, stromatoporoids, and corals. Furthermore, the dominant bryozoans include similar abundances of both encrusting (binder guild) and dendroid/ramose (baffler guild) growth forms in the southern Appalachians. In the Chazyan reefs, however, bryozoans were primarily binders/encrusters (Table 12.2). Elsewhere, tabulate corals dominated Early Caradocian reef-building guilds with binding bryozoans of minor volumetric importance (Cuffey, 1977; Cuffey and Davidheiser, 1980).

The Caradocian also marks another major turning point in the evolution of mid-Paleozoic reef communities. Those from the southern Appalachians appear to be nearly the youngest that were dominated by bryozoans, in contrast to most other Caradocian reefs which were dominated by stromatoporoids and corals. In addition, the Caradocian marks the appearance of the problematical *"Wetheredella* Group," the last component of "Ordovician Flora" of Chuvashov and Riding (1984). However, this "group" seldom became a major contributor to middle Paleozoic reefs (cf. Copper, 1976).

The rising importance of the Tabulata and appearance of the Rugosa during the Caradocian were of major consequence in the constructor guild of reef communities until the Late Devonian. Although tabulates were sporadically present as constructors and binders in reefs as old as Tremadocian, they were volumetrically overwhelmed by algae in Early Ordovician and bryozoans in Middle Ordovician reefs. During the Late Ordovician and Early Silurian, tabulate diversity and corallum volume increased, but not as rapidly as in the Stromatoporoidea, so that tabulates remained subordinate to stromatoporoids as builders of most reefs.

Very early Rugosa included both solitary and colonial forms from level-bottom communities of Late Llandeilan or Early Caradocian Age in eastern North America (Hill, 1981, pp. F49–F50; Neuman, 1984). By the Late Caradocian, rugosans were firmly established as important members of the constructor guild, a distinction held with varying degrees of importance until the Early Carboniferous. Thus, in the Late Caradocian, a basic building guild structure was instituted that was remarkably stable at higher taxonomic levels until almost the end of the Late Devonian (Frasnian Stage), an interval of nearly 100 million years. This is approximately the same duration as from the earliest skeletal reefs of the Tommotian (Example 11.1) through the bryozoan-dominated reefs of the Llanvirnian (Example 12.2). In contrast to the overall stability and uniformity of higher taxa, there was considerable evolutionary change at the family–species levels during both the Tommotian–Llanvirnian and Caradocian–Frasnian intervals.

This basic Caradocian–Frasnian building guild structure consisted of varying proportions of stromatoporoids, tabulates, rugosans, and algae belonging to the "Ordovician Flora" plus some elements of the "Cambrian Flora" (e.g., *Renalcis*) of Chuvashov and Riding (1984). In most Caradocian–Frasnian reefs, either stromatoporoids or tabulates are volumetrically dominant and belong to either the constructor or binder guild; rugosans are almost exclusively constructors and generally third in volumetric importance. Virtually all algae are binders and, except for local concentrations, are much less important than metazoan builders. In the Caradocian, the relative importance of the constructor guild increased dramatically at the expense of both the binder and baffler guilds.

During the Silurian and particularly in the Devonian, there was important expansion in abundance and diversity of the destroyer guild. Kobluk et al. (1978) reported 7 form-genera of borers from the Middle Silurian and 12 from the Devonian; they suggested that the Devonian rise was due to general expansion in abundance and distribution of reef communities.

Although the major expansion in family-level diversity of the dweller guild had been completed by the Caradocian (Sepkowski and Sheehan, 1983), there was a sharp but brief (2–3 million years) decline at the end of the Ordovician ("Hirnantian Crisis" of some authors) followed by rising diversity through the Silurian to new maxima in the Early and Middle Devonian. The Middle Devonian marks the all-time peak in genus/species diversity of reef-dwelling brachiopods, chiefly Spirferida and Strophomenida.

Six examples of Caradocian–Frasnian reef guild structures are discussed below; they have been selected to emphasize both similarities and differences.

Example 12.3: Late Caradocian; Steinvika Limestone, Norway. The oldest stromatoporoid/coral-dominated reefs in Europe occur in the Late Caradocian Steinvika and Mjfsa Limestones near Oslo (Harland, 1981). The volume of stromatoporoids (too poorly preserved to identify at genus/spe-

TABLE 12.3. Taxonomic Composition and Guild Structure of Reefs in the Steinvika Limestone (Caradocian), Langesund–Skien District, Southern Norway

Constructor Guild	Binder Guild	Baffler Guild	Dweller Guild
Stromatoporoidea genus/species unknown	Algae	"Cystoids"	Algae: 3 spp.
	Spongiostroma? Stromatoporoidea genus/species unknown	*Heliocrinites Hemicosmites papaveris*	Tabulata *Eofletcheria subparallela*
Tabulata *Eofletcheria irregularia Lyopora favosa*	Pelmatozoa	Crinoidea genus/species unknown	Rugosa *Streptelasma* spp.
Rugosa *Tryplasma basaltiforme*		Tabulata *Eofletcheria irregularis* Ramose Bryozoa genus/species unknown	Bryozoa *Diplotrypa* sp.; fronds/ sheets
			Brachiopoda: 3 spp.?
			Bivalvia: ? spp.
			Gastropoda: 5 spp.
			Cephalopoda: ? spp.
			Trilobita: 2 spp.
			Ostracoda: ? spp.

Source: After Harland, 1981.

cies level) exceeds that of either tabulates or rugosans (Table 12.3; Fig. 12.3). Although rugosans are less important than tabulates, these reefs are notable as being among the oldest in which rugosans, especially those with cerioid coralla (constructor guild), play a significant role in any of the building guilds. Stromatoporoids included both massive–domal (constructors) and laterally expanded (binders) growth forms; tabulates included both fasciculate and dendroid forms (constructors/bafflers).

There is a well-developed vertical biotic zonation of the patch reefs which Harland (1981) regarded as a true autogenic ecological succession. However, because the same sequence of organisms is present both vertically and laterally from the presumed point of origin of the reef, the autogenic interpretation remains unproven (see Ecological Succession, Chap. 3). Nonetheless, initial stabilization of the level-bottom substrate beneath the Steinvika reefs was the result of current baffling by abundant pelmatozoans and binding by algal mats (Spongiostromata?). The intermediate stage in the faunal sequence included the first tabulate constructors, cystoid and bryozoan bafflers, and considerably diverse dwellers.

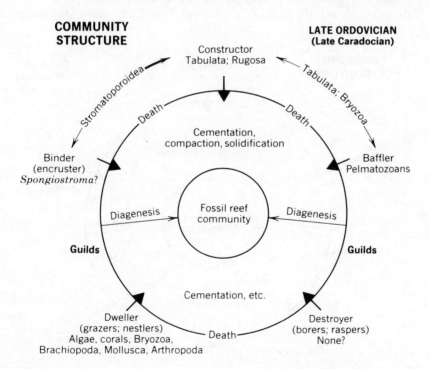

Figure 12.3. Guild structure of Late Ordovician (Late Caradocian) reefs in the Steinvika Limestone, Langesund–Skien District, Norway. The builders, in order of decreasing importance, were Stromatoporoidea, Tabulata, and Rugosa. There was also considerable overlap by these same higher taxa among the constructor, binder, baffler, and dweller guilds based on differences in growth form and packing density (cf. Table 12.3). Main guild membership indicated by thick arrow, and guild overlap by thin arrows (around circle).

Stromatoporoids were important only during the presumed climax stage, which consists of closely packed, large stromatoporoids, tabulates, and colonial rugosans that together form an almost continuous layer across the tops of the reefs.

Example 12.4: Silurian (Wenlockian); Western England. In the area of Wenlock Edge, Shropshire, the upper 12 m of the Wenlock Limestone contains numerous patch reefs (cf. Abbott, 1976) averaging about 4.5 m in thickness and 12 m in diameter. They had an estimated original topographic relief from a few tens of centimeters to as much as 3 m (Scoffin, 1971; Abbott, 1976; Riding, 1981, pp. 45–51).

Previous authors have disagreed regarding the reef or mud-mound origin of these structures, whether or not they are biotically zoned, and the relative importance of various physical factors in controlling the occurrence of organisms in them. The following discussion is based largely on the conclusions of Scoffin (1971) and Riding (1981) who considered them reefs. Guild membership of most genera and species is more clearly defined (less guild overlap) than in any of the previous examples (Fig. 12.4).

Tabulates, especially *Heliolites* spp. and *Thecia expatiata*, dominate the

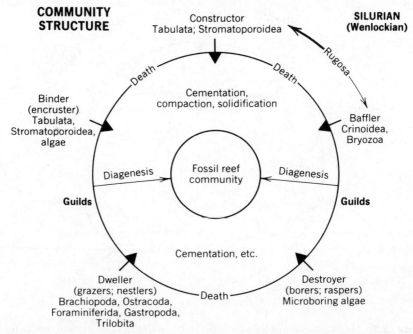

Figure 12.4. Guild structure of Silurian (Wenlockian) reefs in the Wenlock Limestone at Wenlock Edge, Shropshire, England. Note the low level of guild overlap compared with other examples of reef communities described in Chapters 11 and 12 (cf. Table 12.4). Main guild membership indicated by thick arrow, and guild overlap by thin arrow (around circle).

TABLE 12.4. Taxonomic Composition and Structure of the Reef-building Guilds in the Wenlock Limestone (Silurian; Wenlockian), Wenlock Edge, Shropshire, England[a]

Constructor Guild	Binder Guild	Baffler Guild
Tabulata	Tabulata	"Crinoids"
Heliolites barrandei	*Thecia expatiata*	
H. parvistella	*Alveolites*	Bryozoa
Favosites		*Fenestella*
Stromatoporoidea	Stromatoporoidea	*Hallopora*
Actinostroma	*Labechia*	*Rhombopora*
Stromatopora	*Stromatopora*	*Fistulipora*
Rugosa	Algae	
Entelophyllum	*Girvanella*	
	Rothpletzella	
	Wetheredella	
	Spongiostromata?	

[a]Taxa arranged in approximate order of importance in each guild.

constructor and binder guilds in the earlier-formed parts of the reefs and a *Favosites*/stromatoporoid association dominates their later development (Table 12.4). *In situ* tabulates comprise 10–20% of the rock volume; stromatoporoids, rugosans, and bryozoans are of secondary abundance and importance in the building guilds (Scoffin, 1971, Figs. 22–24).

Stromatolitic "crusts" and "domes" several centimeters thick were the most important binders; locally, other algae (e.g., *Rothpletzella, Wetheredella, Girvanella*) and laminar tabulates and stromatoporoids were also members of the binder guild. The algae and some bryozoans line the insides of the reef cavities as evidence of a cryptic subcommunity and bind/encrust the upper layers of sediment and metazoan skeletons (Scoffin, 1971, Figs. 19, 20; Riding, 1981, p. 50).

Pelmatozoan skeletal debris is abundant both below the reef framework and in the sediment within reef cavities; Abbott (1976) regarded densely packed crinoids as very important for initial stabilization of the level-bottom substrate and baffling and trapping of internal sediment. He also estimated that skeletal debris from all sources plus lime mud amounted to over 75% of the rock volume, and largely on this basis, interpreted the Wenlock "structures" as mud mounds rather than reefs.

Reefs of generally similar age, composition, and structure have also been described in detail from: (1) the Great Lakes region of the United States (Cumings and Shrock, 1928; Lowenstam, 1957; Ingels, 1963); and (2) Gotland, Sweden (Hadding, 1950; Manten, 1971; Riding, 1981).

Example 12.5: Silurian (Ludlovian); Somerset Island, Arctic Canada. In the Late Silurian (Ludlovian) rocks of the Douro Formation in Arctic

Canada, there are numerous, small (5–15-m thick; 5–35-m dia) reefs dominated by lithistid demosponges (Fig. 12.5), especially the genera *Somersetella* and *Haplistion* (Table 12.5; Narbonne and Dixon, 1984). Although the sponges are poorly skeletonized, they are commonly in growth position and constitute about 35% of the rock volume. The most common growth forms are thin-walled cones and cylinders up to 12 cm high which overlap the baffler (erect growth; fragile skeletons) and constructor (dense-packing) guilds. Other lithistids are disk-shaped, tabular, or encrusting and because of their dense packing, overlap the binder and constructor guilds.

Lithistid-dominated reefs are quite uncommon in the Paleozoic. Their earliest significant membership in any of the reef-building guilds was in the Early Ordovician (Example 11.7). In addition to the present example in the Late Silurian, the only other episode of significant siliceous sponge

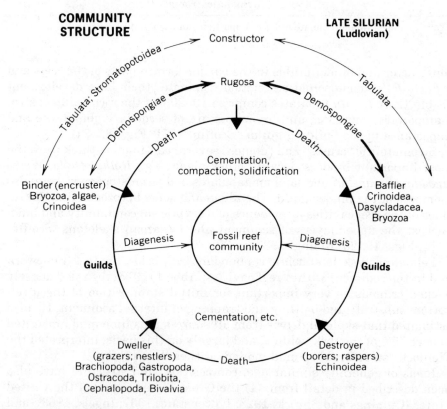

Figure 12.5. Guild structure of Late Silurian (Ludlovian) reef communities in the Douro Formation, Somerset Island, Arctic Canada. These communities are unique among middle Paleozoic reefs in that domination of the building guilds, especially the overlapping baffler/constructor guilds, is by lithistid demosponges (cf. Table 12.5). Main guild membership indicated by thick arrows, and guild overlap by thin arrows (around circle).

influence over reef-building was in the Permian (Chap. 13). Because of the general fragility of demosponge skeletons, their primary function in reef-building is current baffling and sediment trapping. But when they are densely packed, as in the Douro Formation reefs, they may also become participants in construction (Fig. 12.5).

Tabulate and rugose corals are the next highest contributors to skeletal volume (2–3% of the framework; >20% of the internal sediment); some hemispherical *Favosites* coralla are more than 50 cm in diameter but rarely closely enough packed to have formed an interlocking skeletal framework. Sediment binding was performed by laterally expanded growth forms, including lithistids, tabulates, stromatoporoids, bryozoans, algae, and crinoid holdfasts; volumetrically, however, their skeletons are subordinate to the bafflers.

The relative importance of various building taxa in the Douro Formation reefs varies stratigraphically as well as within each reef. Narbonne and Dixon (1984, pp. 36–44) recognized three stratigraphic subdivisions (zones; growth stages) within each typical reef. They attribute the stabilization of the substrate to a pioneer community dominated by crinoids

TABLE 12.5. Taxonomic Composition and Structure of the Reef-building Guilds in the Douro Formation (Late Silurian; Ludlovian), Somerset Island, Arctic Canada[a]

Constructor Guild	Binder Guild	Baffler Guild
Demospongiae: *Haplistion*[b]	Demospongiae	Demospongiae
Tabulata	*Somersetella*[b]	*Somersetella*[b]
Favosites[b]		
Heliolites	Tabulata	Tabulata
Rugosa	*Alveolites*	*Coenites*
Cerioid; fasciculate	*Aulopora*	*Syringopora*
Stromatoporoidea	*Muvophyllum*	Bryozoa
Diplostroma	Stromatoporoidea	*Fenestella*
	Plexodictyon	*Monotrypa?*
	Bryozoa	*Eridotrypa*
	Monotrypa?[b]	Dasycladacea
	Eridotrypa[b]	Crinoidea[b]
	Cyclotrypa?[b]	Camerata
	Fistulipora?[b]	Inadunata
	Algae	
	Sphaerocodium	
	Spongiostromata[b]	
	Crinoid holdfasts	

Source: After Narbonne and Dixon, 1984.
[a] Maximum species diversity: approx. 50.
[b] Dominant reef-builders.

(their holdfasts acted as sediment traps and binders), with additional binding provided by bryozoans and solenoporaceans. The next stage (colonization) was dominated by lithistids of the baffler guild and a few corals in the constructor guild. Species diversity reached a maximum in the upper parts of the reefs (diversification stage) which were dominated by corals and subordinate numbers of sponges, algae, bryozoans, and stromatoporoids.

During reef growth, there was a progressive increase in overall rigidity of the reefs due to an increase in the relative volume of well-skeletonized constructors. Narbonne and Dixon (1984, pp. 39–43) estimated that the maximum topographic relief was about 3 m and occurred during the diversification growth stage.

Example 12.6: Middle Devonian (Eifelian); Ontario, Canada. Reefs of the Devonian Formosa Reef Limestone in southwestern Ontario were the subject of continuous study by Fagerstrom during the period 1961–1983. Individual reefs are small (up to about 10 m thick and 75 m in diameter) and clustered in a reef system of uncertain stratigraphic and geographic dimensions.

The reef and level-bottom faunas were collected with approximately equal intensity and major skeletal macrofaunal elements of both the reefs and level-bottom have been described to species level (Fagerstrom, 1961, 1971, 1982). From these data, it is possible to determine species-level composition and guild membership of the reef communities (Table 12.6;

TABLE 12.6. Taxonomic Composition and Guild Structure of the Formosa Reef Limestone (Middle Devonian; Eifelian), Ontario[a]

Constructor Guild	Baffler Build	Binder Guild	Dweller Guild
Stromatoporoidea: 18 spp.	Tabulata: 5 spp.	Stromatoporoidea: 18 spp.	Brachiopoda: 43 spp.
Rugosa: 9? spp.	Rugosa: 4 spp.	Bryozoa: 2 spp.	Gastropoda: 16 spp.
Tabulata: 7 spp.	Bryozoa: 5 spp.		Bivalvia: 3 spp.
	Crinoidea: ? spp.		Rostroconcha: 3 spp.
			Cephalopoda: 8 spp.
			Trilobita: 7 spp.

Source: After Fagerstrom, 1961, 1971, 1982, 1983.
[a]Minimum species diversity: 130.

Fig. 12.6) and interpret the relative importance of reefs and level-bottoms as habitats for speciation, endemism, and extinction (Fagerstrom, 1983).

Skeletal macrofauna of the Formosa Reef Limestone is exceedingly diverse and highly endemic in comparison to adjacent level-bottom communities and contemporaneous reef communities in eastern North America. Laterally expanded (laminar/tabular) stromatoporoid coenostea dominate the fauna and comprise 20–40% of the rock volume (Pl. 20*b*); their packing density is so high that they also dominate both binder and constructor guilds (Fig. 12.6). The analogous relations between binder/constructor guild overlap by stromatoporoids in the Formosa reefs and the crustose coralline algae in Holocene algal ridges are nearly perfect (cf. Pl. 24 and Pl. 36*a*). Lateral growth rates of Devonian stromatoporoids and Cenozoic coralline algae appear to be quite similar, enabling each to bind "pockets" and lenses of lime mud and skeletal debris rapidly into

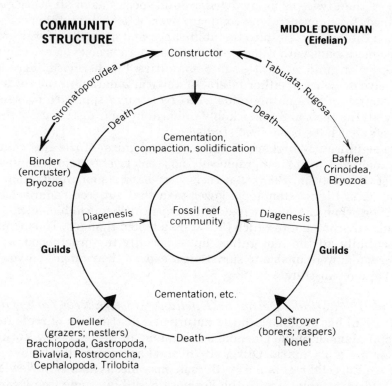

Figure 12.6. Guild structure of the Middle Devonian (Eifelian) Formosa Reef Limestone, southwestern Ontario, Canada. This community is dominated by densely packed, laminar–tabular stromatoporoids that overlap the binder and constructor guilds. The reef-building roles of corals and bryozoans are much less important than those of the stromatoporoids (cf. Tables 12.6 and 12.7 and Fig. 12.7). Main guild membership indicated by thick arrows, and guild overlap by thin arrow (around circle).

the internal sediment and the organic frameworks of both reefs and algal ridges.

Hemispherical tabulate coral skeletons up to 1 m in diameter are second in volumetric importance, followed by solitary and domal/colonial rugosans and thick-branched favositids; all were members of the constructor guild. Nearly all the stromatoporoids, cerioid tabulates, and rugosans are reasonably complete and in growth position, whereas almost all other taxa are broken and not in growth position. Crinoid columnals are the main skeletal component of the internal sediment and thus it may be inferred that they dominated the baffler guild; other bafflers included delicately branched tabulates (auloporoids; *Cladopora*), fenestrate–ramose bryozoans, and phaceloid rugose corals.

As is typical of nearly all well-documented reef communities, regardless of their age, species diversity of the dweller guild in the Formosa Reef Limestone is much higher than for any of the other guilds. In fact, there are more than twice as many dweller guild species as in all other guilds combined; brachiopods alone comprise over 35% of the total species diversity (Table 12.6). Despite the abundance and diversity of well-skeletonized metazoans with rapid growth rates, there is no evidence of either the destroyer guild or cryptic subcommunities. Furthermore, there is no conclusive evidence of either lateral or vertical zonation in the reefs; the most abundant stromatoporoids (*Anostylostroma* spp.) are present in nearly all the reefs and remarkably uniform in their distribution within the reefs that have been most studied.

The significantly higher diversity and endemism of the reef communities compared with stratigraphically adjacent level-bottom communities suggest (Fagerstrom, 1983) that reefs were habitats for rapid, allopatric speciation of highly stenotopic lower taxa that suffered rapid selective extinction when the narrowly defined physical/chemical/biological reef-building environment to which they were adapted changed. The members of essentially all the reef guilds, but especially the brachiopods of the dweller guild, were unable to survive and expand their ranges on younger level-bottom substrates.

Example 12.7: Middle Devonian (Eifelian); Western New York. Oliver (1954; 1976) has summarized the nature and distribution of reefs in the Edgecliff Member of the Onondaga Limestone in western New York and adjacent areas of Ontario; Oliver (1976) and Fagerstrom (1983) have compared the Edgecliff reef faunas with contemporaneous faunas in New York and Ontario, especially with the Formosa Reef Limestone (see Example 12.6). These comparisons clearly demonstrate a very pronounced difference in the composition of the building guilds in reefs only about 200 km apart despite the overall similarity in their sizes and geologic age.

The best studied Edgecliff reef occurs near Buffalo (Locality 108 of Oliver, 1976; see also his Table 41 and Pl. 1). It demonstrates the predominance of colonial rugose corals, especially those with large, phaceloid and astreoid, lenticular–domal coralla (Fig. 12.7; Table 12.7). These data also indicate the enormous importance of the constructor guild relative to the other building guilds and an apparent low species diversity of non-coral components (approx. 25 spp.) relative to the non-stromatoporoid components (approx. 110 spp.) of the Formosa Reef Limestone (Table 12.6). Examples 12.6 and 12.7 and the data of Oliver (1954; 1976) and Fager-strom (1983) show several important aspects of these contemporaneous reef communities:

a.   Composition (at all taxonomic levels) and guild structure may change drastically in relatively short distances. Despite these changes, species diversity of reef communities exceeds that of adjacent level-bottom communities.

b.   The relative importance of one or more of the frame-building guilds may change drastically among contemporaneous reefs. The virtual absence of both baffler and binder guilds in the Edgecliff reefs (Table 12.7) con-

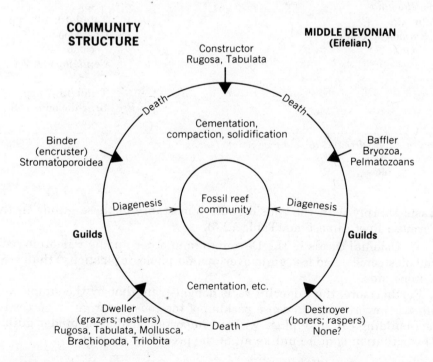

Figure 12.7.   Composition and guild structure of reef communities, Edgecliff Member, Onondaga Limestone (Middle Devonian; Eifelian), western New York. These communities are dominated by colonial rugose corals of the constructor guild. Baffler and binder guilds were relatively unimportant in the construction process (cf. Tables 12.7 and 12.6 and Fig. 12.6).

TABLE 12.7. Taxonomic Composition and Guild Structure of Reef Communities in the Edgecliff Member, Onondaga Limestone (Middle Devonian; Eifelian) Near Buffalo, New York

Constructor Guild	Baffler Guild	Binder Guild	Dweller Guild
Rugosa (colonial)	Bryozoa	Stromato-	Rugosa (colonial)
Actinophyllum	Fenestrate	poroidea:	_Synaptophyllum_
stramineum	Pelmatozoans: 3	(2 spp.)	_arundinaceum_
A. segregatum	spp.		_Cylindrophyllum:_
Asterobillingsa	Tabulata		2 spp.
magdisa steorra	Branching coral-		_Asterobillingsa_
Cyathocylindricum	la: ? spp.		_magdisa mag-_
opulens			_disa_
C. gemmatum			_Grewgiphyllum_
Heliophyllum			_colligatum_
monticulum			_Heliophyllum_
Rugosa (solitary)			_magnaprolifer-_
Heliophyllum halli			_um_
Siphonophrentis			Rugosa (solitary): 8?
elongata			spp.
Tabulata			Tabulata: 14? spp.
Emmonsia epider-			Gastropoda:
mata			7 spp.
			Cephalopoda: 2 +
			spp.
			Trilobita: ? spp.
			Brachiopoda: 7–8
			spp.

Source: After Oliver (1976) and Fagerstrom (1983).

trasts sharply with the considerable importance of these guilds in the Formosa Reef Limestone (Table 12.6).

c. Colonial corals in the Devonian (and other middle Paleozoic reefs and biostromes) had less guild overlap (morphologic plasticity) than stromatoporoids.

Furthermore, the Edgecliff reefs demonstrate that by the simple volumetric importance and dense packing of the constructor guild, successful reef-building can take place without important baffler or binder guilds. This situation is quite unlike all of the preceding examples.

Example 12.8: Late Devonian (Frasnian); Canning Basin, Western Australia. Compared with the ancient reefs discussed so far in Part III, reef complexes along the northwestern margin of the Canning Basin are immensely larger and far more varied both sedimentologically and paleoecologically. They extend in a northwest–southeast trending reef system for nearly 300 km and are up to 50 km wide. (By comparison, the Holocene Great Barrier Reef system is nearly 2000 km long and up to 300 km wide.) Comparably large and varied Frasnian reef complexes occur in Alberta, Canada (Playford, 1969; Wray and Playford, 1970; Jameison, 1971), the Ardennes Mountains of Belgium (Tsien, 1971, 1977, 1979), and the Rhenish Schiefegebirge in West Germany (Krebs and Mountjoy, 1972; Krebs, 1966, 1974; Burchette, 1981).

The general tectonic settling, stratigraphy, and sedimentology of the Canning Basin have been described in numerous publications (e.g., Playford and Lowry, 1966; Playford, 1969, 1980); in the present example, only the reef communities are considered. The Canning Basin reef system had a long and relatively stable sedimentologic history but a more varied biologic history. Reef building began in the Middle Devonian (Givetian) and extended to nearly the end of the Devonian (Famennian), an interval of 15 million years of almost continuous biologically controlled growth. In this example, only the Frasnian communities are discussed, but in Chapter 13, the Famennian communities are compared (see Example 13.1).

The Canning Basin reef complexes formed on a broad continental shelf (Lennard Shelf) and include a relatively wide reef flat/lagoon, a narrow (35–600+ m wide) reef crest and seaward slope with an original relief (crest to base of slope) that varied from a few tens of meters to more than 300 m. There was a full range of reef shapes, including fringing, patch, barrier (Pl. 13*b*) and atolls (Pl. 12*b*) as well as deep-water (>100 m) stromatolite reefs in both the lagoonal and seaward slope areas (Pl. 41*a*).

The thickest and most vigorous reef development occurred at the crest. This main barrier reef mass comprises the Windjana Limestone, which is discontinuously exposed along nearly the entire length of the reef system. However, the best exposures are present in the gorge of the Windjana River where it crosses the Napier Range (Pl. 13*b*; Playford and Lowry, 1966, pp. 105–113). The gorge exposures include not only the Windjana Limestone but also the lagoonal and seaward slope limestone facies. The lateral and vertical facies successions contain a variety of distinctive sedimentological (lithofacies) and paleoecological (biofacies) units indicative of a broad range of environmental factors (depth, turbulence, salinity, etc.; see Chap. 3), simultaneous sedimentological and biological processes (see Chap. 4), and contemporaneous reef communities and subcommunities (see Chap. 5) from the shoreline across the shelf to the deep seaward slope. In many ways, these facies successions are remarkably similar to those of the Holocene Great Barrier Reef; the chief differences are biological (taxonomic, morphologic, and ecologic), and these are emphasized in the following discussion.

Most dominant organisms in the Windjana Limestone are in their original growth positions. Generally, either *Renalcis* or stromatoporoids or

Renalcis and stromatoporoids intimately intergrown in approximately equal volumes (Pl. 28) dominated the building guilds (Fig. 12.8; Table 12.8; Playford and Lowry, 1966, Figs. 9–11). *Renalcis* lived as a binder forming clusters in the mud matrix or as rims on skeletons and fragments, but where its packing density was high, it strongly overlapped with the constructor guild (Pl. 41*b*). This Frasnian abundance of *Renalcis* represents a major resurgence of this element of the binder/constructor guild that was so important in early Paleozoic reefs, especially Early Cambrian (Fig. 7.1; Chuvashov and Riding, 1984).

Stromatoporoid coenostea varied in growth form from very large domes and hemispheres (constructors) to very small, erect, digitate–ramose forms that were most abundant near the reef crest–reef flat margin (bafflers) to thin, laminar sheets (binders) also most abundant near the crest–flat margin (Playford and Lowry, 1966, Figs. 12, 13). Cockbain (1984, pp. 7–8) has described the lateral distribution of 22 stromatoporoid species collected near the southeastern end of the reef system, including both reef

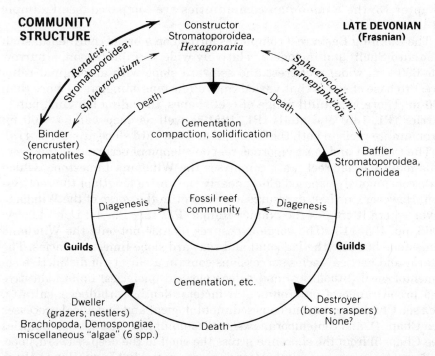

Figure 12.8. Composition and guild structure of the Late Devonian (Frasnian) Windjana Limestone marginal to the Canning Basin, Western Australia. The reef-building guilds include a variety of higher taxa but are dominated by skeletal algae (especially *Renalcis*) and stromatoporoids; both of these higher taxa are commonly so densely packed that they overlap the constructor guild. Some stromatoporoid coenostea are so large that they are also important constructors with no guild overlap (cf. Table 12.8 and Fig. 13.1). Main guild membership indicated by thick arrows, and guild overlap by thin arrows (around circle).

TABLE 12.8. Taxonomic Composition of the Reef-building Guilds in the Windjana Limestone (Late Devonian: Frasnian), Canning Basin, Western Australia

Constructor Guild	Baffler Guild	Binder Guild
Stromatoporoidea	Algae	Algae
Rugosa	*Sphaerocodium*	*Renalcis*
Hexagonaria	*Paraepiphyton*	*Sphaerocodium*
hullensis	Stromatoporoidea	Stromatolites
	Crinoidea	Stromatoporoidea

Source: After Playford and Lowry (1966), Wary (1967; 1977, pp. 133–134), Cockbain (1984).

crest and reef flat/lagoon areas. He found that species were divisible into three major groups and that their distributions were very comparable to scleractinian-dominated crest and flat subcommunities of Holocene reef systems. Stromatoporoids in the seaward slope deposits consisted of a mixture of *in situ* and transported coenostea that were too difficult to unscramble for establishment of bathymetric stromatoporoid subcommunities from the crest to the basin. The delicate, ramose cylindrical coenostea of *Amphipora, Stachyodes,* etc. are almost never found in growth position and are presumed to have lived in dense thickets in quiet water near the crest–flat margin and in lagoonal patch reefs and fringing reefs. During the Early Frasnian, cerioid, domal coralla of *Hexagonaria hullensis* were locally important constructors.

Other algae, including stromatolites, *Sphaerocodium,* and *Paraepiphyton,* are also of local importance in one or more of the building guilds (Fig. 12.8). Lateral distributions of other less abundant skeletal algae in both lagoonal and seaward slope deposits are discussed by Wray (1967; 1977).

Crinoids were locally important as bafflers, judging from the abundance of skeletal debris in the internal sediment. Elsewhere, internal sediment consists largely of whole, disarticulated, and fragmental reef-dwelling brachiopods. The destroyer guild is very poorly represented or absent.

Both the reef crest and the seaward slope deposits contain abundant evidence of initial rigidity and early submarine cementation of the framework. This evidence includes: (1) large reef crest blocks incorporated in toe-of-slope and basin debris flows; (2) very long and wide fractures subparallel to the original trend of the crest; (3) large (up to 30-cm dia.) spheres of layered radiaxial calcite cement, oolite, etc., within the fractures forming "neptunian dikes and sills" that are petrologically distinct from the enclosing organic framework; and (4) *in situ* cryptic subcommunities within the fractures dominated by encrusting *Renalcis* and stromatolites (Playford et al., 1984a).

Other algal-dominated subcommunities of the reef system include (Playford et al., 1976):

a.   Locally abundant, shallow-water (reef crest and reef flat), variably spaced (touching to 10 + cm apart) columnar stromatolites (Pl. 27) enclosed by massive reef framework limestone.

b.   Seaward slope, deep-water (35–100 + m) *Sphaerocodium*-capped oncolites (Playford and Cockbain, 1969) and sediment-binding *Renalcis, Sphaerocodium,* and cryptalgal structures,

c.   Deep-water (100 + m) drowned algal–stromatoporoid patch reef pinnacles with massive, "giant" stromatolite caps that are best developed in the reef flats/lagoons and large stromatolite crusts on debris flow blocks.

In summary, the Frasnian Canning Basin reef complexes are sufficiently large for the development of a spectrum of reef sizes, shapes, and shelf locations that is as complete as in any other reef complex, regardless of geologic age. Within this reef complex, there was an environmentally controlled set of reef and level-bottom communities and subcommunities. These included lateral arrangements of the major shallow-water building guild taxa (algae and stromatoporoids) from the reef crest to the reef flat and lagoon area and bathymetrically arranged cryptic shallow-to-deep-water algal-dominated subcommunities. Such an array of reefs and communities/subcommunities could only have developed in relation to a wide continental shelf with a well-defined seaward margin or crest and steep (30–35°) seaward slope.

The main differences between similarly large but younger shelf reef complexes (e.g., Permian, Triassic, Jurassic, to be discussed in Chaps. 13 and 14; Cenozoic, discussed in Part I) and the Canning Basin (Frasnian only) are:

a.   Much lower species diversity in the Devonian reefs and hence the poorer development of lateral and bathymetric biotic zonations.

b.   General biological simplicity of the higher taxa involved in the Devonian reef-building guilds (algae, stromatoporoids, and a few corals).

CONCLUSIONS

The middle Paleozoic (Llanvirnian–Frasnian), especially the Middle Ordovician, Middle Silurian, and Middle Devonian, was an extended interval (about 100 million years) of unsurpassed overall importance of reef-building in geologic history. Most of these reefs were small patch reefs (10–20 m thick), except for the very large Frasnian reef system of the Canning Basin. However, mid-Paleozoic reefs were generally larger than early Paleozoic reefs, exceedingly numerous, widely distributed (Figs. 3–6 of Flügel, 1975, generally show distribution of middle Paleozoic reefs), and dominated by a much greater diversity of well-skeletonized higher taxa.

After the Early Llanvirnian, there was a general similarity in the higher taxonomic composition of reef-building organisms; they were built by varying proportions of stromatoporoids, tabulate and rugose corals, and algae. Only rarely did a single higher taxon dominate the reef-building guilds in the way that scleractinians dominate most Late Cenozoic reefs. Early Llanvirnian reefs were dominated by binding/encrusting bryozoans and algae, a combination that did not become important again until the Late Paleozoic.

Trophic Structure

Copper (1974, pp. 379–383) and Kapp (1975, pp. 200–203) have described the trophic structure of generalized mid-Paleozoic reef communities. Although Kapp's schematic diagram (Fig. 12.9) was intended for Middle Llanvirnian communities (Example 12.2), it generally applies to most mid-Paleozoic reefs; the chief differences involve the relative importance of higher taxa and wholly different lower taxa.

The most significant aspects of Figure 12.9 to be emphasized here include:

a. Placement of stromatoporoids near the sponges as "filterers" and herbivores.

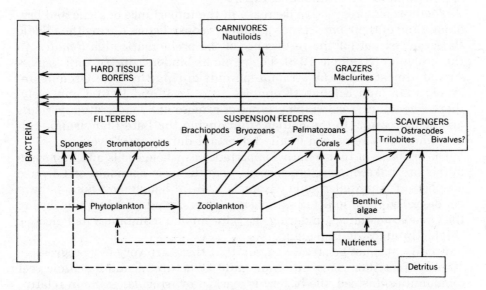

Figure 12.9.   Reconstruction of trophic relations in typical middle Paleozoic reef communities. Solid lines represent solid food, and broken lines dissolved substances. "Fishes" (not shown) would be "carnivores," "scavengers," and perhaps also "grazers" and, along with phytoplankton and zooplankton, are poorly represented as fossils. (From Kapp, 1975, © 1975 the Lethaia Foundation.)

b. Subdivision of "herbivores" (largest box) into "filterers" (passive "strainers") and "suspension feeders" (more active "grabbers"). Food sources (phytoplankton vs. zooplankton) are rarely represented in the fossil record. Many mid-Paleozoic reef communities also contain suspension-feeding bivalves (not shown).

c. "Grazers" commonly include many genera of gastropods, not just *Maclurites*.

d. "Carnivores" probably included a variety of "fishes"; they were also present as "scavengers" despite their very poor representation as fossils.

Guild Structure

By comparison to early Paleozoic reefs, those of the middle Paleozoic were built by well-skeletonized organisms and therefore the relative significance of the constructor guild is greater. Nonetheless, most mid-Paleozoic reefs are still dominated by the binder guild and are classified as boundstones; the chief exceptions are those reefs containing large, densely packed, domal–hemispherical stromatoporoids and corals such as Examples 12.2, 12.3, and 12.7, which are framestones. No pre–Middle Llanvirnian reefs are framestones. In addition, the degree of guild overlap among the dominant higher taxa remained very high in most mid-Paleozoic reef communities. There is evidence of increasing guild specialization, however, particularly in those containing a high volume of corals (e.g., Examples 12.3, 12.4, and 12.7).

There was a progressive decrease in the importance of algae and bryozoans and of their importance as binders/constructors during the middle Paleozoic, except for the resurgence of the problematic alga *Renalcis* in the Frasnian (Example 12.8). Their role as binders/constructors was assumed almost solely by stromatoporoids during the Late Ordovician, Wenlockian, and Eifelian (Examples 12.3, 12.4, and 12.6). Conversely, there was an increase in importance of ramose and fenestrate bryozoans and pelmatozoans in the baffler guild during the Late Llanvirnian–Silurian and they remained locally important during the Devonian.

On the basis of their relative importance as whole shells and fragments in the internal sediment, brachiopods were the most abundant and diverse members of the dweller guild (Example 12.6), although most authors have not described them in detail. Brachiopod diversity increased rapidly during the Ordovician and again during the Silurian and maintained its Paleozoic "high" through the Frasnian.

Finally, it must be stressed again that there are very few progressive "trends" in either composition or guild structure of mid-Paleozoic reef communities. Instead, the history is marked by irregular shifts in relative importance of the (1) higher taxa involved in reef-building, (2) building guilds, and (3) degrees of guild overlap. Taxa and guilds unpredictably rose and fell in importance temporally and also varied enormously among reefs of the same age (cf. Examples 12.6 and 12.7).

Extinction Events

The family-level data on extinction rates for Phanerozoic marine proto-zoans, invertebrates, and vertebrates of Raup and Sepkoski (1982) and Sepkoski and Sheehan (1983) indicate that there were two mass extinction events during the middle Paleozoic: first during the Late Ordovician (Ashgillian), when standing familial diversity dropped by 12%, and second during the Middle and Late Devonian (Givetian through Frasnian), with a drop of 14%. Interestingly, the latter extinction appears to be spread over an interval of about 15 million years and so does not produce a well-defined, statistically significant peak in extinction rates comparable to that for the Ashgillian. These data are based on all families, regardless of their paleoecology, and provide an interesting contrast to the evolutionary history of reef communities.

Late Ordovician (Ashgillian Stage, Hirnantian Substage). By the Late Caradocian, the general middle Paleozoic reef community structure dominated by stromatoporoids, tabulate and rugose corals, and non-skeletal algae was firmly established (Example 12.3). In addition, the dweller guild and level-bottom diversity had gone through a period of about 50 million years of rapid increase, especially by articulate brachiopods and gastropods. Thus, the presumed ecologic stability attendant to high diversity had been achieved for reef, level-bottom, and pelagic communities and continued into the Ashgillian.

However, at the end of the Ashgillian (Hirnantian), the first mid-Paleozoic mass extinction event occurred. Although the event was neither sudden nor catastrophic (McLaren, 1983, p. 319), it was highly selective in terms of the taxa involved and their respective paleoecologies. Level-bottom and reef dweller guild bryozoans, articulate brachiopods, and trilobites suffered considerable extinction, as did crinoids, graptoloids, and cephalopods (summarized by Sepkoski and Sheehan, 1983, pp. 676–678). Conversely, the diversity of well-skeletonized members of the reef-building guilds (stromatoporoids and corals) actually increased from the Hirnantian to the Early Silurian (Llandoverian); they continued to dominate building guilds of most Early Llandoverian reef communities (Copper and Fay, 1984). Thus, the Ashgillian/Hirnantian mass extinction event had far greater impact on composition and structure of level-bottom and pelagic communities that on the building guilds of reef communities. The greatest impact on reef communities was on the diversity of dweller (brachiopods; trilobites) and baffler (some bryozoans; "pelmatozoans") guilds.

Nevertheless, the abundance and geographic range of reef communities were considerably reduced during the Early Llandoverian, an interval of about 5–8 million years. By the Late Llandoverian, however, the return to vigorous reef-building was well underway. Wenlockian reefs are larger, more numerous, and more widespread than those of the Ashgillian and have essentially the same higher taxon composition and guild structure as those of the Ashgillian (Example 12.4). Wenlockian taxonomic diversity in the dweller and destroyer guilds and in level-bottom and pelagic communities (i.e., brachiopods, cephalopods, crinoids) was again comparable to diversities before the Hirnantian biological crisis.

Early Devonian. During the Early Devonian, reef communities suffered a decline that rarely appears on typical compilations of extinction rates or standing taxonomic diversity, either because of the "coarseness" of chronostratigraphic units or the taxonomic level used by the compiler. Reef communities did not become "extinct" nor did any higher taxa in the building guilds. Instead, there was merely a very significant decline in size and number of reefs and in species diversity of stromatoporoids from the Late Silurian to the Early Devonian (Stearn, 1983). Smith (1983) reported the global totals of Early Devonian reefs as 7 for the Gedinnian, 8 for the Siegenian, and 18 for the Emsian; these figures are in sharp contrast to the more than 100 patch reefs (not all shown in Flügel, 1975, Fig. 5) and reef systems that are very widely distributed in the Middle Devonian. Stearn (1982b) estimated stromatoporoid species diversity for the Late Silurian at about 130, for the Early Devonian at about 50, and for the Middle Devonian at about 230.

Therefore, reef communities and the lower level taxa that build reefs may enjoy their own evolutionary history of success and vigor, as well as decline and failure, that may be only loosely related to the success and failure of the global marine biota. In some ways, reef communities and ecosystems appear to operate almost independently from contemporaneous communities; this is particularly true for members of the frame-building guilds (see below and also Chap. 15).

Late Devonian (Frasnian). In a succession of reports, McLaren (1970, 1982, 1983, 1984, 1985) has discussed the nature, duration, and potential causes of the mass extinction event that occurred during the Middle–Late Devonian (Givetian–Frasnian). The family-level data of Raup and Sepkoski (1982) show a statistically insignificant trend of increased levels of extinction (i.e., above the "background" rate) that begin in the Eifelian and continue through the Frasnian; they produced progressively lower standing diversities in the Frasnian and Famennian. Thus, overall familial diversity was lower in the Frasnian than in the Middle Devonian, but Famennian diversity was sharply depressed from the Frasnian.

The end of the Frasnian mass extinction was both taxonomically and paleoecologically extensive. The higher taxa involved include:

a.   Virtually all stromatoporoids. However, there was a brief, minor revival at the end of the Devonian and the beginning of the Carboniferous ("Strunian" in France and Belgium; see also Shilo et al., 1984).

b.   Virtually all corals, but especially the Rugosa. Of the 43 rugosan genera present in the Frasnian, only 14 also occur in the Famennian,

and of the 50 Famennian genera, 34 arose during the Famennian. Furthermore, of the 148 shallow-water Frasnian rugose species, only 6 survived into the Famennian, whereas 4 of 10 deep-water species did survive
(Pedder, 1982). Most Famennian rugosans were solitary or weakly colonial; large, frame-building colonial corals did not reappear in reef communities until the Middle Visean (Example 13.2) and they are not direct
phylogenetic descendants of any Famennian forms.

  c.   Among the brachiopods, Orthacea, Pentameracea, Atrypacea, and
Stropheodontidae became extinct at the end of the Frasnian; all of these
had long and diverse pre-Frasnian evolutionary histories. In fact, the
Atrypacea were one of the major taxa in the Frasnian sessile benthos. Of
71 Frasnian genera or "generic groups," only 10 survived into the Famennian.

  Other less catastrophic changes involved the extinction of tentaculitids
(virtually absent from reef communities, regardless of age), substantial
reduction of trilobite diversity from the Givetian through the Frasnian,
and high taxonomic turnover among ammonoid cephalopods.

  The higher taxa involved were generally important members of level-
bottom, pelagic (ammonoids), and reef communities. The effect on reef
communities was of crisis proportions. Frasnian reefs were large, widespread, and built by a diverse assemblage of algae, stromatoporoids, and
corals with membership in the constructor, binder, and baffler guilds (Example 12.8). Famennian reefs are relatively rare (best developed the
Canning Basin, Western Australia, with modest development in Alberta)
and were built by algae alone, albeit in enormous biomass (Example 13.1).
Generally, algal forms (*Renalcis, Sphaerocodium,* and stromatolites) that
were very important in the binder/constructor guilds in Frasnian reefs
survived the extinction event and assumed even greater importance in
the same guilds in Famennian reefs. Continuation of large-scale reef-
building in the Famennian of the Canning Basin suggests that, in this
area at least, the chemical–physical–geological environmental factors
maintained or returned to their pre-extinction conditions and remained
conducive to the reef-building process for another 4–7 million years.

  Previous authors have disagreed on the global synchroneity of the
event, the abruptness of the mass extinction, and the nature and duration
of the causal factor(s). Of considerable importance for dating the event
is the fact that conodonts did not undergo significant change during the
end of Frasnian extinction.

  Diversity at lower taxonomic levels for most higher taxa that were
adversely affected by the late Frasnian event had begun to decrease from
their mid-Devonian maxima well before the end of the Frasnian. Yet, at
many widespread localities, the event can be determined as precisely as
a single bedding plane separating a relatively diverse Frasnian fauna
from a depauperate Famennian fauna. Such an abrupt faunal change occurs in the Canning Basin within a 12-cm thick algal-rich layer located

chronostratigraphically at the base of the Upper *Palmatolepis triangularis* Zone (Playford et al., 1984b). However, in western Europe, cessation of reef-building seems to have occurred somewhat earlier, during deposition of the *P. gigas.* Zone (Eder and Franke, 1982). McLaren (1982; 1983) has estimated that the mass extinction occurred during the time interval of one conodont zone (uppermost *P. gigas* to *P. triangularis* Zones in the global conodont sequence or approx. 0.5–1 million years). However, Johnson et al. (1985, p. 581) suggested that the duration of the event extended through both conodont zones (perhaps as long as 2 million years).

Discussion of potential causes for this and other mass extinctions of reef communities is reserved for Chapter 15. However, the history of middle Paleozoic reef communities discussed in the present chapter clearly indicates that the factor(s) involved during this 100-million year interval (Middle Ordovician–Frasnian) and their biological effects:

a.   Varied from slow (Early Devonian "decline") to intermediate (Ashgillian) to rapid (Frasnian).

b.   Varied from minor (Ashgillian) to intermediate (Early Devonian) to catastrophic (Frasnian) in terms of their effect on composition and structure of reef communities.

c.   Were selective in their effects on reef-vs.-level-bottom communities; the Ashgillian extinction affected level-bottom more than reef communities, whereas the Early Devonian affected reefs more than level-bottoms.

d.   Were selective in their effects on shallow-water-vs.-deep-water organisms. The Frasnian extinction had less effect on deep- than on shallow-water corals and almost no effect on shallow-water algae and on conodont-bearing "fishes."

13

Late Paleozoic Reef Communities

LATE DEVONIAN–LATE PERMIAN

Subsequent to the Frasnian mass extinction of middle Paleozoic metazoans, algae (especially the skeletal forms) underwent an important revival in their abundance, diversity, and contribution to the frame construction processes. The history of late Paleozoic reef-building contributions by algae may be divided into ethree phases: Famennian–Early Carboniferous, mid–Late Carboniferous, and Permian. The mid–Late Carboniferous represents the time when diversity of higher taxa of skeletal algae was the greatest in all of earth history (Chuvashov and Riding, 1984, Text-Fig. 8) and of the greatest relative importance of algae to the reef-building process since the Cambrian and Early Ordovician (Fig. 7.1).

During the middle Paleozoic, algae in reef communities were generally overshadowed by better-skeletonized metazoans. Because of their typical poor skeletonization or lack of skeletons, late Paleozoic algae were largely confined to the binder and baffler guilds; in local cases of high packing density, they also became important constructors. Thus, most late Paleozoic reefs are boundstones and bafflestones rather than framestones. The only metazoans that were significant contributors to late Paleozoic reef-building guilds were poriferans (Fig. 8.1), bryozoans, and brachiopods (Fig. 10.1).

Famennian–Tournaisian Algae
Except for the well-developed Famennian reefs and reef systems in the Canning Basin, Western Australia, the smaller reefs in Alberta and in the Omolon Region of northeastern Russia (Shilo et al., 1984), mud mounds

of the "Waulsortian facies" are much more numerous than skeletal framework reefs during the Famennian and Tournaisian. All components of the Cambrian and Ordovician floras of Chuvashov and Riding (1984, Text-Figs. 1, 2) continued into the Famennian from the Frasnian. However, the Cambrian and Ordovician floral components of reef communities suffered a major decline at the end of the Famennian; there was no comparable decline in skeletonized metazoans at the end of the Famennian. Thus, the decline in reef-building algae postdates the mass extinction of reef-building metazoans by nearly 10 million years. Of the 6 "groups" of reef-building calcareous algae present in early and middle Paleozoic reefs, 3 became extinct at the end of the Devonian (Famennian), 2 during the Early Carboniferous, and the remaining "group" (Receptaculitales) was absent from all reef-building guilds from the end of the Devonian to the mid-Permian (Chuvashov and Riding, 1984, pp. 493–494). The "Renalcis–Shuguria Group" and a few solenoporaceans were the only skeletal algae present in the Tournaisian and most were confined to mud-mound and level-bottom communities.

"Mid–Late" Carboniferous Algae and Metazoans

Beginning in the Middle Visean, there is a reversal in the relative abundance of mud mounds and skeletal framework reefs. However, most Visean builders were metazoans and non-skeletal algae rather than skeletal algae. By mid-Carboniferous, the earliest reef-building components of the "Carboniferous Flora" of Chuvashov and Riding (1984) had evolved; by the Late Carboniferous (Moscovian) there were six major algal groups contributing significantly, or even predominantly in some situations, to the building guilds (Fig. 7.1).

During the Visean, the Chaetetida began a major period of expanding importance in the constructor and binder guilds that continued to the Permian (Fig. 8.1). They were joined in these same guilds by brachiopods in the latest Carboniferous. Fenestrate bryozoans also were prominent members of the baffler guild during the Late Carboniferous.

Permian Algae and Metazoans

By the Early Permian, the diversity of reef-building algae was reduced to five major groups (Fig. 7.1) and all remained important until the Late Permian.

The Early and mid-Permian marked the culmination of fenestrate bryozoans (baffler guild) and brachiopods (constructor guild; Fig. 10.1). During the Middle Permian, the Chaetetida decreased in importance and were largely confined to the binder guild; various other higher poriferan taxa, however, achieved considerable importance as bafflers and binders. Finally, during the Late Permian, there was a progressive global decline in abundance and size of reefs leading to cessation of the reef-building process and mass extinction of numerous higher reef-building taxa, both algal and metazoan (Figs. 7.1–10.1) at the end of the Permian.

Reef Communities

Late Devonian (Famennian)

Example 13.1: Late Devonian (Famennian); Canning Basin, Western Australia. After the major metazoan extinction event at the end of the Frasnian, there was continued reef-building on the margin of the Canning Basin in approximately the same general areas as the older Devonian (Givetian–Frasnian; see Example 12.8) reef systems. The physical aspects (sizes, shapes, and abundance) of Famennian reefs of the Windjana Limestone are generally comparable to those of the preceding Frasnian reefs.

However, the taxonomic composition of the Famennian communities is much simpler due to the complete absence of stromatoporoids and corals from the reef-building guilds and the drastic reduction in abundance and diversity of brachiopods in the dweller guild (Fig. 13.1). Thus, the frame-building processes, both biological and inorganic, continued unabated from

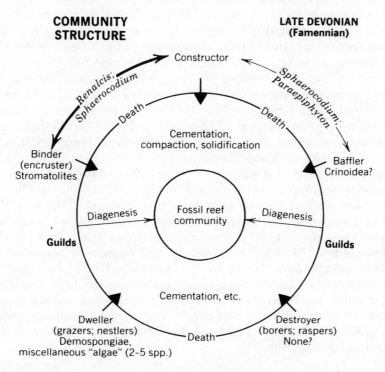

Figure 13.1. Composition and guild structure of the Late Devonian (Famennian) Windjana Limestone marginal to the Canning Basin, Western Australia. All reef-building guilds are dominated by a taxonomically simple assemblage of algae; *Renalcis*, and locally *Sphaerocodium*, are so densely packed that they overlap with the constructor guild (cf. Fig. 12.8). Main guild membership indicated by thick arrows, and guild overlap by thin arrows (around circle).

the Frasnian to the Famennian with the algal components of the building guilds (chiefly *Renalcis, Sphaerocodium,* and both shallow- and deep-water stromatolites; Fig. 13.1) simply filling the niches left vacant by the extinction of stromatoporoids and corals. The complete domination of building guilds, especially the binder guild, by *Renalcis* and other algae is very comparable in both composition and structure to the earliest Cambrian (Tommotian; Fig. 11.1) and Late Cambrian–Early Ordovician (Figs. 11.3, 11.4, 11.5) reef communities, all of which are algal reefs in the full sense of the term. *Renalcis* and *Sphaerocodium* continued to dominate the building of organic frameworks to the end of the Famennian; locally, *Renalcis,* or its taxonomic associates, continued into the Early Carboniferous in mud-mound and level-bottom communities (cf. Chuvashov and Riding, 1984, Text-Figs. 1, 3).

Early Carboniferous

Example 13.2: Early Carboniferous (Mid–Late Visean); Akiyoshi Limestone, Japan. In the southern part of Honshu Island, Japan, the Akiyoshi Limestone Group contains an atoll system (about 17 km in maximum diameter) that persisted with relatively minor changes in the physical/ chemical/geological environmental factors from the Visean to the Middle Permian (Ota, 1968; Ota, 1977). The remarkable aspect of the atoll system is the nearly continuous record of biological evolution of reef and level-bottom communities that inhabited the seaward slope, reef crest, and reef flat/lagoonal areas. Examples 13.2 through 13.4 review the evolutionary history of the reef crest frame-building guilds during part of this interval.

The reef system began to grow on the summit of a quiescent volcano in an actively subsiding eugeosynclinal belt. The earliest sediments (Late Tournaisian) consisted of submarine basic tuffs and breccias interbedded with oolites containing the productoid brachiopod *Marginatia.* The initial organic framework of the reef crest dates from about the mid–Late Visean and was dominated by tightly intergrown dendroid rugose corals which comprise about 75% of the megascopic individual fossils and 10–15% of the rock volume (Pl. 42*a*); well-skeletonized colonies of *Nagatophyllum* and *Hiroshimaphyllum* (Haikawa and Ota, 1978; Fig. 13.2*a, b* and Table 13.1 herein) are by far the most important corals and dominate the constructor guild. Less abundant solitary rugosans are accessory members of the constructor guild and rare rugose and tabulate corals are included with chaetetids and brachiopods as dwellers. Binders consisted of bryozoans and stromatolites.

Example 13.3: Early Carboniferous (Visean). Although organic framework reefs are much less common than mud mounds in Lower Carboniferous rocks, algal-dominated (Wolfenden, 1958) and bryozoan-dominated (Orme, 1971) frameworks are present in a shelf margin (barrier reef) and reef

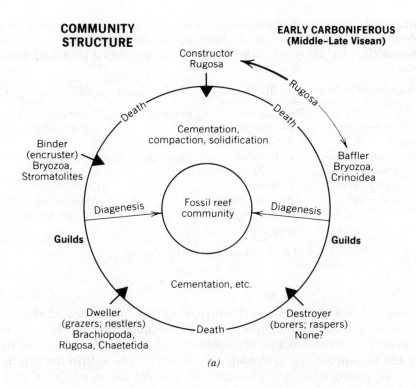

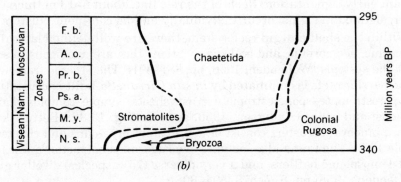

Figure 13.2. (a) Composition and guild structure of Early Carboniferous (mid–late Visean) rugose coral-dominated reef crest subcommunity, Akiyoshi Limestone Group, southern Honshu Island, Japan (cf. Table 13.1). Main guild membership indicated by thick arrow, and guild overlap by thin arrow (around circle). (b) Schematic diagram showing temporal changes in the relative importance of taxa belonging to binder and constructor guilds in reefs of the Akiyoshi Limestone Group (Carboniferous), southern Honshu Island, Japan. Nam. = Namurian. Zonal index species (Ota, 1977): N. s. = *Nagatophyllum satoi* (Rugosa) and the fusulinellids M. y. = *Millerella yowarensis;* Ps. a. = *Pseudostaffella antiqua;* Pr. b. = *Profusulinella-beppensis;* A. o. = *Akiyoshiella ozawai;* F. b. = *Fusulinella biconica.* (M. Ota, May 1983, personal communication.) Approximate duration for this sequence was 45 million years; it is conformable except for a probable hiatus between the *M. yowarensis* and *Pseudostaffella antiqua* Zones.

TABLE 13.1. Taxonomic Composition and Guild Structure of the Early Carboniferous (Mid–Late Visean; *Nagatophyllum satoi* Zone) Reef Crest Community of the Akiyoshi Limestone Group, Southern Honshu Island, Japan

Constructor Guild	Baffler Guild	Binder Guild	Dweller Guild
Rugosa	Bryozoa	Bryozoa	Rugosa
Nagatophyllum satoi	*Fenestella*	*Fistu-lipora"*	*Polycoelia japon-ica*
Hiroshimaphyllum enorma	*Meekoporella*	Stromatolites	*Amygdalo-phylloides?*
Echigophyllum? atetsuense	*Prismopora*		Chaetetida
	Tabulipora"		Brachiopoda
	Polypora		*Gigantoproductus*
	Acanthocladia		
	Streblotrypella"		
	Crinoidea		

Source: After Ota (1977) and Haikawa and Ota (1978).
*"*Guild assignment uncertain.

flat/lagoonal reef system in Derbyshire, England. The incipient shallow-water barrier reefs are elongate (up to 300 m long), narrow (10 m wide), and up to 33 m thick with an original relief of about 125 m from the reef down the seaward slope to the adjacent basin. Voids within the original organic framework contain abundant fibrous calcite as evidence of important early cementation. Reefs of the reef flat, about 6–13 m thick with poorly defined margins, occur individually and as confluent clusters.

Within the shelf margin reef system, there are well-defined lateral petrographic, geomorphic, and ecologic zonations that are analogous to some Holocene systems (Wolfenden, 1958, pp. 881–891). The organic framework of the barrier reefs is dominated by *in situ Girvanella*-built encrustations and porostromate–spongiostromate crusts/sheets, simple–complex domes, columns, and cones (Anderson, 1950; see also Fig. 13.3*a*). Better-skeletonized binders/encrusters consist of fistuliporoid bryozoans and chaetetids (Table 13.2). The fauna also includes one rugosan constructor, a few lithistid demosponge bafflers, and a very diverse (75 + species) dweller guild (Wolfenden, 1958, pp. 877–878, 894–898).

The reef flat/lagoon reefs also contain abundant *Girvanella*-bound layers and encrustations and fenestrate bryozoans (chiefly *Fenestella* spp.). The porostromate binders/encrusters and the fenestrate bafflers formed an open, loose framework of uncertain rigidity with abundant voids, now filled with lime mud, "algal dust," and fibrous calcite (early? cement) spar (Orme, 1971).

In the Akiyoshi Limestone Group in southwestern Japan, the reefs of the Late Visean (Early Namurian?) *Millerella yowarensis* Zone contain a fossil assemblage that is quite similar to those of Derbyshire. In the area of the reef crest (B-I facies of Ota et al., 1969), the organic framework

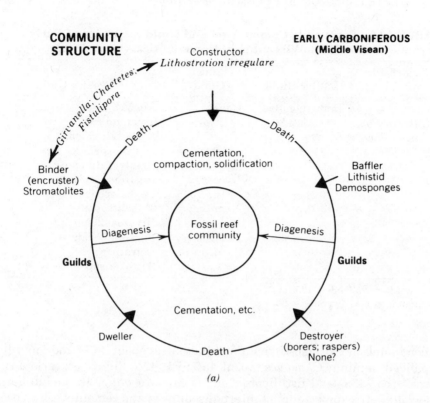

COMMUNITY STRUCTURE

EARLY CARBONIFEROUS
(Middle Visean)

Constructor
Lithostrotion irregulare

Girvanella; Chaetetes; Fistulipora

Death — Death

Binder (encruster) Stromatolites

Cementation, compaction, solidification

Baffler Lithistid Demosponges

Diagenesis → Fossil reef community ← Diagenesis

Guilds   **Guilds**

Cementation, etc.

Dweller

Death

Destroyer (borers; raspers) None?

(a)

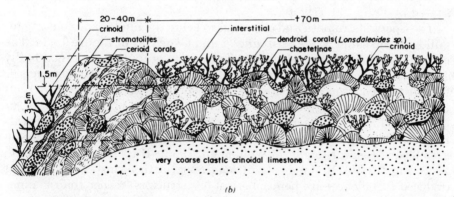

20–40m — +70m

crinoid
stromatolites
cerioid corals

interstitial
dendroid corals(*Lonsdaleoides sp.*)
chaetetinae
crinoid

1.5m

3–5m

very coarse clastic crinoidal limestone

(b)

Figure 13.3. (*a*) Composition and guild structure of Early Carboniferous (middle Visean) shelf margin (barrier) reefs in Derbyshire, England. The chief builders were cyanophytes ("Porostromata"/*Girvanella* and "Spongiostromata"/stromatolites) with lesser contributions by encrusting *Fistulipora* (Bryozoa), *Chaetetes* (Chaetetida), and *Lithostrotion* (Rugosa) (cf. Table 13.2). Main guild membership indicated by thick arrows (around circle). (After Wolfenden, 1958.) (*b*) Schematic reconstruction of the reef system, lower Akiyoshi Limestone Group (Early Carboniferous), Sumitomo Quarry, southwestern Honshu Island, Japan. The 20–40-m wide reef crest is dominated by stromatolites and laminar Chaetetinae, whereas the 70 + -m lagoonal area is dominated by dendroid rugose corals and hemispherical Chaetetinae. "Interstitial" refers to internal reef sediment. (From Ota, 1968.)

TABLE 13.2. Taxonomic Composition and Guild Structure of Early Carboniferous (Middle Visean) Reef Communities, Derbyshire, England[a]

Constructor Guild	Baffler Guild	Binder Guild	Dweller Guild
Rugosa	Demospongiae	Algae	Rugosa: 3 spp.
Lithostrotion	Lithistids:	*Girva-*	Tabulata
irregulare	3 + spp.	*nella;*	*Michelinia* sp.
		stroma-	Brachiopoda: 42 spp.
		tolites	Bivalvia: 13 spp.
		Bryozoa	Gastropoda: 3 spp.
		Fistulipora	Cephalopoda: 2 spp.
		minor	Tribolita: 4 + spp.
		Chaetetida	Bryozoa: 2 spp.
		Chaetetes	Foraminiferida
		depres-	Ostracoda
		sus	Algae: 2 spp.

Source: After Wolfenden, 1958.
[a]Minimum species diversity ≅ 85.

is dominated by Spongiostromata (stromatolites; about 45%) and laterally expanded, laminar *Chaetetes* (about 45%; Pl. 42*b*; Fig. 13.3); cerioid rugosans (Pl. 43*a*) and fistuliporoid bryozoans are minor frame-builders. The volumetric importance of internal sediment and cement was not presented by Ota et al. (1969).

The Spongiostromata and *Chaetetes* overlap the binder and constructor guilds in the same way as *Girvanella* and *Chaetetes* in Figure 13.3*a*. The cerioid rugosans in the *Millerella* Zone reefs of Japan are functionally comparable to *Lithostrotion irregulare* in Derbyshire, but bryozoans appear to have played a somewhat greater role as binders in the Derbyshire reefs than in Japan.

In both Japan and Derbyshire, the relative importance of rugose corals in the building guilds increases from the reef crest to the reef flat/lagoon area ("back reef" or "shelf" of Wolfenden, 1958; "B-II" facies of Ota et al., 1969; Fig. 13.3*b*). In Japan, the *Chaetetes* growth forms in the reef flat (reduced turbulence) are hemispherical (constructors) rather than laminar (binders) and the relative volumetric importance of the building guilds is about 8% dendroid rugosans and 12% *Chaetetes;* the remaining 80% includes abundant crinoidal debris (baffler guild), cerioid rugosans (constructors), dwellers (genera/species listed by Ota, 1977, pp. 10–11), and internal sediment.

Example 13.4: Late Carboniferous (Moscovian); Chaetetid-dominated. In the Moscovian age, reefs of the Akiyoshi Limestone Group (*Profusulinella beppensis* Zone–*Fusulinella biconica* Zone of Ota, 1977), there is a progressive increase in the relative importance of chaetetids in the building guilds from about 50% to 60% of the organic framework and a comparable decrease in rugose corals and stromatolites (Fig. 13.2*b*). Crinoids continue to be important as bafflers, bryozoans as binders or dwellers, and fusulinids as dwellers.

The history of reef community guild evolution depicted in Figure 13.2*b* is regarded as complete, except for a probable brief hiatus between the *Millerella* and *Pseudostaffella* Zones. It is a record of gradual shifts in relative importance of the main taxa involved in building the organic framework over an interval of about 45 million years. The sharp rise in importance of chaetetids during the Visean–Moscovian is in accord with their overall global history (Fig. 8.1); this rise marks the change from predominantly algal-rich mud mounds in the earliest Carboniferous to well-skeletonized framestones and boundstones in the mid–Late Carboniferous.

The post-*Fusulinella biconica* Zone Akiyoshi Limestone crest and marginal lagoon reef frameworks are very poorly exposed (Ota, 1968, Fig. 17, Table 6), so it is impossible to determine the composition and structure of the building guilds. The record of the central lagoon level-bottom communities is much more complete but is not considered here. However, the Akiyoshi Limestone atoll system with all its facies from its inception in the Middle–Late Visean to its final cessation in mid–Late Permian (about 80 million years) is a remarkably complete record of abiotic environmental stability and gradual community evolution; it is not duplicated in such a small area (approx. 100 km^2) elsewhere in the world, regardless of geologic age!

In central and south-central United States, chaetetid-dominated reefs and biostromes occur in limestones of the Atoka (Sutherland, 1984) and Desmoinesian (West and Clark, 1984) Stages (= Moscovian). The reefs are mostly small (up to 5 m in diameter and 3 m thick), but the degree of chaetetid domination is much greater than in the Akiyoshi Limestone atoll.

The reef-building chaetetids occur in several growth forms from laminar (Pl. 25*a*) to low domical, hemispherical, and columnar (Pl. 7*b*). Individual specimens are remarkably large and densely packed; laminar and domal forms up to 2 m in diameter and hemispheres and columns as much as 1.5 m high are locally common. The packing of hemispherical and columnar forms may be so dense that there is almost no internal sediment; their skeletons are in such close contact that they originally were mutually supporting to prevent overturning or toppling in high turbulence. In some cases, the chaetetid density is so high that nearly all other taxa are excluded (e.g., lower part, Type II, Sutherland, 1984).

Because of their excellent skeletonization, dense packing, and varied growth forms, the chaetetids dominated the constructor and binder guilds of these reefs (Fig. 13.4); although the hemispherical–columnar forms

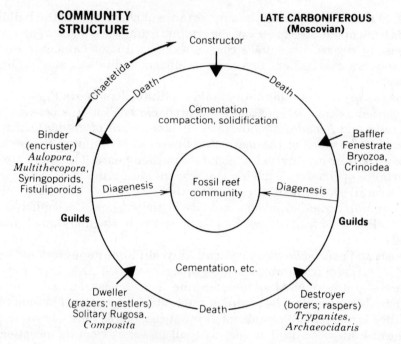

COMMUNITY STRUCTURE

LATE CARBONIFEROUS
(Moscovian)

Constructor

Chaetetida

Death

Death

Cementation
compaction, solidification

Binder
(encruster)
Aulopora,
Multithecopora,
Syringoporids,
Fistuliporoids

Baffler
Fenestrate
Bryozoa,
Crinoidea

Diagenesis

Fossil reef
community

Diagenesis

Guilds

Guilds

Cementation, etc.

Dweller
(grazers; nestlers)
Solitary Rugosa,
Composita

Death

Destroyer
(borers; raspers)
Trypanites,
Archaeocidaris

Figure 13.4. Composition and guild structure of Late Carboniferous (Moscovian) chaetetid-dominated reefs in the south-central United States. The contributions of other builders (tabulate corals; bryozoans) to the construction process are quite minor. (After West and Clark, 1984; Sutherland, 1984.)

baffled the currents, their high degree of skeletalization excludes them from the baffler guild. The columnar forms (Pl. 7*b*) are analogous to similarly shaped Precambrian (Fig. 7.2) and Late Devonian (Pl. 27; Example 12.8) stromatolites and Middle Silurian stromatoporoids (Kershaw, 1981, Figs. 3E, 3F, 7); the domal forms are analogous to middle Paleozoic and Mesozoic–Cenozoic corals.

Example 13.5: Late Carboniferous–Early Permian; Algal-dominated. In a very large area of the central and southwestern United States (Wray, 1968, Figs. 1, 2), the Late Carboniferous and Early Permian rocks contain algal-dominated level-bottom/biostromal (e.g., Toomey, 1976, 1979) and reef communities (commonly described as mounds or banks; e.g., Heckel and Cocke, 1969; Heckel, 1972; Toomey, 1977, 1980) of uncertain rigidity and topographic relief (Ball et al., 1977, pp. 256–258). There are two higher algal taxa (Codiacea and Rhodophyta; see Chap. 7) that are abundant in these communities and both produced lightly calcified, leaflike (phylloid) thalli that are rarely preserved in growth position.

The most common codiaceans are *Eugonophyllum, Ivanovia,* and *An-*

chicodium; Wray (1977) and Toomey (1976; 1979) believe that they grew upright as blades and cups (Pl. 29*a*). If this is correct, they functioned as baffles and were members of the baffler guild. The most common rhodophytes were two species of *Archaeolithophyllum:* an encrusting form and an undulose or umbrella-shaped form (Pl. 30). Both were members of the binder guild. Because of the fragility of their thalli, these codiaceans and rhodophytes are at least as common as transported fragments in biostromes (Pl. 4*b*) and "shell heaps" (grainstones–packstones) as they are in reefs (Ball et al., 1977). Furthermore, even when they are in growth position, they may form biostromes rather than mound-shaped structures. Finally, their original, living packing density apparently was so high that they nearly excluded all other skeletal organisms (Toomey, 1980).

An additional complication in interpreting the origin of these structures is their enormous original porosity. The pore volume is now reduced by variable amounts of calcite spar (Pl. 30*b*), much of it botryoidal and perhaps of early submarine origin (James et al., 1984). Thus, the initial rigidity of these structures may have been due to both an organic (algal) and inorganic (early cement) framework.

Toomey (1976; 1979) has discussed the community paleoecology of two types of phylloid algal level-bottom/biostromal communities: (1) a Late Carboniferous rhodophyte/sphinctozoan (see also Fagerstrom, 1984b, p. 375) and (2) an Early Permian codiacean. In both cases, the fossils appear to be essentially in growth position and species richness is higher than for comparable non-algal level-bottom assemblages or for many other phylloid algal reefs.

Kotila (see Wray, 1977, pp. 135–136) has described lateral and bathymetric zonations of phylloid algae, other algae, and invertebrates in a carbonate bank complex that suggest a close relationship between subtle differences in environmental factors and the distribution of subcommunities. Although total species diversity is not presented, the structure seems zoned like most Cenozoic scleractinian-dominated reef systems.

There are well-developed cryptic subcommunities (Bonem, 1977, pp. 77–79) in numerous, small (1–2-m thick; 2–3-m dia.) algal/bryozoan-dominated reefs having initial rigidity and topographic relief (up to 1.1 m) from the Late Carboniferous (Morrowan; = Bashkirian) of Oklahoma. The cavities are now filled with shale but originally were up to 1 m long with walls and ceilings encrusted by bryozoans and highly bored by clionid? sponges. The cavity floors and the bases of the walls are lined by tabulate corals, and erect rugosans grew toward the cavity centers. Toomey (1980) has described a very simple lateral zonation and vertical allogenic succession in a phylloid algal-dominated reeflike community in the Late Carboniferous (Moscovian) of New Mexico.

Zonations and successions based on non-transported fossil associations and cryptic subcommunities such as those described above are presumptive evidence for reef communities rather than current-produced shell heaps and mounds. Thus, contrary to the conclusion of Ball et al. (1977), the present author regards a great many of these late Paleozoic algal-dominated structures as reefs with well-developed baffler and binder guilds. Each case must be judged according to its own features, however.

The Moscovian reeflike structure in New Mexico (Toomey, 1980) occurs near the middle of the regressive phase of a typical late Paleozoic cyclic shelf sequence. Accretion of the reef and lowered sea level subjected the reef crest and contemporaneous sediments to repeated subaerial exposure during its growth history. The community was dominated by the upward-growing plates and blades of the codiacean *Ivanovia tenuissima* (Table 13.3), which was primarily a baffler; however, arched fragments on the substrate also stabilized and bound internal sediment (Fig. 13.5). Despite the fragility of the plates and blades, the packing density of *I. tenuissima* was so great that it also overlapped the constructor guild. Among the most numerous and diverse members of the community were foraminifera that encrusted (living?) *Ivanovia* thalli. The main constituents of the dweller guild were three species of large brachiopods, various foraminifera, and a few other higher taxa (Table 13.3).

As noted by Toomey (1979; 1980; 1981, pp. 50–52) and Fagerstrom (1984b, p. 375), the total species diversity (approx. 40 + spp.) of the New Mexican community seems significantly lower than comparable level-bottom/biostromal communities. Similarly, other Moscovian mound/bank-

TABLE 13.3. Taxonomic Composition and Guild Structure of Late Carboniferous (Moscovian) Reef Community, La Pasada Formation, New Mexico[a]

Baffler Guild	Binder Guild	Dweller Guild
Codiacae	Codiacea	Foraminiferida
Ivanovia tenuissima	*Ivanovia tenuissima*	Small, vagile:
Bryozoa	Foraminiferida: 5 spp.	6 + spp.
Fenestrates	Bryozoa	Fusulines: 5 spp.
	Fistuliporid	Agglutinated:
	Annelida	3 spp.
	Spirorbis sp.	Brachiopoda: 5 spp.
		Algae: spores?; others:
		4? spp.
		Ostracoda
		Bryozoa: 2 spp.
		Conodonts
		Poriferan spicules
		"Fish and sharks"
		Gastropoda: 2 + spp.
		Bivalvia

Source: After Toomey, 1980.
[a]Minimum species diversity ≅ 40.

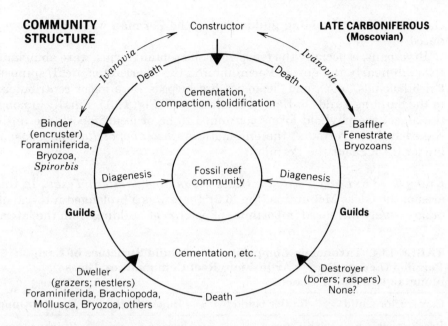

Figure 13.5 Composition and guild structure of a Late Carboniferous (Moscovian) reef community, La Pasada Formation, New Mexico. The erect-growing blade/platelike thalli of the codiacean alga *Ivanovia* belong primarily to the baffler guild but are so densely packed that they overlap with the constructor guild (cf. Table 13.3). Main guild membership indicated by thick arrow, and guild overlap by thin arrows (around circle).

shaped structures dominated by binding/encrusting rhodophytes (*Archaeolithophyllum* spp.) also appear to be less diverse than adjacent level-bottom communities. Thus, the dominance of phylloid algae in the communities they characterize is so complete that only a few other forms can survive on, under, and between the thalli, a situation quite similar to the chaetetid-dominated reef communities described above and the Holocene low diversity reefs described in Chapter 1.

Early Permian

Introduction. Flügel and Stanley (1984, pp. 177–179) reviewed the nature and distribution of Permian reefs and emphasized the dramatic increase in the importance of Sphinctozoa, Inozoa (Fig. 8. 1), and the enigmatic alga (?) *Tubiphytes* (Fig. 7.1) compared with Late Carboniferous reefs. Although the Sphinctozoa had a long pre-Permian history in level-bottom communities, it was not until the Early Permian that they became both abundant and diverse in reef communities (Fagerstrom, 1984b, pp. 375–377). In Late Permian reefs, they were joined by increasingly abundant siliceous sponges and inozoans (Fig. 8.1). Conversely, the contribution of chaetetids to the building guilds during the Permian was markedly reduced.

Bryozoans, especially the fenestrate and reptant forms, were abundant through nearly the entire Permian, and the aberrant conical, spinose ("richthofenids," etc.), and "leptodid" brachiopods were major contributors to the building guilds of Early Permian reefs (Fig. 10.1). Finally, among the algae, the phylloid forms continued to be of local importance until the early Late Permian; the enigmatic *Archeolithoporella* was a major binder throughout the Permian.

Example 13.6: Early Permian; Glass Mountains, Western Texas. In the area of the Glass Mountains (Fig. 6.3), there was a prolonged interval of progressively increased importance of patch reef-building from the latest

TABLE 13.4. Taxonomic Composition and Guild Structure of Early Permian (Leonardian; ≅ Artinskian) Reef Communities, Glass Mountains, Western Texas

Constructor Guild	Baffler Guild	Binder Guild	Dweller Guild
Brachiopoda: ("Major contributors; coralliform; clusters held by spines" |Grant, 1971, p. 1450|)	Sphinctozoa *Girtyocoelia* *Fissispongia* spp.? *Stylopegma* *Cystothalamia* *Guadalupia* sp.? Inozoa *Catenispongia* *Stratispongia* "*Virgola*" Demospongiae *Coelocladiella philoconcha* *Haplistion megalochetus* Brachiopoda Fragile valves, erect growth form Bryozoa: Fenestellidae; ramose zoaria Crinoidea	Algae Bryozoa Brachiopoda ("held by cementation" |Grant, 1971, p. 1450|) Sphinctozoa *Guadalupia* sp.?	Brachiopoda: "Ubiquitous" |Grant, 1971, p. 1450|) Terebratulacea Demospongiae *Heliospongia vokesi* Hexactinellida *Stereodictyum orthoplectum* Gastropoda Tabulata Rugosa Foraminiferida Fusulinacea Ammonoidea

Source: After Finks (1960, 1970, 1983) and Grant (1971).

Carboniferous to the latest Early Permian (about 30 million years). The peak development in size (5 to about 25 m thick and more than 20 m in diameter), abundance, and biotic diversity (Grant, 1971, Fig. 20) was in the Road Canyon Formation (Leonardian of local usage; ≅ Artinskian).

The building guilds are dominated by erect-growing calcareous sponges (especially sphinctozoans), fenestrate bryozoans, algae, and a very diverse assemblage of aberrant brachiopods (P1. 43*b*; discussed in Chap. 10). The volumetric importance of each of these building taxa varies considerably from reef to reef. Although the species diversity of sponges and algae is low, they usually predominate (locally up to 50% of the rock volume) in densely intergrown, nearly monospecific masses. Elsewhere, the brachiopods were the chief builders, or the sponges and brachiopods formed an intergrown rigid framework (Finks, 1960, P1. 8, Figs. 2–4).

Most of the calcareous sponges are sphinctozoans of erect, cateniform growth form (bafflers); the earliest member of the Family Guadalupiidae

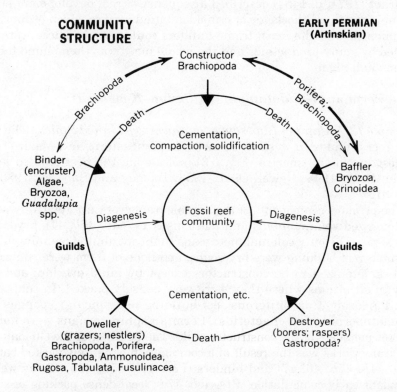

Figure 13.6. Composition and guild structure of Early Permian (Leonardian; ≅ Artinskian) reef communities, Glass Mountains, western Texas. The chief builders were poriferans, brachiopods, and bryozoans. Brachiopods were exceedingly abundant, morphologically diverse, and included members in each of the frame-building guilds as well as the dweller guild. Dwellers also included an incredible diversity of molluscs (cf. Table 13.4). Main guild membership indicated by thick arrows, and guild overlap by thin arrows (around circle).

with sheet-to-cuplike shapes (binders) appear in Leonardian reefs (Fagerstrom, 1984b, p. 376). The Inozoa and the siliceous sponges were also erect, cylindrical-to-vase-shaped bafflers.

Grant (1971, pp. 1450–1453) has summarized the taxonomic and morphologic diversity of brachiopods and their varied roles in the frame-building process. Their diversity appears to exceed the that of any other higher taxon; the most important forms are distributed among the building guilds on the basis of the skeletal features noted in Chapter 10 (Brachiopoda) and Table 13.4. There is strong overlap among constructor, baffler, and binder guilds (Fig. 13.6). The highest species diversity is in the "normal" brachiopods attached to the reef surface by a pedicle; nearly all of these belong to the dweller guild. Other dwellers are listed in Table 13.4 (see also Fagerstrom, 1984b, p. 377). Total diversity of the reef communities exceeds the diversity of the adjacent level-bottom communities by several times (e.g., Grant, 1971, pp. 1474–1475).

Grant (1971, p. 1454) described a sequence of reef development stages beginning with a lithoclastic or crinoidal hardground to which pedunculate brachiopods and the main frame-builders could attach. These were succeeded by spiny productoids and the whole mass was then bound by bryozoans and algae.

Late Permian (Guadalupian; ≅ Ufimian–Kazanian)

Example 13.7: Capitan Limestone, Southwestern United States. The Capitan reef complex in western Texas and southeastern New Mexico is the largest in North America (Fig. 6.3) and among the best studied in the world (King, 1948; Newell et al., 1953; Toomey and Babcock, 1983, pp. 228–316).

The primary components of the organic framework are relatively poorly skeletonized sphinctozoans and inozoans (Pls. 44b, 45b, 47), bryozoans, and algae. The only colonial metazoans that contributed meaningfully to Permian reef-building were bryozoans, and none of them were sufficiently well-skeletonized to be constructors except by guild overlap, and then only in situations where they were very densely packed. In contrast to mid-Paleozoic–Carboniferous reef-building non-spicular sponges (i.e., stromatoporoids and chaetetids), Permian sphinctozoans were not important members of the constructor guild. The building of the Guadalupian reef frameworks was the result of a combination of densely packed bafflers (Pls. 44b, 45b, 46, 47) and binders (Pls. 44b, 45a, 46b, 48) as well as abundant early cementation (Pls. 45b, 47a); local dense packing produced overlap of both bafflers and binders with the constructor guild (Fig. 13.7a). Except for the abundance of sphinctozoans and inozoans and hence the relatively greater importance of the baffler guild, the frameworks of the huge Capitan reefs are remarkably similar to the Late Carboniferous algal-dominated reefs described in Example 13.5 in biotic composition, structure, and early cementation.

The algae and algal-like taxa of the Capitan Limestone, especially the upper part, were studied in detail by Babcock (1977); he identified and characterized 9 genera/forms (Table 13.5) included in the Rhodophyta, Chlorophyta (Pl. 46a), Cyanophyta, 2 questionable algae (*Archaeolith-oporella*, Pls. 44b, 45a, 46a; *Tubiphytes*: see Chap. 7), and 2 other problematic forms ("*Solenopora*" *texana*, *Collenella*, Pl. 46b) that may have closer affinities to animals than to plants.

Finks' (1960) study of Guadalupian and other late Paleozoic sponges emphasized the siliceous non-reef taxa of the Delaware Basin but also included some important observations on the calcareous and siliceous sponges of some seaward slope patch reefs (see Finks, 1960, pp. 22–26, 30). Finks did not study in detail those of the Capitan Limestone, so his listing of about 12 patch reef genera/species (p. 30) may reflect smaller sample sizes than the somewhat higher species diversity of Newell et al. (1953, p. 227, Pls. 22–23) for the Capitan reefs.

The Capitan Limestone marks a major increase in the abundance, diversity, and morphologic complexity of the sphinctozoans, particularly the Family Guadalupiidae, in the reef-building guilds (Fagerstrom, 1984b, p. 376). The level of sphinctozoan and inozoan skeletonization and their effectiveness as bafflers increased dramatically from Early Permian reefs, and the variety of guadalupiid growth forms (sheets, Pls. 34b, 48a; cups and vases, Pl. 45a) made them important members of both binder (Pl. 48) and baffler (Pl. 47) guilds (Table 13.5). The Late Permian also marks an important increase in the abundance and diversity of the relatively well-skeletonized, cateniform Inozoa (bafflers); earlier inozoans were confined to level-bottoms.

The Capitan Limestone reefs are ecologically zoned both laterally and bathymetrically (Newell et al., 1953, pp. 201–203; cf. Yurewicz, 1977, pp. 61–63) and the Capitan Limestone massive is zoned from the bottom to top (Yurewicz, 1977; Babcock, 1977). The latter (stratigraphic/vertical) zonation is most apparent with regard to the algae. Babcock (1977, pp. 22–35) discovered a remarkable increase in their abundance, diversity, and frame-building importance in the upper Capitan reefs; the only algae in the lower and middle Capitan reefs are the problematic *Tubiphytes* and *Archaeolithoporella*. The higher invertebrate taxa are grossly similar in their distributions throughout the Capitan reefs. However, the algal distributions and sedimentological features indicate that the lower–middle Capitan reefs grew in deeper water (below wave base?) than the algal-rich upper Capitan reefs.

Within the upper Capitan, there is an autogenic (?) succession of three algal/sponge/*Collenella*-built frameworks plus the nearly ubiquitous *Archaeolithoporella*/nodular boundstone (Babcock, 1977, pp. 6, 22–35; Pl. 29b, Fig. 13.7b herein) and a very clearly defined lateral algal/invertebrate zonation from the reef crest to the reef flat or shelf (Toomey and Babcock, 1983, pp. 292–316). The erect, fragile dasycladacean *Mizzia* locally dominated the baffler guild in the less turbulent water near the crest–flat

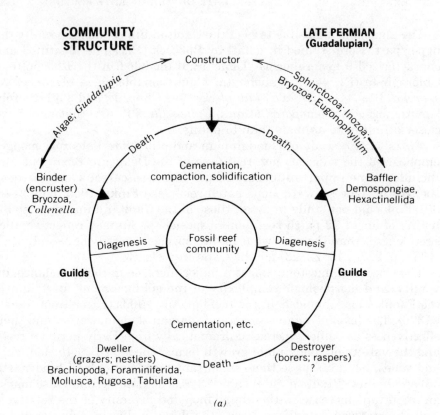

COMMUNITY STRUCTURE

LATE PERMIAN (Guadalupian)

Constructor

Algae: Guadalupia

Sphinctozoa: Inozoa;
Bryozoa: Eugonophyllum

Death

Death

Cementation,
compaction, solidification

Binder
(encruster)
Bryozoa,
Collenella

Baffler
Demospongiae,
Hexactinellida

Diagenesis

Fossil reef
community

Diagenesis

Guilds

Guilds

Cementation, etc.

Dweller
(grazers; nestlers)
Brachiopoda, Foraminiferida,
Mollusca, Rugosa, Tabulata

Destroyer
(borers; raspers)
?

Death

(a)

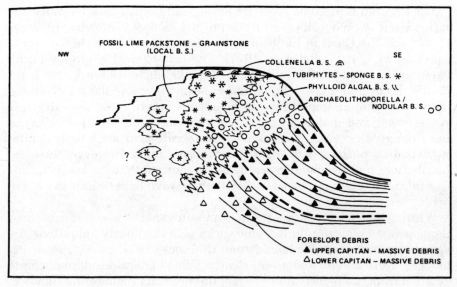

NW

FOSSIL LIME PACKSTONE – GRAINSTONE
(LOCAL B. S.)

SE

COLLENELLA B. S.
TUBIPHYTES – SPONGE B. S.
PHYLLOID ALGAL B. S.
ARCHAEOLITHOPORELLA /
NODULAR B. S.

?

FORESLOPE DEBRIS
▲ UPPER CAPITAN – MASSIVE DEBRIS
△ LOWER CAPITAN – MASSIVE DEBRIS

(b)

TABLE 13.5. Taxonomic Composition and Guild Structure of Late Permian (Guadalupian; ≅ Ufimian–Kazanian) Reef Communities, Capitan Limestone (Massive), Guadalupe Mountains, Western Texas and Southeastern New Mexico[a]

Baffler Guild	Binder Guild	Dweller Guild
Sphinctozoa[b]	Problematic algae[b]	Brachiopoda
Girtyocoelia	*Tubiphytes*	Numerous other
Cysto-	*Archaeolithoporella*	higher taxa
thalmiae	Rhodophyta	(see Newell et
Stylopegma	*Archaeolitho-*	al., 1953, (pp.
Guadalupia	*phyllum*	227–232), e.g.:
Inozoa	*Parachaetetes,* etc.	Foraminiferida
Virgola, etc.	Chlorophyta	Mollusca
Demospongiae:	*Hedstromia*	Ostracoda
5+ spp.	*Pseudovermiporella*	Tabulata
Hexactinellida	Cyanophyta	Rugosa
Stioderma,	*Girvanella*	Tribolita
etc.	Stromatolites, etc.	
Codiacea	Sphinctozoa	
Eugono-	*Guadalupia*[b]	
phyllum?[b]	Bryozoa/Problemati-	
Bryozoa	ca	
Fenestrate[b];	*"Solenopora" tex-*	
ramose	*ana/Acanthocla-*	
growth	*dia guadalupen-*	
habit	*sis* "Consor-	
Crinoidea	tium"; other	
	sheetlike growth	
	forms	
	Collenella	

Source: After Finks (1960, 1983), Newell et al. (1953), Babcock (1977), Yurewicz (1977).
[a]Minimum species diversity: >380.
[b]Most important reef-builders.

◁

Figure 13.7. (*a*) Composition and guild structure of Late Permian (Guadalupian; ≅ Ufimian–Kazanian) reef communities in the Capitan Limestone ("massive"), Guadalupe Mountains, southeastern New Mexico and western Texas. The building guilds of these communities are characterized by the absence of large, well-skeletonized, colonial metazoan members of the constructor guild; framework construction resulted from dense packing of bafflers, binders, and abundant early submarine cement (cf. Table 13.5). Main guild membership indicated by thick arrows, and guild overlap by thin arrows (around circle). (*b*) Stratigraphic distribution of algal and *Collenella*-dominated reef limestones in the upper Capitan Limestone reefs, Guadalupe Mountains. (Petrographic terms packstone, grainstone, boundstone, after Dunham, 1962; B.S. = boundstone). (From Babcock, 1977.)

transition, but current-transported thallus fragments and fusulinids also occur in the bedded shelf deposits. Unlike many large Holocene and ancient reef complexes, the Capitan reef crest–reef flat transition is very abrupt (Toomey and Babcock, 1983, pp. 292–316) and the flat does not contain patch reefs; instead, the shelf area was an intermittently hypersaline lagoon of low biotic diversity. The above discussion of builders and guilds and the data of Table 13.5 indicate that the Capitan reef complex includes 5 of the 7 reef types listed by Flügel and Stanley (1984, pp. 177–179; missing are *Palaeoaplysina* and coral reefs). In addition, many of them are in remarkably close juxtaposition within the "massive" Capitan and reflect the varied, steep, and diverse environmental gradients that existed during the life of the reef complex.

Although not studied in detail, the species diversity of the dweller guild in the Capitan reefs is truly enormous (approx. 350 spp.) compared with those of the level-bottom and pelagic communities of the adjacent reef flat, seaward slope, and basin. The most striking difference between the Capitan reefs and those of the Glass Mountains (Leonardian; Example 13.6) involves the brachiopods. The aberrant, reef-building forms of the Leonardian (reef-dwelling of Grant, 1971, p. 1450, "reef" of Fig. 18, and "bioherms" of Capitan, Fig. 20) are of minor abundance and diversity and played no building role in the Capitan reefs. The dominant dwelling guild brachiopods are the "normal," pedunculate *species* ("neutral" of Grant, 1971, Figs. 18, 22) which are more diverse than in Early Permian reefs. Conversely, the *generic* diversity of Capitan reef brachiopods is lower than in Early Permian reefs and even contemporaneous seaward slope and basin deposits (i.e., Bell Canyon Formation; Grant, 1971, p. 1474).

Other contemporaneous and younger Permian calcispongē, algal- and bryozoan-dominated reef communities in Yugoslavia (Flügel et al., 1984b), Hubei Province, southern China (Fan and Zhang, 1985) and Greece (Flügel and Stanley, 1984) have been described. Such communities persisted locally to the end of the Permian. Paleozoic reef-building in North America ended with the death of the upper Capitan Limestone reefs by encroachment of hypersaline water from the shelf lagoon and Delaware Basin.

CONCLUSIONS

In contrast to the middle Paleozoic (Llanvirnian–Frasnian), which in terms of reef communities was the "age of stromatoporoids and corals," the late Paleozoic (Late Devonian: Famennian–Permian) was the "age of algae, sponges, and bryozoans." During this latter interval of nearly 130 million years, both skeletal and non-skeletal algae of various types were continuously of major importance in the reef-building guilds, followed in order of their overall contribution to the building process by calcareous sponges, bryozoans, and briefly during the Early Permian by aberrant brachiopods. Although late Paleozoic reefs are generally not as abundant, widespread, or as firmly constructed by well-skeletonized organisms as middle Paleozoic reefs, they were built by a greater diversity of higher taxa and locally, as in the Permian of the southwestern United States, were as large or larger.

Trophic Structure

Unlike a large number of mid-Paleozoic reef communities which contain no fossil record of the producer trophic level or in which the producer trophic level is very subordinate to the consumers (especially herbivores), the producers dominate the record of most late Paleozoic communities; in some cases, there is a surprising paucity of consumers (e.g., Toomey, 1979). Toomey (1976, pp. 9–15) has extensively discussed the trophic structure of an Early Permian, and Babcock (1977, pp. 35–36) a Late Permian (Guadalupian) reef community, emphasizing the overwhelming functional roles of benthic skeletal algae.

Guild Structure

Not only did algae control the trophic structure of most late Paleozoic reef communities, but their skeletal forms also dominated the structure of the building guilds. Of the seven examples of reef guild structures described in this chapter, algae were the dominant builders in four of them; the others were specially selected to demonstrate variation in the composition of the building guilds (e.g., Examples 13.2: Rugosa; 13.4: Chaetetida; 13.6: Brachiopoda). The bryozoans were generally less important than the algae; nonetheless, they were prominent members of the baffler (fenestrate and ramose zoaria) and binder/encruster guilds throughout the late Paleozoic and were the only colonial, skeletal metazoan builders of Late Permian reefs.

Porifera had an interesting and varied evolutionary history in late Paleozoic reef communities. After a long and inconsequential pre-Carboniferous history, the very well-skeletonized chaetitids rapidly increased in importance to become major contributors to Late Carboniferous constructor and binder guilds. In fact, these chaetitid-dominated reefs are the only ones to rival those of the mid-Paleozoic in rigidity.

By the Early Permian, the Sphinctozoa, which also had a long early and middle Paleozoic history in level-bottom communities, had suddenly shifted their preferred habitat to reefs and replaced chaetitids as the dominant reef sponges. In Permian reefs, the sphinctozoans expanded rapidly in diversity and morphological complexity and became major components of the baffler and binder guilds, a position they maintained until the end of the Permian (Fan and Zhang, 1985). The sphinctozoans were joined as bafflers in the late Early Permian by erect, cateniform Inozoa, Demospongiae, and Hexactinellida.

During the latest Carboniferous and Early Permian, brachiopod evolution produced a great variety of unusual (aberrant) and highly specialized forms that briefly dominated all building guilds in some reef communities. This evolutionary "experiment" only lasted about 15–20 million years (Fig. 10.1).

Thus, three major characteristics of late Paleozoic reef communities are evident from the guild structure examples described in this chapter:

a.   A much greater diversity of higher taxa was involved in reef-building than in the early (Chap. 11) or middle (Chap. 12) Paleozoic. These taxa included both algae and metazoans.

b.   Relatively rapid rates of rise, short episodes of domination, and rapid decline characterize several of these higher taxa (i.e., accelerated rates of turnover of both taxonomic composition and community structure). These were more true of the metazoans than of the algae.

c.   There was no progressive or predictable increase in biological complexity of reef-building taxa or in guild structure of reef communities, either from the middle to late Paleozoic or during the late Paleozoic. Instead, reef-building resulted from a staggered succession of ecological "opportunists" belonging to several higher taxa.

These characteristics make late Paleozoic reef communities more varied than reefs of any other comparable interval of geological history and strikingly different from Cenozoic reefs described in Part I.

Permian Extinctions

Whether measured by the sharply increased rate of familial extinctions or as the change in family standing diversity (Raup and Sepkoski, 1982), the Late Permian mass extinction "is perhaps the most severe of any in the (geologic) record" (McLaren, 1983, p. 320). Furthermore, in contrast to the middle Paleozoic extinction events (Chap. 12), the Late Permian event was equally catastrophic on reef as well as non-reef communities. There appear to be no Early Triassic reef communities, well-developed *in situ* biostromes, or even mud mounds. The following summary of the effect of this catastrophic extinction event is largely confined to the Late Permian reef-building taxa and their effects on community structure.

Algae. Chuvashov and Riding (1984) recognized a total of 18 Paleozoic algal "groups," 13 of which are present in the Permian. Of the 13, 2 became extinct during the early Late Permian and 4 at the end of the Permian. Seven "groups" of more typical Paleozoic algae continued into the Mesozoic and 5 of these were also present in the Cenozoic. Thus, for the Paleozoic algae as a whole, the end of the Permian was not catastrophic but instead merely a steep decline. Despite the diversity of higher algal taxa in the Triassic, they were all quite rare in the Early Triassic.

However, for the 5 major groups of Permian reef-building algae (Spongiostromata, phylloid Codiacea, Peyssonneliacae, *Archeolithoporella,* and *Tubiphytes;* Fig. 7.1), the end of the Permian was indeed catastrophic.

TABLE 13.6. Stratigraphic Distribution of Bryozoan Generic Diversity During the Late Permian (Kazanian and Tatarian Stages) and Early Triassic (Scythian Stage)

	Total	Cysto-porata	Crypto-stomata	Trepo-stomata	Cteno-stomata
Triassic (Scythian)					
Survivors	5	0	3	2	0
Permian					
Standing					
Diversity	105	25	58	19	3
Tatarian	17–21	4–5	8–9	5–7	0
Kazanian	73–74	14–15	39	19	1

Source: After Ross, 1978.

Archeolithophyllum (the most important late Paleozoic phylloid Peysson-neliacae) and the phylloid Codiaceans became extinct. Early Triassic spongiostromates were confined to level-bottoms, and there is a gap in the stratigraphic record of the problematic *Archaeolithoporella* and *Tub-iphytes* from the end of the Permian until the Middle Triassic (Flügel and Stanley, 1984, p. 180).

Porifera. Four higher poriferan taxa contributed to the building of Late Permian reefs (Sphinctozoa, Inozoa, Demospongiae, and Hexactinellida; Figs. 8.1 and 13.7) and all suffered near-extinction at the end of the Per-mian (Finks, 1960, p. 9–13; Wendt, 1980a, pp. 173–177). Sphinctozoa and Inozoa are almost unknown from the Early Triassic, and although siliceous sponges are more common than calcareous, they are indeed rare and of low diversity.

Others. The end of the Permian brought the extinction of all rugosans and tabulates (Fig. 9.1), all reef-building bryozoans, brachiopods, and cri-noids and the near-extinction of all level-bottom bryozoans and brachio-pods as well (Fig. 10.1). For example, the data on stratigraphic distribution of Permian bryozoans summarized in Table 13.6 clearly demonstrate the enormity of the Late Permian extinction event; these data also show that for all orders, the decline from the Kazanian to Tatarian was numerically greater than that from the Tatarian to Scythian.

In summary, the Late Permian mass extinction event affected all sur-viving late Paleozoic reef-building higher taxa and resulted in the absolute collapse of the structure of all existing reef communities. The collapse was equally catastrophic for level-bottom and pelagic communities, but the rate of mass extinction was by declining diversity (Rhodes, 1967; Schopf, 1974) rather than by instantaneous annihilation of thriving li-neages. The total rebuilding of the structure of Mesozoic reef communities is the subject of Chapter 14.

14

Mesozoic Reef Communities

Following the Late Permian mass extinction event, there was an approximately 8-million year lacuna in the evolution of reef communities. There are no Early Triassic (Scythian) reefs anywhere in the world! In fact, there is almost no Scythian fossil record of any skeletal, colonial/gregarious potential frame-builders of any sort such as algae, poriferans, corals, or bryozoans.

The early Middle Triassic (Anisian) marked the initial stage in the slowly developing evolutionary history of the rebuilding of reef communities; this stage continued through the Middle Jurassic, an interval of about 75 million years. It may be divided into two phases:

a.   Gradual reestablishment of calcareous sponges (Sphinctozoa, Inozoa) and *Tubiphytes* as the dominant reef-builders during the Middle and early Late Triassic (Fig. 8.1).

b.   The appearance of the first scleractinians during the Middle Triassic, their establishment as major reef-builders during the late Late Triassic (Norian), and their domination of the building guilds in shallow-water reef communities during the latest Triassic (Rhaetian)–Early Cretaceous (Fig. 9.1). Stanley has suggested (1980; 1981) that scleractinian–zooxanthellae symbiosis began in the Norian/Rhaetian, based largely on the increased sizes of both colonial coralla and reefs of these ages.

Late Jurassic and early Early Cretaceous (Neocomian) reef-builders were taxonomically heterogeneous; guilds and guild structures included skeletal and non-skeletal algae, a considerable variety of both calcareous and siliceous poriferans, scleractinians, and the rapidly emerging hippuritacean (rudist) bivalves. By the late Early Cretaceous (approx. Albian), the taxonomically diverse and structurally complex older reef communities had been displaced and overwhelmed by rudists, which dominated the constructor guild until the end of the Cretaceous (Fig. 10.1). At this same time, crustose coralline algae appeared for the first time in reef communities and increased in importance as binders (Fig. 7.1) but were volumetrically unimportant compared with rudists. The scleractinians, rudists, and coralline algae were the only higher taxa of Mesozoic reef-builders that were not also late Paleozoic reef-builders. In both composition and structure, Middle Triassic reef communities are remarkably similar to those of the late Paleozoic. Late Triassic–Early Cretaceous shallow-water reefs are dominated by scleractinians and are the earliest to have a "modern" aspect (both composition and structure). In the Middle Jurassic, reefs of somewhat deeper-water origin (= 25–100 m) built by siliceous sponges, or by sponges and algae, first became abundant and continued to the end of the Jurassic. Rudist-dominated (Late Cretaceous) reefs are unique in the evolutionary history of reef communities.

The early Mesozoic reefs were dominated by bafflers and binders like those of the Late Permian, but the increasing importance of first the scleractinians and later the rudists resulted in larger, constructor-dominated Late Triassic, Middle Jurassic, and Cretaceous reefs. The progressive increase in importance of well-skeletonized reefs was also accompanied by widespread increase of the destroyer guild, especially borers, and encrusting epibionts.

TRIASSIC

The most detailed research on Triassic reefs has been done in the Alps, where the largest and most abundant reefs occupied shelf-edge or barrier reef locations marginal to the Tethyan trough; patch reefs were located in seaward slope, reef flat, or lagoon/shelf/platform locations (Flügel, 1982, pp. 307–309). However, reefs are also widely distributed in Asia and western North America and extend in age from Early Anisian continuously through the Triassic (Flügel, 1982, Figs. 1, 2). Early Jurassic reefs are smaller, less common, and not as well-studied, but by the Middle Jurassic, reefs were again well-developed, especially in Europe and Asia.

In terms of reef community composition and structure, the Late Triassic marks an important transition. Anisian through Early Carnian communities were dominated by sphinctozoans, inozoans, and various encrusting algae and are of relatively low species diversity. In Late Carnian and Early Norian reefs, sphinctozoans, inozoans, and scleractinians are about equally important and total community diversity is higher. In latest Triassic (Rhaetian in western Europe) through Middle Jurassic, scleractinians, stromatoporoids, and chaetetids generally predominate (Stanley, 1981; Flügel, 1982; Flügel and Stanley, 1984).

Middle Triassic–Carnian

Organisms

Anisian and some Ladinian reef communities are dominated by "taxonomic holdovers" from the Late Permian. They survived the mass extinction at the end of the Permian, found refuge in Early Triassic level-bottom communities, and then emerged and diversified again during the Middle Triassic. Flügel and Stanley (1984, p. 180) have discussed the algal and problematic "holdovers," the most important of which are crust-forming Spongiostromata and Porostromata and *Tubiphytes*. These forms functioned to stabilize and bind sediments and metazoans into the reef framework.

Finks (1960, pp. 9–10), Ott (1967), and Wendt (1980a, pp. 173–177) have summarized the late Paleozoic–early Mesozoic histories of Sphinctozoa and Inozoa. In the Permian rocks of western Texas, Finks identified 15 genera (in 5 families) of sphinctozoans and 4 genera (1 family) of inozoans, all of which survived the end of the Permian mass extinction and "reemerged" as "holdovers" in the Triassic, mostly in mid–Triassic Alpine reef communities. During the Ladinian and Carnian, both sphinctozoans and inozoans diversified rapidly in both species diversity and in guild membership. Most of the "holdovers" were poorly skeletonized, digitate bafflers, but the newly evolved forms, inozoans in particular, were more massive and better-skeletonized constructors. Sphinctozoans also included forms with thin, encrusting skeletons that functioned as binders (Fagerstrom, 1984b, pp. 377–378).

Anisian scleractinians included a few reef dwellers, but most were members of level-bottom or seaward slope communities (Qi, 1984; Fois and Gaetani, 1984). Although they increased slightly in abundance and diversity during the Ladinnian, the scleractinians were confined to the dweller guild until the Late Carnian, when, for the first time, they were sufficiently abundant and had large enough coralla to be regarded as constructors.

Reef Communities

Example 14.1: Late Anisian; Dont Formation, Dolomite Mountains, Italy. Gaetani et al. (1981, pp. 26–32) and Fois and Gaetani (1984) have described small (up to 10 m thick, 10 m in diameter) mud-rich mounds and patch reefs with diverse frame-building communities dominated by cyanophytes, sphinctozoans, *Tubiphytes*, and bryozoans (Table 14.1). The moderately well-skeletonized, probable sphinctozoans *Olangecoelia otti* and *Celyphia zoldana* dominated the baffler and binder guilds, respectively, during the early stages of reef development. Other major binders included cyanophytes, *Tubiphytes,* and trepostome bryozoans. Specimens of all the above taxa are mostly in growth position and may locally form

**TABLE 14.1. Taxonomic Composition and Guild Structure of Middle
Triassic (Anisian) Mud-rich Mounds and Patch Reefs, Dont Formation,
Eastern Dolomite Mountains, Northern Italy**

Baffler Guild	Binder Guild	Dweller Guild
Sphinctozoa?	Cyanophyta	Porostomata
Olangocoelia otti	Spongiostromata	*"Garwoodia*-like"
	Porostromata	Rhodophyta
Other Sphincto-	Sphinctozoa?	*Solenopora:* 2 spp.
zoa: 5 genera	*Celyphia zoldana*	Scleractinia:
Inozoa: 2 genera	Problematica	10? spp.
Crinoidea	*Tubiphytes*	Foraminiferida
	Ladinella	Annelida
	Bryozoa	Bivalvia
	Trepostomata	

Source: After Fois and Gaetani, 1984.

small, sheltered cavities containing simple cryptic subcommunities. In
addition, they are of sufficient abundance to overlap the constructor guild
(Fig. 14.1). Although scleractinians are remarkably diverse, well-skeletonized and predominantly colonial, they are not abundant enough to be
considered constructors.

One of the compelling arguments for regarding these mound structures
as reefs is the fact that, despite their small size, there is a vertical succession of dominant taxa regarded by Fois and Gaetani (1984, pp. 197–198)
as a three-stage "growth sequence." Cyanophytes and *Tubiphytes* were
the initial mud substrate stabilizers and continued to play a major role
in binding throughout the sequence. As noted above, the sphinctozoans
(?) *O. otti* and *C. zoldana* were also "pioneers." Species diversity, skeletonization, and framework rigidity increase upward with the successive
addition of bryozoans, inozoans, other sphinctozoans, and scleractinians;
concurrently, the mud content decreases upward.

Example 14.2: Ladinian–Middle Carnian; Northern Yugoslavia. Ladinian
and Carnian patch reefs, up to 100 m thick, are abundant and widely
distributed in Slovenia (Turnšek et al., 1984). They are of two types: (1)
smaller, mud-rich reefs that grew on uplifted fault blocks in the deeper
water of the Slovenian Trough; and (2) larger, spar-rich reefs of the adjacent shallower-water shelf-platform north of the trough. Despite differences in age and geologic setting, the communities of these reefs are
quite similar and so are discussed together.

The Yugoslavian communities rather clearly demonstrate the increasing importance of scleractinians and of the constructor guild in comparison
to the Anisian reefs discussed in Example 14.1. In the Ladinian–Carnian
reefs, scleractinians comprise 40% of the fauna; about 30% of the fauna

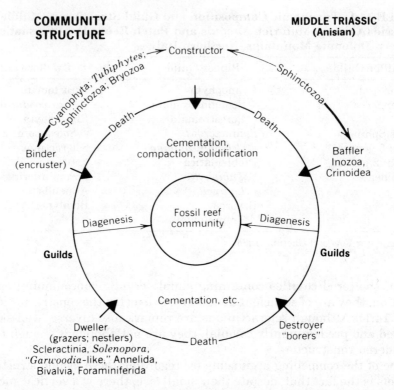

Figure 14.1. Composition and guild structure of Middle Triassic (Anisian) reef communities, Dont Formation, eastern Dolomite Mountains, northern Italy. Building guilds were dominated by densely packed cyanophytes, *Tubiphytes*, sphinctozoans, and bryozoans (cf. Table 14.1). Main guild membership indicated by thick arrow, and guild overlap by thin arrows (around circle).

is sponges (mostly Sphinctozoa). Various microproblematic forms total 12%, foraminifera 12%, and algae, stromatoporoids (?) and mollusc fragments about 6%; all these taxa are dwellers because of their low abundance (Fig. 14.2). The reduction in importance of algae, especially binding cyanophytes, from Example 14.1 to 14.2 is as notable as the rise of corals. Locally, the sponges may exceed corals in volume, but this is uncommon because of the generally larger size of coral coralla. Corals comprise 30–60% of the organic framework of the reefs and about 15–30% of the total reef volume.

The Ladinian–Carnian coral fauna consists of 27 species: 14 solitary, 10 dendroid or phaceloid, 2 cerioid, and 1 meandroid. Because of their apparent abundance in at least one locality (Turnšek et al., 1984, Text-Fig. 5) and well-skeletonized coralla, 18 species were probably constructors and 9 were dwellers (Fig. 14.2); Turnšek et al. (1984) gave no indication of corallum sizes for any of these species, but many of them are described

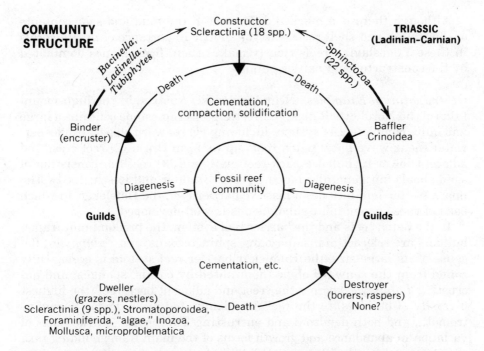

Figure 14.2. Composition and guild structure of late Middle (Ladinian)–early Late (Carnian) Triassic reefs, Slovenia, northern Yugoslavia. Building guilds are dominated by diverse, abundant scleractinians and erect, cateniform sphinctozoans. Main guild membership indicated by thick arrows, and guild overlap by thin arrows (around circle). (After Turnšek et al., 1984; Senowbari-Daryan, 1981; Turnšek et al., 1982; Ramovš and Turnšek, 1984.)

in Turnšek et al. (1982) and are quite small. Therefore, the guild assignment given above is based on their overall volume and apparent packing density in the organic framework rather than on the volume of individual coralla.

Unfortunately, Turnšek et al. (1984) provided no comparable taxonomic or morphological data for calcareous sponges. However, all 5 of the sponges noted in their Text-Fig. 3 are sphinctozoans and belong to the baffler guild; at least 1 species *(Cryptocoelia zitteli)* overlaps with the constructor guild. From a single, rather small mud-rich reef, at least 22 species of sphinctozoans and 2 inozoans have been identified (Senowbari-Daryan, 1981; Turnšek et al., 1982); some of the larger, massive sphinctozoans (up to 10 cm dia.) were as important volumetric contributors to the constructor guild as the corals.

In the larger, spar-rich shelf reefs, Ramovš and Turnšek (1984) reported members of the binder/encruster guild that included spongiostromate crusts and the encrusting microproblematic forms called *Bacinella, Ladinella,* and *Tubiphytes.*

Although there is a marked difference in the mud and spar contents of the trough and shelf reefs, the volumetric importance of *in situ* corals in these Yugoslavian reefs clearly makes them framestones dominated by the constructor and baffler guilds.

Other Ladinian Examples. Near Innsbruck, Austria, in the high mountains of the Nordkette Range, the Wetterstein Limestone contains a large and quite complete reef system, including (1) seaward slope with deeper-water (near wave base) patch reefs up to 40 m thick, (2) reef crest and adjacent lower turbulence back-reef area, and (3) reef flat consisting of sand shoals but generally lacking reefs (Bradner and Resch, 1981). The upper Wetterstein includes a massive barrier reef, the Hafelekar, in which each of these geomorphic subdivisions is well-developed.

In the patch reefs and the barrier reef system, the predominant frame-builders are scleractinians, inozoans, sphinctozoans, and *Tubiphytes*. Because of its large size, the Hafelekar barrier reef system is ecologically zoned from the seaward slope (dominated by corals, sponges, and encrusting *Tubiphytes*) across the crest and adjacent back-reef (the highest diversity of builders) to the reef flat (dominated by inozoans, Spongiostromata, and both dendroid and encrusting *Tubiphytes*) on the basis of variation in abundance and growth forms of the main frame-building taxa (Bradner and Resch, 1981, pp. 212–222). In terms of community composition and structure, the chief importance of the Wetterstein reefs lies in their intermediate nature between the cyanophyte/*Tubiphytes*/sphincto-zoan boundstones of the Anisian (Example 14.1) and the scleractinian/sphinctozoan framestones of the Ladinian–Carnian (Example 14.2) and younger Triassic reef communities (Ott, 1967). In the Wetterstein reefs, the roles of algae and sphinctozoans are less important than in the Anisian (Example 14.1) and the role of scleractinians is less than in the Ladinian–Carnian (Example 14.2).

Neither Fois and Gaetani (1984; Example 14.1), Ramovš and Turnšek (1984; Example 14.2), nor Bradner and Resch (1981; Wetterstein) mentioned the presence of serpulid annelids in Anisian–Carnian reefs. To exemplify the fact that essentially contemporaneous ancient reef communities may have strikingly different compositions and structures, the Ladinian reefs in southern Spain were dominated by gregarious serpulids (*Sarcinella* spp.) of the constructor guild (Flügel et al., 1984a). Neither corals nor sponges contributed significantly to the framework. Binders included *Archaeolithoporella* and *Tubiphytes*.

Example 14.3: Cassian Formation (Carnian); Eastern Dolomite Mountains, Italy. At Alpe di Specie (Seelandalpe) and near Carbonin in northern Italy, there are numerous, small (1–20-m thick; 10–100-m dia.) patch reefs, most of which occur as displaced blocks in bedded, deep-water, seaward slope, and basin shales and volcanic rocks (Fürsich and Wendt, 1977;

Wendt, 1980b, 1982). These reefs are among the youngest that were built primarily by calcareous sponges (about 70% of the organic framework and 15–30% of the total reef volume).

The diverse calcareous sponges include (in order of volumetric importance) at least 6 species of stromatoporoids, 19 species of inozoans, 13 sphinctozoans, and 32 sclerosponges (Fürsich and Wendt, 1977, Table 1). These reefs represent the reemergence of stromatoporoids after an absence of 140 million years from reef communities (Fig. 8.1); as a group, they are so large and densely packed that they were the chief constructors of the Cassian reefs. Other members of the constructor guild were Scleractinia (*Thecosmilia* and *Thamnasteria* "types" plus numerous other species), inozoans (at least 3 species) and sclerosponges (Table 14.2; Fig. 14.3). The most abundant sphinctozoans *(Cryptocoelia; Euophocoelia)* were bafflers, but other species were binders. Several other higher taxa also contain species belonging to more than one guild; so, for the community as a whole, there is considerable guild overlap (Fig. 14.3).

Fürsich and Wendt (1977) and Wendt (1980b) have described a temporal (autogenic?) succession in the building of the organic framework that began with the establishment of the main calcisponge–coral constructor guild. Then, cavities within the constructor-built framework were occupied

TABLE 14.2. Taxonomic Composition and Guild Structure of Late Triassic (Carnian) Patch Reefs, Cassian Formation, Eastern Dolomite Mountains, North Italy[a]

Constructor Guild	Baffler Guild	Binder Guild	Dweller Guild
Stromatoporo-idea	Inozoa	Sclerospongiae:	Brachiopoda:
Cassi-anostroma kupperi	*Sestrostomella robusta*	Numerous spp.	19 spp.
	Peronidella loretzi	"Stromatolites"	Gastropoda: 400 spp.
Other spp.	*Precorynella capitata*	Foraminiferida	Bivalvia:
Scleractinia: 30 +? spp.	Other spp.	Sphinctozoa	29 spp.
Inozoa	Sphinctozoa	Serpulidae	Echinodermata: 17 spp.
Sestros-tomella robusta	*Cryptocoelia zitteli*	Bryozoa	Scaphopoda
	Enoplocoelia armata	Solenoporacea	Foraminiferida
Stellispongia manon	Other spp.	*Solenopora*	Serpulidae
Peronidella	Bryozoa	*Para-chaetetes*	Scleractinia?
Sclerospongiae		Scleractinia?	Hexactinellida

Source: After Fürsich and Wendt (1977) and Wendt (1980b, 1982).

[a]Species diversity; >1000; taxa in each guild listed in approximate order of volumetric importance.

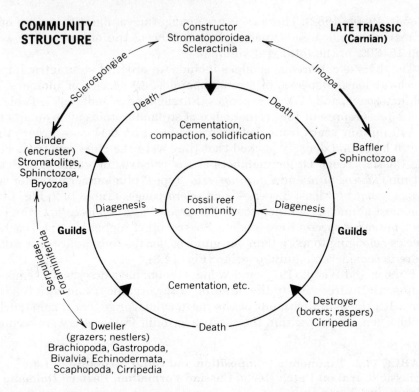

Figure 14.3.   Composition and guild structure of Late Triassic (Carnian) patch reefs, Cassian Formation, eastern Dolomite Mountains, northern Italy. Building guilds are dominated by a great varity of calcareous sponges and corals. Guild overlap is remarkably high and especially important in the Inozoa, Sphinctozoa, and Sclerospongiae (cf. Table 14.2). Main guild membership indicated by thick arrows, and guild overlap by thin arrows. (After Fürsich and Wendt, 1977; Wendt, 1980b, 1982.)

by (in order of abundance) various (semicryptic?) inozoans, sclerosponges, sphinctozoans, corals, and bryozoans. Finally, the reef surface was encrusted by stromatolites, sphinctozoans, sclerosponges, bryozoans, foraminifera, serpulids, and solenopores. Thus, there seems to be a succession of guilds from constructor to baffler to binder that may have been influenced by temporal changes in turbulence (low to high) during reef growth.

Despite the small sizes of these reefs, species diversity of all guilds is much higher than for other Mesozoic reefs; Wendt (1980b) estimated total community diversity at over 1000 species! As is typical of most reef communities, the highest diversity is in the dweller guild (Table 14.2). Despite the overwhelming diversity of gastropods, brachiopods were of greater volumetric/numerical importance.

Norian–Rhaetian

Reef Communities

Numerous Late Triassic reefs in the Northern Calcareous Alps, Austria, and in Bavaria are among the most carefully documented reefs in the world, due in large part to the detailed work of the "Erlangen Reef Research Group" directed by Erik Flügel (Flügel, 1981). These reefs vary considerably in size, proportions of mud and framework, and paleoecology. The latter depends on their location (seaward slope, shelf margin, and reef flat), water depth, temperature, and degree of exposure to high turbulence. Both the large, shelf margin barrier reefs with original topographic relief from crest to base of the seaward slope of 160 m and slope dips of 30° (Piller, 1981; Wurm, 1982; Stanley, 1980) of the Dachstein (Zankl, 1969; Wurm, 1982) and Steinplatte–Hochkonig (Piller, 1981) systems and the smaller, shelf patch reefs (Senowbari-Daryan, 1980a; Schäfer and Senowbari-Daryan, 1981) are ecologically zoned in relation to variation in depth and turbulence and as ecological successions.

Organisms. In most Late Carnian–Middle Jurassic reefs, scleractinians with erect, dendroid–phaceloid coralla were the predominant framebuilders. Calcareous sponges, particularly inozoans during the Norian and sphinctozoans during the Rhaetian, were typically second in volumetric importance in the organic framework; various algae and problematical forms were third. In many reefs, inorganic cement is a significant aspect of the initial framework and provided rigidity in much the same manner as in many late Paleozoic reefs (Chap. 13).

Regardless of size, there is remarkable similarity, even at the genus/species level, in composition (Flügel, 1981, Tables 2, 3, 7, 9, 11, Fig. 22) and guild structure of the various Norian and Rhaetian communities. Thus, the following discussion is based primarily on the excellent summary by Flügel (1981) with references to particular patch reefs from Senowbari-Daryan (1980a), Schäfer and Senowbari-Daryan (1981), and Schäfer (1984) and to the larger Steinplatte–Hochkonig complex from Piller (1981).

Example 14.4: Northern Calcareous Alps; Guild Structure. Dendroid–placeloid coralla of the morphologically diverse genus *"Thecosmilia"*(Pl. 49a) dominate the constructor guild (Table 14.3); Stanley (1980, p. 892) noted that in large Rhaetian reefs, individual coralla of *Thecosmilia* attained heights of up to 10 m! Other coralla were lenticular or sheetlike members of the binder guild. Flügel (1981, Tables 3, 5) listed 32 other species from 9 carefully studied Norian–Rhaetian Alpine reefs, described 6 "growth form groups" of constructor guild corals, and assigned 14 species to these "groups." (Unfortunately, Flügel provided no data on corallum

TABLE 14.3. Taxonomic Composition and Guild Structure of Late Triassic (Norian–Rhaetian) Reef Communities in the Northern Calcareous Alps, Austria, and Bavaria[a]

Constructor Guild	Baffler Guild	Binder Guild	Dweller Guild
Scleractinia	Sphinctozoa	Sphinctozoa	Brachiopoda
"*Thecosmilia*" spp.	*Paradenigeria*	*Colospongia* sp.	Rhyn-
Numerous other	*alpina*	*Salzburgia* sp.	chonellida
spp.	Numerous	*Follicatena ir-*	Terebra-
Sphinctozoa	other spp.	*regularis*	tulida
Annaecoelia spp.	Inozoa	Cyanophyta	Bivalvia
Cryptocoelia sp.?	*Peronidella*	Spongiostromate	Gastropoda
	fischeri	"crusts"	Ammonoidea
	Other spp.?	Porostromata	Ophiuroidea
	Spongiomor-	*Garwoodia*	Holothuroidea
	phida	*Girvanella*	Echinoidea
	Spongio-	*Cayeuxia*	"fish"
	morpha	*Ortonella*	Reptilia
	ramosa	*Zonotrichites*	Dasycladacea
	Crinoidea	*Apophoretella*	*Heteroporella*
		Solenoporacea	*Diplopora*
		Solenopora	*Gripho-*
		Parachaetetes	*porella*
		Bryozoa	Crustacea
		Foraminiferida	Foraminiferida
		miliolids	Fusulinina
		Problematica	Textularina
		"Tabulozoans"	Rotaliina
		"Disjecto-	Sclerospongiae
		porids"	
		Microprob-	
		lematica	
		Microtubus	
		communis	
		Radiomura	
		cautica	
		Bacinella irre-	
		gularis	
		Lamellata	
		wahneri	
		Lithocodium	
		aggregatum	
		Serpulida	

Source: After Flügel (1981), Senowbari-Daryan (1980a, 1980b), Schäfer and Senowbari-Daryan (1981), Schäfer (1984), Piller (1981), Würm (1982).
[a]Species diversity; ≅ 225.

sizes or packing densities, so guild membership for some coral species is uncertain.) Coral diversity appears to be higher in the Rhaetian patch reefs than in the larger Norian reefs; 24 coral species are present in 1 reef (Rötelwand) less than 1000 m long.

Domal, cushion-shaped, and dendroidal sphinctozoans are also important constructors, especially in the central reef areas protected from high turbulence by the more massive scleractinians. For example, Senowbari-Daryan (1980a, pp. 124–130) found that in the central, sponge-rich areas of some patch reefs, the volumetric importance of calcareous sponges (Pl. 49b) was much greater than that of corals and approximately equal to the volume of all other contributors to the organic framework combined. Locally, bulbous solenopores and gymnocodiaceans may contribute to the constructor guild, but various combinations of corals, inozoans, and sphinctozoans are the main volumetric constituents of most reefs (Flügel, 1981, p. 322).

Erect, cylindrical sphinctozoans and inozoans were the dominant bafflers living on muddy substrates, suggestive of lower turbulence; dendroidal spongiomorphids and crinoids were in higher turbulence locations (Pl. 50a). The binder guild was taxonomically diverse and volumetrically important. A variety of sphinctozoans, including *Colospongia, Follicatena irregularis,*and *Salzburgia,* were important binders of both internal sediment and the skeletons of various frame-builders. Other important members of the binder guild were spongiostromate and porostromate cyanophytes, solenoporaceans, questionable codiaceans, bryozoans, and problemetical forms such as "Tabulozoans" (Sclerospongiae?), *Lamellata wahneri* (Pl. 50b), "microproblematica," and miliolid foraminifera (Flügel, 1981, pp. 307–317). Encrusters were generally more abundant and diverse on inozoans and sphinctozoans than on corals, but there were numerous exceptions. Sponges with two or more generations of encrusters (Zankl, 1969; Flügel, 1981, pp. 328–330, Fig. 16) strongly suggest that the encrustations formed after death of the sponge.

In Rhaetian shallow-water shelf patch reefs of similar sizes, Schäfer and Senowbari-Daryan (1981, pp. 243–245) recognized two types of organic frameworks: (1) those dominated by colonial corals, lightly encrusted "by epizoans and epiphytes," and containing considerable internal sediment, much of it mud; and (2) those with a more densely packed organic framework dominated by calcareous sponges, solitary corals, and heavily encrusted by microorganisms. They also summarized other stratigraphic and sedimentologic variations among different patch reefs (their Table 2) and lateral variation in faunal content in individual reefs (their Figs. 6–9) and attributed most variation to local differences in water turbulence. Thus, well-skeletonized corals were dominant in areas of high turbulence such as the reef margins, and the more fragile sponges and spongiomorphids in areas of lower turbulence such as reef centers (lagoons?).

Other framework variations were due to:

a.   Bathymetric occurrence. Piller (1981, pp. 267–268) recognized four seaward slope subcommunities in the Steinplatte barrier reef system. Each was characterized by differences in abundance and diversity of sphinctozoans, massive to dendroidal corals, and encrusting "hydrozoans." In contrast, the reef crest was less diverse and dominated by very large (up to 2 m tall), thick-branched phaceloid corals, especially *"Thecosmilia" clathrata,* and contained relatively fewer frame-building sponges and binders/encrusters. Conversely, in the Gosaukamm shelf margin (barrier?) reef of the Dachstein Limestone, Wurm (1982) found that low-growing calcareous sponges and heavy algal crusts predominated. Even among small patch reefs, the relative importance of different coral growth forms (e.g., "tall vs. short") may vary (Senowbari-Daryan, 1980a, p. 28). In both the Steinplatte and Gosaukamm reefs, radial fibrous calcite (probable early submarine cement) is abundant near the crest and mud-rich internal sediment increases in importance downslope.

b.   Ecological succession. Senowbari-Daryan (1980a, pp. 5, 147–153), Flügel (1981, pp. 344–347), and Shäfer (1984) have described vertical sequences of fossil assemblages from Rhaetian patch reefs. The sequences are different and, because the reefs are so small, it is difficult to judge whether or not the sequences are truly autogenic ecological successions and why they should be different in reefs that otherwise appear to be quite similar.

c.   Cryptic subcommunities appearing to be rather important in at least some reefs. They include the small, cateniform sphinctozoan *Cheilosporites tirolensis* (Senowbari-Daryan, 1980b), encrusting microproblematical forms (e.g., *Muranella sphaerica, Baccanella floriformis),* bryozoans, miliolid foraminifera *(Ophthalmidium, Galeanella, Sigmiolina),* "tabulozoans and hydrozoans" (Flügel, 1981, pp. 307, 317, 320, 327).

Among the sphinctozoans, there is considerable guild overlap (Fig. 14.4) but morphological plasticity at the genus/species level appears to be minimal (Table 14.3). The degree of guild overlap among scleractinians in uncertain due to the lack of published data on corallum sizes and packing densities for the less common species. Despite the diversity of higher taxa in the binder guild, they are not as volumetrically important as either the constructors or bafflers.

The highest diversity at all taxonomic levels is in the dweller guild (Table 14.3). Many taxa are known primarily from fragments in the internal reef sediment, and numerous identifications (e.g., algae and foraminifera) are based on thin sections (Senowbari-Daryan, 1980a, pp. 30–31). In the 4 small patch reefs described by Schäfer and Senowbari-Daryan (1981), the total species diversity of these communities was about 225, over 100 species of which were dwellers. By comparison, Flügel's (1981) less complete tabulations of species diversities from 4 Dachstein and 5

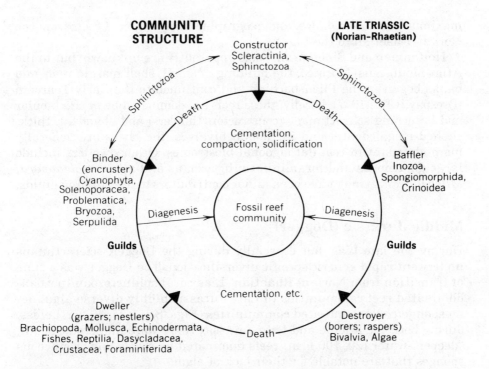

COMMUNITY STRUCTURE

LATE TRIASSIC (Norian-Rhaetian)

Constructor Scleractinia, Sphinctozoa

Sphinctozoa

Sphinctozoa

Death

Death

Cementation, compaction, solidification

Binder (encruster) Cyanophyta, Solenoporacea, Problematica, Bryozoa, Serpulida

Baffler Inozoa, Spongiomorphida, Crinoidea

Diagenesis

Fossil reef community

Diagenesis

Guilds

Guilds

Cementation, etc.

Dweller (grazers; nestlers) Brachiopoda, Mollusca, Echinodermata, Fishes, Reptilia, Dasycladacea, Crustacea, Foraminiferida

Death

Destroyer (borers; raspers) Bivalvia, Algae

Figure 14.4. Composition and guild structure of Late Triassic (Norian–Rhaetian) reef communities, Northern Calcareous Alps, Austria, and Bavaria. Building guilds are dominated by dendroid–phaceloid scleractinians, sphinctozoans, and inozoans; various algae and problematical forms are also important as binders (cf. Table 14.3).

Rhaetian reefs emphasize members of the building guilds; he found inozoans (4 spp.), sphinctozoans (35 spp.), corals (37 spp.), dasycladaceans (11 spp.), and solenoporaceans (6 spp.). Senowbari-Daryan (1980a, pp. 31–33) listed over 130 species from 2 patch reefs. The destroyer guild is represented by large (up to 1-cm dia.) and microscopic borings; Flügel (1981, p. 318) attributed the former to lithophagous bivalves having a preference for massive corals and the latter to endolithic algae and fungi.

JURASSIC

The Early Jurassic (Lias) was a time of sharply reduced abundance and diversity of most of the skeletonized metazoans that were frame-builders of Late Triassic reefs (i.e., sphinctozoans, inozoans, stromatoporoids; Wendt, 1980a, p. 174; Fig. 8.1; scleractinians; Beauvais, 1984, pp. 222–223; Stanley, 1981; Fig. 9.1). Most Lias corals are relatively small and solitary. Consequently, there was an accompanying sharp reduction in maximum size, abundance, and geographic distribution of reefs from the Norian–Rhaetian to the Lias.

Hettangian and Sinemurian reefs apparently are unknown, but in the Atlas Mountains, Morocco, the building of small, shelf margin reefs and banks began in the Pliensbachian and continued to the Early Toarcian (Dresnay, 1971, 1977). Locally, these reefs are dominated by *in situ* tabular and branching scleractinians (constructors; binders) and abundant, thick-shelled megalodontid and isognomid bivalves; the latter are generally more abundant in reef flat/lagoonal biostromes. Other dwellers include large gastropods and foraminifera; bryozoans and algae *(Solenopora; Mitchelldeania)* may have been minor contributors to the building guilds.

Middle Jurassic (Dogger)

During the late Lias, but especially during the Dogger, scleractinians underwent rapid generic/specific diversification. The Dogger was a time of transition from Norian–Rhaetian–Lias coral/sphinctozoan/inozoan-dominated reef communities to Late Jurassic highly diverse algal/de-mosponge/coral-dominated communities (Figs. 8.1, 9.1). Nevertheless, during both the Middle and Late Jurassic, there were numerous, small, "deeper"-water (20–100+ m) reefs dominated by corals and/or siliceous sponges that are notable for their lack of algae.

Reef Communities

Example 14.5: Middle Jurassic (Early Bajocian) Patch Reefs; Northeastern France. Near the village of Malancourt (12 km northwest of Metz) in Lorraine, there are several small (8–16-m thick; 11–33-m dia.), coral-dominated patch reefs in what is locally called the "Lower Coral Limestone" (Hallam, 1975; Geister, 1984c); similar reefs occur in Luxembourg and southwestern France (Lathuliere, 1982).

The species diversity of the constructor and binder guilds is remarkably low, consisting of densely packed, flat, lenticular, and bulbous coralla of *Isastrea* and *Thamnasteria* (Table 14.4). The flat coralla are up to 1 m in diameter and several centimeters thick. The bulbous forms are smaller and less abundant. Most of the non-scleractinian binders encrust the corals and include abundant serpulids, bivalves (*Lopha* spp.), and bryozoans; bafflers and algae are notably absent (Fig. 14.5).

These reefs appear to be too small to have been ecologically zoned and had a maximum original topographic relief of only 2 m. Geister (1984c) attributed the preponderance of flat–lenticular coralla to low light intensity, either from water depths exceeding 20 m or high turbidity. The small size, low diversity, and lack of algae support Geister's deeper-water interpretation.

TABLE 14.4. Taxonomic Composition and Guild Structure of Middle Jurassic (Early Bajocian) Patch Reef Communities, Malancourt, Northeastern France (Lorraine) and Luxembourg[a]

Constructor Guild	Binder Guild	Dweller Guild	Destroyer Guild
Scleractinia	Scleractinia	Scleractinia	Bivalvia
Isastrea: 3–4 spp.	*Isastrea*	*Clado-*	*Lithophaga*
Thamnasteria	*Thamnasteria*	*phyllia*	Porifera
	Serpulida	*Montlivaltia*	*Cliona?*
	Bivalvia	Bivalvia	Echinoidea:
	Lopha spp.	*Chlamys*	2–3 spp.
	Bryozoa: 3–5	Other spp.	
	spp.	Brachiopoda	

Source: After Hallam (1975) and Geister (1984c).
[a]Maximum species diversity: ≅ 30.

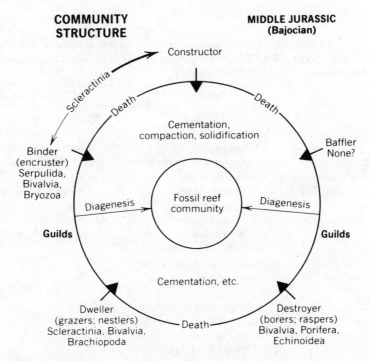

Figure 14.5. Composition and guild structure of Middle Jurassic (Early Bajocian) patch reef communities, Malancourt, northeastern France (Lorraine). The constructor and binder guilds are dominated by large, densely packed, flat–lenticular coralla of *Isastrea* spp. and *Thamnasteria*. The baffler guild aparently was not represented in the community and there were no algae (cf. Table 14.4). Main guild membership indicated by thick arrow, and guild overlap by thin arrow (around circle).

Example 14.6: Middle Jurassic (Late Bathonian) Patch Reefs; North-western France. At Saint Aubin-sur-Mer near Caen in Normandy, there are several small (up to 2.5 m thick and 2–4-m dia.) patch reefs built largely by the lithistid demosponge *Platychonia magna* (Palmer and Für-sich, 1981). The reefs are particularly interesting because the organic framework was built in two steps by two vastly different building guilds and taxa:

   a.   The original framework was constructed exclusively by *P. magna.* The lithistid framework consists of densely packed, cup/bowl/saucer-shaped skeletons up to 35 cm in diameter (mean ≅ 10–20 cm) that were firmly cemented together for enhanced rigidity (Table 14.5). Palmer and Fürsich (1981, p. 10) discovered a single, poorly preserved scleractinian corallum and suggested that the lack of scleractinians in the community resulted from a selective loss of aragonitic forms (e.g., scleractinians and bivalves) during diagenesis rather than their small numbers in the original community.

TABLE 14.5. Taxonomic Composition and Guild Structure of Middle Jurassic (Late Bathonian) Patch Reef Communities, Saint Aubin-sur-Mer, Northwestern France (Normandy)[a]

Baffler Guild	Binder Guild	Dweller Guild
Inozoa	Bivalvia	Brachiopoda
Peronidella pistillifor-mis	*Atreta retifera*	*Crania ponsorti*
Eudea cribraria	*Lopha costata*	*Rioultina triangularis*
Limnorea mammillosa	*Spondylus consobrinus*	3–4 other spp.
Trachyphlyetia helvel-loides	*Plicatula* sp.	Bivalvia
Elasmostoma palma-tum	*Nanogyra* sp.	*Chamys viminea*
Corynella tuberosa	Inozoa: 10–20 spp.	*Plagiostoma* sp.
Sclerospongiae	Sclerospongiae	Decapoda
Neuropora sp.	*Neuropora spinosa*	Annelida: 3 spp.
	Bryozoa: Cyclostomata	
	Hyperosopora typica	
	Mesenteripora undula-ta	
	Approx. 9 other spp.	
	Annelida	
	Spirorbula sp.	
	Serpula: 2 spp.	

Source: After Palmer and Fürsich, 1981.

[a]Species diversity: ≅ 55; The only member of the constructor guild (not listed) is the lithistid demosponge *Platychonia magna;* all members of the binder guild were hard-surface encrusters and all except *Atreta retifera* were members of the cryptic subcommunity inhabiting the undersurfaces of dead *Platychonia magna* skeletons. Taxa are listed in approximate order of relative abundance in each guild.

b. Following the death of the individual sponges, their surfaces, especially the lower surface, were heavily encrusted by a variety of metazoans in layers of successive "generations" up to 10 mm thick. The sponges could not have grown so large unless encrustation had followed the death of the sponge. Furthermore, Palmer and Fürsich (1981, p. 13) noted that overturned bowl/saucer-shaped (convex upward) sponge skeletons were much more heavily encrusted on the underside in the same manner as the *in situ* skeletons. In Table 14.5, the binder guild consists only of encrusters of the original sponge-constructed framework; apparently there were no sediment binders.

In the following discussion of the guild structure of the reefs, emphasis is on the exceedingly important and taxonomically diverse cryptic subcommunity composed almost entirely of encrusters. The only important encruster of the upper, better-illuminated surface, was the plicatulid bivalve *Atreta retifera* (Table 14.5). As noted by Palmer and Fürsich (1981, p. 13), there is a remarkably "modern" aspect to the composition and structure of the cryptic subcommunity; most higher taxa, and even 2–3 genera, in the Saint Aubin reefs are also characteristic of Holocene cryptic subcommunities (see Chap. 5). In both the Bathonian and Holocene, the subcommunities are dominated by successively layered encrusters, strongly suggestive of comparable degrees of competition for substrate space. Because most of the cryptic taxa are absent–rare in the adjacent level-bottom fauna at Saint Aubin and because of the distinct difference between the cryptic and non-cryptic encrusters, Palmer and Fürsich (1981, pp. 1, 13, 20) reasoned that these reefs grew in "shallow" water "in the lower photic zone, below normal wave-base" and that the cryptic taxa at such depths were confined to poorly lighted cavities. The complete absence of algae from both the reef and level-bottom communities also supports the "lower photic zone" interpretation. There is no obvious explanation for very low diversity of the upper-surface encrusting forms unless the one species involved *(Atreta retifera)* simply out-competed all other potential non-cryptic encrusters for substrate space.

Due to the apparent monotypic nature of the constructor guild and the sequential domination of the building guilds (first constructor, then binder), there is little guild overlap by the building taxa (Fig. 14.6). The functional role of the six erect inozoans listed as bafflers in Table 14.5 is quite uncertain because all were cryptic; in such communities, the baffling process is much less important than at the upper surface of the reef.

Finally, it is important to note the overall "modern" aspect of the destroyer guild. Endolithic algae and sponges plus "fish" are the only important groups of destroyers in Holocene reef communities that were not reported by Palmer and Fürsich at Saint Aubin. Fish are exceedingly rare in all fossil reef communities, even Cenozoic, due to the general fragility of their skeletons, and microborings in highly altered siliceous sponge

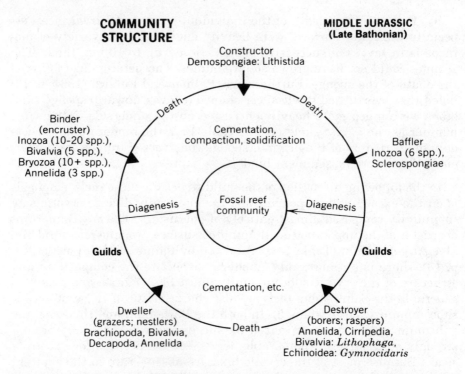

COMMUNITY STRUCTURE

MIDDLE JURASSIC (Late Bathonian)

Constructor
Demospongiae: Lithistida

Death   Death

Binder
(encruster)
Inozoa (10-20 spp.),
Bivalvia (5 spp.),
Bryozoa (10+ spp.),
Annelida (3 spp.)

Cementation,
compaction, solidification

Baffler
Inozoa (6 spp.),
Sclerospongiae

Diagenesis   Fossil reef
community   Diagenesis

Guilds   **Guilds**

Cementation, etc.

Dweller
(grazers; nestlers)
Brachiopoda, Bivalvia,
Decapoda, Annelida

Death

Destroyer
(borers; raspers)
Annelida, Cirripedia,
Bivalvia: *Lithophaga*,
Echinoidea: *Gymnocidaris*

Figure 14.6.   Composition and guild structure of Middle Jurassic (Late Bathonian) patch reef communities, Saint Aubin-sur-Mer, northwestern France. The constructor guild consists only of the lithistid demosponge *Platychonia magna*. Upon death of these sponges, highly diverse encrusters and bafflers colonized their skeletons (cf. Table 14.5).

skeletons such as *Platychonia magna* could be very difficult to distinguish from the canal system of the sponge.

Late Jurassic (Malm)

Reefs of Malm age are more numerous, widespread, compositionally varied, and commonly somewhat larger than those of the Lias and Dogger. The most carefully studied Malm reefs grew in shallow water at the margins of shelf/platform basins in western Europe north of the Tethyan trough, in somewhat deeper water near the shelf–seaward slope margin or on platforms within the trough (J. L. Wilson, 1975, pp. 261–266; Flügel, 1975, Fig. 10; Beauvais, 1973). The Malm in Europe was characterized by general regression over the shelf and shelf–slope margin, so that the younger reefs occur in southern Europe and contain deeper-water reefs capped by shallow water reefs.

Reef Communities

There are two strikingly different frame-building communities in the Malm of Europe:

   a.   A scleractinian/stromatoporoid-dominated assemblage (Type 1, Beauvais, 1973, p. 319) of shallow-water (<25 m) origin present in the Oxfordian in England, northern Yugoslavia, and Switzerland (Arkell, 1935; Turnšek, 1969; J. L. Wilson, 1975, pp. 267–271), the Kimmeridgian of the French Jura Mountains (Pl. 44a; Bernier, 1984, pp. 668–675), and the Tithonian of southern Germany (Swabia and Franconia).

   b.   A siliceous sponge/crustose cyanophyte-dominated assemblage of presumed deeper water (25–150 m) or sponge-dominated assemblage of deep-water (>100 m) origin. This assemblage occurs in the Oxfordian of the French Jura (Gaillard, 1983) and the Kimmeridgian–Tithonian of Swabia (Gwinner, 1976).

Example 14.7: Late Jurassic (Oxfordian); Coral Rag, England. In the vicinity of Oxford and northward to Yorkshire, the rocks of the Coral Rag contain numerous small patch reefs ("coral thickets") dominated by large (up to 1.5-m dia.) colonial scleractinians (Arkell, 1935) most of which are in growth position. The coral-rich units occur in sheets (biostromes?) 6–12 m thick that extended laterally as barriers to circulation for as much as 5 km interbedded with oolitic and shell fragment limestones (Teichert, 1958, p. 1078).

   Corals of the constructor and binder guilds were the chief frame-builders and dwellers (Table 14.6; Fig. 14.7). The large colonial coralla constructed rigid framestones of low topographic relief. The reef-dwelling corals were less numerous and some species had erect, branching coralla. Other dwellers included a variety of invertebrates.

   The reef-building corals contain abundant evidence (chiefly borings) of a well-developed destroyer guild, including lithophagid bivalves, sponges, and urchins; the internal sediment contains evidence of burrowing. There is no evidence of either a baffler guild, except possibly a few small, solitary sponges, or of a cryptic subcommunity.

Other Coral-Dominated Reefs. The Kimmeridgian reefs of the French Jura Mountains were much larger than those of the English Oxfordian. Extensive barrier reefs of shallow-water origin were built by massive and branching corals, domal stromatoporoids, and *Tubiphytes;* dwellers included rudists, brachiopods, gastropods, and varied dasycladaceans (Bernier, 1984).

   Regression during the Tithonian in Swabia and Franconia, southern Germany, caused reversal in the relative importance of algae, siliceous

TABLE 14.6 Taxonomic Composition and Guild Structure of Late Jurassic (Oxfordian) Patch Reefs, Coral Rag, Central England[a]

Constructor Guild	Binder Guild	Destroyer Guild	Dweller Guild
Scleractinia	Scleractinia	Bivalvia	Scleractinia
Thecosmilia	*Thamnasteria:*	*Lithophaga*	*Rhabdophyllia*
annularis	1–2 spp.	Porifera	*phillipsi*
Isastrea explan-	"Red algae?"	Echinoidea	*Cladophyllia*
ata	Spongiomor-		*conybeari*
Thamnasteria:	phida?		5 other spp.
1–2 spp.	Bryozoa		Mollusca
			Pectins; oys-
			ters; grazing
			gastropods
			Brachiopoda
			Thecideids
			Terebratulids
			Serpulidae
			Foraminiferida

Source: After Arkell (1935), Teichert (1958), McKerrow (1978), Anderton et al. (1979).
[a]Listed in approximate order of decreasing importance.

Figure 14.7. Composition and guild structure of Late Jurassic (Oxfordian) coral-dominated patch reef communities, Coral Rag, central England (cf. Table 14.6). Main guild membership indicated by thick arrow, and guild overlap by thin arrow (around circle).

sponges, and corals in the frame-building guilds (Gwinner, 1976, pp. 45–49). Pre-Tithonian reefs were built by algae and sponges, whereas by the mid-Tithonian such corals as *Microphyllia, Stylina,* and *Placophyllia* had become the dominant builders. The world-renowned micritic (lithographic) limestones of the Solnhofen–Eichstätt area of southern Franconia were deposited during the early Tithonian (Malm Zeta 2) in small (atoll?) lagoons surrounded by dead Kimmeridgian algal–sponge reefs (Barthel, 1972, 1978; Gall, 1983, pp. 167–177). Locally toward the east in Bavaria, coral-capped reefs lived simultaneously with deposition of the Solnhofen Limestone.

Stromatoporoid-dominated Reefs. The Late Jurassic was the time of maximum abundance and diversity of Mesozoic stromatoporoids. They commonly occur in close association with corals, or locally, as in the Oxfordian Torinosu Limestone, Naradini (near Kochi), Shikoku Island, Japan, they may be the sole frame-builders (Pl. 7a).

Example 14.8: Late Jurassic (Oxfordian–Kimmeridgian) Sponge–Algal Reef Communities; Jura Mountains, France and Southern Germany. In deeper water ($\cong$ 50–150 m) of low turbulence and turbidity along the northern margin of the Tethyan trough, sponge–algal reefs were abundant during the Late Jurassic from western France and northeastern Spain to eastern Romania (Gaillard, 1983, pp. 271–278, Fig. 44). The most carefully studied are those of the Oxfordian in the French Jura (Gaillard, 1983) and Kimmeridgian of southern Germany (Gwinner, 1976). The French Oxfordian reefs are rather small (maximum dimensions: 10 m thick; 8 m in diameter) with a maximum original topographic relief of 2 m (Pl. 10a). The German reefs are best developed in Swabia, where they attain thicknesses of over 150 m, have coalesced, and extend laterally to form barriers to circulation covering several square kilometers (Flügel and Steiger, 1981, Fig. 3) with topographic relief of 50–100 m. Because of their general biologic similarity, these reef communities are discussed together, with greater emphasis on the sponges and cryptic subcommunities in the French Jura and on the algae in Germany.

The biologic development of the reefs involved a complex two-stage sequence beginning with luxuriant growth of siliceous sponges (Pl. 51a). Upon death, their surfaces provided a firm substrate for the attachment of various encrusters (the second stage; Flügel and Steiger, 1981, Fig. 5). The reef communities generally lack well-skeletonized, large constructors such as scleractinians; the destroyer guild consists of a few echinoids, and the dweller guild is locally abundant and taxonomically diverse.

The diagenetic history of the siliceous sponges is very complex (Gaillard, 1983, pp. 257–262) but their preservation, especially the canal system and spicules, is much better in the French Oxfordian, so that it is possible to identify specimens to lower taxonomic levels than in the German material. In the small reefs of the Couches de Birmensdorf in the French Jura, Gaillard (1983) identified 53 species of siliceous sponges; 80% were hexactinellids and 90% are in life position. They are concentrated near the base of the reefs, vary from about 10 to 30 cm in maximum dimension, and comprise 20–25% of the rock volume. Only rarely are adjacent sponges conjoined (pseudocolonial) in branching, "plocoid," or "meandroid" forms. Instead, they consist chiefly of dispersed solitary, plate/cup/vase-shaped ("en coupe" of Gaillard) forms of the baffler and binder guilds (Pl. 51a; Table 14.7); cups and vases dominate early reef growth, and plates are most common near the tops of the reefs. The sponges are too poorly skeletonized to be members of the constructor guild, but because of their size and abundance, both the bafflers and binders overlap the constructor guild (Fig. 14.8a). Thus, the size, shape, and packing density of sponges was a major factor in the baffling, trapping, and stabilization of muds in the internal sediment. The sediment in turn provided stability to the upward growing sponges.

After death and toppling of the sponges, their upper surfaces were selectively encrusted by various algae and foraminifera (Pl. 51a). There are two types of algal crusts in the Swabian reefs: thrombolites and stromatolites. Thrombolites on flat sponges occur as sheets up to a few centimeters thick or as erect branches up to 10 cm tall; on toppled cylinders, they grew as branches from the upper surface and as crusts on the lower side of the spongocoel (Gwinner, 1976, Fig. 19). Stromatolites are of similar importance as the thrombolites and grew in broadly domal to columnar shapes (Gwinner, 1976, Figs. 21, 22). Many sponges were first encrusted by thrombolites and then by stromatolites. During the mid–late Kimmeridgian, stromatolites totally replaced thrombolites in some reefs.

TABLE 14.7. Guild Membership of Living Siliceous Sponges, Couches de Birmensdorf (Oxfordian), French Jura Mountains

Baffler Guild	Binder Guild	Dweller Guild
(Contains "solitary bowl-, top-, horn-, and cut-off shapes that are very abundant, abundant or quite abundant")	(Contains "solitary plate shapes that are very abundant, abundant or quite abundant")	(Contains all "colonies" and all "solitary" forms that are of "little abundance or very little abundance")
Hexactinellida Dictyida: 2 spp. Lychniskida: 2 spp.	Hexactinellida Dictyida: 5 spp. Lychniskida: 1 spp.	Hexactinellida Dictyida: 20 spp. Lychniskida: 14 spp.
Demospongiae Lithistida: 1 sp.	Demospongiae Lithistida: 1 sp.	Demospongiae Lithistida: 9 spp.

Source: Compiled from Gaillard, 1983, pp. 192–197.

The thrombolites and stromatolites are of greater volumetric importance (up to 50% of rock volume) than the sponges; the remainder (20–40%) is mostly lime mud (Gwinner, 1976, pp. 24–25, Fig. 66). Thus, the living sponges played the overlapping roles of current bafflers and sediment binders (Fig. 14.8a), whereas the dead sponges provided a firm substrate for the considerably greater role of algal binding/encrustation. The resulting reef limestones began as sponge bafflestones and boundstones but were subsequently transformed by laterally expanded crusts joining two or more sponges into algal boundstones prior to burial. Because of their considerable volume, varied growth forms, and dense packing, the thrombolite- and stromatolite-building algae (probably Cyanophyta; Behr and Behr, 1976) played multiple roles as members of the binder and baffler guilds (Table 14.8) and also overlapped the constructor guild (Fig. 14.8a).

Hexactinellids and, to a lesser degree, lithistids, also dominate the dweller guild. The species from the Couches de Birmensdorf assigned here

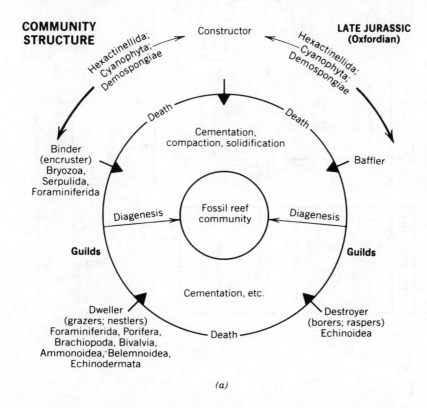

Figure 14.8a. Composition and guild structure of Late Jurassic (Oxfordian–Kimmeridgian) sponge–algal reefs, French Jura Mountains and southern Germany (cf. Table 14.7). Main guild membership indicated by thick arrows, and guild overlap by thin arrows (around circle).

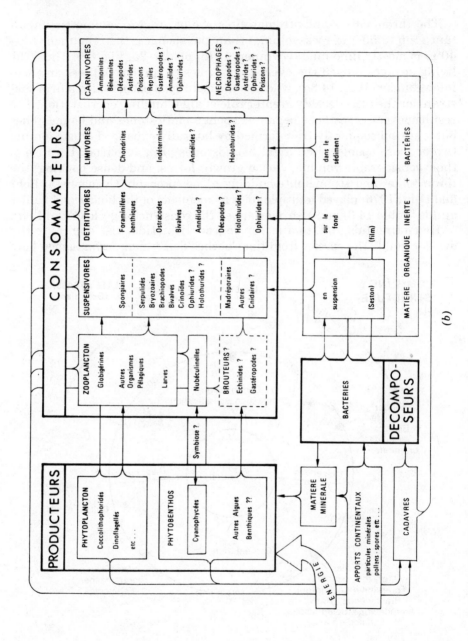

Figure 14.8b. Reconstruction of trophic structure of Late Jurassic (Oxfordian) sponge-algal reef ecosystem, French Jura Mountains. See text for discussion and translation of terms. (From Gaillard, 1983.)

TABLE 14.8 Composition and Guild Structure of Non-Sponge Taxa, Late Jurassic (Oxfordian–Kimmeridgian) Reef Communities, French Jura Mountains and Swabian Alb, Germany[a]

Binder Guild	Baffler Guild	Dweller Guild
Cyanophyta?	Cyanophyta?	Ammonoidea
Thrombolitic–	Thrombolitic–	Bivalvia
stromatoli-	stromatoli-	Brachiopoda[b]
tic crusts,	tic erect	Echinoder-
sheets, domes	branches,	mata
Foraminiferida	columns	Gastropoda
Nubeculinella	Bryozoa	Bryozoa
Serpulida[b]: 11 spp.	Branching	Foramini-
Bryozoa[b]: 4 spp.	Crinoidea	ferida
		Ostracoda
		Serpulida
		Scleractinia
		"Fish" teeth

Source: After Gwinner (1976) and Gaillard (1983).
[a]Listed in approximate order of decreasing volumetric importance.
[b]Includes members of cryptic subcommunity.

to the dweller guild (Table 14.7) are taxonomically diverse but too uncommon (low skeletal volume) to be regarded as frame-builders; locally, they may have overlapped both the binder and baffler guilds.

Although the volumetric importance of encrusters of the lower sponge surfaces (cryptic subcommunity) is much less than the upper surfaces, their taxonomic diversity is much higher (Gaillard, 1983, pp. 201–206; Table 14.8). Both abundance and diversity of cryptic encrusters are inversely proportional to presumed water depth. In the French Couches de Birmensdorf, serpulids are the most abundant and diverse; other cryptic taxa consist of bryozoans, brachiopods (3 spp.), and sponges (2 spp.; Gaillard, 1983, pp. 202–207). In addition, Gaillard (1983, pp. 212–214) recognized a considerable number and variety of foraminifera within the canal system of the sponges, most of which entered the canals after death of the sponges.

Members of the non-cryptic dweller guild living in close association with the sponges are abundant in both the Oxfordian Couches de Birmensdorf (Gaillard, 1983, pp. 215–232) and in the Swabian Kimmeridgian reefs (Gwinner, 1976, pp. 33–38). They include a great variety of foraminifera, ostracods, ammonites, bivalves, brachiopods, and echinoderms; rare specimens of scleractinians, serpulids, bryozoans, and fish teeth (Table 14.8) are also present locally.

Other Sponge–Algal Reefs. Sponge–algal reef communities essentially the same as those of Example 14.8 have been described from the Oxfordian of Franconia, southeastern Germany, by Flügel and Steiger (1981) and the Smackover Formation in the subsurface of the U.S. Gulf Coast by Baria et al. (1982). In the Franconian example, sponges are relatively more important than algal crusts, whereas in the Smackover, algae (including *Tubiphytes*) and, locally, corals are more important than sponges.

Trophic Structure (Sponge–Algal Reefs)

One of the best-documented trophic diagrams showing the complex energy (nutritional) pathways in any reef ecosystem, regardless of age, is the one prepared by Gaillard (1983, pp. 233–235) for the Oxfordian sponge–algal reefs described above (Example 14.8) in the French Jura Mountains (Fig. 14.8b). Gaillard has assigned each of the higher taxa actually present (solid boxes) or believed to have been present (dashed boxes) to one or more "principal trophic groups," some of which have been subdivided on the basis of where the organisms lived (e.g., phytoplankton vs. phytobenthos and zooplankton vs. zoobenthos). Gaillard further subdivided the herbivorous zoobenthos into suspension feeders (suspensivores), epifaunal deposit feeders (détritivores), and infaunal deposit feeders (limivores). The suspension feeders dominated the consumer trophic level and were subdivided by Gaillard into microphagous (sponges through holothuroids, Fig. 14.8b) and macrophagous forms (corals or "madréporaires" and other cnidarians). The scavengers (nécrophages) derived energy from all of the preceding trophic groups, as indicated by the flow of arrows from left to right as well as from dead larger organisms (cadavres). Gaillard did not distinguish between major and minor energy pathways. However, the major controls over energy transfer in these reef ecosystems involved the cyanophytes, nubeculinells (foraminifera), and sponges.

There are four important differences between Oxfordian sponge–algal ecosystems and late Cenozoic coral–algal ecosystems (described in Part I):

a.   The contribution of coral–zooxanthellae symbiosis in the transfer of energy and nutrients in the Oxfordian reefs is almost insignificant and thus not shown in Figure 14.8b. The potential role of corals as suspension-feeding carnivores is also not shown in Figure 14.8b. As discussed in Chapter 2, the coral–zooxanthellae symbiosis and carnivorous nutrition of corals are very important in Holocene shallow-water reef ecosystems and were almost certainly significant in Oxfordian coral-dominated shallow-water reefs (e.g., Example 14.7).

b.   The preservation of large volumes of cyanophytes (thrombolites, stromatolites, and porostromates) in the Oxfordian sponge–algal reefs is very unusual. Cyanophyte primary production was surely of major importance in many pre-Cenozoic reef ecosystems, but rarely can it be quantitatively assessed as in the Late Jurassic sponge–algal reefs. Conversely, numerous Cenozoic benthic algal producers are skeletal and so their trophic significance can be determined; skeletal algae are rare in the Jura Mountains Oxfordian reefs.

c.   In Oxfordian sponge–algal ecosystems, the suspension-feeding herbivores are both abundant and diverse and so must have provided a very efficient filtering system for gathering, using, and recycling nutrients of varied compositions and sizes (a form of niche segregation to reduce interspecific competition; Gaillard, 1983, pp. 235–236). Furthermore, the sponges *may* have been hosts to various symbiotic cyanophytes, bacteria, and zooxanthellae, as they are in Holocene reef ecosystems (discussed in Chap. 2).

d.   The Oxfordian sponge–algal reefs contain surprisingly little evidence (borings, scratch marks, body fossils) of an effective destroyer guild, and the dweller guild does not include numerous grazers (brouteurs in Fig. 14.8*b*). In contrast, both destroyers and grazers are abundant and diverse in Cenozoic reefs (Chap. 5). The general lack of well-skeletonized constructors in Oxfordian sponge–algal reefs partly explains the paucity of destroyers and grazers. In contrast, borers, raspers, and grazers are abundant and varied in Oxfordian coral-dominated reefs (Table 14.6).

CRETACEOUS

Organisms

Compared with the considerable diversity of higher taxa involved in the building guilds in Late Jurassic reefs, Cretaceous building guilds are remarkably simple. They were dominated during most of the Early Cretaceous by scleractinians, and during the latest Early and Late Cretaceous by rudist bivalves. However, other higher taxa typical of older reef communities were also present in Cretaceous reefs and are briefly discussed first.

Algae

The end of the Jurassic marked the extinction of the long-ranging, problematical *Tubiphytes* (Fig. 7.1), and, during the Cretaceous, there was a gradual decline in importance of the Solenoporacea. Although the crustose Corallinacea first appeared in Early Jurassic reefs and were also present in Early Cretaceous reefs, they did not become significant until the Late Cretaceous. Steneck (1983) has suggested that increased herbivory by rasping echinoids during the Cretaceous may have selectively caused the decline of the less well-skeletonized solenoporaceans and allowed better-skeletonized corallinaceans to expand into vacated niches in the binder/encruster guild. The Cretaceous was also a period of moderate expansion of codiaceans, which probably lived attached to reef frameworks and contributed to the internal sediment.

Porifera

There was a sharp decline of the importance of both calcareous and siliceous sponges in the building guilds from the Late Jurassic to the Cretaceous (Fig. 8.1). The enormous shallow-water carbonate continental shelves of the Cretaceous were especially inhospitable to deeper-water siliceous forms (Rigby, 1971). During the Early Cretaceous, the chaetetids and stromatoporoids (Turnšek and Masse, 1973) were locally important, as were inozoans and sphinctozoans during the Late Cretaceous (Wendt, 1980a).

Scleractinia

There was a brief decrease in generic diversity of corals during the early Early Cretaceous (Berriasian–Valanginian) but, for the remainder of the Cretaceous, diversity rose rapidly (Stanley, 1981, Fig. 2); during the Albian, there were about 50 genera and over 100 in the Maastrichtian. Their rise in diversity during the Early Cretaceous was accompanied by a rise in their domination of the building guilds (Fig. 10.1). By the Albian, rudists had displaced corals as the dominant builders, despite the rapidly increasing coral diversity. The Albian–Maastrichtian coral diversity peak for the Mesozoic is an excellent example of the occasional lack of correlation between diversity of a potential reef-building taxon and its actual importance in one or more of the building guilds. Furthermore, those corals that did belong to Late Cretaceous building guilds were neither large, abundant, nor diverse. Thus, much of the genus/species level diversification of Late Cretaceous corals did not occur in reef communities, which is very atypical for most reef-building higher taxa.

Binder Guild

Cretaceous reef communities contained several higher taxa that were potential binders (e.g., Solenoporacea, Corallinacea, Chaetetidae, Stromatoporoidea, Inozoa, Demospongiae, Scleractinia, Spongiomorphida, and Bryozoa). Yet one important characteristic of most Cretaceous reefs, especially mid–Late Cretaceous, is the lack of or poor development of the binder guild (cf. Achauer and Johnson, 1969). In numerous Cretaceous reef complexes, the binder guild is better-developed in the seaward slope and reef flat deposits than in the reef crest (Turnšek and Masse, 1973). Furthermore, biostromes are commonly more tightly bound than the adjacent reefs, and, very commonly, corals rather than algae or sponges dominated the binder guild, especially in pre-Albian reef communities (Masse and Philip, 1981, pp. 409–418).

The poor development of the binder guild in rudist-dominated reefs has been a major factor in the ongoing argument of whether these structures are in fact reefs (see below). The virtual absence of binding algae and poriferans from such reefs is difficult to explain, but certainly rudists and binders were not ecologically compatible. Kauffman and Sohl (1974) suggested that at least some rudists may have repelled some potential encrusters with biochemical toxins or may have aggressively excluded binders by movements of their mantle margins.

Hippuritacea (Rudists)

Although rudists were present in Late Jurassic reef communities (Fig. 10.1), they were minor components of the dweller guild in most cases (Pl. 44*a*). However, at the beginning of the Cretaceous, their volumetric importance (individual skeletal volume and packing density) dramatically increased in level-bottom communities and in some reeflike structures (see below). During the Cretaceous, the overall importance of rudists continued to increase progressively in these communities; by the Albian, they had displaced corals as the dominant taxon in all central Tethyan shallow-water reef environments. This rising importance included the size of individuals, packing density, and taxonomic diversity at all levels (discussed in Chap. 10). In addition, some rudists provide evidence of increasing adaptive morphologic plasticity as they evolved from ancestral level-bottom forms to reef frame-builders.

Rudists produced various organic structures unique to the Cretaceous. From the viewpoint of guild structure, both binder and baffler guilds are commonly absent or poorly represented in rudist-dominated communities. Virtually all reef-building rudists were constructors by virtue of their presumed rapid growth rates, large skeletons, and erect, gregarious growth habit (Pl. 37*b*). Recumbent coiled and disklike growth forms were dominant in level-bottom lagoonal communities and biostromes but uncommon in the constructor guild of mature reef communities. Furthermore, many rudists were atypical contructors because the erect growth forms were poorly supported and thus easily toppled prior to final burial. The total community species diversity of most well-developed rudist-dominated structures is remarkably low. Many rudist species were supremely successful opportunists, especially in the constructor guild, producing reef communities with low guild overlap. In the Late Cretaceous, they also may have been symbionts with the major ecosystem producers (see Chap. 10). Low rudist species diversity is a characteristic of most rudist-dominated reef and level-bottom communities; on level-bottoms, total community diversity commonly exceeds diversity of the adjacent reefs.

Both lateral/bathymetric and vertical (stratigraphic) zonations are other common characteristics of rudist-dominated reef and biostromal communities (J. L. Wilson, 1975, pp. 323–325). The nature of these zonations depends on the geologic age, taxonomic composition, and location (geomorphic and paleobiogeographic) of individual communities (Masse, 1979). Furthermore, some zones are almost monospecific. Just as for Holocene reefs (see Chap. 3), there are no "universal" species-level zonations, either lateral or vertical, that apply to Cretaceous rudist reefs.

Kauffman and Sohl (1974, pp. 457–464) have described in detail a model for lateral zonation of both organism subcommunities and the enclosing sedimentary matrix (largely volcaniclastic) for Caribben Aptian–Albian and Santonian–Maastrichtian reefs and biostromes from the shoreline across the reef flat/lagoon to the shelf edge and seaward slope. They recognized nine sedimentologic–subcommunity "zones," with differences between adjacent zones attributed to such factors as geomorphic location, water depth, and turbulence.

General vertical sequences (ecological successions?) of rudist subcommunities and sedimentary matrices have also been described for the Late Cretaceous of the Caribbean by Kauffman and Sohl (1979, pp. 726–727) and for individual reefs and biostromes (Huffington, 1984). During the Cretaceous, the complexity of rudist-dominated successions increased in the Caribbean from early morphologically uniform, small structures ("thickets" and "coppices") to larger, morphologically diverse, Late Cretaceous "banks" and reefs (Kauffman and Sohl, 1974, pp. 437–449).

Coral-dominated vertical sequences (successions?) have also been described from the Early Cretaceous (Masse and Philip, 1981, pp. 417–418; Scott, 1981, p. 463). Taxonomically "complex or mixed" sequences in "buildups" of the Early Cretaceous Edwards Limestone in Texas commonly begin with a coral-dominated *(Cladophyllia* or *Microsolenia)* assemblage, overlain in turn by two rudist assemblages (first a caprinid-rich and then a radiolitid-rich); finally, the structure is covered by a densely packed assemblage dominated by the non-rudist bivalve *Chondrodonta*. Elsewhere, *Chrondrodonta* may be the dominant substrate stabilizer in the earliest stage of an ecological succession.

Terminology

The number of terms that have been used to describe coral and rudist-rich "buildups" and the differences in usage of many of these terms by various workers generally exceeds the number in use for pre-Cretaceous reefs. In many ways, Cretaceous reefs *(sensu lato)* are unique and many aspects of their descriptive terminology are also unique. For example, numerous North American researchers use the undefined term "frameworks" to describe some of these structures. The result has been quite confusing; the terminology itself has been part of the problem in recognizing which structures are indeed reefs and which are not. Although some rudist-rich assemblages that are clearly level-bottom communities are similar to the early stages of reef successions, they are not be discussed here (see Chap. 10).

Attributes that are characteristic of more typical Cenozoic and pre-

Cretaceous reefs but are poorly developed in rudist-dominated structures include:

a. Rigidity and wave/current resistance. Despite the large skeletal volume and dense packing of many rudists, the lack of binders or evidence of an important early inorganic (cement) framework has led many workers to conclude that rudists rarely produced rigid reefs. (For comparison of the importance of early cement, see discussion of Capitan Limestone, Chap. 6.) However, many Late Cretaceous rudists were cocemented to their neighbors for increased support and rigidity. Furthermore, rudist structures comparable to reefs commonly have a high lime mud content which probably indicates poor support for erect-growing rudists and hence generally low rigidity. Finally, in those shelf margin structures containing abundant, erect rudist growth forms, individuals commonly are not in their original growth position, suggesting that they may be current-transported shell heaps.

b. The original topographic relief was typically low in most rudist-dominated structures; this has led some workers to call them banks, lenses, or biostromes rather than reefs (e.g., Masse and Philip, 1981, Fig. 17A, B). In addition, dipping flank beds consisting of reef-derived skeletal debris are commonly absent or poorly developed, especially in Late Cretaceous reefs.

Thus, each coral and rudist-dominated possible reef structure must be judged primarily on the field criteria discussed in Chapter 1, with the understanding that the Cretaceous contains a broader spectrum of reef to non-reef forms than rocks of any other geologic system. (The difficulty of the reef/non-reef judgment increases considerably in the subsurface for potential reef structures, regardless of geologic age.) Judgment must be based on such biologic attributes as skeletal volume, packing density, growth form, habit, and position, and presence/absence of lateral and vertical zonations. If such zonations are present, the causative physical–chemical–geological–biological factors (Chap. 3) must be interpreted. In addition, judgment must consider evidence for or against original rigidity and topographic relief. For a structure to be a reef does not require shallow water and wave resistance; deeper-water, current-resistant structures may also be classified as reefs. The mere location of a thick coral or rudist structure in a carbonate matrix in a shelf margin location with 100 or more meters of relief to the adjacent basin floor does not make it a reef.

Cretaceous rocks contain numerous reefs of various sizes (Bein, 1976, p. 265, reported a possible subsurface rudist reef system in Israel up to 300 m thick, 1000 m wide, and more than 13 km long), shapes, geomorphic locations, taxonomic compositions, and paleoecologic community structures. Each reef represents a separate challenge to the field and especially to the subsurface geologist, and its recognition requires the integration of multiple criteria.

Occurrence

Coral and rudist-dominated reefs and biostromes are an important characteristic of the Cretaceous Tethyan tropical–subtropical realm. The area of tropical–subtropical reef-building organisms and carbonate-producing continental shelves and platforms was latitudinally much expanded from its earlier (Triassic and Jurassic) and later (Cenozoic) limits. Tethyan reefs, banks, and biostromes are widely distributed in the western hemisphere around the margins of the Gulf of Mexico and the Antillean islands and in the eastern hemisphere from southwestern Europe through the Mediterranean and Middle East to the Himalayas (Coates, 1973, p. 169).

The wide Cretaceous continental shelves/platforms contain coral and rudist assemblages from the upper seaward slope to the shoreline. Depending on local factors, they included barrier, patch, and fringing reef systems and biostromes; many of the older Indo-Pacific guyots are capped by Late Cretaceous rudist reefs. Coral-dominated reefs generally occupied higher turbulence shelf margin locations and rudist-dominated reefs and rudist subcommunities were in lower turbulence locations behind reef crests and in reef flat/lagoonal locations (Philip, 1972; J. L. Wilson, 1975, pp. 319–324; Masse and Philip, 1981).

Masse and Philip (1981, pp. 401–407) have reviewed the nature and distribution of coral/rudist-dominated structures *(sensu lato)* in France and adjacent areas. They occur almost continuously in these shelf deposits from earliest to latest Cretaceous, with minima in the Late Valanginian, Late Albian–Early Cenomanian, Early Turonian, Campanian, and Late Maastrichtian. Maxima came in the Barremian and Coniacian.

Other regions had different minima/maxima patterns based on different environmental factors. For example, in the Gulf of Mexico, reef and biostromal development extended from the Barremian–Cenomanian with the maximum in the Albian. In contrast, in the Antillean region, coral-rudist structures range in age from Barremian to Maastrichtian with maximum development in the Campanian–Maastrichtian (Kauffman and Sohl, 1974, pp. 449–457; Coates, 1977).

Early Cretaceous

Southern France

The Lower Cretaceous rocks of Provence and adjacent areas lack reefs but do contain abundant coral-built and local rudist-built biostromes (Masse and Philip, 1981, Figs. 17A, 18, 19, 23, pp. 414–420; Masse, 1977). The coral biostromes are best developed in the Barremian–Early Aptian and were built by highly diverse (at least 78 species in 53 genera) and morphologically varied coral assemblages belonging to the families Microsolenidae, Stylindae, Calanophyllidae, Thamnasteriidae, and Montlivalliidae (constructors/binders), encrusting foraminifera, coralline algae, calcareous sponges, and serpulids. Bafflers included globular and ramose bryozoans.

Masse and Philip (1981, pp. 418–420) recognized two types of rudist-dominated communities:

a. Large, thick-shelled, loosely associated forms of higher generic diversity; particularly characteristic of the Barremian–Albian.

b. smaller, thin-shelled, more densely packed, longer ranging genera (mostly requienids and monopleurids) of lower diversity.

Other members of these communities include encrusting bivalves (*Liostrea, Chondrodonta*) and chaetetids, nerineid gastropods, and rare scleractinians.

North America

Example 14.9: Early Cretaceous (Early Albian) Mural Limestone, Arizona. The Mural Limestone in southeastern Arizona contains small (3–28-m thick) shelf patch reefs built by corals, algae, and rudists that are zoned both laterally and vertically (Scott, 1981). Corals comprise about 10–60% of the rock volume, various algae encrust the coral-dominated framework, and rudists (approx. 10–15% of volume) are concentrated between the coral colonies and in leeward or back-reef areas.

There is considerable niche and guild overlap of corals (Table 14.9; Fig. 14.9). Coralla of *Actinastrea* spp. are tabular–massive constructors, whereas those of *Microsolena texana* range from massive (up to 1 m thick) to tabular (0.5–4.5 cm thick; 20–300 cm in diameter) or V-shaped (vase-like?; Scott, 1981, Text-fig. 3). *Calamophyllia sandbergi* grew in erect, branching coralla up to 30 cm high.

Within the reefs, the relative importance of rudists increases upward as well as laterally. The surface of the reefs toward the reef flat/lagoon is commonly dominated by coiled, recumbent valves of *Coalcomana ramosa* and the rather elongate, conical valves of *Petalodontia felixi* (climax subcommunity?). In life, *P. felixi* was erect, partially buried in the substrate, or attached to other shells in densely packed, mutually supporting, cocemented, interlocked "thickets." *Caprinuloidea gracilis* formed small "clusters" between the predominant corals in the reef centers and *Monopleura* cf. *M. mardica* formed clusters and thickets ("cluster" and "thicket" terminology after Kauffman and Sohl, 1974, pp. 424, 431–437). Because of their large skeletal size and local dense packing, all the above rudists belonged to the constructor guild but were volumetrically less important than the constructor/binder corals.

Stromatolites were the most important encrusters of dead corals, es-

TABLE 14.9. Taxonomic Composition and Guild Structure of Early Cretaceous (Early Albian) Patch Reef Communities, Mural Limestone, Southeastern Arizona[a]

Constructor Guild	Binder Guild	Destroyer Guild
Scleractinia	Scleractinia	"Borers"
Actinastrea sp.	*Microsolena texana*	"Algae/fungi"
Microsolena texana	*Actinastrea* sp.	Porifera
Calamophyllia sandbergi	Cyanophyta	Bivalvia
Bivalvia: Hippuritacea	Stromatolite crusts[b]	"Litho-
Coalcomana ramosa	Ostreidae	phagids"
Petalodontia felixi	Chlorophyta	
Caprinuloidea gracilis	*Polystrata*	
Monopleura cf. *M. mar-*	*Lithocodium*	
cida	Corallinacea[b]	
	Bryozoa[b]	
	Foraminiferida	

Source: After Scott, 1981.
[a]Taxa in each guild listed in approximate order of importance.
[b]Locally cryptic.

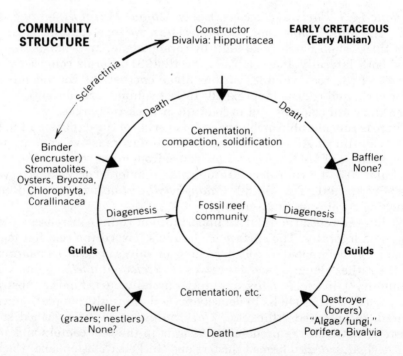

Figure 14.9. Compositon and guild structure of Early Cretaceous (Early Albian) patch reef communities, Mural Limestone, southeastern Arizona. Scleractinians of varied corallum morphologies (tabular, massive, branching, etc.) are the dominant frame-builders and overlap the constructor and binder guilds. Rudist bivalves (Hippuritacea) comprise 10–15% of the reef volume and lived between the scleractinians (cf. Table 14.9). Main guild membership indicated by thick arrow, and guild overlap by thin arrow (around circle).

pecially *Microsolena texana,* forming complex masses of broadly hemispherical laminae (5 + mm thick). The other non-scleractinian members
of the binder guild are volumetrically much less important. The upwardly
branching scleractinians (e.g., *M. texana; Calamophyllia sandbergi*) were
too well-skeletonized to be members of the baffler guild, and Scott (1981)
did not discuss the dwellers; destroyers are indicated in Table 14.9.

Example 14.10: Early Cretaceous (Middle Albian); Glen Rose Formation,
Central Texas. During the medial Cretaceous, nearly the entire Gulf of
Mexico was bordered by a wide continental shelf that was subdivided into
several subsiding basins and platforms and more positive uplifts (J. L.
Wilson, 1975, pp. 323–327). Barrier and patch reefs were commonly present at or near the shelf margin, which may have had an original relief
of nearly 1000 m above the adjacent Gulf of Mexico. Patch reefs and biostromes of various types (sizes, shapes, paleoecology) were abundant across
almost the entire shelf. Albian reefs and biostromes are well-exposed in
northeastern Mexico (e.g., Valles Platform) and central Texas (San Marcos
Platform), where they have been intensely studied because of the economic
significance of their subsurface counterparts (and associated reef complex;
e.g., Golden Lane [Poza Rica in Mexico]).

The Glen Rose Limestone in central Texas contains numerous rudist-
dominated shelf or reef flat/lagoonal biostromes and lagoonal–shelf margin
barrier and patch reefs (Perkins, 1974). The reef flat/lagoonal biostromes
of the Glen Rose are relatively thin (0.15–1.7 m thick) but very extensive
and composed of clusters, inverted cones ("bouquets," Pl. 37*a*) and isolated
specimens of monopleurid and requienid rudists and oysters; gastropods,
varied foraminifera, serpulids, and burrowing bivalves are also present.
The monopleuirds (*Monopleura* spp.) predominate and grew in sheets,
branching clusters, and bouquets up to 1 m high and 1 m in maximum
diameter. Individual shells are slender (1–3 cm in diameter; 3–9 cm long)
and attached only by their apexes to adjacent shells; neighboring shells
were not in extended vertical contact. The requienids (*Toucasia* spp.) were
coiled, with a small attachment base, but closely spaced on the lime mud
substrate (Perkins, 1974, Text-Fig. 21).

The shelf margin patch reefs, built by caprinid rudists, are 5–15 m
thick and had an original topographic relief of 3–5 m. The caprinid-dominated framework trapped both lime mud and skeletal debris as internal
sediment and is surrounded by dipping beds (aprons) of skeletal debris.

The chief builder was the caprinid rudist *Coalcomana texana* (Table
14.10). Its shells are up to 45 cm long and 5 cm in diameter and packed
so densely that adjacent individuals commonly are in self-supporting mutual contact for most of their length to form erect clumps or clusters over
3 m high (Pl. 37*b*). Thus, in the Glen Rose Limestone, the contrast between
biostromes and reefs largely results from the different growth forms of
dominant rudists. Shallow-water (reef flat) biostromal monopleurids grew

TABLE 14.10. Taxonomic Composition and Guild Structure of Early Cretaceous (Middle Albian) Patch Reef Communities, Glen Rose Limestone, Central Texas[a]

Constructor Guild	Binder Guild	Dweller Guild
Bivalvia: Hippurita- cea	Scleractinia	Bivalvia: Hip- puritacea
Coalcomana texana	*Meandrophyllia*	Radiolitidae
Scleractinia	*Polyphylloseris*	Caprotinidae
Actinastrea		Requeiniidae
Muriophyllia		*Toucasia*
Montastrea		Caprinidae
Thamnasteria		Scleractinia
		Gastropoda
		Nerineidae
		Cerithiidae
		Bivalvia
		Ostrea
		Foraminiferida
		Coskinolina sunnilan- densis
		Orbitolina tex- ana

Source: After Perkins, 1974.
[a]Taxa in each guild listed in approximate order of importance.

in more loosely packed, upwardly divergent bouquets or inverted conical clusters (Perkins, 1974, Text-Figs. 7, 18, 19), whereas reef-building caprinids grew in more densely packed, erect clusters of parallel touching, mutually supporting shells.

Perkins (1974, pp. 145–147) also suggested that differences in salinity, turbulence, and turbidity controlled the distributions of monopleurids and caprinids and therefore the nature of biostromal and reef communities. He regarded monopleurids as the most euryhaline and adapted to generally lower turbulence and to periodic episodes of higher turbidity. The caprinids were more stenohaline (normal marine to slightly brackish) and adapted to high turbulence/low turbidity. Scleractinians are second in importance as builders and only rarely found in close association with rudists; in a few reefs, constructor guild corals (Fig. 14.10) are nearly as abundant as rudists, and in such cases, radiolitids rather than caprinids are the most common rudists.

Salinity was probably the main factor that determined the relative abundances of rudists, especially caprinids, and corals in Glen Rose reefs (Perkins, 1974, p. 147). Caprinids may have been tolerant to somewhat more brackish water than corals, and so the caprinid-dominated reefs

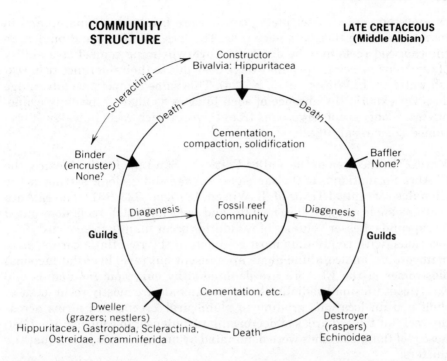

**COMMUNITY
STRUCTURE**

**LATE CRETACEOUS
(Middle Albian)**

Constructor
Bivalvia: Hippuritacea

Scleractinia

Death

Death

Cementation,
compaction, solidification

Binder
(encruster)
None?

Baffler
None?

Diagenesis

Fossil reef
community

Diagenesis

Guilds

Guilds

Cementation, etc.

Dweller
(grazers; nestlers)
Hippuritacea, Gastropoda, Scleractinia,
Ostreidae, Foraminiferida

Death

Destroyer
(raspers)
Echinoidea

Figure 14.10. Composition and guild structure of Early Cretaceous (Middle Albian) patch reef communities, Glen Rose Limestone, central Texas. The chief frame-builder of most reefs is the caprinid hippuritacean *Coalcomana texana*. However, in some other reefs, various corals and a few radiolitids were the main builders. Note the absence of bafflers, poor development of the binder guild, and guild overlap (thin arrows around circle) of Scleractinia and Hippuritacea (rudists) (cf. Table 14.10).

lived in environments where they acted as opportunists and out-competed the corals. This advantage was diminished in normal marine water where corals, and locally, radiolitids, could out-compete the caprinids.

Scleractinian corallum shapes include "massive heads – , branching colonies . . . , and platy colonies" (terminology of Perkins, 1974, p. 142); the heads and branches belonged to the constructor guild and the plates to the binder guild (Table 14.10). However, in most reefs, corals are so rare that they must be regarded as dwellers. Furthermore, for Glen Rose reefs as a whole, coral species diversity (approx. 20 spp.) is much higher than for rudists; in the *Coalcomana texana*-built reefs, *all* other potential rudist builders are so rare that they are here placed in the dweller guild. Other dwellers are listed in Table 14.10.

Perhaps the most unusual aspect of the Glen Rose reefs, both rudist-rich and coral-rich, is the nearly complete absence of binders and poorly skeletonized bafflers. The lack of bafflers is typical of most Cretaceous reefs and thus is not as surprising as the lack of important binders. The rudist reefs contain no encrusting algae or macroinvertebrates except for rare oysters; only a few "platy" corals were involved in binding and in many reefs even these are very rare. The lack of bafflers and binders in the caprinid reefs may be due to the overwhelming competitive ability of caprinids, which in turn may have been due to their tolerance to brackish water (J. L. Wilson, 1975, p. 324). This same competitive advantage does not explain the absence of such binders as algae, especially cyanophytes, sponges, and bryozoans from the coral-rich reefs in water of presumed normal salinity.

Mexico. In the area of the Valles Platform, San Luis Potosi, Mexico, the El Abra Formation is of the same general age and geologic setting as the Glen Rose of central Texas (J. L. Wilson, 1975, pp. 323–331). The El Abra contains shelf margin "barrierlike" and lagoonal patch reefs dominated by caprinids. Lesser volumes of radiolitids occur mainly in seaward slope locations, with requienids most common in the reef flats; corals, stromatoporoids, and coralline algae are present but rare. Reef flat/lagoonal biostromes of the El Abra are dominated by eurytopic requienids and rarely contain small radiolitids. The requienids are mostly recumbent in shelf margin locations grading to planispiral–erect/coiled forms across the reef flat toward areas of decreasing turbulence. In contrast, the Glen Rose reef flat biostromes were dominated by monopleurids in bouquetlike clusters.

Late Cretaceous

Southern France

In contrast to the Early Cretaceous, when both corals and rudists formed only biostromes, during the Late Cretaceous, corals and associated rudists (chiefly caprinids, radiolitids, or hippuritids) formed shelf/platform margin patch reefs up to 20 m thick and 100+ m in diameter (Pl. 51*b*; Masse and Philip, 1981, pp. 415–417). In addition to their association with corals in reefs, rudists also formed important reef flat/lagoonal/near-shore "banks, lenses, biostromes and bioconstructions" in which corals are quite rare but not "typical reefs" (terminology from Masse and Philip, 1981, pp. 414–421).

Masse and Philip (1981, pp. 418–421) recognized three types of Late Cretaceous rudist communities:

a.   Isolated clusters or bouquets 1–2 m thick composed of cylindrical or long conical hippuritids and/or radiolitids.

b.   Loosely packed biostromes composed of the same rudists as in the above clusters.

c.   "Tabular buildups" (biostromes) composed of the same rudists as the above clusters plus recumbent caprinids.

Italy; Yugoslavia

The Upper Cretaceous rocks in east-central Italy (Carbone and Sirna, 1981) and northeastern Yugoslavia (Polsak, 1981) were deposited in tectonically unstable shelf environments quite different from the examples discussed above. In both these areas, coral- and rudist-dominated barrier and patch reefs and biostromes formed in shelf margin locations. The relative proportions of corals and rudists are highly varied; some reefs/ biostromes contain almost nothing but corals, others almost nothing but rudists, and others a mixture of corals and rudists. Carbone and Sirna (1981, pp. 433–437) have reviewed in detail the rudist composition of these structures during the Late Cretaceous in Italy. Species diversity is strikingly higher than that in the Early Cretaceous (Albian) reefs described above, some of which contained fewer than 5 rudist species. Rudist species diversity in the Italian structures (not single reefs/biostromes, but totally) was at a maximum during the Cenomanian (24 spp.) and declined in the Turonian (8 spp.) and Coniacean–Maastrichtian (4 spp.). This local decline in diversity is opposite to the increasing generic diversity of Late Cretaceous rudists in the Antilles (Kauffman and Sohl, 1974, pp. 449–457) and global familial diversity (Coogan, 1969, p. N767).

In the Santonian–Early Campanian barrier reefs of Yugoslavia, the coral- and rudist-dominated communities are stratigraphically separated. At Donje Oresje, the corals underlie the rudists (Polsak, 1981); only rarely are they present in the same stratigraphic unit. Polsak (p. 449) identified 15 coral species in 12 genera which included both massive/domal and branching/dendroidal coralla of the constructor guild. Their packing density varies from isolated coralla to loosely–densely packed, forming level-bottom, biostromal/lenticular, and reef communities. The binder guild is poorly developed and consists of coralline algae and bryozoans. Polsak did not discuss taxa in the baffler, destroyer, or dweller guilds.

The overlying rudist-dominated communities are composed primarily of hippuritids; radiolitids and carpinids are present as dwellers. Polsak identified 1 genus (Hippurites), 2 subgenera (Vaccinites; Orbignya), and 16 species of hippuritids. The rudists are encrusted by rare coralline algae and attached small coral colonies; bafflers and destroyers were apparently also rare, but the internal reef sediment contains fragments of reef-dwelling gastropods, dasycladaceans, and benthic foraminifera.

Jamaica

The Upper Cretaceous carbonate rocks of Jamaica contain a variety of coral and rudist-dominated reefs and biostromes:

a. Coral-dominated biostromes composed of massive flat/laminar coralla more than 20 cm high and 40 cm in diameter (Association 5 of Coates, 1977a).

b. Rudist-dominated lenses, biostromes, reefs, and "frameworks" (Kauffman and Sohl, 1974) in which corals grew between rudists as laterally expanded binders/encrusters and as tall (>15-cm), branching constructors (Association 3 of Coates, 1977b).

c. Rudist-dominated (mostly radiolitids) "frameworks" in which small (7–10-cm maximum dia.) encrusting and low branching corals fill the interstices between rudist shells (Association 2 of Coates, 1977a; Coates' Associations 1 and 4 are here regarded as members of level-bottom communities).

Among the corals there is considerable guild overlap. In (a) and (b) above, they are constructors; in (b), they are binders; in (c), they are dwellers. The genus *Multicolumnastrea* has considerable intercolony variation, including low-to-tall branching forms, as well as "tuberous" and encrusting forms (Coates, 1977a, Fig. 2). Neither Coates (1977a, 1977b) nor Kauffman and Sohl (1974; 1979) stressed the non-coral and non-rudist components of these Jamaican structures; however, they did note the presence of such dwellers as dasycladaceans, ostracods, non-rudist bivalves, gastropods, and the overall lack of a non-coral binder guild.

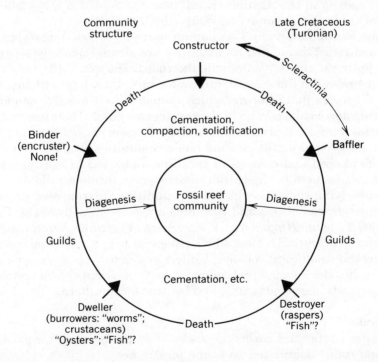

Figure 14.11. Compositon and guild structure of a Late Cretaceous (Turonian) deep-water coral thicket–coppice, Blue Hill Shale Member, near Lamay, New Mexico. The sole framebuilder is the oculinid scleractinian *Archohelia dartoni,* which grew in densely packed colonies composed of long, slender, fasciculate, erect branches. Species diversity of the community was very low. Main guild membership indicated by thick arrow, and guild overlap by thin arrow (around circle).

United States

Example 14.11: Late Cretaceous (Turonian), New Mexico. Coates and Kauffman (1973) described a very small (12–18-cm thick; 1.3-m dia.) coral-dominated "thicket–coppice" (terminology from Squires, 1964) from the Western Interior seaway of North America. The structure was built exclusively by the oculinid scleractinian *Archohelia dartoni*. The coralla consist of slender (approx. 5–10-mm dia.), densely packed, fasciculate, erect branches of uncertain length which overlapped the constructor and baffler guilds (Fig. 14.11).

Archohelia dartoni is phylogenetically related to the Holocene zooxanthellate/non-zooxanthellate scleractinian *Oculina* (discussed in Chap. 2). This relationship, the absence of algae, and the finely laminated shale of the surrounding matrix suggested to Coates and Kauffman (1973, p. 966) that the structure grew in the aphotic zone (150–2850 m).

CONCLUSIONS

In contrast to the late Paleozoic (Late Devonian: Frasnian–Permian) reef communities which were characterized in Chapter 13 as algal/sponge/bryozoan-dominated, the Mesozoic was the "age of algal, sponge, coral, and rudist reef communities." Algae were of major importance, especially in the binder guild, from the Middle Triassic through the Late Jurassic and much less important in the Cretaceous. Calcareous sponges were major contributors to all building guilds during the Middle–Late Triassic. Siliceous sponges were the dominant builders of some Middle Jurassic and most Late Jurassic reefs, especially those in deeper water.

The Mesozoic history of scleractinian corals consists of a succession of "ups and downs." They appeared in the Middle Triassic and by the end of the Triassic had displaced calcareous sponges and algae as the volumetrically dominant reef-builders. Their dominance continued to the Middle Jurassic, when siliceous sponges began to displace corals as the dominant builders of deeper-water reefs. Corals regained their dominance during the Early Cretaceous but were again displaced during the Late Cretaceous in most shallow-water reef environments by rudists. Corals and rudists together dominated earlier Cretaceous (Neocomian) reef-building, but during the Albian there was a turnover in their relative importance; pre-Aptian and some Aptian reefs were coral-dominated, and post-Albian reefs were rudist-dominated.

The Mesozoic rise in importance of well-skeletonized colonial scleractinians and the Late Jurassic–Cretaceous rise of rudists led to the increasing significance of the constructor guild at the expense of the coral-, algal-, and sponge-dominated binder and baffler guilds. Late Cretaceous reefs built by large, densely packed (gregarious) rudists represent the culmination in the domination of the constructor guild in all of geologic history. The overwhelming success of the rudists apparently excluded virtually all poorly skeletonized bafflers and all binders except for coralline and solenoporacean algae (Rhodophyta), and these were only of very local significance. The domination by the constructor guild provided moderate rigidity to Cretaceous reefs but not much topographic relief. Cretaceous reef complexes are generally mud-rich; therefore, except for the rudist framework, mud comprised a large portion of the internal sediment, flanking deposits, and the adjacent level-bottoms. These muddy sediments provided little support for the heavy rudist framework. Instead, the internal muds may have partially filled the spaces between individual erect rudists to prevent toppling, so that the apical ⅓ to ½ of the attached valve was submerged in mud during life.

The morphology and paleoecology of the Late Cretaceous rudists (especially the hippuritids) and Early Permian richthofeniacean brachiopods were similar in several ways:

a. Aberrant morphological adaptations for success in the constructor guild. In both groups, the growth habit was erect and the dominant growth direction vertical. In addition, both developed cup-shaped attached valves and lidlike free valves. In a few taxa of both hippuritids and richthofeniaceans, the free valve also was sievelike. Thus, the morphological convergence and functional adaptations of these taxa for life as constructors are remarkably similar to some other erect constructors. The skeletonization of rudists is much higher than any other pre-Cenozoic constructor taxon.

b. Part of their success was due to their gregarious habit. This resulted in densely packed (bouquetlike) clusters of shells that provided mutual support during life and resistance to destruction and transportation after death.

c. The period of their success as major reef constructors was geologically brief compared with most other higher taxa in this guild. The Richthofeniacea were important constructors for only about 15–20 million years and the rudists (Hippuritacea) for about 30–35 million years (Fig. 10.1). By comparison, Middle Paleozoic stromatoporoids and tabulate corals were of major importance for nearly 100 million years, rugose corals for 60 million years, chaetetids for 50 million, sphinctozoans for 60 million, and inozoans for about 70 million years (Figs. 8.1, 9.1). Several higher taxa of algae (e.g., cyanophytes, solenoporaceans, *Tubiphytes*) were important for even longer periods (Fig. 7.1). Brief success in the constructor guild appears related to aberrant morphology (the "price" of ecological "opportunism"), whereas extended success is related to low levels of biologic complexity and conservative morphology and evolutionary development.

Mesozoic Extinction Events

The familial-level extinction rate and standing diversity data of Raup and Sepkoski (1982; 1984) and Sepkoski (1984) clearly indicate that there were four mass extinction events during the Mesozoic: one at the end of the Triassic (Norian), the second at the end of the Jurassic (Tithonian), the third at the end of the Cenomanian, and the last at the end of the Cretaceous (Maastrichtian). The evolutionary history of reef communities was influenced by all these events, but the latter involved a considerably more profound taxonomic turnover than the others.

Norian Extinctions

Late Norian (Rhaetic in Europe) reefs varied in size from major barrier reef systems and complexes to small, reef flat patch reefs. Their communities were dominated by scleractinians, calcareous sponges, and skeletal and non-skeletal algae organized into highly integrated guild structures including constructors, bafflers, and binders (Fig. 14.4). Species diversity was high in all guilds, but especially among the bafflers, binders, and dwellers (Table 14.3). These reefs were the culmination of a long (>30 million years), gradual reestablishment of sponges as important members of each of the building guilds and the appearance, rise, and domination of corals in the constructor guild.

The extinction event at the end of the Triassic was selective in its effect on the major reef-building higher taxa. The algae suffered least (Fig. 7.1); no major groups became extinct, but there was considerable extinction at the genus/species levels. The calcareous sponges suffered most (Fig. 8.1); after the Triassic, sphinctozoans never again were important members of any of the reef-building guilds. The end of the Triassic also brought a drastic change in composition and significance of the binder guild. Binding by various algae and calcareous sponges was a significant aspect of the frame-building process in Late Triassic reefs (Fig. 14.4); in Early Jurassic (Lias) and Bajocian reefs, however (Fig. 14.5), neither algae nor sponges were important binders and the significance of binding in the whole building process was much reduced.

The Norian extinction event was intermediate in its effect on scleractinians (Fig. 9.1). By the Late Norian, the scleractinians had supplanted sphinctozoans and inozoans as the volumetrically dominant reef-builders; when reef-building began again in the Late Lias, scleractinians were still the dominant builders. The Norian extinction represents a pause in the increasing dominance of scleractinians in the building of Late Triassic and Early Jurassic reefs.

Early Jurassic (Lias) reefs are known only from the Pliensbachian and Toarcian. Both Inozoa (Wendt, 1980a, pp. 173–174) and Scleractinia (Stanley, 1981, Fig. 2) were present in Hettangian–Sinemurian level-bottom communities, but they did not build reefs. In fact, most Liassic scleractinians were solitary, and the Pliensbachian and Toarcian reef-builders had small, tabular and branching rather than domal/cerioid coralla.

Thus, the Late Norian extinction event was relatively abrupt and a true biological crisis for reef communities. The Pliensbachian and Toarcian recovery involved a very gradual increase in size of coralla and a rise in importance of colonial corals. None of the algae or calcareous sponges that had been so important in Late Triassic reef communities participated in any building guilds of Liåssic reefs. However, a variety of algae and calcareous and siliceous sponges were important builders of Middle and Late Jurassic reefs, where they commonly exceed corals in both volume and diversity.

Tithonian Extinctions

The end of the Jurassic was marked by a remarkable change in the composition and structure of reef-building guilds. The encrusting/binding cyanophytes that were of considerable volumetric importance in Late Jurassic deeper-water reefs (Example 14.8) persisted into the Early Cretaceous but were not as important (Example 14.9). The long-ranging and locally important binder *Tubiphytes* became extinct at the end of the Jurassic.

Among the sponges, of particular significance was the extinction of numerous lower taxa of the Hexactinellida that were so very important as encruster substrates in deeper-water Late Jurassic reefs. After the Jurassic, neither hexactinellids nor demosponges were important members of any of the building guilds (Fig. 8.1). The Inozoa and Stromatoporoidea reached their Mesozoic acmes of genus/species diversity in the Late Jurassic but were only of local importance as builders in both Late Jurassic and Early Cretaceous reefs (Wendt, 1980a).

For the Scleractinia, the end of the Jurassic brought no extinctions at the family level, but of the 12 extant families at this time, 6 decreased and 5 increased in generic diversity across the Jurassic–Cretaceous boundary (Newell, 1971, Fig. 2). Beauvais (1984, p. 223) noted that reefs were generally rare in Tithonian rocks except in southern Germany and France and in Czechoslovakia; most of these were coral-built rather than sponge–algal reefs that were more typical of the Oxfordian and Kimmeridgian (Gwinner, 1976).

Although rudists decreased in generic diversity at the end of the Jurassic (Coogan, 1969, Fig. E234), they were dwellers, not builders, so this decline had minimal effect on reef communities.

Cenomanian Extinctions

Kauffman (April 1986, personal communication) has estimated that about 70% of the Cenomanian mollusc species, 35% of the mollusc genera, and 40% of the planktonic foraminiferal species became extinct at or near the end of the Cenomanian. By the Cenomanian, the rudist displacement of the scleractinians as the chief builders in reef communities was complete and so their history at the Cenomanian–Turonian boundary controls the history of reefs.

The data of Coogan (1969, Fig. E234) indicate that of the two reef-building Cenomanian rudist families, there was a sharp reduction in generic diversity of the Caprinidae and a slight increase in the Radiolitidae at this boundary. The Turonian marks the appearance of the reef-building Hippuritidae, which, along with the Radiolitidae, expanded in diversity during the succeeding stages of the Late Cretaceous to reach their generic maxima in the Maastrichtian. In the Antillean region (Kauffman and Sohl, 1974, pp. 449–457) and in France (Masse and Phillip, 1981, Fig. 14), the building of rudist/coral reefs and biostromes virtually ceased during the Early Turonian despite the presence of five rudist families in level-bottom communities of this age (Coogan, 1969, Fig. E234).

Maastrichtian Extinctions

Now we come to the 'type extinction' at the end of the Cretaceous.
(McLaren, 1983, p. 321)

The extinction event at the end of the Cretaceous (end of the Maastrichtian) was profound by any measure of the taxa involved and was catastrophic in its effects on virtually all marine communities and ecosystems, regardless of whether they were level-bottom, reef, or pelagic. However, the effects were not uniform; Tethyan (tropical) taxa suffered higher extinction rates than non-Tethyan (temperate); nannoplankton, planktonic foraminifera, and ammonoids suffered higher extinction than deeper-water benthic taxa. In terrestrial communities, vertebrates suffered higher extinction than vascular plants. Newell (1971, pp. 13–15) has discussed the extinction's effects on reef communities and speculated on its cause, and McLaren (1983) has reviewed evidence suggesting that it was of remarkably brief geologic duration (i.e., its effects can be recognized at a single bedding plane). However, Kauffman (1979; 1984, pp. 185–190) has argued that complete stratigraphic sections containing the Maastrichtian–Paleocene boundary are very rare and that most rudists were extinct as much as two million years *before* the end of the Maastrichtian. Numerous other authors (summarized by McLaren, 1983) have discussed possible causes for this extinction event (see also Chap. 15).

Maastrichtian reef communities were dominated by rudists, especially Radiolitidae and Hippuritidae; encrusting solenoporacean and coralline algae were minor contributors to the binder guild. The abundance, diversity of higher taxa, and overall significance of the baffler, dweller, and destroyer guilds was low relative to Late Jurassic–Early Cretaceous reef communities and also to many Late Cretaceous level-bottom communities. Thus, the abrupt cessation of photic zone reef-building near the end of the Cretaceous directly resulted from the extinction or near-extinction of rudists, scleractinians, solenoporaceans, and corallinaceans.

The Maastrichtian was the time of maximum familial and generic diversity of the reef-building rudists (Caprinidae, Radiolitidae, Hippuritidae; Coogan, 1969, Fig. E234); no rudists, either in reef or level-bottom communities, survived to the Paleocene (Fig. 10.1). Solenoporaceans and corallinaceans did survive the extinction, but at vastly reduced abundance and diversity; solenopores finally became extinct during the Miocene (Fig. 7.1) after nearly 500 million years of association with reef communities. The rapid post-Eocene expansion of corallinaceans was at least partially a delayed refilling of niches vacated by the post-Jurassic decline and extinction of solenoporaceans. The initial niche filling was in the Late Cretaceous.

Late Cretaceous was also the time of highest familial diversity of Scleractinia in their entire evolutionary history (Wells, 1956, p. F363). At the end of the Cretaceous, only 2 families became extinct, whereas during the Early Cenozoic, 5 additional families that had survived the Maastrichtian extinction became extinct. Only 4 new families appeared during the entire Cenozoic. At the genus level, scleractinian diversity abruptly dropped from about 90–110 to about 30–45 (Stanley, 1981, Fig. 2; Newell, 1971, Fig. 5). Unfortunately, the changes in proportions of colonial/solitary species/genera from the Maastrichtian to the Paleocene are not shown or discussed by Coates and Oliver (1973, Figs. 1, 2, pp. 6, 7).

Although poriferans were unimportant in Maastrichtian frame-building reef guilds, they were present in adjacent level-bottom communities in reduced abundance from their earlier (Late Jurassic–Early Cretaceous) maxima (Fig. 8.1). The Maastrichtian marked the extinction of Stromatoporoidea and the near-extinction of Sphinctozoa, Inozoa, Demospongiae, and Hexactinellida; no sponges were important in the building of pre-Quaternary Cenozoic reefs. Sclerosponges and chaetetids are locally important as builders of Holocene reefs, and demosponges are of major importance in Holocene baffler, binder, and destroyer guilds (discussed in Part I). Nonetheless, there was no immediate filling of niches during the Cenozoic that became vacant by the extinction of rudists and solenoporaceans or by the reduction in abundance and diversity of scleractinians by any higher sponge taxa. Instead, the Paleocene–Early Eocene was a time of major reorganization of both composition and structure of photic zone reef communities prior to their major expansion in the Middle and Late Eocene.

15
Overview and Conclusions

DO COMMUNITIES EVOLVE?

Strictly speaking, ecological systems as such do not evolve.

(May, 1978, p. 161)

Evolutionary Time Scales

Biological evolution, in the very broad sense of change through time, can be viewed on different time scales as well as different areas and levels of integration of the ecological units involved. The time scales, areas, and ecological units are discussed below.

Ecological Time

Scope. A few tens of generations; a local area, such as a single reef or reef system; a relatively small number of species populations.

Discussion. These changes are regarded as short-term adjustments, displacements, and replacements in the sizes and ranges of populations and the diversities and boundaries of communities in response to brief stochastic events. They are relatively rapid and reach an ecological equilibrium in a matter of a few tens of generations, as in island populations, communities (numerous examples in Cody and Diamond, 1975), recurrent ecological successions (e.g., some reef communities; discussed in Chap. 3) in individual reefs, and allogenic ecologic successions.

As individuals, populations, and communities undergo perturbations from stochastic events, they may be differentially selected for short-term, local success or failure. These changes during ecological time may initiate later evolutionary speciation, but the duration of ecological time is too brief for full speciation to occur.

Evolutionary Time

... natural selection acts almost invariably on individuals or groups of individuals. Populations, much less communities of interacting populations, cannot be regarded as units subject to Darwinian evolution.

(May, 1978, p. 161)

Populations that live together evolve together. Populations evolutionarily shape one another.

(Roughgarden, 1979, p. 451)

Scope. A few hundreds or thousands of generations; a regional area containing numerous species populations.

Discussion. This time scale includes the classical and synthetic Darwinian evolution, microevolution (Goldschmidt, 1940), and phyletic gradualism and punctuated equilibria (Eldredge and Gould, 1972). It results from individual selection, may involve coevolution, symbiosis, and commensalism of paired taxa (so very important in Holocene reef communities), and is rather randomly distributed through geologic time. Evolutionary time also involves complete (global) extinction of species; these extinction events are also rather randomly distributed in geological time (background extinction; Raup and Sepkoski, 1982). Background extinctions generally do not require major reorganization of ecological systems.

Most species of reef-builders are characterized by slow speciation rates, but some reef environments seem to have been favorable sites for local speciation events (Fagerstrom, 1983). The long-term phyletic evolution of numerous higher reef-building taxa has occurred in reef communities. However, most stratigraphic sequences containing reef communities are not sufficiently long or complete to provide adequate documentation to support phyletic gradualism. Instead, reef species seem to appear suddenly, maintain morphologic stasis through extended periods, and become extinct without obvious direct descendants (i.e., punctuated equilibria).

Geological Time

... the forces shaping natural selection among individuals involve all manner of biological interactions with other species ... Therefore in a sense constellations of species can be viewed as evolving together within a conventional

Darwinian framework . . . evolution produces patterns at the level of ecological systems . . . patterns (in ecological systems) are anchored in the interplay of biological relations that act to confer specific advantages or disadvantages on individual organisms.

(May, 1978, p. 161)

Scope. Tens of thousands to millions of years; areas of provincial to global scale involving hundreds or thousands of species and numerous higher taxa.

Discussion. This type of evolution results from species selection (Stanley, 1975) and/or community selection and may involve macroevolution (Goldschmidt, 1940; Stanley, 1979) and quantum evolution (Simpson, 1944). It is well-documented by the fossil record; some aspects appear to have been random in geologic time, whereas others occurred at times of rapid diversification of taxa at both high and low levels. Conversely, there are also well-documented records of both random (background) and rapid (mass) extinction events that affected taxa at high and low levels (Padian et al., 1984). The pace of evolutionary radiation of higher taxa was generally much slower than that of mass extinction. Slow radiation produced relatively gradual changes in the organization of ecological systems. In contrast, some mass extinction events were geologically brief, produced catastrophic disorganization of ecological systems, and had recovery times lasting millions of years. The periods between mass extinction events are much longer than the periods of extinction or recovery and are characterized by relatively stable community composition (higher taxa) and structure.

The emphasis in Part I was on the evolution of Holocene reef communities at the scale of ecologic time; in Parts II and III, emphasis was on evolution at the scale of geologic time.

Level-bottom Community Evolution

The evolution of marine invertebrate communities in geologic time has been examined for both level-bottom and reef communities. Among the earliest was an attempt to establish recurrent associations of high level taxa having prolonged stratigraphic ranges, subdivide these associations into shorter-range communities, and broadly outline the relative longevities of the associations and communities (Bretsky, 1968). Bretsky's study was confined to Late Ordovician–Late Permian level-bottom communities. He recognized five "associations" of variable duration that were closely related to substrate grain size and presumed location with respect to the shoreline. He concluded that associations and communities living on fine-grained substrates (offshore?) evolved more slowly than those living on coarser-grained (onshore?) substrates (cf. Taylor and Sheehan, 1968) and that environmental instability was correlated with association/community longevity.

Other studies of the evolution of level-bottom communities (e.g., Sep-koski and Sheehan, 1983) indicate that "... major new community types appeared first in nearshore settings and then expanded into offshore set-tings, despite higher rates of species-level evolution in the offshore hab-itats" (Jablonski, et al., 1983) of higher species diversity. However, the enormous data on the classical level-bottom Ordovician faunas of Wales includes eight communities of variable duration and diversities (Lockley, 1983) but fails to support either the conclusions of Bretsky (1968) or Sep-koski and Sheehan (1983). The British brachiopod-dominated communities also occur in a spectrum of substrates from coarse to fine-grained, but there is little evidence that they shifted substrates (except for the *Dal-manella* Community; Lockley, 1983, pp. 139–141) during their strati-graphic range. The highest taxonomic diversity occurred on substrates of intermediate grain sizes (calcareous silts and muds) in mid-shelf locations. Furthermore, the most stable and persistent associations/communities included those of low diversity in relatively offshore, deeper-water loca-tions; others of high diversity were in mid-shelf, shallower-water (not near-shore) locations. The most rapid community evolution occurred in those communities that occupied coarse substrates in shoreline locations.

The above contradictory examples suggest that it may still be somewhat premature to generalize concerning such aspects of geological evolution of level-bottom communities as (1) location of high or low diversity com-munities, (2) which communities have high or low rates of speciation (cf. Lewin, 1983), and (3) which types and locations of communities are geo-logically most durable. Can reef communities provide any more satisfac-tory answers to these and other important questions?

REEF COMMUNITY EVOLUTION

Patterns in Geologic Time

> ... the history of (reef) communities is not simply a quiet and gradual prolif-eration of lineages ... (it) involves dramatic and disconnected episodes, repeated radiations, stagnation, replacement of dominant groups ... selective extinction and even worldwide obliteration of entire communities leaving ecological vac-uums ...
>
> (Newell, 1971, p. 7)

Community evolutionary patterns (Fig. 15.1) consist of an interplay among extinction, recovery/radiation, and stability of composition and structure. Reef communities are among the oldest communities (at least two-billion

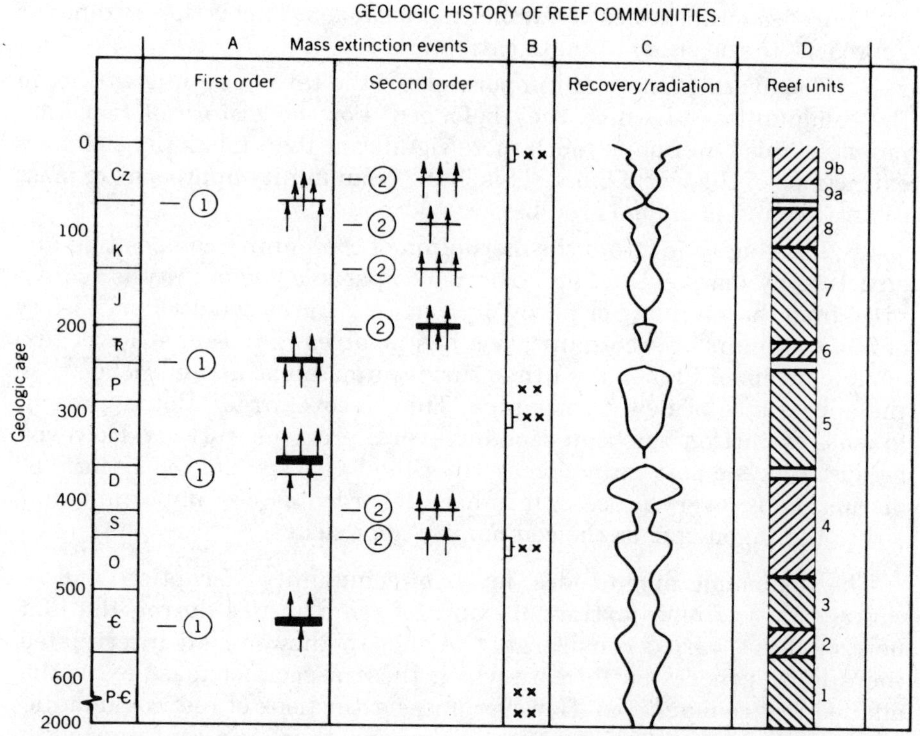

GEOLOGIC HISTORY OF REEF COMMUNITIES.

Figure 15.1. Summary of evolutionary history of reef communities through geologic time. A. Reefs and first/second order mass extinction events; arrows indicate extinction/continuity of reef-building higher taxa; blackened bars indicate brief episodes of global extinction of reef communities. B. Brief episodes and longer intervals (in brackets) of continental glaciation. C. Intervals of recovery/radiation and stabilization. D. Major reef ecologic–evolutionary units. Absolute age in hundred million years. Symbols for geologic periods conventional; C = Carboniferous, Cz = Cenozoic.

years old) on earth and have had a nearly continuous history of overall stability punctuated by several short-term episodes of disruption and reorganization. Each of these aspects of reef history (extinction, recovery, stability) will be considered separately before discussion of their interrelations.

Extinction; Disruption

The magnitude and effects of mass extinction events may be assessed by three different but interrelated criteria:

a. The number of taxa involved, their level in the taxonomic hierarchy, and the rate of their extinction. This has been the approach taken by most previous workers. Thus, the extinction of the last species in a slowly declining higher taxon is weighted as heavily as the simultaneous extinction of several species of another higher taxon. This is the "taxonomic approach" to the study of mass extinction.

b.   The overall functional importance of the taxa becoming extinct in the communities to which they belonged. For the history of reef communities, this criterion is much more significant than tabulations of mass extinctions of the world biota. This is the "community approach" to mass extinction and is emphasized below.

c.   The "lag time" from the disruption of community composition and structure by mass extinction before a comparable community is reorganized from the surviving or newly evolved taxa. In the evolutionary history of reef communities, reorganization has involved radiation at lower taxonomic levels of higher taxa that survived mass extinction rather than the appearance of new higher taxa. This "recovery/radiation approach" to mass extinction has been used by several previous workers. However, because this is a post-extinction or "after-the-fact" aspect of the extinction–disruption–recovery process, it is here regarded as less important than either the taxonomic or the community approaches.

The taxonomic magnitudes, levels of community disruption, and recovery times of mass extinctions on reef communities during the Phanerozoic have varied considerably. Although they are all interrelated, there is no general pattern by which these aspects of mass extinction affected reef communities. However, mass extinctions of reef communities can be conveniently (not "naturally" because there is a continuous gradation in their severity and effect on reef communities) subdivided into two levels of magnitude:

a.   *First order extinctions.* These were characterized by high extinction rates or "near-extinction" of higher taxa that were dominant members of one or more reef-building guilds. As a result, the level of community disruption was so great that its effect is best described as a *collapse,* and reorganization of the community required major *rebuilding.* This level of mass extinction is here termed the "annihilation/collapse/rebuild scenario."

b.   *Second order extinctions.* These were characterized by high extinction rates of lower taxa that were important members of one or more reef-building guilds. The level of disruption of the community may be described as a *crisis* and its reorganization as a *revival* in the abundance and diversity of surviving or new lower taxa. This level is here termed the "high impact/crisis/revival scenario."

Annihilation/Collapse/Rebuild: Examples. During the Phanerozoic there were four first order mass extinction events (Fig. 15.1A): the first came near the end of the Early Cambrian (end of the Botomian Stage), the second during the Late Devonian, the third at the end of the Permian

TABLE 15.1. Characteristics of Four First Order Mass Extinction Events During the Phanerozoic Evolution of Reef Communities

Annihilation Stage	Higher Taxa Involved[a] (Extinction/Near-extinction)	Rebuilding Time[b]
A. Maastrichtian	Hippuritacea, Scleractinia, Stromatoporoidea, other Porifera	Virtually none
B. Tatarian	Several calcareous algae, various sponges, Bryozoa	Scythian Stage ($\cong$ 5 ma)[b]
C. Late Devonian (Frasnian–Famennian)	Stromatoporoidea, Tabulata, Rugosa	Tournaisian Stage ($\cong$ 8 ma)[b]
D. Botomian	Archaeocyatha	Middle Cambrian ($\cong$ 10 ma)[b]

[a]In order of decreasing importance as reef-builders.
[b]ma = million years.

(Tatarian/Dzhulfian/Guadalupian Stage), and the last near the end of the Cretaceous (Maastrichtian Stage). Newell (1972) was the first to recognize and characterize these four mass extinctions. The features of each of these events that were important to reef communities are summarized in Table 15.1 and discussed below.

At the end of the Botomian, a sharp reduction (not extinction) in abundance and diversity of archaeocyathids was accompanied by a reduction (not cessation) in abundance and size of reefs. Archaeocyathids did not become extinct until the Late Cambrian, and algae of several types continued to build reefs during the Middle Cambrian–Early Ordovician that had guild structures quite similar to Precambrian reefs.

Although the taxa involved were different, the pattern of the Frasnian extinctions was quite similar to that of the Early Cambrian. Stromatoporoids, various algae, and corals in different proportions had built reefs during the Late Ordovician–Middle Devonian. During the Frasnian, the importance of stromatoporoids and corals declined; at the end of the Frasnian, nearly all stromatoporoids and most corals became extinct and almost everywhere the building of reefs also ended. However, locally (e.g., Canning Basin, Western Australia), a variety of algae continued to build reefs of surprisingly large sizes during the Famennian and it was not until the earliest Carboniferous (Tournaisian) that reef-building completely ceased.

In both the end of the Early Cambrian and Frasnian extinction events, it was algae, particularly *Renalcis,* and stromatolites that kept the reef construction process going. However, in the Frasnian crisis, there was a delayed but real cessation of reef-building during the Tournaisian, whereas reef-building on a modest scale apparently continued unbroken during the decline and eventual extinction of the archaeocyathids during the Middle–Late Cambrian. Late Paleozoic (Visean–Tatarian) reefs were built by organisms only remotely related to builders of middle Paleozoic reefs.

Late Permian reef-building guilds were dominated by sphinctozoans, inozoans, a smaller number of demosponges of the baffler guild, rhodophyte and codiacean ("phylloid") algae, and problematic algal-like forms *(Tubiphytes; Archaeolithoporella,* etc; binder guild). These taxa are almost unknown from Lower Triassic rocks, and no Early Triassic reefs are known in the world (a period of about 5–6 million years). When reef-building resumed in the Middle Triassic, many of the same *lower* taxa of sphinctozoans and inozoans and some demosponge higher taxa "reappeared" as the chief builders. Phylloid algae and *Archaeolithoporella* were never important after the Permian and *Tubiphytes* was not important in the earliest Mesozoic Alpine reefs.

Late Cretaceous (Maastrichtian) reefs were dominated by the radiolitid and hippuritid rudists. Scleractinians, coralline algae, and locally stromatoporoids were present, but much less important than the rudists. During the Maastrichtian, the rudists and stromatoporoids became extinct.

The Maastrichtian extinction scenario is essentially the same as for the preceding first order extinctions with two exceptions:

a.   Extinction of rudists that dominated Late Cretaceous constructor guilds was final. The "survivors" that continued the reef-building process in the early Cenozoic were chiefly scleractinians (constructor guild) belonging to families with long Mesozoic histories and crustose coralline rhodophytes.

b.   Cessation of reef-building during the Paleocene did not occur. Wray (1969; 1977, pp. 136–137) mentioned algal-rich Paleocene reefs in Libya; small, coral–algal reefs near Vigny in northwestern France (Cros and Lucas, 1982), and also near Banija, Yugoslavia (Babić et al., 1976), have been dated as Paleocene. Small, bryozoan-built deep-water reefs were also locally present in Denmark (Thomsen, 1983).

In summary, each of these four "annihilation/collapse/rebuild" extinction events differs from the others with regard to (1) the higher taxa involved and the magnitude of the "taxonomic impact," (2) the rate of extinction and the degree of collapse and structural disruption of the community, and (3) the time required to rebuild a new reef community. Thus, there was no uniform pattern among the three aspects of this first order mass extinction scenario.

High Impact/Crisis/Revival: Examples. During the Phanerozoic, there were six (or seven) second order mass extinction events in the history of

TABLE 15.2. Characteristics of Six Second Order Mass Extinction Events During the Phanerozoic Evolution of Reef Communities

Time of High Impact	Taxa Involved	Time for Revival[a]
A. Late Eocene	Scleractinia	Early Rupelian ($\cong$ 2–3 ma)[a]
B. Late Cenomanian	Hippuritacea	Turonian ($\cong$ 2 ma)[a]
C. Tithonian	Several algae, siliceous sponges, Scleractinia	Early Berriasian ($\cong$ 3–5 ma)[a]
D. Norian/Rhaetian	Calcareous sponges, Scleractinia	Hettangian–Sinemurian ($\cong$ 10 ma)[a]
E. Late Silurian	Stromatoporoidea, colonial corals	Early Gedinnian ($\cong$ 3–5 ma)[a]
F. Ashgillian/Hirnantian	Bryozoa, Crinoidea, Solenoporacea	Llandoverian ($\cong$ 5–8 ma)[a]

[a]ma = million years.

reef communities (Fig. 15.1A; Table 15.2). Each was characterized by important declines in the diversity of lower taxa and continuity of higher taxa ("root stocks") of reef-builders and generally brief periods of reduced size and abundance of reefs before their revival.

The Cenozoic history of Scleractinia is a particularly interesting example of two types of second order scenarios, neither of which appeared in the compilation of marine mass extinctions by Raup and Sepkoski (1982). Of the 18 families present in the Eocene, 4 became extinct at the end of the Eocene, 3 decreased in generic diversity, and 5 continued into the Oligocene relatively unchanged (Newell, 1971, Fig. 2). Six Eocene families increased in generic diversity in the Oligocene and 1 new family appeared. There was a total of about 72 Middle Eocene scleractinian genera and about 68 in the Middle Oligocene (Newell, 1971, Fig. 5). By contrast, generic diversity dropped from about 80 in the Middle Miocene to about 60 in the Middle Pliocene (Newell, 1971, Fig. 5; cf. Stanley, 1981, Fig. 2). So, for the corals, the end of the Eocene was a family-level extinction event and the Miocene–Pliocene was a genus-level event. However, despite these fluctuations in coral diversity, the reef-building process was generally continuous throughout the Cenozoic.

Background Extinctions. In the history of all communities, there is the rather uniform and continuous (unclumped; normal; background) extinction and relaylike replacement of lower taxa in the framework of evolutionary time. This short-term gradualistic process produces almost no disorganization–reorganization of community structure. In the intervals between mass extinction events, this extinction–replacement process can rarely be distinguished from the common (often random) processes of emigration/immigration, punctuated equilibria, pseudo-extinction, ecologic succession, or even incomplete sampling of the community.

Extinction Rates. Raup and Sepkoski (1982) distinguished between background extinction (2–4.6 families/million years) and mass extinction rates (about 11–19 families/million years). Some mass extinctions appear to be remarkably short events (reviewed by McLaren, 1983), whereas others represent a much more gradual reduction in diversity, commonly with an abrupt termination at a major stratigraphic boundary (Kauffman, 1979; 1984). Most interpretations of mass extinction events and the data upon which they are based certainly emphasize the abrupt, short-duration examples. Unfortunately, the stage-by-stage analysis of reef communities presented in Chapters 11–14 provides little new data regarding extinction rates of reef-building higher taxa. Data on extinction rates of reef-building families were comingled with the larger data-base by Raup and Sepkoski (1982) and McLaren (1983).

Periodicity. The data in Tables 15.1 and 15.2 for changes in composition and structure of most reef communities clearly indicate their overall correlation with mass extinctions of the earth's total biota. Numerous authors have suggested that these biotic changes and their causative factor(s) occur in a cyclic or periodic manner (many such cycles are described in Holland and Trendall, 1984).

The best-documented (taxonomically and temporally) mass extinction event was at the end of the Cretaceous; it was brief and produced a virtual collapse of nearly all terrestrial and marine ecosystems, including reefs. Using this as a temporal baseline (65–66 million years ago), Raup and Sepkoski (1984; also discussed by Kitchell and Pena, 1984; Hoffman, 1985; and Gould, 1985) described several types of greater-than-average extinction rates for families of marine organisms; they were spaced at approximately 26-million year intervals during the Mesozoic and Cenozoic. The general "fit" of extinction rates to the 26-million year cycle is variable among the cycles during the earlier Mesozoic but is nearly perfect during the Late Cretaceous–Miocene.

Between the end of the Permian and the beginning of the Paleocene, there are 8 of these 26-million year "events" of presumed mass extinction. Two of them (end of Permian; end of Cretaceous) precisely coincide with first order extinctions for reef communities and 2 (end of Tithonian; end of Cenomanian) precisely coincide with second order reef extinctions. Another comes very close to the Norian/Rhaetic second order reef extinction, but the remaining 3 (Pliensbachian, Callovian, Aptian) 26-million year "events" appear to have had little influence on reef community evolution.

There are two 26-million year intervals during the Cenozoic (end of

Eocene; middle of Miocene) that had mixed effects on communities and ecosystems. The Eocene–Oligocene boundary marks one of the most profound taxonomic turnovers in the entire history of terrestrial mammalian evolution. For reef-building scleractinians, turnover at the family level was relatively minor and so far as generic diversity is concerned, this boundary was rather inconsequential (Newell, 1971, Figs. 2, 5; Stanley, 1981, Fig. 2). The fossil record of Oligocene crustose coralline algae is poor (Steneck, 1983, Fig. 1), despite the general abundance of Caribbean reefs of this age.

By contrast, the most recent of the Raup and Sepkoski (1984) mass extinction events (mid-Miocene) had virtually no effect on terrestrial mammals. For corals, however, this was a time of rapid decline for generic, but not familial, diversity. However, in the Mediterranean, the most important decline in reef-building was in the Late Miocene (Messinian) and resulted from hypersalinity; in the Caribbean, important reef-building was generally continuous during the Ologocene–Holocene (albeit at progressively decresed generic/specific diversity since the Miocene).

Causes. Numerous causal factors have been invoked to explain mass extinctions (reviewed by Herman, 1981; Stanley, 1984b, pp. 71–74). The suggested causes can be divided into those that are largely biotic (discussed below) and those that are largely abiotic. The general abruptness of mass extinctions, their apparent geological synchroneity, global extent, and the diversity of the taxa and communities involved have led most previous authors to favor abiotic causes (Table 15.3). During the last decade, several symposia and conferences have been convened to consider the merits of various abiotic causal factors (e.g., Silver and Schultz, 1982; Berggren and Van Couvering, 1984; Holland and Trendall, 1984). These meetings have adjourned with a better understanding of the problems involved but without substantial agreement regarding the factors chiefly responsible. More than one factor is still championed for every mass extinction event. However, a general consensus appears to be emerging which is that the impact of a large extraterrestrial object (bolide) was involved in the end of the Cretaceous event.

Of the two major controls over sea-level change (diastrophic; glacial eustatic; Table 15.3) and the attendant transgressions and regressions across continental shelves, there is little doubt that diastrophism has been more important. During Pleistocene glacial maxima, there was only a 6% reduction of the area of continental shelves covered by seas; by contrast, Schopf (1974) estimated a 30% reduction at the end of the Permian due to diastrophic causes. These include movements of spreading ridges, buckling of continental margins, emplacement of granitic plutons, isostatic subsidence of volcanic cones, and epeirogeny of cratons.

There have only been 6 major glacial periods: 2 in the Precambrian (approx. 2100 and 675 million years ago) and those in the Late Ordovician,

TABLE 15.3. Suggested Abiotic Causal Factors for Global Mass Extinction Events During the Phanerozoic

Causal Factors	Geologic Boundary; General	Selected Ref.
I. Extraterrestrial (bolides: asteroids, meteorites; others)		
	a. Eocene–Oligocene	Alvarez et al., 1982
	b. Cretaceous–Cenozoic	Alvarez et al., 1980
	C. Frasnian–Famennian	McLaren, 1984; 1985
	d. General	Silver and Schultz, 1982; McLaren, 1983
II. Terrestrial		
A. Sea-level fluctuations		
1. Diastropic		
	a. Triassic–Jurassic	Hallam, 1981a
	b. Permo-Triassic	Schopf, 1974; Forney, 1975
	c. Frasnian–Famennian	Johnson et al., 1985
	d. General	Newell, 1967; Vail et al., 1977; Hallam, 1984
2. Glacial eustatic	a. Pleistocene	Wise and Schopf, 1981; Hopley, 1982, pp. 158–171; Chapter 6 herein
	b. Neogene	Stanley, 1982
	c. Ordovician–Silurian	Berry and Boucot, 1973; Sheehan, 1973, 1975
B. Temperature		
	a. General	Fischer and Arthur, 1977; Stanley, 1984a, 1984b
C. Chemical		
1. Salinity		
	a. Late Miocene	Adams et al., 1977; Benson, 1984
	b. Permo-Triassic	Fischer, 1965; Stevens, 1977; Benson, 1984
2. Dissolved oxygen		
	a. Jurassic (Toarcian)	Hallam, 1981b
	b. Frasnian–Famennian	Eder and Franke, 1982
D. Mixed factors		
	a. Cretaceous–Cenozoic	Kauffman, 1984

Late Carboniferous, mid-Permian, and the late Cenozoic (Fig. 15.1B). Only the Late Ordovician glaciation coincides with a mass extinction event.

Significant globally synchronous changes in temperature, salinity, and dissolved oxygen of the world ocean share a common problem: the general physical/chemical stability of such an enormous volume of water. If marine mass extinctions are as rapid as some current data suggest, it becomes difficult to establish mechanisms to produce the necessary rapid changes in either temperature or water chemistry. Pleistocene glacial temperatures in the tropics were just a few degrees (2–3°C?) lower than interglacial temperatures and generally within the tolerance limits of most Holocene coral and coralline algal species. The waxing and waning of Pleistocene glacial ice had little effect on the salinity of tropical water because the volume of glacial melt water was so small relative to that of seawater.

Biotic Causes. Similarly, the world biota is so large, complex, and subdivided into so many subsystems (provinces, communities, and other smaller units) that it slowly "absorbs" or modifies most purely biotic impacting events or relegates their effects to local or regional areas. For example, an outbreak of large populations of the starfish *Acanthaster planci* that occurred over a large area of the Indo-Pacific during the 1960s to 1980s inflicted severe damage to numerous reefs. Although geologically "instantaneous" and locally catastrophic, it did not produce mass extinction of any reef-building species and had no effect on Atlantic Province reefs. In many Indo-Pacific reefs, the effects from this outbreak were comparable to the damage and recovery from a major cyclone or tsunami. Thus, biologic factors such as predation and competition may account for much of the background extinction of Raup and Sepkoski (1982) but have not been consequential agents of global mass extinction of reef communities.

Recovery/Radiation (Fig. 15.1C)

The reorganization and recovery aspect of the evolution of populations and communities following mass extinction is generally called radiation or adaptive radiation (for a general discussion see Bambach, 1985, pp. 240–249). It involves the reestablishment of a stable structure, and in reef communities, the commencement of the building process. Once recovery is complete, the community may maintain remarkable stability for extended geological intervals. The pace of reestablishment and recovery usually is gradual and progressive, with diversification and taxonomic turnover of lower taxa by micro- and macroevolutionary processes (gradualism; punctuated equilibrium) and background extinction.

Gradualism. Slow radiation of reef communities, in a geologic time-frame, has taken three forms:

a.   Immigration of established stocks of higher taxa from level-bottoms to reefs followed by rapid diversification, guild overlap, and niche partitioning. For example, the Sphinctozoa had a long, relatively uneventful mid-Paleozoic history in level-bottom communities but appear suddenly in Early Permian reefs (Fig. 8.1), where they rapidly diversified to become major building taxa in two guilds (baffler; binder). The history of the Chaetetida is essentially the same but less dramatic (Fig. 8.1).

b. The gradual diversification, guild overlap, and niche partitioning of lower taxa within a higher taxon (root stock) that was already well-established in reef communities. Thus, the Hexactinellida have a very long history in reef communities but had three episodes of diversification and increased importance in the building guilds (Ordovician; Permian; Jurassic; Fig. 8.1). The same general pattern of decline and later radiation took place in the reef-building scleractinians during the Jurassic, Late Cretaceous–Early Eocene, Late Eocene–Oligocene, and, to a lesser degree, in the Late Miocene–Holocene intervals (Fig. 9.1).

c. The intracommunity appearance, reappearance, or increased importance of new adaptive forms from coexisting different higher taxa. These new forms typically display considerable guild overlap. For example, the histories of evolutionary diversification and guild membership (as bafflers and binders) of the Sphinctozoa, Inozoa, and Demospongiae in Permian–Triassic reef communities are remarkably similar (Fig. 8.1). They appear to be broadly convergent, simultaneously successful adaptations to the reef environment by different higher taxa. A different situation involved the slow displacement of the Scleractinia by the coexisting rudists as the dominant members of the constructor guild in Early Cretaceous reefs; by the Late Cretaceous, rudists had replaced scleractinians as the dominant constructors.

Punctuated. The evolutionary histories of several higher taxa are intimately tied to the building guilds of reef communities. Their earliest, or nearly earliest, members appear (presumably by macroevolution) in reef communities, commonly as dwellers; they increase in importance there and are only rarely of significance in level-bottoms. For most of these higher taxa, their history as reef-builders consists of sudden appearance, followed by diversification, dominance, and decline or mass extinction (Herman, 1981, p. 106).

The rates of diversification of lower taxa within these phyletic lineages and their guild membership are highly varied. During the approximately 25-million year interval from the first appearance of the Scleractinia as dwellers in Middle Triassic (Anisian) reefs to their domination of the constructor guild in the Late Triassic (Norian; Rhaetian), they increased in both diversity (to about 30 genera and 70 species) and in corallum size (Fig. 9.1). The occurrence and evolutionary histories of the Stromatoporoidea and most algae are also directly linked to their presence in reef communities. Even among separate phyletic lineages, such as the morphologically convergent codiacean and rhodophyte "phylloid" algae of the

Carboniferous–Permian, their main evolutionary history and greatest abundance occurred in reef communities.

Stability (Fig. 15.1C)

Subsequent to mass extinction and recovery/radiation, the geologic history of reef communities is characterized by extended intervals of overall stability in their higher taxonomic composition and guild structure. The best example of such prolonged stability of skeletal reefs is the stromatoporoid/coral/algal/bryozoan reefs of the Middle Ordovician (Llanvirnian) through early Late Devonian (Frasnian), an interval of about 100 million years (Chap. 12). By contrast, non-skeletal stromatolitic/thrombolitic Precambrian reefs persisted for nearly one billion years (Chap. 7) and small, poorly skeletonized Early Cambrian archaeocyathid reefs for only about 20 million years (Chap. 11).

The chief exception to the above generalization regarding stability came during the Late Paleozoic (Famennian–Permian; Chap. 13). Famennian reefs were built by various algae (Example 13.1). There are virtually no Tournaisian reefs. Visean reefs were built by rugose corals, non-skeletal algae, chaetetids, and bryozoans (Examples 13.2, 13.3). Late Carboniferous reefs were built by chaetetids and phylloid algae (Examples 13.4, 13.5), Early Permian reefs by aberrant brachiopods and calcareous sponges (Example 13.6), and Late Permian by a great variety of taxa (Example 13.7). Various skeletal algae played a continuously important role throughout the Late Paleozoic as important members of binder and baffler guilds and overlapped the constructor guild.

Middle Triassic–Early Cretaceous reef-building also had a history of moderate instability in composition and guild structure; in those communities, however, the fluctuations in relative importance primarily involved scleractinians (Fig. 9.1) and poriferans (both calcareous and siliceous; Fig. 8.1). Rudists (Fig. 10.1) dominated Late Cretaceous reef construction and provided nearly 50 million years of overall stability to the building guilds.

Interrelations

The overall pattern of evolution of skeletal Phanerozoic reef communities is spindle-shaped, consisting of a succession of mass extinctions resulting in reduced abundance (and usually in the reduced size of reefs), followed by variously prolonged periods of radiation and stability (Fig. 15.1C). Rates of extinction are generally rapid relative to radiation, and stability is usually longer than either extinction or radiation.

Most of the "spindles" have narrow bases, broaden slowly upward (temporally), and have sharply truncated (pinched) tops (Fig. 15.1C). The narrowness of the bases and the degree of pinching reflect the order (first; second) of the extinction event and its rate. The "flare" of the spindle reflects the recovery/radiation rate and the size, abundance, and skeletonization of the subsequent reefs. The "shoulder" of the spindle indicates the duration of the ensuing period of general community stability.

The history of reef community evolution may also be regarded as a "relaylike" succession of opportunistic communities, dominated by a variety of opportunistic higher taxa that filled ecological and evolutionary "vacuums" created by mass extinction. Following mass extinction, reef communities reorganized into guild and niche structures that were generally quite different from their predecessors.

COMPARISON WITH LEVEL-BOTTOMS

> The geologic history of reefs has a similar pattern to that . . . for level-bottom communities.
>
> (Sheehan, 1985, p. 48)

Most studies of the Phanerozoic history of life on earth inevitably emphasize the higher taxa (families, orders, classes) of level-bottom marine invertebrates because they are the most abundant and diverse and best-skeletonized.

However, Boucot (1983) distinguished between level-bottoms and reefs. He subdivided the Phanerozoic into 12 continuous level-bottom "ecologic–evolutionary units" and 5 "major reef community complexes," separated by 4 global non-reef intervals of varying duration. Earlier, Newell (1972) had also subdivided Phanerozoic history into 5 reef-building intervals and 4 short periods of "collapse." The building intervals and non-reef/collapse intervals of Boucot and Newell were only partially coincident in time (occurrence) and duration. Subsequently, Sheehan (1985) recognized 7 "reef intervals," 5 of which coincide with Boucot's "major reef community complexes"; Sheehan subdivided the single Mesozoic–Cenozoic "complex" of Boucot into 3 parts.

After comparing the data from mass extinction episodes (e.g., Raup and Sepkoski, 1982), Sepkoski's 3 Phanerozoic "Faunas," Boucot's (1983) 12 "ecologic–evolutionary units," and his own 7 "reef intervals," Sheehan reached the conclusion quoted at the beginning of this section. However, interpretation of the data presented here (Parts II and III) lead to a quite different conclusion.

Comparison of Reefs to the Three Phanerozoic Faunas

Sepkoski's (1979, 1981, 1984) "Faunas," based solely on skeletonized marine metazoans, are recognized by the following criteria:

a. *Cambrian Fauna:* contains classes that attained maximum familial diversity during the Cambrian (i.e., Trilobita, Inarticulata, Hyolitha, Monoplacophora, Eocrinoidea, and Pogonophora). He excluded all the important reef-builders because they are not metazoans (i.e. algae) or because he regards them as *perhaps* not metazoans (i.e., Archaeocyathida). There is essentially no relationship, then, between the history of Sepkoski's Cambrian Fauna and the evolution of reef communities.

b. *Paleozoic Fauna:* contains classes that reached their greatest familial diversity during the Ordovician–Permian. The classes containing reef-builders are Anthozoa, Sclerospongiae (i.e., Stromatoporoidea), Stenolaemata, Calcarea, and Crinoidea; the Fauna also contains 22 classes that have no reef-building families. Except for the important omission of algae, Sepkoski included all the Paleozoic reef-builders in this Fauna. However, the Calcarea were at least as important in building Mesozoic reefs as in building Paleozoic reefs.

c. *Mesozoic–Cenozoic Fauna:* includes a number of classes with their maximum familial diversities in the late Cenozoic. This fauna includes neither Scleractinia nor Rhodophyta, the chief reef-builders during this interval; the fauna thus bears little relation to the evolution of Mesozoic–Cenozoic reef communities. The Scleractinia reached their maximum familial diversity during the Late Cretaceous rather than the late Cenozoic and so are not included in *any* of Sepkoski's familial diversity curves.

Comparison of Reefs With Phanerozoic Floras

From the viewpoint of reef communities, the most serious flaw in Sepkoski's analyses is his exclusion of algae. This omission can be partly corrected by use of data from Chuvashov and Riding (1984). They recognized three Paleozoic floras based on the associations and relative importances of calcareous algae:

a. *Cambrian Flora:* dominated by reef-building Cyanophyta, possible Cyanophyta (Fig. 7.1), and non-reef-building Solenoporacea. This algal association was of major importance in early Paleozoic (Chap. 11) and mid-Paleozoic (Chap. 12) reef communities; in each case, it was accompanied by vastly different metazoan higher taxa.

b. *Ordovician Flora:* a higly varied association of reef-building algae, many of uncertain biological affinities. Although the association was present in most mid-Paleozoic reefs, it was nearly always of less importance than frame-building metazoans.

c. *Carboniferous Flora:* a varied association including "phylloid" Codiacea and Rhodophyta and several problematic forms (Fig. 7.1). This flora was very important in the building guilds of virtually all late Paleozoic reefs.

Chuvashov and Riding (1984, pp. 496–497) also noted that there were marked differences in the radiation and extinction rates for each of these Paleozoic floras and that the rates were generally much slower than for reef-building metazoans. Furthermore, there was a sharp reduction in importance of "reef-forming" and "debris-producing" calcareous algae during the Late Carboniferous–Early Permian interval (Chuvashov and Riding, 1984, Text-Figs. 5, 7, 9) that was not accompanied by increased metazoan extinction or radiation rates.

Two post-Paleozoic algal floras may be distinguished and both are intimately related to the evolution of reef communities (Fig. 7.1):

a. A Middle Triassic–Jurassic assemblage of Cyanophyta, the revived "groups" of Solenoporacea, and the problematical *Tubiphytes*. All these forms were important in Paleozoic reefs; they were decimated by the end of the Permian mass extinction event and radiated again in the Triassic and Jurassic (Fig. 7.1). They suffered only a decline in importance during the Late Triassic mass extinction, which had its chief impact on non-reef metazoans.

b. Cretaceous–Holocene algal floras are dominated by Chlorophyta and Rhodophyta; both groups are of major importance in reef communities and calcareous chlorophytes are also very significant in tropical level-bottom communities. The reef-building rhodophytes were present but volumetrically overwhelmed by rudists and corals during the Cretaceous. However, during the Eocene, they diversified to become the chief members of the binder guild in middle–late Cenozoic reef communities. The Eocene–Holocene revival and diversification of crustose Corallinacea are almost equally important to the success of Cenozoic reefs as the revival and diversification of Scleractinia at this same time. Unlike scleractinians, which briefly declined in importance at the end of the Eocene, the Eocene–Holocene record of calcareous algae is one of rather continuous expansion in abundance and diversity.

Reefs and Phanerozoic Poriferan Faunas

The Phanerozoic history of the Porifera may be subdivided into five natural assemblages that closely correspond to the evolution of reef communities (Fig. 8.1):

a. *Early Cambrian: Archaeocyathida.* The near-extinction of archaeocyathids at the end of the Early Cambrian and their final extinction during the Late Cambrian do not coincide with the extinction of many other higher taxa (Sepkoski, 1979, Figs. 3, 4).

b. *Middle Paleozoic (Early Ordovician–Late Devonian: Frasnian): Demospongiae and Stromatoporoidea.* The Late Ordovician second order mass extinction (Fig. 15.1A) had limited impact on these poriferan higher taxa.

c. *Carboniferous: Chaetetida.* Their near-extinction at the Carboniferous–Permian boundary is unrelated to the decline of any other major reef-building higher taxa.

d. *Permian; Middle Triassic: Sphinctozoa, Inozoa, and Demospongiae.*
Despite the decimation of these taxa at the end of the Permian, they revived during the Middle Triassic to dominate the reef-building guilds (Fig.
8.1). There is a reciprocal relation between the rising importance of Scleractinia during the Late Triassic and a general decline in importance of
sponges. Whether the relationship is one of cause and effect is uncertain.
The end of the Triassic (Norian) mass extinction coincides with the end
of sphinctozoans (but not of either inozoans or demosponges) as important
reef-builders.

e. *Middle Jurassic–Early Cretaceous.* A "grand revival" of numerous
higher sponge taxa with long prior histories as major reef-builders (Fig.
8.1). The end of the Cretaceous brought an abrupt end to the role of sponges
as important members of any reef-building guild.

Reefs and Phanerozoic Coral Faunas

Although the Phanerozoic evolution of corals is closely related to the evolution of reef communities, the relationship is not as close as as for either
algae or sponges. There were intervals of varying duration (e.g., Carboniferous–Permian, Middle Triassic, Late Cretaceous) when corals generally
were more important in level-bottom communities than in reefs. Furthermore, during the same intervals, reef corals were largely confined to
the dweller guild or overshadowed as constructors by other higher taxa.

However, during the Middle Ordovician–Late Devonian (Frasnian) and
Late Triassic–Early Cretaceous, corals were of major importance as reef-
builders and they have completely dominated the constructor guild since
the Early Eocene (Fig. 9.1). The earliest, or nearly the earliest, members
of each of the main coral taxa (Tabulata; Rugosa; Scleractinia) were reef
dwellers but quickly entered one or more of the building guilds.

Conclusions

The geologic history of reef communities is naturally subdivided into major
temporal units on the basis of their taxonomic composition and guild
structure. Boundaries between some of these units coincide with mass
extinction events of the world biota. Other boundaries coincide with major
macroevolutionary events in the geologic histories of the major reef-
building higher taxa. Still others are gradational and based on slow displacement of old communities by new ones of different composition and
guild structure.

Most previous analyses of the complete fossil record have emphasized
Phanerozoic skeletal, level-bottom metazoans and their mass extinctions;
these analyses have either ignored reef communities as separate ecologic
and evolutionary units or tried to make reef history conform to the extinction–recovery/radiation pattern of level-bottom communities. How-

ever, more careful analysis indicates that the evolutionary history of reef communities conforms rather poorly to most existing models.

Reefs and Extinction Events (Fig. 15.1A)

The end of the Permian and the Cretaceous first order "annihilation/collapse" events were indiscriminant as far as their impact on marine biotas was concerned. Reef communities were affected at least as powerfully as level-bottom and other communities. The recovery of reef communities during the Triassic was even longer than for level-bottom communities (5 million years vs. 1–2 million years). Conversely, the ends of the Early Cambrian and Frasnian extinctions seem to have affected reef communities more than non-reef communities. Extinction of higher reef-building taxa was more widespread and caused greater restructuring of reef communities than in level-bottoms.

Finally, the Late Ordovician (Ashgillian), Late Triassic (Norian) and Late Eocene extinctions affected non-reefs more than reef communities. The Eocene–Oligocene taxonomic turnover for higher taxa of terrestrial mammals was greater than for higher taxa of marine organisms but does not appear in the analysis of extinction by Raup and Sepkoski (1982). The high rate of genus-level turnover of reef corals from the Middle Miocene to the Pliocene has been recognized by only a few authors.

Thus, the four first order "annihilation/collapse" mass extinction events profoundly affected reef history and subdivided the evolution of reef communities into major ecologic–evolutionary units. However, the second order "high impact/crisis" extinctions had much less effect and are not as important in subdividing reef community evolution.

Reefs and Recovery/Radiation–Stabilization Events (Fig. 15.1C)

The evolution of reef communities is also strongly influenced by the history of macroevolutionary events in several reef-building higher taxa. These macroevolutionary events, followed by relatively rapid radiation and longer-term stability, have produced other major reef ecologic–evolutionary units that are not closely related to extinction events. The units based on radiation are:

a.   Precambrian radiation of stromatolite/thrombolite-forming algae about 2 billion years ago to form large reefs (boundstones and bafflestones) in rocks from 1.8-billion years old to the beginning of the Cambrian (570 million years ago). During the Early Cambrian, this flora was joined by a diverse group of problematic and porostromate cyanophytes that continued as major reef-builders until the Middle Ordovician, when they were displaced by skeletal metazoans. This same stable, algal-dominated, frame-building ecologic–evolutionary unit occurs in both the Precambrian and Middle Cambrian–Early Ordovician. It was interrupted during the Early Cambrian by archaeocyathid–algal reefs but survived the Early

Cambrian (Botomian) mass extinction almost unchanged by the loss of archaeocyathids. The origin–radiation–near-extinction of archaeocyathids during the Early Cambrian is like a "brief" (30-million year!) interlude within the 1.5-billion year (Precambrian–Early Ordovician) domination of reef-building processes by the Cyanophyta and problematic algae.

b.   Middle Ordovician origin and radiation of numerous higher taxa of skeletal frame-building metazoans. The first were bryozoans, then in rapid succession came stromatoporoids, demosponges, solenoporaceans, and tabulate and rugose corals. By the Late Ordovician, these skeletal metazoans had almost completely displaced the earlier algal-dominated reef communities.

c.   Middle Triassic and early Late Triassic reefs were built by calcareous sponges and algae that had survived the end of the Permian collapse of reef communities. These survivors underwent a second radiation during the Middle Triassic and were slowly displaced as the chief frame-builders by Scleractinia during the Late Triassic.

d.   During the Early–Late Cretaceous, the radiation of rudist bivalves gradually displaced scleractinians as the dominant frame-builders (constructor guild). The end of the Cenomanian second order mass extinction came after rudists had attained dominance, so that the Turonian was merely a pause of two million years in the history of rudist reef-building, followed by their revival during the Coniacean–Maastrichtian.

Reef Ecologic–Evolutionary Units

In summary, the geologic history of reef-building consists of 10 temporal units, each characterized by the establishment, radiation, stabilization, and extinction/decline of a characteristic association of higher taxa which comprise the reef community building guilds. These major reef-building units and reef-building higher taxa (in order of approximate volumetric importance) are (Fig. 15.1D):

a.   *Precambrian (2000–570 million years ago):* stromatolite and thrombolite-forming Cyanophyta (Unit 1).

b.   *Early Cambrian:* Archaeocyatha and problematic skeletal Cyanophyta (Unit 2).

c.   *Middle Cambrian–Early Ordovician:* spongiostromate and porostromate Cyanophyta, varied problematic Cyanophyta, and Demospongiae (Unit 3).

d.   *Middle Ordovician–early Late Devonian (Frasnian):* Stromatoporoidea, Tabulata, Rugosa, algae, and Bryozoa (Unit 4).

e.   *Late Devonian (Famennian)–Late Permian:* communities of highly varied taxa (including Chaetetida, Sphinctozoa, Inozoa, Demospongiae, Bryozoa, Brachiopoda, Crinoidea, and a great variety of algae), mostly members of the binder and baffler guilds; construction was chiefly by guild overlap (Unit 5).

 f. *Middle Triassic–Late Triassic (Carnian):* Sphinctozoa, Inozoa, and algae (Unit 6).

 g. *Late Triassic (Norian)–Early Cretaceous (Aptian):* Scleractinia in shallow water and a great variety of Porifera and several algae in deeper water (Unit 7).

 h. *Early Cretaceous (Albian)–Late Cretaceous:* Hippuritacea (Bivalvia) and Scleractinia (Unit 8).

 i. *Paleocene–Eocene:* Scleractinia and Corallinacea (Unit 9a).

 j. *Oligocene–Holocene:* Scleractinia (different families and genera from Unit 9a), Milleporina, crustose Corallinacea, and Codiacea (Unit 9b).

These 10 units are recognized on the basis of the overall similarity of higher taxa and on their guild structure. Their chronostratigraphic distribution is related to major global extinction events, macroevolutionary and radiation events, and prolonged ecologic stability. Their number and stratigraphic occurrences do not agree with the "reef community complexes" of Boucot (1983) or the "reef intervals" of Sheehan (1985). Furthermore, the geologic history of reef communities presented above has a distinctly different pattern than the history of level-bottom communities (or any others for that matter). However, three of the four "annihilation/collapse" extinction events (Fig. 15.1A) in reef community evolution (excluding the Cambrian: Botomian extinction) do indeed coincide with the global mass extinction events of other communities and ecosystems and so generally support extraterrestrial-caused mechanisms proposed by numerous previous authors.

The chief difference between the geologic history of reef communities and that of other communities is that reefs underwent major changes in composition and structure between mass extinctions that did not coincide with changes in other communities. Those changes were the macroevolutionary events in the histories of members of the frame-building guilds which are variably related to macroevolutionary events for non-reef higher taxa. In addition, reef communities survived some of the mass extinction events with only minor reorganization and radiation during the ensuing recovery/radiation–stabilization phase (end of Early Cambrian, Ordovician, Triassic, Eocene).

GENERAL ASPECTS

Evolution of Guild Structures

The geologic history of the guild structure of Phanerozoic reef communities indicates three important, interrelated, but discontinuous trends:

a.   Generally increased taxonomic diversity within each guild. Unfortunately, the intraguild species richness for numerous reef communities is poorly known; for reefs containing abundant non-skeletal algae or various problematic taxa (especially those that are "algal-like"), guild diversity may never be known. In addition, diversity of the destroyer guild is based on trace fossil form genera and therefore rather poorly related to true biological diversity. Although the fossil record of cryptic subcommunities extends back to the Early Cambrian, it is also very poorly known in most pre-Cenozoic reefs. The most dramatic increase in diversity was in the dweller guild and generally corresponds with the overall increase in diversity of marine biota during the Phanerozoic.

b.   General decrease in the amount of niche and guild overlap. Broadly adapted, slowly evolving lower taxa typified Paleozoic reef-building guilds; many taxa of uncertain biological affinities (e.g., *Renalcis; Tubiphytes*) had remarkably long geologic histories as members of more than one guild.

c.   The taxonomic distinction between reef and level-bottom communities increased during geologic history. During most of this history, the greatest similarity was between the dweller guild and level-bottom vagile species. Reefs with an important binder guild resisted destruction by waves, currents, and organisms; such reefs generally retain their essential community composition and structure after death and before burial (hence their dissimilarity to level-bottom communities).

Frame-building Guilds

The geologic histories of the binder, constructor, and baffler guilds and their relative importance in reef construction are summarized in Fig. 15.2A). This figure is based on data and interpretations presented in Chapter 7 (Precambrian) and the selected examples of reef community composition and structure presented in Chapters 11–14 for pre-Cenozoic and in Part I for Cenozoic reefs. Other curves based on other examples probably would have other shapes.

The most subjective aspect of Figure 15.2A involves the baffler guild; temporal variations in its importance are based on the presumed abundance of demosponges, sphinctozoans, inozoans, erect bryozoans, and crinoids. In many pre-Cenozoic reefs, judgments of the importance of the constructor guild were partly based on the amount of overlap with binder and baffler guilds. The overall rigidity of the reefs is related to the importance of the binder plus constructor guilds. Reefs with important baffler guilds are less rigid and are gradational with mud mounds (excluded from the figure).

Despite the subjective nature of many aspects of Figure 15.2A, it does indicate some major features of reef community evolution:

a.   Most Paleozoic reefs were dominated by the binder guild; exceptions include mid-Paleozoic coral-built reefs (Example 12.7) and Late Carbon-

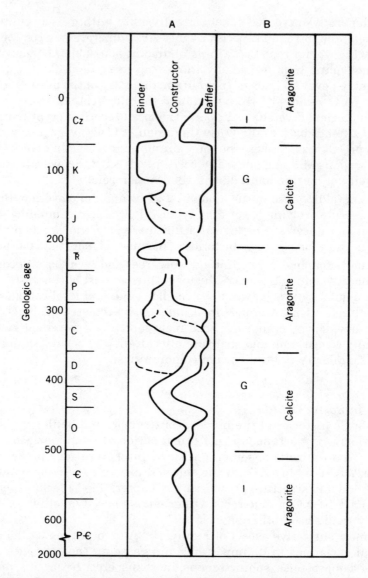

Figure 15.2. Summary of evolutionary history of reef community building guilds through geologic time. A. Relative importance of binder (left), constructor (center), and baffler guilds. Solid lines in Devonian, Carboniferous, and Jurassic based on Examples 12.6, 13.4, and 14.7, respectively; dashed lines based on Examples 12.7, 13.5, and 14.8. B. Occurrence and duration of "Icehouse/Greenhouse (I/G)" global climatic supercycles and "aragonite/calcite ooid/cement" intervals. Absolute age in hundred million years. Symbols for geologic periods conventional; C = Carboniferous, Cz = Cenozoic.

iferous chaetetid-built reefs (Example 13.4). In contrast, most Mesozoic and Cenozoic reefs were dominated by the constructor guild.

b.   There is a general increase in relative importance of the constructor guild during the two-billion year history of reef-building. This overall trend may be further subdivided into three segments, each with increasing constructor importance: Precambrian–Carboniferous, Middle Triassic–Middle Jurassic, and Cenozoic.

c.   None of the changes in relative importance of guilds were continuous over the entire history of reefs or even over several tens of millions of years. These temporal fluctuations correspond to the macroevolutionary history of higher reef-building taxa and their varied degrees of skeletonization; they also exemplify the general lack of orderly progression even within the same higher taxon. Instead, these fluctuations reflect a history of successive "opportunistic" reef-building higher taxa that entered the guild structure of these communities, flourished for varied intervals, and were decimated by mass extinction/decline events or displaced by another even more "opportunistic" higher taxon.

d.   Even among reefs of the same age, the relative importance of building guilds may vary considerably, depending on the nature and abundance of the taxa involved. For example, in most mid-Paleozoic reefs dominated by stromatoporoids, the binder guild is the most important (Example 12.6), whereas, if corals dominate, the constructor guild is most important (Example 12.7). Similarly, in Late Carboniferous reefs built by phylloid algae, the binder or baffler guilds predominate (Example 13.5), but in others, the chaetetids of the constructor guild dominate the building process (Example 13.4).

Guilds: Skeletonization; Reef Size

The general degree of rigidity and skeletonization of reefs is related to the relative importance of the binder plus constructor guilds. However, the binder guild may contain a variety of non-skeletal and weakly skeletonized algae and problematic algae (e.g., Precambrian and Middle Cambrian–Early Ordovician building guilds) and form reefs comparable in size to younger reefs dominated by the constructor guild. Thus, despite the generally increasing skeletonization and rigidity of reefs during geologic time, the overall size of reefs is more strongly influenced by their geologic–structural location than by their degree of skeletonization; shelf margin reefs are generally much larger than reef flat or cratonic reefs, regardless of their age, and Precambrian stromatolitic/thrombolitic reefs are commonly as large as skeletal Early Cambrian archaeocyathid reefs or many Triassic–Jurassic sponge–coral reefs.

Climatic Supercycles. Although there are mixed correlations between the evolutionary history of reef communities and the "icehouse–greenhouse" supercycles of Fischer (1982, 1984; i.e., the supercycle boundaries miss the first order Permo–Triassic and Cretaceous–Cenozoic collapse–rebuild extinction events), there is a very general relation between the supercycles and the degree of overall skeletonization of reef-building organisms and reefs (Fig. 15.2B). The "icehouse" supercycles were extended intervals (approx. 150 million years) of reduced concentrations of atmospheric CO_2, cooler climates, and stronger latitudinal thermal gradients. The "greenhouse" supercycles were of comparable duration but were characterized by warmer climates and weak latitudinal thermal gradients. The relation between the supercycles and reef skeletonization is as follows:

a.   Fischer recognized three "icehouse" supercycles extending from the Late Precambrian to the Late Cambrian, Late Devonian to the Late Triassic, and from the Oligocene to about 100 million years into the future. During the first two "icehouse" intervals, reefs were characteristically poorly skeletonized, non-rigid structures. During the Late Precambrian–Late Cambrian, this was at least partly due to the low numbers and diversity of large, colonial, well-skeletonized metazoans. However, this argument is not satisfactory for the Late Devonian–Late Triassic interval, when numerous skeletal algae, sponges, and corals were present; except for the Late Carboniferous chaetetids, metazoans did not build well-skeletonized reefs during the Late Paleozoic–Middle Triassic "icehouse" supercyle.

b.   Fischer's two "greenhouse" supercycles (Late Cambrian–Late Devonian and Jurassic–Eocene) were times of generally well-skeletonized reef-builders and rigid reef structures. In both "greenhouse" intervals, the builders included the same higher taxa (skeletal algae, sponges, and corals) as the Late Paleozoic–Middle Triassic "icehouse" interval but very different lower taxa; the Cretaceous "greenhouse" reef-builders included rudist bivalves, perhaps the best-skeletonized constructors that ever lived.

The chief difficulty in applying these supercycles to reef skeletonization and rigidity involves the Oligocene–Holocene "icehouse." Despite the onset of cooler climates in the mid-Cenozoic and their culmination in the Pleistocene glacial stages, reef-building scleractinians (chief constructors) and crustose coralline algae (chief binders) continued to build progressively larger and better-calcified skeletons. Furthermore, the organic frameworks of these reefs are among the most rigid reefs in the entire two-billion year history of reef community evolution. Only the mid-Paleozoic stromatoporoid–coral, Late Carboniferous chaetetid, and Late Cretaceous rudist reefs rival the Late Cenozoic scleractinian–crustose coralline algal reefs in rigidity.

Aragonite–Calcite Intervals. Sandberg (1983) has distinguished other long-term intervals in earth history in which the mineralogy of ooids and carbonate cements has alternated between predominantly aragonite and predominantly calcite. The "aragonite-facilitating" episodes conform quite closely with Fischer's (1982; 1984) "icehouse" cycles, and his "aragonite-inhibiting" episodes conform with "greenhouse" cycles (Fig. 15.2B). So, the better-skeletonized reefs of the mid-Paleozoic and Jurassic–Eocene/Oligocene corresond to "aragonite-inhibiting" episodes.

Mistiaen (1984) noted the general link between these "aragonite-inhibiting" episodes and the disjunct stratigraphic distribution of stromatoporoids (Fig. 8.1); he suggested that the Carboniferous–Triassic/Jurassic "gap" merely represents an interval when the stromatoporoids failed to secrete a massive calcareous skeleton and suggests that their skeletons may have been aragonite. Numerous previous authors have proposed that the large skeletons of the Cretaceous rudists were formed of aragonite in warm water; this represents an important anomaly or flaw in the predominantly calcite interval of Sandberg (1983).

Biologic Displacement. In cases where older reef-building higher taxa and guilds are slowly displaced by other more opportunistic higher taxa, the "new" taxa are biologically more complex and better-skeletonized than the "old" taxa. For example, during the Early Cambrian, the skeletal cyanophytes and archaeocyathids displaced the non-skeletal cyanophytes. During the Middle Ordovician, the bryozoans, stromatoporoids, and corals slowly displaced the algae. In the Middle–Late Triassic, scleractinians displaced sponges and in the Cretaceous, rudists displaced scleractinians.

Reef Community Species Diversity

Another significant characteristic of reefs, regardless of age, is their typically high species diversity compared with adjacent level-bottom communities. Unfortunately, species diversity is one of the more elusive aspects of reef community synecology because only rarely has the total biota of entire reefs, reef systems, and reef complexes been studied, and even less commonly, both reef and adjacent level-bottom biotas. Species diversity is strongly affected by the background of the investigator ("lumper/splitter"), goal of the study, preservation potential of various taxa (e.g., corals vs. algae), and overall diversity of the biogeographic province to which the communities belong. Furthermore, in numerous reef and level-bottom communities, species diversity changes by processes of ecologic succession, brief/local catastrophes, and by apparently incomplete sampling (all discussed in Chap. 3).

Evolution of Diversity

For the above reasons, the data on reef community species diversity presented in Figure 15.3 are very incomplete, do not show any long-term uniform trend in the Phanerozoic history of species diversity, and are not easily compared with more complete data for level-bottom communities

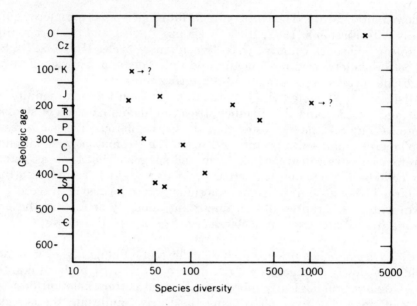

Figure 15.3. Summary of species diversity (logarithmic scale) in selected reef communities described in Part III through geologic time. Absolute age in hundred million years. Symbols for geologic periods conventional; C = Carboniferous, Cz = Cenozoic.

(Bambach, 1977). The chief obstacle in such comparisons is the difference in sizes of units that are collected and in the collecting methods. Reef communities typically occupy smaller areas and have shorter durations than adjacent level-bottom communities. In addition, the methods for collecting large, colonial fossils in reef frameworks are quite different than for small individuals in level-bottoms. Therefore, comparisons of within-habitat species diversity (reef to reef) through time show rapid fluctuations; between-habitat (reef to level-bottom) comparisons of synchronous communities are usually even more spurious unless considerable attention is given to matters involving sample uniformity (i.e., size/area; sampling method/collecting intensity, etc.). Even for the Holocene, there are surprisingly few data that may be used with confidence to compare species diversity in reefs and level-bottoms.

Despite these problems, ecologists and paleoecologists usually acknowledge the significantly higher divesity of reef communities compared with level-bottom communities. The chief exceptions include the Late Carboniferous algal- and chaetetid-dominated reefs and the Late Cretaceous rudist-dominated reefs. Although the diversity of the non-skeletal or poorly skeletonized algal reefs of the early Paleozoic is very uncertain, it appears to have been much lower than that of the adjacent level-bottoms.

Speciation Sites

It is exceedingly difficult to pinpoint the sites of origin of fossil species. Vagaries in distribution of outcrops and subsurface samples and incompleteness of stratigraphic sections and collecting and the like are the usual explanations for the problem of speciation sites (e.g., reefs vs. level-bottoms, near-shore vs. off-shore). Cases where it can be documented that a species originated in either a reef or level-bottom community and then migrated to the other are indeed rare. Nonetheless, the high species diversity and general endemism of reef communities are strong presumptive evidence that reefs are important speciation/micro- /macroevolutionary sites (Fagerstrom, 1983). Holocene reefs are largely confined to the tropics or deep-water environments characterized by general stability of the chemical, physical, and geological factors and are dominated by stenotopic species in highly integrated niche and guild structures. The same generally benign environmental factors (abiotic and biotic) also characterized ancient reefs. However, this conclusion contrasts with interpretations for level-bottom communities (Bretsky, 1968; Sepkoski and Sheehan, 1983; Jablonski et al., 1983; Lewin, 1983) which have emphasized ecologically unstable environments as speciation sites.

Macroevolutionary Sites

It is similarly difficult to determine the preferred locations (reef vs. level-bottom) for macroevolutionary events. However, the evolutionary histories of most reef-building higher taxa are so closely linked to reef environments that it is reasonable to assume that most of them originated and speciated there. Within the Cenozoic tropical reef belt, each of the Miocene–Holocene scleractinian provinces has a near-equatorial high diversity center containing a higher proportion of geologically "young" genera: Jamaica in the Atlantic Province and Indonesia for the Indo-Pacific Province (Stehli and Wells, 1971; Levinton, 1982, pp. 439–441). There are at least two explanations for these higher diversity centers:

a. The genera originated in these centers and migrated toward the periphery of each province. The presence of several "young" genera in these centers and the higher proportion of "old" genera near the periphery support this alternative. But nearly all peripheral genera and species are also present in the high diversity centers and may have migrated there from the periphery.

b. Before the Miocene, scleractinian genera were uniformly distributed in the pantropical reef belt. With the uplift of the Panamanian isthmus and cooling climates during the Miocene–Pleistocene, the latitudinal and longitudinal limits of the reef belt contracted and the higher diversity centers became environmentally benign "havens" for the most stenotopic "young" genera and species.

The fossil record has not been documented carefully enough in either province to rule out either of the above alternatives. Nor has it been determined whether the genera and species involved appeared first in reef or level-bottom communities.

CONCLUSIONS

Several questions, each relating to a key word in the title, have been presented and discussed throughout this book. These questions can now be restated to finalize the main concepts relating to "The Evolution of Reef Communities."

What is a Reef?

A reef is chiefly a biological phenomenon. It has numerous features that distinguish it from other marine phenomena, including:

a. Structural rigidity and topographic relief produced by the rapid growth of large, colonial/gregarious skeletal organisms living in close proximity to one another.

b. High taxonomic diversity compared with adjacent non-reef areas.

There may be exceptions to these features, especially with regard to diversity. Furthermore, it is important to note that the recognition of a reef is not based on water depth or geologic location. Finally, all aspects of the reef phenomenon have changed in varied ways during geologic history (e.g., there is little similarity in size, composition, structure, rigidity, topographic relief, and the like between early Paleozoic and Holocene reefs); it is then virtually impossible to formulate a simple definition of a reef (see Chap. 1 and Glossary).

What is a Community?

It is just as difficult to define an ecologic community. Numerous ecologists doubt the validity of the community concept. However, for the great majority of reef ecologists and paleoecologists, the concept is *real!* A reef community has numerous features that distinguish it from non-reef communities, including:

a. A characteristic taxonomic composition and structure (trophic, guild, niche).

b. Relatively objective boundaries.

c. A restricted set of controlling environmental factors (chemical, physical, geological, biological).

Thus, the composition and structure of a reef community are distinctly different from all other contemporaneous communities. Their boundaries can be objectively mapped and are generally coincident with strong environmental gradients (see Chap. 5).

Do Reef Communities Evolve?

The history of reef communities clearly indicates that they have changed in composition, structure, and occurrence through ecologic (short-term), evolutionary (intermediate), and geologic (long-term) time periods. Changes through geologic time are the focus of this book (especially Parts II and III) and if the concept of evolution is extended to this scale, the answer to the question of community evolution is a resounding "Yes!" In fact, evolutionary changes of reef communities through geologic time are the most profound (in both composition and structure) and therefore the most interesting. This interest is further heightened by the fact that there are no simple means or patterns of reef community evolution and that the histories of reef communities and non-reef communities are only partly interrelated (see Chap. 15). A reef community is a very complex, highly integrated biological system *and* phenomenon. As such, ancient reef communities are characterized by long periods of surprising stability punctuated by shorter episodes of more rapid change resulting from mass extinction and organic macroevolutionary events.

The purpose of this book will have been achieved if the reader has begun to understand "The Reef Phenomenon" and the full meaning of Revelle's (1954) characterization:

Of all earth's phenomena, coral reefs seem best calculated to excite a sense of wonder.

References

Abbott, B. M., 1973. Terminology of stromatoporoid shapes. *J. Paleontol.*, **47**, 805–806.

Abbott, B. M., 1976. Origin and evolution of bioherms in Wenlock Limestone (Silurian) of Shropshire, England. *Am. Assoc. Pet. Geol. Bull.*, **60**, 2117–2127.

Abele, L. G. and Walters, K., 1979. Marine benthic diversity: a critique and alternative explanation. *J. Biogeogr.*, **6**, 115–126.

Achauer, C. W., 1969. Origin of Capitan Formation, Guadalupe Mountains, New Mexico and Texas. *Am. Assoc. Pet. Geol. Bull.*, **53**, 2314–2323.

Achauer, C. W. and Johnson, J. H., 1969. Algal stromatolites in the James reef complex (Lower Cretaceous), Fairway Field, Texas. *J. Sediment. Petrol.*, **39**, 1466–1472.

Adams, C. G. et al., 1977. The Messinian salinity crisis and the evidence of Late Miocene eustatic changes in the world ocean. *Nature (London)*, **269**, 383–386.

Adey, W. H., 1978. Coral reef morphogenesis: a multidimensional model. *Science*, **202**, 831–837.

Adey, W. H. and Burke, R. B., 1977. Holocene bioherms of Lesser Antilles-geologic control of development. *Am. Assoc. Pet. Geol. Stud. Geol.* **4**, 67–81.

Adey, W. H. and Macintyre, I. G., 1973. Crustose coralline algae: a re-evaluation in the geological sciences. *Geol. Soc. Am. Bull.*, **84**, 883–904.

Adey, W. H. and Vassar, J. M., 1975. Colonization, succession and growth rates of tropical crustose coralline algae (Rhodophyta, Cryptonemiales). *Phycologia*, **14**, 55–69.

Agassiz, A., 1894. A reconnaissance of the Bahamas and of the elevated reefs of Cuba. Harvard Univ., *Mus. Comparative Zool. Bull.*, **26**, 203 pp.

Aharon, P., 1983. 140,000-yr. isotope climatic record from raised coral reefs in New Guinea. *Nature (London)*, **304**, 720–723.

Ahr, W. M., 1971. Paleoenvironment, algal structures, and fossil algae in the Upper Cambrian of central Texas. *J. Sediment. Petrol.*, **41**, 205–216.

Ahr, W. M., 1973. The carbonate ramp: an alternative to the shelf model. *Trans. Gulf Coast Assoc. Geol. Soc.*, **23**, 221–225.

Ahr, W. M. and Stanton, R. J., 1973. The sedimentologic and paleoceologic significance of *Lithotrypa*, a rock boring barnacle. *J. Sediment. Petrol.*, **43**, 20–23.

Aitken, J. G., 1967. Classification and environmental significance of cryptalgal limestones and dolomites, with illustrations from the Cambrian and Ordovician of southwestern Alberta. *J. Sediment. Petrol.*, **37**, 1163–1178.

Alberstadt, L. P. et al., 1974. Patch reefs in the Carters Limestone (Middle Ordovician) in Tennessee and vertical zonation in Ordovician reefs. *Geol. Soc. Am. Bull.*, **85**, 1171–1182.

Ali, O. E., 1984. Sclerochronology and carbonate production in some Upper Jurassic reef corals. *Palaeontology*, **27**, 537–548.

Alldredge, L. R. et al., 1954. Magnetic structure of Bikini Atoll. *U.S. Geol. Surv. Prof. Pap.*, **260-L.**

Alvarez, L. W. et al., 1980. Extraterrestrial cause for the Cretaceous-Tertiary extinction. *Science*, **208**, 1095–1108.

Alvarez, W. et al., 1982. Iridium anomaly approximately synchronous with terminal Eocene extinctions. *Science*, **216**, 886–888.

Anderson, F. W., 1950. Some reef-building calcareous algae from the Carboniferous rocks of northern England and southern Scotland. *Proc. Yorkshire Geol. Soc.*, **28**, pt. 1, 5–27.

Anderton, R. et al., 1979. *A dynamic stratigraphy of the British Isles*. Allen & Unwin, London, 301 pp.

Andrews, P. B., 1964. *Serpulid reefs, Baffin Bay, southeast Texas*. In *Depositional environments south central Texas coast*. Gulf Coast Association of Geological Societies. Field trip guidebook for annual meeting, Austin, TX.

Arkell, W. J., 1935. On the nature, origin and climatic significance of the coral reefs in the vicinity of Oxford. *Geol. Soc. London Quart. J.*, **91**, 77–110.

Atkinson, M., 1981. Phosphate flux as a measure of net coral reef flat productivity. *Proc. Fourth Int. Coral Reef Symp.*, **1**, 417–418.

Atkinson, M. J. and Grigg, R. W., 1984. Model of a coral reef ecosystem II. Gross and net benthic primary production at French Frigate Shoals, Hawaii. *Coral Reefs*, **3**, 13–22.

Awramik, S. M., 1971. Precambrian columnar stromatolite diversity: reflection of metazoan appearance. *Science*, **174**, 825–827.

Babcock, J. A., 1977. Calcareous algae, organic boundstones, and the genesis of the Upper Capitan Limestone (Permian, Guadalupian), Guadalupe Mountains, west Texas and New Mexico. In Hileman, M. E. and Mazzullo, S. J. (eds.), Upper Guadalupian facies, Permian reef complex, Guadalupe Mountains, New Mexico and west Texas: Permian Basin Sect. Soc. Econ. Paleontol. Mineral. Spec. Publ. **77–6**, 3–44.

Babić, L. and Zupanic, J., 1981. Various pore types in a Paleocene reef, Banija, Yugoslavia. In Toomey, D. F. (ed.), European fossil reef models. *Soc. Econ. Paleontol. Mineral. Spec. Publ.*, **30**, 473–482.

Babić, L. et al., 1976. Paleocene reef-limestone in the region of Banija, central Croatia. *Geol. Vjesn.*, **29**, 11–47.

Bachmann, G. H., 1979. Bioherme der Muschel *Placunopsis ostracina* v. Schlotheim und ihre diagenese. *Neues Jahrb.Geol. Paläontol. Abh.* **158,** 381–407.

Bak, R. P. M. et al., 1982. Complexity of coral interactions: influence of time, location of interaction and epifauna. *Mar. Biol.,* **69,** 215–222.

Baker, P. A. and Weber, J. N., 1975. Coral growth rate: variation with depth. *Earth Planet. Sci. Lett.,* **27,** 57–61.

Ball, S. M. et al., 1977. Importance of phylloid algae in development of depositional topography-reality or myth? *Am. Assoc. Pet. Geol. Stud. Geol.,* **4,** 240–259.

Bambach, R. K., 1977. Species richness in marine benthic habitats through the Phanerozoic. *Paleobiology,* **3,** 152–167.

Bambach, R. K., 1983. Ecospace utilization and guilds in marine communities through the Phanerozoic. In Tevesz, M. J. S. and McCall, P. L. (eds.), *Biotic interactions in recent and fossil benthic communities.* Plenum, New York, pp. 719–746.

Bambach, R. K., 1985. Classes and adaptive variety: the ecology of diversification in marine faunas through the Phanerozoic. In Valentine, J. W. (ed.), *Phanerozoic diversity patterns.* Princeton University Press, Princeton, NJ, pp. 191–253.

Bardach, J. E., 1961. Transport of calcareous fragments by reef fishes. *Science,* **133,** 98–99.

Baria, L. R. et al., 1982. Upper Jurassic reefs of Smackover Formation, United States Gulf Coast. *Am. Assoc. Pet. Geol. Bull.,* **66,** 1449–1482.

Barnes, D. J., 1972. The structure and formation of growth-ridges in scleractinian coral skeletons. *Proc. R. Soc. London,* **182,** 331–350.

Barnes, D. J., 1973. Growth in colonial scleractinians. *Bull. Mar. Sci.,* **23,** 280–298.

Barnes, D. J. and Devereux, M. J., 1984. Productivity and calcification on a coral reef: a survey using pH and oxygen electrode techniques. *J. Exp. Mar. Biol. Ecol.,* **79,** 213–231.

Barthel, K. W., 1972. The genesis of the Solnhofen lithographic limestone (Lower Tithonian): further data and comments. *Neues Jahrb. Geol. Palaontol. Monatsh.,* **3,** 133–145.

Barthel, K. W., 1977. A spur and groove system in Upper Jurassic coral reefs of southern Germany. *Third Int. Coral Reef Symp.,* **3**(2), 201–208.

Barthel, K. W., 1978. *Solnhofen: ein blick in die Erdgeschichte.* Ott-Verlag, Thun, 378 pp., 80 pls.

Bates, R. L. and Jackson, J. A. (eds.), 1980. *Glossary of geology.* American Geological Institute, 2nd ed., 749 pp.

Battistini, R. et al., 1975. Elements de terminologie recifale Indopacifique. *Tethys,* **7,** 111 pp.

Beauvais, L., 1973. Upper Jurassic hermatypic corals. In Hallam, A. (ed.), *Atlas of paleobiogeography.* Elsevier, Amsterdam, pp. 317–328.

Beauvais, L., 1984. Evolution and diversification of Jurassic Scleractinia. *Palaeontogr. Am.,* **54,** 219–224.

Behr, K. and Behr, H.-J., 1976. Cyanophyten aus oberjurassischen Algen-Schwamm-Riffen. *Lethaia,* **9,** 283–292.

Bein, A., 1976. Rudist fringing reefs of Cretaceous shallow carbonate platform of Israel. *Am. Assoc. Pet. Geol. Bull.*, **60**, 258–272.

Benavides, L. M. and Druffel, E. R. M., 1986. Sclerosponge growth rate as determined by ^{210}Pb and ^{14}C chronologies. *Coral Reefs*, **4**, 221–224.

Benson, R. H., 1984. The Phanerozoic "crisis" as viewed from the Miocene. In Berggren, W. A. and Van Couvering, J. A. (eds.), *Catastrophes in earth history*. Princeton University Press, Princeton, NJ, pp. 437–446.

Berggren, W. A. and Van Couvering, J. A. (eds.), 1984. *Catastrophes in earth history*. Princeton University Press, Princeton, NJ, 464 pp.

Bernier, P., 1984. Les formations carbonatées du Kimméridgien et du Portlandien dans le Jura méridional. *Doc. Lab. Geol. Fac. Sci. Lyon*, **92**, 802 pp., 36 pls.

Berry, W. B. N. and Boucot, A. J., 1973. Glacio-eustatic control of Late Ordovician–Early Silurian platform sedimentation and faunal changes. *Geol. Soc. Am. Bull.*, **84**, 275–284.

Beus, S. S., 1980. Devonian serpulid bioherms in Arizona. *J. Paleontol.*, **54**, 1125–1128.

Bloom, A. L., 1974. Geomorphology of reef complexes. In Laporte, L. (ed.), *Reefs in time and space*. *Soc. Econ. Paleontol. Mineral. Spec. Publ.*, **18**, 1–8.

Boardman, R. S., 1983. Genetic and environmental control, colony integration and classification. In Boardman, R. S. et al. (eds.), *Treatise on invertebrate paleontology, Part G (rev.), Bryozoa*. Geological Society of America, Boulder, CO, and University of Kansas Press, Lawrence, KS, pp. 125–137.

Boardman, R. S. et al., 1973. Introducing coloniality. In Boardman, R. S. et al. (eds.), *Animal colonies*. Dowden, Hutchinson & Ross, Stroudsburg, PA, pp. V–IX, 603 pp.

Boardman, R. S. et al., 1983. *Treatise on invertebrate paleontology, Part G (rev.), Bryozoa*. Geological Society of America, Boulder, CO, and University of Kansas Press, Lawrence, KS.

Bockschoten, G. J. and Bijma, J., 1982. Living bryozoan-stromatolite reefs in the southwestern Netherlands. *Int. Soc. Reef Stud. Second Ann. Meeting Leiden*, The Netherlands, p. 8.

Bonem, R. M., 1977. Comparison of cavities and cryptic biota in modern reefs with those developed in Lower Pennsylvanian (Morrowan) bioherms. *Proc. Third Int. Coral Reef Symp.*, 75–80.

Borel Best, M. et al., 1984. Species concept and ecomorphvariation in living and fossil Scleractinia. *Palaeontogr. Am.*, **54**, 70–79.

Bosence, D. W. J., 1983a. Coralline algal reef frameworks. *J. Geol. Soc. London*, **140**, 365–376.

Bosence, D. W. J., 1983b. Coralline algae from the Miocene of Malta. *Palaeontology*, **26**, 147–173.

Bosence, D. W. J., 1984. Construction and preservation of two modern coralline algal reefs, St. Croix, Caribbean. *Palaeontology*, **27**, 549–574.

Boucot, A. J., 1983. Does evolution take place in an ecological vacuum: II. *J. Paleontol.*, **57**, 1–30.

Bradner, R. and Resch, W., 1981. Reef development in the Middle Triassic (Ladinian and Cordevolian) of the northern limestone Alps near Innsbruck, Austria. In Toomey, D. F. (ed.), European fossil reef models. Soc. Econ. Paleontol. Mineral. Spec. Publ., **30**, 203–232.

Brakel, W. H., 1983. Depth-related changes in the colony form of the reef coral *Porites astreoides*. In Reaka, M. L. (ed.), The ecology of deep and shallow coral reefs. *Natl. Oceanic Atmos. Adm. Symp. Ser. Undersea Res.*, **1**, 21–26.

Braithwaite, C. J. R., 1973. Reefs: just a problem of semantics. *Am. Assoc. Pet. Geol. Bull.*, **57**, 1100–1116.

Breitburg, D. L., 1984. Residual effects of grazing: inhibition of competitor recruitment by encrusting coralline algae. *Ecology*, **65**, 1136–1143.

Bretsky, P. W., 1968. Evolution of Paleozoic marine invertebrate communities. *Science*, **159**, 1231–1233; see also **161**, 491 (1970).

Bretsky, P. W. and Lorenz, D. M., 1970. An essay on genetic-adaptive strategies and mass extinctions. *Geol. Soc. Am. Bull.*, **81**, 2449–2456.

Bromley, R. G., 1975. Comparative analysis of fossil and Recent echinoid bioerosion. *Palaeontology*, **18**, 725–739.

Brown, B. E. and Dunne, R. P., 1980. Environmental controls of patch-reef growth and development. *Marine Biol.*, **56**, 85–96.

Buddemier, R. W. and Kinzie, R. A. III, 1976. Coral growth. *Ann. Rev. Oceanography Marine Biol.*, **14**, 183–225.

Burchette, T. P., 1981. European Devonian reefs: a review of current concepts and models. In Toomey, D. F. (ed.), European fossil reef models. *Soc. Econ. Paleontol. Mineral. Spec. Publ.*, **30**, 85–142.

Burchette, T. P. and Riding, R., 1977. Attached vermiform gastropods in Carboniferous marginal marine stromatolites and biostromes. *Lethaia*, **10**, 17–28.

Buss, L. W., 1979. Habitat selection, directional growth and spatial refuges: Why colonial animals have more hiding places. In Larwood, G. and Rosen, B. R. (eds.), Biology and systematics of colonial organisms. *Syst. Assoc. Spec. Publ. 11*. Academic, London, pp. 459–497.

Buss, L. W. and Jackson, J. B. C., 1979. Competitive networks: non-transitive competitive relationships in cryptic coral reef environments. *Am. Nat.*, **113**, 223–234.

Cairns, S. D., 1979. The deep-water Scleractinia of the Caribbean Sea and adjacent waters. *Studies Fauna Curacao*, **57**, 1–341.

Cairns, S. D. and Stanley Jr., G. D., 1981. Ahermatypic coral banks: living and fossil counterparts. *Proc. Fourth Int. Coral Reef Symp.*, **1**, 611–618.

Carbone, F. and Sirna, G., 1981. Upper Cretaceous reef models from Rocca di Cave and adjacent areas in Latium, central Italy. In Toomey, D. F. (ed.), European fossil reef models. *Soc. Econ. Paleontol. Mineral. Spec. Publ.* **30**, 427–445.

Carpenter, R. C., 1983. Effect of herbivore grazing intensity on coral reef algal communities: biomass and primary productivity. *Am. Zool.*, **23**, 948.

Caspers, H., 1950. Die Lebensgemeinschaft der Helgolander Austernbank. *Biol. Anst. Helgoland, Helgolander Wiss. Meerestunders. List (Sylt)*, **3**, 119–169, 15 figs.

Chalker, B. E., 1983. Calcification by corals and other animals on the reef. In Barnes, D. J. (ed.), *Perspectives on coral reefs*. Australian Institute of Marine Science, Townsville, and Brian Clouston, Canberra, Australia, pp. 29–45.

Chamberlain, J. A. Jr., 1978. Mechanical properties of coral skeleton: compressive strength and its adaptive significance. *Paleobiology*, **4**, 419–435.

Chappell, J., 1980. Coral morphology, diversity and reef growth. *Nature (London)* **286**, 249–252.

Chappell, J., 1983. Sealevel changes and reef growth. In Barnes, D. J. (ed.), *Perspectives on coral reefs*. Australian Institute of Marine Science, Townsville, and Brian Clouston, Canberra, Australia, pp. 46–55.

Chave, K. et al., 1972. Carbonate production by coral reefs. *Mar. Geol.*, **12**, 123–140.

Chevalier, J.-P., 1981. Reef Scleractinia of French Polynesia. *Proc. Fourth Int. Coral Reef Symp.*, **2**, 177–186.

Choi, D. R., 1981. Quaternary reef foundations in the southernmost Belize Shelf, British Honduras. *Proc. Fourth Int. Coral Reef Symp.*, **1**, 635–642.

Choi, D. R., 1984. Succession of coelobites in rubble. *Mar. Sci.*, **37**, 72–78.

Choi, D. R. and Ginsburg, R. N., 1983. Distribution of coelobites (cavity-dwellers) in coral rubble across the Florida reef tract. *Coral Reefs*, **2**, 165–172.

Choquette, P. W., 1983. Platy algal reef mounds, Paradox Basin. In Scholle, P. A. et al. (eds.), Carbonate depositional environments. *Am. Assoc. Pet. Geol. Mem.*, **33**, 454–462.

Chornesky, E. A., 1983. Induced development of sweeper tentacles on the reef coral *Agaricia agaricites:* a response to direct competition. *Biol. Bull.*, **165**, 569–581.

Church, S. B., 1974. Lower Ordovician patch reefs in western Utah. *Brigham Young Univ. Res. Stud. Geol. Ser.*, **21**, 41–62.

Chuvashov, B. and Riding, R., 1984. Principal floras of Paleozoic marine calcareous algae. *Palaeontology*, **27**, 487–500.

Clausade, M. et al., 1971. Morphologie des recifs coralliens de la region de Tulear (Madagascar): elements de terminologie recifale. *Tethys Suppl.*, **2**, 76 pp.

Clausen, C., 1971. Effects of temperature on the rate of [45]calcium uptake by *Pocillopora damicornis*. In Lenhoff, H. M. et al. (eds.), *Experimental coelenterate biology*. University of Hawaii Press, Honolulu, pp. 246–259.

CLIMAP Project Members, 1976. The surface of the ice-age earth. *Science*, **191**, 1131–1137.

Cloud Jr., P. E., 1952. Facies relationships of organic reefs. *Am. Assoc. Pet. Geol. Bull.*, **36**, 2125–2149.

Cloud, P. E., 1959. Geology of Saipan, Mariana Islands. 4. Submarine topography and shoal water ecology. *U.S. Geol. Surv. Prof. Pap.*, **280-K**, 361–445.

Cloud, P. E. and Semikhatov, M. A., 1969. Proterozoic stromatolite zonation. *Am. J. Sci.*, **267**, 1017–1061.

Cloud, P. E. et al., 1962. Environment of calcium carbonate deposition west of Andros Island, Bahamas. *U.S. Geol. Surv. Prof. Pap.*, **350**, 138 pp., 10 pls.

Cloud, P. E. et al., 1974. Giant stromatolites and associated vertical tubes from the Upper Proterozoic Noonday Dolomite, Death Valley region, eastern California. *Geol. Soc. Am. Bull.*, **85**, 1869–1882.

Coates, A. G., 1973. Cretaceous Tethyan coral-rudist biogeography related to the evolution of the Atlantic Ocean. *Spec. Pap. Palaeontol.*, **12**, 169–174.

Coates, A. G., 1977a. Jamaican Cretaceous coral assemblages and their relationships to rudist frameworks. Second symposium internationale sur les coraux et recifs coralliens fossiles. *Bull. Bur. Rech. Géol. Minières (Fr.)*, **89**, pp. 336–341.

Coates, A. G., 1977b. Jamaican coral-rudist frameworks and their geologic setting. *Am. Assoc. Pet. Geol. Studies Geol.*, **4**, 83–91.

Coates, A. G. and Kauffman, E. G., 1973. Stratigraphy, paleontology and paleoenvironment of a Cretaceous coral thicket, Lamy, New Mexico. *J. Paleontol.*, **47**, 953–968.

Coates, A. G. and Oliver Jr., W. A., 1973. Coloniality in zoantharian corals. In Boardman, R. S. et al. (eds.), *Animal colonies*. Dowden, Hutchinson & Ross, Stroudsburg, PA, pp. 3–27.

Cockbain, A. E., 1984. Stromatoporoids from the Devonian reef complexes Canning Basin, Western Australia. *Bull. Geol. Surv. W. Aust.*, **129**, 108 pp.

Cody, M. L. and Diamond, J. M. (eds.), 1975. *Ecology and evolution of communities*. Belknap Press, Harvard University, Cambridge, MA, 545 pp.

Connell, J. H., 1978. Diversity in tropical rainforests and coral reefs. *Science*, **199**, 1302–1310.

Connell, J. H. and Slatyer, R. O., 1977. Mechanisms of succession in natural communities and their role in community stability and organization. *Am. Nat.*, **111**, 1119–1144.

Coogan, A. H., 1969. Evolutionary trends in rudist hard parts. In *Treatise on invertebrate paleontology, Part N, Bivalvia*. Geological Society of America, Boulder, CO, and University of Kansas Press, Lawrence, KS, pp. N766–N776.

Coogan, A. H., 1977. Early and Middle Cretaceous Hippuritacea (rudists) of the Gulf Coast. *Bur. Econ. Geol. Univ. Texas Rept. Invest.* **89**, 32–70.

Cooper, G. A., 1954. Brachiopods (Bikini and nearby atolls). *U.S. Geol. Surv. Prof. Pap.*, **260-G**.

Copper, P., 1974. Structure and development of Early Paleozoic reefs. *Proc. Second Int. Coral Reef Symp.*, **1**, 365–386.

Copper, P., 1976. The cyanophyte *Wetheredella* in Ordovician reefs and off-reef sediments. *Lethaia*, **9**, 273–281.

Copper, P., 1985. Fossilized polyps in 430-M yr-old *Favosites* corals. *Nature (London)*, **316**, 142–144.

Copper, P. and Fay, I., 1984. Early Llandoverian (Silurian) bioherms of Ontario, Canada. Palaeontogr. Am., **54**, 413.

Cowen, R., 1970. Analogies between the recent bivalve *Tridacna* and the fossil brachiopods Lyttoniacea and Richthofeniacea. *Palaeogeogr. Palaeoclimatol. Palaeoecol.*, **8**, 329–344.

Cowen, R., 1983. Algal symbiosis and its recognition in the fossil record. In Tevesz, J. J. S. and McCall, P. L. (eds.), *Biotic interactions in Recent and fossil benthic communities*. Plenum, New York, pp. 431–479.

Crame, J. A., 1980. Succession and diversity in the Pleistocene coral reefs of the Kenya coast. *Palaeontology*, **23**, 1–37.

Cribb, A. B., 1973. The algae of the Great Barrier Reefs. In Jones, O. A. and Endean, R. (eds.), *Biology and Geology of coral reefs*, Vol. 2. Academic Press, New York, pp. 47–75.

Cros, P. and Lucas, G., 1982. Le récif coralligene à algues de Vigny (Danien, environs de Paris). *Sci. Terre Nancy*, **25**, 3–37.

Crossland, C. J., 1981. Seasonal growth of *Acropora* cf. *formosa* and *Pocillopora damicornis* on a high latitude reef (Houtman Abrolhos), Western Australia. *Proc. Fourth Int. Coral Reef Symp.*, **1**, 663–667.

Crossland, C. J., 1983. Dissolved nutrients in coral reef waters. In Barnes, D. (ed.), *Perspectives on coral reefs*. Australian Institute of Marine Science, Townsville, and Brian Clouston, Canberra, Australia, pp. 56–68.

Cuffey, R. J., 1972. The roles of bryozoans in modern coral reefs. *Geol. Rundsch.*, **61**, 542–550.

Cuffey, R. J., 1973. Bryozoan distribution in the modern reefs of Eniwetok Atoll and the Bermuda platform. *Pac. Geol.*, **6**, 25–50.

Cuffey, R. J., 1974. Delineation of bryozoan constructional roles in reefs from comparison of fossil bioherms and living reefs. *Proc. Second Int. Coral Reef Symp.*, **1**, 357–364.

Cuffey, R. J., 1977a. Bryozoan contributions to reefs and bioherms through geologic time. *Am. Assoc. Pet. Geol. Stud. Geol.* **4**, 181–194.

Cuffey, R. J., 1977b. Mid-Ordovician bryozoan reefs in western Newfoundland. *Geol. Soc. Am. Abstr. (with Program)*, **9**, 253.

Cuffey, R. J., 1977c. Modern tidal-channel bryozoan reefs at Joulters Cays (Bahamas). *Proc. Third Int. Coral Reef Symp.*, **2**, 339–345.

Cuffey, R. J., 1985. Expanded reef-rock textural classification and the geologic history of bryozoan reefs. *Geology*, **13**, 307–310.

Cuffey, R. J., 1985. Personal communication. Pennsylvania State University, University Park, PA.

Cuffey, R. J. and Davidheiser, C. E., 1980. Morphologic variability in relation to paleoenvironmental position—the coral *Labyrinthites* and the bryozoan *Diplotrypa* in the Middle Ordovician Long Point reef complex of west-central Newfoundland. *Geol. Soc. Am. Abstr. (with Program)*, **12**, 30.

Cuffey, R. J. and Foerster, B., 1975. Autecology of the cyclostome bryozoan *Crisia ebuonia* in the modern reefs of Bermuda. Bryozoa 1974. *Doc. Lab. Geol. Fac. Sci. Lyon*, **3**(2), 357–368.

Cuffey, R. J. and Fonda, S. S., 1979. Bryozoan species assemblages in the modern bryozoan-rich reefs at Joulters Cays (Bahamas)—general character and paleoenvironmental implication. *Geol. Soc. Am. Abstr. (with Program)*, **11**, 407–408.

Cuffey, R. J. and Kamandulis, M. A., 1985. Trepostome bryozoan reef-mounds in the Upper Ordovician near Maysville, Kentucky. *Geol. Soc. Am. Abstr. (with Program)*, **17**, 283.

Cuffey, R. J. and McKinney, F. G., 1982. Reteporid cheilostome bryozoans from the modern reefs of Eniwetok Atoll, and their implications for Paleozoic fenestrate bryozoan paleoecology. *Pac. Geol.*, **16**, 7–13.

Cuffey, R. J. et al., 1977. Modern tidal-channel bryozoan reefs at Joulters Cays (Bahamas). *Proc. Third Int. Coral Reef Symp.*, **2**, 339–345.

Cuif, J.-P., 1974. Role des sclerosponges dans la faune récifale du Trias des Dolomites (Italie du Nord). *Geobios, **7**(2), 139–153.

Cuif, J.-P. et al., 1979. Comparison de la microstructure du squelette carbonate non spiculaire d'éponges actuelle et fossiles. In Levi, C. and Boury-Esnault, N. (eds.), Biologie des spongiaires. *Colloq. Int. C. N. R. S.* **291**, 459–465.

Cumings, E. R., 1932. Reefs or bioherms? *Geol. Soc. Am. Bull.*, **43**, 331–352.

Cumings, E. R. and Schrock, R. R., 1928. Niagaran coral reefs in Indiana and adjacent states and their stratigraphic relations. *Geol. Soc. Am. Bull.*, **39**, 519–620.

Cushman, J. A. et al., 1954. Recent Foraminifera of the Marshall Islands. *U.S. Geol. Surv. Prof. Paper*, **260-H**, 319–384, pls. 82–93.

Dabrio, C. J. et al., 1981. The coral reef of Nijar, Messinian (Uppermost Miocene), Almeria Province, S. E. Spain. *J. Sediment. Petrol.*, **51**, 521–539.

Dalrymple, D. W., 1965. Calcium carbonate deposition associated with blue-green algal mats, Baffin Bay, Texas. *Texas Inst. Mar. Sci.*, **10**, 187–200.

Darwin, C., 1842. *The structure and distribution of coral reefs*. Smith, Elder and Co., London, 214 pp., 3 pls. (Reprinted 1962, University of California Press, Berkeley, CA.)

Davies, P. J., 1983. Reef growth. In Barnes, D. J. (ed.), *Perspectives on coral reefs*. Australian Institute of Marine Science, Townsville, and Brian Clouston, Canberra, Australia, pp. 69–106.

Davies, P. J. and Hutchings, P. A., 1983. Initial colonization, erosion and accretion on coral substrate. *Coral Reefs*, **2**, 27–35.

Davies, P. J. and Marshall, J. F., 1985. *Halimeda* bioherms—low energy reefs, northern Great Barrier Reef. *Proc. Fifth Int. Coral Reef Congr.*, **2**, 97.

Davies, P. S., 1977. Carbon budgets and vertical zonation of Atlantic reef corals. *Proc. Third Int. Coral Reef Symp.*, **1**, 391–396.

Davies, P. S., 1984. The role of zooxanthellae in the nutritional energy requirements of *Pocillopora eydouxi*. *Coral Reefs*, **2**, 181–186.

Dawes, C. J., 1981. *Marine botany*. Wiley-Interscience, New York, 607 pp.

Debrenne, F., 1983. Archaeocyathids: morphology and affinity. In Rigby, J. K. and Stearn, C. W. (orgs.), Sponges and spongiomorphs—notes for a short course. *Univ. Tennessee Stud. Geol.*, **7**, 178–190.

Debrenne, F. and James, N. P., 1981. Reef-associated archeaocyathans from the Lower Cambrian of Labrador and Newfoundland. *Palaeontology*, **24**, 343–378.

Debrenne, F. and Rozanov, A., 1983. Paleogeographic and stratigraphic distribution of regular Archaeocyatha (Lower Cambrian fossils). *Geobios*, **16**, 727–736.

Debrenne, F. and Vacelet, J., 1984. Archaeocyatha: Is the sponge model consistent with their structural organization? *Palaeontogr. Am.* **54**, 358–369.

Debrenne, F. et al., 1984. Upper Cambrian Archaeocyatha from Antarctica. *Geol. Mag.*, **121**, 291–299.

Dechaseaux, C., 1969. Classification. In *Treatise on invertebrate paleontology, Part N, Bivalvia*. Geological Society of America, Boulder, Colorado, and Univ. Kansas Press, Lawrence, Kansas, p. N766.

Diamond, J. M., 1978. Niche shifts and the rediscovery of interspecific competition. *Am. Sci.*, **66**, 322–331.

Dieci, G. et al., 1968. Le spunge Cassiane (Trias Medio-Superiore) della regione Dolomitica Attorno a Cortina d'Ampezzo. *Boll. Soc. Paleontol. Ital.*, **7**, 94–155, Pls. 18–33.

Dieci, G. et al., 1977. Occurrence of spicules in Triassic chaetitids and cerato-porellids. *Boll. Soc. Paleontol. Ital.*, **16**, 229–238.

Dobrin, M. B. and Perkins Jr., B., 1954. Seismic studies of Bikini Atoll. *U.S. Geol. Surv. Prof. Pap.*, **260-J.**

Dodge, R. E. and Lang, J. C., 1983. Environmental correlates of hermatypic coral *(Montastraea annularis)* growth on the East Flower Gardens Bank, northwest Gulf of Mexico. *Limnol. Oceanogr.*, **28**, 228–240.

Dollar, S. J., 1982. Wave stress and coral community structure in Hawaii. *Coral Reefs*, **1**, 71–81.

Done, T. J., 1982. Patterns in the distribution of coral communities across the central Great Barrier Reef. *Coral Reefs*, **1**, 95–107.

Done, T. J., 1983. Coral zonation: its nature and significance. In Barnes, D. J. (ed.), *Perspectives on coral reefs*. Australian Institute of Marine Science, Townsville, and Brian Clouston, Canberra, Australia, pp. 107–149.

Dons, C., 1944. Norges korallrev. *Forhandlungen K. Norske Vidensk. Selsk.*, **17**, 37–82.

Dravis, J. J., 1983. Hardened subtidal stromatolites. *Science*, **219**, 385–386.

Dresnay, R. du, 1971. Extension et développement des phénomènes récifaux jur-assiques dans le domaine attasique marocain, particulièrement au Lias moyen. *Bull. Soc. Géol. Fr.*, **13**(7), 46–56.

Dresnay, R. du, 1977. Le milieu récifal fossile du Jurassique inférieur (Lias) dans le domaine des Chaînes altasiques du Maroc. Second symposium interna-tionale sur les coraux et récifs coralliens fossiles. *Bull. Bur. Rech. Géol. Min-ières Mem. (Fr.)*, **89**, 296–312.

Drew, E. A., 1983. Halimeda biomass, growth rates and sediment generation on reefs in the central Great Barrier Reef province. *Coral Reefs*, **2**, 101–110.

Duncan, H., 1957. Bryozoans-annotated bibliography. In Ladd, H. S. (ed.), *Pa-leoecology. Geol. Soc. Am. Mem.* 67, **2**, 783–799.

Dunham, R. J., 1962. Classification of carbonate rocks according to depositional texture. *Am. Assoc. Pet. Geol. Mem.*, **1**, 108–121.

Dunham, R. J., 1970. Stratigraphic reefs versus ecologic reefs. *Am. Assoc. Pet. Geol. Bull.*, **54**, 1931–1932.

Eder, W. and Franke, W., 1982. Death of Devonian reefs. *Neues Jahrb. Geol. Paläontol. Abh.*, **163**, 241–243.

Eldredge, N., 1974. Stability, diversity and speciation in Paleozoic epeiric seas. *J. Paleontol.*, **48**, 540–548.

Eldredge, N. and Gould, S. J., 1972. Punctuated equilibria: an alternative to phyletic gradualism. In Schopf, T. J. M. (ed.), *Models in paleobiology.* Freeman, Cooper, San Francisco, pp. 82–115.

Elias, G. K., 1963. Habitat of Pennsylvanian algal bioherms, Four Corners area. In Bass, R. O. (ed.), Shelf carbonates of the Paradox Basin. *Four Corners Geol. Soc. Fourth Field Conf.*, 185–203.

Elliott, G. F., 1950. The Genus *Hamptonina* (Brachiopoda) and the relation of post-Paleozoic brachiopods to coral-reefs. *Ann. Mag. Nat. Hist. Ser. 12*, **3**, 429–446.

Elliott, G. F., 1979. Influences of organic reefs on the evolution of post-Paleozoic algae. *Geol. Mag.*, **116**, 375–383.

Embry III, A. F. and Klovan, J. E., 1971. A Late Devonian reef tract on northeastern Banks Island, N.W.T. *Bull. Can. Pet. Geol.*, **19**, 730–781.

Emery, K. O., 1956. Marine geology of Johnston Island and its surrounding shallows, central Pacific Ocean. *Geol. Soc. Am. Bull.*, **67**, 1505–1519.

Emery, K. O., et al., 1954. Geology of Bikini and nearby atolls. *U.S. Geol. Surv.*, Prof. Paper 260-A, 265 p., 73 pls.

Emiliani, C., 1951. On *Homotrema rubrum. Cushman Found. Foraminiferal Res. Contrib.*, **2**, 143–147.

Endean, R. 1976. Destruction and recovery of coral reef communities. In Jones, O. A. and Endean, R. (eds.), *Biology and geology of coral reefs*, Vol. 3. Academic, New York, pp. 215–254.

Endean, R., 1982. *Australia's Great Barrier Reef.* University of Queensland Press, St. Lucia, London, 348 pp.

Epstein, S. A. and Friedman, G. M., 1982. Processes controlling precipitation of carbonate cement and dissolution of silica in reef and near-reef settings. *Sediment. Geol.*, **33**, 157–172.

Esteban, M. 1979. Significance of the Upper Miocene coral reefs of the western Mediterranean. *Palaeogeogr. Palaeoclimatol. Palaeoecol.*, **29**, 169–188.

Fagerstrom, J. A., 1961. The fauna of the Middle Devonian Formosa Reef Limestone of southwestern Ontario. *J. Paleontol.*, **35**, 1–48.

Fagerstrom, J. A., 1964. Fossil communities in paleoecology: their recognition and significance. *Geol. Soc. Am. Bull.*, **75**, 1197–1216.

Fagerstrom, J. A., 1971. Brachiopods of the Detroit River Group (Devonian) from southwestern Ontario and adjacent areas of Michigan and Ohio. *Bull. Geol. Surv. Can.*, **204**, 112 pp.

Fagerstrom, J. A., 1982. Stromatoporoids of the Detroit River Group and adjacent rocks (Devonian) in the vicinity of the Michigan Basin. *Bull. Geol. Surv. Can.*, **339**, 81 pp.

Fagerstrom, J. A., 1983. Diversity, speciation, endemism and extinction in Devonian reef and level-bottom communities, eastern North America. *Coral Reefs*, **2**, 65–70.

Fagerstrom, J. A., 1984a. The paleobiology of sclerosponges, stromatoporoids, chaetetids, archaeocyathids and non-spicular calcareous sponges. *Palaeontogr. Am.*, **54**, 303–304.

Fagerstrom, J. A., 1984b. The ecology and paleoecology of the Sclerospongiae and Sphinctozoa *(sensu stricto):* a review. *Palaeontogr. Am.*, **54**, 370–381.

Fagerstrom, J. A., 1985. Comparison of processes and guild structures in Holocene and ancient reef communities. *Proc. Fifth Int. Coral Reef Congr.*, **2**, 126.

Fagerstrom, J. A. and Burchett, R. R., 1972. Upper Pennsylvanian shoreline deposits from Iowa and Nebraska: their recognition, variation and significance. *Geol. Soc. Am. Bull.*, **83**, 367–388, 8 figs.

Fairbridge, R. W., 1950. Recent and Pleistocene coral reefs of Australia. *J. Geol.*, **58**, 330–401.

Fan, J. and Zhang, Wei, 1985. Sphinctozoans from Late Permian reefs of Lichuan, West Hubei, China. *Facies*, **13**, 1–44.

Finks, R. M., 1960. Late Paleozoic sponge faunas of the Texas region. *Bull. Am. Mus. Nat. Hist.*, **120**, 1–160.

Finks, R. M., 1970. The evolution and ecologic history of sponges during Paleozoic times. *Zool. Soc. London Symp.*, **25**, 3–22.

Finks, R. M., 1983. Pharetronida: Inozoa and Sphinctozoa. In Rigby, J. K. and Stearn, C. W. (Orgs.), Sponges and spongiomorphs—notes for a short course. *Univ. Tennessee Stud. Geol.*, **7**, 55–69.

Fischer, A. G., 1961. Latitudinal variations in organic diversity. *Am. Sci.*, **49**, 50–74.

Fischer, A. G., 1965. Brackish oceans as the cause of the Permo-Triassic marine faunal crisis. In Nairn, A. E. M. (ed.), *Problems in palaeoclimatology*. Wiley, New York, pp. 566–574.

Fischer, A. G., 1982. Long-term climatic oscillations recorded in stratigraphy. In Berger, W. (ed.), *Climate in earth history*. Natl. Research Council, Studies in Geophysics, Washington, D.C., pp. 97–104.

Fischer, A. G., 1984. The two Phanerozoic supercycles. In Berggren, W. A. and Van Couvering, J. A. (eds.), *Catastrophes in earth history*. Princeton University Press, Princeton, NJ, pp. 129–150.

Fischer, A. G. and Arthur, M. A., 1977. Secular variations in the pelagic realm. *Soc. Econ. Paleontol. Mineral. Spec. Publ.*, **25**, 19–50.

Fischer, J.-C., 1970. Revision et essai de classification des Chaetetida (Cnidaria) post-Paleozoiques. *Ann. Paleontol. Invertebrates*, **56**, 151–217.

Fisher, J. H. (ed.), 1977. Reefs and evaporites—concepts and depositional models. *Am. Assoc. Pet. Geol. Stud. Geol.*, **5**, 196 pp.

Flood, P. G., 1985. Oxygen isotope ratios of *Tridacna* shell material from the southern Great Barrier Reef and their interpretation as paleotemperature indicators. *Proc. Fifth Int. Coral Reef Congr.*, **3**, 147–152.

Flood, P. G. et al., 1978. An analysis of the textural variability displayed by inter-reef sediments of the impure carbonate facies in the vicinity of the Howick Group. *Philos. Trans. R. Soc. London Ser. A*, **291**, 73–83.

Flügel, E., 1975. Fossile hydrozoen-kenntnisstand und problem. *Paläontol. Z.*, **49**, 369–406.

Flügel, E., 1981. Paleoecology and facies of Upper Triassic reefs in the northern calcareous Alps. In Toomey, D. F. (ed.), European fossil reef models. *Soc. Econ. Paleontol. Mineral. Spec. Publ.*, **30**, 291–359.

Flügel, E., 1982. Evolution of Triassic reefs: current concepts and problems. *Facies*, **6**, 297–328.

Flügel, E. and Stanley Jr., G. D., 1984. Reorganization, development and evolution of post-Permian reefs and reef organisms. *Palaeontogr. Am.*, **54**, 177–186.

Flügel, E. and Steiger, T., 1981. An Upper Jurassic sponge-algal buildup from the northern Frankenalb, West Germany. In Toomey, D. F. (ed.), European fossil reef models. *Soc. Econ. Paleontol. Mineral. Spec. Publ.* **30**, 371–397.

Flügel, E. et al., 1984a. Middle Triassic reefs from southern Spain. *Facies*, **11**, 173–218.

Flügel, E. et al., 1984b. A Middle Permian calciosponge/algal/cement reef: Straza near Bled, Slovenia. *Facies*, **10**, 179–256, Pls. 24–42.

Flügel, H. W., 1976. Ein spongienmodell für die Favositidae. *Lethaia*, **9**, 405–419.

Fois, E. and Gaetani, M., 1984. The recovery of reef-building communities and the role of cnidarians in carbonate sequences of the Middle Triassic (Anisian) in the Italian Dolomites. *Palaeontogr. Am.*, **54**, 191–200.

Folk, R. L., 1959. Practical petrographic classification of limestones. *Am. Assoc. Pet. Geol. Bull.*, **43**, 1–38.

Folk, R. L., 1962. Spectral subdivision of limestone types. *Am. Assoc. Pet. Geol. Mem.*, **1**, 62–84.

Folk, R. L. and Robles, R., 1964. Carbonate sands of Isla Perez, Alacran Reef complex, Yucatan. *J. Geol.*, **72**, 255–292.

Forney, G. G., 1975. Permo-Triassic sea-level change. *J. Geol.*, **83**, 773–779.

Foster, A. B., 1979. Phenotypic plasticity in the reef corals *Montastraea annularis* (Ellis and Solander) and *Siderastrea siderea*. *J. Exp. Mar. Biol. Ecol.*, **39**, 25–54.

Foster, A. B., 1980. Environmental variation in skeletal morphology within the Caribbean reef corals *Montastraea annularis* and *Siderastrea siderea*. *Bull. Mar. Sci.*, **30**, 678–709.

Foster, A. B., 1983. The relationship between corallite morphology and colony shape in some massive reef-corals. *Coral Reefs*, **2**, 19–26.

Fricke, H. W. and Hottinger, L., 1983. Coral bioherms below the euphotic zone in the Red Sea. *Marine Ecol., Progress Ser.*, **11**, 113–117.

Friedman, G. M. et al., 1976. Dissolution of quartz accompanying carbonate precipitation and cementation in reefs: example from the Red Sea. *J. Sediment. Petrol.*, **46**, 970–973.

Fritz, H. C. et al., 1983. Coral recruitment at moderate depths: the influence of grazing. In Reaka, M. L. (ed.), The ecology of deep and shallow coral reefs. *Natl. Oceanic Atmos. Adm. Symp. Ser. Undersea Res.*, **1**, 89–96.

Froelich, A. S., 1983. Functional aspects of nutrient cycling on coral reefs. In Reaka, M. L. (ed.), The ecology of deep and shallow coral reefs. *Natl. Oceanic Atmos. Adm. Symp. Ser. Undersea Res.*, **1**, 133–139.

Frost, S. H., 1972. Evolution of Cenozoic Caribbean coral faunas. *Caribb. Geol. Congr. Trans.*, **6**, 461–464.

Frost, S. H., 1977a. Oligocene reef coral biogeography Caribbean and western Tethys. *Second symposium internationale sur les coraux et récifs coralliens fossiles. Bull. Bur. Rech. Géol. Minières Mem. (Fr.)*, **89**, 342–352.

Frost, S. H., 1977b. Cenozoic reef systems of the Caribbean. In Frost, S. H. et al. (eds.), Reefs and related carbonates—ecology and sedimentology. *Am. Assoc. Pet. Geol. Stud. Geol.*, **4**, 92–110.

Fry, W. G., 1979. Taxonomy, the individual and the sponge. In Larwood, G. and Rosen, B. R. (eds.), Biology and systematics of colonial organisms. *Syst. Assoc. Spec. Publ. 11*, Academic, London, pp. 49–80.

Frydl, P. and Stearn, C. W., 1978. Rate of bioerosion by parrotfish in Barbados reef environments. *J. Sediment. Petrol.*, **48**, 1149–1158.

Fürsich, F. T. and Wendt, J. W., 1977. Biostratinomy and paleoecology of the Cassian Formation (Triassic) of the southern Alps. *Palaeogeogr. Palaeoclimatol. Palaeoecol.*, **22**, 257–323.

Futterer, D. K., 1974. Significance of the boring sponge *Cliona* for the origin of fine-grained material of carbonate sediments. *J. Sediment. Petrol.*, **44**, 79–84.

Gaetani, M. et al., 1981. Nature and evolution of Middle Triassic carbonate build-ups in the Dolomites (Italy). *Mar. Geol.*, **44**, 25–47.

Gaillard, C., 1983. Les bioherms a spongiaires et leur environment dans l'Oxfordien du Jura méridional. *Doc. Lab. Géol. Fac. Sci. Lyon*, **90**, 515 pp., 187 figs., 42 pls.

Gall, J. C., 1983. *Ancient sedimentary environments and life style, introduction to paleoecology.* Springer-Verlag, Berlin, 248 pp.

Galloway, J. J., 1957. Structure and classification of the Stromatoporoidea. *Bull. Am. Paleontol.*, **37**, 345–470.

Gandin, A. and Debrenne, F. 1984. Lower Cambrian bioconstructions in southwestern Sardinia (Italy). *Geobios Spec. Mem.*, **8**, 231–240.

Gangloff, R. A., 1983. Archaeocyathids: paleoecology and biogeography. In Rigby, J. K. and Stearn, C. W. (orgs.), Sponges and spongiomorphs—notes for a short course. *Univ. Tennessee Stud. Geol.*, **7**, 191–200.

Gardiner, J. S., 1902. The formation of the Maldives. *Geog. J.*, **19**, 277–301.

Garrett, P., 1969. The geology and biology of large cavities in Bermuda reefs. *Bermuda Biol. Stat. Spec. Publ.*, **2**, 77–88.

Garrett, P., 1970. Phanerozoic stromatolites: non-competitive ecologic restriction by grazing and burrowing animals. *Science*, **169**, 171–173.

Garrett, P. et al., 1971. Physiography, ecology and sediments of two Bermudan patch reefs. *J. Geol.*, **79**, 647–668.

Gebelein, C. D., 1969. Distribution, morphology and accretion rate of Recent subtidal algal stromatolites, Bermuda. *J. Sediment. Petrol.*, **39**, 49–69.

Geister, J., 1977. The influence of wave exposure on the ecological zonation of Caribbean coral reefs. *Proc. Third Int. Coral Reef Symp.*, **1**, 23–29.

Geister, J., 1980. Calm-water reefs and rough-water reefs of the Caribbean Pleistocene. *Acta Palaeontol. Pol.*, **25**, 541–556.

Geister, J., 1983. Holozäne westindische korallenriffe: geomorphologie, ökologie und fazies. *Facies*, **9**, 173–284.

Geister, J. 1984a. Récifs Pleistocenes de la Mer des Caraibes: aspects geologiques et paleoecologiques. In Geister, J. and Herb, R. (eds.), *Geologie et paleoecologie des récifs, 3ème cycle romand en sciences de la terre.* Institute de Geologie, Université de Berne, Switzerland, pp. 3.1–3.34.

Geister, J., 1984b. Les récifs a *Plaucunopsis ostracina* dans le Muschelkalk du Bassin Germanique. In Geister, J. and Herb, R. (eds.), *Geologie et paleoecologie des récifs, 3ème cycle romand en sciences de la terre.* Institute de Geologie, Université de Berne, Switzerland, pp. 19.1–19.8.

Geister, J. 1984c. Geomorphologie, ecologie et facies des récifs actuels des Caraibes: consequences pour l'interpretation des récifs fossiles. In Geister, J. and Herb, R. (eds.), *Geologie et paleoecologie des récifs, 3ème cycle romand en sciences de la terre.* Institute de Geologie, Université de Berne, Switzerland, pp. 1.1–1.15.

Geister, J., 1984d. Récifs a coraux du Bajocien du Grand-Duche des Luxembourg et de Malancourt en Lorraine. In Geister, J. and Herb, R. (eds.), *Geologie et paleoecologie des récifs, 3ème cycle romand en sciences de la terre.* Institute de Geologie, Université de Berne, Switzerland, pp. 12.1–12.16.

Ginsburg, R. N., 1956. Environmental relationships of grain size and constituent particles in some south Florida carbonate sediments. *Am. Assoc. Pet. Geol. Bull.,* **40**, 2384–2427.

Ginsburg, R. N., 1960. Ancient analogues of Recent stromatolites. *Int. Geol. Congr. 21st,* Pt. 22, 26–35.

Ginsburg, R. N., 1983. Geological and biological roles of cavities in coral reefs. In Barnes, D. J. (eds.), *Perspectives on coral reefs.* Australian Institute of Marine Science, Townsville, and Brian Clouston, Canberra, Australia, pp. 148–153.

Ginsburg, R. N. and Choi, D. R., 1984. Coral content of Quaternary reef limestones. *Am. Assoc. Pet. Geol. Ann. Conv.,* abst.

Ginsburg, R. N. and James, N. P., 1974. Holocene carbonate sediments of continental shelves. In Burk, C. A. (ed.), *The geology of continental margins.* Springer-Verlag, New York, 137–155.

Ginsburg, R. N. and Schroeder, J. H., 1973. Growth and submarine fossilization of algal cup reefs, Bermuda. *Sedimentology,* **20**, 575–614.

Gladfelter, E. H., 1984. Skeletal development in *Acropora cervicornis:* III. A comparison of monthly rates of linear extension and calcium carbonate accretion measured over a year. *Coral Reefs,* **3**, 51–57.

Gladfelter, E. H., 1985. Metabolism, calcification and carbon production. II. Organism-level studies. *Proc. Fifth Int. Coral Reef Congr.,* **4**, 527–539.

Glynn, P. W., 1973. Aspects of the ecology of coral reefs in the western Atlantic region. In Jones, O. A. and Endean, R. (eds.), *Biology and geology of coral reefs,* Vol. 2. Academic, New York, pp. 271–324.

Glynn, P. W. and Stewart, R. H., 1972. Pacific coral reefs of Panama: structure, distribution and predators. *Geol. Rundsch.,* **61**, 483–519.

Goldring, W., 1938. Algal barrier reefs in the Lower Ozarkian of New York. *N.Y. State Mus. Bull.,* **315**, 75 pp.

Goldschmidt, R., 1940. *The material basis of evolution.* Yale University Press, New Haven, CT, 436 pp.

Golubic, S. et al., 1975. Boring micro-organisms and microborings in carbonate substrates. In Frey, R. W. (ed.), *The study of trace fossils*. Springer-Verlag, New York, pp. 229–260.

Goreau, T. F., 1959. The ecology of Jamaican coral reefs I. Species composition and zonation. *Ecology, 40,* 67–90.

Goreau, T. F. and Goreau, N. I., 1959. The physiology of skeleton formation in corals II. Calcium deposition by hermatypic corals under various conditions in the reef. *Biol. Bull., 117,* 239–250.

Goreau, T. F. and Goreau, N. I., 1973. The ecology of Jamaican coral reefs II. Geomorphology, zonation and sedimentary phases. *Bull. Mar. Sci., 23,* 403–464.

Goreau, T. F. et al., 1979. Corals and coral reefs. *Sci. Am., 241,* 124–136.

Gotto, R. V., 1969. *Marine animals: Partnerships and other associations.* Am. Elsevier Co., New York, 96 pp.

Gould, S. J., 1965. Is uniformitarianism necessary? *Am. J. Sci., 263,* 223–228.

Gould, S. J., 1984. Toward the vindication of punctuational change. In Berggren, W. A. and Van Couvering, J. A. (eds.), *Catastrophes in earth history.* Princeton University Press, Princeton, NJ, pp. 9–34.

Gould, S. J., 1985. All the news that's fit to print and some opinions that aren't. *Discover,* **6**(11), 86–91.

Gram, R., 1968. A Florida Sabellariidae reef and its effects on sediment distribution. *J. Sediment. Petrol., 38,* 863–868.

Grant, R. E., 1971. Brachiopods in the Permian reef environment of west Texas. *Proc. N. Am. Paleontol. Conv. Part J,* 1444–1481.

Grassle, J. F., 1973. Variety in coral reef communities. In Jones, O. A. and Endean, R., (eds.), *Biology and geology of coral reefs,* Vol. 2. Academic, New York, pp. 247–270.

Graus, R. and Macintyre, I. G., 1982. Variation in growth form of the reef coral *Montastraea annularis* (Ellis and Solander). A quantitative evaluation of growth response to light distribution using computer simulation. In Rützler, K. and Macintyre, I. G. (eds.), The Atlantic barrier reef ecosystem at Carrie Bow Cay, Belize. *Smithson. Contrib. Mar. Sci., 12,* 441–464.

Graus, R. R. et al., 1977. Structural modification of corals in relation to waves and currents. In Frost, S. H. et al. (eds.), Reefs and Related Carbonates-Ecology and Sedimentology. *Am. Assoc. Pet. Geol. Stud. Geol.* **4,** 135–153.

Graus, R. R. et al., 1984. Computer simulation of the reef zonation at Discovery Bay, Jamaica: hurricane disruption and long-term physical oceanographic controls. *Coral Reefs, 3,* 59–68.

Gray, D. I., 1980. Spicule pseudomorphs in a new Palaeozoic chaetetid, and its sclerosponge affinities. *Palaeontology, 23,* 803–820.

Grigg, R. W., 1981. Coral reef development at high latitudes in Hawaii. *Proc. Fourth Int. Coral Reef Symp., 1,* 687–693.

Grigg, R. W., 1982. Darwin Point: a threshold for atoll formation. *Coral Reefs, 1,* 29–34.

Grigg, R. and Margos, J., 1974. Recolonization of hermatypic corals on submerged lava flows in Hawaii. *Ecology,* **55,** 387–395.

Grigg, R. W. et al., 1984. Model of a coral reef ecosystem; III. Resource limitation, community regulation, fisheries yield and resource management. *Coral Reefs,* **3,** 23–27.

Gwinner, M. P., 1976. Origin of the Upper Jurassic limestones of the Swabian Alb (southwestern Germany). *Contrib. Sedimentol.,* **5,** 75 pp.

Hadding, A., 1950. Silurian reefs of Gotland. *J. Geol.,* **58,** 402–409.

Haikawa, T. and Ota, M., 1978. A Lower Carboniferous coral reef found in the *Nagatophyllam satoi* Zone of the Akiyoshi Limestone Group, southwest Japan. *Bull. Akiyoshi-dai Mus. Nat. Hist.,* **13,** 14 pp., 8 pls.

Hallam, A., 1975. Coral patch reefs in the Bajocian (Middle Jurassic) of Lorraine. *Geol. Mag.,* **112,** 383–392.

Hallam, A., 1981a. The end-Triassic bivalve extinction event. *Palaeogeogr. Palaeoclimatol. Palaeoecol.,* **35,** 1–44.

Hallam, A., 1981b. *Facies interpretation and the stratigraphic record.* Freeman, Oxford, UK, 282 pp.

Hallam, A., 1984. Pre-Quaternary sea-level changes. *Ann. Rev. Earth Planet. Sci.,* **12,** 205–243.

Halley, R. B. et al., 1977. Recent and relict topography of Boo Bee Patch reef, Belize. *Proc. Third Int. Coral Reef Symp.,* **2,** 29–35.

Handfield, R. C., 1971. Archaeocyatha from the Mackenzie and Cassair Mountains, Northwest Territories, Yukon Territory and British Columbia. *Geol. Surv. Can. Bull.,* **201,** 119 pp.

Harland, T. L., 1981. Middle Ordovician reefs of Norway. *Lethaia,* **14,** 169–188.

Harms, J. C., 1974. Brushy Canyon Formation, Texas: a deep water density current deposit. *Geol. Soc. Am. Bull.,* **85,** 1763–1784.

Harrison III, J. T., 1983. Metabolism of interreef sediment communities. In Reaka, M. L. (ed.), The ecology of deep and shallow coral reefs. *Natl. Oceanic Atmos. Adm. Symp. Ser. Undersea Res.,* **1,** 145–149.

Hartman, O., 1954. Marine annelids from the northern Marshall Islands. *U.S. Geol. Surv. Prof. Pap.,* **260-Q.**

Hartman, W. D., 1977. Sponges as reef builders and shapers. *Am. Assoc. Pet. Geol. Stud. Geol.,* **4,** 127–134.

Hartman, W. D., 1979. A new sclerosponge from the Bahamas and its relationship to the Mesozoic stromatoporoids. In Levi, C. and Boury-Esnault, N. (eds.), Biologie des spongiaires. *Colloq. Int. C. N. R. S.,* **291,** 467–474.

Hartman, W. D., 1984. Astrorhizae, mamelons and symbionts of Recent sclerosponges. *Palaeontogr. Am.,* **54,** 305–314.

Hartman, W. D. and Goreau, T. F., 1966. *Ceratoporella,* a living sponge with stromatoporoid affinities. *Am. Zool.,* **6,** 563–564.

Hartman, W. D. and Goreau, T. F., 1970. A new Pacific sponge: homeomorph or descendent of the tabulate "corals?" *Geol. Soc. Am. Abstr. (with Program),* **2,** 570.

Hartman, W. D. and Goreau, T. F., 1972. *Ceratoporella* (Porifera: Sclerospongiae) and the chaetetid "corals." *Trans. Connecticut Acad. Arts Sciences*, **44**, 133–148.

Hartman, W. D. et al. (eds.), 1980. Living and fossil sponges—notes for a short course. *Sedimenta VIII.* Comparative Sedimentology Laboratory, University of Miami, Miami, FL, 274 p.

Hatcher, A. I. and Frith, C. A., 1985. The control of nitrate and ammonium concentrations in a coral reef lagoon. *Coral Reefs*, **4**, 101–110.

Hatcher, A. I. and Hatcher, B. G., 1981. Seasonal and spatial variation in dissolved inorganic nitrogen in One Tree Reef lagoon. *Proc. Fourth Int. Coral Reef Symp.*, **1**, 419–424.

Hatcher, B. G., 1983. The role of detritus in the metabolism and secondary production of coral reef ecosystems. In *Proceedings of the inaugural Great Barrier Reef conference.* James Cook University, Townsville, Australia, pp. 317–325.

Hayward, A. B., 1982. Coral reefs in a clastic sedimentary environment: fossil (Miocene, S.W. Turkey) and modern (Recent, Red Sea) analogues. *Coral Reefs*, **1**, 109–114.

Heckel, P. H., 1972. Pennsylvanian stratigraphic reefs in Kansas, some comparisons and implications. *Geol. Rundsch.*, **61**, 584–598.

Heckel, P. H., 1974. Carbonate buildups in the geologic record: a review. *Soc. Econ. Paleontol. Mineral. Spec. Publ.*, **18**, 90–154.

Heckel, P. H. and Cocke, J. M., 1969. Phylloid algal-mound complexes in outcropping Upper Pennsylvanian rocks of Mid-Continent. *Am. Assoc. Pet. Geol. Bull.*, **53**, 1058–1074.

Hedberg, H. D. (ed.), 1976. *International stratigraphic guide.* International Union of Geological Scientists, Commission on Stratigraphy. Wiley, New York, 200 pp.

Hein, F. J., and Risk, M. J., 1975. Bioerosion of coral heads: inner patch reefs, Florida reef tract. *Bull. Mar. Sci.*, **25**, 133–138.

Henderson, R. S., 1981. *In situ* and microcosm studies of diel metabolism of reef flat communities. *Proc. Fourth Int. Coral Reef Symp.*, **1**, 679–686.

Henson, F. R. S., 1950. Cretaceous and Tertiary reef formations and associated sediment in the Middle East. *Am. Assoc. Pet. Geol. Bull.*, **34**, 215–238.

Herman, Y., 1981. Causes of massive biotic extinctions and explosive evolutionary diversification throughout Phanerozoic time. *Geology*, **9**, 104–108.

Hess, H. H., 1933. Submerged river valleys of the Bahamas. *Am. Geophysical Union, Trans. 14th Ann. Meeting*, 168–170.

Hiatt, R. W. and Strasburg, D. W., 1960. Ecological relationships of the fish fauna on coral reefs of the Marshall Islands. *Ecol. Monogr.*, **30**, 65–127.

Hidaka, M. and Yamazato, K., 1984. Intraspecific interactions in a scleractinian coral, *Galaxea fascicularis:* induced formation of sweeper tentacles. *Coral Reefs*, **3**, 77–85.

Highsmith, R. C., 1979. Coral growth rates and environmental control of density banding. *J. Exp. Mar. Biol. Ecol.*, **37**, 105–125.

Hill, D., 1972. Archaeocyatha. *Treatise on invertebrate paleontology, Part E*, 2nd ed. Geological Society of America, Boulder, CO, and University of Kansas Press, Lawrence, KS, 158 pp.

Hill, D., 1981a. Rugosa. In Teichert, C. (ed.), *Treatise on invertebrate paleontology, Part F, Suppl. 1, Coelenterata*. Geological Society of America, Boulder, CO, and University of Kansas Press, 762 pp.

Hill, D., 1981b. *Coelenterata:* Anthozoa Subclasses Rugosa, Tabulata. *Treatise on invertebrate paleontology, Part F*, Suppl. 1. Geological Society of America, Boulder, CO and University of Kansas Press, Lawrence, KS, pp. 1–429.

Hill, D. and Wells, J. W., 1956. Hydroida and Spongiomorphida. In *Treatise on invertebrate paleontology, Part F, Coelenterata*. Geological Society of America, Boulder, CO, and University of Kansas Press, Lawrence, KS, pp. F81–F89.

Hill, D. et al., 1956. *Coelenterata*. In *Treatise on invertebrate paleontology, Part F*. Geological Society of America, Boulder, CO, and University of Kansas Press, Lawrence, KS, 498 pp.

Hillis-Colinvaux, L., 1980. Ecology and taxonomy of *Halimeda:* primary producer of coral reefs. *Adv. Marine Biol.*, **17**, 1–327.

Hillis-Colinvaux, L., 1986. *Halimeda* growth and diversity on the deep fore-reef of Enewetak Atoll. *Coral Reefs*, **5**, 19–21.

Hixon, M. A., 1983. Fish grazing and community structure of reef corals and algae: a synthesis of recent studies. In Reaka, M. (ed.), The ecology of deep and shallow coral reefs. *Natl. Oceanic Atmos. Adm. Symp. Ser. Undersea Res.*, **1**, 79–87.

Hoffman, A., 1979. Community paleoecology as an epiphenomenal science. *Paleobiology*, **5**, 357–379.

Hoffman, A., 1982. Community evolution and stratigraphy. *Newsl. Stratigr.*, **11**, 32–36.

Hoffman, A., 1985a. Biotic diversification in the Phanerozoic: diversity independence. *Palaeontology*, **28**, 387–391.

Hoffman, A., 1985b. Patterns of family extinction depend on definition and geological timescale. *Nature (London)*, **315**, 659–662.

Hoffman, P., 1967. Algal stromatolites: use in stratigraphic correlation and paleocurrent determination. *Science*, **157**, 1043–1045.

Hoffman, P., 1974. Shallow and deepwater stromatolites in Lower Proterozoic platform-to-basin facies change, Great Slave Lake, Canada. *Am. Assoc. Pet. Geol. Bull.*, **58**, 856–867.

Hoffman, P., 1976. Stromatolite morphogenesis in Shark Bay, Western Australia. In Walter, M. R. (ed.), *Stromatolites*. Elsevier, Amsterdam, pp. 261–273.

Hoffmeister, J. E. and Ladd, H. S., 1944. The antecedent-platform theory. *J. Geol.*, **52**, 388–502.

Hoffmeister, J. E. and Multer, H. G., 1964. Growth rate estimates of a Pleistocene coral reef of Florida. *Geol. Soc. Am. Bull.*, **75**, 353–357.

Hoffmeister, J. E. and Multer, H. G., 1965. Fossil mangrove reef of Key Biscayne, Florida. *Geol. Soc. Am. Bull.*, **76**, 845–852.

Holland, H. D. and Trendall, A. F., 1984. *Patterns of change in earth evolution*. Springer-Verlag, Berlin, 431 pp.

Hopley, D., 1982. *The geomorphology of the Great Barrier Reef: quaternary development of coral reefs.* Wiley-Interscience, New York, 453 pp.

Hopley, D., 1983. Morphological classifications of shelf reefs: a critique with special reference to the Great Barrier Reef. In Barnes, D. J. (ed.), *Perspectives on coral reefs.* Australian Institute of Marine Science, Townsville, and Brian Clouston, Canberra, Australia, pp. 180–199.

Hopley, D. et al., 1983. Nearshore fringing reefs in north Queensland. *Coral Reefs,* **1,** 151–160.

Horodyski, R. J., 1983. Sedimentary geology and stromatolites of the Middle Proterozoic Belt Supergroup, Glacier National Park, Montana. *Precamb. Res.,* **20,** 391–425.

Hottinger, L., 1984. Les organismes constructeurs sur la plateforme du Golfe d'Aqaba (Mer Rouge) et les méchanismes régissant leur répartition. *Geobios, Mém. Spéc.* **8,** 241–249.

Hsu, K. J., 1972. Origin of saline giants: a critical review after the discovery of the Mediterranean evaporite. *Earth Sci. Rev.,* **8,** 371–396.

Hubbard, D. K. et al., 1981. Preliminary studies of the fate of shallow-water detritus in the basin north of St. Croix, U.S.V.I. *Proc. Fourth Int. Coral Reef Symp.,* **1,** 383–387.

Huffington, T. L., 1984. Faunal zonation of Cenomanian (Middle Cretaceous) rudist reef, Paso del Rio, Colima, Mexico. *Am. Assoc. Pet. Geol. Book Abstr.*

Hughes, T., 1983. Life histories and growth of corals over a depth gradient. In Reaka, M. L., (ed.), The ecology of deep and shallow coral reefs. *Natl. Oceanic Atmos. Adm. Symp. Ser. Undersea Res.,* **1,** 17–20.

Hunter, I. G., 1977. Sediment production by *Diadema antillarum* on a Barbados fringing reef. *Proc. Third Int. Coral Reef Symp.,* **2,** 105–109.

Huston, M., 1979. A general hypothesis of species diversity. *Am. Nat.,* **113,** 81–101.

Hutchings, P., 1983. Cryptofaunal communities of coral reefs. In Barnes, D. J. (ed.), *Perspectives on coral reefs.* Australian Institute of Marine Science, Townsville, and Brian Clouston, Canberra, Australia, pp. 200–208.

Hutchings, P. A., 1986. Biological destruction of coral reefs: a review. *Coral Reefs,* **4,** 239–252.

Ingels, J. J. C., 1963. Geometry, paleontology, and petrography of Thornton reef complex, Silurian of northern Illinois. *Am. Assoc. Pet. Geol. Bull.,* **47,** 405–440.

Jaap, W. C., 1983. Community structure of stony corals (Scleractinia and Milleporina) in southeast Florida reef communities. *Int. Soc. Reef Stud. Ann. Colloq. Nice, France.*

Jaap, W. C., 1985. An epidemic zooxanthellae expulsion during 1983 in the lower Florida Keys coral reefs: hyperthermal etiology. *Proc. Fifth Int. Coral Reef Congr.,* **2,** 194.

Jablonski, D. et al., 1983. Onshore-offshore patterns in the evolution of Phanerozoic shelf communities. *Science,* **222,** 1123–1125.

Jackson, J. B. C., 1977. Competition on marine hard substrata: the adaptive significance of solitary and colonial strategies. *Am. Nat.,* **111,** 743–767.

Jackson, J. B. C., 1979. Morphological strategies of sessile animals. In Larwood, G. and Rosen, B. R. (eds.), Biology and systematics of colonial organisms. *Syst. Assoc. Spec. Publ. 11,* Academic, London, pp. 449–555.

Jackson, J. B. C., 1983. Biological determinants of present and past sessile animal distributions. In Tevesz, M. J. S. and McCall, P. L. (eds.). Biotic interactions in Recent and fossil benthic communities, Plenum, New York, pp. 39–120.

Jackson, J. B. C. and Winston, J. E., 1982. Ecology of cryptic coral reef communities. I. Distribution and abundance of major groups of encrusting organisms. *J. Exp. Mar. Biol. Ecol., 57,* 135–147.

Jackson, J. B. C. et al., 1971. Recent brachiopod-coralline sponge communities and their paleoecological significance. *Science, 143,* 623–625.

Jameison, E. R., 1971. Paleoecology of Devonian reefs in western Canada. *Proc. N. Am. Paleontol. Conv. Chicago Part J,* 1300–1340.

James, N. P., 1979. Reefs. In Walker, R. B. (ed.), Facies models. *Geosci. Repr. Ser., 1,* 121–132.

James, N. P., 1983. Reef environment. In Scholle, P. A. et al. (eds.), Carbonate depositional environments. *Am. Assoc. Pet. Geol. Mem., 33,* 346–440.

James, N. P. and Debrenne, F., 1980. Lower Cambrian bioherms: pioneer reefs of the Phanerozoic. *Acta Palaeontol. Pol., 25,* 655–668.

James, N. P. and Kobluk, D. R., 1978. Lower Cambrian patch reefs and associated sediments, southern Labrador. *Sedimentology, 25,* 1–35.

James, N. P. et al., 1977. The oldest macroborers: Lower Cambrian of Labrador. *Science, 197,* 980–983.

James, N. P. et al., 1984. Calcification of encrusting aragonitic algae: implications for origin of Late Paleozoic reefs and cements. *Am. Assoc. Pet. Geol., Book Abstr.*

Jell, J. S., 1984. Cambrian cnidarians with mineralized skeletons. *Palaeontogr. Am., 54,* 105–109.

Jenkins, R. J. F., 1984. Interpreting the oldest fossil cnidarians. *Palaeontogr. Am., 54,* 95–104.

Johannes, R. E. et al., 1972. The metabolism of some coral reef communities: a team study of nutrient and energy flux at Eniwetok. *Bioscience, 22,* 541–543.

Johnson, G. A. L. and Nudds, J. R., 1975. Carboniferous coral geochronometers. In Rosenburg, G. D. and Runcorn, S. K. (eds.), *Growth rhythms and the history of the earth's rotation.* Wiley, New York, pp. 27–41.

Johnson, J. G. et al., 1985. Devonian eustatic fluctuations in Euramerica. *Geol. Soc. Am. Bull., 96,* 567–587.

Johnson, M. W., 1954. Plankton of northern Marshall Islands. *U.S. Geol. Surv. Prof. Pap., 260-F,* 301–314.

Jokiel, P. L., 1980. Solar ultraviolet radiation and coral reef epifauna. *Science, 207,* 1069–1071.

Jokiel, P. L., 1984. Long distance dispersal of reef corals by rafting. *Coral Reefs, 3,* 113–116.

Jones, A. R., 1984. Sedimentary relationships and community structure of benthic crustacean assemblages of reef-associated sediments at Lizard Island, Great Barrier Reef. *Coral Reefs, 3,* 101–111.

Jones, D. S. and Hasson, P. F., 1985. History and development of the marine invertebrate faunas separated by the Central American isthmus. In Stehli, F. G. and Webb, S. D. (eds.), *The great American interchange*. Plenum, New York, pp. 325–355.

Joubin, L., 1922. Les coraux de mer profonde nuisables aux chalutiers. *Notes et Mémoires, Office Scientifique et Technologique des Pêches Maritimes*, **18**, 16 pp., 1 map.

Kanwisher, J. W. and Wainwright, S. A., 1967. Oxygen balance in some reef corals. *Biol. Bull. Mar. Biol. Lab. Woods Hole*, **133**, 378–390.

Kapp, U., 1975. Paleoecology of Middle Ordovician stromatoporoid mounds in Vermont. *Lethaia*, **8**, 195–207.

Kapp, U. S. and Stearn, C. W., 1975. Stromatoporoids of the Chazy Group (Middle Ordovician), Lake Champlain, Vermont and New York. *J. Paleontol.*, **49**, 163–186.

Kauffman, E. G., 1969. Form, function and evolution. In *Treatise on invertebrate paleontology, Part N, Bivalvia*. Geological Society of America, Boulder, CO, and University of Kansas Press, Lawrence, KS, pp. N129–N205.

Kauffman, E. G., 1976. Basic concepts of community ecology and paleoecology. In Scott, R. W. and West, R. R. (eds.), *Structure and classification of paleo-communities*. Dowden, Hutchinson & Ross, Stroudsburg, PA, pp. 1–28.

Kauffman, E. G., 1979. The ecology and biogeography of the Cretaceous-Tertiary extinction event. In Christensen, W. K. and Birkelund, T. (eds.), *Symposium, Cretaceous-Tertiary boundary events, Proceedings*, University of Copenhagen, Copenhagen, pp. 29–37.

Kauffman, E. G., 1984. The fabric of Cretaceous marine extinctions. In Berggren, W. A. and Van Couvering, J. A. (eds.), *Catastrophes in earth history*. Princeton University Press, Princeton, NJ, pp. 151–246.

Kauffman, E. G., April 1986. Personal communication. Univ. of Colorado, Boulder, CO.

Kauffman, E. G. and Johnson, C. C., 1984. The evolution and adaptive value of shell wall structure in rudist bivalves. *Geol. Soc. Am. Abstr. (with Program)*, **16**, 555.

Kauffman, E. G. and Scott, R. W., 1976. Basic concepts of community ecology and paleoecology. In Scott, R. W. and West, R. R. (eds.). *Structure and classification of paleocommunities*. Dowden, Hutchinson and Ross, Stroudsburg, PA, 1–28.

Kauffman, E. G. and Sohl, N. F., 1974. Structure and evolution of Antillean Cretaceous rudist frameworks. *Verh. Naturforsch. Ges. Basel*, **84**, 399–467.

Kauffman, E. G. and Sohl, N. F., 1979. Rudists. In Fairbridge, R. W. and Jablonski, D. (eds.), *The encyclopedia of paleontology; encyclopedia of earth sciences*, Vol. 7. Dowden, Hutchinson & Ross, Stroudsburg, PA, pp. 723–737.

Kázmér, M., 1982. Microfacies investigation of the Upper Eocene limestone at Budapest, Hungary. Ph.D. dissertation, Eotvas University, Hungary, as reported in *Reef Newsl.*, **9**, 24.

Kaźmierczak, J., 1974. Lower Cretaceous sclerosponge from the Slovakian Tatra Mountains. *Palaeontol. London*, **17**, 341–347.

Kaźmierczak, J., 1976. Cyanophycean nature of stromatoporoids. *Nature (London)*, **264**, 49–51.

Kaźmierczak, J., 1979. Sclerosponge nature of chaetetids evidenced by spiculated *Chaetetopsis favrei* (Deninger 1906) from the Barremian of Crimea. *Neues Jahrb. Geol. Paläontol. Mineral. Abh.*, **2**, 97–108.

Kaźmierczak, J., 1980. Stromatoporoid stromatolites: a new insight into evolution of cyanobacteria. *Acta Palaeontol. Pol.*, **25**, 243–251.

Kaźmierczak, J., 1981. Evidences for cyanophyte origin of stromatoporoids. In Monty, C. (ed.), *Phanerozoic stromatolites*. Springer-Verlag, Berlin, pp. 230–241.

Kaźmierczak, J., 1984. Favositid tabulates: evidence for poriferan affinity. *Science*, **225**, 835–837.

Kaźmierczak, J. and Krumbein, W. E., 1983. Identification of calcified coccoid cyanobacteria forming stromatoporoid stromatolites. *Lethaia*, **16**, 207–214.

Kershaw, S. J. 1981. Stromatoporoid growth form and taxonomy in a Silurian biostrome, Gotland. *J. Paleontol.*, **55**, 1284–1295.

Kershaw, S. J. and Riding, R., 1978. Parameterization of stromatoporoid shape. *Lethaia*, **11**, 233–242.

Kershaw, S. J. and Riding, R., 1980. Stromatoporoid morphotypes of the Middle Devonian Torbay reef complex at Long Quarry Point, Devon. *Proc. Ussher Soc.*, **5**, 13–23.

King, P. B., 1948. Geology of the southern Guadalupe Mountains, Texas. *U.S. Geol. Surv. Prof. Pap.*, **215**, 183 pp.

Kinsey, D. W., 1981. The Pacific/Atlantic reef growth controversy. *Proc. Fourth Int. Coral Reef Symp.*, **1**, 493–498.

Kinsey, D. W., 1985. Metabolism, calcification and carbon production. I. Systems level studies. *Proc. Fifth Int. Coral Reef Congr.*, **4**, 505–526.

Kinsey, D. W. and Davies, P. J., 1979. Inorganic carbon turnover, calcification and growth in coral reefs. In Trudingar, P. and Swaine, D. (eds.), *Biogeochemistry of mineral forming elements*. Elsevier, Amsterdam, pp. 131–162.

Kinsman, D. J. J., 1964. Reef coral tolerance of high temperatures and salinities. *Nature (London)*, **202**, 1280–1282.

Kinzie III, R. A., 1973. The zonation of West Indian gorgonians. *Bull. Mar. Sci.*, **23**, 95–153.

Kirkland, D. W. et al., 1966. Origin of Carmen Island salt deposit, Baja California, Mexico. *J. Geol.*, **74**, 932–938.

Kirtley, D. W. and Tanner, W. F., 1968. Sabellariid worms: builders of a major reef type. *J. Sediment. Petrol.*, **38**, 73–78.

Kitchell, J. A. and Pena, D., 1984. Periodicity of extinctions in the geologic past: deterministic versus stochastic explanations. *Science*, **226**, 689–691.

Klement, K. W., 1967. Practical classification of reefs and banks, bioherms and biostromes. *Am. Assoc. Pet. Geol.*, **51**, 167–168.

Klement, K. W., 1968. Studies on the ecological distribution of lime-secreting and sediment-trapping algae in reefs and associated environments. In Silver, B. A. (ed.), *Symposium and guidebook*. Permian Basin Section, Soc. Econ. Paleontol. Mineral., pp. 36–48.

Klovan, J. E., 1974. Development of western Canadian Devonian reefs and comparison with Holocene analogues. *Am. Assoc. Pet. Geol. Bull.*, **58**, 787–799.

Knowlton, N. et al., 1981. Evidence for delayed mortality in hurricane-damaged Jamaican staghorn corals. *Nature (London)*, **294**, 251–252.

Kobluk, D. R., 1977. Calcification of filaments of boring and cavity-dwelling algae, and their construction of micrite envelopes. In Romans, R. C. (ed.), *Geobotany*. Plenum, New York, pp. 195–207.

Kobluk, D. R., 1980. The record of cavity-dwelling (coelobientic) organisms in the Paleozoic. *Can. J. Earth Sci.*, **18**, 181–190.

Kobluk, D. R. and James, N. P., 1979. Cavity-dwelling organisms in Lower Cambrian patch reefs from southern Labrador. *Lethaia*, **12**, 193–218.

Kobluk, D. R. and Risk, M. J., 1977. Micritization and carbonate-grain binding by endolithic algae. *Am. Assoc. Pet. Geol. Bull.*, **61**, 1069–1082.

Kobluk, D. R. et al., 1977. Disorientation of Paleozoic hemispherical corals and stromatoporoids. *Can. J. Earth Sci.*, **14**, 2226–2231.

Kobluk, D. R. et al., 1978. Initial diversification of macroboring ichnofossils and exploitation of the macroboring niche in the lower Paleozoic. *Paleobiology*, **4**, 163–170.

Kornicker, L. S. and Boyd, D. W., 1962. Shallow-water geology and environments of Alacran Reef Complex, Campeche Bank, Mexico. *Am. Assoc. Pet. Geol. Bull.*, **46**, 640–673.

Krebs, W., 1966. Der Bau des oberdevonischen Langenaubach-Breitscheider Riffes und seine weitere Entwicklung im Oberkarbon (Rheinisches Schiefergebirge). *Abh. Senckenb. Naturforsch. Ges.*, **511**, 105 pp.

Krebs, W., 1974. Devonian carbonate complexes of central Europe. In Laporte, L. (ed.), Reefs in time and space. *Soc. Econ. Paleontol. Mineral. Spec. Publ.*, **18**, 155–208.

Krebs, W. and Mountjoy, E., 1972. Comparison of central European and western Canadian Devonian reef complexes. *Twenty-fourth Int. Geol. Congr. Sect. 6*, 294–309.

Kuenen, P. H., 1950. *Marine geology*. Wiley, New York.

Laborel, J., 1960. Contribution à l'ètude directe des peuplements sciaphiles sur substrates rocheux en Mediterranee. *Recl. Trav. St. Mar. Endoume-Marseille Fasc. Hors Ser. Suppl.*, **20**, 117–173.

Ladd, H. S., 1973. Bikini and Eniwetok Atolls, Marshall Islands. In Jones, O. A. and Endean, R. (eds.), *Biology and geology of coral reefs*, Vol. 1, Academic, New York, pp. 93–110.

Ladd, H. S. et al., 1950. Organic growth and sedimentation on an atoll. *J. Geol.*, **58**, 410–425.

Ladd, H. S. et al., 1953. Drilling on Eniwetok Atoll, Marshall Islands. *Am. Assoc. Pet. Geol. Bull.*, **37**, 2257–2280.

Land, L. S., 1976. Early dissolution of sponge spicules from reef sediments, North Jamaica. *J. Sediment. Petrol.*, **46**, 967–969.

Lane, N. G., 1971. Crinoids and reefs. *Proc. N. Am. Paleontol. Conv. Part J*, 1430–1443.

Lang, J., 1973. Interspecific aggression by scleractinian corals. 2. Why the race is not only to the swift. *Bull. Mar. Sci.*, **23**, 260–279.

Lang, J. C., 1974. Biological zonation at the base of a reef. *Am. Sci.*, **62**, 272–281.

Lang, J. C., 1984. Whatever works: the variable importance of skeletal and of non-skeletal characters in scleractinian taxonomy. *Palaeontogr. Am.*, **54**, 18–44.

Lang, J. C. and Neumann, A. C., 1980. Lithoherm faunal zonation and mound growth. *Geol. Soc. Am. Abstr. (with Program)*, **12**, 468.

Lang, J. C. et al., 1975. Sclerosponges: primary framework constructors on the Jamaican deep fore-reef. *J. Mar. Res.*, **33**, 223–231.

Lasker, H., 1976. Effects of differential preservation on the measurement of taxonomic diversity. *Paleobiology*, **2**, 84–93.

Lathuliere, B., 1982. Bioconstructions bajociennes à madréporaires et faciès associés dans l'île Cremieu (Jura du Sud, France). *Geobios (Lyon)*, **15**(4), 491–504.

LeDanois, E., 1948. *Les profondeurs de la mer*. Paris, 303 pp.

Lelatkin, V. A. and Zvalinsky, V. I., 1981. Photosynthesis of coral zooxanthellae from different depths. *Proc. Fourth Int. Coral Reef Symp.*, **2**, 33–37.

Levin, S. A. and Paine, R. T., 1974. Disturbance, patch formation and community structure. *Proc. Natl. Acad. Sci. U.S.A.*, **71**, 2744–2747.

Levinton, J. S., 1982. *Marine ecology*. Prentice-Hall, Englewood Cliffs, NJ, 526 pp.

Lewin, R., 1983. Origin of species in stressed environments. *Science*, **222**, 1112.

Lewis, J. B., 1977. Processes of organic production on coral reefs. *Biol. Rev.*, **52**, 305–347.

Liddell, W. D. et al., 1984. Community patterns on the Jamaican fore-reef (15–56m). *Palaeontogr. Am.*, **54**, 385–389.

Lidgard, S., 1985. Zooid and colony growth in encrusting cheilostome bryozoans. *Palaeontol. London*, **28**, 255–291.

Liebezeit, G. et al., 1984. Estimation of algal carbonate input to marine aragonitic sediments on the basis of xylose content. *Mar. Geol.*, **54**, 249–262.

Lighty, R. G., Macintyre, I. G. and Stuckenrath, R., 1982. *Acropora palmata* reef framework: a reliable indicator of sea level in the western Atlantic for the past 10,000 years. *Coral Reefs*, **1**, 125–130.

Lindsley-Griffin, N., 1977. Paleogeographic implications of ophiolites: the Ordovician Trinity Complex. In Stewart, J. H. et al. (eds.), *Paleozoic paleogeography of the western United States. Pacific Section Soc. Econ. Paleontol. Mineral. Paleogeogr. Symp.*, **1**, 409–420.

Lindsley-Griffin, N. and Griffin, J. R., 1983. The Trinity Terrane: an early Paleozoic microplate assemblage. In Stevens, C. H. (ed.), *Pre-Jurassic rocks in western North American suspect terranes*. Pacific Section Soc. Econ. Paleontol. Mineral., 63–75.

Lipps, J., 1984. Personal communication. University of California, Davis, CA.

Littler, M. M. et al., 1983. Algal resistance to herbivory on a Caribbean barrier reef. *Coral Reefs*, **2**, 111–118.

Lloyd, A. R., 1973. Foraminifera of the Great Barrier Reef bores. In Jones, O. A. and Endean, R. (eds.), *Biology and geology of coral reefs*, Vol. 1. Academic, New York, pp. 347–366.

Lockley, M. G., 1983. A review of brachiopod dominated palaeocommunities from the type Ordovician. *Palaeontol.* **26,** 111–145.

Logan, A., 1981. Sessile invertebrate coelobite communities from shallow reef tunnels, Grand Cayman, B. W. I. *Proc. Fourth Int. Coral Reef Symp.,* **2,** 735–744.

Logan, A., 1984. Interspecific aggression in hermatypic corals from Bermuda. *Coral Reefs,* **3,** 131–138. .

Logan, A. et al., 1984. Sessile invertebrate coelobite communities from reefs of Bermuda: species composition and distribution. *Coral Reefs,* **2,** 205–213.

Logan, B. W., 1961. *Cryptozoon* and associate stromatolites from the Recent, Shark Bay, Western Australia. *J. Geol.,* **69,** 517–533, 2 pls.

Logan, B. W. et al., 1969. Carbonate sediments and reefs, Yucatan Shelf, Mexico. *Am. Assoc. Pet. Geol. Mem.,* **11,** 198 pp.

Logan, B. W. et al., 1974. Algal mats, cryptalgal fabrics and structures, Hamelin Pool, Western Australia. *Am. Assoc. Pet. Geol. Mem.,* **22,** 140–194.

Longman, M. W., 1981. A process approach to recognizing facies of reef complexes. *Soc. Econ. Paleontol. Mineral. Spec. Publ.,* **30,** 9–40.

Lowenstam, H. A., 1948. Marine pool, Madison County, Illinois, Silurian reef producer. Structure of typical American oil fields. *Am. Assoc. Pet. Geol.,* **3,** 153–188.

Lowenstam, H. A., 1950. Niagran reefs of the Great Lakes area. *J. Geol.,* **58,** 430–487.

Lowenstam, H. A., 1957. Niagran reefs in the Great Lakes area. *Geol. Soc. Am., Mem. 67,* **2,** 215–249.

Ludwick, J. C. and Walton, W. R., 1957. Shelf-edge, calcareous prominences in northeastern Gulf of Mexico. *Am. Assoc. Pet. Geol. Bull.,* **41,** 2054–2101.

Lyons, W. B. et al., 1984. Calcification of cyanobacterial mats in Solar Lake, Sinai. *Geology,* **12,** 623–626.

MacGeachy, J. K. and Stearn, C. W., 1976. Boring by macro-organisms in the coral *Montastrea annularis* on Barbados reefs. *Int. Rev. Ges. Hydrobiol.,* **61,** 715–745.

Macintyre, I. G., 1984. Extensive submarine lithification in a cave in the Belize Barrier reef platform. *J. Sediment. Petrol.,* **54,** 221–235.

Macintyre, I. G. et al., 1974. Carbon flux through a coral reef ecosystem: a conceptual model. *J. Geol.,* **82,** 161–171.

Macintyre, I. G. et al., 1981. Core holes in the outer fore reef off Carrie Bow Cay, Belize: a key to the Holocene history of the Belizean barrier reef complex. *Proc. Fourth Int. Coral Reef Symp.,* **1,** 567–574.

MacNeil, F. S., 1954. Organic reefs and banks and associated detrital sediments. *Am. J. Sci.,* **252,** 385–401.

Macurda Jr., D. B. and Meyer, D. L., 1983. Sea lilies and feather stars. *Am. Sci.,* **71,** 354–365.

Maksimova, S. V., 1972. Coral reefs in the Artic and their paleogeographical interpretation. *Int. Geol. Rev.,* **14,** 764–769.

Mann, P. et al., 1984. Subaerially exposed coral reef, Enriquillo Valley, Dominican Republic. *Geol. Soc. Am. Bull.,* **95,** 1084–1092.

Manten, A. A., 1971. *Silurian reefs of Gotland.* Elsevier, Amsterdam, 539 pp.

Mao, H.-L. and Yoshida, K., 1955. Physical oceanography in the Marshall Islands area. *U.S. Geol. Surv. Prof. Pap.,* **260-R,** 645–684.

Margulis, L., 1982. *The five kingdoms.* W. H. Freeman, San Francisco, 338 pp.

Marsh, L. M. et al., 1984. Determination of the physical parameters of coral distributions using line transect data. *Coral Reefs,* **2,** 175–180.

Marshall, J. F., 1983. Marine lithification in coral reefs. In Barnes, D. J. (ed.), *Perspectives on coral reefs.* Australian Institute of Marine Science, Townsville, and Brian Clouston, Canberra, Australia, pp. 231–299.

Marshall, J. F. and Davies, P. J., 1982. Internal structure and Holocene evolution of One Tree Reef, southern Great Barrier Reef. *Coral Reefs,* **1,** 21–28.

Marshall, J. F. and Davies, P. J., 1984. Last interglacial reef growth beneath modern reefs in the southern Great Barrier Reef. *Nature (London),* **307,** 44–46.

Marshall, J. F. and Jacobson, G., 1985. Holocene growth of a mid-Pacific atoll: Tarawa, Kiribati. *Coral Reefs,* **4,** 11–17.

Masse, J.-P., 1977. Les constructions à Madrépores des calcaires urgoniens (Barrémian-Bédoulien) de Provence (SE de la France). Second symposium internationale sur coraux et récifs coralliens fossiles. *Bull. Bur. Rech. Géol. Miniéres Mém. (Fr.),* **89,** 322–335.

Masse, J.-P., 1979. Les rudistes (Hippuritacea) du Crétacé inférieur. Approche paléoécologique. *Geobios (Lyon) Mém. Spec.* **3,** 277–287.

Masse, J.-P. and Philip, J., 1981. Cretaceous coral-rudist buildups of France. In Toomey, D. F. (ed.), European fossil reef models. *Soc. Econ. Paleontol. Mineral. Spec. Publ.,* **30,** 399–426.

Matthews, R. K., 1974. A process approach to diagenesis of reefs and associated limestones. In Laporte, L. F. (ed.), Reefs in time and space. *Soc. Econ. Paleontol. Mineral. Spec. Publ.,* **18,** 234–256.

Maxwell, W. G. H., 1968. *Atlas of the Great Barrier Reef.* Elsevier, Amsterdam, 258 pp.

Maxwell, W. G. H., 1973. Sediments of the Great Barrier Reef Province. In Jones, O. A. and Endean, R. (eds.), *Biology and geology of coral reefs,* Vol. 1. Academic, New York, pp. 299–346.

Maxwell, W. G. H. et al., 1961. Carbonate sedimentation on the Heron Island Reef, Great Barrier Reef. *J. Sediment. Petrol.,* **31,** 215–230.

Maxwell, W. G. H. et al., 1964. Differentiation of carbonate sediments in the Heron Island Reef. *J. Sediment. Petrol.,* **34,** 294–308.

May, R. M., 1978. The evolution of ecological systems. *Sci. Am.,* **239,** 160–175.

Mazzullo, S. J. and Cys, J. M., 1978. *Archaeolithoporella*-boundstones and marine aragonite cements, Permian Capitan reef, New Mexico and Texas. *Neues Jahrb. Geol. Paläontol. Monatsh.,* **10,** 600–611.

McCloskey, L. R. and Muscatine, L., 1984. Production and respiration in the Red Sea coral *Stylophora pistillata* as a function of depth. *Proc. R. Soc. London,* **222,** 215–230.

McKee, E. D. et al., 1959. Sedimentary belts in lagoon of Kapingamarangi Atoll. *Am. Assoc. Pet. Geol. Bull.,* **43,** 501–562.

McKerrow, W. S. (ed.), 1978. *The ecology of fossils*. Duckworth, London, 384 pp.

McLaren, D. J., 1970. Time, life and boundaries. *J. Paleontol.*, **44**, 801–815.

McLaren, D. J., 1982. Frasnian-Famennian extinctions. *Geol. Soc. Am. Spec. Pap.*, **190**, 447–484.

McLaren, D. J., 1983. Bolides and biostratigraphy. *Geol. Soc. Am. Bull.*, **94**, 313–324.

McLaren, D. J., 1984. Abrupt extinctions. *Terra Cognita,* **4**, 27–32.

McLaren, D. J., 1985. Mass extinction and iridium anomaly in the Upper Devonian of Western Australia: a commentary. *Geology,* **13**, 170–172.

McNutt, M. K. and Menard, H. W., 1978. Lithospheric flexure and uplifted atolls. *J. Geophys. Res.,* **83**, 1206–1212.

Méndez-Bedia, I. and Soto, F., 1984. Paleoecological succession in a Devonian organic buildup (Miniello Am., Cantabrian Mountains, NW Spain). *Geobios Mém. Spéc.,* **8**, 151–157.

Menge, B. A. and Sutherland, J. P., 1976. Species diversity gradients: synthesis of the roles of predation, competition, and temporal heterogeneity. *Am. Nat.,* **110**, 351–369.

Meyer, F. O., 1981. Stromatoporoid growth rhythms and rates. *Science,* **213**, 894–895.

Middleton, G. V., 1973. Johannes Walther's Law of the Correlation of Facies. *Geol. Soc. Am. Bull.,* **84**, 979–988.

Mistiaen, B., 1984a. Comments on the caunopore tubes: stratigraphic distribution and microstructure. *Palaeontogr. Am.,* **54**, 501–508.

Mistiaen, B., 1984b. Dispartition des stromatopores paléozoïques ou survie du groupe: hypothèse et discussion. *Géol. Soc. Fr. Bull.,* **24**, 1245–1250.

Montaggioni, L., 1977. Structure interne d'un récif corallien Holocène (Île de la Réunion, Océan Indien). Second symposium internationale sur les coraux et récifs coralliens fossiles. *Bull. Bur. Rech. Géol. Minières Mém. (Fr.),* **89**, 456–466.

Montaggioni, L. F. and Pirazzoli, P. A., 1984. The significance of exposed coral conglomerates from French Polynesia (Pacific Ocean) as indicators of recent relative sealevel changes. *Coral Reefs,* **3**, 29–42.

Monty, C. L. V., 1967. Distribution and structure of Recent stromatolitic algal mats, eastern Andros Island, Bahamas. *Ann. Soc. Geol. Belg.,* **90**, 55–100.

Monty, C. L. V., 1977. Evolving concepts on the nature and the ecological significance of stromatolites. In Flügel, E. (ed.), *Fossil algae*. Springer-Verlag, Heidelberg, pp. 15–35.

Mori, K., 1982. Coelenterate affinity of stromatoporoids. *Stockholm Contrib. Geol. (Hessland vol.),* 167–179.

Mori, K., 1984. Comparison of skeletal structures among stromatoporoids, sclerosponges and corals. *Palaeontogr. Am.,* **54**, 354–357.

Muller, P. H., 1974. Sediment production and population biology of the benthic foraminifer *Amphistegina madagascariensis*. *Limnol. Oceanogr.,* **19**, 802–809.

Mullins, H. T. and Lynts, G. W., 1977. Origin of the northwestern Bahama Platform: review and interpretation.*Geol. Soc. Am. Bull.,* **88**, 1447–1461.

Mullins, H. T. et al., 1981. Modern deep-water coral mounds north of Little Bahama Bank: criteria for recognition of deep-water coral bioherms in the rock record. *J. Sediment. Petrol.*, **51**, 999–1013.

Multer, H. G. and Hoffmeister, J. E., 1968. Subaerial laminated crusts of the Florida Keys. *Geol. Soc. Am. Bull.*, **79**, 183–192, 3 pls.

Multer, H. G. and Milliman, J. D., 1967. Geologic aspects of sabellarian reefs, southeastern Florida. *Bull. Marine Science*, **17**, 257–267.

Muscatine, L., 1973. Nutrition of corals. In Jones, O. A. and Endean, R. (eds.), *Biology and geology of coral reefs*, Vol. 2. Academic, New York, pp. 77–115.

Muscatine, L., 1980. Productivity of zooxanthellae. In Falkowski, P. G. (ed.), *Primary productivity in the sea*. Plenum, New York, pp. 381–402.

Muscatine, L. et al., 1981. Estimating the daily contribution of carbon from zooxanthellae to coral animal respiration. *Limnol. Oceanogr.*, **26**, 601–611.

Myers, D. A., et al., 1956. Geology of the Late Paleozoic horseshoe atoll in west Texas. *Texas University Publication 5607*, University of Texas Press, Austin, TX, 113 pp.

Nagai, K., 1985. Reef-forming algal chaetetid boundstone found in the Akiyoshi Limestone Group, southwest Japan. *Bull. Akiyoshi-dai Mus. Nat. Hist.*, **20**, 1–15, 6 pls.

Narbonne, G. M. and Dixon, O. A., 1984. Upper Silurian lithistid sponge reefs on Somerset Island, Arctic Canada. *Sedimentology*, **31**, 25–50.

Nelson, H. F. et al., 1962. Skeletal limestone classification. *Am. Assoc. Pet. Geol. Mem.* **1**, 224–252.

Neuman, B. E., 1984. Origin and early evolution of the Rugosa. *Palaeontogr. Am.*, **54**, 119–123.

Neumann, A. C., 1966. Observations on coastal erosion in Bermuda and measurements of the boring rate of the sponge, *Cliona lampa. Limnol. Oceanog.*, **11**, 92–108.

Neumann, A. C. and Land, L. S., 1975. Lime mud deposition and calcareous algae in the Bight of Abaco, Bahamas: a budget. *J. Sediment. Petrol.*, **45**, 763–786.

Neumann, A. C. et al., 1977. Lithoherms in the Straits of Florida. *Geology*, **5**, 4–10.

Newell, N. D., 1955a. Depositional fabrics in Permian reef limestones. *J. Geol.*, **63**, 301–309.

Newell, N. D., 1955b. Bahamian platforms. *Geol. Soc. Am. Spec. Pap.*, **62**, 303–316.

Newell, N. D., 1956. Geological reconnaissance of the Raroia (Kon Tiki) Atoll, Tuamotu Archipelago. *Bull. Am. Mus. Nat. Hist.*, **109**, 315–372.

Newell, N. D., 1967. Revolutions in the history of life. In Albritton, C. C. (ed.), Uniformity and simplicity. *Geol. Soc. Am. Spec. Pap.*, **89**, 63–91.

Newell, N. D., 1971. An outline history of tropical organic reefs. *Am. Mus. Novit.*, **2465**, 37 pp.

Newell, N. D., 1972. The evolution of reefs. *Sci. Am.*, **226**, 54–65.

Newell, N. D. and Rigby, J. K., 1957. Geological studies on the Great Bahama Bank. *Soc. Econ. Paleontol. Mineral. Spec. Publ.*, **5**, 15–72.

Newell, N. D. et al., 1951. Shoal water geology and environments, eastern Andros Island, Bahamas. *Am. Mus. Nat. Hist. Bull.*, **97**, 1–30.

Newell, N. D. et al., 1953. *The Permian reef complex of the Guadalupe Mountains region, Texas and New Mexico*. W. H. Freeman, San Francisco, 236 pp., 32 pls.

Nicholson, H. A., 1886–1892. A monograph of the British stromatoporoids, Parts I–IV. *Palaeontograph. Soc. London*, **39**, 1–130; **42**, 131–158; **44**, 159–202; **46**, 203–234.

Nicol, D., 1962. The biotic development of some Niagaran reefs—an example of an ecological succession or sere. *J. Paleontol.*, **36**, 172–176.

Norris, R. M., 1953. Buried oyster reefs in some Texas bays. *J. Paleontol.*, **27**, 569–576.

Odum, E. P., 1971. *Fundamentals of ecology*. W. B. Saunders, Philadelphia, 574 pp.

Odum, H. T. and Odum, E. P., 1955. Trophic structure and productivity of a windward coral reef community on Eniwetok Atoll. *Ecol. Monogr.*, **25**, 291–320.

Ogden, J. C., 1977. Carbonate-sediment production by parrot fish and sea urchins on Caribbean reefs. In Frost, S. H. et al. (eds.), Reefs and related carbonates—ecology and sedimentology. *Am. Assoc. Pet. Geol. Stud. Geol.*, **4**, 281–288.

Oliver, J. K., 1984. Intra-colony variation in the growth of *Acropora formosa:* extension rates and skeletal structure of white (zooxanthellae-free) and brown-tipped branches. *Coral Reefs*, **3**, 139–147.

Oliver Jr., W. A., 1954. Stratigraphy of the Onondaga Limestone (Devonian) in central New York. *Geol. Soc. Am. Bull.*, **65**, 621–652.

Oliver Jr., W. A., 1976. Noncystimorph colonial rugose corals of the Onesquethaw and Lower Cazenovia Stages (Lower and Middle Devonian) in New York and adjacent areas. *U.S. Geol. Surv. Prof. Pap.*, **869**, 156 pp.

Oliver Jr., W. A., 1979. Sponges they are not. *Paleobiology*, **5**, 188–190.

Oliver Jr., W. A., 1980. The relationship of the scleractinian corals to the rugose corals. *Paleobiology*, **6**, 146–160.

Oliver Jr., W. A., 1983. Symbioses of Devonian corals. *Mem. Assoc. Aust. Palaeontol.*, **1**, 261–274.

Orme, G. R., 1971. The D_2-P_1 "reefs" and associated limestones of the Pin Dale-Bradwell moor area of Derbyshire. *C. R. Sixth Congr. Int. Strat. Géol. Carbonif.*, **3**, 1249–1262.

Orme, G. R., 1977a. The Coral Sea Plateau—a major reef province. In Jones, O. A. and Endean, R. (eds.), *Biology and geology of coral reefs*, Vol. 4. Academic, New York, pp. 267–306.

Orme, G. R., 1977b. Aspects of sedimentation in the coral reef environment. In Jones, O. A. and Endean, R. (eds.), *Biology and geology of coral reefs*, Vol. 4. Academic, New York, pp. 129–182.

Ota, M., 1968. The Akiyoshi Limestone Group: a geosynclinal organic reef complex. *Bull. Akiyoshi-dai Sci. Mus. Nat. Hist.*, **5**, 44 pp., 31 pls.

Ota, M., 1977. Geological studies of Akiyoshi; Part I, General geology of the Akiyoshi Limestone Group. *Bull. Akiyoshi-dai Mus. Nat. Hist.*, **12**, 1–33.

Ota, M., 1983. Personal communication. Kitakyushu Museum, Kitakyushu, Yamaguchi Prefecture, Japan.

Ota, M. et al., 1969. Reef deposits in the *Millerella* Zone of the Akiyoshi Limestone Group. *Palaeontol. Soc. Jpn. Spec. Pap.* **14**, 12 pp., 3 pls.

Ott, E., 1967. Segmentierte Kalkschwämme (Sphinctozoa) aus der Alpinen Mittletrias und ihre bedeutung als riffbildner in Wettersteinkalk. *Bayer. Akad. Wiss. Math. Naturwissen. Kl. Abh.*, **131**, 96 pp.

Padian, K. et al., 1984. The possible influences of sudden events on biological radiations and extinctions. In Holland, H. D. and Trandall, A. F. (eds.), *Patterns of change in earth evolution.* Springer-Verlag, Berlin, pp. 77–102.

Page, H. et al., 1984. The size of solitary corals as a possible indicator of zooxanthellate symbiosis. *Palaeontogr. Am.*, **54**, 522.

Palmer, T. J. and Fürsich, F. T., 1981. Ecology of sponge reefs from the Upper Bathonian of Normandy. *Palaeontol. London*, **24**, 1–23.

Pandolfi, J. M., 1984. Environmental influence on growth form in some massive tabulate corals from the Hamilton Group (Middle Devonian) of New York state. *Palaeontogr. Am.*, **54**, 538–542.

Pang, R. K., 1973. The ecology of some Jamaican excavating sponges. *Bull. Mar. Sci.*, **23**, 227–243.

Park, R., 1976. A note on the significance of lamination in stromatolites. *Sedimentology*, **23**, 379–393.

Park, R. K., 1977. The preservation potential of some Recent stromatolites. *Sedimentology*, **24**, 485–506.

Parker, G. M., 1984. Dispersal of zooxanthellae on coral reefs by predators on cnidarians. *Biol. Bull.*, **167**, 159–167.

Patterson, B. and Pascual, R., 1972. The fossil mammal fauna of South America. In Keast, A. et al. (eds.), *Evolution, mammals and southern continents.* State University Press, Albany, NY, Chap. 6.

Patton, W. K., 1976. Animal associates of living reef corals. In Jones, O. A. and Endean, R. (eds.), *Biology and geology of coral reefs*, Vol. 3. Academic, New York, pp. 1–35.

Patzold, J., 1984. Growth rhythms recorded in stable isotopes and density bands in the reef coral *Porites lobata* (Cebu, Philippines). *Coral Reefs*, **3**, 87–90.

Pedder, A. E. H., 1982. The rugose coral record across the Frasnian–Famennian boundary. *Geol. Soc. Am. Spec. Pap.*, **190**, 485–490.

Perkins, B. F., 1974. Paleoecology of a rudist reef complex in the Comanche Cretaceous Glen Rose Limestone of central Texas. In Perkins, B. F. (ed.), Aspects of Trinity Division geology. Louisiana State University, *Geosci. Man*, **8**, 131–173.

Philip, J., 1972. Paléoécologie des formations à rudistes de Crétacé supérieur l'example du sud-est de la France. *Palaeogeogr. Palaeoclimatol. Palaeoecol.*, **12**, 205–222.

Pichon, M., 1978. Recherches sur les peuplements à dominance d'anthozoaires dans les récifs coralliens de Tuléar (Madagascar). *Atoll Res. Bull.*, **222**, 447 pp.

Pichon, M., 1981. Dynamic aspects of coral reef benthic structures and zonation. *Proc. Fourth Int. Coral Reef Symp.*, **1**, 581–594.

Pichon, M., 1985, personal communication. James Cook Univ., Townsville, Australia.

Piller, W. E., 1981. The Steinplatte reef complex, part of an Upper Triassic carbonate platform near Salzburg, Austria. In Toomey, D. F. (ed.), European fossil reef models. *Soc. Econ. Paleontol. Mineral. Spec. Publ.*, **30**, 261–290.

Pisera, A., 1985. Paleoecology and lithogenesis of the Middle Miocene (Badenian) algal-vermetid reefs from the Roztocze Hills, south-eastern Poland. *Acta Geol. Pol.*, **35**, 89–155.

Pitcher, M., 1964. Evolution of Chazyan (Ordovician) reefs in eastern United States. *Bull. Can. Pet. Geol.*, **12**, 632–691.

Pitcher, M., 1971. Middle Ordovician reef assemblages. *Proc. N. Am. Paleontol. Conv. Part J*, 1341–1357.

Playford, P. E., 1969. Devonian carbonate complexes of Alberta and Western Australia: a comparative study. *Geol. Surv. W. Aust. Rept.*, **1**, 43 pp.

Playford, P. E., 1980. Devonian "Great Barrier Reef" of Canning Basin, Western Australia. *Am. Assoc. Pet. Geol. Bull.*, **64**, 814–840.

Playford, P. E. and Cockbain, A. E., 1969. Algal stromatolites: deepwater forms in the Devonian of Western Australia. *Science*, **165**(3897), 1008–1010.

Playford, P. E. and Lowry, D. C., 1966. Devonian reef complexes of the Canning Basin, Western Australia. *Geol. Surv. W. Aust. Bull.*, **118**, 150 pp.

Playford, P. E. et al., 1976. Devonian stromatolites from the Canning Basin, Western Australia. In Walter, M. R. (ed.), *Stromatolites*. Elsevier, Amsterdam, pp. 543–563.

Playford, P. E. et al., 1984a. Neptunian dikes and sills in Devonian reef complexes of Canning Basin, Western Australia. *Am. Assoc. Pet. Geol. Book Abstr.*

Playford, P. E. et al., 1984b. Iridium anomaly in the Upper Devonian of the Canning Basin, Western Australia. *Science*, **226**, 437–439.

Polan, K. P. and Stearn, C. W., 1984. The allochthonous origin of reefal facies of the Stuart Bay Formation (Early Devonian), Bathurst Island, arctic Canada. *Can. J. Earth Sci.*, **21**, 657–668.

Polovina, J. P., 1984. Model of a coral reef ecosystem I. The ECOPATH model and its application to French Frigate Shoals. *Coral Reefs*, **3**, 1–11.

Polšak, A., 1981. Upper Cretaceous biolithic complexes in a subduction zone: examples from the Inner Dinarides, Yugoslavia. In Toomey, D. F. (ed.), European fossil reef models. *Soc. Econ. Paleontol. Mineral. Spec. Publ.*, **30**, 447–472.

Porter, J. W., 1974. Community structure of coral reefs on opposite sides of the Isthmus of Panama. *Science*, **186**, 543–545.

Potts, D. C., 1985. Sea-level fluctuations and speciation in Scleractinia. *Proc. Fifth Int. Coral Reef Congr.*, **4**, 127–132.

Powell, E. N. and Stanton Jr., R. J., 1985. Estimating biomass and energy flow of molluscs in palaeocommunities. *Palaeontol. London*, **28**, 1–34.

Pratt, B. R., 1979. Early cementation and lithification in intertidal cryptalgal structures, Boca Jewfish, Bonaire, Netherlands Antilles. *J. Sediment. Petrol.*, **49**, 379–386.

Pratt, B. R., 1982a. Stromatolitic framework of carbonate mud-mounds. *J. Sediment. Petrol.*, **52**, 1203–1227.

Pratt, B. R., 1982b. Stromatolite decline—a reconsideration. *Geology*, **10**, 512–515.

Pratt, B. R., 1984. *Epiphyton* and *Renalcis*-diagenetic microfossils from calcification of coccoid blue-green algae. *J. Sediment. Petrol.*, **54**, 948–971.

Pratt, B. R. and James, N. P., 1982. Cryptalgal-metazoan bioherms of early Ordovician age in the St. George Group, western Newfoundland. *Sedimentology*, **8**, 543–569.

Pray, L. C., 1958. Fenestrate bryozoan core facies, Mississippian bioherms, southwestern United States. *J. Sediment. Petrol.*, **28**, 261–273.

Pray, L. C. and Wray, J. L., 1963. Porous algal facies (Pennsylvanian) Honaker Trail, San Juan Canyon, Utah. In Bass, R. O. (ed.), Shelf carbonates of the Paradox Basin. *Four Corners Geol. Soc. Fourth Field Conf.*, 204–234.

Pruvot, G., 1894. Essai sur la topographie et la constitution de fonds sous-marin de la region Banyuls. *Arch. Zool. Exp. Gen. Ser. 3*, 599–672, 1 map.

Pruvot, G., 1895. Coup d'oeil sur la distribution generale des invertebres dans la region de Banyuls (Golfe de Lion). *Arch. Zool. Exp. Gen. Ser. 3*, 629–658.

Purdy, E. G., 1974. Reef configurations: cause and effect. In Laporte, L. (ed.), Reefs in time and space. *Soc. Econ. Paleontol. Mineral. Spec. Publ.*, **18**, 9–76.

Qi, W., 1984. An Anisian coral fauna in Guizhou, South China. *Palaeontogr. Am.*, **54**, 187–190.

Raitt, R. W., 1954. Seismic-refraction studies of Bikini and Kwajalein atolls. *U.S. Geol. Surv. Prof. Pap.*, **260-K.**

Ramovš, A. and Turnšek, D., 1984. Lower Carnian reef buildups in the northern Julian Alps (Slovenia, NW Yugoslavia). *Slov. Akad. Znan. Umet. Razpr.*, **25**(4), 161–200, 15 pls.

Rasmussen, K. A. and Brett, C. E., 1985. Taphonomy of Holocene cryptic biotas from St. Croix, Virgin Islands: information loss and preservational biases. *Geology*, **13**, 551–553.

Raup, D. M., 1976. Species diversity in the Phanerozoic: an interpretation. *Paleobiology*, **3**, 289–297.

Raup, D. M. and Sepkoski Jr., J. J., 1982. Mass extinctions in the marine fossil record. *Science*, **215**, 1501–1503.

Raup, D. M. and Sepkoski Jr., J. J., 1984. Periodicity of extinctions in the geologic past. *Proc. Natl. Acad. Sci. U.S.A.*, **81**, 801–805.

Read, B. C., 1980. Lower Cambrian archaeocyathid buildups, Pelly Mountains, Yukon. *Geol. Surv. Can. Pap.*, **78-18**, 54 pp.

Read, J. F., 1982a. Carbonate platforms of passive (extensional) continental margins: types, characteristics and evolution. *Tectonophysics*, **8**, 195–212.

Read, J. F., 1982b. Geometry, facies, and development of Middle Ordovician carbonate buildups, Virginia Appalachians. *Am. Assoc. Pet. Geol. Bull.*, **66**, 189–209.

Reed, J. K., 1980. Distribution and structure of deep-water *Oculina varicosa* coral reefs off central eastern Florida. *Bull. Mar. Sci.*, **30**, 667–677.

Reed, J. K., 1981. *In situ* growth rates of the scleractinian coral *Oculina varicosa* occurring with zooxanthellae on 6-m reefs and without on 80-m banks. *Proc. Fourth Int. Coral Reef Symp., 2,* 201–206.

Reed, J. K., 1983. Nearshore and shelf-edge *Oculina* coral reefs: the effects of upwelling on coral growth and on the associated faunal communities. In Reaka, M. L. (ed.), The ecology of deep and shallow coral reefs. *Natl. Oceanic Atmos. Adm. Symp. Ser. Undersea Res., 1,* 119–124.

Reid, R. E. H., 1968. Bathymetric distributions of Calcarea and Hexactinellida in the present and the past. *Geol. Mag., 105,* 546–559.

Reiswig, H. M., 1973. Population dynamics of three Jamaican Demospongiae. *Bull. Mar. Sci., 23,* 191–226.

Reitner, J. and Engeser, T., 1985. Revision der Demospongiaer mit einem thalamiden, aragonitischen Basalskelett und trabekulärer Internstruktur ("Sphinctozoa" pars). *Berl. Geoweissen. Abh. A, 60,* 151–193.

Revelle, R., 1954. Forward. *U.S. Geol. Surv. Prof. Pap., 260-A,* III–VII.

Rezak, R., 1957a. Stromatolites of the Belt Series in Glacier National Park and vicinity, Montana. *U.S. Geol. Surv. Prof. Pap., 294-D,* 127–154, Pls. 18–25.

Rezak, R., 1957b. *Girvanella* not a guide to the Cambrian. *Geol. Soc. Am. Bull., 68,* 1411–1412, 1 pl.

Rhodes, F. H. T., 1967. Permo-Triassic extinction. In Harland, W. B. et al. (eds.), The fossil record. *Geol. Soc. London,* 57–76.

Richard, G., 1982. Growth and reproduction of mollusks in French Polynesian ecosystems. *Int. Soc. Reef Stud. Second Ann. Meeting Leiden (abstr.).*

Richardson, J. L., 1977. *Dimensions of ecology.* Williams & Wilkins, Baltimore, MD, 412 pp.

Riding, R., 1977. Problems of affinity in Paleozoic calcareous algae. In Flügel, E. (ed.), *Fossil algae.* Springer-Verlag, Berlin, pp. 202–211.

Riding, R., 1981. Composition, structure and environmental setting of Silurian bioherms and biostromes in northern Europe. In Toomey, D. F. (ed.), European fossil reef models. *Soc. Econ. Paleontol. Mineral. Spec. Publ., 30,* 41–83.

Riding, R., 1982. Cyanophyte calcification and changes in ocean chemistry. *Nature (London), 299,*(5886), 814–815.

Riding, R., 1983. *Reef Newsl., 9,* p. 43.

Riding, R. and Brasier, M., 1975. Earliest calcareous foraminifera. *Nature (London), 257*(5523), 208–210.

Riding, R. and Toomey, D. F., 1972. The sedimentological role of *Epiphyton* and *Renalcis* in Lower Ordovician mounds, southern Oklahoma. *J. Sediment. Petrol., 46,* 509–519.

Riding, R. and Voronova, L., 1982. Calcified cyanophytes and the Precambrian-Cambrian transition. *Naturwissenschaften, 69,* 498–499.

Riding, R. and Voronova, L., 1985. Morphological groups and series in Cambrian calcareous algae. In Toomey, D. F. and Nitecki, M. H. (eds.). *Paleoalgology: contemporary research and applications.* Springer-Verlag, Berlin, 56–78.

Riding, R. and Watts, N., 1983. Silurian *Renalcis* (?cyanophyte) from reef facies in Gotland (Sweden). *Neues Jahrb. Geol. Paläontol. Monatsh., 4,* 242–248.

Rigby, J. K., 1957. Relationships between *Acanthocladia guadalupensis* and *Solenopora texana* and the bryozoan-algal consortium hypothesis. *J. Paleontol.*, **31**, 603–606.

Rigby, J. K., 1971. Sponges and reef and related facies through time. *Proc. N. Am. Paleontol. Conv. Chicago Part J*, 1374–1388.

Rigby, J. K. and Stearn, C. W. (orgs.), 1983. Sponges and spongiomorphs—notes for a short course. *Univ. Tennessee Stud. Geol.*, **7.**

Risk, M. J. and MacGeachy, 1978. Aspects of bioerosion of modern Caribbean reefs. *Rev. Biol. Trop. (Suppl.)*, **26**, 85–105.

Roberson, D. S., 1972. The paleoecology, distribution and significance of circular bioherms in the Edwards Limestone of central Texas. *Baylor Geol. Stud. Bull.*, **23**, 34 pp.

Roberts, H. H., 1974. Variability of reefs with regard to changes in wave power around an island. *Proc. Second Int. Coral Reef Symp.*, **2**, 497–512.

Roberts, H. H., 1980. Physical processes and sediment flux through reef-lagoon systems. *Proc. Seventeenth Coastal Eng. Conf. Sydney Aust.*, 946–962.

Roberts, H. H. and Murray, S. P., 1983. Controls on reef development and the terrigenous-carbonate interface on a shallow shelf, Nicaragua (Central America). *Coral Reefs*, **2**, 71–80.

Roberts, H. H. and Suhayda, J. N., 1983. Wave-current interactions on a shallow reef (Nicaragua, Central America). *Coral Reefs*, **1**, 209–214.

Roberts, H. H. et al., 1975. Physical processes in a fringing reef system. *J. Mar. Res.*, **23**, 233–260.

Roberts, H. H. et al., 1977. Physical processes on a fore-reef shelf environment. *Proc. Third Int. Coral Reef Symp.*, **2**, 507–515.

Roberts, H. H. et al., 1981. Lagoon sediment transport: the significant effect of *Callianassa* bioturbation. *Proc. Fourth Int. Coral Reef Symp.*, **1**, 459–465.

Robertson, R., 1970. Review of the predators and parasites of stony corals, with special reference to symbiotic prosobranch gastropods. *Pac. Sci.*, **24**, 43–54.

Rogers, C. S. et al., 1984. Scleractinian coral recruitment patterns at Salt River submarine canyon, St. Croix, U.S. Virgin Islands. *Coral Reefs*, **3**, 69–76.

Root, R. B., 1967. The niche exploitation pattern of the blue-gray gnatcatcher. *Ecol. Monogr.*, **97**, 317–350.

Rosen, B. R., 1975. The distribution of reef corals. *Rept. Underwater Assoc.*, **1**, 1–16.

Rosen, B. R., 1977. The depth distribution of recent hermatypic corals and its palaeontological significance. Second symposium internationale sur les coraux et récifs coralliens fossiles. *Bull. Bur. Rech. Géol. Minières Mem.* (Fr.), **89**, 507–517.

Rosen, B. R., 1979. Modules, members and communes: a postscript introduction to social organisms. In Larwood, G. and Rosen, B. R. (eds.), Biology and systematics of colonial organisms. *Syst. Assoc. Spec. Publ. 11*, Academic Press, London, XIII–XXXV.

Rosen, B. R., 1981. The tropical high diversity enigma—the corals' eye view. In Forey, P. L. (ed.), Chance, change and challenge; The evolving biosphere. *Br. Mus. Nat. Hist. Publ.*, 103–129.

Ross, C. S., 1972. Biology and ecology of *Marginopora vertebralis* (Foraminiferida), Great Barrier Reef. *J. Protozool.*, **19**, 181–192.

Ross, J. P., 1964. Morphology and phylogeny of early Ectoprocta (Bryozoa). *Geol. Soc. Am. Bull.*, **75**, 927–948.

Ross, J. P., 1972. Paleoecology of Middle Ordovician ectoproct assemblages. *Twenty-Fourth Int. Geol. Congr. Proc. Sect. 7*, 96–102.

Ross, J. P., 1981. Ordovician environmental heterogeneity and community organization. In Gray, J. et al. (eds.), *Communities of the past*. Hutchinson Ross, Stroudsburg, PA, pp. 1–33.

Roughgarden, J., 1979. *Theory of population genetics and evolutionary ecology: an introduction*. Macmillan, New York, 634 pp.

Roux, A., 1985. Introduction à l'étude des algues fossiles Paléozoïques. . . . *Bull. Centres Rech. Expl. Prod. Elf-Aquitaine*, **9**, 465–699.

Rowland, S. M., 1981a. Archaeocyathid bioherms in the lower Poleta Formation, Esmeralda County, Nevada. In Taylor, M. E. and Palmer, A. R. (eds.), Cambrian stratigraphy and paleontology of the Great Basin and vicinity, western United States. Second international symposium on Cambrian system guidebook, field trip 1. *U.S. Geol. Surv. Int. Union Geol. Sci.*, 44–49.

Rowland, S. M., 1981b. Archaeocyathid reefs of the southern Great Basin. In Taylor, M. E. (ed.), Short papers for second international symposium on the Cambrian system. *U.S. Geol. Surv. Open-File Rept.*, **81-743**, 193–197.

Rowland, S. M., 1984. Were there framework reefs in the Cambrian? *Geology*, **12**, 181–183.

Rozanov, A. and Debrenne, F., 1974. Age of archaeocyathid assemblages. *Am. J. Sci.*, **274**, 833–848.

Rudwick, M. J. S., 1961. The feeding mechanism of the Permian brachiopod *Prorichthofenia*. *Palaeontol. London*, **3**, 450–471.

Rudwick, M. J. S., 1965. Ecology and paleoecology. In Treatise on invertebrate paleontology, Part H, Brachiopoda. Geological Society of America, Boulder, CO, and University of Kansas Press, Lawrence, KS, pp. H199–H214.

Rudwick, M. J. S., 1970. *Living and fossil brachiopods*. Hutchinson University Library, London, 199 pp.

Rudwick, M. J. S. and Cowen, R., 1968. The functional morphology of some aberrant strophomenide brachiopods from the Permian of Sicily. *Boll. Soc. Paleontol. Ital.*, **6**, 113–176.

Runcorn, S. K., 1966. Corals as paleontological clocks. *Sci. Am.*, **215**, 26–33.

Ruppel, S. C. and Walker, K. R., 1984. Petrology and depositional history of a Middle Ordovician carbonate platform: Chickamauga Group, northeastern Tennessee. *Geol. Soc. Am. Bull.*, **95**, 568–583.

Rützler, K. and Macintyre, I. G., 1978. Siliceous sponge spicules in coral reef sediments. *Mar. Biol.*, **49**, 147–159.

Rützler, K. and Macintyre, I. G., 1982. The habitat distribution and community structure of the barrier reef complex at Carrie Bow Cay, Belize. *Smithson. Contrib. Mar. Sci. Spec. Issue*, **9-45**, 260–269.

Rützler, K. and Rieger, G., 1973. Sponge burrowing: fine structure of *Cliona lampa* penetrating calcareous substrata. *Mar. Biol.*, **21**, 144–162.

Ryland, J. S., 1970. *Bryozoans.* Hutchinson University Library, London, 175 pp.

St. Jean Jr., J., 1971. Paleobiologic considerations of reef stromatoporoids. In Reef organisms through geologic time. *Proc. N. Am. Paleontol. Conv. Part J,* 1389–1429.

Sale, P. F., 1977. Maintenance of high diversity in coral reef fish communities. *Am. Nat.,* **111,** 337–359.

Sandberg, P. A., 1983. An oscillating trend in Phanerozoic non-skeletal carbonate mineralogy. *Nature (London),* **305,** 19–22.

Sandberg, P. A., 1984. Recognition criteria for calcitized skeletal and non-skeletal aragonites. *Palaeontogr. Am.,* **54,** 272–281.

Sanders, H. L., 1968. Marine benthic diversity: a comparative study. *Am. Nat.,* **102,** 243–282.

Sanders, H. L., 1969. Benthic marine diversity and the time-stability hypothesis. In Woodwell, G. M. and Smith, H. H. (eds.), Diversity and stability in ecological systems. *Brookhaven Symp. Biol.,* **22,** 71–81.

Sarà, M. and Vacelet, J., 1973. Ecologie des démosponges. In Grasse, P. (ed.), *Traité de zoologie,* Vol. 3. Masson, Paris, pp. 462–576.

Sarg, J. F., 1981. Petrology of the carbonate-evaporite facies transition of the Seven Rivers Formation (Guadalupian, Permian), southeastern New Mexico. *J. Sediment. Petrol.,* **51,** 73–96.

Sargent, M. C. and Austin, T. S., 1954. Biologic ecology of coral reefs. *U.S. Geol. Surv. Prof. Pap.,* **260-E,** 293–300.

Schäfer, P., 1984. Development of ecologic reefs during the latest Triassic (Rhaetian) of the Northern Limestone Alps. *Palaeontogr. Am.,* **54,** 210–218.

Schäfer, P. and Senowbari-Daryan, B., 1981. Facies development and paleoecologic zonation of four Upper Triassic patch-reefs, northern calcareous Alps near Salzburg, Austria. In Toomey, D. F. (ed.). European fossil reef models. *Soc. Econ. Paleontol. Mineral. Spec. Pub.,* **30,** 241–259.

Scheltema, R. S., 1972. Dispersal of marine invertebrate organisms: paleobiogeographic and biostratigraphic implications. In Kauffman, E. G. and Hazel, J. E. (eds.). *Concepts and methods of biostratigraphy.* Dowden, Hutchinson and Ross, Stroudsburg, PA, 73–108.

Schmidt, V., 1977. Inorganic and organic reef growth and subsequent diagenesis in the Permian Capitan Reef Complex, Guadalupe Mountains, Texas, New Mexico. In Hileman, M. E. and Mazzullo, S. J. (eds.), Upper Guadalupian facies, Permian reef complex, Guadalupe Mountains, New Mexico and west Texas. Permian Basin Section Soc. Econ. Paleontol. Mineral. Publ., **77-6,** 93–131.

Schopf, J. W., 1977. Biostratigraphic usefulness of stromatolitic Precambrian microbiotas: a preliminary analysis. *Precamb. Res.,* **5,** 143–173.

Schopf, T. J. M., 1974. Permo-Triassic extinctions: Relation to sea-floor spreading. *J. Geol.,* **82,** 129–143.

Schopf, T. J. M., 1978. Fossilization potential of an intertidal fauna: Friday Harbor, Washington. *Paleobiology,* **4,** 261–270.

Schröder, J. and Purser, B. H., 1986. *Reef diagenesis.* Springer-Verlag, Berlin, 450 pp.

Schuhmacher, H., 1976. *Korallenriffe: ihre Verbreitung, Tierwelt und Ökologie.* BLV Verlagsgesellschaft, Munich, 275 pp.

Schuhmacher, H., 1984. Reef-building properties of *Tubastraea micranthus* (Scleractinia; Dendrophylliidae), a coral without zooxanthellae. *Mar. Ecol. Prog. Ser.,* **20,** 93–99.

Schuhmacher, H. and Plewka, M., 1981a. Mechanical resistance of reefbuilders through time. *Oecologia Berlin,* **49,** 279–282.

Schuhmacher, H. and Plewka, M., 1981b. The adaptive significance of mechanical properties versus morphological adjustments in skeletons of *Acropora palmata* and *Acropora cervicornis* (Cnidaria, Scleractinia). *Proc. Fourth Int. Coral Reef Symp.,* **2,** 121–128.

Schuhmacher, H. and Zibrowius, H., 1985. What is hermatypic? A redefinition of ecological groups in corals and other organisms. *Coral Reefs,* **4,** 1–9.

Schwan, W. and Ota, M., 1977. Structural tectonics of the Akiyoshi Limestone Group and its surroundings (Southwest Japan). *Akiyoshi-dai Mus. Nat. Hist. Bull.,* **12**(Part II), 35–110.

Scoffin, T. P., 1970. The trapping and binding of subtidal carbonate sediment by marine vegetation in Bimini Lagoon, Bahamas. *J. Sediment. Petrol.,* **40,** 249–273.

Scoffin, T. P., 1971. The conditions of growth of the Wenlock reefs of Shropshire (England). *Sedimentology,* **17,** 173–219.

Scoffin, T. P., 1981. Aspects of the preservation of deep and shallow water reefs. *Proc. Fourth Int. Coral Reef Symp.,* **1,** 499–501.

Scoffin, T. P. and Stoddart, D. R., 1978. The nature and significance of microatolls. *Philos. Trans. R. Soc. London Ser. B,* **284,** 99–122.

Scoffin, T. P. et al., 1978. The Recent development of the reefs in the Northern Province of the Great Barrier Reef. *Philos. Trans. R. Soc. London Ser. B,* **294,** 129–139.

Scott, R. W., 1976. Trophic classification of benthic communities. In Scott, R. W. and West, R. R. (eds.), Structure and classification of paleocommunities. Dowden, Hutchinson & Ross, Stroudsburg, PA, pp. 29–66.

Scott, R. W., 1981. Biotic relations in Early Cretaceous coral-algal-rudistid reefs, Arizona. *J. Paleontol.,* **55,** 463–478.

Scrutton, C. T., 1965. Periodicity in Devonian coral growth. *Palaeontol. London,* **7,** 552–558.

Scrutton, C. T., 1978. Periodic growth features in fossil organisms and the length of the day and month. In Brosche, P. (ed.). *Tidal friction and the Earth's rotation.* Springer-Verlag, Berlin, 154–191.

Scrutton, C. T., 1984. Origin and early evolution of tabulate corals. *Palaeontogr. Am.,* **54,** 110–118.

Scrutton, C. T. and Powell, J. H., 1980. Periodic development of dimetrism in some favositid corals. *Acta Palaeontol. Pol.,* **25,** 477–491.

Searle, D. E. et al., 1981. Significance of results of shallow seismic research in the Great Barrier Reef province between 16°10'S and 20°05'S. *Proc. Fourth Int. Coral Reef Symp.,* **1,** 531–539.

Seilacher, A., 1962. Die Sphinctozoa, eine Gruppe fossiler Kalkschwämme. *Akad. Wiss. Lit. Mainz Abh. Math. Phys. Naturwiss. Kl.*, **11**, 725–790.

Senowbari-Daryan, B., 1980a. Fazielle und palaontologische Untersuchungen in oberrhatischen Riffen (Feichtenstein-und Gruberriffe bei Hintersee, Salzburg, Nördliche Kalkalpen). *Facies*, **3**, 1–237.

Senowbari-Daryan, B., 1980b. *Cheilosporites tirolensis* Wähner-systematische Stellung und fazielle Bedeutung. *Facies*, **2**, 229–240.

Senowbari-Daryan, B., 1981. Zur paläontologie des riffes innerhalb der Amphy-clinen-Schichten bei Hudajuzna, Slowenien. *Slov. Akad. Znan. Umet. Razpr.*,Classis IV, Razred **23**(3) 99–118, 10 pls.

Sepkoski Jr., J. J., 1979. A kinetic model of Phanerozoic taxonomic diversity II. Early Phanerozoic families and multiple equilibria. *Paleobiology*, **5**, 222–251.

Sepkoski Jr., J. J., 1981. A factor analytic description of the Phanerozoic marine fossil record. *Paleobiology*, **7**, 36–53.

Sepkoski Jr., J. J., 1982. A compilation of fossil marine families. *Milwaukee Publ. Mus. Contrib. Biol. Geol.*, **51**, 1–125.

Sepkoski Jr., J. J., 1984. A kinetic model of Phanerozoic taxonomic diversity. III. Post-Paleozoic families and mass extinctions. *Paleobiology*, **10**, 246–267.

Sepkoski Jr., J. J. and Sheehan, P. M., 1983. Diversification, faunal change, and community replacement during the Ordovician radiations. In Tevesz, M. J. S. and McCall, P. L. (eds.), *Biotic interactions in recent and fossil benthic communities*. Plenum, New York, pp. 673–717.

Sepkoski Jr., J. J., et al., 1981. Phanerozoic marine diversity and the fossil record. *Nature (London)*, **293**, 435–437.

Sheehan, P. M., 1973. The relation of Late Ordovician glaciation to the Ordovician-Silurian changeover in North American brachiopod faunas. *Lethaia*, **6**, 147–154.

Sheehan, P. M., 1975. Brachiopod synecology in a time of crisis (Late Ordovician-Early Silurian). *Paleobiology*, **1**, 205–212.

Sheehan, P. M., 1977. Species diversity in the Phanerozoic: a reflection of labor by systemists. *Paleobiology*, **3**, 325–328.

Sheehan, P. M., 1985. Reefs are not so different—they follow the evolutionary pattern of level-bottom communities. *Geology*, **13**, 46–49.

Shepard, F. P., 1977. *Geological oceanography*. Crane, Russak Co., New York, 214 pp.

Sheppard, A. L. S., 1984. The molluscan fauna of Chagos (Indian Ocean) and an analysis of its broad distribution patterns. *Coral Reefs*, **3**, 43–50.

Sheppard, C. R. C., 1982. Coral populations on reef slopes and their major controls. *Mar. Ecol. Prog. Ser.*, **7**, 83–115.

Shier, D. E., 1969. Vermetid reefs and coastal development in the Ten Thousand Islands, southwest Florida. *Geol. Soc. Am. Bull.*, **80**, 485–508.

Shilo, N. A. et al., 1984. Sedimentological and paleontological atlas of the Late Famennian and Tournaisian deposits in the Omolon Region (NE-USSR). *Ann. Geol. Soc. Belg.*, **107**, 137–247.

Shinn, E. A., 1966. Coral growth rate: an environmental indicator. *J. Paleontol.*, **40**, 233–240.

Shinn, E. A., 1983. Birdseyes, fenestrae, shrinkage pores and loferites: a reevaluation. *J. Sediment. Petrol.*, **53**, 619–628.

Shinn, E. A. and Robbin, D. M., 1983. Mechanical and chemical compaction in fine-grained shallow-water limestones. *J. Sediment. Petrol.*, **53**, 595–618.

Shinn, E. A. et al., 1981. Spurs and grooves revisited: construction versus erosion, Love Key Reef, Florida. *Proc. Fourth Int. Coral Reef Symp.*, **1**, 475–483.

Shipek, C. J., 1962. Photographic survey of sea floor in southwest slope of Eniwetok Atoll. *Geol. Soc. Am. Bull.*, **73**, 805–812.

Signor, P. W. III, 1982. Species richness in the Phanerozoic: compensating for sampling bias. *Geology*, **10**, 625–628.

Silver, L. T. and Schultz, P. H. (eds.), 1982. Geological implications of impacts of large asteroids and comets on the earth. *Geol. Soc. Am. Spec. Pap.*, **190**, 528 pp.

Simpson, G. G., 1944. *Tempo and mode in evolution.* Columbia University Press, New York, 237 pp.

Skelton, P. W., 1976. Functional morphology of the Hippuritidae. *Lethaia*, **9**, 83–100.

Skelton, P. W., 1978. The evolution of functional design in rudists (Hippuritacea) and its taxonomic implications. *Philos. Trans. R. Soc. London Ser. B*, **284**, 305–318.

Skelton, P. W., 1979a. Preserved ligament in a radiolitid rudist bivalve and its implication of mantle marginal feeding in the group. *Paleobiology*, **5**, 90–106.

Skelton, P. W., 1979b. Gregariousness and proto-cooperation in rudists (Bivalvia). In Larwood, G. and Rosen, B. R. (eds.), Biology and systematics of colonial organisms. *Syst. Assoc. Spec. Publ. 11.* Academic, London, pp. 257–279.

Smith, G., 1983. Untitled, informal report. *Reef Newsl.*, **9**, p. 46.

Smith, S. V., 1973. Carbon dioxide dynamics: a record of organic carbon production, respiration, and calcification in the Eniwetok reef flat community. *Limnol. Oceanogr.*, **18**, 106–120.

Smith, S. V., 1978. Coral-reef area and the contributions of reefs to processes and resources of the world's oceans. *Nature (London)*, **273**, 225–226.

Smith, S. V., 1983a. Net production of coral reef ecosystems. In Reaka, M. L. (ed.), The ecology of deep and shallow coral reefs. *Natl. Oceanic Atmos. Adm. Undersea Res. Prog.*, **1**, 127–131.

Smith, S. V., 1983b. Coral reef calcification. In Barnes, D. J. (ed.), *Perspectives on coral reefs*. Australian Institute of Marine Science, Townsville, and Brian Clouston, Canberra, Australia, pp. 240–247.

Smith, S. V. and Marsh, J. A., 1973. Organic carbon production on the windward, reef flat of Eniwetok Atoll. *Limnol. Oceanogr.*, **18**, 953–961.

Sorauf, J. E. and Jell, J. S., 1977. Structure and incremental growth in the ahermatypic coral *Desmophyllum cristagalli* from the North Atlantic. *Palaeontol. London*, **20**, 1–19.

Soroka, L. G. and Cuffey, R. J., 1979. Modern Bermuda reef-dwelling lichenoporoids (Cyclostomata, Bryozoa)—ecologic distributions as comparative data for the paleoecology of reef deposits. *Geol. Soc. Am. Abstr. (with Program)*, **11**, 257.

Sorokin, Y. I., 1981. Aspects of the biomass feeding and metabolism of common corals of the Great Barrier Reef, Australia. *Proc. Fourth Int. Coral Reef Symp.*, **2**, 27–32.

Squires, D. F., 1959. Results of the Puritan-American Museum of Natural History expedition to western Mexico. *Am. Mus. Nat. Hist. Bull.*, **118**, 367–432.

Squires, D. F., 1964. Fossil coral thickets in Wairarapa, New Zealand. *J. Paleontol.*, **38**, 904–915.

Squires, D. F., 1965. Deep-water coral structure on the Campbell Plateau, New Zealand. *Deep-water Res.*, **12**, 785–788.

Stach, L. W., 1936. Correlation of zoarial form with habitat. *J. Geol.*, **44**, 60–65.

Staff, G. et al., 1985. Biomass: is it a useful tool in paleocommunity reconstruction? *Lethaia*, **18**, 209–232.

Stanley Jr., G. D., 1980. Triassic carbonate buildups of western North America: comparison with the Alpine Triassic of Europe. *Rev. Ital. Paleontol.*, **85**, 877–894.

Stanley Jr., G. D., 1981. Early history of scleractinian corals and its geological consequences. *J. Geol.*, **9**, 507–511.

Stanley, S. M., 1975. A theory of evolution above the species level. *Proc. Natl. Acad. Sci. U.S.A.*, **72**, 646–650.

Stanley, S. M., 1979. *Macroevolution*. Freeman, San Francisco, 332 pp.

Stanley, S. M., 1982. Glacial refrigeration and Neogene regional mass extinction of marine bivalves. In Gallitelli, E. M. (ed.), *Palaeontology, essentials of historical geology*. S.T.E.M. Mucchi, Modena, Italy, pp. 179–191.

Stanley, S. M., 1984a. Temperature and biotic crises in the marine realm. *J. Geol.*, **12**, 205–208; see also *J. Geol.*, **12**, 741–742 (1984), and **13**, 157–158 (1985).

Stanley, S. M., 1984b. Marine mass extinctions: a dominant role for temperature. In Nitecki, M. H. (ed.), *Extinctions*. University of Chicago Press, Chicago, IL, pp. 69–117.

Stanton, R. J., 1967. Factors controlling shape and internal facies distribution of organic carbonate buildups. *Am. Assoc. Pet. Geol. Bull.*, **51**, 2462–2467.

Stearn, C. W., 1972. The relationship of the stromatoporoids to the sclerosponges. *Lethaia*, **5**, 369–388.

Stearn, C. W., 1975. The stromatoporoid animal. *Lethaia*, **8**, 89–100.

Stearn, C. W., 1975. Stromatoporoid assemblages, Ancient Wall reef complex (Devonian), Alberta. *Can. J. Earth Sci.*, **12**, 1631–1667.

Stearn, C. W., 1982a. The shapes of Paleozoic and modern reef-builders: a critical review. *Paleobiology*, **8**, 228–241.

Stearn, C. W., 1982b. The unity of the Stromatoporoidea. *Proc. Third N. Am. Palæontol. Conv. Montreal*, 511–516.

Stearn, C. W., 1983. Stromatoporoids from the Blue Fiord Formation (Lower Devonian) of Ellesmere Island, Arctic Canada. *J. Paleontol.*, **57**, 539–559.

Stearn, C. W., 1984. Growth forms and macrostructural elements of the coralline sponges. *Palaeontogr. Am.*, **54**, 315–325.

Stearn, C. W. and Riding, R., 1973. Forms of the hydrozoan *Millepora* on a Recent coral reef. *Lethaia*, **6**, 187–200.

Stearn, C. W. et al., 1977. Calcium carbonate budget of a fringing reef on the west coast of Barbados. I. Zonation and productivity. *Bull. Mar. Sci.,* **27**, 479–510.

Steers, J. A., 1937. The coral islands and associated features of the Great Barrier Reefs. *Geogr. J.,* **89**, 1–28, 119–146.

Steers, J. A. and Stoddart, D. R., 1977. The origin of fringing reefs, barrier reefs and atolls. In Jones, O. A. and Endean, R. (eds.), *Biology and Geology of coral reefs,* Vol. 4. Academic, New York, pp. 21–57.

Stehli, F. G. and Webb, S. D., (eds.), 1985. *The great American interchange,* Plenum, New York, 532 pp.

Stehli, F. G. and Wells, J. W., 1971. Diversity and age patterns in hermatypic corals. *Syst. Zool.,* **20**, 115–126.

Steneck, R. S., 1983. Escalating herbivory and resulting adaptive trends in calcareous algal crusts. *Paleobiology,* **9**, 44–61.

Steneck, R. S., 1985. Adaptations of crustose coralline algae to herbivory: patterns in space and time. In Toomey, D. F. and Nitecki, M. H. (eds.). *Paleoalgology: contemporary research and applications.* Springer-Verlag, Berlin, 352–366.

Steneck, R. S. and Adey, W. H., 1976. The role of environment in control of morphology in *Lithophyllum congestum,* a Caribbean algal ridge builder. *Bot. Mar.,* **19**, 197–215.

Stenzel, H. B., 1971. Oysters. In Moore, R. C. (ed.), *Treatise on invertebrate paleontology, Part N.* Geological Society of America, Boulder, CO, and University of Kansas Press, Lawrence, KS, N953-N1224.

Stephenson, T. A. et al., 1931. The structure and ecology of Low Isles and other reefs. *Sci. Rept., Great Barrier Reef Exped.,* **3**, 17–112, 27 pls.

Stetson, T. R. et al., 1962. Coral banks occurring in deep water on the Blake Plateau. *Am. Mus. Nat. Hist. Novit.,* **2114**, 39 pp.

Stevens, C. H., 1977. Was development of brackish oceans a factor in Permian extinctions? *Geol. Soc. Am. Bull.,* **88**, 133–138.

Stockman, K. W. et al., 1967. The production of lime mud by algae in South Florida. *J. Sediment. Petrol.,* **37**, 633–648.

Stoddart, D. R., 1969. Ecology and morphology of Recent coral reefs. *Biol. Rev.,* **44**, 433–498.

Stoddart, D. R. and Johannes, R. E. (eds.), 1978. *Coral reefs: research methods.* United Nations Educational, Scientific and Cultural Organization, New York, 581 pp.

Storr, J. F., 1964. Ecology and oceanography of the coral-reef tract, Abaco Island, Bahamas. *Geol. Soc. Am. Spec. Pap.,* **79**, 98 pp.

Suchanek, T. H. et al., 1983. Sponges as important space competitors in deep Caribbean coral reef communities. In Reaka, M. L. (ed.), The ecology of deep and shallow coral reefs. *Natl. Oceanic Atmos. Adm. Undersea Res. Prog.,* **1**, 55–60.

Sutherland, P. K., 1984. *Chaetetes* reefs of exceptional size in Marble Falls Limestone (Pennsylvania), central Texas. *Palaeontogr. Am.,* **54**, 543–547.

Sutton, M., 1983. Relationships between reef fishes and coral reefs. In Barnes, D. J. (ed.), *Perspectives on coral reefs.* Australian Institute of Marine Science, Townsville, and Brian Clouston, Canberra, Australia, pp. 248–255.

Swart, P. K., 1983. Carbon and oxygen isotope fractionation in scleractinian corals: a review. *Earth Sci. Rev., 19*, 51–80.

Swart, P. K. and Coleman, M. L., 1980. Isotopic data for scleractinian corals explain their palaeotemperature uncertainties. *Nature (London) 283*, 557–559.

Swart, P. K. et al., 1983. Oxygen isotope variation on a lagoonal platform reef, Heron Island, Great Barrier Reef. *Aust. J. Mar. Freshwater Res., 34*, 813–819.

Swinchatt, J. P., 1965. Significance of constituent composition, texture, and skeletal breakdown in some Recent carbonate sediments. *J. Sediment. Petrol., 35*, 71–90.

Talbot, F. H., 1965. A description of the coral structure of Tutia Reef (Tanganyika Territory, East Africa) and its fish fauna. *Proc. Zool. Soc. London, 145*, 431–470.

Tayama, R., 1935. Table reefs, a particular type of coral reef. *Proc. Imper. Acad. Tokyo, 11*, 268–270.

Tayama, R., 1952. Coral Reefs in the South Seas. *Bull. Hydrogr. Japan, 11*, 220–285 (translated by Engineer Intelligence Div., U.S. Army, 1955).

Taylor, M. E. and Sheehan, P. M., 1968. Evolution of fossil invertebrate communities: additional factors. *Science, 161*, 491.

Teichert, C., 1958. Cold- and deep-water coral banks. *Am. Assoc. Pet. Geol. Bull., 42*, 1064–1082.

Ten Hove, H. A., 1979. Different causes of mass occurrence in serpulids. In Larwood, G. and Rosen, B. R. (eds.), Biology and systematics of colonial organisms. *Syst. Assoc. Spec. Publ. 11*, Academic, London, pp. 281–298.

Thiel, E. C., 1962. The amount of ice on planet earth. Antarctic Research, National Research Council Publ. 1036, *Geophys. Monogr., 7*, 172–175.

Thom, B. G. and Chappell, J., 1975. Holocene sealevels relative to Australia. *Search, 6*, 90–93.

Thomassin, B. A., 1974. Soft bottom carcinological fauna sensu lato on Tulear coral reef complexes (SW Madagascar): distribution, importance, roles played in trophic food-chains and in bottom deposits. *Proc. Second Int. Coral Reef Symp., 1*, 297–320.

Thomsen, E., 1977. Phenetic variability and functional morphology of erect cheilostome bryozoans from the Danian (Paleocene) of Denmark. *Paleobiology, 3*, 360–376.

Thomsen, E., 1983. Growth of Paleocene reef-mounds. *Lethaia, 16*, 165–184.

Todd, R. and Post, R., 1954. Smaller Foraminifera from Bikini Atoll drill holes. *U.S. Geol. Surv. Prof. Pap., 260-N.*

Toomey, D. F., 1970. An unhurried look at a Lower Ordovician mound horizon, southern Franklin Mountains, west Texas. *J. Sediment. Petrol., 40*, 1318–1334.

Toomey, D. F., 1976. Paleosynecology of a Permian plant dominated marine community. *Neues Jahrb. Geol. Paläontol. Abh., 152*, 1–18.

Toomey, D. F., 1979. Role of archaeolithophyllid algae within a Late Carboniferous algal-sponge community, southwestern United States. *Bull. Cent. Rech. Expl. Prod. Elf-Aquitaine, 3*, 843–853.

Toomey, D. F., 1980. History of a Late Carboniferous phylloid algal bank complex in northeastern New Mexico. *Lethaia,* **13,** 249–267.

Toomey, D. F., 1981. Organic-buildup constructional capability in Lower Ordovician and Late Paleozoic mounds. In Gray, J. and Boucot, A. J. (eds.), *Communities of the past.* Hutchinson Ross, Stroudsburg, PA, pp. 35–68.

Toomey, D. F. and Babcock, J. A., 1983. Precambrian and Paleozoic algal carbonates, west Texas and New Mexico. *Col. Sch. Mines Prof. Contrib.,* **11,** 345 pp.

Toomey, D. F. and Ham, W. E., 1967. *Pulchrilamina,* a new mound-building organism from Lower Ordovician rocks of west Texas and southern Oklahoma. *J. Paleontol.,* **41,** 981–987.

Toomey, D. F. and Klement, K. W., 1966. A problematical micro-organism from the El Paso Group (Lower Ordovician) rocks of west Texas and southern Oklahoma. *J. Paleontol.,* **40,** 1304–1311.

Toomey, D. F. and Nitecki, M. H., 1979. Organic buildups in the Lower Ordovician (Canadian) of Texas and Oklahoma. *Fieldiana Geol. New Ser.,* **2,** 181 pp.

Toomey, D. F. et al., 1977. Evolution of Yucca Mound Complex, Late Pennsylvanian phylloid-algal buildup, Sacramento Mountains, New Mexico. *Am. Assoc. Pet. Geol. Bull.,* **61,** 2115–2133.

Tracey Jr., J. I. et al., 1948. Reefs of Bikini, Marshall Islands. *Geol. Soc. Am. Bull.,* **59,** 861–878.

Tracey, J. I., June 1985. Personal communication. *U.S. Geol. Surv.,* Washington, D.C.

Trench, R. K. et al., 1981. Observations on the symbiosis with zooxanthellae among the Tridacnidae (Mollusca: Bivalvia). *Biol. Bull.,* **161,** 180–198.

Trichet, J. et al., 1984. Stratigraphy and subsidence of the Mururoa Atoll (French Polynesia). *Mar. Geol.,* **56,** 241–257.

Trudgill, S. T., 1976. The marine erosion of limestones on Aldabra Atoll, Indian Ocean. *Z. Geomorphol. Suppl.* **26,** 201–210.

Tsien, H. H., 1971. The Middle and Upper Devonian reef-complexes of Belgium. *Pet. Geol. Taiwan,* **8,** 119–173.

Tsien, H. H., 1977. Morphology and development of Devonian reefs and reef complexes in Belgium. *Proc. Third Int. Coral Reef Symp.,* **2,** 191–200.

Tsien, H. H., 1979. Palaeoecology of algal-bearing facies in the Devonian (Couvinian to Frasnian) reef complexes of Belgium. *Palaeogeogr. Palaeoclimat. Palaeoecol.,* **27,** 103–127.

Tsien, H. H., 1981. Ancient reefs and reef carbonates. *Proc. Fourth Int. Coral Reef Symp.,* **1,** 601–609.

Tsien, H. H., 1984. Organisms: their ecology and function in carbonate construction. *Palaeontogr. Am.,* **54,** 415–420.

Turmel, R. J. and Swanson, R. G., 1976. The development of Rodriguez Bank, a Holocene mudbank in the Florida reef tract. *J. Sediment. Petrol.,* **46,** 497–518.

Turnšek, D., 1968. Some hydrozoans and corals from Jurassic and Cretaceous strata of southwestern Jugoslavia. *Slov. Akad. Znan. Umet. Razpr.,* Classis IV, Razred **11,** 351–376, 9 pls.

Turnšek, D., 1969. A contribution to the palaeoecology of Jurassic hydrozoa from Slovenia. *Slov. Akad. Znan. Umet. Razpr.*, Classis IV, Razred **12**, 211–237, 1 pl.

Turnšek, D., 1970. The Devonian stromatoporoid fauna from the Karavanke Mountains. *Slov. Akad. Znan. Umet. Razpr.*, Classis IV, Razred **13**, 165–192, 14 pls.

Turnšek, D. and Masse, J. P., 1973. The Lower Cretaceous Hydrozoa and Chaetetidae from Provence (southeastern France). *Slov. Akad. Znan. Umet. Raspr.*, Classis IV, Razred **16**, 217–244, 27 pls.

Turnšek, D. et al., 1982. Carnian coral-sponge reefs in the Amphiclina Beds between Hudajužna and Zakriž (western Slovenia). *Slov. Akad. Znan. Umet. Raspr.*, Classis IV, Razred **24**(2), 48 pp., 12 pls.

Turnšek, D. et al., 1984. The role of corals in Ladinian-Carnian reef communities of Slovenia, Yugoslavia. *Palaeontogr. Am.*, **54**, 201–209.

Twenhofel, W. H., 1950. Coral and other organic reefs in geologic column. *Am. Assoc. Pet. Geol. Bull.*, **34**, 182–202.

Vacelet, J., 1979. Description et affinites d'une éponge sphinctozoaire actuelle. *Colloq. Int. C. N. R. Sci.*, **291**, 483–493.

Vacelet, J., 1983. Les éponges calcifiées et les récifs anciens. *Pour Sci.*, 14–22.

Vacelet, J., 1985. Coralline sponges and the evolution of Porifera. In Morris, S. C. et al. (eds.), The origins and relationships of lower invertebrates. *Syst. Assoc. Spec. Vol. 28*, Clarendon Press, Oxford, UK, pp. 1–13.

Vail, P. R. et al., 1977. Seismic stratigraphy and global changes of sealevel, Part 4. In Peyton, C. E. (ed.), Seismic stratigraphy. *Am. Assoc. Pet. Geol. Mem.*, **26**, 83–97.

Valentine, J. W., 1968. Climatic regulation of species diversification and extinction. *Geol. Soc. Am. Bull.*, **79**, 273–275.

Valentine, J. W., 1969. Niche diversity and niche size patterns in marine fossils. *J. Paleontol.*, **43**, 905–915.

Valentine, J. W., 1984. Neogene climatic trends: implications for biogeography and evolution of shallow sea biota. *J. Geol.*, **12**, 647–650.

Vaughan, T. W., 1911. Physical conditions under which Paleozoic coral reefs were formed. *Geol. Soc. Am. Bull.*, **22**, 238–252.

Vaughan, T. W., 1915. The geologic significance of the growth rate of Floridinian and Bahaman shoal-water corals. *J. Wash. Acad. Sci.*, **5**, 591–600.

Vaughan, T. W., 1919. Corals and the formation of coral reefs. *Smithson. Inst. Ann. Rept. for 1917*, 189–328.

Veeh, H. H. and Green, D. C., 1977. Radiometric geochronology of coral reefs. In Jones, O. A. and Endean, R. (eds.), *Biology and geology of coral reefs*, Vol. 4. Academic, New York, pp. 183–200.

Vella, P., 1964. Foraminifera and other fossils from the Late Tertiary deep-water coral thickets, Wairarapa, New Zealand. *J. Paleontol.*, **38**, 916–928.

Veron, J. E. N., 1974. Southern geographic limits to the distribution of Great Barrier Reef hermatypic corals. *Proc. Second Int. Coral Reef Symp.*, **1**, 465–473.

Veron, J. E. N. and Done, T. J., 1979. Corals and coral communities at Lord Howe Island. *Aust. J. Mar. Freshwater Res.*, **30**, 203–236.

Veron, J. E. N. and Pichon, M., 1976. Scleractinia of eastern Australia, Part I. families Thamnasteriidae, Astrocoeniidae, Pocilloporidae. *Aust. Inst. Mar. Sci. Monogr.*, **1**, 86 pp.

Vogel, K., 1963. Riff, bioherm, biostrom-versuch einer begriffserklärung. *Neues Jahrb. Geol. Paläontol., Monatsh.*, **12**, 680–688.

Vogel, K., 1974. Endosymbiotic algae in rudists. *Palaeogeogr. Palaeoclimatol. Palaeoecol.*, **17**, 327–332.

Walker, K. R. and Alberstadt, L. P., 1975. Ecological succession as an aspect of structure in fossil communities. *Paleobiology*, **1**, 238–257.

Walker, K. R. and Ferrigno, K. F., 1973. Major Middle Ordovician reef tract in east Tennessee. *Am. J. Sci.*, **237A**, 294–325.

Walter, M. R., 1972. Stromatolites and the biostratigraphy of the Australian Precambrian and Cambrian. *Spec. Pap. Palaeontol.*, **11**, 268 pp.

Walter, M. R. (ed.), 1976. Stromatolites. *Dev. Sedimentol.*, **20**, 790 pp.

Walther, J., 1888. Die Koralriffe der Sinaihalbinsel. *Abh. Sächs Akad. Wiss.*, **14**, 437 pp.

Ward, P. and Risk, M. J., 1977. Boring pattern of the sponge *Cliona vermifera* in the coral *Montastraea annularis*. *J. Paleontol.*, **51**, 520–526.

Warme, J. E., 1977. Carbonate borers—their role in reef ecology and preservation. *Am. Assoc. Pet. Geol., Stud. Geol.*, **4**, 261–279.

Weber, J. N. and White, E. W., 1977. Caribbean reef corals *Montastrea annularis* and *Montastrea cavernosa*—long-term growth data as determined by skeletal x-ray. In Frost, S. H. et al. (eds.), Reefs and related carbonates—ecology and sedimentology. *Am. Assoc. Pet. Geol. Stud. Geol.*, **4**, 171–179.

Wefer, G., 1980. Carbonate production by algae. *Halimeda, Penicillus* and *Padina. Nature (London)*, **285**, 323–324.

Weinberg, S., 1978. The minimal area problem in invertebrate communities of Mediterranean rocky substrates. *Mar. Biol.*, **49**, 33–40.

Wellington, G. M., 1982. Depth zonation of corals in the Gulf of Panama. *Ecol. Monogr.*, **52**, 223–241.

Wells, J. W., 1933. Corals of the Cretaceous of the Atlantic and Gulf coastal plains and western interior of the United States. *Bull. Am. Paleontol.*, **18**, 85–288.

Wells, J. W., 1954a. Recent corals of the Marshall Islands. *U.S. Geol. Surv. Prof. Pap.*, **260-I**, 385–459.

Wells, J. W., 1954b. Fossil corals from Bikini Atoll. *U.S. Geol. Surv. Prof. Pap.*, **260-P**, 609–617.

Wells, J. W., 1955. A survey of the distribution of coral genera in the Great Barrier Reef region. *Rept. Great Barrier Reef Comm.*, **6**, 21–29.

Wells, J. W., 1956. Scleractinia. In Moore, R. C. (ed.), *Treatise on Invertebrate Paleontology, Part F, Coelenterata*. Geological Society of America, Boulder, CO, and University of Kansas Press, Lawrence, KS, pp. F328–F444.

Wells, J. W., 1957a. Coral reefs. *Geol. Soc. Am. Mem. 67*, **1**, 609–631.

Wells, J. W., 1957b. Corals. *Geol. Soc. Am. Mem. 67*, **2**, 773–782.

Wells, J. W., 1963. Coral growth and geochronometry. *Nature (London)*, **197,** 948–950.

Wells, J. W., 1967. Corals as bathometers. *Mar. Geol.*, **5,** 349–365.

Wells, J. W., 1970. Problems of annual and daily growth-rings in corals. In Runcorn, S. K. (ed.), *Palaeogeophysics.* Academic, New York, pp. 3–9.

Wells, J. W. and Lang, J. C., 1973. Systematic list of Jamaican shallow-water Scleractinia. *Bull. Mar. Sci.*, **23,** 55–58.

Wendt, J., 1975. Aragonitische stromatoporen aus der alpinen Obertrias. *Neus Jahrb. Geol. Paläont. Abh.*, **150,** 111–125.

Wendt, J., 1979. Development of skeletal formation, microstructure, and mineralogy of rigid calcareous sponges from the Late Paleozoic to Recent. In Levi, C. and Boury-Esnault, N. (eds.), Biologie des spongiaires. *Colloq. Int. C. N. R. Sci.*, **291,** 449–457.

Wendt, J., 1980a. Calcareous sponges—development through time. In Hartman, W. D. et al., Living and fossil sponges—notes for a short course. *Sedimenta VIII.* Comparative Sedimentology Laboratory, University of Miami, Miami, FL, pp. 169–178.

Wendt, J., 1980b. Coral-sponge reefs in the South Alpine Upper Triassic. In Hartman, W. D. et al., Living and fossil sponges—notes for a short course. *Sedimenta VIII.* Comparative Sedimentology Laboratory, University of Miami, Miami, FL, pp. 241–252.

Wendt, J., 1980c. Sponge reefs of the German Upper Jurassic. In Hartman, W. D. et al., *Living and fossil sponges—notes for a short course. Sedimenta VIII.* Comparative Sedimentology Laboratory, University of Miami, Miami, FL, pp. 122–130.

Wendt, J., 1982. The Cassian patch reefs (Lower Carnian, southern Alps). *Facies*, **6,** 185–202.

Wendt, J., 1984. Skeletal and spicular mineralogy, microstructure and diagenesis of coralline calcareous sponges. *Palaeontogr. Am.*, **54,** 326–336.

West, R. R. and Clark II, G. R., 1984. Paleobiology and biological affinities of Paleozoic chaetetids. *Palaeontogr. Am.*, **54,** 337–348.

Wiebe, W. J. et al., 1981. High latitude (Abrolhos Islands) reef community metabolism: what sets latitudinal limits on coral reef development? *Proc. Fourth Int. Coral Reef Symp. (Abstr.),* **1,** 721.

Wiedenmayer, F., 1978. Modern sponge bioherms of the Great Bahama Bank. *Eclog. Geol. Helv.*, **71,** 699–744.

Wiedenmayer, F., 1980a. Shallow-water sponges of the Bahamas. In Hartman, W. D. et al., Living and fossil sponges—notes for a short course. *Sedimenta VIII.* Comparative Sedimentology Laboratory, University of Miami, Miami, FL, pp. 146–168.

Wiedenmayer, F., 1980b. Modern sponge bioherms of the Great Bahama Bank and their likely ancient analogues. *Colloq. Int. C. N. R. Sci.*, **291,** 289–296.

Wiedenmayer, F. and Cuffey, R. J., 1980. Modern sponge-built mounds off Joulters Cays (Bahamas)—general character and paleoecological implication. *Geol. Soc. Am. Abstr. (with Program),* **12,** 260–261.

Wiens, H. J., 1962. *Atoll environment and ecology.* Yale University Press, New Haven, CT, 532 pp.

Wilkinson, C. R., 1983. Role of sponges in coral reef structural processes. In Barnes, D. J. (ed.), *Perspectives on coral reefs.* Australian Institute of Marine Science, Townsville, and Brian Clouston, Canberra, Australia, pp. 263–274.

Willenz, P. and Hartman, W. D., 1985. Calcification rate of *Ceratoporella nicholsoni* (Porifera: Sclerospongiae): an *in situ* study with calcein. *Proc. 5th Int. Congr. Coral Reefs,* **5,** 113–118.

Wilson, J. B., 1975. The distribution of the coral *Caryophyllia smithii* S. & B. on the Scottish continental shelf. *J. Mar. Biol. Assoc.,* **55,** 611–625.

Wilson, J. B., 1979. "Patch" development of the deep-water coral *Lophelia pertusa* (L.) on Rockall Bank. *J. Mar. Biol. Assoc. U.K.,* **59,** 165–177.

Wilson, J. L., 1974. Characteristics of carbonate-platform margins. *Am. Assoc. Pet. Geol. Bull.,* **58,** 810–824.

Wilson, J. L., 1975. *Carbonate facies in geologic history.* Springer-Verlag, New York, 471 pp.

Wilson, W. B., 1950. Reef definition. *Am. Assoc. Pet. Geol. Bull.,* **34,** 181.

Winston, J. E., 1976. Experimental culture of the estuarine ectoproct *Conopeum tenuissimum* from Chesapeake Bay. *Biol. Bull.,* **150,** 318–335.

Wise, K. P. and Schopf, T. J. M., 1981. Was marine faunal diversity in the Pleistocene affected by changes in sealevel? *Paleobiology,* **7,** 394–399.

Wolfenden, E. B., 1958. Paleoecology of the Carboniferous Reef Complex and shelf limestones in northwest Derbyshire, England. *Geol. Soc. Am. Bull.,* **69,** 871–898.

Wood, R. A. and Reitner, J., 1986. Poriferan affinities of Mesozoic stromatoporoids. *Palaeontology,* **29,** 469–473.

Wood-Jones, F., 1910. *Coral and atolls.* Lovell Reeve & Co., London, 392 pp.

Woodley, J. D. et al., 1981. Hurricane Allen's impact on Jamaican coral reefs. *Science,* **214,** 749–755.

Wray, J. L., 1964. *Archaeolithophyllum,* an abundant calcareous alga in limestones of the Lansing Group (Pennsylvanian), southeastern Kansas. *Geol. Surv. Kansas Bull.,* **170,** 1–13.

Wray, J. L., 1967. Upper Devonian calcareous algae from the Canning Basin, Western Australia. *Col. Sch. Mines Prof. Contrib.,* **3,** 76 pp.

Wray, J. L., 1968. Late Paleozoic phylloid algal limestones in the United States. *Proc. Twenty-Third Int. Geol. Congr.,* **8,** 113–119.

Wray, J. L., 1969. Paleocene calcareous algae from Libya. *Symp. Geol. Libya Univ. Libya,* 21–22.

Wray, J. L., 1971. Algae in reefs through time. *Proc. N. Am. Paleontol. Conv. Part J,* 1358–1373.

Wray, J. L., 1977. Calcareous algae. *Dev. Palaeontol. Stratigr.,* **4,** Elsevier, Amsterdam, 185 pp.

Wray, J. L. and Playford, P. E., 1970. Some occurrences of Devonian reef-building algae in Alberta. *Can. Pet. Geol. Bull.,* **18,** 544–555.

Wulff, J. L., 1984. Sponge-mediated coral reef growth and rejuvenation. *Coral Reefs*, **3**, 157–163.

Wulff, J. L. and Buss, L. W., 1979. Do sponges help hold coral reefs together? *Nature (London)* **281**, 474–475.

Wurm, D., 1982. Microfacies, paleontology and paleoecology of the Dachstein reef limestone (Norian) of the Gosaukamm Range, Austria. *Facies*, **6**, 203–296, 15 pls.

Yonge, C. M., 1930. Studies on the physiology of corals. 1. Feeding mechanisms and food. *Sci. Rept. Great Barrier Reef Exped. 1928–1929*, 13–57.

Yonge, C. M., 1973. The nature of reef-building (hermatypic) corals. *Bull. Mar. Sci.*, **23**, 1–15.

Yonge, C. M. et al., 1932. Studies on the physiology of corals. VI. The relationship between respiration in corals and the production of oxygen by their zooxanthellae. *Sci. Rept. Great Barrier Reef Exped.* **1**, 135–176.

Yurewicz, D. A., 1977. Origin of the massive facies of the Lower and Middle Capitan Limestone (Permian), Guadalupe Mountains, New Mexico and west Texas. In Hileman, M. E. and Mazzullo, S. J. (eds.), Upper Guadalupian facies, Permian reef complex, Guadalupe Mountains, New Mexico and west Texas, Permian Basin Sect. *Soc. Econ. Paleontol. Mineral. Spec. Publ.*, **77-6**, 45–92.

Zankl, H., 1969. Der Hohe Göll: Aufbau und Lebensbild eines Dachsteinkalk-Riffes in der Obertrias der nördlichen Kalkalpen. *Sencken. Naturforsch. Ges.*, **519**, 1–123.

Zhang, Z. and Li, Z., 1984. Noctidiurnal growth rhythm of filamentous cyanophytes from the Gaoyuzhuang Formation (Changchengian System) of north China. *Kexue Tongbao*, **29**, 1132–1133.

Zhuravleva, I. T. and Miagkova, Y. I., 1977. Morphology of fossil elementary organogenous buildings. *J. Palaeontol. Soc. India*, **20**, 89–96.

Ziegler, A. M. et al., 1981. Cambrian world paleogeography, biogeography and climatology. In Taylor, M. E. (ed.), Short papers for second international symposium on Cambrian system. *U.S. Geol. Surv. Open-File Rept.*, **81-743**, 252.

Zimmerman, L. C. and Cuffey, R. J., 1985. Acanthoclad-fenestrate-trepostome frame-thickets (Permian, west Texas), a model for Late Paleozoic bryozoan reefs. *Proc. Fifth Int. Coral Congr.*, **6**, 587–592.

Glossary

In several places in the text (e.g., Preface, Chaps. 3, 6) reference is made to the problems of reef terminology. Although the following glossary is very incomplete, it contains most of the terms regarded here as basic; other such terms and a discussion of them may be located in the text by referring to the Index.

The glossary includes both geologic (see Chaps. 3, 4, 6) and biologic (see Chaps. 3, 5) terms. The terms are followed by definitions appropriate to the reef community context; many are thus somewhat modified from the source indicated for each and the definitions are generally given in chronological order. The definitions have often been selected to demonstrate the varied, inconsistent, and often contradictory usage of the same term. The glossary also may be useful to readers comparing terms used in the general reef literature because it contains a few terms not used in the present volume but commonly used elsewhere.

Numerous terms pertaining to reefs and not included here may be found in Bates and Jackson (1980), the glossary in Levinton (1982, pp. 445–460), and in James (1983, pp. 346–397).

Algal Ridge Low ridge at seaward margin of reef flat, largely composed of skeletons of calcareous algae (modified from Bates and Jackson, 1980).

Antecedent Platform Any bench or platform at proper depth within the equatorial reef zone; a potential reef foundation (Hoffmeister and Ladd, 1944).

Apron Reef Initial stage of a fringing reef; discontinuous, covers a small area (Tayama, 1952).

Atoll 1. First used by Micronesians as a descriptive term for large circular platform reefs in Maldive Islands; originally spelled atollen (Tracey, June 1985, personal communication); 2. a more-or-less continuous emerged or slightly submerged calcareous reef surrounding a distinctly deeper lagoon(s) lacking emerged volcanic islands, which stand apart from other islands, and whose upper seaward slopes rise steeper than repose angle of loose sediments (Wiens, 1962, p. 8); 3. coral reef appearing in plan view as roughly circular (sometimes elliptical or horseshoe-shaped); surmounted by a chain or ring of low islets that nearly encircle a shallow lagoon in which there is no preexisting land; surrounded by deep water of open sea, either oceanic or shelf (Bates and Jackson, 1980).

Back-reef   Landward side of a reef, including the area and sediments between the reef crest/algal ridge and the land; corresponds to reef flat and lagoon of barrier reef and platform margin reef systems (modified from Bates and Jackson, 1980).

Bafflestone   1. Carbonate rocks containing *in situ* stalk-shaped fossils which trapped sediment during deposition by acting as baffles (i.e., reducing the rate of water flow, thus causing deposition; Embry and Klovan, 1971); 2. carbonate rocks formed by the baffling process as indicated by abundant minimally transported members of the baffler guild.

Baffling   Process by which velocity of waves and currents is reduced by erect obstructions above general level of substrate; occurs in reef and level-bottom substrates as a prelude to sediment deposition/trapping/binding.

Bank   1. Structure formed by organisms incapable of raising their substrate; unconsolidated sediments; exerts minimal influence over environment (Lowenstam, 1950); 2. any type of feature at sufficient depth as to not pose a hazard to navigation (MacNeil, 1954); 3. (for "coral bank") a bioherm far below effective wave base (modified from Teichert, 1958); a large (500 m across), coral-built topographic feature in deep water; solidly filled with trapped fine sediment and coral skeletal debris near the base (modified from Squires, 1964); 4. consists of organisms unable to erect a rigid three-dimensional framework; may be formed in place or by transported skeletons; wave-resistant (Klement, 1967); 5. (in oceanography) relatively flat-topped elevations of seafloor at shallow depth (<200 m), typically on continental shelf or near an island (Bates and Jackson, 1980); 6. mound- or ridgelike deposit of skeletal matter, largely unbroken, formed *in situ* by organisms lacking ecological potential to build rigid, wave-resistant structure; lacks structural framework of a reef; may develop in cold, deep waters far from true reefs (Bates and Jackson, 1980).

Bank Deposits   Shoal-water, local mounds, ridges, and terraces of sediments rising above surrounding sea bottom (Newell et al., 1953).

Bank-reef   Large reef growths, generally irregular in shape, which developed over submerged highs of tectonic or other origin and are more or less completely surrounded by deeper water (Henson, 1950).

Barrier Reef   Long, narrow coral reef roughly parallel to shore and separated from it by a lagoon of considerable depth and width; may enclose (wholly or partially) a volcanic island or may lie at a great distance from a continental coast; generally follows continental coasts for long distances, often with short interruptions, termed passes or channels (Bates and Jackson, 1980).

Basin   Low area of earth's crust, of tectonic origin, in which sediments have accumulated in considerable thickness (modified from Bates and Jackson, 1980).

Binding   Process by which laterally expanded organisms hold loose sediment and support or brace large *in situ* skeletons of reef framework; unites organic framework and internal sediment to enhance reef rigidity; includes "encrusting" (cf. Klement, 1967; Heckel, 1974, p. 96).

Bindstone   Carbonate rocks containing *in situ*, tabular, or lamellar fossils which encrusted and bound sediment during deposition; the matrix, not the *in situ* fossils, forms the supporting framework of the rock; fossils may form as little as 15% of the rock volume (Embry and Klovan, 1971).

Bioerosion   Erosion by organism activities such as boring, scraping, chewing (Neumann, 1966).

Bioherm   1. Dome-, moundlike, or otherwise circumscribed mass built by sedentary organisms and enclosed in normal rocks of different lithology (Cumings and Shrock, 1928); 2. reef, bank, or mound; reeflike, moundlike, lenslike, or otherwise circumscribed structure of strictly organic origin (Cumings, 1932); 3. accumulation of lime mud inferred to have been caused by growth of organisms no longer preserved (Heckel, 1974, p. 92).

Biomass   Amount (weight) of living matter (cells, tissues, etc., excluding shells, skeletons, etc.) per unit area or volume; syn.: standing crop.

Biostrome   1. Distinctly bedded structure that does not swell into lens- or reeflike form; consists mainly of remains of organisms (Cumings, 1932); 2. diverse assemblage of living organisms and organic structures intimately associated with bioclastic debris largely derived from those organisms (Kauffman and Sohl, 1974, p. 435).

Bioturbation   The churning and stirring of sediment by organisms (Bates and Jackson, 1980).

Boundstone   1. Carbonate rock showing signs of original components being bound during deposition; signs of binding are specific and occur within sample being classified (Dunham, 1962); 2. autochthanous limestone in which the specific mode of binding cannot be recognized (Embry and Klovan, 1971).

Buildup Organic carbonate masses which represent predominantly in-place accumulation of largely skeleton-derived carbonate sediment and which had some topographic expression above seafloor during growth; includes reef, bioherm, organic reef, biohermal reef, and mound (Stanton, 1967); 2. carbonate mass which differs from equivalent deposits and surrounding and overlying rocks; typically thicker than equivalent carbonate rocks; includes oolites, transported shell accumulations, reefs, etc. (Heckel, 1974, p. 91); cf. organic buildup.

Calyptra Organogenous buildings (<0.5—1 m in diameter); occurs either as independent formations or as component parts of larger and more complex buildings (biostromes, bioherms); built by algae and other organisms growing one upon another; a large colony (usually of Stromatoporoidea or Tabulata) may play the role of calyptrae too (Zhuravleva and Miagkova, 1977).

Cateniform 1. Coralla of tabulate (rarely rugose and scleractinian) corals in which corallites are erect and laterally united to form palisades which appear chainlike in cross section; 2. skeletons of typical erect sphinctozoan and archaeocyathid sponges in which chambers are added in a linear series; beaded/beadlike; syn.: moniliform, catenulate (Finks, 1983).

Cay Small, low, coastal island or emergent reef of sand or coral; flat mound of sand and admixed coral fragments built up on a reef flat at or just above high-tide level; used in West Indies where it is pronounced "key"; syn.: key, as used in southern Florida (Bates and Jackson, 1980).

Cement Chemically precipitated $CaCO_3$ present in spaces within skeletons or between individual grains of internal sediment; binds framework and internal sediment together to enhance rigidity.

Chronostratigraphy Branch of stratigraphy that deals with the age (time of origin) of strata and their time relations (Hedberg, 1976).

Coelobite Organism living in voids or pores within a reef; includes "cryptic habitat" and "sciaphile" (shade-loving) of previous authors (Ginsburg and Schroeder, 1973, p. 589).

Coevolution Simultaneous evolution of interacting populations (Roughgarden, 1979, p. 451).

Commensalism A situation in which organisms live together, with no harm to either, and generally share a source of food; the process of obtaining food is usually carried out by one partner (host), so advantages of the association are to the other partner (commensal); commensal may live on surface or inside body of host (Gotto, 1969).

Continental Shelf   That part of continental margin located between the shoreline and the continental slope; characterized by its very gentle slope (approx. 0.1°; Bates and Jackson, 1980).

Coppice   Stage of development of a deep-water coral thicket at which skeletal debris begins to accumulate about the base in amounts adequate for animals requiring food and shelter provided by the debris and fine organic and inorganic material in the interstices of the broken coral branches (Squires, 1964); dia.: approx. 15 m; cf. thicket.

Coral Knoll (or **Knoll**)   1. Small reef within the lagoon or on shallow shelves (Darwin, 1842; Stoddart, 1969, pp. 452–453); 2. isolated mound of coral rising steeply from bottom; may be more than 1.6 km in diameter at base; nearly reaches sea level (Ladd et al., 1950); 3. rise from lagoon floor; varies from pinnaclelike structure to broad, flat-topped, or mushroom-shaped mound; 4. when lagoonal coral knolls reach or nearly reach water surface they become patch reefs (Wiens, 1962); 5. isolated, more-or-less circular area of carbonate accumulation in deeper water below wave base (J. L. Wilson, 1975, p. 22).

Craton   Part of earth's crust that has attained stability; usage restricted to continental areas; the extensive central areas of continents (Bates and Jackson, 1980).

Cryptalgal   Pertains to rocks formed by non-calcareous blue–green (Schizophyta) and green (Clorophyta) algae; influence of algae in the rock-forming process is more commonly inferred than observed; rocks originate through sediment-binding and/or carbonate-precipitating activities of non-skeletal algae; may include filamentous or unicellular structures due to non-skeletal algae (Aitken, 1967).

Cryptofauna   Animals living in coral substrates and certain fauna living on the substrate surface; consists of borers and bore hole dwellers (Hutchings, 1983).

Dendroid   1. In colonial corals, irregularly branching fasciculate coralla; 2. in non-coral higher taxa, any branching growth habit; syn.: ramose.

Diagenesis   All chemical, physical, and biologic changes undergone by sediment after its initial deposition, and during and after its lithification, exclusive of weathering and metamorphism; includes compaction, cementation, leaching, etc. (Bates and Jackson, 1980).

Diastrophism   General term for all movement of earth's crust produced by tectonic processes; orogeny and epeirogeny are major subdivisions; syn.: tectonism (Bates and Jackson, 1980).

Ecophenotype An environmentally induced growth form; syn.: ecomorph.

Encrusting An aspect of binding performed by laterally expanded skeletal organisms attached to hard substrates.

Endoecism A biologic relationship in which one animal habitually lives within the tube or burrow of another animal (Gotto, 1969).

Epeirogeny A form of diastrophism that has produced the larger features of the continents and oceans (e.g., plateaus and basins); movements are primarily vertical, either upward or downward (Bates and Jackson, 1980).

Epizoism A biologic relationship in which one animal (epizoite) lives (attached or free) on surface of another (host); may involve marked substrate preference and/or provision by host of a favorable environment (Gotto, 1969).

Erect Dominant growth direction of organisms is vertical or generally perpendicular to substrate surface; cf. reptant.

Eucaryote Morphologically advanced organism characterized by cellular organelles, including the nucleus, bounded by membranes (Wray, 1977, p. 164); cf. procaryote.

Eustasy Worldwide sea-level regime and its fluctuations, caused by absolute changes in the quantity of seawater (i.e., by continental ice-cap fluctuations; Bates and Jackson, 1980).

Faro 1. First used as a descriptive term for small circular platform reef in Maldive Islands (Tracey, June 1985, personal communication); 2. small, ring-shaped basin with small lagoon; occurs on rims of barrier reefs and atolls; lagoon well-defined and rarely greater than 20 m deep (Gardiner, 1902); 3. large, ring-shaped patch reef at atoll margin (Scoffin and Stoddart, 1978).

Fasciculate In colonial corals, coralla with erect–horizontal cylindrical corallites which are somewhat separated from one another but may be joined by connecting tubules.

Fenestrate In bryozoans, erect zoaria with reticulate network formed by branches and dissepiments.

Floatstone Carbonate rock containing greater than 10% of grains larger than 2 mm with grains not in contact with each other (i.e., they "float" in finer-grained matrix); used to describe and classify internal sediment of a reef or sediment of adjacent level-bottom (Embry and Klovan, 1971); cf. rudstone.

Foliaceous   1. Colonial scleractinian coralla in the form of thin, laterally expanded, overlapping sheets with small basal attachment (Wells, 1956, p. F352); 2. thin, sheetlike, or "wrinkled" bryozoan zoaria; 3. recumbent rudists with frills on major growth lines (Philip, 1972).

Fore-reef   Seaward side of reef, including area and sediments of seaward slope.

Form   The size and shape of an organism.

Framestone   Carbonate rock containing *in situ* massive fossils which constructed a rigid three-dimensional framework during deposition; *in situ* fossils form the supporting framework (Embry and Klovan, 1971).

Framework (or **Reef Framework**)   1. Rigid, wave-resistant, calcareous structure built by sedentary organisms, such as sponges, corals, and bryozoans, in a high energy environment (Bates and Jackson, 1980); 2. rigid, organism-built component of reef with potential to resist waves; a fulcrum for reef complex by acting as both site for abundant sediment production and wave baffle to allow reef-associated non-framework facies to be deposited in adjacent areas (Longman, 1981, p. 12).

Fringing Reef   A reef directly attached to or bordering the shore, having a rough, tablelike surface exposed at low tide; may be more than 1 km wide with its seaward edge sloping sharply down to seafloor; syn.: shore reef (Bates and Jackson, 1980).

Frondescent   Bryozoan zoaria in the form of erect, leaflike branches and blades; syn.: foliaceous of some authors.

Functional Morphology   Form and structure of an organism in relation to its adaptation to a specific environment and/or survival under specific conditions; morphology of an organism as it responds to environmental changes and conditions (Bates and Jackson, 1980).

G   Gross $CaCO_3$ production per unit area; usually expressed as kg $CaCO_3$/m^2/yr (Chave et al., 1972).

Guild   A group of species that exploit the same class of environmental resources in a similar way; species that overlap significantly in their niche requirements (Root, 1967, p. 335).

Guyot   1. Flat-topped seamount (Bates and Jackson, 1980); 2. a deeply submerged (drowned) inactive volcano in the open ocean.

Habit (or **Growth Habit**)   The orientation, form, and structure of an organism with respect to substrate; chiefly erect (upright) or lateral (reptant).

Habitat   Place where an organism lives; local environment in that place.

Hardground   A submerged hard surface of skeletons, rocks, or wood; a reef is a type of hardground.

Inquilinism   A biological relationship in which two organisms of different species live together, one within the other, the former using host mainly as a refuge; protection is the keynote; host does not suffer from the association (Gotto, 1969); cf. parasitism.

Internal Sediment   Sedimentary grains, chiefly skeletal fragments, deposited within the pores of the reef framework.

Isocryme   A line of equal minimum (winter) temperature of sea surface waters.

Key   See cay.

Knoll Reef   A knoll of organic frame-built growth; used to identify individual buildups of shelf margins or in basins (J. L. Wilson, 1975, p. 22); cf. coral knoll; syn.: reef knoll.

Lagoon   1. Shallow water between an offshore (barrier) reef and the shore; overlies reef flat; 2. shallow water within rim of an atoll (Bates and Jackson, 1980).

Level-bottom   Sediment-covered seafloor adjacent to a hardground.

Lithoherm   Deep (below photic zone) muddy carbonate buildup formed by constructive interaction of penecontemporaneous submarine lithification and organism attachment (Neumann et al., 1977).

Lithology   Description of rocks, especially in hand specimen and outcrop, on the basis of such characteristics as color, mineral composition, and grain size (Bates and Jackson, 1980); includes fossil content.

Massive   1. Coralla of colonial rugose corals in which corallites are in contact with one another on all sides; corallites in central part of corallum erect, subhorizontal near corallum margin; 2. scleractinian colonial coralla in form of more-or-less thick masses or heads (Wells, 1956, p. F352); 3. domal–hemispherical growth form in non-anthozoan reef-builders and dwellers.

Microatoll   1. Circular colonial corallum (chiefly *Heliopora*, *Porites*, *Millepora*) up to 1 m tall and 4 m in diameter with growth chiefly lateral and top composed of dead coral veneered by algal mat and foraminiferal sand; upward growth stopped by aerial exposure (Wood-Jones, 1910).

Mini-atoll   Ring-shaped patch reef with central area (lagoon) containing sand (Scoffin and Stoddart, 1978).

Motu   Polynesian name for a vegetated sand cay.

Mound   1. Organic structure built by fossil colonial organisms, such as crinoids (*sic:* Bates and Jackson, 1980); 2. an equidimensional or elliptical buildup (J. L. Wilson, 1975, p. 21).

Mud Mound   Mound-shaped mass of carbonate mudstone–wackestone; fossils, if present, are not in growth position and skeletons are not large or of major volumetric importance.

Mutualism   An association between individuals of different species involving reciprocal benefit or mutual advantage; partners are not ultimately dependent on one another in a physiological sense (Gotto, 1969).

N   Net $CaCO_3$ production; amount of $CaCO_3$ permanently retained by a reef system; usually expressed as kg $CaCO_3/m^2/yr$ (Chave et al., 1972).

Niche   1. Functional role or "profession" of a species in a community; the set of conditions that permit a species to exist in a particular biotope (Root, 1967); 2. the resources a species uses, where it finds them, and the strategy by which it harvests them (Diamond, 1978); 3. position and role of a species in a community: how and when it feeds, what it feeds on, where it lives, its preferred combination of physical and chemical conditions, and the range of those conditions that it can tolerate (Richardson, 1977, p. 72); 4. the range of environmental space occupied by a species (Levinton, 1982, p. 453).

Off-reef   Syn.: fore-reef, seaward slope; back-reef of some authors.

Organic Buildup   Carbonate body composed primarily of fossil organisms, regardless of shape or mode of origin; reef, bank, bioherm, and biostrome are specific types of organic buildups depending on shape and mode of origin (Embry and Klovan, 1971); cf. buildup.

Orogeny   Originally: the process of forming mountains; presently: the process by which structures within fold-belt mountainous areas were formed (Bates and Jackson, 1980).

Parasitism   An intimate association between individuals of different species in which one partner profits and the other is harmed or debilitated (Gotto, 1969).

Patchiness   1. Condition where organisms occur in aggregations (Levinton, 1982); can occur on geographic scales from individual reefs to reef complexes or from a reef to the adjacent level-bottom.

Patch Reef   1. Independent coral growths in lagoons of barriers and atolls; ranges in size and shape from pillars or mushroom-shaped growths consisting of a single large colony to several kilometers across; small patch reefs called "knolls" (Kuenen, 1950, p. 426); 2. small, subequidimensional or irregularly shaped reefs that are typically part of reef complexes (Cloud, 1952); 3. scattered reefs in shallow parts of atoll lagoons; dia.: a few meters to a few thousand meters (Wells, 1957a, pp. 621, 623); 4. moundlike or flat-topped organic reef generally less than 1 km across, less extensive than a platform reef, and frequently part of a reef complex (Bates and Jackson, 1980).

Petrology   Origin, occurrence, structure, and history of rocks (Bates and Jackson, 1980).

Phaceloid   Fasciculate coralla having erect, subparallel corallites.

Phanerozoic   That part of geologic time represented by rocks in which evidence of metazoan life is abundant, i.e., Cambrian and later (modified from Bates and Jackson, 1980).

Pinnacle Reef   Subcylindrical reefs with nearly vertical sides; up to 200 m in diameter and 50 m tall (modified from Ludwick and Walton, 1957, p. 2055; cf. Bates and Jackson, 1980).

Platform   1. A flat or gently sloping underwater erosional surface extending seaward from the shore (Bates and Jackson, 1980); 2. (as "carbonate platform") huge carbonate body built-up with a more-or-less horizontal top and abrupt shelf margins where "high energy" sediments occur (J. L. Wilson, 1975, p. 21).

Platform Reef   1. Reef in shallower parts of continental shelves, in barrier reef lagoons; flat-topped, without lagoons, ovate with long axis parallel to prevailing wind in barrier reef lagoon or perpendicular to wind if located near open ocean; size range: small reef knolls to 25 km across; depth of upper surface: wave base to awash at low tide; active coral growth only on margins (Wells, 1957a, p. 625); 2. a reef with a flat upper surface, sometimes forming an island; more extensive than patch reef (i.e., several km across; Bates and Jackson, 1980).

"Porostromata"   An artificial group of algae containing forms with definite microstructure consisting of filaments of unknown systematic position, but probably either green or blue–green (Wray, 1977, p. 35).

Predator   A vagile animal that consumes another living organism; includes some herbivores but are mostly carnivores.

Procaryote   Morphologically primitive organisms (bacteria and blue–green algae; mostly single cells or simple filaments) which do not have DNA separated by cytoplasm or an envelope (Wray, 1977, p. 166); cells lack nucleus and chromatophores.

Productivity   Rate of increase of biomass in a community or ecosystem; may be subdivided into (1) gross (total productivity, not including losses by respiration) and (2) net (total productivity minus amount consumed by respiration) or into (1) primary (productivity by plants) and (2) secondary (productivity by consumers). Productivity by consumers may be subdivided into (1) secondary (productivity by herbivores) and (2) tertiary (productivity by carnivores).

Province   1. Large, biogeographic area with a characteristic set of species or a characteristic percentage representation by given species (Levinton, 1982); larger area than a community; 2. sometimes used for area of Great Barrier Reef, Australia.

Ramose   See dendroid.

Ramp (or **Carbonate Ramp**)   1. Sloping surface connecting two levels with no break in slope; sloping surface on which carbonate facies are deposited while subject to open ocean conditions from surf zone to depths of hundreds of feet (Ahr, 1973); 2. huge carbonate bodies built away from positive areas and down gentle regional paleoslopes; no striking break in slope exists (J. L. Wilson, 1975, p. 21).

Rampart   1. Narrow, wall-like ridge 1–2 m high built by waves along seaward edge of a reef flat; consists of boulders, shingle, gravel, or reef rubble, commonly capped by dune sand; 2. wall-like ridge of unconsolidated material formed along a beach by strong waves and currents (Bates and Jackson, 1980).

Reef (Inorganic)   1. Originally from Old Norse word "rif," meaning "rib"; applied by sailors to narrow rock ridges, shingle, or sand near enough to surface for a vessel to run aground (Heckel, 1974, p. 93); 2. any impediment to travel or navigation (i.e., a canyon such as Capital Reef, Utah, or a mountain such as Castle Reef, Montana); 3. a local (or provincial) term for a metalliferous mineral deposit, especially gold-bearing quartz (e.g., a saddle reef; Bates and Jackson, 1980).

Reef (Organic)   Countless authors, almost exclusively geologists, have defined organic reefs; these definitions are so inconsistent, contradictory and inconclusive that it would be pointless and futile to include them here (see discussion in Chap. 1). However, the interested reader may wish to consult the following representative sample of such definitions: Vaughan (1911, p. 238; 1919, p. 238); Cumings (1932); Lowenstam (1950); Wilson (1950); Cloud (1952); Newell et al., (1953); MacNeil (1954); Kornicker and Boyd (1962); Nelson et al., (1962); Stoddart (1969, p. 473); Dunham (1970); Heckel (1974); Schuhmacher (1976, pp. 12–15); Bates and Jackson (1980, pp. 440, 525); Geister (1984c, p. 3).

Reef-builders   Organisms that participate in the reef construction process, that is, contribute to the organic framework of the reef; include members of constructor, baffler, and binder guilds of the reef community, but exclude members of destroyer and dweller guilds.

Reef Complex   1. The entire reef structure, including reef surface, lagoon deposits, and off-reef deposits (Henson, 1950); 2. aggregate of $CaCO_3$-secreting and frame-building organisms, the associated biota, and mainly biogenetic sediments (Cloud, 1959, p. 387); 3. solid reef and heterogeneous and contiguous material derived from it by abrasion; aggregate of reef, fore-reef, back-reef, and interreef deposits, bounded on seaward side by basin sediments and on landward side by lagoonal sediments (Bates and Jackson, 1980).

Reef Crest   Sharp break in slope at seaward margin or edge of reef flat (Bates and Jackson, 1980).

Reef Flat   1. Any relatively flat area behind a reef (Stoddart, 1969); 2. relatively flat zone immediately behind reef crest characterized by water depths of 0–2 m; with scattered framework organisms and associated algae but generally lacking extensive organic framework in mature reef complexes (Longman, 1981, p. 12).

Reef Mound   Structure that lacks characteristics of a reef (e.g., diversification and domination stages of reef succession) because the environment was not conducive to growth of large, skeletal metazoans or because metazoans did not exist at the time the structure was formed; rich in skeletal organisms; consists of poorly sorted lime mud with minor amounts of organic boundstone; formed in quiet water (James, 1979).

Reef Patch   Coral growth formed independently on a shelf of less than 70 m depth, often in lagoon of a barrier reef or atoll, ranging from an expanse several km across down to that of a single colony (Bates and Jackson, 1980).

Reef System   A cluster of reefs.

Reptant   1. In colonial corals: corallites with horizontal, creeping growth habit growing attached along one side of corallum to some foreign body; syn.: reptoid; 2. in non-anthozoans: dominant growth habit horizontal or lateral; cf. erect.

Ribbon Reef   1. Located along seaward edge of Great Barrier Reef platform; forms rampart 300–500 m wide with broad scallops 5–35 km long with ends curved into lagoonlike horns of a sand spit (Fairbridge, 1950, p. 338); 2. reef growing from linear foundations that are either discrete antecedent platforms or higher rims on much larger and usually deeper platforms (Hopley, 1982, p. 254).

Rudstone   Carbonate rock containing greater than 10% of grains larger than 2 mm; grains are in mechanical contact with each other (i.e., they support each other); used to describe internal sediment of a reef or the level-bottom (Embry and Klovan, 1971); cf. floatstone.

Seamount   An elevation of seafloor, 1000 m or higher (Bates and Jackson, 1980); cf. guyot.

Seaward Slope   Area of a barrier reef or atoll seaward from reef crest; includes spurs, grooves, terraces, reef walls, caverns, etc.

Shelf   That part of continental margin between shoreline and continental slope; syn.: continental shelf; 2. a stable cratonic area that was periodically flooded by shallow marine waters and received a relatively thin, well-winnowed cover of sediment (Bates and Jackson, 1980); 3. an area on top of a ramp or platform (J. L. Wilson, 1975, p. 21).

Spar   Cement of carbonate rock; consists of calcite in large transparent–translucent crystals.

"Spongiostromata"   An artificial group of algae containing forms lacking any microstructure; includes all stromatolites (Wray, 1977, p. 35).

Spurs and Grooves   System of shallow ridges (spurs) separated by deep channels (grooves) oriented perpendicular to reef crest and extending down upper seaward slope; spurs = "buttresses" of some authors.

Stereome   Calcareous skeletal deposit in some scleractinian corals that covers and thickens parts of corallite.

Stromatolite   Structure produced by mechanical accumulation of fine-grained carbonate sediment on organic films or mats generated by colonies of non-skeletal filamentous and coccoid algae; distinctly laminated with pronounced vertical relief (Wray, 1977, p. 6).

Table Reef   1. Small coral reef without a central island or lagoon (Tayama, 1935; 1952); 2. small, isolated, flat-topped reef; with or without islands; does not enclose a lagoon (Bates and Jackson, 1980).

Tectonic   Of or pertaining to forces involved in the outer part of the earth, or the resulting large-scale (regional) structures or features thereof (modified from Bates and Jackson, 1980).

Thallus   The whole algal plant body, including cells, tissues, and skeleton (if present).

Thicket (or **Coral Thicket**)   Aggregation of closely associated coral colonies approximately 5–7 m across; monotypic or polytypic in biologic composition; characterized by definable extent and continuity of coral both laterally and vertically (modified from Squires, 1964); first stage in ecologic succession of deep-water reefs; cf. coppice.

Thrombolite   Cryptalgal structure related to stromatolite but lacking lamination and characterized by a macroscopic clotted fabric (Aitken, 1967).

Tower Karst   Type of tropical karst characterized by isolated, steep-sided limestone hills that may be flat-topped and are surrounded by a flat plain usually underlain by alluvium (Bates and Jackson, 1980).

Trapping   Process of holding loose surficial sediment on level-bottom substrates by soft-bodied organisms; syn.: stabilization; cf. baffling, binding.

Trophic   Pertaining to nutrition or use of energy.

Trophic Level   In a food chain, a level containing organisms of identical feeding habits with respect to the chain (e.g., herbivore; Levinton, 1982).

Unconformity   A substantial break or gap in the geologic record where a rock unit is overlain by another that is not next in the stratigraphic succession; an interruption in the continuity of a depositional sequence of sedimentary rocks; implies uplift or eustasy and erosion (Bates and Jackson, 1980).

Register of Age and Localities for Plates

(All photos taken and samples collected by author unless otherwise indicated.)

1. Holocene. Makatea Island, French Polynesia.
2. Late Permian; upper Capitan Limestone. Mouth of Walnut Canyon, Guadalupe Mountains, White City, New Mexico.
3. Pleistocene. Windley Key quarry, Florida.
4. Pleistocene. Makatea Island, French Polynesia.
5. Early Permian; Cottonwood Limestone. Approximately 9 km west of Eureka, Greenwood County, Kansas.
6. Late Carboniferous; Akiyoshi Limestone. Southwestern Honshu Island, Japan.
7. Holocene. Heron Island, southern Great Barrier Reef, Queensland, Australia.
8. Jurassic; Torinosu Limestone. Naradini, near Kochi, Skikoku Island, Japan.
9. Late Carboniferous (Pennsylvanian: Virgilian); Altamont Limestone. Valeda, west of Coffeyville, Labette County, Kansas.
10. Holocene–Pleistocene. San Pedro Channel, Los Angeles County, California.
11. Early Cretaceous (Albian); lower Glen Rose Limestone. Pipe Creek, Bandera County, Texas.
12. Late Cambrian; Point Peak Member, Wilberns Formation. White's Crossing, Llano River, Mason County, Texas.
13. Late Jurassic (Oxfordian); Couches de Birmensdorf. St. Claude, eastern Jura Mountains, France.
14. Huahine, a "high" volcanic island, French Polynesia.

15. Late Permian. North side, Pine Spring Canyon, Guadalupe Mountains, Culberson County, Texas.

16. Late Carboniferous (Pennsylvanian); Holder Formation. North side, Dry Canyon, Sacramento Mountains, Otero County, New Mexico.

17. Pingelap Atoll, Caroline Islands. Photo courtesy of J. Ayres.

18. Late Devonian. Lloyd Hill Atoll, Laidlaw Range, Canning Basin, Western Australia.

19. Late Devonian; Windjana Limestone. Windjana Gorge, Napier Range, Canning Basin, Western Australia.

20. Bora Bora, French Polynesia.

21. Late Devonian. Teichert Hills Atoll, near Lawford Range, Canning Basin, Western Australia.

22. Capricorn Group, southern Great Barrier Reef, Queensland, Australia.

23. Holocene. Near Hikkaduwa, Sri Lanka. Photo courtesy of R. Bromley.

24. Holocene. Moorea Island, French Polynesia.

25. Middle Devonian; Formosa Reef Limestone. Approximately 9 km west of Walkerton, Ontario.

26. Holocene. Near Sandy Lane, Holetown, Barbados. Photo courtesy of R. Bromley.

27. Holocene. Florida Keys. Photographer unknown.

28. Miocene. Makatea Island, French Polynesia.

29. Late Carboniferous (Pennsylvanian: Virgilian). West of Coffeyville, Montgomery County, Kansas.

30. Early Cambrian; Poleta Formation. Near Lida, Esmeralda County, Nevada.

31. Late Carboniferous (Pennsylvanian: Virgilian): Ozawkie Limestone. Bartlett, Mills County, Iowa.

32. Late Devonian. Elimberrie Bioherm #2, Oscar Range, Canning Basin, Western Australia.

33. Late Devonian. Bugle Gap, Canning Basin, Western Australia.

34. Late Devonian. McWae Ridge, Lawford Range, Canning Basin, Western Australia.

35. Late Devonian; Virgin Hills Formation. McIntrye Knolls, Canning Basin, Western Australia.

36. Late Carboniferous (Pennsylvanian: Virgilian); Ervine Creek Limestone. Approximately 6 km south of Madison, Greenwood County, Kansas.

37. Late Carboniferous (Pennsylvanian: Virgilian); Spring Hill Limestone. Approximately 2 km west of Neodesha, Wilson County, Kansas.

38. Late Permian; upper Capitan Limestone. Mouth of Dark Canyon, Guadalupe Mountains. Approximately 14 km southwest of Carlsbad, Eddy County, New Mexico.

39. Late Permian; Capitan Limestone, seaward slope. Guadalupe Peak Trail, Guadalupe Mountains, Culberson County, Texas.

40. Early Cretaceous (mid-Albian); El Abra Limestone (seaward slope, Valles Platform), Taninul quarry, Querareto Road, west of El Abra, northeastern Mexico. Collected by C. Johnson.

41. Early Cretaceous; Edwards Limestone. Near Crawford, McLennan County, Texas.

42. Early Cretaceous (Albian); lower Glen Rose Limestone. Near Sisterdale, Kendall County, Texas.

43. Early Cretaceous (Albian); lower Glen Rose Limestone. "The Narrows," Blanco River, Hays County, Texas.

44. Late Cambrian; Point Peak Member, Wilberns Formation. Section I (Ahr, 1971), Mason County, Texas.

45. Late Ordovician; Grant Lake Formation. Washington, Mason County, Kentucky. Photo courtesy of R. Cuffey.

46. Early Carboniferous (Visean); Akiyoshi Limestone. Southwestern Honshu Island, Japan.

47. Late Jurassic (Kimmeridgian); Calcaires de Tabalcon. Cluse de la Balme, near Yenne, southern Jura Mountains, France.

48. Late Triassic (Norian/Rhaetian); Adnet reef. Tropf quarry, near Salzburg, Austria. Collected by P. Schäfer.

49. Late Triassic (Norian/Rhaetian); Rötelwand reef. Gaissau, near Salzburg, Austria. Collected by P. Schäfer.

50. Late Triassic (Norian); Dachstein Limestone. Hoher Göh, Berchtesgaden, West Germany. Collected by P. Schäfer.

51. Late Jurassic (Oxfordian); Calcaires lites. Bouvesse-Quirieu quarry, near Montalieu, southern Jura Mountains, France. Collected by C. Gaillard.

52. Late Cretaceous (Cenomanian). Corniche de la Marcouline, near Cassis, Bouches du Rhone, France. Photo courtesy of R. West.

Plate 1. (a) Fissure in approximately 5000-yr BP reef flat flagstone. Scale: hammer. Loc. 1. (b) Fissure filled with encrusting cryptic subcommunity and early submarine cement (cf. Pl. 3a). Scale: hammer. Loc. 2.

Plate 2. (a) Massive coral (*Diploria?*) in growth position surrounded by internal sediment; framestone. Scale: pen. Loc. 3. (b) Branching corals and encrusting coralline algae in growth position; framestone. Loc. 4.

Plate 3. (a) Close-up of fissure margin in Plate 1b with calcareous sponge encrusting wall (center) and algal (?) (*Archaeolithoporella*)-rich cement (top). Scale: cm. Loc. 2. (b) Early submarine cement (radial fibrous; dark) and phylloid algal laminae (light); cementstone. Scale: mm. Loc. 2.

Plate 4. (a) Transported/abraided coral fragments in beachrock flagstone; 5300-yr BP rudstone "shell heap." Scale: hammer. Loc. 1. (b) Minimally transported and broken phylloid algal *(Andchicodium)* thalli in biostrome; bafflestone "leaf pile." Coin dia.: 18 mm. Loc. 5.

Plate 5. (a) Internal sediment containing abundant bivalve and coral fragments. Width of photo: 25 cm. Loc. 3. (b) Internal sediment containing abundant crinoid columnals and skeletal sand. Width of photo: 10 cm. Loc. 6.

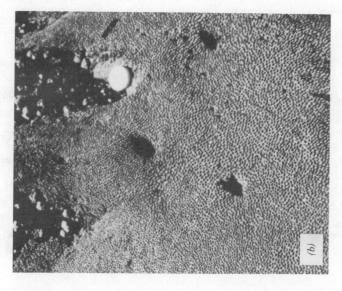

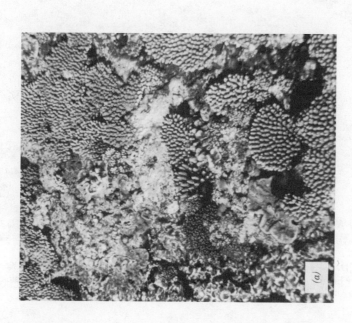

Plate 6. (a) Reef crest with densely packed corals and encrusting coralline algae (center; upper left). Width of photo: 1 m. Loc. 7. (b) Mass of sabellid (Polychaeta) tubes. Lens-cover dia.: 4 cm.

543

Plate 7. (a) Densely packed domal stromatoporoids in growth position; framestone. Scale: hammer head. Loc. 8. (b) Densely packed columnar chaetetids in growth position; framestone. Scale length: 15 cm. Loc. 9.

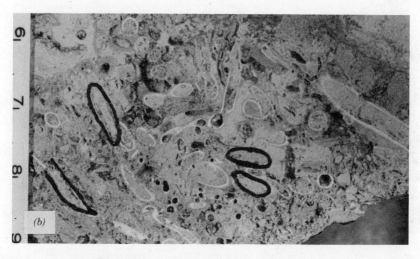

Plate 8. (a) Entwined serpulid (Polychaeta) tubes; framestone. Scale: cm/mm. Loc. 10. (b) Serpulid tubes (some outlined) in mudstone matrix; polished surface; reef flat framestone. Scale: cm. Loc. 11.

Plate 9. (a) Margin of 1.9-m thick (below man's shoulder) chaetetid framestone lacking dipping flank beds (left) and draped overlying beds. Loc. 9. (b) Domal algal reef with poorly developed internal bedding, draped overlying beds (evidence of topographic relief), and inward dipping subjacent beds (evidence of differential compaction). Loc. 12.

Plate 10. (a) Inverted conical sponge/algal reef; inward dipping flank beds near base of cone formed by differential compaction. Loc. 13. (b) Arcuate crest, barrier reef algal ridge (breaking surf), reef flat with continuous elongate reef (dark), and lagoonal sediments (light). Loc. 14.

Plate 11. (a) Basinward (to right) migration of reef (unbedded; upper center) overlying older seaward slope (dipping; left center) and basin (horizontally bedded; lower left) deposits. Loc. 15. (b) Multiple patch reefs (cliff-forming) at different stratigraphic levels. Scale: highway along bottom of photo. Loc. 16.

Plate 12. (a) Atoll with well-developed geomorphic zonation (algal ridge, reef flat, islands, central lagoon). Maximum dia.: 3 km. Loc. 17. (b) Atoll (dark) with seaward slope and central lagoon patch reefs. Maximum dia.: 1.5 km. Loc. 18.

Plate 13. (a) Margin of atoll with possible surge channel (right) and horizontally bedded lagoonal deposits (foreground). Loc. 18. (b) Shelf margin barrier reef (unbedded; center) and associated seaward slope (dipping; left) and reef flat (horizontal; right) deposits. Loc. 19.

Plate 14. (a) Crest of algal ridge nearly at low tide; reef flat to left, seaward slope to right (cf. Pl. 14b). Loc. 20. (b) Close-up of above. Dark areas are brown *(Turbinaria)*, light are crustose coralline *(Porolithon)* algae.

Plate 15. (a) Probable spur and groove system viewed from seaward slope. Loc. 21. (b) Reef flat at low tide with exposed tops of corals and crustose coralline algae. Loc. 7.

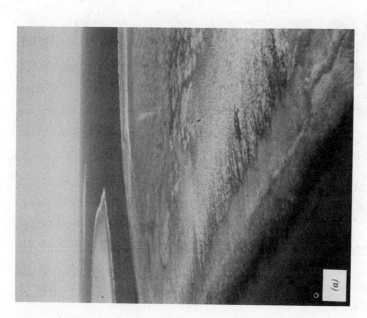

Plate 16. (a) Continental shelf patch reef complex surrounded by deep water. Living reefs (dark areas) elongate perpendicular to bank margin currents (center foreground), irregularly shaped in lagoon center, and parallel to margin on upper seaward slope (lower left). Light areas are calcareous sediments. Loc. 22. (b) Cliff with two levels of wave-cut notches. Lower notch (+6 m) formed 120,000 yr BP partly filled by speleothems. Upper notch (+25 m) formed 200,000 years BP. Loc. 1.

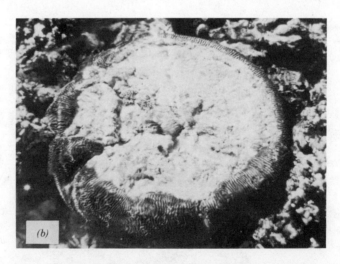

Plate 17. (a) Wave-cut notch (+1–2 m) formed 5300 years BP and seaward dipping beachrock flagstone of transported skeletal fragments (cf. Pl. 4a). Loc. 1. (b) Microatoll; upper surface marks low tide. Dia.: 0.8 m; height: 0.4 m. Loc. 7.

Plate 18. (a) "Combat Zone" (light-gray bare corallum) and damaged polyp tissue; shallow reef (−2 m). Width of photo: 10 cm. Loc. 23. (b) Corallum *(Diploria?)* in growth position bored by bivalves. Scale: cm. Loc. 3.

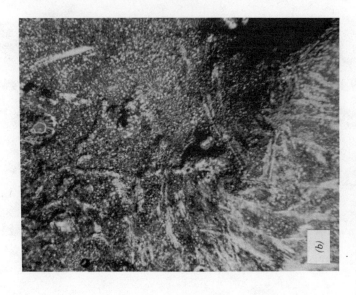

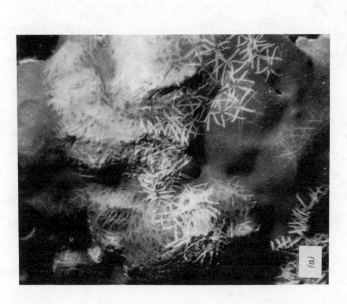

Plate 19. (a) Star-shaped rasp marks made by echinoid (*Diadema*) into encrusting coralline algae (~5 m). Width of photo: 5 cm. Loc. 23. (b) Linear rasping traces made by limpets on encrusting coralline algae; shallow reef (~2 m). Width of photo: 10 cm. Loc. 23.

556

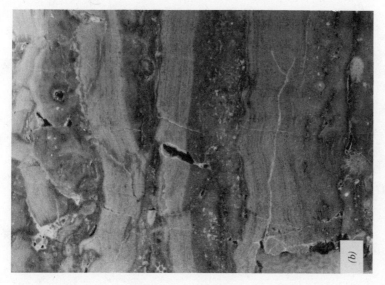

Plate 20. (a) Boring bivalve (*Lithophaga?*) tubes in coralline algal (*Porolithon?*) crust. Scale: pen. Loc. 24. (b) Densely packed tabular/laminar stromatoporoids (medium gray) and interlayered mudstone/wackestone; boundstone; polished surface. Scale: mm. Loc. 25.

557

(a)

(b)

Plate 21. (a) Foliaceous coral *(Agaricia)* (−25 m). Binder guild; chief growth direction lateral. Loc. 26. (b) Branching corals *(Acropora palmata,* left; *A. cervicornis,* right); shallow water. Constructor guild. Loc. 27.

Plate 22. (a) Poorly skeletonized, flexible gorgonians (Alcyonaria); shallow water. Baffler guild; fans oriented perpendicular to prevailing currents. Loc. 27. (b) Rigid hydrozoans *(Millepora);* shallow water. Baffler guild; blades oriented perpendicular to prevailing currents. Loc. 27.

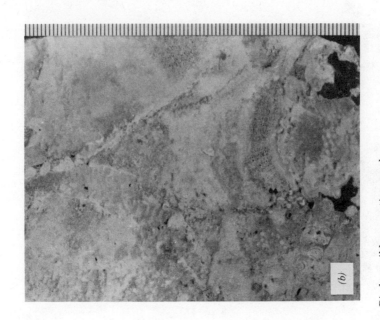

Plate 23. (a) Algal ridge subcommunity; vertical view. Binder guild: encrusting coral (center), coralline algae (left). Baffler guild: erect brown alga (*Turbinaria?*; dark "stars"). Scale: cm/mm. Loc. 20. (b) Guild overlap. Constructor: corals (lower center and right). Binder: crustose coralline algae (light–medium gray). Polished surface, framestone/boundstone. Scale: mm. Loc. 28.

Plate 24. Guild overlap, algal ridge subcommunity. Binder–constructor: crustose coralline alga in sheet and nodular growth form. Width of photo: 40 cm. Loc. 20. (b) Interlayered crustose coralline alga (light gray) and fibrous early submarine (?) cement (medium gray); porous boundstone/cementstone; polished surface. Scale: mm. Loc. 24.

Plate 25. (a) Tabular/laminar chaetetid coenostea (medium gray; upper right and base of photo); boundstone. Scale: hammer head. Loc. 29. (b) Thrombolite; non-skeletal algae (dark) and mudstone (light); boundstone; outcrop surface. Scale: cm/mm. Loc. 30.

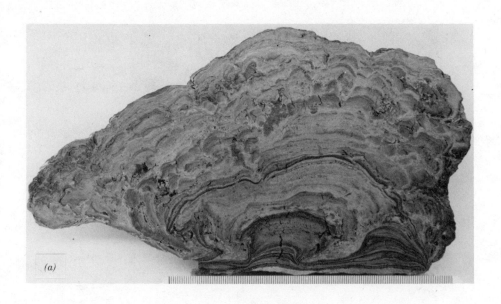

(a)

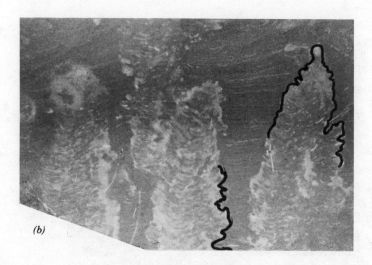

(b)

Plate 26. (a) Domal stromatolite; polished surface; boundstone. Scale: mm. Loc. 31. (b) *Sphaerocodium* (light gray; skeletal cyanophyte?) forming digitate stromatolites; polished surface. Width of photo: 7.7 cm. Loc. 32.

Plate 27. (a) Columnar stromatolites (dark) and laminated internal sediment; bound-stone/bafflestone; vertical outcrop surface. Scale: 15 cm long. Loc. 33. (b) Upper ends of densely packed columnar stromatolites; boundstone/bafflestone; oblique outcrop surface. Scale: hammer. Loc. 34.

Plate 28. (a) Irregular masses of *Renalcis* (skeletal cyanophyte?; light) in mudstone matrix (dark); boundstone; polished surface. Scale: mm. Seaward slope, Loc. 18. (b) Cylindrical stromatoporoids (*Stachyodes?*; white) encrusted by *Renalcis* (light gray) in mudstone matrix (medium gray); boundstone; polished surface. Scale: mm. Loc. 35.

(a)

(b)

Plate 29. (a) *Anchicodium* (Codiacea) "cups" in erect growth position; baffler guild (cf. Pl. 4b). Scale: cm. Loc. 5. (b) *Archaeolithoporella* (alga?) in nodular growth form (white lines) in abundant early submarine cement; boundstone/cementstone; outcrop surface. Width of photo: 10 cm. Loc. 2.

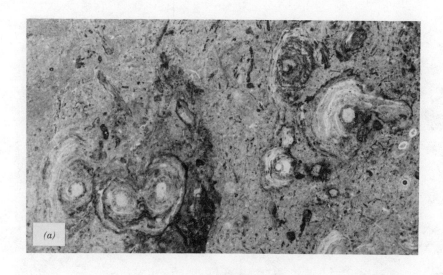

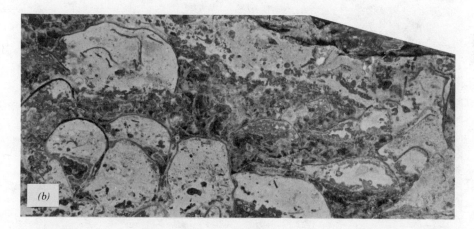

Plate 30. (a) *Archaeolithophyllum lamellosum* (red alga) encrusting sphinctozoan sponges in wackestone matrix; polished surface. Width of photo: 9.5 cm. Loc. 36. (b) *Archaeolithophyllum missouriense* (red alga) "umbrellas" in growth position (thin, dark lines) covering mudstone fillings (light gray) and spar (dark); boundstone; polished surface. Width of photo: 10 cm. Loc. 37.

Plate 31. (a) Large fragments of archaeocyathid walls (center) of uncertain shapes (discoid/cup?) and smaller dendroid (?) forms in mud-rich thrombolite boundstone; outcrop surface. Scale: cm/mm. Loc. 30. (b) Cateniform–dendroid colonial archaeocyathids; bafflestone; outcrop surface. Scale: cm/mm. Loc. 30.

(a)

(b)

Plate 32. (a) Multilayered *Chaetetes* (Sclerospongiae?) coenosteum overgrowing (binder guild) mud-filled brachiopod (lower right) and flattened oncolite? (center); polished surface. Scale: cm. Loc. 9. (b) Sheetlike growth form of sphinctozoan (Porifera: Family Guadalupiidae) with chambers of irregular sizes and shapes; binder guild. Width of photo: 16 cm. Loc. 2.

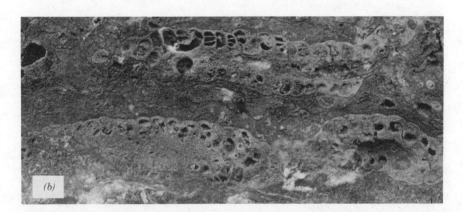

Plate 33. (a) Domal *Chaetetes* (Sclerospongiae?) coenosteum overgrowing mudstone; boundstone. Scale: cm. Loc. 9. (b) Toppled cateniform sphinctozoans (Porifera) with internal chamber walls; bafflestone; outcrop surface. Width of photo: 13.5 cm. Loc. 2.

Plate 34. (a) Multibranched sphinctozoan (Porifera) in growth position; baffler guild; outcrop surface. Scale: cm. Loc. 38. (b) Sheetlike growth form of sphinctozoan (Porifera: Family Guadalupiidae) with regularly arranged, vertically elongate chambers; binder guild; outcrop surface. Width of photo: 11 cm. Loc. 39.

Plate 35. (a) Tabular/laminar stromatoporoids enclosing lenses of bioclastic internal sediment indicative of rapid lateral growth; boundstone; outcrop surface. Scale: pen. Loc. 25. (b) Erect cluster of rudists (Bivalvia: Hipputitacea) with vertical partitions in mantle cavity and interlocking ornament (upper right); framestone; transverse polished section. Width of photo: 16 cm. Loc. 40.

Plate 36. (a) Tabular/laminar stromatoporoids that performed the same binder—constructor function as crustose coralline algae in Cenozoic reefs (guild overlap; cf. Pl. 24); boundstone. Width of photo: 50 cm. Loc. 25. (b) Thick-walled, heavy rudists (Bivalvia: Hipputitacea) in erect growth position in wackestone matrix; framestone; polished surface. Scale: mm. Loc. 41.

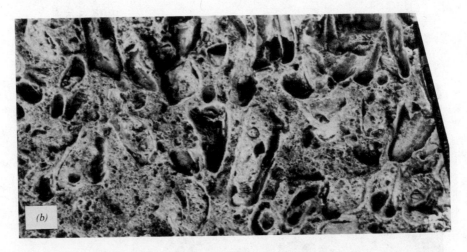

Plate 37. (a) Monopleurid (Bivalvia: Hippuritacea) rudist bouquet in growth position; constructor guild; outcrop surface. Scale: hammer. Loc. 42. (b) Bouquet of leached rudists (Bivalvia) in erect growth position; constructor guild. Scale: pen. Loc. 43.

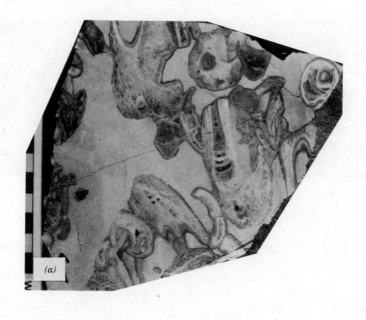

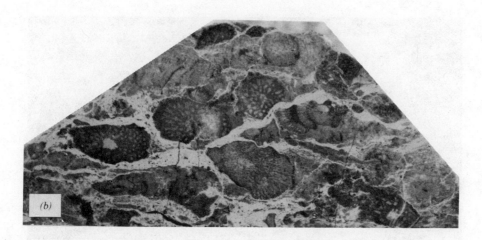

Plate 38. (a) Conical–cylindrical rudists (Bivalvia: Hipputitacea) with tabulate mantle cavity (center) and thick, porous/canaliculate shells in mudstone matrix; framestone; polished surface. Scale: cm. Loc. 40. (b) Densely packed, toppled, cylindrical archaeocyathids; bafflestone; outcrop surface. Width of photo: 55 cm. Loc. 30.

Plate 39. (a) Mottled fabric formed by thrombolitic algae in low turbulence. Width of photo: 6.5 cm. Loc. 44. (b) Dome of coalesced stromatolites. Scale: hammer. Loc. 44.

576

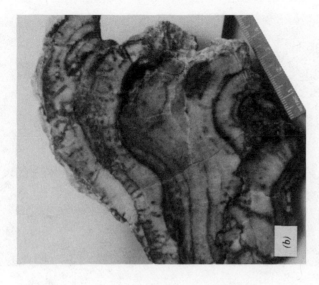

Plate 40. (a) "Reef" (maximum dimensions: 40 cm thick; 3.5 m dia.) built by domal trepostome bryozoans; framestone (cf. Pl. 7a). Scale: hammer. Loc. 45. (b) Domal zoarium of "reef"-building trepostome (*Stigmatella personata*) shown in Plate 40a; polished surface. Scale: cm/mm. Loc. 45.

Plate 41. (a) Elimberrie Bioherm #2 (looking southwest) built by deep-water stromatolites with prominent, steep seaward slope. Maximum width: 250 m. Loc. 32. (b) Intergrown *Renalcis* (skeletal cyanophyte?; right center), *Actinostroma?* (Stromatoporoidea; upper left), and *Amphipora* (Stromatoporoidea; upper right); boundstone; outcrop surface. Scale: pen. Loc. 19.

Plate 42. (a) Densely packed dendroidal Rugosa in oolite matrix; framestone; outcrop surface. *Nagatophyllum satoi* Zone. Coin dia.: 19 mm. Loc. 46. (b) Intergrown chaetetids (light gray) and stromatolites (dark gray); binder guild; polished surface. *Millerella yowarensis* Zone. Loc. 46.

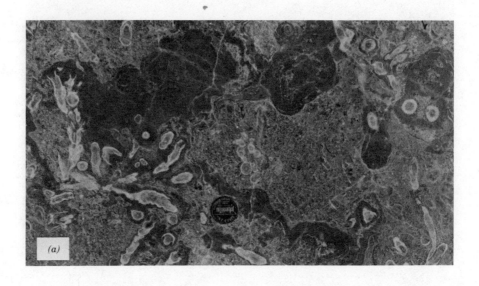

Plate 43. (a) Dendroidal Rugosa (light gray) encrusted by chaetetids (dark gray) in packstone matrix (medium gray); framestone/boundstone; transverse polished section. Coin dia.: 19 mm. *Millerella yowarensis* Zone. Loc. 46. (b) Artist's reconstruction, clustered coralliform richthofenaceans (Brachiopoda) held erect by spines, with depressed operculiform brachial valves surrounded by spines to "strain" incurrent water and surrounded by rhynchonellid and strophomenid brachiopods, ramose Bryozoa (left center), and solitary Rugosa. University of Nebraska State Museum, Lincoln. Width of photo: 15 cm.

580

Plate 44. (a) Stromatoporoid (lower half)–scleractinian (upper half) framestone in fragmental rudist (Bivalvia: Hippuritacea) packstone matrix; vertical outcrop surface. Scale: in./cm. Loc. 47. (b) Cateniform calcareous sponges encrusted by *Archaeolithoporella* (alga?; dark gray) in radial fibrous, early submarine cement (upper right); outcrop surface. Coin dia.: 19 mm. Loc. 2.

Plate 45. (a) Huge, vase-shaped (?) calcareous sponge (light gray) in abundant radial fibrous, early submarine cement (right); bafflestone/cementstone. Scale: in./cm. Loc. 2. (b) Calcareous sponges of varied taxa and growth forms encrusted by *Archaeolithoporella* (alga?); bafflestone/boundstone. Coin dia.: 18 mm. Loc. 2.

Plate 46. (a) *Eugonophyllum?* (Codiacea; thin, dark lines) in erect growth position and baffled mudstone (light gray) encrusted by spar-cemented *Archaeolithoporella* (alga?; dark); presumed current direction left to right; bafflestone/boundstone. Scale: cm. Loc. 2. (b) *Collenella?* (Animalia?) boundstone. Width of photo: 17 cm. Loc. 38.

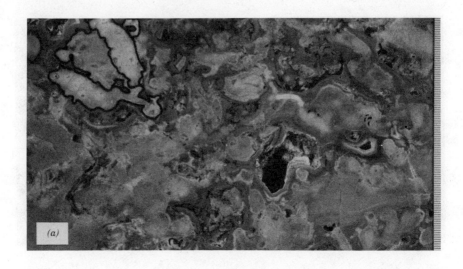

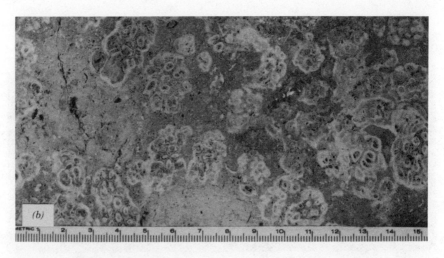

Plate 47. (a) Cateniform Sphinctozoa (Porifera; light gray) in varied orientations enclosed by isopachous rim cement (dark gray) of vadose zone origin; bafflestone/cementstone; polished section. Scale: mm. Loc. 15. (b) Clusters of densely packed Sphinctozoa (Porifera) with thickened walls and internal chamber plates in wackestone matrix; bafflestone; transverse polished section. Back-reef facies. Scale: cm/mm. Loc. 38.

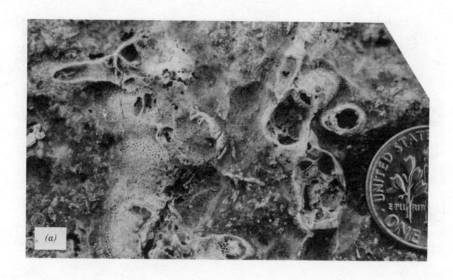

Plate 48. (a) Sheetlike and cateniform Sphinctozoa (Porifera) in wackestone matrix; boundstone/bafflestone. Coin dia.: 18 mm. Back-reef facies. Loc. 38. (b) Toppled cateniform Sphinctozoa (Porifera) enclosed by *Archaeolithoporella* (alga?) and early radial fibrous cement; bafflestone/boundstone/cementstone; outcrop surface. Back-reef facies. Width of photo: 15 cm. Loc. 38.

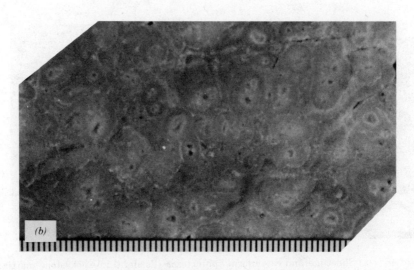

Plate 49. (a) Recrystallized dendroidal *"Thecosmilia"* (Scleractinia) in wackestone matrix; framestone; transverse polished section. Scale: mm. Loc. 48. (b) Densely packed cateniform calcareous sponges; bafflestone; transverse polished section. Scale: mm. Loc. 49.

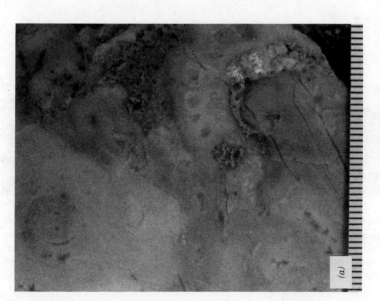

Plate 50. (a) Sphinctozoa (Porifera; right half) and Spongiomorphida (Coelenterata; left half); bafflestone; polished section. Scale: mm. Loc. 48. (b) Macroscopic binder guild (upper left and lower center); taxa not identified; polished section. Scale: mm. Loc. 50.

Plate 51. (a) Siliceous sponges (dark gray) of varied growth forms (sheets, cups, vases) encrusted by stromatolites/thrombolites (medium gray) and *Nubeculinella* (Foraminiferida; white dots) in mudstone matrix (light gray); bafflestone/boundstone; polished section. Scale: mm. Loc. 51. (b) Two coral–rudist (Bivalvia: Hipputitacea) patch reefs (left and center) and adjacent bedded reef flat breccia (base of cliff) and bioclastic limestone. Loc. 52.

Index

Glossary pages in *italics;* plate pages in **bold face.**

ABN 3267